STARS
AND
KEYS

STARS AND KEYS

Folktales and Creolization in the Indian Ocean

Lee Haring

WITH TRANSLATIONS BY

CLAUDIE RICAUD AND DAWOOD AULEEAR

INDIANA UNIVERSITY PRESS

Bloomington and Indianapolis

This book is a publication of

Indiana University Press
601 North Morton Street
Bloomington, IN 47404-3797 USA

http://iupress.indiana.edu

Telephone orders 800-842-6796
Fax orders 812-855-7931
Orders by e-mail iuporder@indiana.edu

The paper used in this publication meets the minimum requirements of American National Standard for Information Sciences—Permanence of Paper for Printed Library Materials, ANSI Z39.48-1984.

Manufactured in the United States of America

Library of Congress Cataloging-in-Publication Data

Haring, Lee.
Folktales and creolization in the Indian Ocean / Lee Haring ; with translations by Claudie Ricaud and Dawood Auleear.
p. cm.
"Translates, for the first time into English, oral tales from the languages of five island groups: Madagascar, Mauritius, Seychelles, Réunion, and the Comoros"—Pref.
Includes bibliographical references and index.
ISBN-13: 978-0-253-34868-5 (cloth)
ISBN-10: 0-253-34868-4 (cloth)
1. Tales—Islands of the Indian Ocean. 2. Creoles—Islands of the Indian Ocean—Folklore. I. Title.
GR360.I743H37 2007
398.20969—dc22

2006033835

1 2 3 4 5 12 11 10 09 08 07

To
Roger D. Abrahams
Regina Bendix
Henry Glassie
John F. Szwed

je leur dois tout

Contents

Preface

Once in Paris, I took a beautiful young French banker out on a date. We went to a production of Gertrude Stein's *Doctor Faustus Lights the Lights,* directed by the American Richard Foreman (in whose film *Strong Medicine* I play a tiny role). When Agnès learned that I was doing research on folklore in Madagascar, she quickly found the *mot juste* for me: "*Très spécialisé,*" very specialized. I felt perceived, though not profoundly understood, like a butterfly on a card, and inarticulate in the face of such precise mastery of language. In the spirit of the staircase, I thought afterwards that I should have translated Paul Goodman's words: "I want to treat the things that make literature important, moving and concernful, to us" (Goodman 1). I was already thinking, but could not say, what Edward Said would write, that I was engaged in "the rediscovery and repatriation of what had been suppressed in the natives' past by the processes of [French] imperialism" (Said 210). Anticipating Said, I could have conceded that European culture was indispensable to the subjugation of Malagasy people, yet that awareness of their own culture was indispensable to their survival today. Or had I been able to translate from memory, I could have quoted Henry Glassie: "folklore (or art or communication) is the central fact of what we call culture, and culture is the central fact of what we call history, and . . . people, as history's force, create the phenomena we study whatever name we give our discipline" (Glassie xiv). But even in English I couldn't explain all that, and certainly not in French.

It was my only date with Agnès.

Her phrase *très spécialisé* came to epitomize, for me, the paradox of all scholarship, not just mine. The small, marginal discipline calling itself folklore speaks to a whole field of practices comprising the varieties of expressive culture. "Literature" and "folklore" are names that certain people chose, for different reasons, to give to certain segments of what occurs in all societies, the ongoing production of art in words (Eagleton, *Literary* 1–16). Now that capturing and transmitting verbal art is so easy, with cheap recorders and the Internet, "literature" and "folklore" will coalesce. The broadening of the literary canon requires a massive program of retrieval, to which this book contributes.

> Literally hundreds of linguistic and literary convergences ("creolizations") remain to be investigated or simply read. The best known of these creolizations are of course contemporary West Indian and African writing in English or French, but there is much more to be assayed. Yiddish writing, Chicano writing, Afro-American literature in North America, writing in Papiamento in the Dutch West Indies, and the various written literatures by the native peoples of Melanesia, Australia, and North and South America. Further along the scale, but products of convergence nonetheless, are Indo-Anglian, Anglo-Irish, Anglo-Scots, Slavo-Italian, Judeo-Spanish—the list reaches on and on. And sooner or later we will be face to face with the fact that the so-called "standard" or "national" literatures are quite often best understood from the point of view of the process of creolization, at least at some points in their development—Middle English literature, for example.

Orally, Southwest Indian Ocean folktales continually manifest that mixing and novelty which John F. Szwed finds in written literature today. "In short," he continues,

> instead of seeing all literatures as genetic products or divergences of other, older literatures, against which the offspring is to be measured, we need to find and assess those that were formed by the meeting and admixture of different languages and literary traditions. At the very least we are likely to find that in the latter literatures the product is a totally new thing, with new features and functions, and thus not properly understandable exclusively in terms of one or the other of its "parent" sources. (Szwed 498)

This retrieval and reading of the world's verbal art should be, in fact, the task of literary criticism in the coming years.

The book translates, for the first time into English, oral tales from the languages of five island groups: Madagascar, Mauritius, Seychelles, Réunion, and the Comoros. Some are cited without interruption; a few are translated only in part, or summarized. Into others I interpolate commentary, as if I were reading to you and then looking up to explain something from time to time.[1] The words of storytellers are in one typeface, the editor's commentary in another, to enable a reader to skip the boring parts (whichever those are). The music of the songs is left for some future CD. As it's a book of stories, it says little about other forms of folklore still to be researched in these islands: riddles, proverbs, poetry, oratory, song, music, dance, costume, cookery. . . . Equally unrepresented are some ethnic and language groups in the islands, such as Chinese in Mauritius and Indians in Réunion. These will have to await future research. Like the novel of nineteenth-century Europe, the creole folktale is the dominant literary form of the Southwest Indian Ocean. It both reflects and influences how people live. Hence it demands attention first.

The title is borrowed from Mauritius, where I did fieldwork for this book. Stella Maris, "Star of the Sea," is the name for a resort in the Bahamas, a Hungarian publisher, a Catholic women's college in Chennai (India), a hotel in Sardinia, a Catholic seamen's mission in Hamburg, an Istituto Scientifico per la Neuropsichiatria dell'Infanzia e dell'Adolescenza in Pisa, a cancer clinic in Tijuana, a 1918 Mary Pickford film made from a novel by William J. Locke, a hotel in Mayo (Ireland), and numerous holiday flats and Roman Catholic churches. The island of Mauritius appropriates the phrase for its own identity, in Latin, as befits a national motto: Stella Clavisque Maris Indici, The Star and Key of the Indian Ocean. On the seas, Mauritius is a starlike point for navigation; the nation sees itself as a key to the important wealth-giving trade routes between the East Indies and Europe. This book appropriates the phrase for storytellers who are stars of performance and verbal art, and for tales which are keys to a creole aesthetic.

Acknowledgments

I began assembling these translations in 1975–76, when I had the honor of being posted to the University of Antananarivo (then the Université de Madagascar) as Fulbright Senior Lecturer in American Literature and Folklore. Unfailingly cordial colleagues in the Department of Modern Languages, especially Yvette Ranjeva, Siméon Rajaona, and Mireille Rabenoro, encouraged my interest in Malagasy oral literature, as did M. César Rabenoro, the President of the Académie Malgache. At the American Cultural Center, G. Michael Razi, Marilyn Hulbert, and Rolland Razafintsalama were constantly helpful, as were librarians of the university and National Library. Subsequent research in Paris was supported by the PSC-CUNY Research Award Program of the City University of New York. Pierre Vérin, Geneviève Calame-Griaule, Brunhilde Biebuyck, and Christiane Seydou showed me innumerable kindnesses; Paul Ottino, Claude Allibert, Robert Chaudenson, and Claude Vogel too have given encouragement directly and through their example, as well as translation permission; librarians of the Institut National des Langues et Civilisations Orientales (INALCO) have helped.

A year in Mauritius (1989–90), under a second Fulbright-Hays grant, initiated research into Mauritian folktales. At the Mahatma Gandhi Institute there, I incurred debts of gratitude to the then director of the institute, Mr. U. Bissoondoyal, and his administrative secretary, Mrs. A. Sibartie, for welcoming me with the finest of working conditions and becoming true friends. In addition to providing transport, recording equipment, and sometimes lodging, the director of the MGI generously brought me together with a trained linguist and ethnomusicologist, Claudie Ricaud, whose collaboration made fieldwork on folktales possible. Her translations appear throughout this book. Nelzir Ventre and Sydney Joseph welcomed us again and again. Pavi Ramhota of the

MGI translated some materials. On subsequent visits, Vinesh Y. Hookoomsing and Danielle Tranquille have been extraordinarily hospitable. I am especially grateful to Dr. Karen W. Gallob for permission to reprint jokes from her dissertation on verbal humor. Others who have sweetened my stays in Mauritius include Prem and Vasanti Saddul, Ramesh Ramdoyal, Gisèle Vardin, Bina Jissurey, Sheila Wong, Sheila Bunwaree, and Shakuntala Hawoldar. Dawood Auleear, through years of assisting foreign researchers in Mauritius and collecting folklore, has shown himself to have a deep respect for Mauritian tradition and an equal determination to help preserve it.

During research in Réunion in 1995, I received a generous welcome from Didier de Robillard, Jean-Claude Carpanin Marimoutou, Claudine Bavoux, and the other members of team URA 1041 of the Centre National de Recherche Scientifique, as well as from Christian Barat and Bernard Champion. Jean-Pierre Domenichini shared his unfathomable knowledge of Madagascar. M. Yves Parent of the Rectorat de La Réunion gave assistance to my project. To my sustained astonishment, Michel Carayol patiently spent many hours evoking informants and styles and helping me turn Réunionnais tales into English. His outline history of the island of Réunion is indispensable. The librarian of the Indian Ocean collection of the Université de la Réunion, Mme Safla, gave much advice and provided invaluable materials. The stay in Réunion was suffused by the warm hospitality of Gilbert and Hélène Martin, Christiane Durand-Gasselin, Philippe Charbonnel and Gwladys Gobale, Dominique and Chantal Girardot, and Chantal Maugueret.

In the Comoros (after getting good advice from Ian Tattersall of the American Museum of Natural History), I was greatly helped by Mme Masséande Chami Allaoui, Moussa Issahaka, and the staff of the Centre National de Documentation et Recherche Scientifique in Moroni, as well as by M. Sahala. Valuable information has also come from the Hon. Mahmoud M. Aboud, ambassador of the Union of the Comoros to the United States and Canada.

In two visits to Seychelles, I have been greatly welcomed and helped by many persons: Mr. Bernard Shamlaye of the president's office; Messrs. Marcel Rosalie, Gabriel Essack, Jean-Claude Mahonne, and Léon Radegonde of the Division of Culture; Mrs. Marie-Thérèse Choppy and her successor as director of Lenstiti Kreol, Mrs. Penda Choppy; Mme Marie-Reine Confait of the Ministry of Education; two successive directors of the National Archives, who gave permission for translations; Jean-Norbert Salomon; and many others, including Roger and Marguerite Mancienne.

After a visit to the Institut d'Études Créoles of the Université d'Aix-Marseille, I could never fully express my longstanding gratitude to Robert Chaudenson, the doyen of creole studies. Among other benevolences, he made available to me his extensive notes on Southwest Indian Ocean and Caribbean folktales. With M. Jacques de Bono of the university's audiovisual center, he allowed me to view videotapes of Gérose Barivoitse and Germain Elizabeth, from his team's extensive collecting project in Réunion. Thanks also to Marie-Christine Hazaël-Massieux, President of l'Association pour l'Information dans le Monde Créole.

Some of these translations were written while I was a Wolfe Institute Fellow of Brooklyn College, where Robert Viscusi and L. S. Asekoff gave encouragement. The English department there and its former chairman, Herbert Perluck; Judith Wild, Nick Irons, and William Gargan of the Brooklyn College Library—all have helped. The book was completed with the priceless aid of a fellowship from the John Simon Guggenheim Memorial Foundation. Maps were drawn and generously contributed by Timothy Warner.

Numerous colleagues and friends have cheered me on. I name a few: Roger D. Abrahams, Cristina Bacchilega, Robert Baron, Dan Ben-Amos, Brunhilde Biebuyck, Michael L. and Nancy B. Black, Dörte Borchers, Robert Cancel, Geneviève Calame-Griaule, Ana Cara, the late Daniel J. Crowley, Bakoly Domenichini-Ramiaramanana, Gillian Feeley-Harnik, Marie-Paule Ferry, Kathleen A. Foster, Rachel Fretz, Henry Glassie, Veronika Görög-Karady, Joanna Komoska, Alison Jolly, Susan Kus, the late Denise Paulme, Philip M. Peek, Pieranna Pieroni, Leslie Prosterman, Rüdiger Schott, Nicholas Spitzer, Sabine Steinbrich, John F. Szwed, Julia Vandevelder, Ann Wollock, and Henry T. Wright, as well as several former University of Pennsylvania students. Dorothy Noyes gave the manuscript a hugely constructive reading. In addition to collaborating in a seminar on translation and several conference presentations, reading drafts, and making innumerable helpful suggestions, Professor Dr. Regina Bendix, of Georg-August-Universität in Göttingen, has given sustained and inestimable encouragement. To all of them my thanks.

I am also grateful to Michael Lundell, Elisabeth Marsh, and the staff of Indiana University Press for their efforts in bringing the book to publication.

Chronology of the Southwest Indian Ocean

Sources: Claude Allibert, Histoire de Mayotte, île de l'archipel des Comores, avant 1841, *dissertation, 3e cycle, Universitè de Paris 1 (Sorbonne) (1977); John Mack,* Madagascar: Island of the Ancestors *(London: British Museum Publications Ltd, 1986), p. 93; Jean-Louis Joubert,* Littèratures de l'Ocèan Indien *(Vanves: EDICEF, 1991), pp. 15–21, 97–101, 193–197, 265–268, 273–278; Pierre Vérin, class lectures at Institut National des Langues et Civilisations Orientales, Paris, November 1982–April 1983; chronology of Rèunion history graciously provided me by Michel Carayol.*

Four island groups treated here are independent nations (Madagascar 1960, Mauritius 1968, Comoros 1975, Seychelles 1976). People in each one do sense their affinity to the other island nations, but their cultural research turns inward, to history, not expressive culture. From outside, a common history and a common culture are visible. The history of the Comoros archipelago, for instance, is said to go back to the era of King Solomon; all the islands have their legends. From earliest times there were contacts.

Settlement Begins

AD 500	Beginnings of settlement in Madagascar. East Africans begin to arrive in the Comoros. Many Malagasy descend from Indonesians who spent time on the African coast, mixing with Africans and later coming in waves to Madagascar and the Comoros.
800–900	Villages exist in northern Madagascar and the Comoros. Fishing, herding, slash-and-burn agriculture in Madagascar. Islamic influence begins to be felt.
1200	Arabs and Shirazi (a group originating in Persia who mixed with Africans) arrive in Madagascar and the

	Comoros, building mosques. In succeeding centuries they reach Mauritius, Réunion, and Rodrigues.
1500	Portuguese explorer Diogo Dias finds Madagascar. Ecological transformations there: the plant kingdom shrinks, forests diminish, and a hundred animal species will disappear, among them the dwarf hippopotamus, the Aepyornis (a sort of wingless ostrich), and some species of diurnal lemurs.
1506	Sakalava from Madagascar and fugitives from Grande Comore arrive in Mayotte.
1511–12	Portuguese explorers Domingos Fernandez and Pero Mascarenhas reach Madagascar. The future Réunion and Mauritius will be called "Mascarene" islands.
1538	Diogo Rodrigue "discovers" Rodrigues, which is given his name.

Europeans Arrive

1598	Taking possession of Cirné ("island of swans," probably meaning the dodo), the Dutch name it Mauritius in honor of Prince Maurice of Nassau.
c. 1500	Most present-day Malagasy ethnic groups are in existence.
c. 1600	Reign of Ralambo in highland Madagascar, which he names Imerina. Ralambo allows eating of beef, introduces guns. His son Andrianjaka takes possession of a high hill that becomes Antananarivo ("town of a thousand"). Beginnings of rice cultivation in Madagascar.
1619	Dutchman Willem Ysbrantsz Bonte-Koe stays three weeks in Rèunion, publishes his account in 1625.
1638–57	Dutch attempt to settle Mauritius, then leave.
1638, 1642	French vessels take possession of Réunion, then called Mascareigne Island.
1646	Twelve Frenchmen exiled to Mascareigne live there for three years.
1650	Sakalava kingdoms expand from northwest Madagascar.
1658	Flacourt publishes his *Histoire de la Grande Isle Madagascar* in Paris, after his seven-year attempt at founding a colony.
1663	French India Company makes Mascareigne the first French base in the Indian Ocean. Settlement follows in 1665. The Malagasy who accompany the French flee

	into the mountainous interior. The island is renamed Ile Bourbon.
1664	Dutch return to Mauritius, abandoning it in 1710.
1700s	French and British pirates use the islands as temporary bases.
1715	France takes possession of Mauritius, renaming it Ile de France.

Slavery

1735	Mahé de la Bourdonnais arrives as governor of Ile Bourbon and Ile de France. He makes Bourbon an agricultural colony and Ile de France the commercial and strategic port of call on the Indian route. The two become seats of French policy against Britain. Both islands begin cultivating sugar; coffee cultivation improves Réunion's economy. To provide labor, La Bourdonnais fosters the slave trade with Madagascar and Portuguese East Africa.
1742	La Bourdonnais effects exploration of Seychelles by commander Lazare Picault, who names the big island Mahé.
1756	France takes possession of the Seychelles archipelago, naming it for Moreau de Séchelles, Louis XV's comptroller.
1765–1820	Betsimisaraka and Sakalava expeditions raid the Comoros and the East African coast. Comoran sultans seek protection from European powers. The white population of Réunion, previously dominant, is now outnumbered by the slaves introduced after 1725. Réunion's white population begins to separate into prosperous and poor.
1770	Settlement of Seychelles, with difficulties: crops fail, settlers quarrel, ecology is damaged with the massacre of tortoises.
1778	Romainville re-establishes order in Seychelles and founds the capital (later named Victoria). Spice cultivation develops for export.
1780	Andrianampoinimerina declared king of Ambohimanga (Madagascar).
1789–90	Revolution in France provokes thoughts of island autonomy in Seychelles and Mauritius, but authority is

	maintained despite the killing of Macnamara, the French commander in the Indian Ocean, in Mauritius.
1794	The decree abolishing slavery falls on deaf ears.
1795–96	Andrianampoinimerina establishes his capital at Antananarivo.
1810	Death of Andrianampoinimerina, succeeded as Merina king by Radama I (d. 1828), who with British military assistance undertakes the conquest of the whole of Madagascar. British blockade and conquest of Ile de France.
1811	Britain takes possession of Seychelles.
1814	British sovereignty over Mauritius assured by the Treaty of Paris. Farquhar, the first governor, maintains the French administrative and legal structure. Maritime and commercial activity decline in Mauritius, as sugar cultivation develops spectacularly. Réunion is returned to France as Ile Bourbon; sugar and spices cultivated there.
1816	Sultan Abdallah I of Anjouan (Comoros) travels to Bourbon to ask protection from Louis XVIII against Malagasy raids.
1818, 1820	British missionaries open first schools at Tamatave and Antananarivo.
1828–61	Ranavalona I succeeds Radama, initiating the high days of the Merina monarchy. Little extension of Radama's conquests; southern Madagascar remains independent. The queen cooperates with Europeans but refuses any concessions or transfer of rights to them, developing an independent politics. Advance of sugar cultivation in Réunion.
1829	Contract laborers from India begin to arrive in Mauritius and Réunion. Colonists resist the anti-slavery movement.
c. 1830	Earliest manuscript of Ibonia (Merina epic) is written.

Abolition, Indenture, Scholarship

1835	Bible translation published in Malagasy. Queen declares profession of the Christian faith illegal. Slavery abolished in Mauritius and Seychelles.
1836	Most Europeans and missionaries leave Madagascar.
1840	B. F. Leguevel de Lacombe, *Voyage à Madagascar et aux îles Comores* (1822–1830), published in Paris.

1842	Abbé Dalmond, *Vocabulaire et grammaire pour la langue malgache,* published in Bourbon.
1848	Slavery abolished in Bourbon, which is again renamed Réunion. Despite ominous expectations, economic and social chaos fails to occur. Poor whites become numerous. Indian indentured laborers are imported.
1853	Raombana writes his history of Madagascar.
1861–63	Radama II rules Madagascar as Merina king. Missionaries return. Sugar cultivation reaches its peak in Mauritius. Prosperity declines in Réunion. About 3,000 liberated Africans arrive in Seychelles.
1863–68	Queen Rasoherina succeeds Radama as Merina sovereign. Modernization in Seychelles (bank, telegraph, hospital, lighthouses established).
1864–85	Père Callet researches the oral history of the Merina.
1868–83	Ranavalona II, Merina queen.
1869	Baptism of Ranavalona II and her husband, the prime minister Rainilaiarivony, who married Ranavalona I and will marry Ranavalona III. Destruction of the traditional *sampy* ("idols"), symbols of royal power.
1866–1900	Malaria, cholera, decline in sugar production, cyclones, prostitution, and a major fire in Port Louis cause deterioration of life in Mauritius and Réunion. Indo-Mauritians, acquiring land, increase to two-thirds of the Mauritian population. Economic improvement in Seychelles, which exports fish, copra, and cinnamon bark.
1872–76	Norwegian missionary Lars Dahle collects oral literature in Imerina.
1875–1900	*Antananarivo Annual,* British missionary publication, edited by Sibree.
1883	Coronation of Queen Ranavalona III. Léon Humblot substitutes himself for the French government to sign a contract with Sultan Saïd Ali of Ngazidja (Grande Comore), awarding him lands and labor.
1885	John Richardson, *A New Malagasy-English Dictionary,* published from the missionary print shop.
1889	Humblot, as "resident" of Ngazidja (Grande Comore), sets up a colonial enterprise that controls the entire Comoran economy.
1893	Gabriel Ferrand, *Contes populaires malgaches.*

The Colonial Period

1895	French establish protectorate in Madagascar. It becomes a full colony in 1896.
1897	Ranavalona III exiled first to Réunion, then to Algiers, dying in 1917. Merina monarchy abolished.
1901	M. K. Gandhi visits Mauritius, inspiring the Indo-Mauritians. His emissary Manilal Doctor continues his work.
1901–21	André Dandouau makes four stays in northwest Madagascar, publishing *Contes populaires des sakalava et des tsimihety* in 1922.
1903	From being a dependency of Mauritius, Seychelles becomes a British colony.
1907–10	Charles Renel collects folklore through the teachers he supervises. *Contes de Madagascar,* 1910.
1907–22	Norwegian missionary Emil Birkeli collects Sakalava folklore. *Folklore sakalava recueilli dans la région d'Analalava,* 1922.
1908	The Comoros are decreed an annex of Madagascar, henceforward suffering neglect and poverty.
1914–18	World War I boosts sugar prices. All the islands send men to fight. Comoran society conserves its customary law, Islamic religious observances, and local powers.
1918	Self-determination implications of the treaty of Versailles provoke a movement to return Mauritius to France, which is defeated in 1921 elections.
1926	Electricity and telephone come to Seychelles.
1938	Return of the remains of Ranavalona III for reburial in Antananarivo. Henri Dubois, *Monographie des betsileo.* Labor unrest threatens the white oligarchy in Mauritius.
1939–45	World War II isolates all the islands. Economic isolation of Réunion leads almost to famine. Poverty of the Réunionnais *petits blancs* reaches a new low. Standard of living in Seychelles declines.

Independence

1946	Réunion becomes an overseas department of France. Population increase creates demographic problems. The Comoros separate from Madagascar, becoming a French overseas territory.

1947	Anti-colonial uprising in Madagascar (the first African liberation movement) brings many thousand deaths in reprisal. Jacques Faublée, *Récits bara*. New constitution in Mauritius.
1958	Comorans vote to remain French.
1960	Madagascar achieves full independence.
1968	Mauritius becomes independent under Sir Seewoosagur Ramgoolam.
1972	First Malagasy Republic falls after discontent at excessive economic and cultural dependence on France. General Gabriel Ramanantsoa initiates reforms.
1975	Assassination of Ramanantsoa, succeeded by Didier Ratsiraka as president (reelected 1982, 1989 despite economic decline). Three of the Comoros (Grande Comore, Mohéli, and Anjouan) decide for independence; Mayotte secedes, becoming a "territorial collectivity" of France. Ali Soilihi comes into power in Comoros, but his secularist reforms prove too radical for a conservative Islamic society.
1976	Seychelles becomes independent.
1977	France-Albert René becomes president of Seychelles. Ministry for Education, Information and Youth (later several times renamed) sponsors cultural research. Ali Soilihi loses prestige in Comoros.
1978	Mercenaries led by Bob Denard unseat Ali Soilihi and reinstall Ahmed Abdallah as authoritarian, paternalistic president of the Comoros. He attempts commercial relations with South Africa.
1982–	Politics in Mauritius becomes more democratic; tourism increases; textile processing plants augment the earnings from the sugar industry. In Réunion, sugar cultivation is profitable and tourism begins, but agriculture does not feed the people, and a lack of resources impedes industrial development. Madagascar's economy declines.
1989	President Ahmed Abdallah of the Comoros assassinated, probably by Bob Denard and his mercenaries.
1995	Abortive coup attempt in Comoros, again led by Bob Denard.
1997	Anjouan unsuccessfully attempts to rebel against central government of Comoros.
2002	Reconciliation of the three Comoros islands, with a new constitution granting greater autonomy.

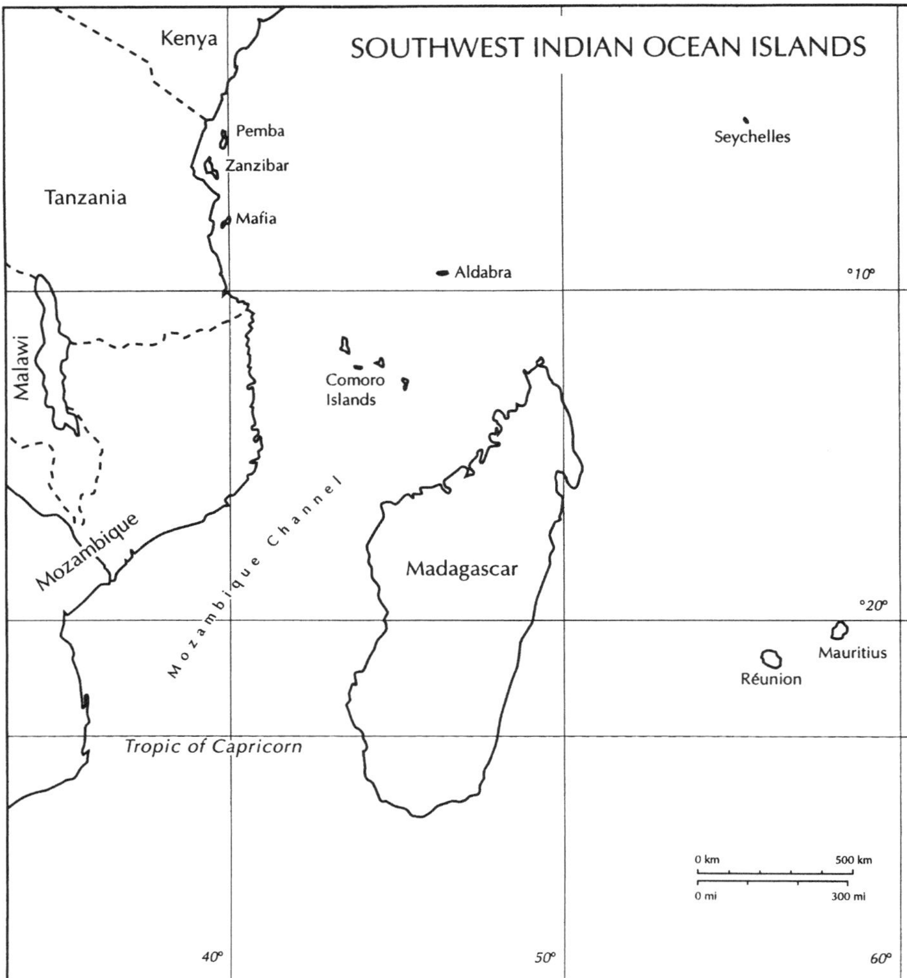

SOUTHWEST INDIAN OCEAN ISLANDS
Kenya
Pemba
Zanzibar
Tanzania
Mafia
Seychelles
Aldabra
°10°
Malawi
Comoro
Islands
Mozambique
Mozambique Channel
Madagascar
°20°
Mauritius
Réunion
Tropic of Capricorn
0 km
500 km
0 mi
300 mi
40°
50°
60°

Timothy Warner

STARS

AND

KEYS

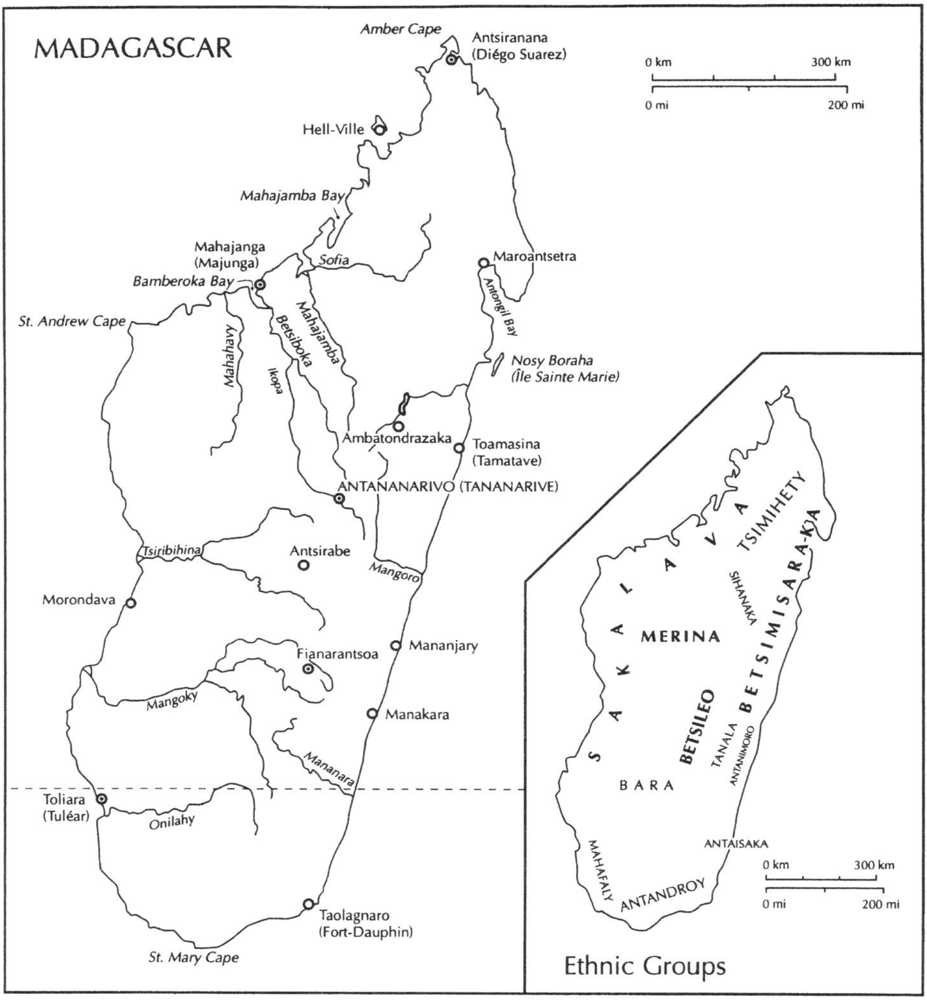
MADAGASCAR
Amber Cape
Antsiranana
(Diégo Suarez)
0 km
300 km
0 mi
200 mi
Hell-Ville
Mahajamba Bay
Mahajanga
(Majunga)
Bamberoka Bay
Sofia
Maroantsetra
Antongil Bay
St. Andrew Cape
Mahahavy
Betsiboka
Mahajamba
Ikopa
Nosy Boraha
(Île Sainte Marie)
Ambatondrazaka
Toamasina
(Tamatave)
ANTANANARIVO (TANANARIVE)
Tsiribihina
Antsirabe
Mangoro
Morondava
Mananjary
Fianarantsoa
Mangoky
Manakara
Mananara
Toliara
(Tuléar)
Onilahy
Taolagnaro
(Fort-Dauphin)
St. Mary Cape
SAKALAVA
TSIMIHETY
SIHANAKA
BETSIMISARAKA
MERINA
BETSILEO
TANALA
ANTANIMORO
BARA
ANTAISAKA
MAHAFALY
ANTANDROY
0 km
300 km
0 mi
200 mi
Ethnic Groups

1
Land of the Man-Eating Tree

A Narrator of the Merina—the Largest and Most Prestigious of Madagascar's ethnic groups–told this story to a schoolteacher of the French colonial time.

1. Origin of the Earth, Living and Inanimate Beings, according to the Tales of the Ancestors

Ambatolampy narrator 1907–10

The earth, they say, was entirely covered with a blanket of water. Only a water monster named Itrimobe lived in it. This monster was the sole inhabitant of this immense ocean, living there unconcerned. One day, they say, he wanted to see light. He put his head out of the water. Charmed by the spectacle before him, he stirred himself towards east, north, west, and south, sniffing everywhere, but he found no way out of the water, which was endless, they say. Then he got the idea to dig five large holes with his claws, to serve as vast reservoirs: three in the middle of the earth and two at each end. When he had finished that task, the waters in the middle flowed into the middle holes and those on the sides into the end holes. Then pieces of land emerged, forming continents and islands. Itrimobe became amphibious and lived alternately on land and under water. But because his eyes were not made to stand the light, they could not see, and soon he died. Dead though he was, his spirit was alive and said, "May my two arms become men to help each other! May my two legs become animals to serve men! May my entrails and lungs become reptiles! My vertebrae, fish to inhabit the seas! May my bones become rocks, my fur, trees and grass!" Thus Itrimobe's arms were transformed into human beings. The right arm became a man, the left, a woman. Man and woman still help each other like two arms. The legs were changed into domestic animals, which serve human beings just like legs. (Renel, *Contes* 3:124–25)[1]

Any western reader would recognize this as a myth, from its thematic content. The earth achieved its present form by the drying-up of primeval water, as it did after Noah's flood. A world-creator (Plato would call him a demiurge) caused the primeval sea to roll back. Unlike the earth-diver of Native American myth, who had to bring mud to the surface from which the world is made, this Malagasy creator made human beings out of the parts of his body. At the end, there is the world we know, where human beings marry, labor, and are served by their animals. That has been one way to define it: an account told as true, about the remote past, usually involving divine characters (Bascom, "Forms" 9).

Europeans define a myth thematically, as a story that conveys "information about decisive, creative events in the beginning of time" (Honko 50): the creation of the world, the creation of human beings, the origin of death, the acquisition of necessities like rice, and the loss of luxuries like God's presence. Creation myths around the world narrate such themes, inviting allegorical interpretation. In Madagascar, a true tale of something that happened in the past, whether in prehistory or the remembered past, has been inherited from the ancestors and is called a *tantara.*

Structure too defines this Merina myth, with its two stages. In stage 1, something we know to exist in the world, such as dry land, or humanity itself, doesn't exist; the myth narrates how it came to exist in stage 2. Or some essential custom like marriage does not yet exist, so the myth brings it into existence. Because the final state of things looks like the world as we experience it, we tend to believe the myth is a true story. Malagasy people tend to believe a *tantara* is true because it has come from the ancestors, the *ntaolo.* Folklorists are fond of saying the Lack has been Liquidated (Propp 53)—hardly the term for draining off all that superfluous water.

Then there is the other kind of myth, in the same class as the "myth" of the hyperactive child, or of the inscrutable Oriental. This one is so splendid that I don't interrupt it by commentary.

2. The Man-Eating Tree

"Carle Liche" 1880s

The Mkodos, of Madagascar, are a very primitive race, going entirely naked, having only faint vestiges of tribal relations, and no religion beyond that of the awful reverence which they pay to the sacred tree. They dwell entirely in caves hollowed out of the limestone rocks in their hills, and are one of the smallest races, the men seldom exceeding fifty-six inches in height. At the bottom of a valley (I had no barometer, but should not think it over four hundred feet above the level of the sea), and near its eastern extremity, we came to a deep tarn-like lake about a mile in diameter, the sluggish oily water of which overflowed into a tortuous reedy canal that went unwillingly into the recesses of a black forest composed of jungle below and palms above. A path diverging from its southern side struck boldly for the heart of the forbidding and seemingly impenetrable forest. Hendrick led the way along this path, I following closely, and behind me a curious rabble of Mkodos, men, women and children. Suddenly all the natives began to cry "Tepe! Tepe!" and Hendrick, stopping short, said, "Look!" The sluggish canal-like stream here wound slowly by, and in a bare spot in its bend was the most singular of trees. I have called it "Crinoida," because when its leaves are in action it bears a striking resemblance to that well-known fossil the crinoid lily-stone or St. Cuthbert's head. It was now at rest, however, and I will try to describe it to you.

If you can imagine a pineapple eight feet high and thick in proportion resting upon its base and denuded of leaves, you will have a good idea of the trunk of the tree, which, however, was not the color of an anana, but a dark dingy brown, and apparently as hard as iron. From the apex of this truncated cone (at least two feet in diameter) eight leaves hung sheer to the ground, like doors swung back on their hinges. These leaves, which were joined at the top of the tree at regular intervals, were about eleven or twelve feet long, and shaped very much like the leaves of the American agave or century plant. They were two feet through at their thickest point and three feet wide, tapering to a sharp point that looked like a cow's horn, very convex on the outer (but now under) surface, and on the under (now upper) surface slightly concave. This concave face was thickly set with strong thorny hooks like those on the head of the teazle. These leaves hanging thus limp and lifeless, dead green in color, had in appearance the massive strength of oak fibre. The apex of the cone was a round white concave figure like a smaller plate set within a larger one. This was not a flower but a receptacle, and there exuded into it a clear treacly liquid, honey sweet, and possessed of violent intoxicating and soporific properties. From underneath the rim (so to speak) of the undermost plate a series of long hairy green tendrils stretched out in every direction towards the horizon. These were seven or eight feet long, and tapered from four inches to a half inch in diameter, yet they stretched out stiffly as iron rods. Above these (from between the upper and under cup) six white almost transparent palpi reared themselves towards the sky, twirling and twisting with a marvelous incessant motion, yet constantly reaching upwards. Thin as reeds and frail as quills, apparently they were yet five or six feet tall, and were so constantly and vigorously in motion, with such a subtle, sinuous, silent throbbing against the air, that they made me shudder in spite of myself, with their suggestion of serpents flayed, yet dancing upon their tails. The description I am giving you now is partly made up from a subsequent careful inspection of the plant.

My observations on this occasion were suddenly interrupted by the natives, who had been shrieking around the tree with their shrill voices, and chanting what Hendrick told me were propitiatory hymns to the great tree devil. With still wilder shrieks and chants they now surrounded one of the women, and urged her with the points of their javelins, until slowly, and with despairing face, she climbed up the stalk of the tree and stood on the summit of the cone, the palpi swirling all about her. "Tsik! Tsik!" (Drink, drink!) cried the men. Stooping, she drank of the viscid fluid in the cup, rising instantly again, with wild frenzy in her face and convulsive cords in her limbs.

But she did not jump down, as she seemed to intend to do. Oh, no! The atrocious cannibal tree that had been so inert and dead came to sudden savage life. The slender delicate palpi, with the fury of starved serpents, quivered a moment over her head, then as if instinct with demoniac intelligence fastened upon her in sudden coils round and round her neck and arms; then while her awful screams and yet more awful laughter rose wildly to be instantly strangled down again into a gurgling moan, the tendrils one after another, like green serpents, with brutal energy and infernal rapidity, rose, retracted themselves, and wrapped her about in fold after fold, ever tightening with cruel swiftness and the savage tenacity of anacondas fastening upon their prey. It was the barbarity of the Laocoön without its beauty—this strange horrible murder. And now the great leaves slowly rose and stiffly, like the arms of a derrick, erected themselves in the air, approached one another and closed about the dead and hampered victim with the silent force of a hydraulic press and the ruthless purpose of a thumb screw. A moment more, and while I could see the bases of these great levers pressing more tightly towards each other, from their interstices there trickled down the stalk of the tree great streams of the viscid honey-like fluid mingled horribly with the blood and oozing viscera of the victim. At sight of this the savage hordes around me, yelling madly, bounded forward, crowded to the tree, clasped it, and with cups, leaves, hands and tongues each one obtained enough of the liquor to send him mad and frantic.

Then ensued a grotesque and indescribably hideous orgy, from which even while its convulsive madness was turning rapidly into delirium and insensibility, Hendrick dragged me hurriedly away into the recesses of the forest, hiding me from the dangerous brutes. May I never see such a sight again.

The retracted leaves of the great tree kept their upright position during ten days, then when I came one morning they were prone again, the tendrils stretched, the palpi floating, and nothing but a white skull at the foot of the tree to remind me of the sacrifice that had taken place there. I climbed into a neighboring tree, and saw that all trace of the victim had disappeared and the cup was again supplied with the viscid fluid. (Osborn 4–9)[2]

Chase S. Osborn, the American explorer-writer who purveyed this fantasy in 1924, refused to uphold it as true, but like me, he could not resist using "Land of the Man-Eating Tree" as the subtitle of his book about Madagascar. Perhaps he liked the *faux*-Poe style, which tells the reader how to react by adjectives such as "strange," "horrible," and "atrocious." Though in reality there's no such tree; though there was never a people called Mkodo in Madagascar; though the supposed writer of the story, a German explorer called "Carle Liche," and the Polish person he is supposed to have sent it to, "Dr. Omelius Fredlowski," are equally imaginary, the story does liquidate one kind of lack. Europeans of the 1880s needed a screen onto which they could project their fantasies about naked savages. Victorian readers liked to read that somewhere out there were savages with no religion and no social obligations, but the Empire had them under control. The story still arouses the ire of those who know Madagascar well. It is a "gross European falsehood," they bellow, "which scholars have had much difficulty in destroying, so great is readers' credulity and thirst for the marvelous" (Molet, *La conception,* 188). You wonder what Malagasy readers have made of it. Gross falsehood, anyway, is another definition of myth, anticipated among the contradictory English translations for *tantara* in the Malagasy-English dictionary of 1885: "A history; a tale; a legend, a fabulous narration" (Richardson 622).

In fact the *tantara* genre, like Lewis Carroll's little crocodile, welcomes little fishes—well, genres—in with gently smiling jaws. *Tantara* may narrate the origin of the social order at the hands of a demiurge, or the introduction of beef cattle by a famous eighteenth-century king. The smile of the genre welcomes definitions that seem contradictory: how can Malagasy not make a separation between prehistory and history? But *tantara* is a genre that will later allow genre-mixing, embedding, reduction, allusion, irony, and parody. All these are elements of the developing creole aesthetic, which characterizes the Southwest Indian Ocean islands today. Because Madagascar was the "hinge" or crossroads of Southwest Indian Ocean cultural history, its myths are the ancestors of other story forms.

The first to doubt the authenticity of a Malagasy myth was an embittered Frenchman, Sieur Étienne de Flacourt, who attempted a settlement in the south in 1648. When it failed miserably, and he'd left behind a stone inscribed *Cave ab incolis,* Beware of the natives, he returned to France to write the first important accounts of the island. He inherited the low opinion of myth that Greece bequeathed to Europe (Haring, "Pieces" 191). Summarizing a story of the Antanosy people, who lived near his settlement, Flacourt says he did not even want to include it in his history of Madagascar, because it was too propagandistic—something the upper class in the district imposed on their black slaves, "in order to humble them."

3. Origin of Social Classes

Antanosy narrator 1640s

It says that after God created Adam out of earth, he cast sleep upon him, during which he drew a woman from his brain. The Roandrian [a clan] descend from her. Another woman from his neck, from whom the Anacandrian descend. Another from his left shoulder, from whom the Ondzatfi issued. Another from his right side, from whom the great Voadziri, who are black, descend. Another from his thigh, from whom the Lohavohits come. Another from his calf, from whom the Ontsoa come, and the last from the sole of his foot, from whom the slaves issue. (Flacourt xxi–xxii; Leroy 106)

The social stratification that the myth explains was quite real. "A group had a higher social status," says the modern historian, "if it [was] closer in religion and genealogy to the Islamic stock," the peoples who had immigrated in the sixteenth century (Vérin 89). The stratification has not disappeared from modern Madagascar.

Flacourt saw another ideological mix: the Malagasy had remodeled the Qur'anic symbol system.

4. Origin of Human Beings; Expulsion from Paradise

Antanosy narrator 1640s

They believe that after God created the heavens and the earth and all creatures, he created Adam out of earth and put him in Paradise, which they believe to be in the moon or sun. After lodging him in Paradise, he forbade Adam to drink and eat, inasmuch as he had no need of it there. Yet there were four rivers—one of milk, another of wine, another of honey, and another of oil—and all sorts of fruits were abundant there. The devil, who was wily, said to Adam, "Why don't you eat of all these good fruits? Why don't you drink this good wine and this milk? And why don't you eat this honey which is so sweet and tasty, and this oil?"

Adam answered that God had forbidden him, and he did not want to disobey him, and more, that he had no need of any food in order to live. At this rebuff the devil went for a walk for about two hours. Then he came to find Adam and said to him that he came on God's behalf to ask permission for him to eat everything he might fancy. Adam, who was tempted to eat, ate his fill. After he had digested, the desire came over him to do his natural necessities, which he was obliged to do in Paradise. The devil immediately went before God to accuse Adam about his ordure. This was the reason God put him out of Paradise and sent him to earth. There an abscess came to be on his calf, which lasted ten months. At the end of that, the abscess opened and a girl came out. Adam sent the angel Gabriel to God to ask him what he should do with this girl. He told the angel to say that he should bring her up carefully, and when she was big and of age, he would make her his wife, naming her Rahauva—that means Eve.

After some time she gave birth to two sons, whom the wicked devil deceived, when they were grown, as follows. He gave them a spear or javelin tipped with iron at both ends and incited them to quarrel so that they both threw themselves on this spear, each one drawing it to slash the other. But as the iron points did not hold fast, they came loose when they were pulled and wounded both of them in the chest. They died of the wounds. These two brothers were Cain and Abel.

Adam had several children who propagated much, but as men became wicked and no longer wanted to know God in any way in the world, God sent the flood on earth and told Noah to make a big ship in which he would withdraw himself, all his friends and servants, women and children, and several animals of each kind, male and female. The whole earth and the rest of the animals were drowned except four mountains. The first is named Zaballicaf in the north, the second Zabellicatoure in the south, the third Zabilliraf in the west, and the fourth Zaballibazani in the east. On these, no one could be saved. When the flood was over, Noah came out of this ship, left it in Jerusalem, and himself went to Mecca.

God gave Noah four kinds of writings, which contain the laws. The first was called Alifurcan, or Alcoran, for Noah; the second was called Soratsi, for Moses; the third was called Azonboura, for David; and the fourth was called Alindzini for Jesus Christ, whom they call Rahissa. They say also that Jesus Christ was put into the world by God without being begotten by any man, born of the Virgin Mary, who brought him forth without pain and remained a virgin. Their name for her is Ramariama. That he was a man and a god and a great prophet, and that he was put on the cross by the

Jews. That God did not allow him to die, but that he wanted the body of a criminal to take his place. There are 4,444 prophets. (Flacourt 57–59; Leroy 94–95)[3]

A Qur'anic authority could unravel the strands of borrowing and creativity in this account, which foreshadows the mixing now called creolization. What might look internally dissonant was evidently quite coherent to Flacourt's informant, who told another origin story too.

5. The Seven Deadly Sins

Antanosy narrator 1640s

In old times the devil was married to a very bad wife, who gave him seven male children, who when they were grown devoted themselves to the vices. Among them there was one who devoted himself to pride, to despising men, and to a thousand wickednesses such as making poisons and spells to bring hail, rains, winds, cyclones, grasshoppers or locusts, and thunder, and spoiling all the earth's goods, and by this means to oblige men to recognize him as a god, though they well knew who he was. Another commenced to steal, rob, and lend at high interest, thereby ruining everyone. Another gave himself to all sorts of wickednesses and lewdnesses, abducted women and girls and enjoyed them by force or willpower. Another gave himself to envy, backbiting, and making up a thousand kinds of wickednesses and lies against honest folk, inciting quarrels, feuds, and fights, so well that by his evil spirit he set everyone on fire and trouble, being angry when he saw men in peace and at rest. And when he saw someone in prosperity, immediately he invented a thousand slanders against him to trouble his rest and prosperity. Another gave himself so much to gluttony that by his bad example, he provoked everyone to imitate him in his expenditures and gluttonies, so well that he was the reason everyone became a bad housekeeper and began to waste all his wealth in filling his stomach and incessantly getting drunk. Another became so angry that on any occasion, he killed and massacred these and those without cause, and instigated quarrels and fights among men over things of little importance; so that by his bad example and bad habits the habits of all men were corrupted, which has caused all the wars that there have been on earth up to now. Another was so lazy that he preferred to leave his lands fallow rather than cultivate them, and urged all men to do the same as he; so that all the Ompilampes or thieves in the Ompizées forest, who are savage and good for nothing, imitate him in such a way that the slaves no longer want to do anything, neither work nor serve their masters.

Thus young men imitated these seven brothers, and each according to his inclination was so attached to all kinds of vices and wickednesses that men, by common consent, deputized the angel Gabriel to present their grievances to God and pray him to deliver them from these seven hateful brothers. God said to Gabriel that he would allow men to destroy and exterminate them. Men surprised these seven brothers and killed them.

From this the devil, being in despair, went to find God and ask him for justice against the men who had killed his children. In deep mourning he asked God that he have the death of his children mourned and that he give him the means for this. God, knowing that his children were the authors of all wickednesses committed on earth, told him that men had done well to exterminate his children, and that it was the mother who had instructed and brought them up so badly who was the cause of their death. That all the same, he gave him the sea to weep for them. Since that time, the devil has always been on the shore of the sea, where he makes his dwelling, and the noise the sea makes against the shore is the devil and his wife weeping for their children. (Flacourt 60–62)[4]

The distrust of foreigners has never died in Madagascar. There's still something gratifying about the idea of throwing them back into the sea from which they emerged. By Flacourt's time, anyway, Madagascar had already become the home of a capacity for cultural mixing and blending.

The same kind of adaptation of scripture shows in a modern narrative. An aged, blind narrator of Betaindambo, near Toliara in the southwest, connects the origin of humanity with the genealogies of his clan's ancestors, and reinterprets Bible characters according to Malagasy tradition. He brings on Andriambilisy (the Islamic devil Iblis, long a turbulent secondary divinity for Malagasy) from the east, where the ancestors came from; prosperity should come from there. He brings on Jesosy from the west, the direction of obscurity and slavery (Gueunier, *L'origine* 55). After they exchange greetings appropriately, Bilisy claims "some people here" as his. Jesosy refutes the claim by showing him a crowd prostrated in the big house. Bilisy goes outside and begins to dance half naked. Jesosy grants him "the ones who look at you," so everybody who doesn't look up to heaven belongs to Bilisy. The old man appears to be spinning off an edifying tale in which Jesus and the devil dispute over human beings. "That's how it is: there are two kinds of people in church. The ones who sleep or talk all are the devil's; the few who listen to the sermon belong to Jesus" (Gueunier, *L'origine* 57–58). Bilisy's followers are too uncontrolled, while churchgoers are excessively controlled (Gueunier, *L'origine* 58n), so victory goes to the Islamic figure associated with the ancestors.

Flacourt was impressed by one aristocratic historical legend, which would still have been locally classified as *tantara*.

6. Rasoanor

Étienne de Flacourt 1661

This Rasoanor [Shining Beauty] was the only son of a very powerful and rich king. His father wanted him to marry the daughter of another neighboring king, who was very beautiful. Rasoanor refused this offer, as well as several other women he was offered, because he was in love with the wife of a great lord, king of an island far removed from that country, where she lived. He was so passionate about her that he decided to have several large pirogues or boats built, to go and see this lord, offer him his service, gain time to win the favors of his mistress, and wait for a chance to be able to take her away.

When his father was alerted to his scheme, he did everything he could to turn him away from it, advising him of the difficulty he would have in bringing it off, the danger he was putting himself into if discovered, and the evil he would do by wanting to carry out such a pernicious scheme. He had his relatives and most trusted friends speak to him about it; he made him other very advantageous offers; finally, as he could not change his mind, he had all the boats broken up and burned and forbade any to be made until his son would change his plan.

Nevertheless, Rasoanor still persevered with his intention. When he saw he could have no boat, he told his father that he would swim to the island where he dear mistress was. He warned his father, his mother, all his beloved kinsmen, and all his father's subjects. He notified them of the day, and came to the seashore with a large crowd of people to see him off. He took leave of his father, his mother, and his tearful relatives, promising them that they would see him come back with his mistress. He threw himself into the sea and swam to where he was nearly out of sight. A whale took him on its back and carried him for three months, all the way to that island, gathering around it a great number of little fish for Rasoanor to live on. He arrived at that island, where the lord received him cordially. After a time, he won the good favors of his mistress and brought her away in a big pirogue, accompanied by twenty slaves. They traveled along the coast as far as his own country, from which he had departed six months before, and he was received with open arms by his father and mother. (Flacourt 62–63)

The risk that the father is pointing to is the risk of dying far from home, hence being unable to be buried in the family tomb. The legendary whale shows up in coastal stories as a dolphin, who carries the hero Borahy to an island that bears his name today (Ferrand, *Contes* 145–46). In central highland narratives, ruling-class ideology sends many a legendary hero over the sea (evidently symbolizing the incest barrier) to win a suitable and exogamous wife (Ottino, P., *L'Étrangère* 9, 51–53, 334).

When narrators, in ensuing centuries, dictated myths on other worldwide themes, such as the invention of wood sculpture by Creator, they often showed unwillingness to commit to the truth of their story. Either in deference to their European audience or disclaiming individual responsibility, they would repeat the word *hono,* "they say."

7. Origin of Mountains, Valleys, and Stones

Bara narrator, from Betroko 1907–10

Formerly, they say, mountains, valleys, and stones did not exist on earth, which was covered with grass, rivers, and pleasant fruit trees.

One day, they say, the children of Creator came down for a walk on the earth. It was very hot; the children went for a swim. Later they continued their walk at pleasure, and suddenly saw, in the grass, a beautiful clay statue. They took it and wrapped it in green leaves to take it back to the sky. Seeing this theft, all the lands were unhappy. Several raised themselves to a great height and ran after the children. Others threw stones after them and made them fall.

This, according to the story, was the origin of mountains, valleys and rocks. The lands that arose into the air formed the mountains, and the stones became the rocks and stones which now are found all over the earth. (Renel, *Contes* 3:8–10)[5]

One narrator keeps repeating *hono;* another expresses his ambivalence by citing other, anonymous speakers.

8. Earth's Battle with Sky

Merina narrator 1872–76

Some of the old people, they say, when they are passing the time by telling stories, say this:

The earth, they say, went off to fight the sky. It called together, they say, all the soils and the rocks, they say, and they made bullets out of stones to throw at the sky. They fixed the time for the fight in the morning. The plain and the valley, which go slowly, they say, started marching. At noontime they ate, and so they arrived too late. The plain, the valley, and the mountaintop, they say, not being on the same level, could not reach the battlefield together, because they all had to travel different distances. So they say the earth and sky did not do battle, because all the different places on the earth are uneven. (Dahle 268–69)[6]

Whoever dictated this piece to Lars Dahle in the 1870s was as reluctant as the explorer Osborn to stand behind the truth of his story. He knew Dahle was a Christian missionary; he probably observed how eager he was to hear *tantara* rather than dirty jokes; he may not have known how accurately Dahle would reproduce those incessant repetitions. But the story has a moral: the impending battle is called off. By occupying different parts of the cosmos, earth and sky initiate the principle of social differentiation, which the narrator has been quietly asserting in his *hono*. Economic and social differentiation went hand in hand in old Madagascar, where one lineage group would become, say, providers of honey and another might provide fuel for fires. Within the family, a rebellious son insisting on his own space might disclaim any subservience to his father; this is the subject of the Earth Hero stories below.

Within a community, what shall be the criteria for leadership? Narrators distance themselves assiduously.

9. The Birds Choose a King

Merina narrator 1872–76

All the flying birds on earth (they say) decided to elect a king and commander. But the owl did not come (they say), for his wife was giving birth. All the birds decided (they say) that when they saw the owl they would not kill him, but they would treat him as an enemy.

The owl does not go around in the daytime, he goes out only at night. When birds see him, they attack and kill him.

It was the big hawk (they say) who tried to have himself named king. He could fill the part, but the crowd did not choose him, and he withdrew before a large number of rivals. When the big hawk sees a bird, he seizes it right away, for he is their enemy. A few, in fact, chose him as their king (they say). Then the widow-bird was chosen, because he is good-natured and has a large crest, and can sing in different ways.

People too (they say) think the widow-bird is the king of the birds. (Ferrand, *Contes* 49–50)[7]

Rejecting candidates who are nocturnal or overbearing, the birds choose the widow-bird, *railovy,*[8] who has the same reputation for high intelligence that the storytellers have: he can imitate bird songs and natural sounds. Bird-fable was another genre the missionaries could recognize. A century later, a university student passed one to me.

10. God Appoints the Cock

Rajaonah (Merina), Antananarivo 1976

Formerly, God used to dwell with animals and human beings. Yet one day, he said that because he was not like human beings, for he was a spirit, he had to go and live somewhere else. But before he left, he told the cock to stay and live with man. He punctured one of the cock's legs with a golden pin, took some blood, asked the cock to drink it, and said, "You will be the 'key of the day.' Every morning when the sun begins to rise you will sing and pull man out of his sleep. Man will take care of you and be kind to you. Every evening he will lock you up in a room and every morning he will set you free. He will give you food so that you cannot starve. In return, you will give him the eggs the hens living with you lay. Don't think that I shall disappear for ever. Every day, it will be possible for you to see my face on the ground and you therefore will never forget me."

The student could have read the myth in an old collection of tales from the Bara, of the south (Le Barbier, "Notes" 128–29), but he attributed it to his own highland Merina people. He ended much as the written text does: "[It] says that that is why a cock sings every morning. Why man takes care of him and eats eggs. Why a cock is most of the time 'working the land' with its legs. He is constantly looking for God's face."[9]

That student may have found his story fanciful, but he told it "straight." Sometimes in colonial Madagascar, the interview situation reduced the style of sacred narratives to a summary with no performance features, a kind of Cliffs Notes, which I could call "antinarrative" (Haring, "Pieces" 199). They did that even when recounting an innocent moment like the introduction of *Bos indicus,* Madagascar's most important animal.

11. Origin of the Ox

Betsimisaraka narrator 1907–10

The Betsimisaraka say that cattle were found long ago by an Antankarana king, in a place called Mann. These cattle lived in the sea and came out to browse on the shore. Sometimes they lay down and the place got the name *Bibiomby* [cattle animals]. They say it's in Diego-Suarez bay, a little west of Antsirane. The Antankarana king took a few of these animals and raised them. Then, when they had increased, he traded them. Among the Betsimisaraka, it was rumored that the Antankarana had got some new animals that were good to eat. Some of them immediately set off to buy some, and that is how cattle were introduced to the country. When cattle low, they go "Mann!" because they remember their place of origin. (Renel, *Contes* 3:87–88)[10]

The Betsimisaraka storyteller doesn't perform; he gives an abstract of the story. Another is even stingier.

12. Origin of Cattle

Southern Betsimisaraka narrator of Fatraomby 1907–10

Cattle first belonged to the *Zazavavindrano* [daughters of water]. They lived in water like their owners. It was the *Zazavavindrano* who gave them to human beings. (Renel, *Contes* 3:87–88)

Schoolteachers collected these unperformed "antinarratives" for supervisor Charles Renel; they were published, unedited, after his death. But not all explanations in colonial times were so parsimonious.

13. Two for the Husband, One for the Wives

Betsileo narrator 1887–1893

One day a man who had several wives caught a tenrec (the Malagasy hedgehog). He ordered one of his wives to roast it. When the meat was cooked, the man skinned it and said to his second wife, "Cut up the tenrec, it is cooked." She obeyed and made three portions.

Seeing this, his first wife said to her, "Let me make the portions. You do not understand how." She divided it into three, as the second wife had done. She took one of the three pieces of the tenrec and said, "This one is for the master. The second piece is for the master too; he will eat it tomorrow morning with his rice. The third," she said, "is for us two, his wives."

"A quick and fine way to share," said the delighted husband. (Ferrand, *Contes* 172–73)[11]

Nothing ambiguous about that, but nothing sacred about it either.

The capacity for maintaining two symbol systems at the same time was not invented by F. Scott Fitzgerald.[12] In religion, a Christian convert might reserve some credence for the sayings of the ancestors. "There were in the beginning only two persons, a male and a female, who were settled in a certain place in the world, most probably in Sakalava country," said one narrator to a Protestant missionary, who already knew this plot.

14. The Fall

Sakalava narrator 1890s

These two people were extremely happy, for they had nothing to do but sit and look at each other, and enjoy themselves from day to day. But one day they were visited by a curious fellow called *Do,* a big serpent. He said this to these two happy people: "Why do you sit in such an inactive manner? Is that the way to grow up to a life of comfort and fortune?" They were very much surprised at his question, but ventured to reply to the great orator that they were happy in their present position, for they had nothing to do but take care and abstain from certain things which were forbidden to them; for such was the law they had received from *Andriananahary.* But the serpent proved to them that those things which were forbidden were the very things that would make them extremely happy. So they listened to the serpent's words, especially as he sneered at their folly; and they transgressed the law they had received from God, and thus became bad in character. (Walen)[13]

The missionary didn't acknowledge that he and his colleagues had fed the myth into tradition in the first place. The laziness and disobedience of the primordial pair reveal that they are the ancestors of his Christian converts. By playing on the stereotype of the lazy native, the narrator demonstrates that capacity for conveying several meanings simultaneously which is so often found among African-derived peoples. In African-American studies, such irony is labeled "signifying" and is usually directed at someone present—in this case, the missionary himself (Mitchell-Kernan). In the Southwest Indian Ocean, the signifying that African slaves brought with them mixes European, Malagasy, and Indian traditions. It is an enduring tool of social critique, always relevant to class and power inequalities, and found in many tales in this book. One reader of this story observed, if "Adam and Eve's state as natives not interested in fortune and self-improvement is represented as virtuous . . . [then] the colonizer/missionaries who stir them up to activity are in fact the agents of the Fall" (Dorothy Noyes, personal communication). Anyway, this narrator's people would not accept the missionary's attempt to correct their theology: "If we were to tell the Sakalava that the evil dispensation was not from God, but from themselves and the serpent, they would reply: 'Well, but God has made us and the serpent also; the character of both is from Him'" (Walen). Religious syncretism was already an old island skill. By the time the missionary collected that story, a syncretic Protestant Christianity had established itself as the religion of many people, especially in the highlands.[14] The missionaries' collections, however, kept native and imported religions separate.

The first serious folklore fieldwork in the Southwest Indian Ocean began when Britain's London Missionary Society (LMS) posted men to Mauritius, then on to Madagascar (1820). The literacy they promoted made it possible for one of their graduates, a member of the emerging bourgeoisie, to write (at least in part) the manuscript of an elaborate epic (Dahle ix; Haring, *Ibonia*). Collecting flourished after W. J. Thoms invented the word *folklore* (1846), and the study of the new subject was blooming in France and Britain (Dorson). Between the return of the British missionaries in 1869 and the outbreak of World War I, collecting Malagasy folklore became the cultural part of subordinating Madagascar to Europe.

At this time too came the French Jesuit Father Callet (1822–1885), who began researching and writing down oral traditions in Imerina in 1868, four years after arriving in Antananarivo. Possessed of "all the qualities desirable in a researcher" (Delivré 58), Callet aspired, by collecting oral histories, to compose a true, objective picture of archaic Malagasy religion (Delivré 36–44). His attention to the beliefs of his prospective converts set him apart from many missionaries (Neill 192), though not from the LMS men. Like them, he used Malagasy words, sayings, and modes of thought in preaching. Vernacular locutions were especially appropriate to an audience largely drawn from the lower stratum of Malagasy society. The *andevo,* slaves, were turning towards Catholicism as the elite turned towards Protestantism under LMS influence (Gow).

As an editor, Callet did not hesitate to rearrange the ethnographic data he was given. (So the Finn Elias Lönnrot, a generation before, had assembled the *Kalevala* from oral sources.) Fortunately for modern historians, Callet did not comment on or interpret (they hope he did not tinker with) the dictated texts of oral history. The legends and oral poetry in his *Tantaran'ny Andriana,* Royal Histories, are as faithfully presented as the *anganon'ny ntaolo,* the tales of the ancestors. Taciturnity was his conscious ideology.

15. Ranoro

Callet's most famous narrative, a historical legend-plus-folktale rather than a myth, is the Malagasy counterpart of a European story: Mélusine, the fairy, married a mortal, on condition he would never visit her on the one day of the week when he might discover her identity as a serpent. He broke his agreement, found out the secret, and lost her forever. Both the Mélusine legend and Callet's story of Ranoro inscribe the origin of a clan. I summarize.

Ranoro, a lady from the sea or river, goes to a mortal's home, marries him, and becomes the ancestral mother of a clan, then immediately returns to the water when her husband breaks her taboo. Taboos against offending a supernatural wife are known all round the world, of course.[15] Ranoro's distinguishing characteristic is her foreignness. She comes from a family whose members cannot be seen or mentioned; even the commonest of words, "salt," a euphemism for their place of residence, cannot be spoken. "Salt lost in water does not come back," says a Merina proverb encapsulating her story. Because she dies in water, Ranoro has no tomb, unlike her descendants. Nor has she any family who might make demands on them in the present. By allying himself to this woman of no family, the symbolic ancestor has rejected normal kinship connections in favor of a contracted alliance, as if to say, "The sovereign has no family; he is above obligations of blood." So the search for a wife, the main plot line of so many European folktales, becomes in legend the assertion that for royalty, blood ties are of less importance than contractual alliances (Kent 294–95). The symbolism connects political life to the female body, like the Statue of Liberty in New York harbor (Babcock, "Taking" 401).

Taciturnity, objectivity, and containment characterized Callet's greatest Protestant contemporary too. So determined to preserve folklore was the Norwegian Lutheran missionary Lars Dahle that he spent four years (1872–1876) amassing materials for his modestly titled *Specimens of Malagasy Folk-lore.* This 4¼" by 6⅜" landmark of folklore study, printing nine genres of verbal art in Malagasy language, has the status of the sole manuscript of *Beowulf,* Percy's *Reliques,* or Bartók's ethnomusicological researches. Dahle must have been convinced that literacy would proceed far and fast and that oral culture was doomed, for his 457-page book contains only eleven paragraphs of English. For the sake of an audience who continually practiced ambiguity and double-entendre, he carefully excised anything "dirty" he could see. Since nearly all Dahle's informants spoke the Merina dialect (into which the LMS missionaries translated the Bible), the book standardized their language as classic. Callet and Dahle became classic Malagasy authors. Under the re-edited title *Anganon'ny Ntaolo,* Tales of the Ancients, the text was hardly ever out of print and was translated piecemeal through the years. The re-edition was finally translated in toto in 1992 (Dahle et al.).

Tantara on themes of the origins of the cosmos, human beings, or death presented the problem of sacred secrecy. Confronted with a *vazaha,* foreigner, who was in a position of authority, a potential narrator had an alternative to "signifying." He could decide that knowing is not saying; that the origin of his group is none of the outsider's business. To perform a story, he knew, would render it a "text." To degrade or undermine that rendering, which has been named "entextualization," and yet not directly refuse to answer questions, he could diminish or distort his performance. A slow, reluctant, or evasive answer could put a distance between interviewer and interviewee, and even withhold the information an outsider wants (Shuman 117).

Thus a storyteller could subvert the effort of a missionary like the Norwegian Emil Birkeli to "reveal to every European, administrative officer, colonist, or missionary the true Sakalava mentality, the motive of all the actions of the natives, the reason for their customs, and the basis of their primitive, rough philosophy" (Birkeli 186–87). Translations like Renel's Origin of Cattle reveal a fragmentary style which, like a pidgin language, has limited communicative function. It inscribes the narrators' artistic decision to be inartistic (Haring, "Pieces" 195–99). Against the effort by *vazaha* to understand myth in order to extirpate it, their poetics was a politics of cultural survival. Still in modern Imerina, as anthropologists vividly recount, information is a scarce good, not something to be readily handed over to outsiders (Keenan and Ochs). Even some of Dahle's texts are reduced in style (Dahle 297) and give only the feeblest impression of live storytelling. More than one of Birkeli's stories do the same, but some reveal poetic features of performance.

16. The Origin of Wood Sculpture

Sakalava narrator 1907–22

When Creator made men, the name of the first one was Ietse [There]. He did no work, but he had plenty to eat. What he did for work was to make statues that looked like him. He made ten statues; they were male statues.

Creator said to one of his women servants, "Go and marry Ietse."
"What if he will not have me?" she said.
"Here, take these ten gourds," Creator said.
"And if he does not want you,
uncork the gourd so the mosquitoes come out.
If he will not have you after that,
then uncork the second one and let out heat.
If he is still unwilling,
then uncork the third one and let out cold,
so that he will not resist you but will come close to you.
But if he is still unwilling,
uncork the fourth one; thirst is in that one,
so he will ask you for water.
But if he is still unwilling,
then uncork the fifth one and let out hunger,
so that he will ask you for food.
If he does not come then, and is still unwilling,
uncork the sixth one and let out the itch,
so that he will ask you to scratch.
If he is still unwilling,
uncork the seventh one and let out eye-mist
so that he will ask you to un-mist him.
If he is still unwilling,
then uncork the eighth one and let out boredom,
so that he will approach you.
If he is still unwilling,
then uncork the ninth one and let out loquacity,
so that he will seek to talk with you.
But if he is still unwilling, after all those things,
then uncork the tenth one, let out laughter."
The woman arrived on earth. Ietse did not receive her.
She uncorked cold; the man approached the fire.
She uncorked heat; he went into the shade.
She uncorked thirst; he chewed sugarcane.
She uncorked hunger; he cooked, so he would not have to eat the food the woman made.
She uncorked the itch; he approached a tree and scratched.
She uncorked eye-mist; he removed it with his hand.
She uncorked boredom; the man cut firewood.
She uncorked loquacity; he yawned.
She uncorked laughter; he pretended to be picking his teeth.
The woman went back and told Creator, "He would not receive me."

Then Creator ordered Ivelo, his daughter: "Go along and become the wife of Ietse."

When Ivelo got there, she turned into a rainbow. "What are you doing here?" Ivelo said.

"I am just here [doing nothing]," Ietse said.

"Where are you going?" Ivelo said.

"I am just going [going nowhere]."

"Come, I will be your wife."

"Very good." Then they got married.

When Ivelo saw the statues Ietse had made, she said, "I am looking at your work. But it touches me that they are only statues. I will go to my father and ask him to animate them." Ivelo went to ask, and she got a gourd full of life. She blew the life on the statues, and all the statues lived—all ten statues.

Ivelo had four children with Ietse. A long time later, she went home and divided the children. "The boys to you," Ivelo said, "the girls to me."

"All right," said Ietse.

The three women returned to heaven.

Ietse died, but his two sons married the children of the statues. They became kings. That was the origin of kings. When a person sneezes, they say "Ietse [*Etse*]!" or "Live [*Velo*]!" to recall the first parents. (Birkeli 346–49)[16]

This storyteller uses balance, antithesis, and symmetry to account for the creation of human beings by a pair of creators, the origin of both kingship and marriage, the engendering of human beings without incest, the necessity of marrying within one's rank, and even the ritual meaning of a sneeze.

At about the same time, another narrator varies the account of man's creation, forgetting neither the sneeze nor the politically correct image of God as the generous chief, which Africa exported all over the Southwest Indian Ocean.

17. Origin of Human Beings; The First Sculptor

Sakalava or Tsimihety narrator 1901–22

Long ago, they say, after Zanahary (God) had created the world, he decided to put a man there. He made one out of nothing, gave him the name *Live* [*velo*], carried him to earth himself and left him there.

At the end of some time, Live had been over all the piece of earth where God left him. He got bored with being alone and went back up to his creator.

"Lord, O God," he said, "I thank you for having created me and placed me on earth. Life there is easy and fine, food is plentiful and interesting, but I'm all alone there. I have nobody to talk to. I am very bored, and I would like you to give me companions."

"That is easy," said God. "I will give you some and you will be their king. Go back down to earth and with your *fitetika* [axe] cut some *sarin'olo* [human images] that look like you, out of tree trunks."

Live went back down and carried out God's command. But his statues were not alive, and he could not talk with them. He went back up to heaven.

"Lord God," he said, "what you ordered me to do is finished. But the *sarin'olo* do not move, do not speak, and I am just as alone as before. Give life to them as you gave it to me."

God answered, "I am willing to animate those *sarin'olo,* who are going to be your subjects. Take this *fanafody* [medicine] and sprinkle your bits of wood with it. They will come to life and speak." Then he went on: "Also, here is my daughter Atsihe, whom I am giving you as a wife. You will live with her and have many children by her. Once the *sarin'olo* are alive, they will marry among themselves. Their descendants will increase and multiply on the earth and become as numerous as the grass on the savanna."

God's words came true, and human beings became very numerous. But the earth became angry because everybody dropped all kinds of refuse on her surface. She complained to God, who brought all men together in a large *kabary* [gathering]. Then he said to earth: "Since men are dirtying you, it is just that they give you a recompense. Here is what I grant to you. When someone dies, he will be given to you. He will be your property, your thing, and you can swallow him if that pleases you."

Everyone applauded these words and found them just. It is since then that the dead are buried.

Kings and queens are the descendants of Atsihe and Live. When someone sneezes, he bends his head and says "*Atsihe!*", which means he is remembering his first queen. Those standing around will always say "*Velo!*" to indicate that her husband, the first king, must be remembered too. That is why Sakalava people always say "*Velo!*" when someone sneezes nearby. (Dandouau, *Contes populaires* 92–94)[17]

Malagasy agree that wood sculpture originated in primordial times (Renel, *Contes* 3:11–12, 17–18, 39–41, 89–91, 95–96, 97, 98, 119–21, 126–32; Dubois 1331; Faublée 344–45), and that creation was the work of two creators, who lie behind the mythology of the rest of the island. Is such material too secret to be fully performed?

18. Sun God Marries Earth

Bara narrator 1938–41

God got married. He went to earth: "You are great, I am great. Let us marry, us two who are great."

"I will marry you, but I do not want to leave people here, because their heads are getting burned."

"I'll send rain," God said, "and people's heads won't get burned. They will dig and work the earth. What are these people you are raising here?" He was speaking of human beings.

"What's it to you, asking questions about my people?" said earth.

"I won't hold on to them. Let us marry. You take half, I'll take half of those who sleep on earth."

Men die; their breath of life goes to God, their bodies into earth. God and earth divided human beings. That is why, when people die, their breath is taken by God, and people are buried in the earth–because they were made out of earthen dolls. (Faublée 344)[18]

"The story," says the collector, "is a truncated version of the motif that earth made statues of men, God gave them life, they argued, and each one took back what he or she had made" (Faublée 345).

This collector, Jacques Faublée, explains the truncation: "Practical necessities of transcription," Faublée writes, "obliged me to write the tales in artificial conditions: the narrator was alone with my Bara collaborator and me. . . . To judge the social value of these tales, I ought to have collected them by night, passing the evening indoors by the light of the hearth" (Faublée 4). Daylight and the absence of a proper audience made for a translation style that unintentionally seems, as one critic remarked of an American novella, "to be presenting us less with an object for judgment than with an example of judgment" (Johnson, B., 1052). Faublée's Bara texts, meticulously transcribed and translated, are as stark, bare, and ungenerous as Renel's highland ones. Fortunately they have much to say about the central importance of wood sculpture.

19. God Makes a Statue

Bara narrator 1938–41

God made a statue, he put it in the road. A man passing saw the statue and tried to turn it over; didn't succeed. Comes another man: "I see that thing, but I can't turn it over. Let's try to turn it." The two men tried to turn it; they didn't manage to turn it.

"We'll look for a lever at God's place, we'll make it turn over."

"Go," said one, "I'll stay here to watch it."

One left, the other turned that thing over. It got turned while the man's companion was away. The one carrying the lever came back.

"Where is my companion?"

"It's my wife," the other one said.

"What will we do with it?" the first one said.

"I'm not giving it up," the other one said, "because I'm the one who turned it over. You only saw it. Although you saw her, I'm the one who turned her over."

"Let's discuss it in front of God."

"I'm the one who saw her," this man said.

God didn't give it to him.

"Although he saw her," the other one said, "he couldn't turn her over. I'm the one who got her to turn over."

"The one who turned her," God said, "is her master."

That's the origin of marriage, because he turned her over. (Faublée 354–56)

The story hinges on a pun on "woman," *vali,* and "turn over," *valiki* (Edmonson 161).[19]

Generically this is a hybrid. It mixes a *tantara* with a dilemma tale. Ordinarily in Africa, the dilemma tale is an interactive game, a riddle posed by the narrator, which the hearers must resolve through discussion (Bascom, *African Dilemma Tales* 48). So also in Madagascar.

20. Repairing an Egg

Betsimisaraka narrator at Antanambao 1907–10

Three men met, they say, where three roads crossed, and asked each other where they were going. "I'm going to practice shooting," said the first. "I'm going to learn woodworking," said the second. "I'm going to learn thievery," said the third. They went their ways and did what they'd said. Having succeeded at their enterprises, they started for home and met at the same crossroads. They saw a *laidronga* [shrike] that had laid eggs. "Shoot at the *laidronga*'s eggs," they said to the shooter. He broke just one. "Go grab the *laidronga*'s eggs without her seeing you," they said to the thief. He went, but he broke them bringing them back. "Repair these broken eggs," they said to the woodworker. He repaired the eggs. When they'd shown what they could do, each one returned home.

Which of the three men was the smartest? (Renel, *Contes* 2:118–19)[20]

The audience is to judge among the three men. The mix of genres becomes clearer in a story that Renel, loyal to French tradition, called a *fabliau*. The characters' names, too unwieldy to translate, denote their extraordinary powers of vision, making magic medicines, and resuscitation.

21. The Three Brothers

Betsimisaraka 1907–10

Three brothers, they say, were out walking one day. The first was named Tarabemahita, the second Imananodiaina, the third Ifaingampandeha. They made their way northward and reached a big village where they took their meal. One of them, Itarabemahita, after he ate, took a few steps and, looking north, said to his two brothers, "Ah, brothers! I see a body over there, its head turned towards the south. Let's go and do what we can to bring it back to life."

Ifaingampandeha asked for the *odiaina* [life-giving charm] from Imananodiaina, and going ahead of his brothers, soon came near the body and brought it back to life quickly. The dead person's relatives were very happy and offered two oxen to the brothers. But dividing it was not easy; the three brothers argued amongst themselves. And you, what do you think? What share should go to each one? It was Itarabemahita who found the body, Imananodiaina who gave the *odiaina,* and Ifaingampandeha who succeeded in resuscitating the dead person.

The descendants of these three brothers became the *ombiasy* [diviners] and makers of *ody mahery* [charms, amulets] for the Zafimisana and Zafindrianambo. (Renel, *Contes* 2:111–12)[21]

The true Malagasy dilemma, an ethical paralysis between alternatives, is narrated as an allegory (doubtless it is many times enacted, too, in private life).

22. The Guinea-Fowl

Merina narrator 1872–1876

The guinea-fowl, it is said, went to visit his relations beyond the forest; but when he came to the thick of the woods he turned giddy and fell, and broke his wing. Then he lamented thus: "I would go on, go on, but cannot; yet if I go back, I long for my relations."

So that, they say, is the origin of the proverbial saying, "Guinea-fowl in the midst of the forest: go forward, he can't; go back, wing broken; stay there, longs for his relatives." (Dahle 298)[22]

The story inscribes a dilemma whose only resolution is in the words of the proverb. The concise, "packed" quality of this 1883 translation is about as literal as can be achieved from Malagasy to English.

In another mixing of genres, the dilemma tale combines with folktale, for instance in this modern example from the Comoros, which are always under Malagasy influence:

23. Four Brothers: Bunku, Mladje, Sumbui, and Laul

Maanli Fayadhinddine, Mayotte 1973–75

There were four brothers living in a village. They loved the same girl but didn't know it. The four brothers were adults, and each one wanted to marry the girl. One Monday morning, the eldest went to the girl's parents to ask for her in marriage. That was Sumbui. The parents answered he should get ready first, and come back on the fifth day.

Bunku came next. The parents told him to come on the fourth day.

Mladjé arrived; they told him to come back the third day (three days from then). As for Laul, he was to come back on the second (the next day).

The time went by and the four brothers, after eating, went to the girl's parents, taking different paths. They reached the girl's yard, each one under one wall. One of them was under the right wall, by the door of the room where the girl's parents were waiting for the young men. The mother saw this boy, called him, and all four came in together. They each sat on a chair and lowered their heads so as not to see the faces of the others. After a few moments the father said to the children, "There are four of you for my only daughter; I can't accept all of you. But I'm going to offer you a solution to help you, because I'd like one of you to marry my daughter. Take a long journey together and come back within three weeks with something interesting and necessary!"

The young men went home and asked their father for money. Then they went far away from their village. They came to four roads. Each took one and reached a small village.

Laul, where he was, met a poor man selling perfume. Laul asked him what this perfume was good for. "It can bring someone dead back to life!" said the man, letting him know the price. Laul bought some and took the road back. Sumbui found a mat that could carry people where they wanted to go. He bought it. Bunku bought a mirror that would tell its owner what was happening far away. Mladjé found a king's ring, which had been lost and was picked up by a poor woman. This ring protected against danger. He bought that as well.

The four brothers went back to the place where they separated, their hand under their shirt because they didn't want to show the others what they'd found. Then they asked what they found. The one with the mirror said to the others, "Come see! The mirror is showing that the beloved is dead!"

"Come sit on this mat and we'll get to her quickly!"

In a short time they were at the village. A group of enemies came to kill them. The one with the ring said to the others, "Get behind me!" He put the ring on his finger and the enemies disappeared. They hurried to the beloved's house. The one with the perfume put it under the girl's nostrils, and she woke up.

The girl's father asked what each one had found. Each young man said what he had and what it was good for. The father couldn't choose among them, and the girl stayed unbetrothed. (Allibert 86–87)[23]

A similar tale from Réunion appears in a later chapter.

These are *angano,* stories, rather than *tantara.* The fragmentary or truncated style of some *tantara* is an ideological statement. In the Caribbean, the attitude behind it has been called an "ambivalent acceptance-rejection syndrome" (Brathwaite 16). A riddler withholds information from his hearer; a riddler is often also a storyteller, who can withhold information from outsiders and guard the ancestral inheritance. Before many Malagasy became historians, family secrets and previously unexploited manuscripts were often talked up to foreigners. Sometimes no manuscript of genealogy or *tantara* existed; concealing it was a strategy (Raison-Jourde 13). Even a most patient ethnographer such as Philippe Beaujard has found a number of topics to be forbidden among the Tanala, who know and trust him: anything to do with slaves, any mistake committed by a forefather, any internal conflict. People tell him that the appropriate person was absent, or that they were not the right person to talk about that, or that the wrong people were listening (Beaujard, *Princes et paysans* 33). Tanala elders, he finds, act equally parsimoniously within the family: if the younger generation are indifferent to family traditions, they simply refuse to pass them on (Beaujard, *Princes et paysans* 28). A need for secrecy is a habit that colonized people develop and don't let go of even for a Beaujard. For colonial governors, secrecy is a matter of course and normal policy.

Myths of the Bara people, in their style so often stark, are a window into older Malagasy symbol systems. They provide a base from which genre-mixing and embedding become visible. The Bara are reputed to be simple. A culture like theirs, fond of bullfighting and other games of physical skill, is expected to be simple in economy and technology and low in political integration, whereas "cultures possessing games of strategy are at a higher level of cultural complexity" (Sutton-Smith and Roberts 332–35). But Bara are not averse to games of strategy.

24. Origin of the Animals, Creation of Various Species

Bara narrator 1913–15

In the beginning heaven and earth were one. Ndriananahary [Lord Creator] lived with man and the other animals.

At that time, all could converse familiarly with Ndriananahary about the conditions of their living, and they could ask him to make needed improvements.

But one day Ndriananahary . . . said to the gathered animals, "Do you want me to stay on among you, or would you rather be free to do what you like without me around?" They all told him he could leave; they were capable of getting out of difficulties without him, if they had everything they needed to live.

Ndriananahary agreed to what they wanted and separated sky from earth. Immediately the sky rose up, carrying Ndriananahary.

When he had reached a certain height, Ndriananahary told the animals who remained on earth to group themselves on an immense plain. They obeyed. He then ordered them to dig many holes at equal distances from each other, in two parallel lines. In each of the holes of the first row, he had them put foods: fodder, seeds, meat, fish, fruits, leaves, tubers—everything to live on. In the holes of the second row he had them put everything needed for covering and clothes: hides in one, feathers in another, wool in the third, *lambas* in the fourth, and so forth. Then he ordered each animal to choose its own food and clothing. The animals lined up: the ox chose fodder and hide, the bird, seed and feathers, the sheep grass and wool, the tortoise cactus, each following its own taste and needs.

God is playing a game with human beings. He has arranged the holes of a giant game board; the foods and clothes are placed like the seeds used in the game of *katra*. This game "has hundreds of names, dozens of versions of play, and is popular throughout Africa, as well as in parts of Asia, in the Philippines, the West Indies and South America" (Zaslavsky 118; de Voogt). Flacourt saw it in the south, in the seventeenth century; its strategy paralleled the devious behavior he complained of in the

Antanosy. In Imerina, it has sometimes been a women's game, though enjoyed elsewhere by both sexes (Decary, *Moeurs* 174). Cribbage it's not.

> It is played on a thick rectangular board, mounted on four low feet and hollowed out with four rows of eight holes. At each end the board is extended with/by a handle that is also hollowed out as a bowl. Sometimes the holes are actually carved in rock, as can be seen in the sandstone of the Isalo *massif* in Bara country. The seeds, which are gray and round, come from the *tsiafakomby* [thorn bush] or *voandelaka* [cape lilac]. Each player holds thirty-two of them which he places in each of his holes, by twos. The rules are somewhat complicated, and they vary. The game is over when one of the players has lost all his seeds, or when he is blocked, unable to advance, and "sleeps." (Decary, *Moeurs* 174)

Katra is a less complex game than the Merina *fanorona,* which has a larger board (victory in *fanorona* is described as "eating" your opponent) (Callet 1:276–78). But both can be drawn on the ground, as God does in the Bara tale (Chauvicourt 3).

When it was man's turn, only grains and fish were left. He was content to accept what fell to him as food, but instantly asked for the *lamba* as clothing. God granted him this favor.

When each of the animals was in possession of what it had to have for life and shelter, Ndriananahary spoke to them: "Now that you have got all you wanted, I shall leave you, and go away for ever. You will not see me again, and you will not be able to speak to me about things you need or ask me for changes in your kind of life. Once you have each chosen, I can change nothing.

"Here is what I have decided about you: You will always remain as you are today. Your descendants will look like you. They will have food and clothing just like yours. As to man, since he is more intelligent and strong than the other animals, he will be your master, and will be able to speak. All animals will be under him, and he can do with them as he likes. I even give him the right to kill any one that tries to disobey him. Moreover, to distinguish him from you, he will not wear clothes all the same, like the other animals. He will use his skill to make varied clothes in different colors and to improve his diet. I have spoken."

With those words, Sky rose very high into the air, and Ndriananahary disappeared from their sight. Each one went its own way to try to earn its living according to its wants and nature.

Since then, Ndriananahary never paid any attention to what men or animals said or did, and no one has seen him again.

Animals ought not to complain of the hard conditions of their living, since they freely chose their sort of life. Even man has not anything to say about that, having received the title of king of the animals and the gift of speech. (Le Barbier, "Contes et légendes" 129–31; Le Barbier, "Notes" 151–52)[24]

If people will just concede that the existing system is fair and stop complaining, the system of class relations will be maintained.

Katra is played all over Madagascar; *fanorona,* which requires more strategy, is Merina property. If the Bara favor a simpler game, are they therefore less sophisticated than the Merina, with their elaborate music and dances and their history of conquest, or is this race prejudice? The simplest tale structures in Madagascar appear among the Bara; is their simplicity an index of Bara culture, an unfortunate result of fieldwork exigencies, or an artistic decision?

25. Mr. Sun and Mrs. Earth

Bara narrator 1950s

Sun and Earth got married. The sun was the husband, the earth the wife. Earth brought forth many offspring; all living things came out of her. All these children got from her the right to eat among themselves, so they owe their existence to being nourished by living beings like themselves. But their mother did not want them to be mistreated, so she gave orders to all living beings. The advice was, "Be careful not to mistreat living beings needlessly or make them suffer for no reason," for we are all kinfolk, born from the same mother. Moreover, Ramasoandro our father [sun] sees our acts every day. (Michel 177)[25]

The unedited Merina myths left behind by Renel are just as simple as this, and other Bara tales are more complex. Any easy correlation between narrative and society is a delusion. Camille Le Barbier, poor fellow, was truly surprised, around 1916, to find practical common sense, natural logic, and acuity of observation in the stories (Le Barbier, "Contes et légendes" 119). He failed to remark on how concerned the Bara were over problems of authority, which his presence doubtless brought to their consciousness.

26. The Bat

Bara narrator 1913–15

Once God called a huge meeting of all birds. The bat sent ten of his children to represent him, but at length they failed to come home. Upset, the bat went to Creator, who disclaimed any knowledge of them. The bat therefore vowed that neither he no his descendants would ever again raise their heads to God. Back on earth, he also forbade his family to drink water, since water comes from heaven. He remained unrelenting despite God's remonstrances. That's why, since that time, bats hang from trees with their heads down; it's to defy God, who formerly tyrannized over their ancestor. (Le Barbier, "Notes" 132)[26]

Though Le Barbier saw in this only a simplistic morality (Le Barbier, "Contes et légendes" 120), the allegory is hard to miss.

An especially definitive Bara myth on the theme of separation sets the fly against God, surely the most dramatic victory of the weak since Tortoise vanquished Hare.

27. Origin of the Fly

Bara narrator 1913–15

In the beginning the fly lived in dark, moist places. Fearing dryness and wind, it went out only in the hot season, because it rains a lot at that time of year and the humidity is nearly constant everywhere.

In vain Ndriananahary ordered it to work. It always answered the creator, "What's the good of working? I only live on garbage and shit, and I find those everywhere with no trouble, and lots of them too. So why should I tire myself out to make a living?"

"Let be like you say," Creator said, and went back to heaven. That's why there are so many flies in summer, and pester men and animals at that time to get food. (Le Barbier, "Notes" 157)[27]

The *tsikotry* (egret), in another Bara tale, is more obedient than the fly and offers to mind cattle. "But in heaven," the narrator remarked, "there isn't much good pasture-land—it's mostly desert and dry rock—so the cattle began to run out of edible grass. Creator thus had to send the herds and the egret to earth." Thus did mankind acquire cattle and the egret acquire the color white, which Creator said would "'distinguish you from earthly herdsmen.' . . . That's why even today the egret is such a brilliant white and follows the herds to pick off their ticks and other parasites. He is continuing to fulfill the divine mission that Creator entrusted to him" (Le Barbier, "Contes et légendes" 142). When this tranquilizing piece was being dictated, twenty years after conquest, a surprising number of Malagasy were continuing to fulfill the mission the French entrusted to them, by fighting and dying in the Great War.

The same theme comes up again in an allegory of the social order, tailored to Le Barbier's position as adjunct colonial administrator.

28. Crocodile, Chameleon, and *Sitry*

Bara narrator 1913–15

In the beginning, the crocodile, chameleon, and *sitry* [lizard] lived in equality on earth. Wanting to acquire a superior rank, the proud chameleon betook himself to Creator, to ask to be made king of the reptiles. Not granting him this, Creator instead gave him the ability to climb trees, so that he could get food the other two could not reach. Upon his return to earth, however, he told the other two that Creator had in fact made him king, and that they had to submit to his authority. The other two, not content with this, agreed only on condition that Chameleon stay in the trees.

One day, Chameleon came down to lay some eggs in the sand. Crocodile and Lizard spotted him breaking his word. He went back to Creator, who said, "I never made you king in the first place. I'm coming down to earth to resolve this." Creator told all three, "Chameleon will keep the power I gave him, of climbing trees, but he will never be your king. He will live like you and work for his wife and family." The other two were grateful.

To mark the story ideologically, the narrator flattered his hearer.

That is why many people among the Bara want to order others around and take the title of *mpanjaka* [king]. But very fortunately, the *vazaha* [foreigners, Europeans] came. They freed the people from the tyranny of kings, and all Bara are now free and equal. It is thanks to popularity and education that certain Bara have acquired a rank superior to their fellows, for the question of origin and caste is now completely secondary, and only merit prevails. (Le Barbier, "Notes" 130–31)[28]

Like many other stories Le Barbier collected, this political myth helps to legitimate the system of colonial power by native symbols. Politics saturates even Le Barbier's animal tales, like the one about the deceptive burning game, a favorite trickster story in which rat gets cat burned to death (Le Barbier, "Notes" 121). In an import from East Africa, the kite carries off chicks to devour them, as the ransom for the needle once lost by their ancestor (Le Barbier, "Notes" 125; Finnegan 338–42). A third piece narrates the permanent rupture of friendship between the crocodile and the dog (Le Barbier, "Notes" 125–26). A bit of natural history, in a fourth tale, puts the ox and crocodile side by side:

29. Ox and Crocodile

Bara narrator 1913–15

Once the ox and the crocodile were water animals, like fish. At that time Crocodile had no teeth and Ox had no tongue, so when they wanted to eat, they couldn't. They betook themselves to Creator to ask for teeth and tongue. Creator was moved by their pleas and offered to remove some of Crocodile's tongue to give to Ox, and take out some of Ox's teeth to give to Crocodile. They agreed to that, and he carried out the double operation so each could have appropriate food. That is why cattle have no incisors in their upper jaw, and why the crocodile has a short tongue, which obliges him to throw his head back so as to swallow his food. (Le Barbier, "Notes" 129–30)[29]

When they are not adapting the breaking of friendship to describe their relations with the neighbors, many of the tales the Bara informants told Le Barbier are about the withdrawal of God's protection. Turtle and tortoise, for instance, lose Creator's protection because they disobeyed him (Le Barbier, "Notes" 138–39). In Africa, narrative is a path to oneness with God (Scheub xvi); in Madagascar, God has withdrawn from his creation and does not interfere with it (Linton). He leaves the animals to fend for themselves.

30. Master of the Earth

Bara schoolboy 1930s

The Bara live in the south of the island. They are one of the most famous tribes, well known to their neighbors for their strength and skill in war. The Zafimanelo are their kings. I talked one day with an old Bara man who gave me the legend of the origin of the superiority and royalty of the Zafimanelo. This is more or less what he said about it.

One day God called all men together to elect the king of their choice.

When everyone was gathered, God dropped various gifts into the middle of this large crowd: cattle, rice, bananas, jewels, gold, weapons, a bit of earth, and other things. Each man hurried to collect cattle, rice, bananas, jewels, gold, weapons, and so on. One man of noble stature humbly picked up the bit of earth, wrapped in an old piece of cloth, to the general scorn of the assembly. When each one had his prize, God appeared and commanded them to be silent. Then all at once, taking the gentleman by the arm—the man who had preferred earth to all the shining gifts—he said, "This is your king. It is he who will command you from now on. I give him more powers than any of you, men as well as women. The reason is that only he owns the earth, which he is immediately going to spread out over the whole rock you live on. Dry rocks will be transformed into fertile earth, where streams will appear and grass will grow for your cattle to feed on." (Decary, *Contes et légendes* 23–24)[30]

If Adam and Eve and the fly were justified in not working—if Malagasy facing Europeans were content to act out the lazy-native stereotype—a substantial number of other narratives feature a culture hero who is the epitome of assertiveness.

31. Self-Created

Sakalava 1907–22

Once, they say, there was a man called Self-Created. This man was not created by any other man, nor had he been created by God. He had created himself and came from under the earth. On earth, there was no rice yet. But for a long time there had been manioc, yams, and many other root crops, which served people and animals for food.

This world seems to be the one we know. If a myth takes place in prehistory, and a legend is "set in a period less remote, when the world was much as it is today" (Bascom, "Forms" 4), either the standard categories of folklorists are too simple, or a story like this, definitely situated between the two, must be a hybrid, a *tantara*. Mankind, in this myth, will acquire rice, surely one mythical theme; the acquisition will result from an Oedipal conflict, surely another. As in the Madagascar of today, the forest presents itself to this hero as a resource for him to exploit.

One day, Self-Created cut down a big forest and chopped the trees into small pieces. When the wood had dried somewhat, he made a huge pile and set fire to it. A great flame sprang up; the seasonal east wind blew it and it rose very high. The thick smoke was so intense that it ascended to the dwelling of the god of the upper regions.

The fire evokes an issue strangely ominous in modern times. People in Madagascar have always depended on forest products, but their consumption of trees has always incurred the wrath of those in authority. By inventing slash-and-burn agriculture, which came to Madagascar from Indonesia with its earliest settlers (Deschamps 22), the mythical hero Self-Created launches what western development experts call an "especially destructive practice . . . the annual burning of grass and brush in the west and in the central highlands of the island" (Wong). The high god doesn't like it either.

Irritated at the smoke, God said, "What is this smoke coming from earth?" He called, "Prince!"

"Here, lord."

"Go down to earth and see what is making this smoke."

"Yes, lord," and Prince went down.

When he looked, he saw Self-Created burning the wood he had cut down. He said, "Who gave you permission to burn the forests and make so much smoke?"

"No one gave me permission and I don't need to ask anyone. I took it. I am Self-Created. I am God; I created myself."

"You are God?"

"Yes, I am God!"

"Very well," said Prince, and went back up to God to let him know what Self-Created had answered.

The collector obscures the favorite device of *da capo* repetition by having Prince say, "Such, such, and such were the words of Self-Created."

"Is that true?" says God.

"Yes, truly," he said.

"Well, if he really is God, we will put him to the test and see how he gets on."

He called together all the other gods of the upper regions into a big meeting for consulting. And when they had deliberated well, God decided to drop a great rain on Self-Created and his fire. It was to last six months and be accompanied by dreadful lightning and thunder. He summoned the clouds, which hurried up, blocking out the sun. Rain fell in torrents and soon covered the soil. Lightning bolts streaked through he clouds; the thunder made terrible roar; the whole earth was overwhelmed.

But as soon as the first clouds appeared, Self-Created went into a big cave with a little of his fire and some dry wood to keep himself going.

The world becomes more and more as we see it today, thanks to the hero's development schemes.

Self-Created guessed God's plan. He improved the approach to his dwelling by making huge piles of earth with roomy caves inside. These are mountains today, like Andranovo, Ampomby, and Marangibato. The rain built up, in the places where Self-Created moved the earth, and it formed the lakes that are still near those mountains today.

As the narrator builds the case for Self-Created as both a *tompon-tany,* owner of the land, and a hero with magic powers, the world looks more and more like the one Malagasy know.

The rain did not touch him. He also performed the "weakening charm" against the storms, which were overcome by the power of his curses and went back up to God. "Why are you here and not there where I sent you?" he said.

"Oh," they answered, "we did go to Self-Created just as you ordered, but he made the weakening charm, he called after us, he took up the red cock, he took up the sword, and he buried the sharp ax in the earth. We had to be his friends, we had to treat him like a blood brother; we could not kill him."

God said nothing. He waited to see what Self-Created was going to do. As soon as the rains stopped, he began cutting down the trees in the forest again and chopping them into little pieces. When they were dry, he made a big pile and burned them. The smoke rose up again, with the flames right behind it, as far as God's house, and bothered him very much.

God again sent Prince to earth. He saw Self-Created again feeding his great fire and singing at the top of his voice in his joy at seeing the flame and smoke rise up to the sky.

"Look here," Prince said, "who permitted you to make a fire like this?"

"No one gave me permission," Self-Created said, "and I did not ask anyone's permission. I, Self-Created, maker of my own body, am the one who made this great fire."

Self-Created, always isolated, sustains his claim to stand outside society until God makes him his son-in-law. God can't be isolated either; later he will replace Prince with a team of emissaries.

Prince went back up to God and told him what he had seen and heard: "This, this, and this were the words of Self-Created." God was very puzzled. He did not know what to do to put a stop to Self-Created. He gathered all the other gods again for a big meeting and told them the situation.

"Look, this Self-Created on earth is resisting me; he goes openly against me. The smoke from the big fires that he lights comes up here and makes our eyes water. I have sent dreadful rains against him, but he hid in a cave with a little of his fire to keep him. I unleashed terrible storms against him, with much lightning and great claps of thunder, but he used the weakening charm and the storms could do nothing against him. What are we going to do with this obstinate person?"

God probably thinks lightning should be the only kind of fire. A cognate story depicts a victory by lightning over the flames of earth (Dandouau, *Contes populaires* 110–12; Molet, *La conception* 1:110–11). Some Malagasy see the fire in their hearth as a small fragment of the sun (Beaujard, *Princes et paysans* 274–75). Such a powerful symbol is inevitably ambivalent. "The gods who had been called to the meeting were old and wise," the narrator remarked. "They thought it over for a long while." Then they come up with a device for bringing both blame (*tsiny*) and retribution (*tody*) on the rebel. Since both *tsiny* and *tody,* as well as the mores of marriage, are already available to the gods (Andriamanjato), the world in the myth becomes more and more recognizable.

Then they said, "If we want to weigh Self-Created down, let us give him First-Wife, Prince's daughter, in marriage. And we will say these words to him: 'Our daughter, whom we are giving you in marriage, eats no food other than rice. If she eats any other food, dreadful calamities will come down on to you.'"

"Yes, that would do. It is well. That is what we shall do."

A food taboo establishes the most rigorous separation between members of different ethnicities. The theme comes in to all kinds of narratives: the *fille difficile* discovers she has married a cannibal, Ranoro's husband is forbidden to say "salt," and so on.

Immediately they sent for First-Wife, Prince's daughter. They put her most beautiful clothes on her, adorned her with her richest jewels, told her to get ready to marry a god who was on earth, and departed.

Still today, Sakalava women, like their Comoran neighbors across the channel, wear a great variety of local and imported gold jewelry. The realism of the thirteen bracelets, necklaces, and earrings which the translator appended to this text prepares for an even more realistic account of a formal marriage proposal. God's messengers open the dialogue with the pacifying phrases appropriate for unifying two non-mythical families of equal rank; Self-Created responds correctly (Haring, *Verbal Arts* 155–65).

When God's envoys reached earth, they looked for Self-Created. They found him in his house, sharpening his good axe so as to cut more trees in the forest. "Hello?" they said.

"Come in," said Self-Created. There were greetings, they sat down on a mat, tobacco was exchanged, and conversation began. "You have something to say to me?" said Self-Created. "Me, I am always sitting here as you see me. Oh, I saw those storms. Yes, they were really very fierce. And that great rain, ugh! I saw that too. But I, Self-Created, I can't die. And how are things at your place?"

"No, no," the envoys said, "we have nothing to say to you. We are here, we too, as you see. We did make that rain fall, but it did not spoil anything. We did send those storms, but they did not harm anyone. We did send someone, but our messenger came back saying, 'That is a smart man, a powerful man—really a god like ourselves.' So we come to see you, and we think that is good."

"Good, I thank you," Self-Created said. "I saw your messenger and I showed him that I am a smart man, a powerful man, a god like those who live above, and since you come to visit me, my heart feels much joy."

With that speech ended, the oldest of the gods went on, "But the reason we have come to see you is not merely to visit you or to take a trip. Our journey has another reason. And this reason is neither war nor argument. It is to offer you First-Wife, daughter of Prince, in marriage—for you are a powerful man, a smart man, a god like ourselves. Come to our place and we will give her to you."

The words in which the bride's family offer her to the hero, especially their instructions to him on her diet, reproduce traditional marriage negotiations between families (Haring, *Verbal Arts* 152–90).

Self-Created accepted the proposal and went up to the sky with the gods of the sky. The marriage took place. The husband and wife lived together several days in a nice house, and they were very happy.

After a week Self-Created wanted to take his wife home with him. God said to him, "Go, take your wife; she is yours. But you must know that our daughter never eats relish [food other than rice]. It is taboo for her. She eats only rice. If she ate anything else, great calamities would come down on her!"

When Self-Created heard that, he was puzzled. He had come out of the earth, and he only had as food what is found in the earth–yams, manioc, and various root crops.

Like other sky-women, the heavenly wife becomes her husband's ally against her father, mediating the opposition between heaven and earth.

He spoke to his wife, who said, "Do not be sad, my dear husband, for I shall do everything I can to help you. Here is how we will manage. You go on without me to get our house ready. When you leave, I will give you a hundred geese, which I will have stuffed with rice in straw. As soon as you get to our place, you will kill the geese, take the paddy rice from their gullets, and sow it just as you have seen done here, at my father's place. When the rice is ripe, you will come back and get me."

"Good," said Self-Created. "Thanks for your good advice. That is what I will do."

He went to find God and told him, "I am going home on my own so as to get a nice house ready for my wife. As soon as it is finished, I shall come back and get her." Then he left, taking his geese.

As soon as he reached home, he killed them all, took the paddy rice from their craws, and sowed it in a plot that was damp and already cleared. That work he did himself, for in those days there were as yet no cattle on earth to tread the ricefields. The rice grew very well; it got big; it ripened. As soon as it was ripe, Self-Created wetted it, cut it down in place and put the whole harvest into the granary. With that done, he went back up to God to get his wife. He let her go without saying a word to her. She came down to earth and brought with her men who would be her slaves, as well as cattle, sheep, and poultry.

A month later, God wanted to see if his daughter was happy, and if she was not eating relish. When he reached his son-in-law's house, he found him sitting on a mat, with his wife beside him, eating a big place of rice seasoned with fish broth. He was very surprised to see this rice; he asked his daughter where she had found it.

Having stolen from her father, she now lies to him. Mastery of language is a woman's forte.

"Oh, father," she said, "you allowed your daughter to travel far. But the rice knew that its duty was to nourish me, and that I could not live without it. So it got here before me. When your servants were carrying your harvest to your granary, some of it escaped through the sky. It fell to earth, on to the ground you see over there, and it grew."

Then God said, "I did not want to give rice to you. I was keeping it as food for myself alone. But since it has reached you just the same, keep it and cultivate it for the two of you and your servants. Since it has sprung up so well as to reach you, may it keep on springing, may it get scattered everywhere, may it spread, as long as you cut it, beat it, eat it, and may it be always in your mouth!" Having said these words, God went back up to the sky.

Then Self-Created said, "All men in the future will cultivate rice, and all will have to offer us the first fruits of their harvest. If they do not, they will be changed into wind, they will be changed into whirlwind!"

Only when the sky-god loses the struggle, and his daughter, does he reluctantly allow rice cultivation, thus tolerating human agriculture for the first time in history. The narrator concludes with explanation.

It is since then, they say, that men cultivate rice and make it their main food, for it is the main food of the gods, and it was they who created it. When they lack it, manioc and yams take its place, and that is an excellent food, for it was the food of Self-Created, who gave it to us.

And all those who cultivate rice must offer their first fruits of their harvest to God. They cook rice that is not yet fully ripe with chicken. When the rice and the chicken are cooked, they divide them into two equal parts, which are spread out on a banana leaf. One of the leaves is laid on the roof of the house; that is the offering to the sky god. The other is laid at the foot of the house, on the earth; that is the offering to Self-Created.

But also, since that moment, when rice is beaten in place, we see rice fly in all directions. It flies again when it is beaten in the mortar with the big blows of the pestle to separate it from the husks and the bran. And when it is cooked and put into the mouth, a few grains again escape and fall on the mat in the form of crumbs, in order to obey the orders of God. (Dandouau, *Contes populaires* 123–32)[31]

The conflict between a culture hero and the gods brings together myth, legend, and folktale in *tantara*. In a later chapter I translate a Réunionnais *kont*, folktale, which draws on this Malagasy narrative and combines it with a well known European tale type. In the closest Sakalava cognate, Ratovoana, "the uncreated one," creates wooden animals until Creator sends a great rain and flood. Not ignorant of how such tests can work, Ratovoana makes a big boat and shelters in it during the forty days of rain (perhaps influenced by a missionary's preaching). After passing two more tests of resourcefulness, he proposes a deal with God, seeing that one of them can make bodies and not life and the other life but not bodies. Creator sends his son for the prized ingredient, "thick liquid, white like *tembo* [sperm] of the coconut tree." Did the narrator really mean to say *trembo,* juice, as the collector thought, or had puns not yet been invented in 1907? The final arrangements: all the animals Ratovoana makes come to life and go to suitable habitats, and he and Creator agree that at death, each will take what belongs to him; burial gives Ratovoana back what he has made (Renel, *Contes* 3:69–74; Dandouau, *Contes populaires* 149–53).

No myth has been more often recorded in Madagascar than this of the separation of body and spirit at the time of death.[32] None has been such a dependable model for ideology, allusion, and adaptation. Ideologically it overcomes the contradiction between alienness and relation (*fihavanana*) which governs all marriages. Mythologically it functions as many narrations and agrarian rituals do, "to collapse the past into the present, re-creating . . . the very conditions that led to the existence of the present community" (Ottino, A. 118).

In Sakalava country, on the northeast coast, where the tale of Self-Created was told, storytellers have long taken advantage of the adaptability of *tantara,* for both history (Feeley-Harnik, *Green Estate* 67–68) and fiction. In the first decade of the twentieth century, the region of Analalava (Longwood), where André Dandouau recorded that piece (1901–10), comprised some 88,000 Sakalava and Tsimihety people. He evokes the aura of a typical storytelling event of those days:

> It is the hottest time of day. Men shelter under a platform covered with leaves and mats, the *fantsina,* to smoke or nap. Here, some play cards. There, others play the board game *katra.* A storyteller begins to speak. The games stop, the sleepers wake up, heads go up, and the men group themselves in a circle around him. When he has finished, he passes the word to another with the formula "*Raha tsy marina izany, tsy zaho mavandy fa Rantaloha,* If what I say isn't true, it is not I who lie but the ancients. *Izay tsy mamaly zeny, may sikiny!* The one who does not answer that, let his clothes burn up." And immediately another story begins. The storyteller's tone and delivery are enhanced by his intonation: some words he says through his nose, others he draws out at the end. A good storyteller is an accurate imitator who makes fun of people's mannerisms and behavior. Though his in-jokes and local references are lost on a visitor, they are appreciated by his attentive audience. Some famous old performers (*mpitantara,* historians) can hold that audience through a whole afternoon. If tellers or audience become tired, they go into riddling, which all can participate in. If a new riddle is posed, and then someone produces a new answer for it, everyone laughs, exclaims, and stirs—and then there is much high-spirited discussion and debate about it. (Dandouau, *Contes populaires* 11–12)

Dandouau caught the variations of pitch, pace, and intonation which link Sakalava performers to their colleagues in East Africa and the Comoros. One told him an *angano,* framing it with a bit of *tantara* from the book of Job.

32. The Ungrateful Beast

Sakalava or Tsimihety 1901–21

God [Zanahary] and Man were inseparable friends. One day, God said to Man, "Go roving about the earth and find us something new to talk about."

Once Man the species leaves God's presence, he becomes the representative man and a folktale hero.

The man left and arrived near some big rocks surrounded by tall trees. Some of the trees had been leveled by fire, and between two trunks, a huge *Rakakabe* [Big Beast] had got caught. The fire was consuming the trunks little by little, coming closer to the monster, who was shrieking horribly. The sight of such danger inspired the man with pity. With much effort he managed to separate the trunks and free the *Rakakabe*—who now said, to reward him, "My friend, I am very hungry, I'm going to eat you straightway." Hearing these words, the man quietly answered, "My friend, you are not worth doing a favor for, you deserve to be punished. Without me, you would be dead, burned alive under those tree trunks that were holding you prisoner."

The animal got angry and said, "Who are you talking to so insultingly? I'm going to really chew you up, accursed man!" And he got ready to throw himself on him. But the man defended himself, saying, "Why do you want to eat me? I have never done you any harm, and I just saved your life. Let me go on my way looking for news, as Zanahary has ordered me to."

"No, no, I'm not crazy enough to let you go, now that I have hold of you."

"You are not right to act so, and no one who knows about it will fail to blame you. If you please, let's keep on going towards the south, and we'll take those we're going to encounter as witnesses. We will listen to their opinion." The *Rakakabe* finally agreed and they started out.

Dandouau's anonymous narrator practices a favorite technique of island storytelling, which can be called *da capo.* Man must make his case to the three witnesses (vegetable, animal, and human) by narrating the incident from the beginning. In Grande Comore, *da capo* is a habit of Comoran narrators: if interrupted, they will run back to the top and start again, as they were taught in Qur'an school.

They came upon a big tree with thick, fresh foliage. The man said to it, "O tree, I must tell you that having been sent by my friend Zanahary to rove about and go in search of news, I saw Rakakabe here, caught between two tree trunks which had been brought down by fire, and in great danger of death. Taken by pity, I pulled him out of this bad place. Once he was free, instead of being grateful to me, he wanted to eat me, saying, 'I'm going to devour you, I'm going to eat you!' "

[Rakakabe:] "You know that for three days I stayed under the tree trunks without eating. I'm hungry and I'm swallowing you today, without chewing."

"I see no objection to that," said the leafy tree. "Look, I am this leafy tree under which everybody takes shade. Nobody passing near me forgets to take shelter under my foliage. They are very happy to rest there. And yet, before leaving, they cut my branches and make deep wounds in my trunk, so that sap flows out abundantly. I only do them good, they answer with evil."

Hearing that, Rakakabe was very happy and got his teeth ready to eat the man, who was very afraid but said, "Our journey is not yet at an end. Let's go on some way, maybe you will change your mind."

"No, no, you must no longer think you are of this world, you are dead, 'Fat-good-to-eat!'" But he begged him so much that Rakakabe allowed himself to bend, and they continued on their way.

They met a big ox browsing by the side of the road. The man said, "Ahh—sir? Ah, sir!"

"*Aaaa,*" said the ox.

"Listen to us a little, for we have something to say to you." When they got close to him, the man continued, "God sent me to earth to fetch news to tell him. On the way I noticed this Rakakabe caught between two tree trunks leveled by fire. It pained me to see him in danger, and I separated the two trunks holding him prisoner. When he was loose, instead of thanking me, he wanted to eat me. 'My friend,' he said, 'I'm eating you today in one mouthful.' "

"Yes, it's really too bad for you, younger brother," the ox answered, "but only look at what happened to me. When the rainy season came, they made me tread the rice-fields by hitting me with big sticks. My whole body was sore, my skin was spotted with bruises. In time of drought, for all happy or unhappy circumstances, for *fêtes* as for funerals, we are killed to be eaten. Our milk is taken. We are separated from our children, who are put to death or sold, without ever taking account of the services we render. Most men on earth do ill to those who do good to them!"

That may not be news to God.

Rakakabe was very happy to hear these words, which authorized him to eat the man. He was very unhappy and saw himself lost. Still he begged him to wait again a bit. The animal said to him, "You ask me too often to wait. I do not want to go farther, and I am going to eat you now."

"Don't do that, elder brother, let's go ahead a little towards the south. We don't have too far to go, and when we have reached, you will eat me if you still desire."

Rakakabe agreed again. After a few moments, they met someone who had been counting his cattle.[33] The man addressed himself to him and said, "I have been charged by God to go and learn the news, to talk about with him. On the road I found this Rakakabe on some big rocks. Some tree trunks, brought down by fire, were crushing him. I took pity on him and separated the tree trunks that were restraining him. But when he was delivered, he wanted to eat me!"

"Is this really true, Rakakabe?" said the other man.

"Yes, that is right, and I still want to eat him, for I am very hungry!"

"If that is it, we are going to go back to those tree trunks. I can only judge fairly if I see well how things happened."

"So, let's go," said Rakakabe.

All three reached near the big rocks. "There, those are the big tree trunks that held you?"

"Yes, that is them!"

"Oh, Rakakabe!"

"Waaa!"

"I don't quite see how you were placed between the trunks. Try putting yourself as you were before, so I can judge." The animal, without thinking, put himself between the trunks, and the two men united their efforts to pull them together as they had been before.

"Move a little," they said.

He tried to budge, but it was impossible.

"Are the tree trunks squeezing you as before?"

"Yes, yes, but you are making a long story out of a short one, friends. Pull me out of here, for I'm hungry and it's a long time since I should have had the good meal that was offered to me."

"Fool! Are we your slaves, that we should extricate you from those tree trunks! Stay there where you are, since you are back in there. We will come back to see you when you are dead and cooked! You did not recognize us. With your inferior ideas and limited intelligence, you were trying to triumph over us. You are a great fool, and we are leaving you to die there."

And the two men went and did not come back. (Dandouau, *Contes populaires* 366–71)[34]

In antiquity, this story of The Ungrateful Animal Returned to Captivity may have been disseminated by a cheap printed collection from India (Thompson, *Folktale* 218). Orally, through the centuries in East Africa, which sent many slaves through Madagascar, it proved a useful allegory of social hierarchy (Macdonald, *Africana* 346–47). The mythical frame is a microcosm of Malagasy secularization.

So is another international tale, recorded not far away and not much later. The missionary collector should have remembered the Grimms' Goose Girl (no. 89), in which a chambermaid forces a princess to change clothes and places with her (Aarne and Thompson 191; Grimm and Grimm 322–27).

33. The Girl Entrusted to a Servant

Tsimihety Mid-1920s

Once a woman went a long time without going to see her parents. She had a daughter who could speak well; she decided to send her to her uncle and to have her accompanied by a slave, who was charged with helping her and carrying her when the road became too difficult. She put beautiful clothes on the girl, loaded her with riches, and sent her off with the slave. But on the way the slave would not help or carry the girl unless she gave her some of her clothing or the ornaments she wore. The slave repeated her demands so often that the girl had nothing left, and the slave had to give her a rag to cover herself. At the end of the trip, the slave deceived the people and, in front of them, she refused to be Ikalo's slave. Everyone was surprised, but the uncle gave the girl a new slave, and they waited to see what would happen.

It was then that time when the rice was ripe but not yet cut. Ikalo and her new slave were sent to watch over the rice and chase away the *fody* birds. One of the *fody* began to speak: "*Oso fody oso* [Away, birds, away]! The mistress has become a slave and the slave has become master!" The slave was surprised, and when he came back with the girl, he recounted what he had heard. The uncle was astounded. He himself went to hear the *fody* sing "*Oso fody oso,* the mistress is a slave . . ."

Then he called everyone together. It was necessary to have a divine judgment [*ordalie*], which would reveal the truth. Either the girl or the slave was lying. The uncle had a long rope stretched out and asked in his invocation to Zanahary that he show what was the truth. The true noble would be the one who could not jump over the rope. The slave came, jumped, jumped again. She could jump very well; she happily continued jumping, without ever falling. She thought that jumping would liberate him from her thefts, for certainly the girl wouldn't jump like her. When the girl's turn came, her feet were numb; she couldn't even lift them. The uncle understood Zanahary's sentence, and the guilty one was condemned. Ikalo got her riches back. (Rusillon 224–26)[35]

"The slave is lost by the force of her interpretation," the collector writes, "but also by her need to affirm that she is in the right. That for the Tsimihety is the comedy in the story. All ends well because Zanahary reestablishes things. The narrator enjoys his effect; the hearers experience the satisfaction of their powerful sense of justice; their sympathy passes from the unfortunate slave, who has become worse than her masters, to the little spoiled girl. And the whole story will be discussed at length" (Rusillon 226). It carries social messages as potent as any myth.

When Comoran storytellers (only 300 kilometers distant) perform this plot, they bring the symbiotic relationship between mothers and daughters into the foreground. Often in their stories, a young orphan girl is mistreated by a female character of lower rank; she may die, really or symbolically; then she is recognized and restored to her high rank when her dead mother (or both parents) supernaturally intervenes. Globalizing influence remolds this plot so that the servant becomes less important. Instead the girl's mother dies, her father remarries, and the villain is a stepmother. Evidently this family dynamic, so familiar in European folktale, corresponds more closely to the internal tensions of present-day society, at least in Mayotte (Blanchy, "Lignée" 44). Mauritius inherited a related plot from India, equally class-related, in which a maid takes the princess's place as she is about to remove the last needles from the eyelids of a sleeping prince. Reduced to menial work, the true wife obtains a black wooden doll to which she sings her story; she is recognized and united with her prince (Ramsurrun 23–28).

A culture-hero narrative such as Self-Created takes a long time to perform. Neither the terseness of Bara storytelling style nor the curtailments of Jacques Faublée's daytime sessions could do much to shorten "Tinaimbuati and God."[36]

34. Tinaimbuati and God

Bara narrator 1935–38

When Tinaimbuati [Not Created by God] was born, he spoke; when he was born, he had teeth. He walked the day he was born, he spoke and walked: "I was not made by God," he said, "for I made my body."

Denial of any family dependence, the first characteristic of these Malagasy heroes, equals provocation. God's messenger tells him, "Look at human beings. He made them all."

"When they are born from their mother," Tinaimbuati replies, "they walk at five months, at six months they start to walk and fall, after a year they walk well. That's not my way. I walked as soon as I was born." That's enough to send the messenger back to God, who imposes tests that allude to other Malagasy symbols. First, God turns three hornless cattle into three generations of heifers; in Imerina, a "mysterious cow without horns had neither owner nor family" (Renel, *Contes* 1:35). The hero must tell them apart, a safeguard against incest that qualifies many a hero (Renel, *Contes* 3:19–21, 69–74; Faublée 433–35; Renel, *Contes* 1:65–76). God concedes that this fellow is very clever, but only then is it revealed that these have been suitor tests. "Will you get God's daughter?" the messenger asks. "It'll be good to get her," he answers. "If I don't get her, she'll stay there. I won't be punished for going for her. I've never sought a wife; not to have got her will be shameful."

Then the Bara storyteller takes his hero through another folktale plot, The Grateful Animals, as popular in Madagascar as everywhere else (Lombard; Haring, "Grateful Animals"). Aided on his journey by a magic charm that flies him to the upper world (as Borahy's dolphin transported him to fetch his bride), Tinaimbuati rescues some fish from drying out. They, a mason wasp (*faraki*), and some termites all offer to help him, saying, "What you do to people they will do to you." They aid him to pass God's suitor tests: the termites eat down a huge tree, and the fish recover a silver bar from under water. "There's what you sent me to get," he says. "It's found."

"You didn't create him," people said. "You sent him to get all kinds of murderous things; he got them all."

"We will go back, I and my wife, for what you told me to do is finished."

Here the genre shifts toward *tafasiry,* a story told for entertainment.

"There's still one little thing stopping you from going. My *pirog* is there, it's cut, but it isn't hollowed out all the way. When you finish that and it's open, you can go."

But that was a stone he had cut, which he was calling a *pirog,* and which he told him to hollow out.

If God wants to play ogre, Tinaimbuati, unaided now by his magic charm, is ready with a "counter-impossible obligation."

He made a basket in the shape of a jug, with a neck and a spout. "Have God come here to get me some drinking water, for I am thirsty from fitting his *pirog* [canoe]."

"Here is my jug, lord, go get some water, for I am thirsty. How is this *pirog* of yours made? It's not getting done quickly. Go get my water, and don't lose any, for this is going to get finished."

God filled the thing up. When he picked it up, the water ran out. "Bring my water quickly, I'm thirsty, and your *pirog* is going to get finished. You're only enjoying yourself there at the edge of the water."

"Enjoying myself? I'm drawing your water, but I can't manage to carry it in this hollow thing. I'm leaving it here, how can I carry water [in it]?"

"I'm terribly thirsty, if you can't bring water I'll leave this thing and it won't be finished. It's stone," he said. "You are tricking me. If you manage to carry water, I'll finish fashioning this stone."

"Go back to the village," said God,

who begins to look even more like a stupid ogre when he pursues the departing couple with lightning. Tinaimbuati, as defiant as ever, mocks God by disguising his body to look like a woman's. Falling for the deception, God kills his daughter and has to resuscitate her. "I am not dead, God, I am not dead!" Tinaimbuati shouts, like a trickster. God turns pharmacist when "life," a bottled liquid, gets spilt on the way home; asked for more, God ordains,

"When your wife is giving birth, take the trees where the 'life' got upset, take them and have her drink them, and make an ointment for your child. It will make him live. It is the water where the 'life' got poured out. When your child is ill, scatter the water towards me here and that'll be your life."

The story ends when Rahinu, about to give birth and discontented with her husband, returns to her father's.

Tinaimbuati was sick with sorrow. Someone came. "Friend, does Rahinu come from here? Something happened there, I don't know what, something that scared me." That's the origin of our saying, "*Rahinu ini,* What's this?" (Faublée 435–49)[37]

The hero's precocity, his challenge to God, and his reliance on an *ody* (charm) are myth elements; the search for a wife who is finally found, the suitor tests, the donor role played by the charm Matahula, and the use of a punning proverb as a formula for ending the piece and re-entering the everyday world—all these are folktale elements. The punning proverb, by the way, is another African device (Bascom, *Ifa Divination* 130). Here *Rahinu ini* means both "What's this?" and "Is it Rahinu?" (Faublée 449). As to belief, the collector is ambivalent: the Bara narrators believed their own stories, he says, but they carry little affective force and "are only rarely associated with man's deepest desires" (Faublée 509). At least in the daytime.

The rebellious hero, however, lurks behind many Malagasy narratives.

35. Looking for Trouble

Sakalava 1907–22

There was once a man who had three children, and one of them was called Youth [*Zatovo*]; he was the eldest. When he was grown, he said to his father, "I've heard, papa, that there is something called 'trouble' and I want to find this trouble and know what it is. Tell me, papa, where to find it, for I want to go look for it."

"Oh, oh," said his father. "I am a dead man. My child is looking for trouble!"

The quest structure of Self-Created surrounds a sequence of trivial adventures with mythical overtones. The youth will pass tests of mastery over insects, reptiles, and wild animals.

"Don't say that, father. As for dying, it's not you who is looking to die. I am the one looking for trouble," said Youth. "And where is this 'trouble'?" His father answered him, "If you are looking for trouble, go play with red honeybees."

Youth set off with his two brothers. They went a long way, for they really wanted to find what they were looking for. Then they saw it and took it. They went back, but those honeybees followed them. They came back to the village and put down the honey for the people there, but the bees stung the people. People said, "Trouble like this, who brought it to us?" And the king scolded him for bringing it. "That's not trouble," said Youth. "It's only a fierce animal." "Yes," the people said, "it *is* trouble. It should never come back to our village."

"Tell me another trouble, papa, because that wasn't trouble!" He went to the fields with his father. As they were coming back, he stepped on a snake. "Ay-day," said his father, "my child will find trouble all right. He stepped on a snake. How will we find a doctor? We are in for big trouble."

"We don't need a doctor, papa, it's only an animal I happened to step on as we were walking. I am the man looking for trouble," he said, "and where is this 'trouble'?"

"If you seek trouble," his father said, "then go kill the white boar."

"Good," said Youth, "now that's what I want."

When the cock next crowed, Youth got up, took three hemp bushes, gave them to his mother, and said, "See those bushes? I am going to hunt the white boar, and if they are shaking, I am fighting him."

"Good," said his mother, "but be careful this time. It means real trouble and it is looking for death."

Youth went with his two brothers, and in the middle of the day they saw the tracks of a hundred boars. Later, the younger two saw and cried, "Here are the white boar's tracks!"

"How do you know?" said Youth.

"It's the white boar for sure, because his belly drags the ground."

They followed the boar's tracks, then killed an ordinary boar for food, and as night was coming on, they went to sleep. At break of day they set out again and looked for the white boar's tracks. And there they were. His belly dragged the ground like a barrel. They found the white boar among a thousand boars, but night came. They went after him, but they couldn't catch up with him. They again had to go to sleep, and when day came they took up the pursuit again. Finally at midday they saw him and went for him. The shrubs started shaking, and his mother did the chant,

> Shaking, shaking are the hemps
> In danger, in danger are my children

The white boar defended himself furiously, and at the end of the day only six dogs were left. (They brought thirty dogs.) Then Youth climbed a tree and threw the spear called Big Tree [named for the wood] and killed the boar.

The three men hauled the boar's body back, but all the other boars were weeping for the white boar, and the ground reverberated where they trod. When they brought the white boar into the village, all the boars came in with them. "Hey," said the people, "what is this? Trouble is coming on us," they all said. "The boars do not usually come into the village in the daytime! This is real trouble, and what confusion!" But soon they all heard that Youth had killed the white boar and that the crowd of boars had followed it weeping.

Instead of the reward or high rank a successful folktale hero would expect, the young man is accused of challenging royal authority.

The king got angry when he heard about it and ordered Youth before him. So Youth came, and the king spoke to him and said, "What is this, Youth? What trouble have you brought in here today?"

"I," Youth said, "am looking for trouble, and when there is something people think is trouble, I go after it."

"I hate that," said the king, "and it is not done in my country because I hate it. You will pay a forfeit of a hundred cattle and ten slaves. Quick, do it now."

"I thank you," Youth said, "for not taking my life." And Youth paid the forfeit of a hundred cattle and ten slaves. Then he said, "That surprises me. I still don't see 'trouble.'"

"That was trouble," his father said. "There is no bigger trouble than that. You are really a surprising person. This looking for trouble is going to kill you, and won't that trouble do for you? I do not see any other trouble to show you."

"Well, as you do not see any trouble to show me," his son said, "I will go see where the day is born. Maybe there I will get a surprise or find some trouble."

But the quest to the upper world is intercepted.

Then he said to his mother, "Please cook me eight loaves of bread, because I am leaving early in the morning." Next time the cock crowed he put his loaves in a basket and left.

At the end of the day, he met God's son and asked him, "Where are you coming from, friend, and where are you going?"

"I am looking for my goats," God's son said. "But you, where are you going, then, and what are you carrying in that basket?"

"Eight loaves of bread for my provision, and I am going to look for where the birth of the day is."

"That is my father's job. Don't be so rash." Then after a moment he said, "Show me your loaves of bread." Youth opened his basket and they were changed to eight goat heads. "I've caught you stealing," said God's son. "You said you had loaves of bread, but you have stolen my eight goat heads. I am tying you up and taking you with me."

"I did not steal," said Youth. "But if you punish me for what I am carrying, what can I do? I will come with you on my own."

When he was tied up, he spoke to God's son and said, "Let me buy myself off. At home I have a silver mortar. I will give it to you as my forfeit."

"All right," said God's son, "but be quick about it."

"Don't be in too much of a rush. I live far away," said Youth. He left and he didn't go back to that place; he went home. There he said to his father, "This time was really trouble. Those eight loaves of bread became eight goat heads!" And he stayed home (after that), because he had found somebody stronger than himself. (Birkeli 198–203)[38]

By lightening the tone of heroic myth, "Looking for Trouble" draws attention to the hero's quest. The contest between a rebellious hero and a disapproving father figure echoes plenty of myths around the world. So do the hero's successes in overcoming the insect, reptile, and animal worlds, and his quest for something more powerful than either father or himself. But the hero's escape by pretending to perform an errand for his captor is trickery of the kind practiced by the twin Malagasy tricksters, Ikotofetsy and Imahaka. And isn't it the *angano* or *tafasiry* genre, corresponding to the ordinary European folktale, that sends the hero home with the object he was searching for? In this case he acquires a fuller understanding of the world, including its distribution of power.

The result is neither hero legend, nor myth, nor ordinary folktale, but a hybrid genre. As in the European context, so here, "the most archaic layer of content," the rebellious earth-god, "continues to supply vitality and ideological legitimation to its later and quite different symbolic function" (Jameson, *Political* 186–87). The content of this hybrid's later function is not cosmological concepts, not heroic virtue, not collective fantasy, but a cultural transition from one system of production to another. The foods that turn into goat-heads, in the final episode, are tubers, the oldest food on the island, part of its most "primitive" economy; their transformation symbolizes the move from a primitive diet to the keeping of livestock and the consequent eating of meat (Faublée 481–512).

Insert, into the Self-Created or Tinaimbuati kind of plot, episodes and minor genres that build up the hero, and the new combination is epic. By mixing genres, highland Madagascar has produced one epic text (Haring, *Ibonia*), whose chronology begins with a manuscript written about 1830 and completed forty years later by dictation to Lars Dahle (Dahle 108–55). He printed a second, shorter version, which follows; three more versions were recorded in 1978, 1991, and 1992 (Noiret 219–67). The outline is consistent with *angano:* a royal hero, born of a queen who was barren until she consulted a diviner, chooses his future wife magically, goes on a quest for her, is tested, receives supernatural aid, and wins over an adversary to bring home the prize. The epic version derives its magnitude from inserted segments of *kabary* (formal oratory) and panegyric flights, which praise both the hero and his adversary. Those high days of the highland monarchy (1780–1896) were the last point in Malagasy history when the totality of experience could be conceptualized. The east coast, being part of the Indian Ocean culture area, knows nothing like Ibonia; it favors smaller, parodic forms.

Once the Lutheran Dahle had collected and published Ibonia and his other "specimens," it was James Sibree, Jr., who led the other missionaries in translating and publishing Malagasy verbal art, by serving as editor of the missionary publication *Antananarivo Annual* throughout its existence (1875–1896). He and several colleagues (Cousins, Parrett, Montgomery, and Richardson) initiated a Malagasy Folk-Lore Society, which published seven small volumes of "tales, fables and allegories, proverbs, public speeches, etc." (Sibree, "Oratory" 210). Though he jibbed at translating the 46-page Ibonia, he didn't mind showing the world the shorter, more easily understood version, which he sent to London for the newly established *Folk-Lore Record* (soon to be renamed the *Folk-Lore Journal*). Except for inserted headings, Sibree's translation is reproduced verbatim.

36. Ibonia

Merina narrator 1872–76

[Conception and Birth of the Hero] Once upon a time there were two sisters who had no children, and so they went to work the divination (*sikidy*) at the house of Ratoboboka. As soon as they came in she asked, "Why have you come here?" The sisters replied, "We are childless, and so have come to inquire by divination here of you." Then said Ratoboboka, "Look into my hair." So the elder one looked and saw only a bit of grass; then she said, "I saw nothing, mother, but this bit of grass." Ratoboboka replied, "Give it me, for that is it." Then the younger girl searched, and saw only a little bit of broken charm, red in colour; so she said, "I saw nothing, mother, but this little bit of a red charm." Ratoboboka replied, "Give it me, for that is it." And upon this, Ratoboboka said, "Go alone to yonder forest to the east; and when you have arrived there the trees will all speak and say, 'I am the sacred child-charm'; but do not you speak for all that, but take the single tree which does not speak there, last of all, and take its root which lies to the east." So the two girls went away.

Fusing the diviner who can effect conception–a male in the epic version—with the female donor who will liquidate a heroine's lack connects this story with more recent tales (Gueunier, *L'Oiseau* 26–49).

And when they came to the forest each of the trees said, "I am the sacred child-charm" (i.e., which causes the barren to bring forth). Nevertheless the sisters passed them all by. And when they came to the single one which did not speak, they dug round the tree, and saw one of the roots which struck eastwards, which they thereupon took away.

And when they were on the road the sisters vowed, saying, "If we should bear boy and girl (i.e., if one have a boy and the other a girl), they shall marry each other." And when they came home they each drank (of the charm). Accordingly the elder one became pregnant; and after a half-year had passed the younger also was with child. And when the time came for her to be delivered the elder sister bore a daughter, and she called its name Rasoamananoro [or Rampelasoamananoro, Beautiful Happy-Making Girl].

In due time came the day for her younger sister to be delivered, so she went to the south of the hearth to bring forth her child. But the child in her womb, they say, spoke and said, "I am not a slave, to be taken here south of the hearth"; so his mother went north of the hearth. But it spoke again, "I am not a prince, to he taken north of the hearth." Then his mother took him to the box but it said, "I do not like to be smoked." After some time, it said, "Make a big fire of wood." So they made it. Then it said again, "Swallow a knife for me, and take me west of the hearth." So he was taken there. And having come there, with the knife his mother had swallowed he ripped up his mother's womb, and then leaped into the fire which burned brightly there, after having patted the wound which he had made by ripping up his mother, so that it was healed. Then his father and mother endeavoured to save him, lest he should be killed through going into the fire; but when they thrust out their hands to take him they were broken and unable to take hold of him; and so it happened with their feet as well.

Other heroes speak before birth or emerge on their own (Renel, *Contes* 1:268–74), but only Ibonia chooses both his birthplace and his name, choices usually made by parents. The parallelisms of panegyric elevate the tone from prose to verse.

[He Chooses a Name] And after a while the child spoke thus: "Give me a name." Then said his mother, "Perhaps you should be called Fozanatokondrilahy [Male Crab], for I hear that he was a strong man." But the child did not like it; so his mother mentioned another name, and said, "Perhaps Ravatovolovoay [Stone Man the Crocodile Killer] then, for he, I understand, was famous for his strength." But he did not like that either. So the child gave himself a name, and said,

"I am Iboniamasy, Iboniamanoro:
breaking in pieces (*manoro*) the earth and the kingdom;
at the point of its horns, not gored;
  beneath its hoofs, not trampled on;
    on its molar teeth, not crushed.
Rising up, I break the heavens;
  and when I bow down the earth yawns open.
My robe, when folded up, is but a span long;
  but when spread out
    it covers the heavens,
  and when it is shaken
    it is like the lightning.
My loin-cloth, when rolled together,
  is but the size of a fist,
but when unfolded
  it surrounds the ocean;
  its tongue (when girded) causes the dew to descend,
  and its tail sweeps away the rocks.
    Ah! I am indeed Iboniamasy, Iboniamanoro."

And having spoken thus he came out from the fire and went upon his mother's lap.

Once born, the hero needs no adolescence. The testing of Ibonia puts looking for trouble in a graver light.

[Villainy; the Hero Looks for Trouble] And after he had grown up he had a dog called Rampelamahavatra [She who makes you jump]. One day while he was hunting in the fields, there came that famous man called Fozanatokondrilahy to seek for Ibonia, and inquired of his parents, "Where is Ibonia?" They replied, "He has gone for pleasure into the forest." So he took Ibonia's dog, for the parents could not prevent it.

And as soon as Ibonia returned from hunting he asked his parents, "Where has my dog gone?" They replied, "Fozanatokondrilahy has taken him." So he said, "I am going to fetch my dog, father." But his father would not let him, for he said, "Why, child, even the crocodiles in the water are sought by Fozanatokondrilahy, and found, and how can you fight with him without coming to harm ?" But his father, seeing that he would not be warned, made him fetch a great stone, in order to see the strength of his son; then he said, "Since I can't persuade you, fetch me yonder big stone to make me a seat." So he went and fetched it. Then his father let him go. So off he went and came up with Fozanatokondrilahy.

[The Test] And when the latter saw him he said, "What are you seeking for here?"

Ibonia replied, "I want my dog."

So he asked him, "Are you strong?"

"Yes," replied Ibonia, "I am strong." And no sooner had he said so than Fozanatokondrilahy seized him, and threw him more than the length of a house. Then Ibonia seized him in his turn, and threw him also as far as the length of a house. And so they went on, first one and then the other, until each had thrown his opponent as far as ten house lengths. Then said Fozanatokondrilahy, "Don't let us throw each other any more, but cast each other down" (a descent). So he lifted Ibonia up and cast him down, but he did not fall, but stuck in the ground as far as his ankles; then he, in turn, cast down Fozanatokondrilahy, who descended as far as his knees. And so they went on with each other until Fozanatokondrilahy was forced completely into the ground, that is, the rock on which they were contending, and Ibonia pressed down the stones upon him so that he was quite covered up.

Then Ibonia called together Fozanatokondrilahy's subjects and asked them, "Will you obey the living, or the dead?" So his wife and people replied, "We will obey the living, sir." So they became Ibonia's subjects, and he departed with all his spoil.

The testing is a rehearsal for the climactic struggle and victory.

[Extraordinary Companions] And on his way back a number of people met him who were each skilled in various ways. Some were swimmers in deep waters, others were able to tie firmly, others again were able to see at great distances, others were able to make alive; and all these Ibonia showed kindness to, and gave them a share of the spoil which he had obtained. So he went on his way back and came to his village.

[Abduction] Arriving there he could not find Rampolasoamananoro, his betrothed wife, for she had been taken by Ravatovolovoay [Stone Man]. So he asked his parents, "Where has my wife gone?" They replied, "She has been taken by Ravatovolovoay." So he said, "I am going to fetch my wife." When they heard that, his parents they warned him, saying, "Don't do that, child, for Ravatovolovoay is extremely powerful" But he would not stay. So at last his father got angry and took gun and spear to kill him, but he could do nothing to harm him, for the spear bent double when he hurled it. Upon that, Ibonia planted some arums and plantain-trees, and said to his parents, "If these grow withered, then I am ill; and if they die, that is a sign that I also am dead."

[Disguise] That being done, he went away and came to an old man who took care of Ravatovolovohy's plantain-trees, and asked him, "What is it you take with you, when you go to visit your master?"[39] The old man replied, "A few plantains, and some rice with honey, my lad."

So in the morning—for he slept there that night–he plucked off the old man's hair from his head so that the whole skin from his body came away with it. Then Ibonia covered himself with it, while he fetched some plantains and prepared rice and honey to take to Ravatovolovoay. So he came presently to his village; and when the people there saw him they said, "The old man's come," for they did not know Ibonia, because he was covered with the old man's skin. Then he said, "I am come, children, to visit you." So they took the plantains and the rice which he had brought to the prince, for Ravatovolovoay was a prince. And they cooked rice for the old man (Ibonia) and gave it to him in the servants' plate, but he would not eat from that, but said, "Fetch me a plantain-leaf on which to eat. You know well enough how well my wife and I live, so why do you give me such a plate as that?"

[An Old Man Becomes Stone Man's Rival] On the day following his arrival, it was announced that the chief would have sport with throwing at a mark with a cross-piece of wood, and so the old man went with the rest. When they came to the place where the mark was set up, the chief aimed at it, but not one of the people could hit it. Then said the old man, "Just give me a cord that I may catch hold of it." So they gave him one, and he was successful with the one the chief had missed. Then the chief said, "This is not the old man, but some one altogether different, so give a spear and gun that I may attack him." But the old man said, "Why, who else is it but me, my son, for I am only showing the strength I used to possess?" So the chief let him off, and went on playing with the cross-piece of wood. And as they went on with the game the old man pressed in with the rest, but did not obtain what he aimed at, for the cross-piece went into the earth and brought up a hedgehog, and dipped into the water and brought out a crocodile. Then Ravatovdlovoay said again, "Did I not tell you that this is not the old man, but some one else?" And again he sought to kill him; but the old man spoke as before, and so Ravatovolovoay again refrained.

On the day following after that again, the chief's orders came saying, "Today we will try the tempers of the oxen,[40] therefore make ropes to catch the stubborn ones." And when they began the game very many of the stronger oxen could not be caught. Then said the old man (Ibonia), "Just give me a rope." So they gave him one, and he caught the strong oxen and held them; and the people wondered when they saw it. And when the chief saw it, he said again, "This cannot be the old man, but some one else." But the people replied, "But who else can it be?" Then the old man answered again as he had done before, viz. that he was no one else, but was merely showing his strength. So the players dispersed.

[Recognition] And upon the following night, Ravatovolovoay went to his other wife; and upon that the old man (Ibonia) went to the house where Rampelasoamananoro was, and said, "Let me lie here by the side of your feet." But she replied, "Why, what a wretch you must be, old man, to say such a thing to me, and speak of lying at my side." But when the people were fast asleep, Ibonia took off the skin of the old man with which he had covered himself, and there was a blaze of light in the house because of the shining of the skin of Ibonia. Then his wife knew him, and said, "Is it you who have come?"

"Yes," said he, "I have come to fetch you." So he bade the people go out of the house. And when they had gone out he bolted and barred the doors, and sat down to wait for the morning, that he might show some marvellous things to the people of the village. Then said Rampela to Ibonia, "How shall we get free from here?" He replied, "Don't be afraid, for we shall get out all right; but take heed what I say: do not speak to me or beckon to me, for if you do either they will kill me." So in the morning, when Ravatovolovoay awoke, he found that the door of the house where Rampela was was locked. Then he said to the people, "Isn't it just as I told you, that this is not the old man, but another person?" So he tried to break open the door; but the door became like a rock, and he could not force it. Then he set fire to the thatch of the roof; but it would not burn, but rather dropped down water. Then he dug round the foundation of the house; but that also became as rock.

And so, all his attempts being unavailing, at last Ibonia and Rampela prepared to go out, and Ibonia caused a profound sleep to fall upon all the people outside the house, so that every one slept. Then he said to her, "Let us go, but do not speak to me or beckon to me."

[Escape and Pursuit] So they went out, and stepped over all the people who slept along the road they travelled. And when they came to the gateway, he beckoned to a lad and bade him awake the people. So the lad awoke and roused up all the people, and Ravatovolovoay as well. Then said he, "Bring quickly guns and spears; and come, let us pursue them!"

So away they went, and shot at them with their guns; but when the smoke rolled away there was the pair going along without any harm. And so they went on without any mischance, until they came to the water-side; but when they got there the wife beckoned to him to ask him where to ford.

But the moment she did so he was struck by a bullet, and fell back into the water and was dead. Then came up Ravatovolovoay to Rampela and asked what she wished to do, to follow the living or the dead? She replied, "I will follow the living, sir," at the same time excusing herself to him.

And so Ibonia met his death, and his parents looked upon the arums and the plantain-trees which he had left with them as a token; and when they saw them dried up they lamented him, because the things were dead which he had given them as a sign about himself. However, his friends to whom he had made presents when he came from conquering Fozanatokondrilahy had by no means forgotten him, and one day Joiner-together and his companions said to the Far-off-seer, "Look out for Ibonia, lest some harm should have befallen him." So he looked and said "Ibonia is dead; and behold, yonder stream is carrying away his bones." Then said they all (Far-off-seer and Joiner-together and Life-giver) to Strong-swimmer: "Do you go and gather together those bones." So he went and gathered all the bones. Then Joiner-together united them, so that they all came together again, and Life-giver made them live. And they continued invoking blessings until flesh grew and a little breath came, and until he could eat a little rice, and so on, until at length he could eat as he had formerly been used to do. And when he was alive again he prepared to go and fetch his wife away from Ravatovolovoay.

So he went off, and when he came to his village there was the chief playing the game called *fanorona* . . . above the gateway. When he saw Ibonia he asked him, "Where are you going?"

Said Ibonia, "To get my wife"; and, having thus answered each other, Ibonia struck him with the palm of his hand, and he became as grease in his hand; so Ibonia got everything that had belonged to Ravatovolovoay. (Sibree, "Malagasy Folk-Tales" 49–55)[41]

The genre of *tantara* resembles myth as a great authority characterizes it: "Myth does not 'travel' very well and, when it does travel, frequently moves from its specific historical and geographical fulcrum into the international realm of legend, folktale, fairy tale, and other debased forms of originally mythical narrative" (Puhvel 3). For a great authority on Madagascar, tales like this of Ibonia are neither epic nor *angano.* They are debased *tantara,* which allegorize royal genealogies. Once their allegory would have been obvious. Malagasy history, he says, does not show us "epistemological ruptures that substitute one paradigm for another in a given space; much rather, a superposition, a sedimentation whereby ancient and more recent symbols continue to influence and color one another reciprocally" (Ottino, P., *L'Étrangère* 389). Thus conventional bits of a story, like the marriage of a woman from the sky-world to a mortal man, preserve symbolic associations that were brought to Madagascar from its contributing lands (Ottino, P., "Mythology of the Highlands"), if not from Indo-European antiquity (Dumézil). Paul Ottino's approach to Dahle's narratives uncovers political conceptions and ideas of kingship—conscious models of social structure—which survived "the conflict between wholly different cultural periods or modes of production" (Limon 181). Itself a hybrid of history, literature, and anthropology, Ottino's reconstruction of Malagasy mythology honors Madagascar's capacity for linguistic and cultural mixing, which occurs when peoples of different traditions and languages come together.

For example, he reads Dahle's *angano* Seeking a Wife from Heaven (Dahle 250–58) as a myth ratifying the social hierarchy. The hero's name, Andrianoro, identifies him as noble. His search for a wife (parallel to the engagement of the hero Self-Created) symbolizes the absolute necessity for the future sovereign to be properly espoused and succeed his father. The sky-woman he seeks, at first reluctant because of dietary differences, allows herself to be captured; she means "to lead him towards the universal sovereignty she personifies" (Ottino, P., *L'Étrangère* 291).[42] By marrying the sky-woman, however, Andrianoro extinguishes his elder sister's hopes of seeing her own son in that place. Only this offense, says Ottino, can explain why her in-laws murder her; of course she is then resuscitated by her noble husband (Ottino, P., *L'Étrangère* 286).

Is the piece truly *tantara,* a true history? In print, Andrianoro's story has all the earmarks of the fictional tale Dahle thought it was, a symbolic composition as "aware of its own fictionality" as a trickster tale or indeed any symbolic construct (Eagleton, *Ideology* 191). But hybrid genres are normal in creolizing societies. Cultures of this region, Ottino says elsewhere, must be expected to be singular amalgams, constituted at different historical periods. Ottino's ideological reconstruction—the reconstituting through oral literature of Hindu, Islamic, and Indonesian concepts in philosophy, politics, and religion—assumes, like the Marxist critic, that "[t]exts are ideologies which hide the realities of power in the kinship system as well as in the organization of labor" (Rossetti 174).

With his close reading, Ottino shifts the key of stories like "Andrianoro." He makes plots and characters into "so many allusions to a *more basic ideological 'sign'* [the class separation] which would have been grasped instinctively by any contemporary reader but from which we are culturally and historically somewhat distanced" (Jameson, *Political* 200). Shifts of attitude or key are indispensable to any society undergoing immigration or deep change. His cultural-historical criticism unlocks secrets Malagasy have striven, for four hundred years, to keep from *vazaha,* outsiders.

Even in a single word, Ottino uncovers multiple meanings. In Richardson's 1885 dictionary, *famoizana* has two meanings: "any medicine or charm used on recovering from illness to prevent a relapse; the last ceremonies performed for the dead" (Richardson 153). The colonial dictionary by Abinal and Malzac adds three meanings: "ceremony to transfer the ill one is suffering on to an object; tears shed on the dead on the morning of the *fandroana;* gift of meat or money given to those present at end of a funeral" (Abinal and Malzac 142). This one word, Ottino writes, "presents us a remarkable example of that constant multiple discourse and ambiguity, obviously deliberate and sought after, that defies all translation" (Ottino, P., *L'Étrangère* 535). Such multiple discourse and ambiguity, part of Madagascar's African-Indonesian heritage persisting today in its language, Ottino also attributes to the Malayo-Polynesian region (Ottino, P., "Un Procédé").

Through most of the history of collecting in Madagascar, "the author" disappeared into "the folk." Callet, Dahle, and Renel kept their informants anonymous representatives of their collectivity. Now the author returns in a displaced form: a European who gives a metatextual account of Malagasy mythmaking activity. Ottino's criticism stands on the border between exegesis–the incessant commentary a culture gives on its symbolism, practices, and stories–and interpretation, which requires distance, perspective, and a nonmythical kind of thinking (Detienne 5). While limiting his scope to Imerina, Ottino explains Malagasy culture as an amalgam. Even the narrative form of Tinaimbuati is a hybrid, as leaky as the basket he hands to God, produced out of the succession of productive systems which is Malagasy history.

Genres leak; that is the moral of Ottino's criticism. Consider the more modern piece called "Réval," which Gérose Barivoitse, of Sainte-Suzanne in Réunion, learned from his Malagasy grandmother. The narratives of the poor whites (*petits blancs*) of Réunion combine French, European, African, and Asian elements, and point to a history of intermarriage and cultural exchange. Amongst them, Gérose Barivoitse was a star. After his usual opening formula, he introduces a childless old couple, who ask God for a child and bring forth a boy with one leg, one arm–half a man. Speaking Kreol, he retains here her Malagasy pronunciation, rolling the *r* in the name Réval and in the sung parts.

37. Half a Man

Gérose Barivoitse, Réunion March 1976

So the guy's name was Réval. Well, the kid grew, grew, grew, grew. One day he says to his papa, "Papa, Mama!"

"Yes, son," he says, "what do you want, Réval?"

So he says, "I'm all grown up," he says, "I'm going far away." His mother says, "My child, how can you go? Look, you're an invalid," she says, "you're half a person, you have one leg, you have one arm, your face is cut in two, you're half a man!" "Yes," he says, "that's the way God made me. So be it. What can I do?" Finally he set out, he went, went, went, went. He found he could make it, for about two or three years.

The half-man who will triumph comes from a popular Malagasy story, which is worth a momentary digression (Dahle 170–78; Dahle et al. 186–95; Sibree, "Malagasy Folk-Tales" 129–32; "Voatovo"; Renel, *Contes* 1:209–14). In a Bara version, he has only a head and neck.

From birth, the child could see and cry. His parents didn't dare throw him out, and raised him tenderly. Around the age of eight months, when he would have walked if he'd had members, he began walking by rolling himself on the mat. Later he could speak like other children and became very intelligent. (Decary, *Contes et légendes* 129)

This deformed hero, in this Sakalava incarnation, must accomplish great deeds against the opposition of jealous brothers, rescue them from monsters, and effect an obstacle flight; yet the brothers still try to claim all the credit with their father the king. As proof, he produces the dead monster. That Malagasy half-man is the ancestor of the precocious Réval of Réunion.

Here, the father and mother, the old mother worried about her son. She sat down and cried. The old man said, "Why are you crying?" "Oh," she said, "Réval's gone away," she says, "we don't see him any more." She says, "The only child we have," she says, "and he's gone. I don't know if he's dead."

Well, one day the old woman said to her husband, "I'm going out." "Where, where are you going?"

"I'm going to look for my child," she says, "because–it's just that I have to go look for him."

The formalist critic of the folktale genre knows she must go on a quest (Propp 36–65). The true Malagasy-Réunionnais mother knows she must be reunited with her child. The performer must get to the songs so as to move the action forward. No wonder she breaks off before explaining her motivation.

So she went, and as she was walking, she sang. She found a man along the road, she felt him, she saw more clearly, she felt him and sang [in Malagasy], "His legs, oh, became a half leg, O Rasoa!"

She felt him. He had two arms, he was healthy. She said to herself, her son had only one arm.

Mr. Barivoitse translates, "*Tongony* is the arm, the hand," and then repeats the song for the leg, then for the face, of this unidentified stranger she has found on the road.

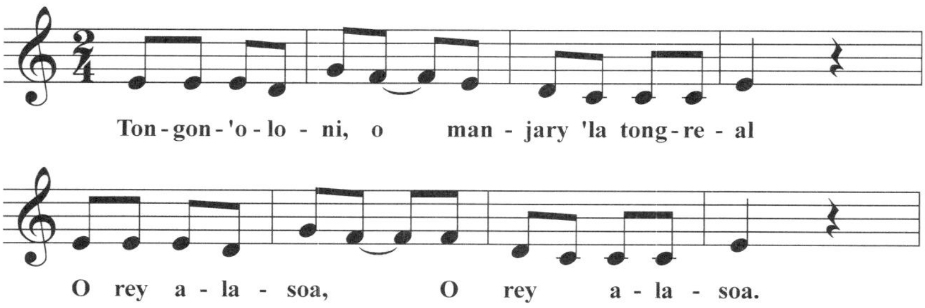
Ton-gon-'o-lo - ni, o man - jary 'la tong-re - al
O rey a - la - soa, O rey a - la - soa.

She felt his leg and sang: "His legs, oh, became a half leg, O Rasoa!"

She said, "That's not my boy." She said, "My boy has just one arm, one leg." She tried the face. "His eyes became one eye, O Rasoa!" She said, "No, that's not my boy," she said. "His face is all there," she said, "but my boy has only half a face, half an arm, half a leg." She left that man there and went on. She found another and did the same thing. But after walking and walking and walking, she came upon her son. She touched his arm, she said, "His arms became half [only one], O Rasoa!"

She said to her son, "I don't see well, I found you, but," she said, "his arm is like your arm." The boy didn't move. She touched his leg. "His legs, oh, became a half leg, O Rasoa!" The boy didn't move. She jumped up and said, "His eyes became one eye, O Rasoa!" "Ah," he said, "mama," he said, "it's you!" He picked up his mother, he carried her, they left, carried her to their house. When they got there, he said, "Papa," he said, "how could Mama walk so far to come find me?" "Oh well," he said, "mama was thinking of you. She went to find you," he said. "Me, what could I say to her? What could I say to her? I didn't know where she was going, walking like a crazy person?"

"Yes," he said, "you see, mama went looking, she came looking for me and she found me."

To finish, Mr. Barivoitse inserts himself into the story. His Malagasy ancestors would have withdrawn themselves.

Well, he stayed with his mama and papa until the two old people died. It wasn't long; finished. I found him, I said, "Réval," I said, "how are you going to eat?" He said, "I'll eat like you," he said. "You have two hands, you can walk, you get things," he said. "I have one arm, one leg. Well, I walk with my arm and my leg; I roll, like this." "OK," I said, "you make out." I said, "You don't do it like me at all."

Réval's fantastic round body becomes a stepping-stone into another piece of Mr. Barivoitse's recurring autobiography (of which more later).

With all that trouble, I managed to go into hospital. They didn't cut my toe off! Good thing, they cut just one finger. The doctor said to me, Dr. Trésak, said to me, "When I finish operating on your leg," he said, "don't move.

Don't go anywhere, because if you move, I'll take your leg off!" I said, "God, better be careful not to get like Réval! I'd be pretty then." Well, that's how it ends. The story is over. (Barat, Carayol, and Vogel 78, 84)[43]

In Réunion as in Madagascar, the half-man is recognizably a folktale hero. He succeeds in retrieving marvelous creatures, after leaving behind a life token; pursued by monsters, he throws back objects that transform into obstacles against them; he rescues his treacherous brothers and brings home a captured ogre. And at one point in the Antandroy version (southern Madagascar), he asks one of the witches for water and it is brought to him. But he refuses to drink, saying that it is not the kind of vessel he is used to drink from. So they bring him different kinds of things, but still he refuses. After some time the witch asks, "What then do you drink from?" He replies that he drinks only out of a net. So the three witches go to fetch water in a net (Sibree, "Malagasy Folk-Tales" 131)[44] —just as God has to do for Tinaimbuati. The deformed hero—another African export to Madagascar (Werner 198–202), found too in Yemen (Ottino, P., *L'Étrangère* 247)—was already a debased mythical character before he migrated to the Mascareignes.

Half a man (evidently a metaphor for paralysis) is not peculiar to the Indian Ocean. For the British social anthropologist Rodney Needham he is a worldwide archetype, "an empirically demonstrable proclivity of the imaginative unconscious" (Needham, *Reconnaissances* 39). Motifs with global distribution like this one are, he says, "relatively steady forms, standing in contrast to the perpetual variation of the languages in which they are uttered and to the exuberant phantasy of the imagination from which they are born" (Needham, *Reconnaissances* 19). But tested evidence for the operation of the imaginative unconscious had not begun to be uncovered when Needham made this declaration (Fauconnier and Turner; Lakoff and Johnson), and his case is not yet proved.

From *tantara* to *angano,* from myth to epic, from any of these to hybrid, from Madagascar to Réunion, mythical material exposes itself to transformations and hybridizations. A generation after the French conquest of Madagascar in 1896, mythic style and structure were used to create a pseudo-myth about how the Europeans were inflicted on the Malagasy for a broken taboo.

38. Why *Vazaha* Are Superior to Malagasy

Sakalava narrator 1907–22

As the old Sakalava tell it, the *vazaha* [Europeans] are almost gods; they are the masters of the whole earth, having no one but God over them.

Here, according to them, is why the Malagasy must submit to their domination.

The Malagasy one day asked Great-Creator, the chief of the gods, for a god who would live on earth with them. "For, O Great-Creator," they said, "you live much too far away, much too high. It needs too much time for our prayers to rise up to you, and your answers reach us too late. Thus we would prefer to have a god here with us. Things would be taken care of much more quickly."

"Good," Great-Creator answered. "I wish to be nice to you and do what you ask. I shall give you a god who will live with you, though under my command. Here he is. He is in this closed box. Above all be careful not to open it. If you do, great misfortunes will happen to you."

Everyone promised never to open the box, and they thanked Great-Creator for his bounty.

But as soon as he had left, curiosity became too strong, and the bolder ones opened the box. There they found a white man; this was a *vazaha* [European], the first *vazaha.* They wanted to close the box right away, but they could not manage to.

Great-Creator, who had foreseen what just happened, had not gone far away, and he was looking on attentively. He came back down to earth, called everyone together, and asked, "Why did you open the box in spite of my forbidding you and your promises? Since you do not want to have a god with you who would be under my command, I shall put this *vazaha* among you. He will be wiser, more clever, and better educated than you in all things. His descendants will be just like him in these respects, and you will obey him." And Great-Creator went back up to heaven, leaving the *vazaha* on earth. He never came to take him back.

It is since then *vazaha* exist and are wiser, more clever, and better educated than Malagasy. (Dandouau, *Contes populaires* 358–59)[45]

The narrator honors tradition by adapting *tantara* to the colonial situation, nicely voicing that "psycho-cultural plurality" found also in the Caribbean (Brathwaite 16). The *tantara* genre invites "misprision" or misreading, the transformation by a strong narrator of what his predecessor has left him (Bloom).

39. The Boyhood of Radama II

Such adaptation, like parody and *hommage,* hybridizes the mythic structure it is honoring. "Whether in literature, art, or music, parody stresses the continuity of a tradition at the same time that it deflates earlier works within the tradition" (Lindenberger 102). Contrived legends mold

Radama II, who was king of the Merina for two years (1861–63) after the death of his bloody-minded mother Ranavalona II, into a mythical hero. When he was three months old and still bearing the name Rakoto, he revealed his royal heritage by generously saying, "Give Blue-Eyes [a cousin] some cattle." At nine months he said, "Go fetch me a big sheep. I will make a toy out of it." They brought him a big ram. "If I can lift this sheep, I can carry it," he said. His mother said, "Well, lift it, then." To everyone's surprise, he lifted the ram three inches off the ground. He looked at his mother and laughed. Rakoto's mother said, "I've never seen the like since I was born. I hardly know what will become of this child. But ever since I conceived him, I've seen really amazing things."[46] Radama had an endearing sense of humor: he would spread out coins on the ground, or scatter them into a flock of chickens, to watch people fight over them; he would pull the wings off chickens, drop them from a great height, and then give them as food to his playmates; sometimes he would smear rum or *eau de Cologne* on one of them and set him afire. For that, at least, his mother would remonstrate with him. He was a keen wrestler and loved the tug-of-war; he knew all the ways to fight before he was fully grown (the narrator ignores the contradiction with the ram episode). When he wanted a *songomby,* a legendary animal, as a pet, people managed only to catch a *fosa* for him, but finally he settled for a crocodile (Rigaud; Haring, *Malagasy Tale Index* 226–27). And in conformity with the hero pattern found in so many mythologies, his quasi-public execution "was widely rumored among the general populace to have failed" (Feeley-Harnik, "Divine Kingship" 285). Rank certainly has privileges.

Radama was a politically motivated hybrid, combining hero and trickster qualities that were especially useful. Now that Radama's royal dynasty had been annihilated by the invaders, the stories could ironically bow towards an honored ancestor by making him a social deviant. The irony accepted the political ideology of the new rulers by publishing these anecdotes from the old regime in a periodical of the colonial school system. Mythicization and trivialization fuse. More than merely activating the disparate reactive associations of two distinct genres (Ben-Porat), these stories typify what became more visible later, an island consciousness that appropriates media images and remolds them "into local repertoires of irony, anger, humor, and resistance" (Appadurai 7).

The descendant of those adversaries of God, who build unauthorized fires and yet attain integration into society, is a folktale hero, the clever lad, who in Madagascar achieves high rank by his power over language. He is both a *mpikabary,* master of words, and a trickster. So it is not surprising to find the international tale of The King and the

Peasant's Son appealing to the Malagasy fondness for verbal skill. Like European poems that are really about poetry ("The Circus Animals' Desertion," "L'Après-midi d'un faune," "In Memory of W. B. Yeats"), the story celebrates the skill of a storyteller whose name, derived from Kiswahili, is also the name of his genre.

40. Ngano

Betsimisaraka narrator 1907–10

Two men lived in neighboring villages, one to the north, the other to the south. The one who lived to the north was rich, the one who lived to the south was poor. The poor man had many children, the other one had no progeny. The one in the northern village was obeyed by the people because he was rich, and was proclaimed king.

Now one day, two boys from the northern village went to play with the children in the southern one. They found no grownups in the village, only a young boy. They asked Ngano: "Where is your father?"

The pairing of the characters is enacted in their alternation of opposed lines, which in classical Greek tragedy bears the name of stichomythia. Malagasy are fond of verbal dueling.

Ngano answered, "He went to kill the living and take the dead."

"Where is your mother?"

"She went to lose wisdom and find madness."

"Where is your uncle?"

"He went to break men's skulls so his skull would get broken by others."

"Where is your elder brother?"

"He went to enter into living bonds; he will take some too."

"Where is your elder sister?"

"She has abandoned the advice of several to take the advice of one."

At those words, the boys went back and said to the king, "Sire, Ngano is insulting us." The king became angry and summoned him to execute him.

Before the king, Ngano said, "May I speak, or not?"

"You may."

"Sire, why have you summoned me? I'm only a child."

"You have insulted me," he said.

"Sire, I have not insulted you. Here is what happened. These two boys asked me where my father was, and I answered, 'He went to kill the living and take the dead.' He went to look for firewood. I also told them that my mother had 'lost wisdom and found madness,' because she went to catch fish in the ricefields. I told them that my uncle went to break men's skulls so his would get broken too, because he went to watch the dancers, and when you go to watch dancers, you get drunk on liquor and then you fight. I said my brother had entered into living bonds and was taking bonds too, because he went to gather rubber. I said my sister had abandoned the advice of several to follow the advice of one, because she got married."

Immediately the king set him free, for he had not insulted him. "You are very smart," he said to Ngano. "Stay here with me." Ngano agreed.

As the mythical hero of the combat myth proves himself by defeating a giant or wild beast, so the *mpikabary* earns high rank through his verbal skill. As the court jester, he has a rich stock of "counter-impossible obligations," like Tinaimbuati.

After a few days, the king said to his followers, "Let's test how smart Ngano is." He sent the boys of the village to bring together all the male cattle in one pen. In the morning, the king said to Ngano, "I want some milk. Go draw me some." When he got to the cattle pen, Ngano was very surprised to see nothing but males. How could he milk them? He thought for a few moments, then ran to the king and arrived all out of breath. The king asked why he had run so hard, and he answered, "Sire, would you allow me to go to my father? He is very ill; he is going to give birth in a few hours. My elder brother came to let me know."

"What are you telling me? How can a man give birth?"

"No doubt, Sire, you know that's not true. But then why did you send me to milk oxen?" The king could not answer.

Some time later, he sent him to make a *pirog* out of stone, because, he said, the crocodiles were so fierce that they could seize and break wooden *pirog*s. The king had him given an axe and several days' ration of rice. Ngano set out, and when he was well away from the village, he built a hut at the foot of a large boulder. First he ate his rations, then gave the rock some blows with the axe, then went back to the king and said, "Sire, the stone *pirog* is almost finished, but I came back to sharpen the axe, which doesn't cut any more. For that you will have to fill this earthen vessel with tears."

The king answered, "How can you want me to do that? A thousand men couldn't fill that vessel with their tears."

"In that case, how can you want me to make a *pirog* out of stone?" The king was again so surprised with that trick that he did not say a word.

A little later, he promised a hundred pieces of money to anyone who would stay all night in cold water. Nobody dared try it but Ngano. He succeeded, but the king, not trusting him, refused to give him the reward. Ngano held a grudge against him for that.

In an Antakarana version of this plot, the king asserts that Ngano's mother has built a fire near the source of the river, which warmed him.

"Can fire warm what is far away?" says Ngano. "Yes," says the king, whose stinginess provides continuity among these unrelated trickster episodes.

One day when the king and his men were clearing some land, Ngano stayed behind to do the cooking. He put all the rice pots on one side and the meat pots on the other, and made the fire between the two rows. At mealtime he told the king he had followed his advice. The king was angry at being tricked; Ngano ran away into the forest. The men the king sent to find him went into the house where he was staying, until he should come back. But Ngano suspected there might be people in his house, and to find out, he used a trick. He climbed up on a little hillock nearby and said, "Oh, my little house, my little house!" Then he listened and looked, but the men didn't answer. Then he cried out again, "Little house, you don't want to answer me because there are people inside you." And he called again, "Oh, my little house, my little house!" This time the men answered, because they believed the house answered when it was called. Ngano made fun of them: "Do you think I'm crazy? When did you ever see a house that answers when it's called? You won't catch me like that."

The king's emissaries told him the trick Ngano had used. He ordered them to go and catch him by night. That's what they did. They caught Ngano and brought him to the king. The king ordered his men to lead Ngano out of the village, tie him up tight in a mat, and then come back at nightfall and throw him into the water. They carried out the order. Once he was tied up in the mat, they left him on the road.

Then a rich man happened to pass by, coming from the north, carrying riches and driving many cattle. From inside the mat Ngano heard him and cried out, "You, the one passing by!" But when the passers-by looked, they didn't see anything. Ngano cried out again; finally the rich man and his followers caught sight of him. Ngano said, "The king wants to make me marry his daughter. I don't want to become a householder. So to force me, he is treating me like this." "Is the girl pretty?" said the rich man. "There's no girl prettier," said Ngano. Immediately the rich man had the mat untied, let Ngano come out, and took his place. They tied him up tight. Ngano took his gun and spear and said to the rich man's followers, "Anybody who doesn't obey me, I kill." They obeyed him, and Ngano set forth with the rich man's men and goods. The king's men arrived at sunset and threw the mat into the water. The rich man was drowned.

A few days after that, Ngano came back and the king was very surprised to see him alive, especially seeing all his wealth. "What did you do to get out of being drowned and to acquire all this wealth?"

"Here's what," Ngano said. "When they threw me in the water, I plugged up my nose and mouth with my fingers so the water wouldn't come in. Then I gathered money and all kinds of things from the bottom of the lake. You, who are the king and rich already, could gather four times as much from there as I did."

Immediately the king, burning to go get wealth from the lake, had a mat woven just like the one they had tied Ngano up in. Then he had himself sewn into the mat and thrown into the water. Bubbles came up from where they threw him in. Ngano said to the others, "He's gathering up the money." Most of them asked to be thrown in too. They had themselves tied into mats and tossed into the lake. By that time there were no more men in the village, which made people afraid.

Ngano went back to his father's village and told him that he was going to be king. He took the people from his own village to the village of the drowned king, and with his gun in hand, walked up and down saying, "Those who don't obey me will die!" Nobody breathed a word. "Those who obey me," Ngano went on, "will keep their property." Everybody in the village came right away and accepted his authority. "Henceforward," Ngano said, "My orders are orders and my laws are everybody's laws." The people agreed, and that's how, thanks to trickery, Ngano became king. (Renel, *Contes* 2:89–95)[47]

Behind the youth's smart-alecking lies his multiple ancestry. He incarnates the rebellious earth hero, descended from the earth goddess (Faublée 497); he has trickster ancestors from East Africa, Indonesia, and India (Thompson and Balys 306–307); he is descended also from The Master Thief, whose story "appears in nearly every collection of tales from Europe and Asia" (Thompson, *Folktale* 174). Now he is a modern hero, who acquires power by deception. If, as Ottino has shown, highland Madagascar became the home of Andriambahoaka ideology, their subordinates, as well as other ethnic groups, also inherited and transformed ideological symbols from their diverse ancestors. In the nineteenth century, the freeman class (*hova*), like any emerging class, "found the mystique of monarchy ready-made for it by a previous ruling class, and adapted it efficiently to its own ends" (Eagleton, *Ideology* 44). Thus did Madagascar acquire a bourgeoisie, while maintaining a narrative repertoire into the colonial era and beyond. Traditional narrative became a theater in which the class struggle could be allegorized (Volosinov 23).

Ngano is a creole if anybody is. Hybridized stories like his provided a conceptual base and a repertoire for creolization. Classification, that European obsession, becomes in Madagascar the logic of the plural and the possible. Narrators unhesitatingly transfer names, characters, incidents, and combinations of episodes from, say, a happy-ending story to a different one ending in a loss or permanent deterioration for the characters. Firm classification of genres is simply impossible.[48] The most closely studied genre terms keep shifting.

> *Tafaširi* can be translated as tale, *takiyati* as tale, legend, narrative precedent or example, *tatara* as historical narrative or legend, *fedrā* as legend or myth. The distinction among these four groupings is theoretical: an amusing story can be an origin story at the same time. Every legendary, historical, or amusing story contains an example. Depending on the narrator, the same narrative has been given to me as *tafasiri, takiyati, tatara, fedra.* Narrative forms vary; only by going back to certain better-preserved variants can one try to retrieve the ancient meaning of a narrative. (Faublée 14)

The plural parentage of Ngano and other hybrid narratives engenders their ambiguities. Ngano has many Indian Ocean relatives. The Master Thief, for one, shows up as Ti Zan in the large repertoire of Alfred Picard, of the village of Plaine des Cafres in Réunion (Carayol 12). Another of Ngano's relatives is evidently of Indian descent: The Clever Peasant Girl.

41. The Clever Peasant Girl

Bhojpuri narrator, Mauritius 1984

In a village, there was a royal couple and their minister. The minister was always loyal and satisfied his master. The king would ask his minister and the latter would give him anything he would ask. So the king was very happy. So one day, the king and minister had a meeting, and on his way out the king said, "I want to drink bull's milk. Bring me a liter." So the minister said yes.

When he got home, he had a problem. He was so worried he stopped eating and drinking. "Where am I going to get bull's milk?" His only daughter brought him food. He said, "Take it away. I will not eat, I will not eat. I'm not hungry."

She said, "Father, aren't you well? Ten o'clock is the last time you ate. What has happened to you? You are a minister. I'll bring the doctor."

He said, "No, don't bring the doctor. I'm sick from worry." He said, "I'll tell you what the king said. He's asked me to bring him bull's milk. Where am I going to get bull's milk?"

She said, "Stay home and don't worry. Sleep quietly. Tomorrow morning I'll give you the bull's milk. Don't worry."

There was a river behind the king's house. At five o'clock in the morning, the minister's daughter brought a pile of clothes and washed them and beat them and washed them. The king sent out some soldiers to see "Who's beating clothes behind my castle?" They saw it was the minister's daughter and said, "It's the minister's daughter." He said, "Call her in right away.

"Why are you washing clothes here today? Nobody ever came here to wash clothes before." The king said, "What is the matter, what's happening that today you're washing clothes at five in the morning?"

The minister's daughter said, "O king, at four this morning my father gave birth to a baby."

"Your father gave birth to a baby?"

"Yes, king. That's why I've come to wash the clothes. What kind of a shame would it be to my house not to have clothes? I have to do them quickly."

"That's not possible," the king said. "That's not possible that my minister has given birth to a baby."

"Well," she said, "you asked for bull's milk. If a bull has milk—if a bull has milk, a minister can give birth to a baby." (Gallob 301–306)[49]

Mythology in and of Madagascar confirms a remark of Claude Lévi-Strauss:

> There are always several kinds of myths simultaneously present in the system, some of them primary (in respect of the moment at which the observation is made) and some of them derivative. And while some kinds are present in their entirety at certain points, elsewhere they can be detected only in fragmentary form. Where evolution has gone furthest, the elements set free by the decomposition of the old myths have already been incorporated into new combinations (Lévi-Strauss, *From Honey* 354).

New combinations are the keys to creolization.

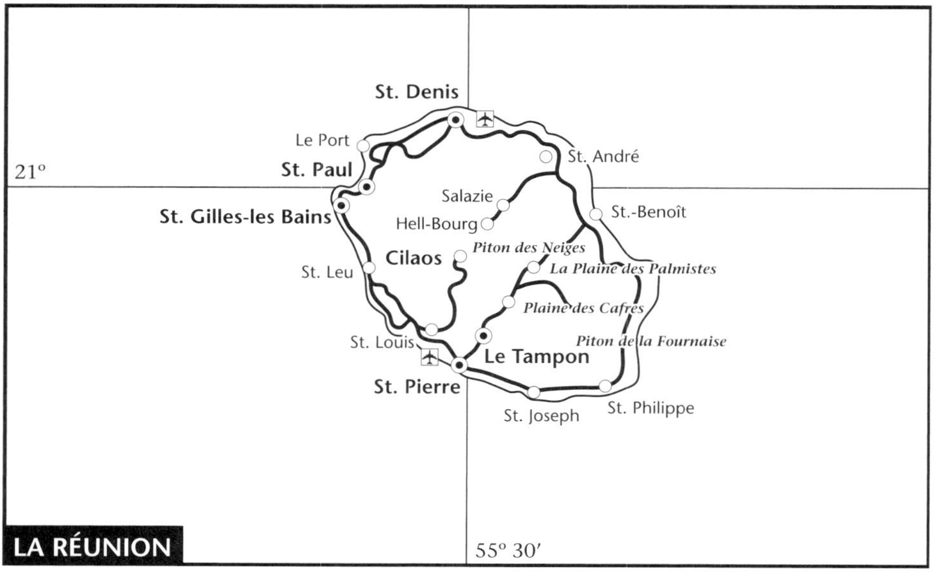
St. Denis
Le Port
St. André
21°
St. Paul
Salazie
St. Gilles-les Bains
Hell-Bourg
St.-Benoît
Piton des Neiges
Cilaos
La Plaine des Palmistes
St. Leu
Plaine des Cafres
Piton de la Fournaise
St. Louis
Le Tampon
St. Pierre
St. Joseph
St. Philippe
LA RÉUNION
55° 30′

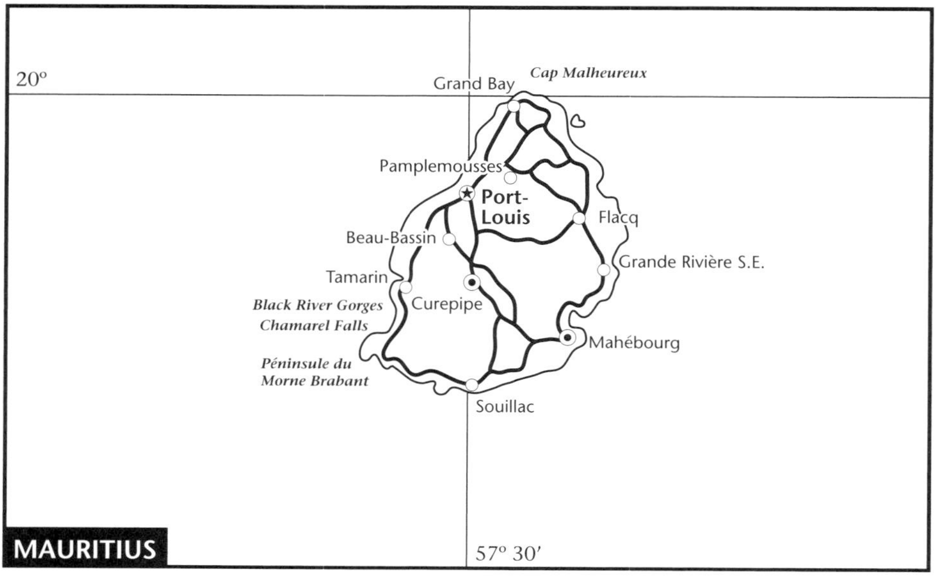
20°
Grand Bay
Cap Malheureux
Pamplemousses
Port-Louis
Flacq
Beau-Bassin
Grande Rivière S.E.
Tamarin
Black River Gorges
Curepipe
Chamarel Falls
Mahébourg
Péninsule du Morne Brabant
Souillac
MAURITIUS
57° 30′

2
Diaspora

42. The Cat and the *Fosa*

After decades of historical research, why are Africa's contributions to world culture still obscure? "There was a cat and a *fosa*," begins a storyteller from northwest Madagascar, only 400 km away from the continent. His story typifies the African animal tales that were taken to the creole islands by merchants, "liberated" slaves, and others. These settlers—some willing, many resistant—implanted a common stock of tradition, which is shared by the "old world" islands of Madagascar and the Comoros, and by the "creole islands" of Mauritius, Réunion, and Seychelles. This chapter samples that common stock. The stories show these islands to be a model of "cultural creolization" (Chaudenson and Mufwene) under Africa's influence. At the outset of Madagascar's history, "the majority or at least a large part of the population of the island was African" (Vérin, *History* 45). Bantu languages contributed vocabulary and word structure to Malagasy language. East Africa contributed much of the Mascareigne population, by way of Madagascar, whose verbal arts are part of the heritage of the other islands (Haring, "Eastward"). Folktales are the proof.

What's a *fosa*? He is a peculiarly vicious feline, whose name is pronounced *foosh'*, with a reputation for destroying people's chickens. In Sakalava country, where this storyteller lived, a colonial officer once killed a guinea-fowl, but "I didn't have time to go fetch it; a *fosa* prowling the area, unperturbed by the gunshot, flew out in front of me and was already carrying it off in his mouth. The southeastern tribes even claim that it goes into their houses to steal newborn babies" (Decary, *Faune* 37). On the other side of the island, this animal is credited with flattening a whole forest, but only in fiction (Fanony 145n). Still, he's not an animal you can expect to be friendly with, even if you're a cat, who should be a cousin. The storyteller plays off the obvious inequality of these two females: "They were very good friends." As always in this sort of plot, the friendship is unstable for a good reason:

The cat had no children, but the *fosa* did have children. There they were, there they were.

—that is, they lived a long time together; doubling the word stretches out the time. From such an unstable relationship, trouble must come.

When she came back, the *fosa* was upset. "Where is my child," she said, "if not here?" She asked the gourds. "We haven't seen him." She asked the pots too. "We haven't seen him." She asked all kinds of things, whatever they were; they all answered in the same words, "We haven't seen him"—because the cat had ordered them not to tell. Finally she also asked a needle with a broken eye, and it gave the news: "That child of yours, it's at cat's house. No use looking around here." The *fosa* set out to chase the cat so as to kill her.

Violation by a subordinate is to be punished, as in all societies where antagonism is chronic.

The theme is dramatized, in this Sakalava story, by means of an African pattern of plotting, which connects such folktales to the history of the islands. The way African tales artistically represent violation and its consequences was pointed out to me once, over lunch, by the late brilliant folklorist Alan Dundes. The molecules of narrative I already knew about: actions like stealing a child, or playing music that magically causes someone to dance, can be analyzed and cataloged as "motifs." That cataloging was a towering achievement by folktale scholars such as Thompson. What organizes actions or motifs into sequences is the universal human capacity for narration. The sequences are plots, which are similar enough to need analysis and cataloging. Plots that are similar are thought of as tale "types," such as The Man on a Quest for his Lost Wife or The Grateful Animals (Uther; Aarne and Thompson). Seen from a greater height, some tale types are clearly not the same plot, yet follow a similar outline, a "structural pattern" like the one Alan Dundes told me about (Dundes, "Making"). What controls this Malagasy story, as it does other narratives I translate below, is such a pattern, the making and breaking of friendship.

The abstract version of the pattern begins with two characters who in real life are permanent enemies. They make a contract with each other for their common benefit. Here, cat agrees to watch *fosa*'s children. Then trickster betrays his or her partner's trust, and the friendship falls apart. The sequence shapes many stories, Dundes said. Later it occurred to me that something else is needed. To move from the abstractness of such structural analysis to the tensions of life as it is lived, another concept is required, more elusive, yet more present to a local audience than an abstract pattern. It would be part of the structure of everyone's feeling (Williams 241). It would permeate the symbolic messages of storytellers about a society. Audiences would apprehend it semi-consciously through the adventures of characters like the *fosa* or the cat. This concept fills a theoretical gap: it opens a path from the static analysis of narrative forms to the historical forces that shape them. Formally it carries what Fredric Jameson calls an "ideologeme" (Jameson, *Political* 185), which I discuss further below. The making-and-breaking of friendship gives the audience a message about the precariousness of interdependence, so important to Africans living in close, face-to-face societies, constantly aware of their need to get along with each other in order to survive. Interdependence was later intensified to the point of pain when they were enslaved.

The conversation with Dundes sent me back to some notes I'd made on stories among the Akamba of Kenya in 1968. Sure enough, I found his pattern there, as well as in New World African-derived narratives (Haring, "Characteristic"). Dundes graciously said that my few examples showed the pattern to be more widespread than he thought. In fact it turns up everywhere Africans have been planted, even among Sakalava who probably would disclaim their connection to Africa, though the connection is obvious in their storytelling style. The pattern must have some ideological weight.

The cat took protection from the king. When the *fosa* came and asked, "Have you seen the cat that took my child?" there was no answer. "Call the people together," said the *fosa*. The people gathered at a tamarind tree. The *fosa* beat the drum. All the people clapped their hands. Only the cat was hiding.

The storyteller switches into a song, which, like some magic musical instrument, causes a person to dance.[1] Both the switch of channels and the effect of the singing are devices of style that Madagascar acquired from Africa. In the 1860s, for instance, in what is now Malawi, Edward Steere found Yao people telling "tales of creatures which when they are played to cannot but dance . . ." (Steere, "On East African" 151).

[Song] The cat that took the *fosa*'s child
Didn't she pass this way?

"I can't stand this," the cat said, trying to get away from the ones who were holding her. "Sing louder!" the *fosa* said. "She'll come out!" The cat leaped out and danced to that music. The people couldn't hold her, she was so eager to dance. When she came out, the *fosa* saw her. "Got you!" she said. The cat had nothing to say, because the *fosa* grabbed her head and squeezed it. They say that's why the cat has a flat head. (Birkeli 334–37)[2]

The Sakalava storyteller (I imagine a woman) brings the fictional past into the real present by ending the tale with an "etiological tag," purporting to explain some present phenomenon. Saying "That's why . . . ," she makes her story allude to myths that narrate the origin of animal characteristics. The device enables her to reassert the normal power relationship between a *fosa* and a domestic cat, as familiar to her audience as, say, the relation between themselves and the Merina, the ethnic group from the highlands, who conquered them in the nineteenth century. In Madagascar as in Africa, "an explanatory ending . . . can apparently be tacked on to almost any plot as a pleasing framework and conclusion fitting in with current literary conventions." The tacking, which is unrelated to the pattern of making and breaking friendship, blurs the boundaries between *tantara* and *angano,* or *tafasiry* (Finnegan 347). But the message about the precariousness of interdependence still comes through.

Like the pattern, the very plot is an African invention, which has migrated around the world and inserted itself into many European tales (Krohn; Dundes, "African and Afro-American" 42). European scholars call it Fox as Nursemaid for Bear. The southern American journalist Joel Chandler Harris published a version of it from the Georgia coast, exclaiming over its parallels with a Xhosa story (Theal 84; Harris xix–xx). The animals have to be familiar locally, so in southern Africa, which has long had commerce and communication with Madagascar, and in eastern Africa, from which many slaves were exported to the Mascareignes, Hare is the nursemaid who eats Lion's cubs (Klipple 52–63). A version collected in Nyasaland (today Malawi) in the 1920s fastens the blame for eating the cubs on Zebra, who starts singing his confession when Rabbit (as the missionary translator named him) teaches him a good tune. On pretext of working with Zebra cooperatively, to sharpen some blunt axes, Rabbit goes to fetch charcoal. He returns with Lion, who is now his confederate in pursuing the child-murderer. He wraps Lion in a bundle of grass and covers him with charcoal. The two of them kill off all but a couple of the zebras, divide their spoils, and start a fire for their common meal. Rabbit has one more trick in store: he persuades Lion to be wrapped in a strip of green bark, which squeezes him so much that finally Lion says, "Rabbit, break the bark."[3] Rabbit confesses the children's murder and kills Lion with a single blow. The missionary collector made clear that among his "natives," tales were told to children to instruct them.

Do you see the guile of the Rabbit, you children? What harm did Lion do that the Rabbit should kill it, along with its cubs? But (you see that) it is (all due to) the badness of the Rabbit. (Young, T. C., 201–207)

The Sakalava storyteller opposed the cat to the *fosa*. Elsewhere in the Indian Ocean, treachery is otherwise personified. In the creole islands—Mauritius, Réunion, and Seychelles—the star of the making-and-breaking pattern is the East African trickster Hare. Not rabbit, as the missionary's translation of the earlier story had it: rabbits don't live in Africa, only hares do (*Lepus europaeus*). But this Hare is fictional. One of Charles Baissac's Mauritian tales, from the 1880s, begins with a contract between Hare and Elephant, which is broken by Hare's trickery. He turns things in his favor when Elephant gives a dance and invites all the other animals except him. When Hare learns that it is Tortoise who is to play the music, he asks Tortoise to hide him in his shell and feed him from time to time (reversing an antagonism these two enact in other stories). From there he gets drunk and begins to sing. When Elephant recognizes his voice, he beats Tortoise to death, but Hare escapes (Baissac, *Folklore* 112–17).[4] Almost always, Hare escapes to be available for another successful trick.

He made his way to the Comoros, too, between Mozambique and Madagascar, where Africans mixed with the Arabo-Persian Shirazi as early as the thirteenth century (see Chronology). There he doubles the making-and-breaking pattern.

43. Cock and Hare

Narrator from Ngazidja (Grande Comore) 1930s

Cock and Hare were great friends. They went out early in the morning to look for food. On the way, they exchanged plenty of jokes, but without making much noise. Once they got home, they talked about the beautiful planting they each would do when the season came. So when summer came, they each planted seeds. Cock's were fine, Hare's were doubtful. Cock was assured a good harvest, Hare a very poor harvest. Hare, unscrupulous as he was, proposed to Cock that at the right time, they should exchange their fields of corn (maize), rice, and beans. Cock accepted the bargain easily. But Cock saw right away that the plantations he was getting wouldn't bring him anything.

After Cock finds he got nothing in the deal, the second half reverses direction. With fake blood, Cock deceives Hare into cutting off his own head.

He wanted a brilliant revenge. One day, he hid his red head under his wing and colored his neck with betel nut. He said to his child, "Don't move from here. Hare is going to come to get me. Let him wait. I'll be back soon." And indeed, Hare arrived looking for his comrade. The little chick reported what his father Cock had said. Hare didn't answer, and waited a bit, worried about his friend's fate.

Just then Cock came back. He still had his head hidden under his wing. Hare, very intrigued, left deep in thought, went back home and asked his wife for a sharp knife; he cut off his head with it. That's how Cock satisfied the hate he had for Hare, such a villainous animal. (Fontoynont and Raomandahy 76–77)

Within one plot that twice breaks friendship, the dual structure reflects the habit of alternating episodes, so that sooner or later, trickster gets his comeuppance.

In Seychelles, a bit farther north near the equator, African culture is the basis of some complicated mixing. We are not surprised that the beloved trickster Soungoula, whose name means hare, is the villain. But—as a schoolteacher?

44. Soungoula, Zako, and Mama Tig

Praslin narrator (Seychelles) 1980s

There was Brer Soungoula who acted bad all the time.[5] He said he would start a school. He said to Mama *Tig* [Tiger] to give him her brood of children to teach in the school. That way her children would learn to read well. Mama Tig said to him, "Yes, I give you my children to have school."

There were seven children in all, and they went to Soungoula's school as if it were a *lekol kolez* [a regular school]. Soungoula said to Mama Tig, "Don't come [too] often to see the children, because they'll get hung up, they'll follow you. Come see them every two weeks."

Soungoula's scheme is topical. At the time this tale was recorded, the Seychelles government's emphasis on education and literacy was in the news. Children from six to sixteen were henceforward to have free primary education. If the old trickster is to represent the new breed of teachers, parents might not want compulsory schooling. They might recall that the schools of the nineteenth century were operated by either emissaries of the landowner class or the Catholic Church (Scarr 56, 68)—not tricksters perhaps, but eating up children in their own way. More likely, however, the story was given to the collector as a sample of repertoire.

Mama Tig came in two weeks. "Hello, hello, hello." Soungoula put his hand out toward Mama Tig and said, "Don't talk loud, the children will hear you. I'll show you."

"A B C K. A B C K." Just then Soungoula had eaten one of Mama Tig's children. Six were left. He said to Mama Tig, "Mama Tig, don't make noise, I'll show you the children. There's one, there's two, there's three, there's four, there's five, there's six," [and] the sixth chimed in, "There's seven."

He went to get a basket of bananas that Mama Tig brought for her children. He saw that bunch of bananas in the road as she was coming. Mama Tig went away very satisfied with Soungoula's work.

Two weeks later, Mama Tig came back. Soungoula saw her coming afar off, he acted as if he didn't see at all. He said, "A B C K. Repeat again." Children: "A B C K." Children: "A B C K." Mama Tig came up and said, "Hello, Soungoula, hello, Soungoula." Soungoula answered, "Hello, Mama Tig, did you come to see the children?" "Yes, I came to see them again." Soungoula said, "Don't make noise or come too close, because the children will get hung up with you."

Now there were just five little ones left, he'd eaten another one. He held them up one by one: "One, two, three, four, five," and held up the fifth one three times: "Six, seven."

Every time Mama Tig came to see the children, Soungoula did the same thing. When just one was left, Soungoula had the gall to say to Mama Tig, "The children are progressing, Mama Tig. I tell you they are well brought up, they are learning well." Mama Tig too was well satisfied with her children learning in the college.

Finally Soungoula ate the one that was left. In two weeks Mama Tig came as usual. When Soungoula saw her coming, he started shouting, "Arrrr! Mama Tig doesn't know how many's on the bench. I ate all her children. Mama Tig will count the bench."

No trick of style could be more African than for the storyteller to imitate animal sounds. The more he does it, the funnier it gets. The animals in folktales gain humor and meaning from being familiar figures (Finnegan 350); in Seychelles their familiarity comes from the world of fiction and mimicry.

Mama Tig came up and said, "Hello, Soungoula."

"Arrrrr!"

"Soungoula, hello."

"Arrrrr!"

"Soungoula, Soungoula, hello!"

"Arrrrr!"

Mama Tig started yelling hello. Soungoula acted as if he didn't hear, he said, "Hello, Mama Tig. Mama Tig, I don't know how to tell you—somebody ate all your children."

Mama Tig is as untamable as the *fosa*.

Instead of weeping, Mama Tig consoled Soungoula, so well could he play murderer. Soungoula wept more than she did. Soungoula said, "Mama Tig, I'll find out for you who ate your children." Mama Tig answered, "Yes, Soungoula, I will be glad to know who ate my children."

One day, Soungoula got his story together. He went to Mama Tig and said, "Mama Tig, O, I will find out for you who ate your children." Soungoula went into the country; he met Brer Zako and said, "Brother Zako, we're going to give a party." Zako said, "Sure." Soungoula said, "Get ready to play the violin. Let me give you your song. When you sing, you have to say,

> I ate Mama Tig's children
> Mama Tig didn't do anything to me down below
> I ate Papa Tiger's children
> Papa Tiger didn't do anything to me up above

They set the date to give the dance for Saturday. Soungoula snuck away, crouched over. Saturday morning he went to find Mama Tig. He said, "Come to the dance, you'll know who ate your children." Mama Tig gladly agreed.

Mama and Papa Tig that night went to the dance. There they both were, eating with the crowd. The dance began.

—and with it, another chance for the storyteller to switch channels.

In Seychelles, as in all the islands, switching from speech to song is a persistent habit carried over from African performance style. Madagascar and Comoros "belong to the pre-colonial Old World of the Indian Ocean, had been peopled by immigrants from the rim of the ocean, and had developed cultures of their own, well before the arrival of the European colonizers" (Houbert 2000:196). There, song is more sacred than in Seychelles. Through song, one communicates with "the beyond, whether that means Heaven or the world of the dead, or between the beyond and the world of the living" (Beaujard, *Mythe et société* 493). In Mayotte, one of the Comoros, when a narrator launches into her story without an opening formula and summarizes it instead of dramatizing, she still switches into full performance of the songs (Gueunier and Said 218). In the "creole" islands like Seychelles, though the sacredness of song is dissipated, it remains a privileged channel for revealing truth in tales. Soungoula in one story sings a song he has learned at a donkey's funeral. When one of the donkeys wants to know where he learned the song, he fastens the blame on tortoise, his dupe (Abel, *Contes et Poèmes* 21–23, *Contes* 22–26). In a closely related story, Soungoula teaches his dupe Kousoupa to confess, at the king's ball, to stealing two hundred coconuts. Interpolated in this performance-of-a-performance are the directions for the *contredanse* that Soungoula, as *komander,* gives to the men (*kavalye*) and lady (*dam*) dancers (Carayol and Chaudenson, *Les aventures* 122–29). Perhaps the audience for the Mama Tig story joins in the singing, as frequently happens in African narration (Okpewho, *African* 134–35). Anyway the people at the king's dance do join in.

All the people were glad to start singing, "Bador, give me Celine, Bador, give me Celine." Waltz, everybody waltzed, *doum doum.* Towards midnight Soungoula said to Zako, "Play music for people to dance to, brother." By then Zako was drunk. He said,

I ate Mama Tig's children
Mama Tig didn't do anything to me down below
I ate Papa Tig's children
Papa Tig didn't do anything to me up above

Mama and Papa Tig ate Zako, then they ate Soungoula too. The two of them got a good start on eating. They started eating all the people, raw.

The story is over, yet this narrator, like his Yao forerunner, thinks the interviewer needs a summary.

Soungoula was no good. He ate Tig's children, then tricked Zako because Zako was so poor in mind. He told Zako they would give a dance and asked him to sing his song. Zako, poor devil, without knowing that Soungoula had eaten Tig's children, sang and thinking to give pleasure, he met his death (Diallo et al., *Veyez 2* 11–15)

Such care from a narrator, to make sure his audience gets all the meaning, entered the rhetoric of fiction long before the days of Dostoevski or Henry James.

Animal tricksters like Soungoula are the most visible contribution of Africa, often by way of Madagascar, to island storytelling. Trickster tales reinforce class boundaries when the trickster undermines the social rules. The making-and-breaking pattern is another such contribution. Through one plot and another and another, it expresses "the importance of friendship, perhaps institutional friendship in African cultures" (Dundes, "Making" 180), displaying it as a cultural ideal, yet simultaneously providing opportunity for both narrator and audience to escape society's norms in fantasy (Bascom, "Four" 290–91). The pattern thus speaks for ideology, which is "indispensable in any society if men [and women] are to be formed, transformed and equipped to respond to the demands of their conditions of existence" (Althusser 235). As the pattern is not verbalized except through varying plots, it lies, analytically, between performance and the more elusive concept of "ideologeme," which the critic Fredric Jameson advances. If an ideologeme is "never given directly in primary verbal form, but must always be reconstructed after the fact, as working hypothesis and subtext" (Jameson, *Political* 185), then in oral literature it must underlie the narrative model for creating stories. Anthropologists have identified what Jameson calls ideologemes under other names: basic premises, cultural axioms, existential postulates, unstated assumptions, cultural postulates, folk ideas (Dundes, "Folk Ideas" 98n5). Sometimes they discover them, sometimes they invent them. The LMS missionaries to nineteenth-century Madagascar looked for these ideas to be directly expressed in proverbs such as *Aza homehy lavo, fa ny tody tsy misy, fa ny atao no miverina,* Don't laugh at the guy who falls down; there's no (divinely appointed) retribution, but what you do does come back on you (Houlder 147). At a less explicit level, after Africans had been forcibly moved to the islands as slaves, their ideologeme about interdependence maintained its vitality through the structural pattern of the making and breaking of friendship. Thus they created meaning, or what the critic Julia Kristeva, writing of European literature, calls signifying (*signifiance*): an "unlimited and unbounded generating process, this unceasing operation of the drives toward, in, and through language; toward, in, and through the exchange system and its protagonists—the subject and his institutions" (Kristeva, *Desire in Language* 17). Seychellois people needed a trickster like Soungoula.

In the switching of channels between speech and song, we hear Africa's most audible contribution to island culture. Another kind of switching moves from the "voice" a performer uses for narration into a "voice" for commentary. It is the oral counterpart of authorial commentary in fiction. The Mauritian narrator Nelzir Ventre, whom I met in 1990, made a point of giving such summaries before he began his stories (which he called *segas*). I suppose he meant to summarize, to mold audience attitudes, and to generalize the significance of the piece (as other subgenres do—for instance, the dumb show before Hamlet's play scene), by connecting its particulars to established norms of morality and value (Booth 169–200). He told a newspaper interviewer in 1980 how important preparation was.

> Let's say I was going to sing a *sega:* I would need the drums, the *maravann* [a percussion instrument] and everything. And I had to first translate [*tradir*] the story—to present all the words before the people listening, do

Nelzir Ventre.
Photo by Lee Haring.

> you understand? Drum players and musicians accompanying me, there's no dancing at that point. *Tradir* means to tell the whole story beforehand, while singing. No dancing, just drumming. Everybody sits down and listens.

These were his rules for proper performance.

For Ton (Uncle) Nelzir, *sega* was a narrative-and-song preceded by a spoken summary, but the various meanings of the word encapsulate the variability effected by creolization. Once, it was a piece of island dance music played on a European instrument, the piano (La Selve 102). Ton Nelzir's traditional songs and anecdotes were strongly local, sung at social gatherings. A scholar would call Ton Nelzir's story-songs *cante-fable.* The dance *sega,* a commercial invention, now entertains tourists at the Royal Palm, Pirogue, Touessrok, and other beach hotels in Mauritius.

One evening in 1990, he explained to Claudie Ricaud and me his order of performing. He always began by singing "Good evening, I'm

here, Good evening, friends"; a chorus had to reply with the same words. "That's it," he explained. "I say good morning to everybody and good evening to everybody, then I start. Now I'll start singing and all that. You understand?" The *mpilalao,* the professional dancers of Madagascar, begin their performances the same way. The head of the troupe speaks a *kabary,* a formal exordium with proverbs and elaborate figurative language, to ask for the audience's favor and announce the subject to be performed (Decary, *Moeurs* 179–80). Is this an accidental parallel, or a bit of culture that Madagascar has sent to Mauritius? Anyway, that evening in Poudre d'Or, Ton Nelzir's friend and neighbor John Brasse was present with his two sons. They could make up the chorus. So Ton Nelzir was ready to narrate and sing a trickster story. "There was King Cat." So he began to perform an example of a literary genre that is as distinct a literary and historical phenomenon as the "well-made play" of nineteenth-century France or the detective story of twentieth-century America. Like those western art-forms, a trickster tale tells an observer significant things about how people see social life, and how they want to see it. Its most obvious theme is reversing power relations. Cat, of all animals, successfully deceives Elephant and Whale into pulling against each other.

45. The Deceptive Tug-of-War

Nelzir Ventre, Poudre d'Or, Mauritius 15 February 1990

There was . . . King Cat. A big cat, a king among cats. Do you hear? Well, that cat, he is very clever, really clever. He goes out, he walks about, and he goes to the seaside. He does like this [*gesture*]. He sees the whale playing in the water. He says, "My, you are really very clean." The whale says, "Yes. Really, in the water, I am the biggest chief there is." He says, "Sure. If you want to bet with me, I'll catch you, I'll put a chain around your neck, I'll pull you and drag you aground." He says, "You, cat, a cat like you?" A big cat like that, I tell you, a king cat. The cat says to him, "I tell you, if I put a chain around your neck, I'll drag you and bring you on, on—"

John Brasse: Aground.

Nelzir Ventre: "In the water. I'll drag you from the sea." He says, "Do you want to bet?" He says, "Yes." He says, "On the fifteenth of August, Assumption Day, well, I'll come and sing. When you hear me singing, you just pull." The cat says to him, I mean the whale says to him, "OK." He says, "Do you hear?" He says yes. Ha-a-a-a-a.

What's going to happen? The elephant. He goes in the woods. He goes to see King Elephant. A big elephant it was, I tell you. He finds the elephant, he says, "My, you! How can you be like this? Look at your size. You are a big elephant.

He says, "Yes, among animals I am the strongest." He says, "Stop bragging," the cat says. "Of course, what do you think?" He says, "Look here, do you want to make a bet that I'll put a chain around your neck, I'll drag you and bring you into the sea." The elephant says, "What?" He says, "I tell you yes. What do you think?" The elephant says to him, "OK." He says, "OK, on the fifteenth of August, well, I'll sing, and as soon as I sing, you just pull."

So in fact, on the fifteenth of August, King Cat went up on a little hill, just like Citadelle, a little mountain. He sits on it and—Ahh-h-h-h-h. He is ready. He sings, he says,

John Brasse, to his sons: You must say.

Nelzir Ventre [*sings*]: I am King Cat, *lelo lelo asiama,*
I am King Cat.

Chorus [John Brasse and his two sons]: *Lelo lelo masiama*

Nelzir Ventre: I am King Cat

Chorus [John Brasse and his two sons]: *Lelo lelo masiama*

After nine more calls and responses, Ton Nelzir stopped the singing with one more "I am King Cat" and his usual transition back into speaking, "Eh-ou, brother."

These two like—that thing—what's its name—

John Brasse: The whale.

Nelzir Ventre: The whale keeps going. It has made a gap in the reefs. And the elephant, the elephant on this side, what can I tell you?

And five more repetitions of the call and response.

Eh-ou. I tell you, they both pull and pull and pull. Do you hear? The whale went through, got from under the table and went through the gap—

John Brasse: On the reef.

Nelzir Ventre: Opened, opened the reef everywhere. It has made a gap.

The two powerful animals are disempowered and embarrassed; the trickster has won the victory. Again the ending is marked by a tag and a shift of voice.

As for me, I passed through here, and I tell you about King Cat.

John Brasse: Story ends. That you know already.

Nelzir Ventre: Are you recording? Is it good?

Claudie Ricaud: Yes, very nice story. How many do you have like that?

John Brasse: A series.[6]

The false tug-of-war, with its two kinds of struggle and victory, is often part of a series. The tales are told one after another; the untold pieces reside in memory as a source for allusions (Paulme, "Quelques Procédés"). Germain Elizabeth of Réunion modeled an unrelated piece on the tug-of-war, as a narrative paradigm. No tale could more directly symbolize the longstanding view from underneath of the tensions between classes. In an Ila version of the story, told in the British colony of Northern Rhodesia (now Zambia) before the First World War, Rhinoceros becomes exhausted from pulling against Hippopotamus and puts his head up out of the water.

"Who is that pulling me?" Said the other: "Why! Shinakambeza, it's you pulling me!" And Chipembele (the Rhino) answered: "It is I." "Why, who was it that tied you up, Chipembele?" Then Rhinoceros answered, "It was Hare. Was it he who tied you up also, Hippopotamus?" Said he: "Yes, it was he."

Once they discover their common enemy, the two are reconciled by agreeing to occupy distinct territories, as different ethnic groups have done.

Rhinoceros and Hippopotamus, when they do not see each other in the flesh, Rhinoceros will drink water in the river where Hippo lives, and Hippopotamus comes out to go grazing where Rhinoceros has his home. (Smith and Dale 2:377–78)

Ila people, knowing this story and experiencing colonial domination, may well have been among the ancestors of Mauritian Kreols like Nelzir Ventre. In the slave culture of Mauritius, as in its counterpart in the New World, the social and psychological usefulness of such a tale kept it alive (Levine 82). Some listeners will have found these seemingly fanciful tales a guide to real-life behavior, especially to how to cope with authorities who were plainly bigger than they were.

Animal tricksters such as Hare or Soungoula model, in their exploits, that chronic combination of pain and resentment that Nietzsche calls *ressentiment.* "The slaves' revolt in morals begins with this," the philosopher writes: "that *ressentiment* itself becomes creative and gives birth to values: the *ressentiment* of those who are denied the real reaction, that of the deed, and who compensate with an imaginary revenge" (Nietzsche, *Genealogy; The Portable Nietzsche* 451). Storytellers and audiences maintain their critique of power through mixing genres in all the forms of verbal art: "rumor, gossip, folktales, jokes, songs, rituals, codes, and euphemisms" (Scott 19). Whatever metaphorical slaves Nietzsche had in mind, the people telling trickster stories were real slaves, or their descendants. So the Indian Ocean trickster tale provides an imaginary, or vicarious, solution to the contradiction between freedom and enslavement. Trickster is the slave in his imagined rebellion against authority and his escape from it; simultaneously he's the Other, who must be punished from time to time to keep him healthy. But he always escapes.

Performance of these tales was Nelzir Ventre's assertion of his own power. The *sega* singer's intense delivery and commanding presence prevailed over his social position, which was low in the nation's eyes and high in the ears of his audiences.

46. Hare at the Animals' Well, 1

Nelzir Ventre 27 February 1990

A couple of weeks later, Nelzir Ventre said,

So—there was another king. He was a great king, the king of animals. So he was a king, a great king of all animals that there were. . . . Well, in his country, there was no water, you hear? There was no water. So what did he do? He invited all those animals to come and dig a well, a pond, that is, a big pond. So really, all the animals, hedgehogs, mongooses—there wasn't one kind of animal that . . . All the animals came to help. The hare didn't come. The king sent a message to tell the hare to come and help. The hare said, "Me? I don't need to. I'll go and—"

and Ton Nelzir broke off; he was a bit slow getting started on this one.

So in his country, there was no water, you hear? There was no water.

I could tell that Tarbaby was coming, remembering an Akamba storyteller I had known in Kenya, who started even more abruptly: "The hare refused to go and dig with the other animals. After the others had worked for some time, they became tired and went to have food. During their absence, the hare came back and started polluting the water."[7] For the plot, Ton Nelzir followed tradition; for performance, he led his little chorus in a call-and-response.

Really, brother, all the animals helped to put in that big pool, that big pond. When that was done, what do you think the hare did? The hare had his calabash. There was honey in his calabash. Well, so, when he came to drink the water, he came:

I, Mr. Hare, the water *kara musa*
I, Mr. Hare
Chorus: the water *kara musa*
[*repeats thirteen times*]
Nelzir Ventre: Eh-ou, brother.

Ton Nelzir's transition from song to story—he always said, "Eh-ou, brother"—helped him switch channels and shift his singers back into an audience role.

Really, as he got there, you see, he went like this [*gesture*]. He saw the pond and the water, which was very clear that day. The hare just took his clothes off and threw himself in the pond. He had a bath and everything, then he left. Then, early in the morning, the king, when the king looked, had people look at the water, the water was all muddy, all stirred up, all the mud there was stirred up. The king said, "What?!"

Ton Nelzir, in this early episode, shows more delicacy than his African ancestors, or than my Akamba storyteller. Later he is more candid—but isn't mud a worldwide euphemism?

Now begins the sequence of pollution-controllers at the pond. My Akamba narrator made the first guardian a hyena, to be followed later by a lion; both are real Kenyan animals. Hare deceives them with honey. Ton Nelzir brings on a tiger—an animal as common in Mauritius as in Seychelles, but only in fiction.

The king woke up the tiger. He is strong. He said to the tiger, "Go and keep watch. Watch out for the hare." The tiger said yes. As he came, really early morning, when the hare came out to get there, he did like this on the road, he did like this [*gesture*]. He saw the tiger. He sang:

Nelzir Ventre: I, young hare
the water *kara musa*
I, young hare
Chorus: the water *kara musa*
[*repeats eight times*]
You hear?

—again the transition functions to keep the audience in contact with the story.

So then, the tiger said to him, "Where are you going, hare? I am going to eat you right now." The hare said, "Hey, you, shut up. Do you want to taste some of this honey?" He just took out of his calabash a little bit of honey and rubbed it on the tiger's lips. The tiger drank it *chuk-chuk-chuk*. "Wow," the tiger said. "Give me some more, please, old man. "OK, that's all right," he said. "Let me tie you up, then we'll see." He said, "OK, old chap." He tied him up, brother, he tied the tiger.

He had a bath, he made water everywhere and spread mud everywhere, shit everywhere and everything. When the king came, well, the king said, "Oh God, it's the hare." And on the next day, he took the elephant, the elephant went the same way. All those who came got caught. They stayed over there. So all those who came . . . the king said, "Well!" All animals, big, big animals [*laughs*], they all got caught with that honey he came with.

Ton Nelzir's laugh points to the essential device of trickster stories: the audience identifies with the self-seeking protagonist. What motivates the laughter is the delight of watching power relations being reversed. Storytellers like Ton Nelzir are even better at those reversals than Hare or Soungoula. After winning every round so far, Hare must get his comeuppance, from a character whose only character trait makes him the opposite of speedy Hare. All folktales put their characters exaggeratedly in contrast with each other, don't they (Olrik 135–36)?

So the tortoise—to the king, he said, "My king, Let me tell you something, king." He said, "What is it?" He said, "Put me on a big cart, take me and leave me near the pond." He said, "You, tortoise? Be quiet. So, you would go to the pond over there? So you would . . . Keep quiet." He said, "No, let me try, I tell you. I will bring the hare back." He said, "You?" He said, "Yes." Really, brother, they got, like, a big truck. They put a big tortoise in it, really big tortoise. They put him in it and they got there.

People around the world know what will happen next: Tortoise will trap Hare in sticky gum; trickster will move from successful deceit, theft, and pollution to public humiliation.

"Everybody" knows this plot. Americans know it from Joel Chandler Harris's "Wonderful Tarbaby Story." Harris's name for the sticky doll adheres to this plot, which became known as The Tarbaby and the Rabbit.[8] Hottentot, Henga, Nyanja, Nyika and other eastern and southern African examples, collected early in the history of European contact, show that the beloved tarbaby was ready to travel when slaves were being captured and brought to Mauritius and Réunion (Klipple 213–33). An Ila version collected before World War I contains an episode found also in Mauritius (Smith and Dale 2:396–98). Near the same time, a Gogo schoolteacher, in what is now Tanzania, collected the tale at the behest of a British missionary (Carnell 35). Kenya knows it today (Kabira and Adagala 85–86; Gecau 107–109). So does Malawi. R. S. Rattray collected it there, in quite a different form, in 1905, when the country was the British Central Africa Protectorate (Rattray 60–62, 139–42). Modern editors give their Malawian version an ingenious symbolic interpretation, connecting it to male-female relations and the perennial theme of selfishness and greed (Schoffeleers and Roscoe 88–91, 97–99).

In variant forms, this tale, which is properly titled The Hare at the Animals' Well (Baer 29–31, 99–101), traveled with Africans everywhere they were enslaved. Tarbaby is common property in modern Mauritius, the Comoros, Réunion, and Seychelles, as it is in the Caribbean and Latin America, and is the plainest evidence of an "African survival." Innumerable versions and variants of Tarbaby have been found in the Caribbean and United States (Crowley, *I Could Talk* 148). The leading authority on Louisiana folklore calls it "the best known animal tale in Louisiana" (Ancelet 6).

What was its origin? An elaborate, Eurocentric hypothesis asserted that the tale originated in India and passed through Arabia to North and East Africa. Only then was it Africanized and exported to the New World (Hattingh). But since the tale is hardly known in India, Arabic-speaking countries, or Europe, and is found in nearly every place to which African slaves were sold, one can't deny its African origin (Duffy; Bremond, "Traitement"). What explains Tarbaby's popularity in all those places is the perennial delight people take in reversing power relations. In these islands the tortoise personifies *ressentiment*.

Now that tortoise was about so high, that tortoise. The tortoise sat down, he said—the king put tar everywhere, very thick layer—that thick, tar. He put it on him. Then around eleven he came, he was singing.

Nelzir Ventre: I, young hare
Chorus: the water *kara musa*
[*repeats nine times*]
Nelzir Ventre: Eh-ou, brother.

He got close, he looked around carefully, he couldn't see anybody. He said, "My my, today, ah-ah, the king likes me very much today. My, my." He took his clothes off, he threw himself in the pond, *bouff!* he had a good swim, everything was perfect. He said, "My, my, aaah. The king has put a rock for me to sit on a throne. Ah, ah, ah, ah."

He came and sat on the tortoise. As soon as he sat down, the tortoise—the tar caught him, ah-ah, caught him. The tortoise moved, ah-ah. He went like this, he said, "Is that you, old buddy?" He said, "Ah-ah, old buddy." He said, "Yes, old buddy, it's me." He said, "Ah-ah, old buddy." He said, "Let me go please, old buddy." He said, "You? I'm going to take you to the king today." He said, "You are stubborn. I'll slug you, I'll finish you off, stubborn!" He slugged him [*laughs*].

Making the contest physical was the high point of the story for my Akamba narrator too, who said, "The hare punched the tortoise on the back with his left hand." Nelzir Ventre, laughing, particularly appreciated this feature.

Ton Nelzir was a contradictory artist. Not all his *segas* had happy endings like this. Some were about oppression and hopelessness, which sounded strange from this forceful, assertive old man. Poor and deprived persons in his *segas* are in hopeless situations, often without resources. One song describes an old man begging: "I have no family, I have no children." Another shows a starving boy hoping, "Yesterday I didn't have food, So Saturday I will have to eat, Tomorrow to have food." In a third song, a man whose hand has been burned by his cruel mother-in-law goes back home to mother, attesting to the value of kin relations over marriage relations. A fourth isolates the main character from all others: the famous Ti Zan, too young to smoke, insists on smoking a cigarette and burns down the house. In only one song does

Nelzir Ventre show a victim fighting back on his own behalf, and that man is a criminal: passing a church, he steals from the poor box. As narratives, these plotless songs give forth mostly pathos.

Ton Nelzir's tales use a worldwide theme—the weak and slow overcoming the strong—to express the contradiction between the social position of creoles and his individual assertiveness. In performance, he was the strong one, displaying as much force as Hare.

He got stuck—like this, I tell you. He caught him from here, right punch—left, stuck. Like this. Now he is like this [*demonstrates*]. He said, "Well, how are you?" The tortoise said to him, "How are you, brother?"

Once caught, the hare always escapes, one way or another. That Akamba narrator, back in Kenya, effected the escape by a deceptive burning game: Hare is captured and taken home by Hyena, whose wife prepares to cook him, until he proposes they take turns throwing each other into the fire. "This went on for some time," the narrator said, "until finally the woman was thrown into the pot, and the hare covered the woman while she was still on the fire." Ton Nelzir's trickster also looks like being cooked.

So he said,
Tortoise my brother, put me in the water, *kan kolombo*
Brother, brother—
Tortoise, brother, put me
Chorus: in the water, *kan kolombo*
Nelzir Ventre: Tortoise, brother, put me
Chorus: in the water, *kan kolombo*
[*repeats twice*]

After some more call-and-response and a transitional "Eh-ou, brother, Eh-ou," Ton Nelzir repeated the call five more times.

He might have included a vivid moment from the version Charles Baissac published (a century before I met Ton Nelzir). Tortoise carries Hare to the king for dinner and says, "Cooked with wine, it's not bad" (Baissac, *Folklore* 2–15). Where Baissac's tortoise in that wisecrack claims the status of a guest at the king's table, Ton Nelzir's tortoise is more workmanlike.

What can I say? The tortoise—the king went like this. The king just called "Hey cook! Put him over there. Soon we'll have a *salmi* [game dish]." Eh-ou.

That one we call the hare, he is really clever. When he saw—when the cook took the hare—you hear?—when he grabbed the hare, the hare *fup!* So the hare ran away. So the hare left. And all the time I see the hare ahead of me.

So I told you that tortoise-and-the-hare one.[9]

If the trickster like Nelzir Ventre's hare is the most common figure in the repertoire of African storytellers—and he surely is that

(Abrahams, *African Folktales* 153)—his character should be as central to island storytelling as the pattern of making-and-breaking-of-friendship. And so he is. The weak overcome the strong in tales around the world; is this character universal to humanity? Yes, according to C. G. Jung: a trickster like the hare "is obviously a 'psychologem,' an archetypal psychic structure of extreme antiquity" (Jung and Kerényi 200). An archetype, according to Jung, is a pattern or form shaping human experience. The idea that archetypes might also be shaping literary works was expounded in the celebrated *Anatomy of Criticism* by Northrop Frye, where it proved to be an enlightening way of classifying literary forms. Anthropologists, who want more from a concept than a mere way of thinking, dismiss Jung's psychology as demonstrably false, but Rodney Needham argues for the antiquity and universality of trickster as much as for that of the half-man (Needham, *Reconnaissances* 17–40). His instance is Seth, from ancient Egyptian mythology, who "does not keep to the boundaries of sex" (Velde 59, 33). East African and Mauritian tricksters are not transgender creatures; instead of transgressing the boundaries of sex, they violate boundaries of the social order, while expressing the storyteller's individuality.

If trickster is an archetype, how does he become visible to real audiences? For archetype to appear in literature or folklore, mediation is necessary (a strange word to use for Nelzir Ventre's *sega*s). Genre and performance are what make pattern and archetype accessible to our experience. Maybe the Indian Ocean trickster is archetypal. Certainly he is a historical symbol, who arrived in the islands with the slaves (Gamaleya, "Contes populaires" [1974]; Diallo, Rosalie, and Essack 10–15, 30–34). The dislocation of these people, as of their successors the Indian indentured laborers, forced them back on inherited tools of psychological survival. Trickster became a guide for their real-life behavior in a particular way. It is not just his violation of social norms that distinguishes him; it's his multivoiced, deliberately ambiguous way of speaking. Trickster taught people how to "signify" (see previous chapter). He modeled their strategy of social critique, in their new situation of cultural convergence. His people, African-descended creoles, displayed a capacity for adapting their culture to a new and oppressive situation that was unhinging their social framework. Their system of signs had to be re-established. "Establishing a sign system," writes Julia Kristeva,

> calls for the identity of a speaking subject within a social framework, which he recognizes as a basis for that identity. Countervailing the sign system is done by having the subject undergo an unsettling, questionable process; this indirectly challenges the social framework with which he

> had previously identified, and it thus coincides with times of abrupt changes, renewal, or revolution in society. (*Revolution* 18)

In the new place, along with creative imitation, the multivalence, plural meanings, and "signifying" come into play.

The West African practice of plural meaning was uncovered by the eminent French Africanist scholar and critic Geneviève Calame-Griaule, who analyzes the ways of speaking among the Dogon of Mali (Calame-Griaule, *Ethnologie*). Her description of the complexities and ambiguities of West African "riddle language" applies not merely to the rest of the continent but also to the westward and eastward African diaspora. Riddling language is a way of hiding one's thought and saying it at the same time. Being a form of politeness, it enables the speaker to allude to delicate, even dangerous matters, but it must also be beautiful, humorous, playful, and a test of intelligence. To hear it properly, one has to be able to decipher its complex codes (Calame-Griaule, "L'Art" 85).

In East Africa, the genre most laden with meaning is the proverb, which uses metaphor as a tool of social control (Kabira and wa Mutahi 37–39; Finnegan 389–425; Okpewho, *African* 226–39). For the Haya of Tanzania, who are copious interpreters of folktales (Seitel, *See So That* 292), "pasturing goats is proverbially the scene for [boys to learn] the verbal arts of repartee and double-entendre" (Seitel, *See So That* 96), and also proverbs such as "The soap of the land is fire" and "He who was not told set out in a clay canoe" (Seitel, "Proverbs" 65, 71). Haya may have been among the slaves exported to the islands. Along the Kenya coast, among many Swahili genres depending on riddling language, the *vugo* song is a highly efficient way of signifying. Mature women sing *vugo* at a wedding to castigate misbehavior, sometimes the misbehavior of specific persons present (Eastman 325–28). Swahili culture, which in early days helped to form Malagasy culture, is now one part of the cultural mosaic of the region. Performance of a tale like Hare at the Animals' Well is itself a way of signifying in both Madagascar and East Africa (Mvula; Mbiti 147–51).

In Madagascar, it is even more important to mediate the contradiction between private thoughts and public expression. Feelings and thoughts, being private to oneself, should be hidden; everybody knows that. From childhood one learns with difficulty to fit oneself into society's way of speaking and to separate informal talk from formal, poetic language (*kabary*). Information is a scarce good (Keenan and Ochs 138). As in the narrative of child development expounded by the French psychoanalytic philosopher Jacques Lacan, the crucial point is the stage where the child enters into language (Lacan). Thenceforward, a common word can take on many meanings: consider *salt* in the legend of Ranoro (in previous chapter).

The contradiction between hiding and revealing is dramatized in a poignant Malagasy poem, an example of the traditional Merina *hainteny*, "word play." A weeping woman is being questioned by a neighbor. Repeatedly she denies that anything is wrong, until finally she is forced by the pressure of the repeated questions to admit, "My child is dead!" Then, the narrator concludes, she bursts into tears and evokes pity from everyone. The moral is, "Do not hide your sorrow" (Fox 296–97; Haring, *Verbal Arts* 130–31). The poem stylizes a tendency to ration information that observers notice among Merina. The *hainteny* genre elaborates plural meaning to its artistic apogee (Haring, *Verbal Arts* 98–151). Readers in France, who got information about their colony through an equally effective rationing by government officers, began to glimpse the poems before World War I, through translations by a young sojourner there who later became famous as a man of letters, Jean Paulhan.

South of Imerina, still in the highlands, the Betsileo consciously know and practice double meanings, which they call "beautiful language." A children's counting game called *kanisa* consists of counting from one to ten using parodic number words (rather like Cockney rhyming slang [Ashley]). *Kanisa* resembles riddling: the game must be based on knowledge the child already has. Thus it doesn't teach counting; it teaches how to mean more than one thing at a time (Michel-Andrianarahinjaka 224–32). A Betsileo story tells of an old man rooting for a tenrec (the Malagasy hedgehog) in a hole where one of the pair of tricksters grabs his hand. They swindle him out of twelve oxen (Dubois 1355). Such stories are told privately, within the family or village community, unlike the formal speaking of *kabary* (Michel-Andrianarahinjaka 295). Perhaps their irony points at one of the listeners, as "signifying" does in African-American culture.

Farther south in the island, the Tanala in tales often use an ambiguous motif: an insect enables the hero to identify his betrothed among other identical women.[10] Multiple meaning explains the frequency of the motif: *voto*, the stinger of a bee or wasp, also means penis (Beaujard, *Mythe et société* 429). Signifying also invokes a concern of Tanala people which comes up again and again in their stories, the establishment and legitimacy of royal power. Verbal ambiguity, as a deliberate weapon in this unspoken debate, is fully present to the Tanala themselves (Beaujard, *Mythe et société* 531). Signifying, finally, is learned early in the zone of Madagascar most closely connected to the other islands, geographically and culturally—the east coast. There one can see boys learning the difference between having feelings and expressing them. The humor of folktale, says one observer, aids Betsimisaraka people to put aside hatreds, murders, and disorder. The boy who performs is learning "how to express himself in public, learning his language and the forge at the same time" (Schrive, *Contes* [1989] 21).

If Madagascar shares with Africa this trademark of "riddle language," it is the "creole islands" that use it most zestfully in narratives. In a Rodrigan version of a well-known African false-friendship tale, Hare deceives Monkey into killing his own mother; Hare gets revenge by incinerating his former friend (Carayol and Chaudenson, *Lièvre* 94–101).[11] Is the punishment so unrealistic? Is the narrator alluding to slavery times? Comparably cruel punishments were common enough in the era when the ancestors of Rodrigans suffered under slavery in Mauritius. Hare is only turning the tables. In a Mauritian false-friendship story, both partners manage to elude the agreement. The final episode is reciprocal like the first: unable to find Hare, Monkey sends his whole *réziman* (troop), but Hare escapes by convincing his captors to place him in his favorite environment, the morning dew (Baissac, *Folklore* 332–37). The derivation of these materials is certain. The use of trickster tales to celebrate the superiority of wit attests to African influence (Neumann).

It also points to those "times of abrupt changes, renewal, or revolution in society" (in Julia Kristeva's words) which brought these island societies into being. Through plural meanings, people remind themselves of their oppression and symbolically overcome it. A Mauritian joke portrayed creole success in the 1980s:

47. The Old Lady at the Bus Station

Bhojpuri narrator 1984

Once an old lady was in the bus station waiting for a bus. The bus was gone already, the old lady didn't know. She asked a Creole man, "What time is it, son?" "Seven o'clock." So she says, "Has the bus gone?" The Creole says, "Maybe [*peut-être*]." But the old lady didn't understand. She went over to two or three men playing cards and said, "Has the bus gone?" They said, "Didn't that Creole you were with tell you?" She said, "He says 'peut-être, peut-être,' I don't know what it means." They say, "Oh, grandmother, 'petet,' you know what it is [fart], he cursed at you." The old lady went and hit the Creole man. (Gallob 264–66)

The creole character has the victory, through his knowledge of languages, but so has the creole storyteller, performing for an American anthropologist.

When these island tales were first published, much remained to be discovered about their African influence. Wondering about the derivation of the making-and-breaking of friendship, Charles Baissac corresponded with the pioneer linguist Hugo Schuchardt about one tale, which is known as Rabbit Rides Fox A-Courting (Baissac, *Folklore* 346–57; Uther 1:65). In his Mauritian version, Hare twice deceives Snail, his dupe, into self-injury. In the third scene, Hare persuades the vengeful Snail that he is so ill, he's not worth killing; instead, he persuades Snail to carry him to the king's house. The story ends with complete victory for the trickster: he forces Snail into the water, where he drowns. Then, returning to the king's daughter, he says he sold Snail because he was such a poor mount.[12] Schuchardt suggested that the Mauritian version was a case of reverse migration, being a combination of three "American Negro" episodes (Baissac, *Folklore* 246). In fact all three were well known in Africa before slavery began (Dundes, "African Tales" 41–42). The Réunion version is simpler than Baissac's. If the cat and the *fosa* were unlikely friends, how about Tortoise as a suitor for the princess? It begins after Tortoise's victory over Hare.

48. Hare Rides Tortoise A-Courting

Réunionnais narrator   1970s

The king thanked Tortoise and put him in the garden of the palace. The king's daughter fell in love with him. And Tortoise, with his stupid little head, passed his hand next to her *soubik* [basket]. The king's daughter had to give it to Tortoise. . . . So the two of them were lovers, like, engaged. Hare was jealous, he came around to break them up.

He remembered that time when Tortoise carried him on his back. So after a while he came down. He went by the king's place.

"Hey, isn't that Hare coming?"

"Yeah, it's me."

"What are you up to, Hare?"

"My king, you are the king, and your daughter is the princess. But how could you allow Tortoise to marry Mademoiselle the princess?"

"Ah, hare, don't go there, it's no business of yours."

"I know it's not my business, but I just tell you, Tortoise is my riding-horse, Tortoise is my riding-horse, I tell you, king."

The king heard. "So Tortoise is your riding-horse?"

"Yes, I tell you, he's my horse."

"Wait."

"No, I'm leaving. I told this to you, [but] Tortoise won't like to hear me [say it]." He knew Tortoise didn't hear him.

Wasn't Hare riding on Tortoise in the Tarbaby story, and isn't he now reframing that shame into his triumph? As trickster's behavior is a model of reversing power relations, the storyteller's performance alludes to his other tricks.

He ran. He went up to his house, among the houses up above. He prepared his plan. Once Hare was gone, the king called his stable-boy. "Bring Tortoise here to the corral." Tortoise was fastened by his fiancée herself. "Tortoise, you didn't tell us Hare was your rider."

"What did you say?"

"Hare just told me you are his riding-horse."

"King! Hare told you that?"

"Sure."

"Wait, I'll go see him."

"Go see him if you want, but if Hare wasn't telling the truth, he should come here."

"No, I'll go to him, I'll bring him."

Challenging something trickster has said doesn't have much chance of success, given his skill at switching registers (sometimes called lying).

He ran up *kokolok kokolok kokolok,* he found Hare up there in his house. "Hey, *konper* Hare!"

Hare went "Oh!"

"What did you just tell the king?"

"I didn't say anything to the king, not me."

"What, you didn't say you were using me as your riding-horse?"

"Ah, *konper,* could I say something like that?"

"The king is angry. Come down a minute and talk to me."

"Yeah, I'm coming." He jumped down. "*Konper,* you take me for a liar, to stop me getting married? I'm no liar, *konper.*"

"Look here, if you're an honest man, a real *konper,* let's go down quick."

"But of course, *konper,* I'll go down."

"Quick."

"Wait a second, I'm getting ready."

Hare will break this agreement as he has broken so many others; that is his game. The storyteller's game is similar. The contradiction between truth and lying, or between history and fiction, is of course a cultural universal, but when Hare shams illness, the real behavior of a clever underling points to the necessity of using one's wits against the oppressor. For the moment, Tortoise is the king's man.

He started moaning, "Ahnnh-ahnnh, ahnnh ahnnh ahnnh, ahnnh-ahnnh." Tortoise said, "What's the matter?"

"I'm not sure I can make it to the king's palace, I'm sick."

"You're sick? I didn't know you were sick. We're going to the king's."

"Yes, *konper,* I hear you, something's wrong with me, I tell you, ahnnh-ahnnh."

"Get up on my back, I say, get up on my back. I'll carry you, you'll straighten things out with the king." (Hare had it figured out.)

"Get up on your back?"

Tortoise said to him, "Yes, get up." He acted so sick, what a sick man! "Get up!" He stopped next to a rock, he climbed up on the rock, he made a little jump, and up he was. So they went off, they went ten yards. Hare started mumbling to himself, "Aya, ahh!"

"What is it?"

"My feet are dragging too much, careful, I might fall to the ground."

"Well, what do you want me to do?"

"Get a little iron thing they call a stirrup, to put your foot in." Tortoise said to him, "I'll get it." Tortoise ran to the smith, got a pair of stirrups, came back and gave them to him. He put his feet in. That was his plan. They went along. He thought the king, when they got there, was going to be shocked. They went on down. At a certain moment, "Dizziness is coming over me, *konper.*"

"*Konper* Hare, you're acting like a child."

"I'm sliding down, I'm falling to the ground."

"What do you want?"

"Don't you know that thing they call 'guide, guide' [a bridle], to put in your mouth?"

Tortoise, poor devil, ran off to look for the "guide." He got back and said, "This?"

"That's the one, open your mouth, *konper.*" Tortoise went "Ahh." He had him!

Tortoise didn't know he was going to be dressed up like that. "Okay, that's good, now let's go."

"We'll get there."

They went along. Went. They went a kilometer to get to the king's palace. "Ah, *konper,* you're all spoilt, you can't possibly go to the king's palace like that, brother, with so much mud on you."

"What do you want?"

"Look for a switch to get the mud off. A nice long one, hey. And strip it." Poor Tortoise looked for a nice switch for him. "There, let's go, *konper.*" He wasn't sick any more, he felt fine. He twirled his moustache. Then he started pulling on the "guide." Tortoise said, "You're hurting me."

"*Konper,* again it looks like I might fall to the ground, that's why I'm pulling the rope there."

"It's fastened good and tight, just don't yank too much."

Ah! the king caught sight of them. The fiancée fainted to the ground. "Father, it's true, Hare really does have Tortoise as his riding-horse!"

That is, he can signify with his dupe's costume as well as with his own words. Clothes unmake the suitor.

The girl was fainting. She saw them, she thought about her flower-basket, how in three days she was going to marry tortoise, a guy like Tortoise who was carrying her flowerbasket . . .

Hare, whack, whack, gave blows with the switch, whack! Tortoise gave a kick, he turned, trying to throw him to the ground. He didn't fall, he held on. Tortoise was beginning to get it now. He straightened up. Hare hung on still more. Arrived before the king. He jumped to the ground. Grabbed the "guide," tied it to a guava tree. Tortoise was streaming with tears. Tortoise wanted to eat him, he wanted to kill him, but he was caught by the neck. The king looked at his daughter, the one looked at the other. It was true!

"When I told you that, king, you didn't believe me. Now you see."

The king said, "Take Tortoise into the corral over there." Once he was there, the king came back and said—now he didn't call him Hare any more, he called him Mr. Hare—"Mr. Hare, what you told me was the truth, he really is your riding-horse. You can be married to my daughter now!"

"It pained my heart to see Tortoise being the princess's fiancé. But I am too young to get married. I did you a favor, but I'll go on being a bachelor." So he let him go, gave him a good sum of money; he took off. He left. He was a bachelor! (Gamaleya, "Contes populaires" [1974] 20–24)[13]

In a characteristically creole move, the Réunionnais storyteller leads his or her audience into the conventional wondertale sequence, in which the hero will pass a test in order to win the princess, and at the last moment switches back to the trickster genre, so that Hare will escape into another adventure. The switching between genres is the narrative parallel of the variability of the local languages, or of many creole languages (Sebba 264–69)—and words like *konper* are derived from French. The mix of traditions in the island gives the victory to Hare, the champion trickster of British East Africa, over his rival. For the moment, the many successful tricks of Tortoise, who in Portuguese East Africa was the second "most conspicuous figure in Bantu folklore," are forgotten (Werner 273–90). If Hare beats Tortoise, and both animals make a fool of the human being, a hierarchy of power is established for a little while, ironically strengthening the ideologeme of subordination. Such narratives look back to inherited culture, too, remembering the earth hero in Madagascar who successfully contended with the sky god. Through such imaginative constructs—symbols, signs, images—ideology works for the powerless. No wonder these stories are still told.

Trickster tales celebrate a playfulness that is a creole response to oppression. It shows in the joke in which the creole man wins a verbal victory over the old lady at the bus station. In another joke, a Mauritian who is the apparent underdog wins, on behalf of his nation, through a pun. It helps to know the Kreol word he is punning on: Mauritians import a certain small dried fish from India and use it as a condiment, which in English is called "Bombay duck."

49. Mauritius's Bomb

Mauritian Kreol speaker 1984–85

There was a conference in the United States where all the countries were represented by the delegates to talk on armament, which country has which kinds of arms in their country. So the American says he has very sophisticated bombs, so he says, "I have nuclear bomb." France says, "I have atomic bomb." Russia says, "Me, I have hydrogen bomb." China says, "I have hydrogen bomb." India says he has underground bomb. Now it comes the turn of Mauritius. What will he say? Each country has said the power of its bomb, what effect their bomb makes. It comes Mauritius's turn, which bomb it has. The Mauritius representative stands up and says, "In my country we have *bomli.*" (Gallob 288–89)

In one word, the Mauritian delegate, recognizing that all the other kinds of power have been taken away from him, out there on his own in this overgrown marketplace—invokes the Indian past of his people, admits their powerlessness, and reclaims their power.

Some European aestheticians see such playfulness underlying all of art. The romantic philosopher Friedrich Schiller is remembered for two things, giving a libretto to Beethoven and declaring, "man only plays when in the full meaning of the word he is a man, and *he is only completely a man when he plays*" (Caillois 163). The Dutch philosopher-historian Johan Huizinga contends that all culture develops out of play. The French scholar Roger Caillois, finding it strange that Huizinga could write about play without looking at games, completes the theory (Huizinga; Caillois). The Danish folklorist Bengt Holbek, noting that "play" and "game" are the same word in Danish, asserts that telling folktales was both play and game (Holbek). For these three writers, play is a separate world. In the folktale world, Holbek asserts, the unresolvable conflicts of real life are solved.

Holbek gives no attention to slave societies or their successors, but his theoretical construction could have been written about them.

> Human societies are organized in power structures originally created through conflicts. The victors have established norm systems which are suitable to their interests, and institutions to propagate and confirm these systems. (Holbek 14)

The "emotional intensity, rapid action and minimal characterization" (Glassie 61) of a trickster tale enable the loser, in the system created by the victors, to win a symbolic victory. As any art-work, according to psychoanalytic theory, is the successful solution to the artist's inner conflict, so the folktale's ending solves, in that separate world, a real-life conflict that never goes away. Sometimes the tale admits that.

50. The Cat and the Water-Rat

Betsimisaraka female narrator 1880s

"The father of the cats one day was on the bank of a river," says a narrator from the east coast of Madagascar, modeling his *angano* on a *tantara*.
He wanted to cross to the other shore. He asked the rat to get him across the river. In the middle of the river, the rat, carrying the cat on his back, slipped away and let him sink. The cat reached shore with much difficulty. When he got on land, he gathered his children and grandchildren. "See what the rat did to me," he said. "It is an insult to all of you. So to get revenge, let us destroy their damned race. Every time one of them gets in our way, let us eat him and kill him." (Ferrand, *Contes* 1–2)[14]

The narrator assumes that rat's character as a trickster is already well known. Unlike many of the stories in Gabriel Ferrand's collection, but like other stories that reluctant "natives" dictated to Europeans, this one is rather sketched than performed. Like the cat-and-*fosa* story, it is structured like myth: a state of the world we know today is shown to originate in the breakdown of an earlier, happier state. Any hearer would foresee, from the present unhappy state of things, that enmity will endure. Genres of verbal art in Madagascar often overlap, as they do all over Africa (Haring, "Classification"; Ben-Amos, "Folklore in African Society" 4–7).

In folktale as in history, Malagasy presence has ever been a force in Comoran history (Vérin, *Les Comores* 88–92), but the politics are different, at least in this example. In the old Merina kingdom, for instance, royal decisions had to be ratified by the advice and consent of the governed (Vérin, *Madagascar* 83–91). Malagasy birds require qualifications in a king other than majesty and size. According to a Merina tale, a number of birds tried to become king, but the one chosen was *railovy*, the drongo, chosen for his good speaking voice, his middle height, and his modesty (Renel, *Contes* 2:160–63; Dahle 290).

51. Hare at the Animals' Well, 2

Comoran narrator 1930s

In the Comoran election story, Elephant must play the royal role by initiating reprisal against trickster Hare, but as so often, the monarch is not the hero.

Once, they say, the animals had an unusually grand gathering during which they decided to elect a king. After many deliberations and hot debates, the elephant was elected, because of his majesty and size. Before separating, the animals planned to build a pond, which they needed in a country where it doesn't rain most of the year. They all agreed except Hare, who declared he didn't want to take part in this job, as he had enough water for the whole year.

So the Comoran storyteller has found a new way to frame the familiar story. The animals, foreseeing the possibility of Hare's depredations, ration the water and station a couple of domestic animals as guardians. Both Donkey and Sheep are decoyed into being tied by Hare's sweet water. Tortoise prepares his strategy by reference to Malagasy trickster tales.

He promised the animal assembly to capture Hare, whom he considered like an Ikotofetsy. "I'll be an Imahaka," he said.

Who? Tortoise is alluding to devious behavior the animals, and the storyteller's audience, will recognize.

The names of Ikotofetsy and Imahaka are well translated as Wiley and Cheatam. These are Madagascar's best-known tricksters, whose tales are told all over the Great Red Island, even when storytellers give them other names (Mamelomana 859–65). Their stories are African in origin but uniquely Malagasy in character structure. Instead of a single trickster who embodies antisocial behavior, like Hare in Kenya or Soungoula in Seychelles, they are a pair of tricksters who carry out all the exploits. They nearly always win. By alluding to Malagasy stories like these, as the Comoran performer does here, a storyteller practices the half-quotation that is the mark of excellence in a performer and sophistication in an audience. Always, such allusion reinforces the connection between himself and all members of his audience; always it marks the boundary between those who know and those who don't. Tortoise will model his behavior on what is known from inherited discourse. His audience can do no less.

"I will be an Imahaka," Tortoise has said. The rest of the Comoran tale stays more true to African tradition than to the Malagasy twin-trickster pattern. He has his shell covered with glue and goes to the bottom of the reservoir; Hare, seeing no watchman, calls out, "No watchman here? I'm going to steal water from your reservoir." No answer. Plunging in, he gets each foot in turn stuck to the shell, Tortoise surfaces, Hare is captured, he is taken to king Elephant and jailed. He escapes with a favorite African deception, convincing his guards to hold up the mountain;[15] again he is captured, again he escapes. His final capture encloses him in a hut to which everybody brings their night-soil. He knows what will happen: the animals will add liquid to the solid. So, legalistically manipulating their authoritarian system to his advantage, Hare complains that the sentence was not accurately carried out and is freed. Elephant is long forgotten. The combination of African and Malagasy influences in this piece is more easily disentangled than the ethnic mix of the Comoran population, whose ancestors intermarried with Malagasy, Arabs, and Persians.

Hare has remarkable survival ability. His predictable behavior survives translation from Yao, Kiswahili, and Nyamwezi to *shimaore* (the main language in the Comoros) and all the Kreol languages of the islands, and from there it survives even a mannered translation to French.

52. Elephant, Hare, Lion

Grande Comore (Ngazidja) narrator 1930s

All the animals except Lion (*simba*) and Cock harbored resentment against Hare, who had so tricked them, and prepared revenge. After long discussions, a death sentence was passed on him. Obviously all the animals could not overcome Hare, so the king himself, Elephant, put himself forward for the arrest. So one day he placed himself close to Hare's hideout. Hare came out early to get food; on his way back in, sniffing a trap, he set himself a little way from his dwelling and cried loudly, "Hey, house! Answer as usual. Are you still there?" Naturally he got no answer.

This "cave call" is a popular trick on its own, originating in Africa, developing into "an Indo-African-Afro/American tale," and migrating to the United States (Baer 132–33). Closer to the Comoros, a Swahili story shows Hare playing the same trick on Lion, who is deceived into answering (Steere, *Swahili Tales* 369).

Giving signs of impatience, he came near the house and knocked loud enough to be heard, and again with a loud voice he said, "Oh, my nice house, be nice, answer me, are you still there? Otherwise I'm leaving for good."

This time a deep voice was heard, full of despair. "Yes, I'm still waiting for you. Welcome." From the first words, Hare was sure a stranger was there and answered mockingly, as he was leaving, "Oh, pal, don't try a trick like that on me, I'm not such an innocent as to let myself get caught as easily as that." Elephant, quite crestfallen, came out of his hiding-place, then went back to his palace, attended by mocking looks and murmuring of his subjects. This misadventure did not dishearten the king, who was irritated at the spiteful attitude of his subjects. He promised not to come back without bringing his enemy.

He went to post himself in a place where Hare usually passed by. He lay down right outside, playing dead. Flies didn't hesitate to invade his big ears and especially his mouth, which was half open. That was proof for Hare. Also, several of his subjects were coming by. They bowed respectfully before the body of their revered king, believing him truly dead. Hare, still distrustful, arrived. He was suspicious of the reality of this death; staying on guard, he cried, "Oh, friend, you can't play that trick on a smart fellow. You think you'll persuade me you are dead so I'll come and get under your paws. You forget, a dead man moves part of his body—an ear or a paw. Let him open one eye and if you are dead, prove it to me by moving some part of your body!" Unthinkingly the supposed dead man moved one paw. That made his clever adversary laugh.

The king saw he was caught and tricked again. He didn't want to deal with the nagging of his subjects again; he went around his palace without going in. But he didn't get discouraged; he waited patiently for the right moment. As for Hare, he knew his enemies were tracking him and took precautions. He moved his house to a safe place, a detail that did not escape the always watchful king. He in turn set up his lair near this new house.

This tale was translated from Comoran in the 1930s, a period when colonial officers were attempting to comprehend, or contain, Malagasy "identity" and "mentality." (Later on, the lion is credited with a "fantasy.") Maurice Fontoynont, one of the translators, was the most eminent physician in Madagascar and was revered for his contributions. His cohort conceived the Comoros as a kind of offshoot of the great island. In retrospect, the tales he published in the *Bulletin de l'Académie Malgache* look like one side of a dialogue, which was meant to resolve what many colonials called the "fundamental misunderstanding between Malagasy and Europeans" (Berthier 27). The Comoran side of the dialogue was translated in a style which embodied the contradictions of colonial society.

Translation, indeed, was the main effort. In this translation, characters such as Hare and Elephant and incidents such as the "cave call" come through recognizably, as they do in other regional trickster tales. But the condescending tone of the vocabulary and sentence structure can affront a politically correct reader of today. At one point, Hare is caught and jailed, for the first of three times, in the sentence, *"Le malheureux lapin fut sans autre forme de procés mis en prison,"* literally, The unfortunate hare was, without other form of trial, put in prison (Fontoynont and Raomandahy 88). The word *malheureux* extends a feigned sympathy to the character; the interpolated phrase *sans autre forme de procès,* drawn from colonialist discourse, creates a sentence structure more complex than oral style usually tolerates. Reinforcing the tone of condescension, the opposition of king and "subjects" (which doesn't appear, for example, in Malagasy oral histories) recurs throughout: *"Il ne voulut pas affronter à nouveau les criailleries de ses sujets* . . . ," He did not want to face again the cries/complaints of his subjects (Fontoynont and Raomandahy 88). The great importance accorded to a king is a distinct touch in the Comoros, where folktales look back on a time when kings were powerful (Abdallah Paune 108–109; Blanchy, "Lignée" 9–11). Of course Fontoynont and his collaborator Raomandahy were under no obligation to reproduce oral style, though their predecessors, such as Lars Dahle in Malagasy and Gabriel Ferrand in French, had done so long before. They choose one of the classic alternatives posed by the German philosopher and translator Friedrich Schleiermacher: a translator can leave "the reader in peace as much as possible" by "moving the author toward him," or he/she can leave "the author in peace," and "move the reader toward him" (qtd in Lefevere 149). The question is, as Humpty Dumpty says to Alice in his explanation of pragmatics, which is to be master. In the Madagascar of the 1930s, the way Fontoynont and his collaborator Raomandahy chose to leave the colonial reader in peace was to invoke a tone that would remind him or her who was master.

Admittedly, translation is my main effort here too. The more direct and colloquial style of my translation is equally domesticating, based on an imaginary reconstruction of the Comoran original. Theoretically perhaps, nothing but difference exists between Comoran and English, and meaning is only produced in the relation between them as signifiers. The signified original—that imagined performance for a village audience—is endlessly delayed and deferred, the more so as the storyteller is long dead. For us there is no primal, undivided state of immediacy;

there is no transparent translation, here or anywhere. The desire for presence, the yearning for immediate contact with an original, animates many people's interest in folktale and myth. That desire is an effect of what Jacques Derrida calls *différance* (Derrida). He coined this playful term to convey simultaneously the production of *difference*(s) with that endless *deferral* of meaning which, Derrida asserts, happens in every signifying system. Pursuing that meaning draws many of us into reading folktales and literature. Fortunately the sequence of trickster incidents forces its way through *différance.*

For a long time Hare lived peacefully with no alarms. He thought he could let go of his suspicions. His adversary jumped for joy, thinking the capture had become easy. One fine evening, Elephant easily entered Hare's place and summoned him to give himself up.

The king's subjects were very worried, not having seen him or had news from him for several days. They decided to send out scouts, who found the king quite soon, a bit tired but bringing back his prisoner. His entry into the village was greeted with cries of joy and applause. Poor Hare was imprisoned without trial.

Soon after, the king assembled his subjects and put before them the situation, which had become alarming as a result of the collusion of Hare and Lion. He sent a certain number of them to Lion's den under orders to take him. But they came back empty-handed. The king thought that only Hare, as Lion's friend, could get him out of the deadlock. He decided to go find him in prison. The prisoner agreed to go in search of Lion; he brought him back with no difficulty.

Hare was put back in prison and Lion was tied up tight. But he easily broke the weak cords the guards used to hold him down—they didn't know his strength—and he took off. The king, when he heard about it, came back to the prison to find Hare. He asked him to go again and find Lion, which he agreed to do.

He left, and stayed away a long time, not because he hadn't been able to find the fugitive, but because the two friends were having such a good time, for six whole days. Finally they both came back before the king. For the third time Hare was put in prison, and Lion was tied up. Next day, following the king's orders, people took Lion and Hare out to the fields, supposedly to work. The subjects were assembled; the king ordered them to kill the lion. One of them came to carry out the sentence, but he'd hardly moved before he was torn to pieces by the lion's claws. Another one took his place. He had the same fate, and so it went, so much that the only one left was the king.

Hare, present at the scene, came up to Elephant and said, "Your turn. You've been so cruel with us that if you try to run away, my friend Lion will pursue you. If you try to put him to death, you'll undergo the same fate as your poor subjects." Elephant jumped in anger, but stayed put, watched by his humble adversary, who preferred to make him suffer as long as possible to satisfy his vengeance, for he wanted to advance his candidacy for kingship. Hare perched on a little mound, laughed with a happy heart, and mocked the king.

Hare has put Elephant in a true dilemma. An older Malagasy tale does the same thing with an irresolute guinea-fowl, as we saw in the preceding chapter. Whether the ethical dilemma is also experienced by Comorans, the guinea-fowl's dilemma echoes the continual frustration of Malagasy confronting the many *fady,* taboos, around them (Ruud). Back to Elephant, Hare, and Lion:

[52, continued] The king's wife, not seeing her lord and master come back, brought him something to eat. It was not her husband but the others who profited from the meal. Even better, once he'd eaten his fill, the lion had the fantasy of killing the wife in the presence of the king her husband. Elephant stayed like that a long time, locked in place by his fear, without taking the least food, enduring the heat of the sun and the rigors of cold. He got visibly thinner. Despairing, he tried to run away while Lion was sleeping. But Lion was not slow to catch him and kill him. The elephant's subjects, from that moment on, recognized the lion as their true and only king. (Fontoynont and Raomandahy 83–86)

In Seychelles, the favorite trickster is Soungoula.

53. Soungoula at the Animals' Well

Seychelles narrator 1970s

Once there was a Soungoula who was very clever in his country.

His name derives from *sungura* in Kiswahili, the coastal language 1600 km to the west. Sungura is known to storytellers in Yao, a major language in the old British Central Africa Protectorate, or Nyasaland (Malawi), one of the shipping points from which slaves were taken to the islands. Playful tales about Soungoula resolve recurrent, permanent sociopolitical issues, in familiar, predictable ways.

After a while, there was a drought, and there was no water. So the king had the drum beaten around the whole country. They announced that everybody had to come lend a hand to dig a well, to get water. Like that, people and animals, they would get water. So all the people and animals came to help and dig. Bird, ox, goat, tortoise, even ant, they all came. But among all those animals, that Soungoula didn't come to lend a hand.

In a country populated by Africans, it was inevitable that Soungoula should be cast as the Hare at the Animals' Well. "Mischievous, good-humoured, a wiseacre as well as a trickster"—he is all those indeed, as a historian says, but you can only visualize him as "more of a monkey" if you ignore his continual duping of the monkey Zako in other stories (Scarr 29–30). Trickster and dupe must be opposites; it's one of the rules of the folktale genre. The binary opposition, the Tarbaby plot, and Soungoula's very name all come from East African trickster tales (Diallo, Rosalie, and Essack 10–15; Werner 252–72). Touches of realism, such as the assumption that community tasks will be carried out cooperatively, the unquestioned authority of a ruler, the ridicule cast on people of small endowments, and the inevitability that rules will be broken, point to a body of ideas which are part of the same heritage. They are why the tale is meaningful.

The same is broadly true for Soungoula's tug-of-war, but its politics are different from the trickster's decisive victory as I heard it in post-independence Africa. In 1968, an Akamba storyteller in Kenya told me,

One day the hare asked the hippo, "How can I know that you are strong?" and the hippo asked, "How can you understand my strength?" Now the hare told the hippo, "You can experience my strength while I am on one side of the hill and you are on the other."

Giving the hippopotamus one end of a rope, the hare goes over the hill and gives the other end to the elephant, who succeeds in pulling the hippo to the top of the mountain. The hippopotamus admits that Hare is the strongest animal. In Soungoula's version, the animals are less equal. Soungoula at the outset is already afraid of elephant, who however is quite willing to have a tug-of-war with an animal so obviously powerless.

54. Soungoula's Tug-of-War

Seychelles Kreol narrator 1970s

So Soungoula left Elephant and went down to the sea and met Brer Whale. He said to Whale, "Ah, how's it going, Brer Whale?" Whale said, "Great, my friend, still living by the seaside." Soungoula said, "Brer Whale, let's have a tug-of-war, see if I can beat you." Whale was glad and said, "Sure, Brer Soungoula, when?" Soungoula said "Monday. Only I'll stay on the other side of the mountain and you stay here in the sea."

He hands the other end of the rope to Elephant and tells him to wait for the sound of a whistle.

Soungoula looked for a big shell and put a hole in it to make a horn. When he got to the mountain, he blew on it three times

—and the narrator imitates the sound. Elephant, cheered on by Soungoula, succeeds in pulling Whale out of the water on to the reef. The narrator sympathizes with Whale's suffering: "Whale broke his whole body." Then comes the post-slavery touch. Both animals admit that Soungoula has beaten them. When Elephant vows revenge, the two animals, who have been set against each other by a common enemy, bond together. Elephant helps Whale get back into the channel, and in a final episode, Elephant catches Soungoula by a pool and breaks his neck. "Soungoula died. That was how the elephant got his revenge," the narrator ends the story ("Creole Stories" 64–65). The solidarity of elephant and whale has a Utopian element of incipient class consciousness.

Soungoula personifies Nietzsche's *ressentiment* as Seychelles has known it through history. Long a dependency of Mauritius (1742–1903), Seychelles received runaway slaves, originally from Mozambique, Madagascar, Somalia, and Tanganyika, who escaped from the Mauritius sugar plantations. Running away was not their only defensive effort: telling and retelling folktales such as the tug-of-war, which they remembered, was another. After slavery was abolished in 1835, the British saw fit to set down the Africans they called "liberated" in Seychelles (and other places). These men and women now became apprenticed to colonial employers. Modern historians have a better name for them: "recaptives" (Carter, Govinden and Peerthum). The descendants of these Africans and Malagasy intermarried with Europeans, Indians, and Chinese to produce the present-day Seychellois population, whose Kreol language, like the related Kreol of Mauritius, is the vehicle for both their inheritance and their innovations. Dislocation and convergence with other populations—marks of a creole society—have sent them back to trickster as a guide for coping with authority, as well as for a few laughs.

Even when Soungoula gets killed, as he sometimes does in Seychelles stories, his death is an African touch. An especially fine Seychellois version of that story mentioned above, in which Cock dupes Hare into cutting off his head—making-and-breaking again, of course—was collected in 1980 in the island of La Digue. The incident is evidently well known in the part of East Africa from which the slaves were seized (Rattray 142–45; Diallo, Rosalie, and Essack 30–34; "Creole Stories" 53). But Soungoula doesn't stay dead for long. He tricks lion into a fatal imitation (Diallo et al., *Veyez 2* 4–5; Payette, *Kont* [1990] 63–64). In another piece, after stealing the king's coconuts, he persuades his dupe Kousoupa to sing a song confessing the crime—a true African touch

(Carayol and Chaudenson, *Lièvre* 122–29, *Contes créoles* 129–33; "Creole Stories" 48–49; Beidelman, "Four Kaguru Tales" 5). As in New World slave tales, "the dominant themes are trickery, subterfuge, and securing as much as possible of a desired item (often food) for oneself" (Kolchin 154). A trickster will send away his companion so that he can eat their common food supply. Soungoula is the victim of this trick, at the hands of Zako the monkey. Their story is again framed by the making and breaking of friendship.

Still in African style, one Seychellois storyteller assembles three old plots of false friendship.

55. The Loose Handle

Seychelles Kreol narrator 1970s

Well, one day there was *Soungoula* and *Lulu* [wolf]. So one day Soungoula said to Brer Lulu, "Let's make a house for the two of us." Brer Lulu said "OK." So Soungoula went down, went to the smith and said to him, "Make me two spades, make the handle out of iron. Don't attach the handle. The one with the iron handle, weld it all around for Brer Lulu, the other one for me, Soungoula."

About four o'clock the spades were ready. Soungoula went to get them. Soungoula made a handle for his out of a stick of manioc. Next morning he went to Brer Lulu and said, "Brer Lulu, let's go start working." As they went along, Soungoula said, "Brer Lulu, let's make a deal [*kondisyon*]. The one whose spade, the handle comes off first, he uses the other one's forehead to put it back on." Lulu said OK. They hardly gave two hits with the spades before the handle of Soungoula's one came off. He said, "Brer Lulu, bring your forehead so I can put my handle back on." In one day Brer Soungoula's spade handle came off eight times.

This incident spins off from a Yao story collected in the 1870s, which is short enough to quote.

> The elephant and the hare formed a friendship. The elephant said, "Friend, let us go and hoe a field." The hare said, "Come let us cut handles for our hoes." When they had cut the handles they said, "Come let us put on our hoes" [Editor's footnote: We should rather speak of putting on the handle.]. When they had put on the hoes, they said, "Come let us hoe." As they were hoeing the hoe of the hare came out, and it said, "I am here, my chief, I have come to you to put in my hoe." The elephant said, "How will you put it in!" The hare said, "I will put it in on your head, I will use it (your head) for a stone. When your hoe comes out,

> you will come to me." The elephant said, "Fix it in." So the hare knocked his hoe in, on the elephant's head. Soon the hare's hoe fell out again and the hare came once more to the elephant and said, "O chief, I have come to put in my hoe on your head," and it put it in on the elephant's head and then went away.
>
> As they hoed, the hoe of the elephant fell out. The elephant said, "Hare, O chief, my hoe has fallen out! I will fasten it in on your head."

The missionary noted, "Simple humour like this is greatly enjoyed by the natives. I suppose their hares (sungula) like English ones, are most easily killed by a stroke on the head."

> The hare said, "Wait for me a little": and it ran off. When the elephant went to look he saw no one. (Macdonald, Duff, *Africana* 353–54)

In the Seychelles story, it takes eight hits from Soungoula before wolf gets the idea, and Soungoula has to think up a second trick, the one called "holding up the rock."[16]

[55, continued] "Brer Soungoula, bring me your forehead so I can put my spade handle back on." Brer Soungoula said, "Brer Lulu, look, the mountain's gonna fall, let's go hold it up." They held it up. When it got to be four o'clock, Brer Soungoula said, "Brer Lulu, keep holding it up, I'm gonna go look for a big fork to hold it up for us." Brer Lulu said OK.

Now the storyteller introduces another character, Kousoupa. When Makua audiences, back in Tanzania, heard this character's name, Hyena, they knew he was Hare's dupe. In Seychelles he has been transformed into a *"lapin dans le folklore seychellois"* a rabbitlike double agent (St. Jorre and Lionnet 149).

Brer Soungoula had a violin made out of coconut wood. He went to his house and played his violin. For three days Lulu kept holding it up. Fourth day, Brer Kousoupa came by and said, "Brer Lulu, what can you be doing there?" Brer Lulu said, "I'm holding up the mountain, it's going to fall otherwise, give us a hand to hold it up so it doesn't fall on us." Kousoupa said, "Lulu, enough of this foolishness, a mountain can't fall on us, those are clouds moving." Lulu said, "No, Kousoupa, it's gonna fall." Kousoupa wickedly gave Lulu a shove and he fell to the ground. When he raised his head, he turned and saw the clouds moving.

Kousoupa asked Lulu how he came to be holding up the mountain. Brer Lulu told him. Kousoupa said, "I came by Soungoula's house, I found him playing his coconut violin, and he had two five-sou pieces under his foot." Lulu said, "I'm gonna go kill him."

But the wolf is deceived when Soungoula pulls the third trick, the "cave call."[17]

Soungoula said, "Brer Lulu, you're not gonna catch me." Another day Lulu put himself in a bundle of grass. When Soungoula came, he said, "Mama always told me not to pick up grass that doesn't move." Brer Lulu budged, budged. Soungoula said, "Ha ha, Brer Lulu, you can't catch me."

One other day, Lulu fell half dead in the middle of the road. Soungoula, as soon as he came, he saw Lulu. He said, "Mama always told me when big animals die, there's always a sign of life, it moves its nose, nose, its eyes, its ears, most of all its tail, to know the truth." Lulu gave a sign of life. Soungoula said, "Ha ha ha, Lulu, you can't catch me."

Makua audiences, back in Mozambique, would have remembered the falcon who tricks a sham-dead rabbit the same way: "I heard from the great ones of old that when a rabbit dies you see him wag his tail, all except this one who does not wag his tail" (Woodward 153). Soungoula ends the three-part Seychelles tale by accident, escaping only in the mind of his dupe.

Soungoula climbed up a boulder. He found a blue pond, but he didn't know there was a rock at the bottom. When he found Lulu coming he said, "Lulu, I'm going away for a couple of weeks." He jumped down into that little blue pond, broke his head and died. Lulu said, "Oh well, you went for a couple of weeks. You'll find a time you're so cunning, you'll give death to your body." ("Creole Stories" 18–19)

As Soungoula usually escapes, his dupe thinks he's still alive. As in West Africa, "Trickster tales remain open. The character is immortal: if he's killed in one tale, he will reappear in the next" (Paulme, *La Statue* 31). And if he cheats people in one island, he will cheat them in another.

In the Comoros, the trickster Bunuaswi carries on much as Soungoula does in Seychelles, though he's a bit more outrageous. Trotrochendijarouai is a master thief. Stories about Bunuaswi were collected in the largest island, Grande Comore (Ngazidja), in the 1930s, and translated by Fontoynont and his collaborator in their accustomed style (Fontoynont and Raomandahy). Others were collected in Mayotte in the 1960s (Allibert). In Madagascar, it's usually the clever lad (called the Peasant's Son in European versions) who shows up the ruler's absurdity, but in Grande Comore, that task falls to the trickster Bunuaswi. His Swahili incarnation, Abu Nuwasi, said to be the favorite poet of the Caliph Haruni Rashidi (Knappert 116), was once directed to build a house in the sky in three days. He made a huge kite shaped like a house, floated it in the sky, and asked the Caliph for additional timbers. When the men saw the thread holding the kite, they refused to walk up it. "No one can," said the Caliph, to which Abu Nuwasi asked, "Why did you order me to build a house in the sky?" (Knappert

119–20). Comoran social structure keeps the rebuke but awards Bunuaswi the honor of an indirect intervention.

56. Bunuaswi the Wise

Narrator of Grande Comore 1930s

One evening some villagers heard the horn resound. In the Comoros, as is known, the hunting horn is used by the *fokon'olona* [village assembly] or the government for communications to be made to the population. The public crier in the king's name informed the population that whoever could remain for a whole night in the cistern situated near the palace would collect the sum of five hundred francs. This cistern contained only thirty centimeters of water, just enough to wet one's legs, but it was the midst of winter and the nights were very cold. Everybody was wary of accepting the challenge except one man, named Lazar, an unfortunate who took the bait of the prize.

Since *lazar,* in languages like French, is a generic word for a pauper or leper, one wonders who gave this *malheureux* his name.

He entered the cistern at nightfall. His mother, a very perspicacious woman with much love for her son, took a position some distance from the cistern. She lit a big wood fire and kept it going.

The gambler stayed all night in the cistern. He was very tired, exhausted, and numb, but no matter; he thought towards the five hundred francs he would soon collect. The king did not want to carry out his contract, on the pretext that the mother's intervention had allowed the son to warm himself and stand the rigors of the cold.

Full of despair, the unfortunate victim put his case before the notables of the village, who sent him to find a certain Bunuaswi, reputed to have an extraordinary mind. Lazar went to him full of hope. Bunuaswi received him amiably and listened to him attentively, then he sent him back, promising to get him out of the affair four days later, on Friday.

On Thursday, Bunuaswi went to the poor man's village, killed an ox and some goats, and had the inhabitants told that before going to the Friday prayers, he was inviting them to a meal that would be prepared. All the inhabitants, very surprised, accepted this invitation at once. Friday morning early, Bunuaswi arrived at the place and had a great quantity of rice put into big pots, with the beef and the goat meat. But he had the pots positioned some distance from the fire. The king, who had agreed to preside over the ceremony, came and was surprised, like many of the inhabitants, at this new way of cooking food. Bunuaswi arrived and said, "Friends, I have guessed your thoughts and I avow you are right. But understand that all this is done by design, to see if fire placed some distance from the pots can cook the rice and the meat." No one dared to speak, for only the king or someone he designated was allowed to. The king arose and said that short of a miracle, the rice would remain hard and the meat uncooked, as long as the pots remained far from the fire.

So Bunuaswi said to the king, "Yourself, my lord, have given the answer. Fire placed a great distance from the pot will never cook either rice or meat, just as a fire being kept up far from the cistern will never heat either the cistern or what is in it." Everyone approved this judgment, and the king promised the assembly to pay Lazar. He became, if not a rich man, at least a comfortable man, thanks to Bunuaswi's wisdom. (Fontoynont, "Le folklore" 75–76)[18]

Mayotte (Maore), the southernmost of the Comoros islands, receives most attention from Europeans, especially since 1975, when it obliged France to keep it as a dependent under the title of a "territorial collectivity." Its Muslim culture and its stock of stories link it to Grande Comore, Anjouan, and Mohéli; its population and its ancient cultural substratum link it to Madagascar and the Swahili coast. One Mahorais narrator, Bwanali Said, strings together seven trickster episodes; the first is a bit like the first episode in the Grimms' "Little Farmer," where the poor but clever hero trades a wooden calf for a real one (Grimm and Grimm 247–62).

57. Bwanawasi

Bwanali Said, Mayotte 1973–75

Once there was, a long time ago, a great trickster, very wily, named Bwanawasi. One day the people in a village wanted to organize a celebration. They wanted to kill an ox. Everybody there knew they wanted to kill an ox. Bwanawasi took his, killed it, and skinned it so as it wouldn't be spoilt. He sold the meat and filled the skin with straw, so it got its shape back. Then he fastened it near the village, all set up. Next he went to the king and said, "I have an ox I can sell you. But be careful, he's very bad-tempered. Only go fetch him at night!" The king gave him the money and he left.

That was in the morning. Bwanawasi walked a long time. That evening, the villagers went to get the ox. As soon as they pulled on the rope, the ox fell over. They went quick to the palace and told the king what had happened. The king ordered them to chase him. Five men went in pursuit. They walked all night. In all the villages they passed, they asked the chief if Bwanawasi was there. They told them no, and they kept going. Finally they reached the place where Bwanawasi was. They found him dressed in a mosque costume, with a cap and a Qur'anic book in his hand. They didn't recognize him. Bwanawasi asked them, "Who are you and where are you coming from?" They told him the adventure. He told them he would give them something to eat and they would sleep in the mosque. The strangers agreed. They ate, then went to sleep. Bwanawasi took some papaya and crushed it till it looked like excrement. Then he put it under the legs of the strangers. In the morning, when they woke up, they saw the papaya there and they thought they had soiled the mosque. So they fled to their village. Thus Bwanawasi could get away.

His next episode is a favorite for Sakalava storytellers of Madagascar, who are the closest neighbors to Mayotte (Birkeli 240–45; Dandouau, *Contes populaires* 216–28), but the highland storytellers know it too (Dandouau, "Contes malgaches"; Renel, *Contes* 1:77–81).

After a few kilometers, he came upon an old woman harvesting. He said to her, "Grandmother, grandmother! I'm a good harvester. I can harvest your whole field right away!" She was an old woman all alone in the country in a little house. The old woman thanked him in advance and blessed him. The old woman's house was two kilometers from her field. She went to make food. Bwanawasi ate a few stalks of sugarcane, then burned the whole field. Next he went back to see the old woman and told her he'd finished. He claimed the meal. The woman gave him food and said, "When you're finished, you can sleep on this bed!" And she went to see her field. Bwanawasi ate, then he took all the plates and pots, put them carefully on the bed, wrapped them in a cloth and left. When the old woman saw the state of her field, she came back. At home she thought Bwanawasi was on/in the bed. She went for a stick to kill him with. Furious, she hit the bed so hard she broke her plates and pots. She thought she'd beaten Bwanawasi black and blue, from head to foot. Then she picked up the cloth. When she saw what she'd done, she began to weep.

What differentiates Bwanawasi from the Tanzanian Hare or the Seychellois Soungoula is the scurrility of his tastes.

Bwanawasi had stolen some cakes from the woman. On the way, he ate some raw sweet-potatoes. They made him gassy, which made him feel very bad. When he wanted to fart, he uncorked a bottle, farted into it, and closed it so the smell didn't come out. He got to a village and bought a bottle of perfume, then went on his way. Soon he got to another village close by, where there was a marriage in progress. He joined the dancing and sprinkled perfume on the women. But the women didn't know what it was, and they all wanted to smell that nice smell. So Bwanawasi said to them, "Find a house with only one door," and he added, "If I put perfume on all of you, the smell will go off and none will be left." The women went and found that house. Once there, Bwanawasi said, "Go in, I'll stay by the door!" The women went in and then Bwanawasi broke the bottle and double-locked the door. Then he left, and most of those women died of asphyxiation.

A trickster episode like this brings up the oldest question in fiction. How is it that trickster characters like Bwanawasi (Bunuaswi) or Soungoula, clever lads like Ti Zan, or noble heroes like Andrianoro are allowed to perform acts that would be forbidden or impossible in everyday life? They are fictional, one says in reply. Even so, if folktales and novels are a mirror of culture, is the mirror image right side up? To what extent and in what ways are Comoran or Malagasy folktales an index of Comoran or Malagasy culture? Psychologists answer that all folktales are collective fantasy; like dreams, they transform real and imaginary experience into symbolic language. All the components of story performance—the content, form, and structure; the social, political, and economic situations surrounding the communication—might be familiar (presented as right side up) or wildly unreal (upside down). It follows that if a serious folktale hero, like Andrianoro (in previous chapter), is superior to you and me in manly virtue, a trickster, like Soungoula or Bwanawasi, is superior to us in wiliness and trickery. Consequently he must stand apart and be society's antagonist, as Andrianoro was society's protector. In slavery times in Réunion and Mauritius, a single runaway slave, Bwanawasi's real-life counterpart, was a threat to the social order. Comorans have clear signposts to separate true narratives from fictional ones. A storyteller introduces the *hale ndrabo*, "lying word," with a formula forbidding the hearer to discuss it: "*Hale ndrabo, namwambiwa kashindana, ye shindana mdrwa mdroni,* The tale is a lie; the hearer does not discuss it; if he discusses it, he is damned to hell" (Allaoui and Haring 54).

Bwanawasi has yet more plans for the village women.

After this outrage, Bwanawasi went to another village, where there was an epidemic. Bwanawasi said that the women could escape from this misfortune if they went to sit on the little thing sticking out of the water near the shore. Then he went and stretched out in the water with only his prick sticking out. All the village women went there and sat, the way Bwanawasi had told them to. Then came the turn of the old lady of the village, who suspected something. She grabbed a needle and stuck Bwanawasi's member as hard as she could. He was discovered and could only run away.

After this last misdeed, Bwanawasi left. By now everybody knew there was a man in the country called Bwanawasi who had to be arrested. In the [next] village he came to, there was a man who knew him. When he got there, the man saw him and went to tell the king. The king summoned him to the palace. The king asked him, "Are you Bwanawasi?" He said yes. The king ordered him to be put in a sack and thrown into the water. Fortunately the sea was low. The king's servants left him on the sand and went back to the palace. Bwanawasi then heard a herdsman going to pasture his cattle. He started yelling, "No, I won't marry her! I'll never marry her! You want me to marry the king's daughter, but I don't want to! You can throw me into the water!" The herdsman heard what Bwanawasi was saying. So he let him out and went into the sack in his place. Bwanawasi closed the sack up well and left with the herd. He went to sell them, then came back to the palace saying, "King, king! I come/came from the sea! The king of the sea is inviting you; he's getting up a *grand mariage.* He told me to come and tell you he's inviting you and you have to come with me. It's really gay in the sea, everybody is happy." He told each one to fasten a rock to his feet to get down to the sea kingdom more quickly. When they got near the coral reef, he made them lean down and told them to listen to the orchestra. It was the sound the sea makes on the corals. He had them jump in one after another.

As only the king's daughter was left, he gave her the choice of marrying him or joining her family. She agreed to marry him and he went back to the king's palace and that one's daughter became his wife. They lived happy and had many children. (Allibert 25–27)[19]

Slyly pulling in the classic folktale ending, in which the hero marries the princess and inherits the throne, and "They all live happily ever after," the Mahorais storyteller Bwanali Said brings an end to this string of Afro-Malagasy tricks.

The translators of the Comoran story of Lion, Elephant, and Hare also bring us the human trickster with the most charming name of all, Trotrochendijarouai, who synthesizes several roles. Their version, in summary, begins with that faint echo of the culture-hero that opens many another story: an old, childless couple at last produce a son, who demonstrates his potency by aspiring to marry the king's only daughter. The king sets him four tasks as her suitor, which can only be accomplished by thieving. First the future son-in-law must bring the king a goat belonging to Jim-Kou, who is king of the devils. Rivalry between kings, typical in precolonial Comoros, motivates the whole piece (Abdallah Paune 109). Trotrochendijarouai has his mother prepare him some good cakes, which he distributes to the goatherds, thus distracting their attention; he steals a goat. The second task renews the rivalry: the suitor must steal an ox belonging to Jim-Kou; again his mother's cakes are a sufficient distraction. Not content, the king now orders a golden cock: Trotrochendijarouai succeeds the same way. Finally he must steal

Jim-Kou's sheet and pillow. For this feat, Trotrochendijarouai consults a *mwalimu,* diviner, who advises him to cut sharp, needle-shaped leaves from the *ouniongo* plant. From under Jim-Kou's bed he pricks the royal couple seven times through their mattress, till they light a lamp and discover him. At this point—like a Swahili hare who persuades Lion to take him where he will find more meat (Arewa 65), or like a couple of Malagasy predecessors who persuade cannibal ogres to wait till they get fat (Ferrand, *Contes* 69–76; Birkeli 294–99)—he escapes death by persuading Jim-Kou to delay killing him till next day, and to do it in public. He obligingly conceals Trotrochendijarouai in a big jug. Throughout, he is both a trickster and the Master Thief, well known in European and New World folklore (Aarne and Thompson 431), while playing a third role, the typical folktale hero on his way to marrying the princess.

Planning to eat his prisoner, Jim-Kou sends out invitations to a banquet. As his wife is cutting firewood, Trotrochendijarouai offers help, then kills her when she lets him out of the jug, dismembers her, and puts her in the jug. But he retains her calf, thigh, and foot, to place in the bed; he sets the head on a piece of furniture and flees back to his king—with the sheet and pillow, of course. When Jim-Kou finds his wife dead, he faints, holding the head. So successful are the suitor's thefts that his king now demands the capture of Jim-Kou himself. Again consulting the *mwalimu,* Trotrochendijarouai learns that Jim-Kou's strength is diminished if he goes near a certain waterfall. To that place he carries a huge metal container and sits down, acting the low-class role of a fisherman. There he captures Jim-Kou, delivers him to his king, and marries the princess (Fontoynont and Raomandahy 80–83).[20] If Bunuaswi stands out as a fighter for the oppressed, Trotrochendijarouai finds it to his interest to submit, be a good soldier, and accomplish what his future father-in-law commands.

We expect a trickster to stand out; how else will he be society's antagonist? But if he lives in a society that teaches a person to avoid standing out, and instead to identify with his or her family or clan, how shall trickster values be remodeled? By cloning. This was Madagascar's unique innovation for trickster: there are two of them.

58. Making True Friendship

Merina narrator 1880s

One day, Wiley and Cheatam met on the way to market. "Where are you going?" Cheatam said.

"Going to sell this cock," he answered.

"Me, I'm going to sell a spade," Cheatam said.

"Well," said Wiley, let's trade my cock for your spade." (Both the cock and the spade were in baskets.)

Thus we meet Madagascar's twin tricksters, Ikotofetsy (Wiley) and Imahaka (Cheatam), who establish their equality by making, breaking, and remaking friendship.

They made the exchange right away, and the two traders each went home. When they opened the baskets, the cock turned out to be a crow, which flew away, and the spade turned out to be made of clay. Our two comrades, who had intended to trick each other, set out to find each other so as to swear blood brotherhood. (Ferrand, *Contes* 201–202)

Thenceforward, these two enact a dependence on each other that will enable them to undermine everybody else's interdependence. Every move by Ikotofetsy and Imahaka proclaims a social value: the importance of working with each other, even if you are violating every other value. This part of their behavior is quite realistic, according to one authority: "If two Malagasy enter into relation, their first move is in some way to *exchange places.* One reflects always as if he were in the place of the other, and reciprocally" (Andriamanjato 49). The Merina storyteller who dictated the story was living on the east coast, away from the highlands he called home, at the time. He made them realistic by localizing the two tricksters, for all the world as if they were historical characters: "Wiley and Cheatam lived in Vonizongo district. Cheatam's tomb is near the village of BareRidge (Andringitra)."[21]

Could they have arrived from East Africa? A story from southwest Tanzania tells of two deceitful men meeting by a tree and a stream, where they trade sugar for coconuts. At home, each is upbraided by his wife and vows revenge; when they meet again, they fight, but then make friends: "Let's not fight, we are brothers." And they go on to trick a dead man's relatives and share the wealth (Mwakasaka 10–17). Which of these two stories came first is difficult to tell. The Tanzanian story was published sixty-five years after the Malagasy one; it could have been recently composed, or told for centuries earlier. As much as the structural pattern of making-and-breaking-friendship or the character of the trickster, this sort of African verbal play prepared the people who became Malagasy, Mauritians, and Réunionnais both to continue performing old tales and to adapt them to their new setting.

Ikotofetsy and Imahaka come from the central highlands of Imerina, as the storyteller said, but they have cousins in other parts of the Great Red Island, including the southeast. The African substratum in Malagasy folktales transpires through the doubling of tricksters like Bolio (Slick) and Bolaotsy (Slippery). We join them in the midst of a sequence of four tricks, which began with the reciprocal trickery we just saw. (The sequence might be the translator's work.)

59. Slick and Slippery

Antaisaka narrator 1960s

Bolio and Bolaotsy were tricky men. After they tricked each other, they made *fatidra* [blood brotherhood], and once they'd done that, they decided to go into far countries and swindle people.

On the way they met an old woman getting in rice from a ricefield, and they said to her, "We come to this place to help people. As you are reaping all by yourself, we'll help you, if you accept." "Gladly," said the old woman. "May God and the ancestors bless you!" After she said that, the old woman went back to her house to cook some rice for those nice rice-harvesters.

As soon as the old woman left, the two friends started selling the rice to people passing by: "Come! come!" they said, "rice for sale! We need money for a circumcision ceremony coming." And the people going by bought rice from Bolio and Bolaotsy. When they'd got some money that way, they left the ricefield and hid in the forest, so as not to be seen if pursuers came looking for them. At noon the old woman came back, carrying some cooked rice. She saw that her ricefield was half harvested, but she didn't find any heap of paddy. She was angry, and she warned the people in the nearest villages. They ran to the ricefield, carrying spears, big knives, axes, sticks, and asked the old woman what happened. She explained to them, "Two men said they'd help me harvest my rice, but while I was in the village, the crooks stole the harvest!"

The villagers followed Bolio and Bolaotsy's tracks. They found them in the middle of the forest at the foot of a tree, counting the money. "What are you guys doing?" the villagers asked them. Bolio and Bolaotsy answered, "We just sold some cattle, and we're counting our money under this tree because it's cool here." "Thieves! thieves!" the pursures said, and jumped on Bolio. Bolaotsy got away at top speed and didn't get caught. Bolio was taken to the old woman's village, with people saying "Thief! thief!"

Isolating one of the pair enables him to deceive a dupe into taking his place.

After the villagers roughed him up, they put him in a big bag and placed it by the river, to throw him in the water later. At mealtime, when the people went back home to eat, there was a woman looking for a lost goat. She passed by the riverbank calling, "*Bengy, bengy* [goat], eh!" "Beh, beh!" went

Bolio inside the bag. "Aaah, what bad people they have in this village," the woman said. "They've put my goat in a bag to kill it." She untied the bag; Bolio got out, tied her up, and put her in the bag instead. He tied the bag back up and ran off. After eating, the villagers went back to where they left Bolio. The woman cried out, "Don't throw me in the water! The man you put in this bag tricked me!" "No, no, you devil, the crow doesn't get fooled twice," the villagers said. They took the bag and threw it into the water.

Bolio went to where Bolaotsy was hiding. They met and said to each other, "Aren't we the kings of devils?"

Their third deception, the "voice from the grave," is known in both central Africa and India (Aarne and Thompson 438; Lambrecht 112–13; Thompson and Balys 338; Beck 18). It gains local emphasis from the enormous Malagasy respect for the dead, who have not departed, but have simply moved into a different part of the belief system. Ancestors "have their corner of the house, are present at all festivals," and are otherwise available to the living (Andriamanjato 42).

Continuing their journey, they heard a big noise in one village, crying and songs together. They asked a man passing by, "Who's dead in the village?" He answered, "A rich man there died, leaving a big herd of cattle, ricefields, fields of manioc, jewels of gold, money. The burial is done already." Bolio hid under the trees growing around the tomb. Bolaotsy ran to the village weeping, "O, Abba [father], O, Abba! Why didn't you wait for me before dying forever? "What, what?" the people said to each other. "Did this dead man have other children than the ones we know?" After weeping according to custom, Bolaotsy responded to the greetings of the people around the tomb by saying, "I am a son of the dead man. I learned of Papa's death. I come to weep for him and see how you have buried him!" Then he asked that the property left by the dead man be divided.

There was a big meeting. The elders decided that the unknown son had no right to inherit, because his name had not been uttered by the dying father. At that, the unknown son asked that they get the word of the dead man himself. The elders agreed to get the word of the dead man himself.

When an ox had been sacrificed at the gate of the tomb, the sacrificer,[22] surrounded by clan chiefs and wearing his red hat, asked the opinion of the dead man thus: "O dead man, listen. Here is a man, he says he is your son and asks for his share of your wealth. Answer if it is all right."

Hardly had the sacrificer finished when a nasal voice was heard from the direction of the tomb. "He is my son. Give him his share of the wealth."

Hearing this voice, Bolaotsy sobbed, groaned, stiffened, shook his feet and hands, and cried, "That is my father's voice!" There was suddenly a great silence. The crowd was amazed. When Bolaotsy had calmed down, he spoke to his father in the tomb: "Oh papa! Speak now. Shall I not be given my share of the wealth?"

And the voice answered, ""Yes, yes, my son! Get your share of the wealth, and take it wherever you like!" The excitement of the crowd was at its peak. They went back to the village. The elders divided the dead man's goods among his children, including Bolaotsy. Then he said to his fellow heirs, "I am taking only the cattle. The ricefields and jewels I leave to you." He led away more than half the herd.

The fourth, fatal deception turns up in many stories around the world, especially The Master Thief, but the Malagasy version features a trickster who knows how to manipulate the belief system.

Bolio left his hiding-place when Bolaotsy was well away from the dead man's village, leading his cattle. They passed near the village where Bolio almost got thrown in the water. The people in that village were surprised to see him again, and asked each other, "Isn't that the man we threw in the river over there, leading those cattle?" "Yes," said some; "no," said others. To put an end to their discussion, they put it to Bolio himself. He answered, "You are too clumsy even to lead cattle. Don't you know that the Water-Princess gives a herd of cattle to whoever goes down to her home at the bottom? It was Water-Princess who gave me these cattle!"

Having heard Bolio with wonder, all the villagers had their wives put them into sacks. The wives threw them in the water, and Bolio and Bolaotsy addressed them: "Be patient, you wives of future rich cattlemen!" They left. The men thrown in the water did not come back.

The translator follows oral tradition in the final administering of justice.

Bolio and Bolaotsy went into another country. Because their bad reputation had spread around, the people watched them. Then one day, they went into a house to spend the night, and the owner burned the house down. The tricksters were burned up.

Late or soon, the evildoer will be caught. The one who does evil to his friends will be hated by God and the ancestors. (Mamelomana 859–65)[23]

Some of the same episodes are told in the highlands about Ikotofetsy and Imahaka, though the splitting of trickster into two characters is not consistent: sometimes one acts alone like his African forebears. For instance, Ikotofetsy, rolled in a mat, substitutes an old woman for himself; later he persuades the prince and all the men of a village to be thrown into the water, to get jewels like his. Other episodes, like the voice from the grave, require the pair to collaborate (Dahle et al. 75–78; Chapus 76–79; Ferrand, *Contes* 226–32). (I preserve Ferrand's variant spelling of Imahaka's name.)

60. They Trick the King

Merina narrator 1880s

Kotofetsy and Mahaka[24] learned that a prince was fond of having cricket fights on a certain hill. One day Kotofetsy had Mahaka go into a hole, leaving him only one opening to put his hand through. Mahaka had a big crab with him, which he held in his hand. When the prince came to play on the hill, he saw the crab and put out his arm to grasp it. Mahaka then took the prince's hand and began to pinch it hard. The prince was frightened and called for help: "I am dying," he cried. Kotofetsy came and said to the people there, "There's a *vazimba* living in that hole."

As the editor, Gabriel Ferrand, explained in 1893, "The *vazimba* are generally considered the aboriginal inhabitants of the highlands, from which they were driven out by the Merina. Today the Malagasy have made them into supernatural beings. They seek their protection by means of prayers, in which they promise offerings of chicken or sheep fat to the *vazimba* if the petitioner is successful" (Ferrand, *Contes* 236). Evidently the word once meant persons who were "part of the first African migrations," but from earliest times they met those who arrived from Indonesia, and thus underwent cultural creolization (Vérin, *History* 48). The word welcomed variant meanings. A century after Ferrand, the enigmatic *vazimba* had become a useful classification to contain "any dead person who does not have descendants to continue his line. . . . [W]herever one goes one might inadvertently step on a Vazimba tomb, the worst thing one can do to a tomb" (Bloch 42). Mahaka sees how useful such a dangerous creature can be to him.

"Much money is needed to make it let go. Give me a large sum and I will have the prince released." The prince offered ten coins, but Kotofetsy refused to work for so little. The animal inside pinched more and more strongly, and the prince cried more from it. The king offered fifty coins to deliver his son. Kotofetsy put the money on the imprisoned hand of the prince and said, "You are the remedy for the pinch. *Vazimba,* if you will release his hand, it can come out; if you don't let go, it will stay there." Mahaka pinched less strongly, but he held on to the hand.

Then Kotofetsy said to the king, "The hand can not be released unless you give a hundred coins. The *vazimba* refused first ten coins, then fifty." The king was so sorry to see his son weeping and suffering that he gave Kotofetsy a hundred coins. He put the money on the prince's hand and the grip was loosened immediately.

"Don't come up close here," he said then to the people. "There is a *vazimba* who will punish you." It was only that he didn't want them to see

Mahaka come out of the hole. When the king, the prince, and the people had left, Mahaka came out of the hole, and the two men were overjoyed to have obtained a hundred coins so easily. A little while later, the people learned with great surprise how the king had been tricked by Kotofetsy and Mahaka. (Ferrand, *Contes* 235–37)[25]

Kotofetsy and Mahaka are profane. Knowing that "Vazimba power is random, unregulated, and potentially disruptive," and that *vazimba* are "rather like nature spirits" (Bloch 42–43), they manipulate sacred power against royal authority, and win. Is religion supposed to be based on the sacred power of idols and amulets? Then they will deceive people into worshiping fake ones.

61. They Sell Pseudo-Magic Objects

Merina narrator 1872–76

One day the two companions went to set up an idol. This was nothing but manioc wrapped in red cloth. The weather just then was overcast; they saw it was going to rain, and the wind was blowing hard. They called the people together into the village square. Then they brought out the idol; the idol did not move. They said, "We brought out the god, but you have not worshiped him. He is angry; he refuses to reveal his glory to you. For that reason it is going to rain in torrents, and the rivers will overflow." They knew that much rain would soon fall and cause the rivers to overflow. That is what happened, and there was a big flood. People were amazed and frightened.

Next they took a snake and wrapped it in red cloth, as they had done with the manioc; they put it in a basket. Then they said to the people, "Here is our god. He was irritated yesterday, but we pleaded with him, and the rain stopped. Now he is going to show himself. So let us all begin to dance, to honor him. Perhaps he too will dance." When they had taken the snake out of the basket, they put it on the ground and it began to stir under the cloth. The people did not stop dancing all day, and everyone gave something as an offering. So that day the two men got about ten thousand pieces of money.

And this is what the two told the crowd there: "If you are sick, O people, come to us and bring twenty-five cents and a red cock as an offering. But if you forget the gods, you will die young." So it was that many people began praying to the idols. There were many who took away bits of the idols, and the two men got rich. (Dahle 296–97)[26]

Is family life supposed to be based on reverence for elders? Then Ikotofetsy and Imahaka calmly discuss killing their own mothers, simply to get people's sympathy.

62. Deceptive Agreement to Kill Mothers

Merina narrator 1872–76

One day when the two friends met, Imahaka said to Ikotofetsy, "My friend?"

"What is it, dear friend?" he said.

Imahaka answered, "Let us go learn to weep, so that we will know what to do if a rich person happens to die."

"Good idea," he said. They applied themselves to that for two months. A long time after that, Imahaka said again, "My friend!"

"What is it, dear fellow?" the other said.

Imahaka answered, "Partner, people talk only of us. People are saying, 'Aren't Ikotofetsy and Imahaka crazy to do nothing but cry, when they have not had a death!' "

"Really?" Ikotofetsy said.

"No, my friend," Imahaka said, "it's too shameful. We must go and kill our mothers. When they are dead, then at least people will have no more to say. Even if we weep for a whole year, people won't have an excuse to make fun of us, because they will say, 'They are weeping for their mother, those two brothers.' "

Ikotofetsy did not guess the trick, and agreed, somewhat in spite of himself. "Let us go then, friend."

Imahaka took him in tow, saying, "Let's go. We'll put ourselves at the edge of the water, you downstream and me upstream. I'll be the first to kill my mother, and when she is dead I'll throw her body into the water. When you see blood downstream, then strike your mother with the spear, because mine is dead." "All right, old friend," said Ikotofetsy.

When the two partners reached the edge of the water, Ikotofetsy followed it. Imahaka got hold of a sheep belonging to somebody and stuck it with his spear, then threw the body in. The water was reddened by the blood. Then Ikotofetsy said to himself, "She is really dead, that clown's mother!" He speared his mother to death, then threw her body into the water. After that, Imahaka declared to Ikotofetsy, "Let's both go and show our mothers' bodies."

"No, mine is dead—how can I show her?" said Ikotofetsy. Then Imahaka showed him his mother. Ikotofetsy was sad and wept, because he knew he wasn't as brave as Imahaka.

Now the pattern repeats: a contract is again broken.

When a year had passed, Ikotofetsy said, "Partner, let's go raise some maize in that fertile patch. It's just the right season."

"All right, good idea," Imahaka said. The two fellows cultivated and got a good crop. When the maize was ripe, Ikotofetsy said, "Come watch it, because there are thieves." The two comrades went to sleep in the field and decided to spear anyone who passed by in the evening.

One day Ikotofetsy came to the village and said to Imahaka's mother, "Come out to the fields in the evening, mother, and get a little maize."

"Thank you very much, my son," said the old woman. When evening had come, at the time when the light makes it hard to recognize people, the old woman came. She went straight to the maize and began to cut some. Ikotofetsy called Imahaka and said, "Hey, partner, watch out! There's a thief."

"Where?" said Imahaka.

"Look over there. I'll take care of him," Ikotofetsy said.

"No," said Imahaka, "I'm the one to hit him." And he began to walk stealthily and when he got near the old woman, he speared her and she fell dead. And Ikotofetsy said, "Soon it will be dark." But when it was day, Imahaka fainted, because there was his mother stretched out dead. Then Ikotofetsy began to cry and jump for joy, saying, "The wife's punishment belong to the wife, the child's punishment belongs to the child!" (Dahle 362–63)[27]

This is the sort of behavior Tortoise, in the Comoran story, expects to practice on Hare. Whatever force it is that keeps Hare alive works also to keep Ikotofetsy and Imahaka in balance. A Chaga version of this same tale from Kilimanjaro (Tanzania) has a different moral: it ends with a counterpunishment that kills off Hyena, Hare's dupe (Fokken 88–90). Similarly, a Kaguru version (also Tanzanian) breaks the friendship permanently as Hyena starves to death (Beidelman, "Hyena"). When this tale type was imported to Madagascar, equilibrium within the dyad had to be preserved: both mothers had to die. Such is the force of this ideologeme of interdependence.

63. How Mahaka Got Cattle for His Mother's Funeral Meal

Merina narrator 1872–76

"Mahaka was very embarrassed after his mother's death," we are told. For a bereaved son not to offer a funeral meal to friends and relatives would be an insult to the memory of the dead.

For he owned no cattle, and consequently could not have any killed according to custom. An idea came to him. He leaned his mother up against the door, sitting up, and put cotton and a spinning-wheel into her hands, to make it look as if she were alive and spinning. Then he rejoined Ikotofetsy and the two began to wait for travelers.

Instead of setting up a corpse to frighten people, as happens in other tales (Dubois 1357; Faublée 137–40; Aarne and Thompson 442), Imahaka will use her corpse to enrich himself.[28]

Some men came along leading cattle which they were going to sell. It was lunchtime, and the herders were looking for a house where they could cook their rice. Mahaka offered them his house, showing them the door: "Push on it to go in; it's not locked." The herders accepted Mahaka's offer, not knowing the trap that was set for them. Arriving at the door, they pushed on it to go in, and caused the old lady's corpse behind it to fall. Mahaka took all the village to witness that these strangers had just killed his mother. "This woman," said he, "was alive and well when Ikotofetsy and I left the house. What's more, the proof is that cotton she was spinning, as she was in the habit of doing every day. Since she has been killed, let these strangers die too. A life for a life."

Mahaka is as ready with a proverbial justification as Ikotofetsy was before.

The herders, trembling with fear, hinted that the old lady might have been already dead when they tried to enter the house. "You lie," Mahaka answered. "My mother was probably about to go out when you came in. But because you pushed the door so violently, she fell backward, and you killed her. The best proof that she was living before you got there is that she's still holding the spinning-wheel and the cotton she was spinning. Since you killed her, you must die. Well—you might be allowed to live, on condition that you turn your cattle over to me. They can be used to carry out the funeral ceremonies."

The village elders applauded these words and asked the herders to decide between losing their lives and abandoning their cattle to become Mahaka's property. The herders accepted the second condition, for "life is sweet" and one looks twice before leaving it. Mahaka had the cattle killed for his mother's funeral meal. The village people, who had witnessed the way he procured them, said, "Truly, that dead woman gave the world one clever man!" (Ferrand, *Contes* 210–12)[29]

The villagers in the story see things as clearly as the audience listening to it.

Some of the British missionaries, in the 1870s when these stories were being collected, convinced themselves that stories like this one proved the Merina were skeptical about their ancient religion. They cited proverbs such as "A good divination isn't for dancing, a bad one isn't for weeping," or similes: "Like a diviner asking too much, for a sick person to dance" (Cousins 6). If idolatry were ridiculed in proverbs, conversion would be easier. But they gave no evidence of how such proverbs were used, or what they meant to their hearers. Much as they enjoyed the trickster stories, the London Missionary Society men could not credit Malagasy with a capacity for varying attitudes, shifting points of view, or irony. In fact, what happened among New World slaves also happened in nineteenth-century Madagascar: the converts selected, rejected, and reshaped Christianity in accordance with the emphases of their culture (Gow 84; Genovese 159–284). As for signifying in words, the Norwegian Dahle understood that ambiguity and plurisignification were essential to Merina ways of speaking (Dahle viii); that was why he had to censor his texts. When Malagasy Christians wrote texts under missionary eyes, they transferred signifying to writing and used "turns of speech which possessed more than one meaning" (Gow 138). But nobody understood double meanings so well as Ikotofetsy and Imahaka.

64. Kotofetsy and Mahaka Trick an Old Man

Merina narrator 1872–76

One day Kotofetsy and Mahaka were carrying a basket containing a turkey. Under the turkey's wings they had put pieces of money. When they arrived in front of the house of an old man, who they knew was rich, they went in and said to the master of the house, "We were passing your door by chance and thought well to come and pay you a visit."

"What are you carrying in that basket?" the man asked.

"A bird that lays money and pearls. The king asked us to bring it to him, to buy it from us."

"Show it to me," the rich man replied. "Whether the king buys it from you or I do, the money will be worth the same. We only have to agree on the price."

"We cannot show it to you," the two comrades said. "The king would be angry if he found out. This bird lays money."

"Does this bird really lay money?" the man asked.

"Yes," answered Kotofetsy and Mahaka. Upon these words, the man offered to buy it, but the two rascals refused to sell. Finally the rich man promised to pay them very dearly if he saw it lay money before his eyes. Kotofetsy and Mahaka immediately took the turkey in the basket and said to it, "Money bird! Pearl bird! Lay some money. There is someone who wants you." And they began to whistle. The turkey immediately agitated its wings, and the pieces of money fell to the ground.

The rich man, astonished, offered ten, twenty, fifty coins successively for the turkey, without getting it.

Next he begged Kotofetsy and Mahaka to begin the experiment again. It happened again, with the same success: a *sikajy* [one-eighth of a coin] fell on to the mat. The man offered a hundred coins for it, after consulting with his wife, who urged him to conclude the bargain. When the sum was paid, Kotofetsy and Mahaka warned the man that the turkey would not lay again that day, but that it would begin laying again the next day, morning and evening, by means of the procedure they had shown him.

The next day, the man took the turkey aside and whistled, as Kotofetsy and Mahaka had done. From its wings dropped a tiny bit of money, very little. But that was all; there was no more of the money they had put under its wing. Hoping that the harvest would be better the next day, the man shut up the turkey, to be sure that the money would not be stolen. It was absolutely no use. The man and his wife perceived that they had been tricked by Kotofetsy and Mahaka. They were all the more put out because they had paid a hundred coins for a bird worth only a farthing. (Ferrand, *Contes* 213–15)[30]

Only in Madagascar is this trick credited to a pair of tricksters. Whether in Grimm tale no. 61, "Little Farmer," when an animal that supposedly drops gold is sold, or in the many appearances of the trick in India (Thompson and Balys 293), or in a Togolese tale (Clarke 350), the deceptive salesman is always working solo.

The assiduous doubling of what was once a single character reinforces a message about not standing alone. In Malagasy thought, especially among the highland Merina, one metaphysical concept dominates: *tsiny,* the invisible force of reproach or blame, which falls on those who offend the ancestors or the community. *Tsiny* affects not what you do (in this case the deception), but the manner in which you do it. "*Tsiny* is like the wind, one doesn't see it, but one feels it" (Paulhan 358–61; Andriamanjato). One avoids *tsiny,* among other ways, by sharing responsibility. In Imerina, where Ikotofetsy and Imahaka are at home, "it would be *exceedingly* unusual . . . for an individual, as such, to initiate an important action and assume responsibility for it. . . . Most actions then are taken by families or the *ray-aman-dreny* [the village elders], not by individuals" (Keenan and Ochs 139–42). Even when Imahaka acts on his own, the audience remembers that he is one of the responsible pair.

65. The Insect That Turned into an Ox

Merina narrator 1870s

One day Mahaka made a bet with a noble that he could arrange for a *sakoririka*[31] to turn into an ox. People made much fun of him. Nevertheless he put his insect inside a stalk of bamboo, which he carried on his shoulder, and he showed it to everyone shouting, "This is my ox! This is my ox!"

He spent the rest of the day that way, walking from village to village, carrying his insect on his shoulder. When night came, he stopped in a house in a village he had passed through earlier. When the people saw him, they began to shout and make fun: "Oh, it's Mahaka! Oh, it's Mahaka!"

"That is my name," he answered, "didn't you know?" And again he said, "This is my ox! This is my ox!" showing his insect all the while.

"Where should we put your animal?" said the owner of the house to Mahaka, when night came.

"Put it in its proper place," he answered.

So the owner put the insect with the chickens, which pecked it to death. Next morning, there was the insect, dead. The owner of the house was worried, and said to his guest, "Mahaka, Mahaka! Your animal is dead!"

"Then whatever killed it will belong to me."

"Oh no, really!"

"Well," said Mahaka, "replace my animal with another just like it. Otherwise whatever killed it will belong to me."

The house owner was intimidated and agreed to give Mahaka a hen to replace the insect.

Next morning, Mahaka left the village, carrying the hen under his arm, and happily went on his way. When the sun went down, he went into the house of an old gentleman with many children. "Hey, Mahaka!, hey, Mahaka!" they shouted.

"Mahaka is my name all right. You know it, of course. Have a look at my ox. This is my ox!" he said, showing them his hen.

"Where should your hen be put?" the owner of the house said.

"Put it in its proper place." The children took the hen and put it with the ducks. But they killed the alien one, as it was the only one of its kind among them.

"I will take whatever killed my animal," Mahaka said. At the same time he scowled at the owner of the house, who was afraid and gave him a big duck in place of his hen.

That evening Mahaka asked for hospitality from a man who raised turkeys. "I ask you to put my animal where it ought to be," he said. The children placed the duck among the turkeys, but next day it was found dead. Under some threats from Mahaka, the man gave him a nice turkey.

Mahaka, with his turkey enclosed in a basket, slept at the house of SheepMan. "Put my animal there in its proper place." The turkey was lodged in a corner of the sheepfold. But the sheep thought that there was grass inside the turkey. They gave it so many strong blows with their horns during the night, to open its stomach, that it died.

"I shall not be satisfied," said Mahaka, pretending to be angry, "until I am given whatever killed my animal."

"It is not my fault," said SheepMan, "but never mind. Take a sheep!"

Mahaka stopped the night in the house of a rich man who owned many cattle.

They put his sheep in a cattle ditch, where there was one animal being fattened. At night Imahaka got up, went into the ditch, killed his own sheep, and hooked it over the ox's horns several times so that they were red with blood. Then he went back to bed and slept in, to allow the owner of the house to find out the accident.

Once he got up, he pretended to go look for his sheep. When he saw it dead, he covered the owner of the ox with reproaches. "The one that killed my animal will become mine. If you do not agree, I shall take a grievance to the king." The debate went on a long time, but under Mahaka's stubbornness, the man finally gave in and let him take an ox.

Then Imahaka went and found the noble who had spoken with him, to tell him his adventures and the tricks he had used to replace his insect with a fine ox. The noble was obliged to pay the bet. (Renel, *Contes* 2:60–63)[32]

The sure sign of a sorcerer's evil qualities is dancing on a tomb; for the ordinary person, it would be the worst of offenses.

As the community comes after Hare to punish him, so some individual was bound to try upsetting the continual victories of the mini-society.

66. The Man Who Thought He Was Cleverer than Kotofetsy and Mahaka

Merina narrator 1872–76

There was once a man who thought he was cleverer than Kotofetsy and Mahaka. He wanted very much to meet them. One day as he was looking for them, Kotofetsy went by with a spade on his shoulder, coming back from the field. "Sir," said the man, who did not know whom he was speaking to, "do you know where those two smart fellows called Kotofetsy and Mahaka live?"

"If you want to see them," answered the peasant, "post yourself at the foot of this tomb. I will go find them and show them to you." Kotofetsy ran to the village elders and told them, "There is a sorcerer dancing on a tomb over there. He is going to begin dancing soon. Let us go and catch him." The villagers armed themselves with heavy sticks and came up on the man. They beat him so hard, he nearly died. Having punished the false sorcerer, the people went back to the village.

Kotofetsy and Mahaka said to the man, "If you aren't smarter than that, do not attack Kotofetsy and Mahaka. You can never resist them. Their mind is as deep as the sea." The man obeyed and went home to cure himself of the blows he had got from those sticks. (Ferrand, *Contes* 233–34)[33]

The remodeling of African trickster tales in Madagascar answers the question, "How can you be an individual in a society that values only a group, family, clan, or village?" Trickster stories ask, "What will become of this individual of unforeseeable behavior, who claims to be self-sufficient and continually courts open defiance? His final fate can only be uncertain. . . ." In West Africa, either he will be reintegrated into society as a benefactor, because he has brought necessities to mankind, or else he will meet his death (Paulme, *La Statue* 53). Are Ikotofetsy and Imahaka the sort of twins so honored in West Africa, where "there is almost no society which has not developed a complex system of representations and rituals about twins" (Dieterlen 33)? Apparently not. Yet some parts of the twin concept echo the behavior of the Malagasy pair. The Dogon sage Ogotemmêli, in faraway Mali, explained to the anthropologist Marcel Griaule, "Trade . . . selling and buying different kinds of things, is exchanging twins," because "the things exchanged must be of the same value" (Griaule 200), like Ikotofetsy's fake cock, which is a crow, and Imahaka's spade made of clay. The property of Dogon twins "multiplied much faster than that of other people," because the ancestral twins were the inventors of trade (Griaule 205–208). But Ikotofetsy and Imahaka acquire property by subterfuge, not equal exchange; they are ridiculed as the Dogon twins are honored. Like other tricksters, they escape even death. Too little historical connection exists between Madagascar and West Africa for these echoes to count for anything more than independent invention.

At the time when the stories about Ikotofetsy and Imahaka were first recorded, Malagasy and Europeans had been confronting each other since Flacourt's day. For many generations these stories had doubtless been told to allude to particular situations that hearers would recognize. Hence the resemblance to African-American signifying. The game of verbal dueling, another mode of signifying, did function in just that way, to enable people to settle arguments and agree on contracts (Haring, *Verbal Arts* 113–16). That game, like the proliferation of metaphor in Madagascar's innumerable proverbs, lent support to using trickster stories to refer to a recognizable situation. Entertaining as they are, a storyteller's performances "are selected for reasons particular to the audience at hand, and often interpretable as interpersonal comment, critique, or admonition" (Mills 123).

Print too was a channel for Ikotofetsy and Imahaka to use for signifying. The fusion of admonition and entertainment characterizes one of the earliest publications in Madagascar. Even before Dahle's anthology put Ikotofetsy and Imahaka in print, John Parrett, a British Quaker missionary, published a collection of trickster folktales by a "native" author, Rabezandrina (pseudonym for Rainandriamampandry) (Rabezandrina). Parrett was one of the second generation of British churchmen, who had been readmitted to Madagascar under the monarchy of Radama II, after the death of his xenophobic predecessor, Ranavalona I. The first generation of missionaries (1820–1836) had introduced writing. This would enable Malagasy people to read the Bible, which the London Missionary Society men had translated (from English, of course, God's language), and printed on a press belonging to their Quaker colleagues (whom they tolerated far better than they did the French Catholics [Heseltine 123]). Parrett and his cohort began their English-language periodical, the *Antananarivo Annual,* the same year as they brought out the forty-two-page collection of trickster tales (Cousins and Parrett; Sibree, *Madagascar*). They saw no message but amusement in the little book.

Yet Rabezandrina's book signified on a situation its readers could have recognized, the growing confrontation between Malagasy and Europeans. It contained the same coded message as that story: "If you aren't smarter than that, do not attack Kotofetsy and Mahaka. You can never resist them." It was a hard-cover celebration of the superiority of wit. It amused its readers with the deceptions and cheats practiced by the twin tricksters, and it addressed an "interpersonal comment, critique, or admonition" to the very British missionaries who printed the book. As ironic as any Trinidadian calypso, the trickster tales declared that deviousness and treachery were approved forms of behavior by the poor towards the rich. The next year, Dahle printed the trickster tales, with all his others. His later re-editors—the book has hardly ever been out of print—were criticized, because the tales were put in sequence

> in such a way as to produce the impression of a progress down the path of coarseness and crime. At first the two comrades are no more than jokesters. Next, they reveal themselves as rascals, and finally criminals. This arrangement seems much more consistent with the views of the missionary who compiled this material than with the reality of feelings. By giving the tales a certain arrangement and presenting them in a progressive order, one runs the risk of making them say more than their hearers understood them to mean. (Chapus 106)

In fact Dahle, always the censor, had bent his efforts to avoid this downward progress, by scattering the trickster stories among animal tales, ordinary folktales, and legends. It was others who rationalized the arrangement, and still others who imitated it (Haring, "Folklore"; Mamelomana).

Entertaining the stories surely were, but the French were no more attentive than the British. They had settled on the east coast two generations earlier; like the British, they wanted to install a protectorate in Madagascar. To assimilate themselves into Malagasy mentality, they would have had to imitate one of their few compatriots who successfully did so. The entrepreneur Jean Laborde set up a manufacturing complex at Mantasoa involving glass, pottery, paper, sugar, soap, and (most important) stonemasonry. He must have understood Malagasy language well. According to anecdote, a hawker sold Laborde a cat telling him it was a rabbit. Instead of showing irritation when he discovered the deception, he made a joke of it. For a moment, it was the European's turn to play the trickster (Vérin, *Madagascar* 109).

Whatever the actual reception of the little book of trickster tales, its author was acting true to Malagasy tradition. "I am not the liar," say many Malagasy storytellers, even about stories that don't portray trickster's continual prevarication; "it's the ancestors who invented the tale." Faced with a cultural invader, Rabezandrina brought the *tenindrazana,* the ancestors' words, to the Quaker missionaries' press and let the ancestors speak. Thenceforward, the zealous collecting and publishing of island folklore from anonymous informants enacted the "death of the author" long before Roland Barthes gave one of his essays that title (Barthes; Haring, "Interpreters").

Not all the characters that the Indian Ocean islands took from Africa are animals; not all the clever characters are tricksters. We turn to the Ile de la Réunion, once Ile Bourbon.

67. Ti Zan of the Red Rag

Gérose Barivoitse, Sainte-Suzanne, Réunion 1976

Gérose Barivoitse: *Kriké!*

Christian Barat: *Kraké,* sir!

Gérose Barivoitse: The key in your pocket, the shit in my bag!

There's one good liver, Mr. La Foi, he eats his liver with a grain of salt. (Barat, Carayol and Vogel 13)

Réunion's master storyteller, Gérose Barivoitse, was of Malagasy extraction. His favorite main character, also of Malagasy extraction, is the clever Ti Zan, the one who eluded Rakakabe's attempts to eat him, in the Sakalava story, by disguising himself and substituting someone else. Self-preservation, in the face of an ogre to whom your mother has promised you, is hardly trickster behavior. It allegorizes social struggle.

In Réunion, social struggle and class conflict imprint themselves on inherited narrative paradigms so as to allude to class. Ti Zan is as witty as Soungoula, but he does not subvert social boundaries; he only rebels against a cannibal's threat. His equally resourceful Sakalava cousin Tsikifo, from Madagascar's west coast, runs no fewer than seven successful tricks against Big Beast, deceives him into sticking a hot poker into his navel, and finally beats his treacherous mother to death before inheriting the cannibal's wealth (Birkeli 258–69). Ti Zan's Antambahoaka cousin Takinga, from Madagascar's east coast, escapes the ogre Trimobe five times and deceives him into eating his own children; finally he cuts the rope Trimobe is climbing to reach him, so that he is impaled and killed on a row of pointed sticks; he too inherits the cannibal's wealth (Ferrand, *Contes* 69–76). Charles Baissac called his Mauritian version one of the most widespread of his island's tales (Baissac, *Folklore* 98–111; Goswami 41–47). He also called it witty, probably because of a moment near the end: the hero, unforgettably named Namcouticouti, outsmarts his treacherous mother for a second time, engineers his father's death at Wolf's hands, and escapes when a phallic wand transforms him into a pebble. His mother throws the pebble across the river, where he resumes human form.[34] Ti Zan has the nerve to say, "*Grand merci, maman; vous même qui fine sauve mo lavie,* Thanks, Ma, you saved my life" (Baissac 111).[35] The Mauritian and Réunionnais versions of "Ti Zan of the red rag" probably came from Madagascar, in fact (Ferrand, *Contes* 69–76; Haring, *Malagasy Tale Index* 329–31; Birkeli 258–69). Many Yao and Makua slaves were transshipped through Madagascar and were joined by Malagasy, who accompanied them to the Mascareignes. The story still carries its parentage through the mix of traditions: the name Ti Zan uses for disguise, Mikuikuik, may derive from Kiswahili *kikoi,* a loincloth; the three Réunionnais tales invoke a southern African image, of a pumpkin in which trickster hides (Werner 205–21; Barat, Carayol, and Vogel 13–18).

Several voices are heard throughout Gérose Barivoitse's tale, as he playfully hops between narration and personal history. The voice from the past is African. Near the same time that Baissac was recording the piece in Mauritius, two missionary collectors noted it in what is now Malawi (Macdonald, D., "Yao and Nyanja Tales" 276–79; Woodward 146–50). Gérose Barivoitse himself recorded it three times in 1976 (Barat, Carayol, and Vogel 13–28). Few examples so definitely show the cultural debt of the Mascareignes to Africa; few tales so obviously appealed to the slaves and their descendants; few performers could be as ebullient.

There was a little boy. His mother always wanted something, she says, "Oh, husband, go find something for me." She wanted a little water with no frogs in it. Well, she says to his father, "Go, go look for it." And the wife was in the family way. Finally the husband, poor bugger, he went, but he didn't know what's water with no frogs. He got to some pool or other, dived in, brought it, got back to his wife, he says, "Here." The wife says "No, that's not what I told you. Water with no frogs!" So he says, "I yelled. I asked if there was any frogs, nobody answered." He goes to see if there's any in there. Only the bugger went in a hurry to get the water, fast. He wanted to get home early.

The Nyanja narrator, back in British East Africa, degraded the woman less than Gérose Barivoitse does. For him (or her), the search for pure water is a bargain; if the wife is pregnant, we aren't told.[36] We look quickly at the Nyanja tale. "There was a woman who had a husband," the narrator began,

> and they went to hoe in the garden and the man sneezed, and the woman said, "What do you want?" The woman said, "I want the eggs of an ostrich." The man said, "I want water where frogs do not croak." They both assented to the bargain. The man went to seek the eggs of an ostrich and brought five, and gave his wife. The woman went to seek water where frogs did not croak. (Macdonald, D., "Yao and Nyanja Tales" 277)

Gérose Barivoitse, in his own voice, always localizes a man's adventures and identifies with him against an annoying wife.

[67, continued] Well, before nightfall he got there. What did he do? He dived in, he arrived, like to the river Sainte-Suzanne there, he dived in, he filled his gourd, went on his way. When he got there, he says to the wife, says, "There, I got it." The wife says "No, I tell you that's not it!" "OK," he says, "if that's not it, better you go yourself. I'm tired, walking since this morning."

So the wife started out. She went on the way, she climbed, more or less, like into the Bagatel forest there. She got up there, ah, ah, she was tired. She did like that, she saw a little running stream, saw how small it was, two steps across. So what she did, she saw some bananas there, there were all kinds of fruit. Then she broke some off. She had a little basket. (Lots of times, I see my little basket, I think that, hey! Little basket like that, very nice.) Filled it with bananas, filled her gourd, went on her way. Went down to her house.

As usual he connects the narrative to himself. The familiar "Fee-fi-fo-fum" motif identifies the ogre.

But along comes that damn Gran Dyab. Uh-uh. He didn't see her, he looked around like this: "Ah-hah," he says, "I smell fresh meat around here." He says, "Someone's been here. Well," he says, "never mind, let 'em go, I'll catch 'em later."

Well, a week later, when she got down to her house, she says to her husband, she says, "I got it." She says, "You, you didn't get all the way there. You're not a real man. Now I get to eat it, I won't give you any." With that she starts arguing with her husband. Finally the husband says, "OK, it's good. You managed to get it, good for you." Then she says, "Taste and see how good it is." The husband tasted, he says, "Hey, that's really good," he says, "is that really water?" the husband says. She says "Yeah, it's running water." The husband says, "Hey, that's not water, that's honey." She says, "Aaah, aaah, honey doesn't run like that. That's water. That's water with no frogs."

(And frogs can't get into something that way. That's oil there. Frogs'd be crazy to bathe in there, hey? Well, onward, enough.)

Next day she went back up again and got some more. But the third day, Gran Dyab says to himself, "No," he says, "they're destroying too much," he says, "I'm gonna keep watch." So he kept watch. The woman got there, did her usual, broke off some bananas. But her stomach was getting big, understand? Beginning two, three days already, getting, see? She filled her gourd with honey, took some bananas, everything she needed, started out. He caught her. He was watching, he found the place. Her basket was full. Ah, he bowed to her, Gran Dyab says, "Well, madame," he says, "You know what you're doing?" "Oh," she says, "no, sir," she says, "I didn't know, I thought it didn't belong to anybody. I came . . ." "Yeah," he says, "you came [here]?" She says yes. He says, "What you got in there?" "Oh," she says, "I'm in the family way, I want it." "Yeah," he says, "me too, I want it too." Then he says, "I don't know," he says, "when you have your baby, you have to give me that baby. Let's agree, OK?"

In world folklore, children are sold, or promised, to ogres or devils for many reasons: money, danger, death, barrenness, or merely a good catch of fish (this is Thompson's motif S220, Reasons for promised sale of child, in *Motif-Index of Folk Literature*). The African motive is more basic; the child is exchanged for water, as Macdonald's Nyanja storyteller said it:

> She went far, far away and found water. At that water she met with Namzimu, the owner, who asked, "What do you want?" The woman replied, "I want water where frogs croak not." Namzimu said, "What do you give in exchange for it." The woman bargained with Namzimu saying, "I am with child; when I bear the child I will give it to you." Then Namzimu said "Draw water."
>
> So she drew water, and went to the village and gave her husband. The husband said, "That is right, my wife."

In the Réunion of the slavery era, as in Mauritius, more than water was involved. Once coffee was introduced (1725) and slaves were being imported from Madagascar, Mozambique, and even India, the substantial loss of life in the trade meant a chronic labor shortage. A boy would be useful; his story remains in the repertoire because it speaks to the tensions of the social order, even if you are white. Reminding his hearer that it's all just a performance, Gérose Barivoitse runs a fanciful version of his formula, and then drives an even greater distance between the *then* of fiction and the *now* of his present moment.

[67, continued] *Kriké!*

Kraké, sir!

The key in your pocket, the shit in my bag! One good liver, two times Mr. La Foi eats his liver with a grain of salt. If he doesn't find it good, you have to have salt to eat it. Because if there's no salt, it's flat.

So! Then, the poor woman, poor devil—devil's not poor—he got her baby. But Gran Dyab, two days, not yet, three days, not yet. "Ah," he says, "it—" he says, finally the woman had her baby. Well, Gran Dyab waited, eight days he had to . . .

(Nowadays a woman has her baby; she has the baby sitting down; next morning she goes out, she goes to the store, she goes to work, she goes walking. But in the old days it wasn't like that, she had to wait eight days before she went out, because . . . people in the old days said, "Ah-ah, be careful!" and it was true. Because today, there's young people who have a baby, she goes out, she comes and goes. As soon as one two three, she starts up again, see? She starts up. But in the old days it wasn't like that. If a family had a baby, ten days she stayed in. Before she'd go out, she'd wrap up well. But when she went out, she'd get her nerves back, all strong, all fixed up. Well, what the hell . . .)

Kriké!

Kraké, sir!

The key in your pocket, the shit in my bag!

Well! So the woman got there the next day. Gran Dyab says to her, "Well, lady, did you have your baby?" She says, "Yes, I had him." "Good," he says, "that baby is for me." "Yes," she says, "OK." "So," he says, "go ahead. Take your honey, take it, it's yours. We made a deal." Then she came, she filled her thing, she went back. But Gran Dyab says to her, "No, now," he says, "tomorrow I'm coming to see your baby." "Yes," she says, "OK." "So," he says, "how'm I going to find him?" She says, "When you get there," she says, "I'm gonna put a little red rag (*langouti*) on him." She says, "When you go by all the children, ask which one is Ti Zan with the red rag." She says, "They'll show you him," she says, "yeah," she says, "take that one."

Every time Gérose Barivoitse switches between the inherited plot and his autobiography, his mode of performance becomes more contradictory, and the voices grow farther apart.

Well, Ti Zan, that SOB, he was smart. Lots of times there's boys called Zan, they're dopes, but many times the one called Zan, mmmmm! he's serious, he's solid, he's smart!

Kriké!

Kraké, sir!

The key in your pocket, the shit in my bag! So, that, that's why I named my boys Zan: Zan Pyer and Zan René. So, I liked this and not that, I say, "OK, maybe, the bugger will be—delayed. Finally I don't know if that'll be, if it's—because . . . not gonna break my head for Gran Dyab. That's how I am . . .

Kriké!

Kraké, sir!

The key in your pocket, the shit in my bag!

So it went on. Gran Dyab, next morning he came down. He sharpened his teeth, he says he wanted to eat. But that Ti Zan was really smart. His mama says to him, "Zan," she says, "go, go to school, go play." He says, "Yes, mama." She says, "don't take off your clothes, huh?" He says no. He gets there with his gang of friends (*kamarad*), he says, "You know?" he says, "I'll tell you something," he says, "each one of you take a piece," he says, "whoever comes, asks which is Ti Zan with the red rag, then say we're all Ti Zan with the red rag." His friends are all loyal. He puts a little red cloth on all of them. "Ah," he says, "good *nwar*!" he says.[37]

Gérose Barivoitse is faithful to the inherited plot. The same story in Rodrigues, the small creole island, changes the garment but keeps the red color: what was a red *lamba* (shawl) in Madagascar or *languti* (loincloth) in Mauritius becomes a thread in Rodrigues. The color alone evokes the era of slavery (Carayol and Chaudenson, *Les aventures* 94–99, *Contes créoles* 97–99).

They were all playing. He ran a trick. That damn Gran Dyab got there: "Hey kids!" They say, "Yes, big daddy!" He says, "Which one is Ti Zan with the red rag?" They say, "We're all Ti Zan with the red rag!" Gran Dyab says, "Oh, oh, oh, oh, oh, oh, oh! To bother an old fool like that! I'll eat you all, I'll eat you all, all! All Ti Zan with the red rag! But which one am I gonna eat?" Finally Gran Dyab took off, went back up. He got up there, found the lady, he says, "It's not like you said," he says. "I asked which one was Ti Zan with the red rag, they said all of them! So am I gonna eat them all? Huh?" he says, "I'm gonna eat all of them?" But the woman says, "I tell you there's only one." He says, "All of 'em there, can't tell anything—all! Aaah," he says, "change your ways, because that's not nice to me, hey! That's my honey you ate. That's my banana, all that fruit is mine that you ate, you are tricking me!"

Kriké!

Kraké, sir!

The key in your pocket, the shit in my bag! Mr. La Foi ate his liver with a grain of salt. Nice grain of coconut! Ah, then he grilled the liver to eat. Claimed he was frying it, it took too long, he grilled it, snap!

Next day, the good lady went up, got up there, she says, "Grandfather," she says, "today you come to my house." She says, "I'll put his food out on the *farfar.*" (In the old days they had the *farfar* [shelf], I don't know, a board. In the kitchen they had a little *farfar* out of bamboo, they put wood there, you could put anything on there for a while; it was a thing to put meat, all like that, she put it.)

Does Gérose Barivoitse believe that the anthropologist Christian Barat, who was recording him, didn't know what a *farfar* (in Malagasy, *farafara*) was, or is this explanation merely another bit of stepping offstage, to assert his consciousness of himself? Looking at all language, the linguist Benveniste declares, "Language is possible only because each speaker sets himself up as a *subject* by referring to himself as *I* in his discourse" (Benveniste 225). It's part of Gérose Barivoitse's art to make idiosyncratic use of such self-reference. He also sets himself up as a *petit blanc,* a poor white, of Réunion, who, like a woman in western culture, is "both produced and inhibited by contradictory discourses" (Belsey 359). Once sugar plantations and other large holdings were introduced after 1815, more and more *petits blancs* withdrew from the coast to the high places of the interior. Descending in social rank, they were exposed at the same time to the revolutionary discourse of *liberté, égalité, fraternité,* which they could only reproduce by diminishing their own liberty and declaring equality and fraternity within their enclaves. By 1848, when slavery was finally abolished, the *petits blancs* represented two-thirds of the free population and posed a class conflict, which has never been resolved and which produces the indirect ironies of signifying.

A microcosmic response to this contradiction is the irresistible way Gérose Barivoitse sets himself up as a subject, over against the fictional Ti Zan—who of course is a subject too—and against his interviewer from the university, by his switching of voices. Any performance, in a creole society, is itself "a symbolic move in an essentially polemic and strategic ideological confrontation between the classes" (Jameson, *Political* 85). But when Gérose Barivoitse annotates the *farfar* with such good humor, he mediates the confrontation. Ti Zan, for his part, has hidden powers of his own.

So she put Ti Zan's food there. He went out to play, came back. His mother told him, "Zan!" He says "Yes?" She says "Your food is there on the *farfar,*" she says, "go get it."

Gran Dyab was waiting there to catch him and eat him. He's sitting there; Gran Dyab did like this [*gesture*]. Before he caught him, ah! he saw Gran Dyab's paw. See, Gran Dyab has a big paw. His paw stuck out, it did like this, he says, "Hey!" he says, "so that's where you are," he says, "don't move." Uh! he turned into a rat, a big rat; he goes into the rice. He says, "There's a rat. It's coming to eat Ti Zan's food, going to eat it all." The rat comes, snap! It was that Ti Zan, only, see, he was kind of—Zan was clever. He comes and eats the whole thing. Eats his food, just like that, and leaves. "Mamma," he says, "here's the plate"—he did like this, he says "here's the plate." Ah, ah, the mother says, "Zan, you ate it?" He says, "Yes, mamma," he says, "I ate it up." But what about it? This guy is cursed! But then Gran Dyab ate more.

As the story goes on and the voices multiply, Gran Dyab becomes more human than cannibal; his dietary restrictions threaten to destroy the bargain. Gérose Barivoitse recovers quickly from a misstep that would have skipped one of the failed captures necessary to the story.

Gran Dyab comes down to the place and starts to argue. "Look," he says, "lady," he says, "what's all this?" he says, "there was a big rat came to eat."

"But," she says, "that was no rat," she says, "that was Ti Zan. You didn't get to eat him."

He says, "Me eat an animal? Huh?" he says, "me eat a rat? Ecch," he says, "I'm changing the deal. If that's how it is, no good any more, the deal where you come to get my stuff up above."

"But," she says, "I told you you had to catch the rat, had to eat him! OK," she says to him, "tomorrow I'll send him up there. Get ready—I'll tell him to go get a bag of charcoal up there, then when he comes, catch him. No—I'll send him to gather *zanbrovat* [pigeon peas] first." She says, "When he gets there, when he's gathering the *zanbrovat,* catch him."

Ti Zan went up, he got there, he came back to eat—she says, "Zan," she says, "go get some *zanbrovat* up above, with—in that field." Gran Dyab hid in the tuft of *zanbrovat* there. Sat down like this, watching for Ti Zan. He sat there, sat there, watched like this.

Finally Ti Zan got there with his basket. Some way away he turned into a black fly. See that bunch of big big black flies there? He stung him, like that. Gran Dyab was watching for him. He buzzed around. Gran Dyab says, "Ow, ow, ow!" he says, "Aie, aie, aie, aie, aie, aie—now—mmm, mmm, mmm! Hurts!" He fills his basket. He watched, watched, watched. He went back. Gran Dyab: "Ooh! Aie, aie, aie, aie! Brother, it hurts. Mm, mm, mm, mm, mm, mm!" He filled his basket with *zanbrovat,* got it. He got back down and says, "Mamma," he says, "here's your basket." She says, "Zan," she says, "you got it?" He says, "Oh, mamma," he says, "nothing else," he says, "I got the stuff."

Gran Dyab came there. His face was all lumpy—the black fly. He was stung, stung, his face swelled up like this. The woman said to him, “Hey,” she says, “what happened to you?”

“Aah,” he says, “you made me get hurt,” he says, “this is no good. Some animal stung me!”

“Yeah,” she says, “that was Zan.”

He says, “The black animal, I’m gonna eat that?” he says, “what do you think? You think I want to sting my tongue?”

“Oh well,” she says, “what’ll I tell you? I told you to catch Zan, you don’t want to do it. Well,” she says, “last thing for you to catch him,” she says, “I’ll send him to fetch charcoal.” She says, “You go in the sack of charcoal, then—no, say, tonight: I’ll shave his head, make his head bald. I’ll put him in the middle of the bed. I’ll put his father in the corner and me on the outside.”

“Good,” he says, “that’ll be good.” (The papa there, the mamma on the outside; one had to be on the outside, one in the corner, one outside, him in the middle.)

She says, “When you come, feel, feel feel him. You’ll find the guy with the bald head. Eat him,” she says, “that’s Zan for sure.”

Ti Zan didn’t hear that, but he was watching, the way he did, chewing his piece of wood. He kept that—you understand, he liked his wood—his thing said to him, “Careful, that guy there, he might eat you tonight.” So—poor Ti Zan—

Kriké!

Kraké, sir!

The key in your pocket, the shit in my bag!

So that night Ti Zan came. His mamma skinned his head, she says, “Here, you’ve got lice,” she says, “we’re going to shave your head clean.”

“OK,” he says, “mamma, shave!” His mamma shaved his head really clean, done, he went to play, that night he came back to sleep. “Hey,” she says, “tonight you sleep in the middle, huh?” she says, “Papa’ll sleep in the corner, me on the outside.”

“OK,” he says, “yes, mamma.” She took the boy, put him in the middle. Madame on the outside, mister in the corner. The time came. He listened well, everybody was asleep. When everyone was asleep, he took the scissors and cut his papa’s hair all off. His father had a big mustache. (Me, mine is short, but his papa, see, he had a nice mustache. If it’s short like this, it’s ugly, but a long time ago they cut it so it stood out. His mustache was tile colored, like Mr. Ango.) So he cut his father’s mustache all off, shaved his head, put it on his own head, and fixed everything up. Took his father’s mustache, zap! Damn Gran Dyab got there, chewing his bit of curry, to put in his mouth. When he thought he caught Ti Zan, he caught the papa. Caught his father, there in the middle; he was in the corner. Gran Dyab felt, felt, felt. "Ah," he says, "I got him." Hard! Ate the father. Nowadays if you ate that, you'd say it was full-grown. "Ah, ah, ah, ah, ah!" he says, "Ti Zan wears down my teeth."

The wife says, "Don't argue, just eat him!"

"I'm doing it," he says, "he's like a root." So which one did he eat? The bugger! Chewed up the grownup.

In the morning, Ti Zan didn't move; he made like his papa. He put his mustache outside the covers, like this. The mamma says, "Hey, get up, get up." He didn't move, he was sleeping. The mustache was like this, the mustache stuck out. Like bad Lyev [Hare], he stayed like that all night. There he was like that, asleep.

Kriké!

Kraké, sir!

The key in your pocket, the shit in my bag!

Next morning the woman called him to wake up. Time for him to go, she says, "Hey, still asleep, aren't you working today?" Ti Zan got up and jumped down to the ground. "Ah, Ti Zan," she says, "oh, my child, you're a curse. You've made your father get eaten by an animal!"

"Yeah," he says, "mamma, the animal did what you said, not me. I don't know about it."

"Eh," she says, "it was you who shaved your father's head, took his mustache and put it on your mouth! Well," she says, "today you go fetch a bag of charcoal for me from up there."

Then Gran Dyab spoke to her; she found Gran Dyab, told him she'd sent him for charcoal. He wanted to get this finished. But he didn't make it! So—

Kriké!

Kraké, sir!

The key in your pocket, the shit in my bag!

Next morning she says, "Go up there," she says, "catch him in the bag of charcoal."

He says, "Right." He went up. Damn Gran Dyab went inside the bag of charcoal. He sat like this. Ti Zan spied him from a distance; he got some Indian arrows. Soon as he did that, he got close, he shot him, zap zap! Gran Dyab said, "Ow, ow, ow! Aie, aie, aie, aie, aie!" He stayed in place. He didn't move. Ti Zan turned around to look; he said, "He's not dead yet." He hit him another shot, fyak! a shot with the Indian arrows. Stabbed Gran Dyab. Gran Dyab: "Oooh, uhhh," he says, "you're gonna kill me today. I'm dead."

So he shot him again. Didn't move. Poor bugger, gave him one more. Looked inside. Gran Dyab rolled, he turned him, he rolled. Gave him another shot in the stomach. But before that, he put some more in his heart. Ti Zan looked at him. He couldn't get out of there. Little bugger looked at him, thwacked him, thwacked him, thwacked him. Oh well, finally, hit him some more, vyoup. Got him right in the stomach. Gran Dyab rolled in the big bag of charcoal, vap! He took and picked up the bag, put it on his back. Ah, got there, he says, "Mamma, OK, here's that bugger you were trying to have kill me. You—" Threw the bag down on mamma. The mother, ah, finished! Poor Ti Zan, he's at liberty, peacefully.

Story is finished, sir.

[If] the story is a lie, I'm not the author, the grandparents long ago said it was true, that's no lie.

Be careful!

And Gran Dyab is still around, so be careful.

Be careful with your kids, because nowadays Gran Dyab is starting up [again].

Finished. (Barat, Carayol, and Vogel 13–18)

To interpret this piece, it's easy to apply the "pragmatic" orientation, the bit of rhetoric that was defined by Anglo-American "New Criticism." It is a "means to an end, an instrument for getting something done" for an audience; its value is measured by "its success in achieving that aim" (Abrams 11–12). The "something" is several things. The hearer, by vicariously experiencing the triumph of the weak over the strong, is given psychic escape and compensation, which help him or her to respond to life's demands (Bascom, "Four"); this is the Freudian answer. Politically, as part of a subordinated population, the Réunionnais hearer has "the need of being anchored in a collective past" (Carayol 10). Performance is a defensive effort to maintain group identity. Psychology and politics make up the social framework Julia Kristeva points to, in her picture of a sign system. Ego psychology will see the hearer's identity being reinforced when Ti Zan proves victorious. Telling the tale to an anthropologist's microphone preserves an inherited artistic genre, thus achieving another end. Finally, performance of the tale is an instrument for Gérose Barivoitse to play out an alternative politics of language, a separation between individual and collective voices. The hearer catches it in his repeated pun on "Mr. La Foi/*foie*," since *foi* means faith and *foie* means liver. If one tale performance can achieve all these aims, it must be rated pretty highly.

Ti Zan often rebels against authority, personified as Gran Dyab, but he is not always the same character (Haring, "African Folktales" 188–89). One Seychelles tale gives him a victory over his father, by means of the "mirror" structure favored by some African storytellers (Paulme, *La Mère* 38–41). In the first episode, Ti Zan retrieves, with the aid of a grateful *karang* fish, a pet *kato* (parrot), of which his father is very jealous. But his father, now aged, fails to play caretaker in return: in a second episode, he loses Ti Zan's pet and goes in search of it until he falls dead (Diallo et al., *Veyez 2* 1–3). Perhaps he is a victim of that mysterious Malagasy force of retribution known as *tody,* which dictates that your deeds always come back on you (Heseltine 76). Anyway, it is not Ti Zan who has directly killed this father, who is a less threatening figure than Gran Dyab.

Like the animal trickster stories, Ti Zan's tales show how well inherited symbol language could dramatize power relations and accept Malagasy and European traditions. When the Malagasy water-princess Ranoro turns up in Seychelles, she is again the answer to poverty, not as a prospective wife or mother, but only as a donor of foreign aid.

68. The Queen of the Sea

Seychelles narrator 1969

Once there was a man and a woman. They were trying to make their living out of the ground to feed their children, but they didn't succeed.

Uncountable folktales around the world begin in such poverty. It has special force in islands where, at best, agriculture must be supplemented by fishing. "To be unemployed in the society of the type that exists in Seychelles," protested the colonial governor in 1960, "is not merely a matter of drawing the dole but is at worst near starvation" (Scarr 166). East African versions of this well-known plot don't mention poverty; the Malagasy ones do. In Europe, a typical French version begins with a prosperous farm couple whose excellent harvest is blown away by the north wind (Delarue and Tenèze 2:414). The north wind still blows through a Réunionnais version collected in 1976 (Decros 47–55). Seychellois landscapes and objects are inserted into the plot, along with imported Christianizing.

So the man went down to the seaside and found a little *pirog* [boat] named *Lak o Poul* [Fowl Lake]. He took this little boat, put it in the water, and tried going fishing. He fished for a week and got nothing. At the beginning of the next week, he said, "I'll try going to the island." On the island, he fished till five o'clock, then he felt a tug on his line. When he pulled it out, he saw the Queen of the Sea. He raised his stick to hit the Queen of the Sea, and she said, "Before you hit me, raise your eyes to *Bondye* [God]."

The Queen of the Sea addresses him like a priest. She, not God or the north wind, will be the donor figure and will recall the bounty expected of an African chief.

"I'll give you a goat. You won't have to come back to the sea; you'll say, 'By the virtue of the goat the Queen of the Sea gave me, I want to see everything I need!' "

Ranoro, the Malagasy water-princess, gave herself to a poor unmarried man, then left him. The Queen of the Sea, a Utopian version of the European Mélusine, resembles that always-hoped-for donor from abroad: she will give this poor husband gifts that will finally lift him out of poverty. But the Seychellois social system interferes with the prospects for foreign aid. The kinship terms *komer* and *komper* (so spelled in Seselwa Kreol), which parallel the French system of fictive kinship, connect a child's godparents to each other in the Seychelles system. The terms bespeak an "extensive network of kinship (both legitimate and illegitimate) and personal relations through which people claim ties of dependence on those economically and politically better placed than themselves" (Benedict and Benedict 66).

But there was a woman who'd been his son's godmother. The *komer* knew that the *komper* didn't have any goat. She went down to the seaside with a little food and said to the *komper,* "You're hungry, you're tired. I brought you some food. Give me your little basket of fish, I'll carry it."

Before he got home, the *komper* had to pass by his *komer*'s house. She said to him, "Stay, sleep." So the *komper* stayed.

The villain of the piece is posed against both the fisherman's wife, always offstage, and the Queen of the Sea, whose gifts she steals. The *komper's* true dependence is on just such a person, the Queen.

The *komer* had a little adoptive daughter living with her; she said to the girl, "Take the *komper*'s goat, put it with ours, take ours, and put it near him." When day came, the *komper* took his goat and went home. When he got there, he said to his children, "Stay back, stay back, I'm starting. By the virtue of the goat the Queen of the Sea gave me, I want to see everything I need!" Well, at those words the goat started defecating in the children's bed. The *komper* said, "Queen of the Sea, tomorrow I must go back."

He went back to the seaside, launched *Lak o Poul* into the water, rowed a little, got to the island, and said, "Queen of the Sea, today I'm going to kill you." The *komper* fished till 5:30, he felt his line get heavy; he looked, he saw the Queen of the Sea. He picked up his stick to hit her. The Queen of the Sea said, "My friend, before you hit me, lift your eyes, look at Bondye. My friend, I'll give you a little snuffbox. Don't come back here again. When you get home, say, 'By the virtue of the snuffbox the Queen of the Sea gave me, I want to see everything.'" In fact the *komper* agreed, but don't forget that the *komer* was there.

The *komper* got to land. His *komer* said, "Poor *komper,* I know you're thirsty; here's a little coffee for you." The *komper* took and drank it. His *komer* said to him, "Give me your basket of fish, I'll carry it." Then they both started back. The *komper* was very tired, he fell down asleep.

What about that snuffbox? Gérose Barivoitse used to tell a tale in which a snuffbox contains all the furnishings a supernatural wife supplies to her mortal husband, rather like the Malagasy water-princess (Barat, Carayol, and Vogel 63–66), or a reverse Pandora.

When the *komer* saw her *komper* asleep, she said to her little girl, "Take the snuffbox next to the *komper,* put it next to ours, take ours, put it next to him." When the *komper* got up in the morning, he took his snuffbox and went home. When they saw him coming, his children and their mother said, "Ah, what's Papa bringing today? Yesterday he brought a goat that shat on us." The *komper* began, "By the virtue of the snuffbox the Queen of the Sea gave me, I want to see everything." Well, bees started coming out of the snuffbox and stinging the children. They yelled, "Aïe, aïe, aïe! The bees are stinging us!" The *komper* said, "Well, today I won't sleep home, I'll sleep at the seaside." The *komper* went down and slept under the boathouse.

When 5:30 struck, he took his *pirog Lak o Poul,* rowed hard, and arrived just near the island. He fished till six o'clock in the evening. He felt his line get heavy, he looked and saw the Queen of the Sea. He raised his stick to strike. The Queen of the Sea said, "My friend! Before you strike me, lift your eyes, look at Bondye. This is the last day you will come here. Today I'm giving you a cane. When you get home, say, 'By the virtue of the cane the Queen of the Sea gave me, I want to see everything.'"

So the *komper* took the cane and left. When he got on land, he saw his *komer.* She said to him, "Poor *komper,* I know you're thirsty, you're hungry. Let's go to my house and eat something." She did the usual, she took the *komper*'s basket and they went along. When they got to her house, the *komper* drank and ate. The *komer* said to him, "Stay, sleep." And sure enough, he stayed. As he was falling asleep, the *komer* said to him, "Give me your cane, I'll put it away." The *komper* said, "No, I'm going to put it next to me." The *komer* waited for the moment when the *komper* was asleep; she said to her little girl, "You know what you have to do! Go take that cane next to the *komper,* put it in our house, take ours, and put it next to the *komper.*" So the girl went; as she grasped the cane, it gave her a hit on the arm. The girl put out her hand again and for the second time the cane hit her. She yelled, "Aïe, aïe! Mama, the cane is hitting me!" The *komer* said to the girl, "You're hungry, go eat out of the pot, I'll go myself." The *komer* picked up her skirts, put her dressing-gown over it/them, and put out her hand. The cane hit her too. When the cane hit her for the third time, she shook the *komper* and said, "Get out of my house! Go!" The *komper* said to his cane, "Do what you have to do." The cane started beating the *komer;* it struck her, struck her; her skirts fell off, she fell down, she said, "*Komper*! I'll give you back your goat, your snuffbox, your cane. Get out of my house! Go!" The *komer* was nearly dead, she'd received so many blows. So the *komper* took all his stuff, his goat, his snuffbox, his cane, and went back home.

When he got home, he said, "By the virtue of the goat the Queen of the Sea gave me, I want to see everything I have to have!" He saw everything he needed arrive in front of him. After that day, the *komper* lived like a rich man with his family.

The other day I met the *komper* and said to him, "*Komper,* do something for me." Pow! He gave me a hit and just then I headed back and left. (Carayol and Chaudenson, *Contes créoles* 135–40)[38]

The closing formula marks the piece as a faithful local adaptation of the old tale which readers of Grimm might remember as "The Magic Table, the Gold Donkey, and the Club in the Sack" (Grimm and Grimm 134–42). The Seychellois tale keeps internationally popular motifs, easily labeled (see Thompson, *Motif-Index*): an animal that fulfills wishes, a neighbor who steals magic objects, a magic cudgel that beats a person and effects the recovery of what was stolen. It encloses the motifs within a poverty-to-riches frame, which hearers in a poor country can always make real for themselves. Frame and plot are easily recognized (Aarne and Thompson 205–206). They, like the motifs, could have reached the islands from East Africa (Arewa 460–64) or Europe. But the tale as told in 1969, with its localizations of setting and social relations, was no standardized import from either place. No cultural product, after all, is imported arbitrarily. The recurrent dream of being lifted out of poverty, in so many folktales, has the special appeal of a hopeless Utopianism, in which the solution to life's problems always resides in fantasy.

If the Queen of the Sea is a projection out of poverty's desire, she has a male counterpart in Mauritius, Prince Lulu, who is the projection of sexual desire.

69. Prince Lulu and the Defiant Girl

Nelzir Ventre, Mauritius 1990

Performing, Nelzir Ventre had to have responses from a chorus. But on one evening in 1990 when he was ready to record it, he didn't have properly trained singers. His tension over achieving a proper performance for our recording echoed the tension between the wife in the story and her wolfman husband, Prince Lulu. This prince, an Indian Ocean Bluebeard, whose name derives from the French *loup,* wolf, and *loup-garou,* werewolf, seems a typical creole synthesis. Ton Nelzir liked him well enough, but from time to time he mixed up whether Ti Zan or his sister Ti Zann was speaking; he interrupted himself impatiently several times.

Nelzir Ventre [*sings*]: Come, fellows! Today I have arrived.

Come, you, come.

[*aside*] So you must hit [with] the song. Give me a little stick.

Patrick Brasse: Yes, yes, here's one.

Nelzir Ventre: [*with sticks*] Come, fellows! Come, fellows! Today I have arrived. Come, you, come!

Eh-ou.

What is this one about? There was a man, he had two kids, a daughter and a son. One was called Ti Zan, one was called Ti Zann. Well, Ti Zann, she is older, Ti Zan is younger. As it went on, one day while they were walking, going to church, Prince Lulu saw Ti Zann and he loved her. So in fact, he courts her at her father's place (and the mother's place and Ti Zan's). After around, let's say, three months, so they got engaged and everything to get married. And in fact. they did a big wedding, you hear, a b-i-g wedding to get married. Well, after the wedding, so, he left, he left for his country in his place.

A man who would agree to live at his wife's place would be dishonorably acting against custom (Fanony 37n2), but consider her plight: this virilocal marriage delivers her, as it does every woman, into an alien land, at the mercy of a strange man and his relatives (Ottino, "Les aventures" 40). But doing without protection is part of this woman's defiance. She tries to use her knowledge of the germ theory of disease to keep her brother at home.

So as he was about to leave, Ti Zan says to Lulu—Prince Lulu, he says, "Well, all right, you come too. You'll come, Ti Zan. See how sick you are, you have this itch, well, over there you will have fresh air, you will—this itch will go away." The girl says, "No, no, you don't need to take him. You're going to spread this *makombin* to the people over there. You don't need to come." They argued, they argued. Ti Zan says to him—Lulu says to him, Prince Lulu says to him, "Let's go."

So he takes them in his carriage. They leave, they come to his castle, a big castle in the forest. They all get down—all of them, you see?

Castles are like elephants in Mauritius, or tigers in Seychelles, elements of fiction, but the separate kitchen is familiar to Ton Nelzir's audience.

So Ti Zann is in the castle, with the prince in the castle, and Ti Zan, they've put him in a small kitchen, in the kitchen. Well, he has that *makombin.* At night he is itchy, you hear? So it's about eleven at night, everybody is sleeping, but Ti Zan is not sleeping. He is very itchy with that itch. So Lulu, prince Lulu, just goes outside, it's about eleven at night, as usual he calls his gang, he says,

> Come, fellows, come fellows! Today I have arrived.
> Come, you, come.
> Come, fellows, come fellows! Today I have arrived.
> Come, you, come.

Eh-ou, wolves! In the yard everywhere, because he is a king, a prince. All sizes of wolves, small, big, all kinds. So Ti Zan, Ti Zan is watching all this. Wolves are all around him, they are circling him. [*aside*] Well? Nobody's hitting.

Patrick Brasse: You tell the story, we hit.

Ton Nelzir went into the next song, in which the prince delays his fellow wolves from eating the two human beings.

Let's eat him, let's eat him

Chorus: Let him grow fatter, let him grow fatter

But Ton Nelzir was still not satisfied: "Not enough people," he said. Patrick Brasse called in another boy: "Come, come. I'll show you. You know how to beat *sega*." Ton Nelzir said, "Just hit that bamboo there. We must have one or two people, then it's OK. Listen carefully to what I say." Three repetitions of the lines of the song took him into the next scene; again he stumbled a bit.

Well, Ti Zan heard very well. All night he didn't sleep; he was thinking until early morning. Tea was made and everything. The prince says, Prince Lulu says to his wife, he says to her, and to Ti Zan, he says to her, "I'm going to work now. Watch the house well." She says, "OK." He goes out, he goes to work. Well, Ti Zan takes advantage to tell his sister—he is scared she might be angry, he says nothing. He says, "I'll just see tomorrow what happens," so really he spent the whole day, the afternoon, he had dinner and everything and went to sleep. Around midnight or eleven o'clock, prince Lulu goes outside, he calls his fellows,

> Come, fellows, come fellows! Today I have arrived.
> Come, you, come.
> Come, fellows, come fellows! Today I have arrived.
> Come, you, come.

It didn't take long, I tell you. Very quickly, there were wolves everywhere. Wolves right around. The wolves want to eat now.

Nelzir Ventre: Let's eat him, let's eat him

Chorus: Let him grow fatter, let him grow fatter [*three more repetitions*]

Eh-ou, brother. It's now about three in the morning, just like before, and prince Lulu tells them, "Let him get very fat, then we will eat him. Right now he is skinny." And Ti Zan is only skin and bones. So it's as if he should grow fatter. So Ti Zan says, after three or four days have gone by like that, he cannot think about it, he calls his sister.

Hearing a car outside, Ton Nelzir thought John Brasse might be arriving to help him, but he wasn't.

So he says, he comes towards the sister, he says, "Sister, I'll tell you something. You won't get angry?" She says, "You are going to tell something? What are you going to tell me? I told you not to come. You come and cause trouble." He says to her, "Sister, listen to my words, sister." He says, "It's been now four or five days. Wolves are around us to eat us. You're not aware of any of it." She says, "What? Are you sure of what you are saying now?" He says, "I say that I am sure, sister, because I am seeing it every day. As for you, you sleep like an animal. I can tell you, like a pig you sleep."

We all laughed.

He says, "I listen to everything that's going on." He says, "Would you believe, sister, what I'm telling you? I'll give you a spool of thread no. 10." This is very strong, that thread. He says, "You take that spool, you take one end, you tie it to your foot, to your toe. As for me, I'll take it in my kitchen over there. Well, when the wolves arrive, I'll pull it, and you will be able to hear." She says, "Are you sure?" He says, "Yes, I tell you, sister."

Prince Lulu by day is quite the ordinary working husband, though Ton Nelzir didn't want to be asked for details of his day job.

Well, when her husband usually comes back, two or three o'clock in the afternoon he comes back, when he comes he eats, drinks, and everything, goes to sleep. They leave. Ti Zan has given the thread and has tied it. Then Ti Zann stays still. Just at eleven o'clock at night, the wolf comes, he calls,

> Come, fellows, come, fellows! Today I have arrived.
> Come, you, come.

The song was repeated several more times.

Nelzir Ventre made the songs essential to the movement of plot, in all his performances. Song was always the high point, used here to heighten tension and excitement. One of his songs of pathos had the same theme as the Prince Lulu story, of rescue from in-laws: a young man, son of a wolf-man, saves his wife from being eaten by the monster-father. Now he focused on the young woman.

Wolves—when she sees the number of wolves in the yard, my, she feels cold. She begins to tremble, you hear? She gets chills of fear. Around four o'clock in the morning, the wolves leave. Early in the morning, prince Lulu has got up. He drinks his tea and everything, yes, to go to work. What work? Nothing; he just meets his gang. He leaves, he goes.

His sister says to him, "Ah, Ti Zan, brother, there were so many wolves last night!" He says, "What did I tell you?" Then he says to her,

Nelzir Ventre [*sings*]: What did I tell you, sister?
See, your husband is a wolf, sister.
Chorus: What did I tell you, sister?
Your husband is a wolf, sister.
Nelzir Ventre: What did I tell you, sister?
See, your husband is a wolf, sister.
Chorus: What did I tell you, sister?
Your husband is a wolf, sister.
Nelzir Ventre: What did I tell you, sister?
See, your husband is a wolf, sister.

Again Ton Nelzir directed one of the boys, "Hey you, hit," and resumed the song for seven more pairs of lines. Then the conflict intensifies.

Eh-ou, wolves! The sister looks at them—Ti Zan says to her, "Sister, I'm leaving. As for you, you stay with your husband. I'm leaving."

"Father left the two of us alone. How can you now leave me behind?"

He says, "Didn't I tell you? You did not believe, you did not believe me." He says, "Sister, [I'll] find a way to bring us back home to our mother's." He says, "All right. You know, when your husband comes back later, tell him to get four big pieces of bamboo—bamboo like this [shows stick]. Take four pieces like this, I'll make a basket." He says, "Do you hear?"

She says this to her husband, really when the husband comes back, she says, "Husband, get four big pieces of bamboo for me. Ti Zan is going to make a basket so we can go for a ride in the air."

He says, "Hey? What's this?"

She says, "Don't worry. My brother is very clever."

He says, "OK, go." Really, shortly afterwards, he went to give the news to his wolves, and they brought four big pieces of bamboo.

Ti Zan cuts, fixes, puts together; he makes a big basket, a b-i-g basket, I tell you. So then, Ti Zan made that basket, he finished making the basket. So Ti Zan says to her, so Zan says to her, "OK, now." He says to prince Lulu, he says to him, "We will go in the basket, we will go for a ride in the air for a little while, in the air." So then, well, that balloon, you must sing for it to go up.

How appropriate, for a *sega* singer who provided his audiences with fantasies of escape from the everyday, that a balloon powered by song will be Ti Zann's means of escape (Baissac, *Folklore* 146–53).

The balloon is as African as all the rest. Alice Werner, whose publications on African folklore ranged over forty years beginning in 1896, found a defiant girl whose brother learns the danger from an *akachekulu* ("gnome"), who makes him a magic drum that floats him in air. With that he fetches his sister and the baby. The drum, as it carries them away, also forces the lion-husband to dance (Werner 192–95; Doke). Werner produced a prototype of the story as it is known in Mauritius, by joining together two Yao versions of the defiant girl, which she collected at different times from different narrators, as if she were herself a creole storyteller. In this synthetic version, the brother makes a *nguli* (a big top), which he causes to rise into the air by singing. He has his sister climb into it and they float home. She remains unmarried (Werner 195–98). Werner's version furnishes a line of descent from East Africa to the Southwest Indian Ocean versions (Ottino, "Les aventures" 40). Her Hyena Bridegroom indeed strongly resembles Nelzir Ventre's tale of Prince Lulu.

So does a tale collected more recently in Malawi. As the editors rewrote it, the boy in the Malawian tale

> always wanted to be with his sister, so much so that she thought him a nuisance. Now the grandmother of the two children was a renowned magician who taught the boy how to get out of difficult places by weaving a grass basked and flying it like an aeroplane. The secret of making the basket fly was contained in a special flying song which she also taught him. (Schoffeleers and Roscoe 215–16)

The boy rescues his sister from dangerous wild animals in the forest, but not before she pleads with him that if he doesn't, "you'll have nobody left in the world" (Schoffeleers and Roscoe 216). Without a defiant girl, this can't be thought of as the same plot as Ton Nelzir's, but it is obviously a cognate (Derive 269). Ton Nelzir never left out the balloon.

So then, really, he placed the balloon, a big balloon, so Ti Zann went in, Ti Zan too, inside.

Then he says, "Don't go too high. When I make a signal, you come back down, do you hear?" He says, "Yes." So he starts, he says, "Sister, go on, you sing.

Balloon, go up, balloon, go up,
balloon, we go *ban nyan nyan*
Balloon, go up, balloon, go up,
balloon, we go *ban nyan nyan*

Then it goes up like this, that thing, that balloon. The balloon has gone up very high. Ti Zan says—King Lulu says, "Come down, come down." So Ti Zan does like this: he says, now he says,

Alo murima muripa, take us to mother's place
Take us, *murima muripa,* take us to mother's place,

murima muripa, take us to mother's place
murima muripa, take us to mother's place
murima muripa, take us to mother's place

Eh-ou. They kept on going like that.

So it's necessary for Prince Lulu to call his fellows to pursue the two, singing the same song, "Come, fellows, come fellows! Today I have arrived." Ti Zan too keeps on singing, "*Mulima mulipa,* take us to mother's place."

Now Ti Zan got tired, so he said to Ti Zann, he said, "Sister, I am too tired. There's a big *tambalakok* tree, let's go on it. Then we will rest a bit. After that we will leave." Really, they did just that, resting on that *tambalakok* tree, a big *tambalakok* tree.[39] The balloon just rested on it.

He said—Lulu gave orders to his general, Lulu, "Eat the wood and leave nothing." So they attacked the tree, and chips fell out of their mouths, like that. What can I tell you? He said,

Goombah, goombah, goombah
Goombah, capa, u'rya
Goombah, goombah—

As the wolves were attacking the tree, Ton Nelzir again broke off, dissatisfied that his regular collaborator John Brasse was not present: "Well, if he were here, he would understand, he would be hitting, you understand? They don't understand. So he would sing here." And he went on with the unintelligible words of this song, which Ton Nelzir called *langage, "Gombah, gombah, la lu ya,"* ten times in all.

Eh-ou, brother.

All the wolves are eating. Ti Zan went like that [looking down]. Half the tree has been eaten. There's still some left. Ti Zan shouts again,

and Ton Nelzir began the Lulu song, then corrected his mistake.

Balloon, go up, balloon, go up,
Up, up we go
to mother's place
to mother's place
Balloon, go up, mama
Balloon, we are going to mother's place

So then, it went. It went, the balloon, it went.
Now he shouts,

Take us to mother's place, Take us to mother's place,
Take us to mother's place, Take us to mother's place,
Take us to mother's place, Take us to mother's place,
Take us to mother's place, Take us to mother's place,

Take us to mother's place, Take us to mother's place,
Take us to mother's place, Take us.

Eh-ou, brother.

The balloon came to rest in front of father's house, father and mother. They are very happy when they see the two children.[40]

"So now this story is finished," Ton Nelzir said, probably relieved. "You've got one now." Indeed we had, despite the singer's frustrations at not being able to alternate speaking with singing properly. The alternation was, for him, the essence of *sega;* the old context of performing was what he called a "bean party." He described this scene of Kreol socializing on another occasion.

Well, long ago, this is how you would sing a *sega.* You have to tell the man's story first. You have to tell his experience. Then after you've finished saying all those words, and everybody has been sitting listening to you, then the drummers start *rule* [riffing on the drum]. Then the chorus would start answering, following you. The *sega* singer would then say what he likes, to make the *sega* amusing. At that point, among the drummers, one man would come out, with his handkerchief or his hat, and he would start dancing. A girl or a woman, whoever feels like it, would come to dance with him. They go to the front and both dance. When the rhythm gets going, the whole night, male dancers would go in front of female dancers. (Ventre)

What made a bean-party succeed was a network of responsibility, which is what has helped African culture survive in these islands (Benedict and Benedict 148). Ti Zan enacts that network. When Ton Nelzir recorded this piece for us, I had no idea that this was the best known African folktale of all, more potent even than Tarbaby, or that he had performed it on national television. Only recently have scholars uncovered the various languages and social settings in which, through multiple and nuanced ideological messages, this narrative teaches young women their most important lesson: what they are not to do (Görög-Karady and Seydou 14).

The Ti Zann of Nelzir Ventre's story can be called a "defiant maid" (Cosentino) or a *fille difficile* (Görög-Karady and Seydou). Her story is told all over Africa and the Southwest Indian Ocean.[41] As Ton Nelzir shows, she refuses many suitors; she defies custom by marrying an attractive man, in reality a supernatural being or animal (here, Prince Lulu the wolfman), who takes her home, accompanied by her scabrous brother. The disguised monster prepares to devour her until the brother rescues her by magic and she returns to her parents (Görög-Karady and Seydou 13). Europeans also know, or used to know, folktales that speak to the same questions about marriage. In Bluebeard, for example, a young woman marries a murderous husband, from whom she is rescued by her brothers; in The Robber Bridegroom, a robber marries a young woman under pretense of being a fine gentleman (Aarne and Thompson 103–104, 338; Uther 1:192–97, 485–86). But Africa is the birthplace of Nelzir Ventre's story. It is current in Kenya, where I heard it in 1968, and Madagascar (Beaujard, "La fille"; Haring, *Malagasy Tale Index* 363–71; Njururi 4–10; Gecau 92–99). It was well known in nineteenth-century Mauritius (Baissac, *Folklore* 146–79). In Réunion it has been recorded eight times, in Seychelles, twice (Gamaleya, "Contes Populaires" [1977]; Barat, Carayol, and Vogel 29–32; Bollée and Neumann). It carries a central message about marriage from pre-slavery oral tradition into the new setting of oppression and the breakup of families.

70. Defiant Girl, TV Version

Performing her story on Mauritius Broadcasting Company television, even at home in Poudre d'Or, may have been a bit stressful too.[42] This was no bean party. "There was a lady and her husband," he began, knowing every member of his audience would be ready to plunge into the imaginary world. "They had a daughter and a son," he went on, reminding his audience of familiar characters. "One was called Ti Zan, the other was called Ti Zann." "Well," Ton Nelzir went on, "that Ti Zann grew up, and many boys want to marry her. She is not satisfied; anyway, they're all too big or too small for her."

An African audience would understand right away. It's not that she is disobedient or capricious, as she is for the Peul in Sénégal or Mali, where her refusal might even be a mark of high social status (Görög-Karady and Seydou 85). In West Africa, she wants "a man without any scar"—a husband who is outside society, untouched by "life," because he has never been circumcised. When, in a Peul tale, an animal disguised as a perfect young man presents himself, a fly (which she regularly employs to inspect her suitors) discourages her, as her family does, but in vain. After the marriage, the husband resumes his shape; then he retransforms in public, at the marriage festivities. The wife—dishonored, isolated, and suicidal—causes herself to be buried in earth by magic song (the element Nelzir Ventre considered essential) (Seydou, "Mariage Sauvage" 90–91). In northern Ghana, Bulsa storytellers portray a defiant girl who wants a man whose skin is perfect, without blemishes—a rare and treasured feature in a land where diseases like yaws leave their marks (Schott 112). Ton Nelzir's Ti Zann doesn't say she is looking for a prince, a rich man, or an uncircumcised man. This girl's demand is sexual: no suitors are the right size for her, until Prince Lulu comes along. His high-status name helps to disguise his animal nature, but he must be using sexual attractiveness as his means of subordinating this woman, because she accepts him without a word.

As in tales about the making and breaking of friendship, the initial incident creates an unstable situation. "It was a very nice wedding," Ton Nelzir said, but a vulnerable marriage, because the woman has chosen raw sex over "the whole yoke of regulations that society has set up, to control this unmediated reality and integrate it into being one of the fundamental mechanisms of its functioning" (Seydou, "La fille" 46). Other family members will intervene; sometimes they have already examined her suitor to make sure he conforms to her requirements. Every time it's told, the defiant-girl story is about sex (animal attraction) and power (a prince who is an ogre). No wonder it has such a grip on storytellers and audiences.

In the TV broadcast, the interviewer wanted to make sure Ton Nelzir was understood, when the necessary third character came in.

Well, after they got married, Ti Zan said to his sister, "I'll come with you." Well, Ti Zan had *makombin,* he had an itch.

Marie-Josée Baudot: You call this *makombin.*

Nelzir Ventre: Yes, *makombin.* Well, his sister said no to him. His sister did not want to take him. Then Prince Lulu said, "Take him. Maybe over there—

Marie-Josée Baudot: —he will be better.

Nelzir Ventre: —it will be a change of air. His sickness will go away." So they took Ti Zan.

Prince Lulu is not merely being hospitable. A Seychelles version explains what Ton Nelzir didn't: *"Mé Frer Loulou i kalkilé, i ana zis Zane; si i ava amene Ti Zan, i a gagne dé dimoune pour li manzé,* Bro Lulu thought, he had only Zann; if he took Ti Zan, he'd get two people to eat" (Bollée and Neumann 58). Ton Nelzir kept going despite the interruption.

Well, as soon as they got there, at night, Lulu, that Prince, announced to the other *lulus* that he had arrived, that he had come today.

Normally, Ton Nelzir would sing the wolf-man's summons to his gang of fellow wolves. Ton Nelzir's interviewer was determined the TV audience wouldn't miss anything.

Well, the sister took Ti Zan and put him to sleep in the kitchen [a separate building]. She did not put him to sleep together with them in the main house. She put him to sleep in the kitchen because he had that itch, in case it would spread to them.

Marie-Josée Baudot: He had *makombin.*

Nelzir Ventre: Yes.

For the television broadcast, Ton Nelzir moved rapidly through the scenario to reveal the extreme dangers that Ti Zann is exposed to by moving to her husband's place. About thirty Poudre d'Or villagers acted as his chorus, more successfully than the handful we recorded later. When it was the moment for Ti Zan to find out Prince Lulu's true nature, the interviewer got help from one of the group, who translated a vernacular word.

They were going around Ti Zan, and Ti Zan had *makombin,* he was not sleeping. Well, as for the sister, in a deep sleep, she *roti roti.*

Marie-Josée Baudot: She what?

Nelzir Ventre: She ate roast meat.

Marie-Josée Baudot: I see. She *roti,* she has *roti.*

Member of audience: She's drunk [or dead tired].

Marie-Josée Baudot: Ah, she is drunk [or dead tired], it means she is drunk [or dead tired].

We were uncertain about this translation, and Ton Nelzir omitted this detail when he recorded it later, but it does tell the audience why Ti Zann does not hear the wolves. Her conflict between family loyalty and marriage intensifies as Ti Zan, still resentful at her former disdain, threatens to leave her until she says, weeping, "Think of father and mother. There's only me and you left. Now you are going to leave me." Without help from her birth family, how is Ti Zann to escape from an impossible marriage? In Baissac's nineteenth-century version, her brother successfully thinks up an excuse: he tells her to invite the wolf and his friends to a dance at their parents' house, where they will be trapped (Baissac, *Folklore* 154–61). In most other tellings, Ti Zan's skin ailment is evidently a sign of magic powers. Once the brother and sister are in the air, they will not get home without being pursued.

Prince Lulu looks at it. He calls his gang, he calls the wolves, he says,

"Come, my gang, come, my gang, come my gang.

"Wolves," he says, "wolves, chase the balloon."

The wolves are up—the balloon is up, the wolves are down. Ti Zan has gone on singing, he has grown weak

—surely something his *sega* singer understood, by this point in the broadcast. The flight is interrupted; so is the singer-storyteller, who curtails the narrative.

He says, "Sister, see, there's a big *tambalakok* tree."

Marie-Josée Baudot: What? What tree?

Nelzir Ventre: *Tambalakok,* a big *tambalakok* tree. Ti Zan—the balloon comes down on it. The wolves—

Marie-Josée Baudot: —get around the tree.

Nelzir Ventre: Get around the tree.

Prince Lulu gives the order to eat down the tree. The wolves sing: *gomba gomba la luya* [*repeated several times*].

Now Ton Nelzir was eager to end this piece.

Eh-ou, eh-ou, brother. The wolves have eaten half the tree down.

Audience member: Too quick!

Nelzir Ventre: Half the tree the wolves have eaten down.

Audience member: Hey, that means two people are there.

Nelzir Ventre: Ti Zan does this way:

Balloon, go up [*repeated several times*]

—and the story is suddenly over, "too quick" in the judgment of at least one of Ton Nelzir's neighbors in the audience. Even on MBC television, old *sega* traditions deserved a bit more time, but shortening the piece was clearly his decision, based on the tensions of the occasion.

Ton Nelzir's defiant girl had a long life before he came along. Everywhere her story asks Freud's question, "What does a woman want?" Even in Europe her African identity is known, through the Nigerian novel *The Palm-Wine Drinkard,* by Amos Tutuola. The exotic happenings and style of this novel won a wide Anglophone audience for its author. Later, critics labeled its style as a creolized English and found that its genre had an important Igbo-language forerunner in the novels of D. O. Fagunwa. The defiant-girl episode in the novel ends when the narrator, an interventionist like Gérose Barivoitse, rescues the lady from the ogre by transforming himself and flying (Tutuola 23–29). Tutuola recontextualizes the defiant girl for European readers, making a powerful ideological vehicle into a neocolonial amusement, of the kind the French call *folklorique* (Görög-Karady 11). In Africa it is a heavier vehicle, one of great variety, performed "for reasons particular to the audience at hand" (Mills 123).

Scholars have established, out of the bewildering variety of narrations, a unifying "tale type" for this narrative. It sets forth the refusal of suitors, marriage to a disguised husband, discovery and rescue. Since no one ever performs and no audience experiences a "type," which is a scholarly abstraction, its meaning is to point to the contradiction, in all the societies that tell the story, between a woman's sexual desire and the regulation of marriage by males.

Ti Zann gets around. In Sierra Leone, Donald Cosentino collected so many Mende versions of the girl's story that it gave him part of his book's title, *Defiant Maids and Stubborn Farmers.* One Mende version makes her no inexperienced girl (as we might expect from her fantastic expectations for a husband) but "a great fornicator." When a spirit courts her, she follows him and the other spirits home, against the spirits' urging. She witnesses him give back all his borrowed human features. At his home place, when they eat what he has caught, the difference between their diets becomes critical. She bears him a child; he sleeps for a year; her child becomes ill and dies. Unable to escape from his iron house, she too dies (Cosentino 164–66). Cosentino's first narrator was followed by a second, Mariatu Sandi, who performed the piece with much more detail and dialogue; she directed occasional commentary at the collector, as Gérose Barivoitse does. Cosentino was reminded of the dialogues and arguments on the same subject of marriage by Chaucer's Wife of Bath, Friar, and their successors. Mariatu Sandi augmented the number of interlopers, who transform themselves into young men, from four to twelve; in her version, the captive woman successfully escapes (Cosentino 166–72). In a third Mende version, an emaciated, scabrous brother accompanies the unfortunate young woman and her sisters, discovers the lover's identity, and effects her escape by magically propelling a boat with his singing (Cosentino 179–86).

Still in West Africa, Peul narrators give the tale various endings: suicide, burial, or escape through her brother's intervention (Seydou, "Mariage Sauvage" 89). "It is thanks to the vigilance and perspicacity of a little brother (as opposed to the sister's total lack of awareness), then thanks to the courage of the leprous brother, that the sister escapes the fate of being devoured by her animal partner, with all the ambiguity of meaning hidden in the image of devouring," writes Christiane Seydou. If the brother, she goes on, can pull his sister out of a bad marriage, the family will benefit: the girl will return to the status of a marriageable daughter and be reintegrated into the regular circulation of women, which society requires (Seydou, "Mariage Sauvage" 95). Her opposite, in some West African tales, is a young woman who makes excessive demands on her suitors: they must either overeat or go without food (Seydou, "Mariage Sauvage" 106–107). One man accomplishes her tests with the aid of grateful animals, marries her, and then kills the wife as punishment (Seydou, "Mariage Sauvage" 109). The brother's role towards his defiant sister, in one story type, and the husband's revenge on the tyrannical wife-to-be, in the other, justify, in West African eyes, the authority of males over women. A woman must learn to temper her desires to achieve the marriage she wants and find a husband equal to her qualities and beauty. There are many more versions: dozens in central Africa (Biebuyck and Biebuyck), and many in East Africa, from which the majority of Africans were seized and enslaved (Gutmann 75; Cagnolo; Doke; Carnell; Werner 192–95).

Until the French Africanists established *la fille difficile* as a tale type, her tale—so well known, focusing so many peoples' concern about marriage—did not fit well into folklorists' classifications. If the scholar strove to be loyal to the system, creole creativity would interfere. For instance, if the refusal comes not from the young woman herself, but from a father who wants to prevent her marrying, that's not the same tale. Then there was the King Thrushbeard type (Grimm no. 52), in which a disdainful princess is obliged to marry a beggar and endure poverty, until the beggar is revealed to be a prince. Obviously not this story. Or one could try the Rescue by the Sister type (Grimm nos. 46 and 66), in which a sister deceives the ogre-captor into carrying three sisters home in a sack or a chest. Another zero. If a brother, a key character in Nelzir Ventre's story, rescues his captive sister by killing the ogre, again that's not this story (though in some Indian Ocean versions, the ogre is finally burned to death).[43] Evidently the defiant girl refuses to be subordinated to the European classification system. Her story spotlights major issues: the fear of any outsider, class and gender difference, and anti-male prejudice.

These concerns explain her persevering history in the Southwest Indian Ocean islands. Fifty years after slavery was abolished in Mauritius, Charles Baissac distinguished two variant forms, both preserving multilingual traditions (Baissac, *Folklore* 146–79; Goswami 20–23). In one, the wolf-husband is a sorcerer, against whom her brother warns her; in the other, the helper is not a relative, but a beautiful woman disguised as a mouse (Baissac, *Folklore* 162–79). Once disenchanted, this beautiful mother-figure gives her an egg, a broom, and a stick to throw behind her when she is pursued, to conceal her escape. This obstacle-flight episode ends many folktales in Europe, Africa (Johnson and Sisoko 117), and Madagascar (Birkeli 240–45; Mamelomana 889–92). Leaving banana trunks in the bed to deceive the ogre is a case of creolization, "a detail reinforced in Madagascar," says Paul Ottino, "by Indonesian symbolism, which makes the banana-tree a vegetable substitute for the human being" (Ottino, "Les aventures" 39). Concern for a proper marriage has rooted the defiant girl's story in all the other islands.

In Madagascar and the Comoros, the defiant girl's story has astonishing vitality, asserting its message again and again among the northern Sakalava, Vezo, Antanosy, and Betsimisaraka (Ramamonjisoa et al.; Fanony 56–73). In one version, the monster husband is a *fosa* in disguise; instead of taking himself apart, he removes some clothes because it's so hot (Fanony 56–73). In another, the husband is a ghost. My prose translation doesn't conceal the rhythm of the west coast storyteller.

71. The Defiant Girl in Madagascar

Antifiheranana narrator 1920s

A young woman was of an age to take a husband.
Chiefs came after her, she would not have them
Rich men came after her, she would not have them
A handsome young man came after her, she would not have him
Princes came after her, she would not have them
and all those men said,

"We went after her, we didn't get her consent. Let's leave her and no longer think about her."

Mandrongana, a *lolo,* a revenant, came to her door.[44] "I have come to get you," he said, "and take you to my place to be my wife." And she left, she left, she left! "Is the village nearby?" she asked him. "Very near." She reached the cemetery, and her companion sang, "*Biby Mandrongana, Biby Mandrongana* [Mandrongana is an animal]!" The woman's sister, who was with them, said to her elder sister, "Don't you hear those words, Biby Mandrongana, Biby Mandrongana?" "You are wrong," her sister answered, "this is my husband taking me home." As they were getting near the cemetery, they heard the *sifaka* (large lemurs) crying, "*Crok, crok, crok,*" and Mandrongana said, "You can hear the men in the village. We've arrived."

"But where are the houses?" said the little sister.

"That's yours," the *lolo* said, pointing to a tomb.

"But we are in a cemetery, not a village," she answered.

"*Biby Mandrongana, Biby Mandrongana,*" the *lolo* sang. Then he picked up a skull and blew on it like on an *antsiva* [a large shell used as the royal trumpet], because he was glad to have got home.

The two women, frightened, ran away and went back to their house at top speed. Their father killed some oxen to thank God for allowing them to escape. And since then, for fear, they no longer were willing to marry. (Grandidier 180)

Elsewhere in Madagascar, the defiant heroine is split into a pair of women, as inseparable as the Malagasy tricksters Ikotofetsy and Imahaka (Haring, *Malagasy Tale Index* 320–22, 324–27, 337–45). These desirable women refuse all rich suitors—*vazaha* (Europeans), Indians, even civil servants—and demand men who don't defecate. "You want men who don't shit?" says the ogre Manjongay. "That's me! I'm not one of those who shit, so you're for me!" The plot unfolds through the dual marriage (the ogre has a friend), rescue by the women's brother in the flying basket, and punishment of the ogres (Ramamonjisoa et al. 69–106).

From Mayotte, twenty-three versions of this story have been published in a single volume (Gueunier and Said). There, where nothing is more important than marriage properly arranged and celebrated, nothing is more dangerous for a woman than becoming isolated from her family. The plot of one Mahorais version turns on understanding language.

72. The Defiant Girl in Mayotte

Antuat Asoghra Abdurahamani 1973–75

There was once a king who had a charming daughter, fairer than the day. This girl, who was already grown, was not yet married. She refused all marriage proposals.

One fine day when she was at her window, she saw a very handsome, well-dressed man wearing a big *kemba* [strip of skin, peel] on his head. She looked at him for a few minutes and thought, "Who's that attractive young man? There's the husband I have to have!" And right away she ran to call her father and showed him the man of her choice. The king summoned him, asked him what his name was, where his family was, and what village he came from. He said his name was Ali Charif, he had old parents, and he lived on the other side [of the island]. The *grand mariage* was celebrated.

The *grand mariage* is the central event in Comoran life, an occasion for the most ostentatious kind of spending. All through life, climactically at the wedding, a person tries to be known as generous and to manifest the values which Comoran society attaches to the sharing and circulating of goods. A great many stories attest to the agonies of poverty (Ahmed-Chamanga and Mroimana). By custom, marriage is uxorilocal; women own the property. So if a man decides to repudiate his wife under Islamic law, he must then leave her house and any furniture or goods he has given her. A Malagasy saying is heard in Mayotte: "*Lahilahy tsisy an'nazy,* No man is at home"—except at his mother's, which he considers "home" (Gueunier and Said 13). Against this social background, the Mahorais narrator dramatizes the dangers of virilocality.

Two weeks later, the man told the king that he wanted to go and introduce his wife to his parents, as they were too old to travel. The king agreed, but said he'd have to wait till they prepared his trip. He added that everything would be ready the next day. They put on a big ceremony at court to send them off. The evening before, the young wife's little sister asked her father to go with her sister, but the sister refused. Her husband begged her to let his sister-in-law come with them, saying she would be alone in the house, but she refused. Early in the morning the couple departed.

Alas, I am sorry to have to say, that man was just a devil who had transformed himself into a nice man when he found out that the king's daughter was not marrying. But as he was well dressed, like a rich man, nobody suspected who he was. When he got to the village, the man showed his wife a great palace which he claimed belonged to him, but which belonged to a king he had swallowed. The devil had eaten the whole population of the village.

The East African swallowing monster appears in as many regional narratives as the obstacle flight, often combining with an Indonesian seven-headed snake (Ottino, "Les aventures" 37).

The wife asked him, "Isn't there anyone living [here]? On this whole trip I didn't see anyone!"

"Yes, there are some people, but you know, now is the season they work in the fields, and the peasants stay in the field to guard their plots," her husband answered. They visited the whole palace. As the wife did not see her husband's parents, which was the purpose of her journey, she asked him, "Where are your parents?"

"They're guarding their plot too," said the man.

"Aren't there any servants here?"

"No."

"Who's going to take care of us?"

"You are. You are my wife and you have to keep house!"

"I never worked at home, and I don't know how to do anything!"

"You'll try to work. That's why I married you, right?"

The wife had no more to say and was silent. As evening had come, they ate what they'd brought with them and went to sleep.

At sunrise, the man said to his wife that he was going to the field and gave her two kilos of rice and a chicken to cook. At noon, when the wife had gone to a lot of trouble to set the table, he came back. They sat down and at the moment when the wife was going to take a spoonful, he caught her arm and said to her, "*Krobala zina kaukani?*" which means "Tell me the name I had in childhood." The wife understood nothing, because this was devil language.

Mayotte is as multilingual as the other Comoros; people switch between Comoran and Kiswahili. In a fragmentary story, an elderly narrator gave the ogre the name *Djaha Romola:* "And this Djaha, he was a man, you must not pronounce his name. Understand? And he went to ask someone else that name, that name, if he knew his name" (Gueunier and Said 276–77). Guessing this supernatural creature's name, becoming the kind of translator many real-life Comoran women are, will give the wife a power over him.

Her husband told her that if she did not answer, she would not eat. She stayed without eating. Fortunately, she'd left a bit of rice in the pot, and while her husband was sleeping, she went to eat it all up. For three days it was the same thing.

The fourth day, she went out and saw a little smoke far away. Right away she set off in that direction. She got to a little cave where the smoke was coming from, and said, "*Hodi!*" The person in the cave answered, "If you are a devil, cave, close up till I feel you are closed. But if you are a person, cave, open!" She saw the cave open wide, and the person inside was surprised to see the young woman. "Ah! What are you doing here, my dear?" The woman told everything and said that every time she went to eat, her husband told her, "*Krobola zina kaukani?*"

"Oh heavens, it's that wicked devil! Poor child! He is the one who ate all the people around here. But I ran away and came to take refuge in this cave. When you called from outside, I thought it was him. That's why I was slow to open."

"And what do you bid me do?"

"What he is saying to you at every meal means that he wants you to tell him his name. This time, when he asks you his name, say, '*Ndindi!*' He will be very surprised and upset, and you'll have a chance to run away, my child!" She thanked the old woman and went back home.

When her husband returned and asked her the question, she answered, "*Ndindi!*"

"Oh, poor me! My wife knows I'm a devil!"

Like the cat hunted by the *fosa,* he cannot keep himself from dancing.

He began to sing and dance: *Ndindi, ndindi-ka*

Tiyana-ka, Ndindi-ka
krobala, Ndindi-ka
zina-ka, Ndindi-ka
ukani, Ndindi-ka
Ndindi, Ndindi-ka, Ndindi, Ndindi-ka!

Which means Devil, devil
She knew, devil
to say, devil
my name, devil,
when I was a child, devil
devil, devil, devil, devil!"

While he was singing, he gradually took back his own shape: horns, tail, fur, all of it. And the wife fled. He came back to devour her but he didn't see anyone. Empty! (Allibert 66–68)

And as the rat, having reached the shore, escaped from the cat, the woman regains her life. While justifying male authority over women, the tale carries a second message: a woman can exercise power over the word. For the Mahorais wife who has risked a virilocal marriage, everything depends on saying the right words. With these she will conquer the lying enemy male. "Ali Charif" is an acceptable Muslim name; his story is as plausible as his raiment; but often in these Comoran tales, the ogre, djinn, or animal tells lies, as this one does, about cultivating his crops. His *langage,* in fact, bizarre though it seems, is only a slight deformation of Kiswahili. When his true name is announced, his power vanishes (Gueunier and Said 206–18, 276–80). Such power of language says everything important about Mahorais social life: marriage must be uxorilocal, a husband must be properly selected, marriage is an initiatory experience (Blanchy, "Le tambour," "Mères"). One narrator adds xenophobia to the fear of virilocal marriage: Madagascar, whence the collector had recently come, is the place where this imprudent girl acquires her ogre of a husband (Gueunier and Said 137). So in one breath the narrator both reminds her guest, a Frenchman, of his outsider status and smears the Great Red Island as a place for ill-fated exogamy.

The defiant-girl tale puts women, quite realistically, at the center of Comoran society; in Africa, it puts their marriages at the center of societies. Many of them gain power by owning their houses, thus being able to compel or prevent divorce. Moreover, the traditional succession of power through the female line links Comorans to Makua of Mozambique and Nyanja of Malawi (Gueunier and Said). As any visitor to Grande Comore (Ngazidja) can see, few women are secluded nowadays. All know the defiant girl. Feminist critics should meet her (Haring, "The Multilingual Subaltern").

Storytellers like these in the Indian Ocean islands are the unacknowledged, unheard legislators of cultural theory, which made the twentieth century an intellectual golden age (Eagleton, *After Theory* 1). They are unheard because they speak a different language. Yet, now that literary criticism, philosophy, linguistics, aesthetics, "pleasure, desire, art, language, the media, the body, gender, [and] ethnicity" (Eagleton, *After Theory* 39) have met on a vast playing field, surely there is room for skilled storytellers from creole societies, the symbolism they employ, and their aesthetic. One vague name for that field is culture; another, not much more precise, is textuality. In criticism, this word has often meant "a potentially infinite and indefinite, all-inclusive series of networks of interrelation whose connections and boundaries are not securable because they are ruled by never-ending movements of linguistic energy that recognize neither the rights of private ownership nor the authority of structuralism's centralized government of interpretive norms" (Lentricchia 189). In real life (if there is such a thing), such networks of interrelation are neither infinite nor indefinite. Postcolonial societies like the Southwest Indian Ocean islands offer a laboratory for mapping them. There, rights of private ownership are seldom exerted over orally performed folktales, but performers like Nelzir Ventre or Gérose Barivoitse receive distinction and acclaim which award them a kind of ownership. No more in those islands than in the world of cultural theory will interpretive norms be agreed on. But since every performer, even the proud Ton Nelzir, learns from others; since each performance is based on somebody's previous performances; since recorded texts reveal what those performances were like, and at least the broad geographical region where they took place, the African contribution to island storytelling is a case of intertextuality, or what might more properly be called "interperformance" (Haring, "Interperformance").

This notion is not all-inclusive, but it is animated by "never-ending movements of linguistic energy"; even in translation, Gérose Barivoitse's tales are enough to demonstrate that. What I mean by "interperformance" is simply the relation of one performance of a tale or proverb or riddle to other performances. It begins from M. M. Bakhtin's idea that "all texts, oral or written, within a given field of expression and meaning, are part of a chain or network of texts in dialogue with each other" (Bauman, "Conceptions" 16). Interperformance asks to have some of the links in the chain identified. In a more complex meaning, though still one that asks for historical verification, interperformance takes on "the transposition of one or more systems of signs into another, accompanied by a new articulation of the enunciative and denotative position" (Kristeva 59–60). Systems of African signs that were transshipped to the islands include plots such as Tarbaby, characters including Soungoula and Ti Zan, structural patterns such as the making-and-breaking-of-friendship, and performance styles such as the alternation of speech and song. Behind these lie the ideologemes of interdependence, marriage rules, and subordination. These too had to undergo that "passage from one signifying system to another [which] demands a new articulation of . . . enunciative and denotative positionality" (Kristeva 59–60). Whatever those last terms mean in semiotics, the position of narrators such as Nelzir Ventre or Gérose Barivoitse is not difficult to discover. They are the inheritors of those "times of abrupt changes, renewal, or revolution in society," which have placed them in the lowest social or economic classes of their islands. From that position, they have anticipated many of the issues that afflict cultural theory: "ambivalence, indeterminacy, the question of discursive closure, the threat to agency, the status of intentionality, the challenge to 'totalizing' concepts, to name but a few" (Bhabha 173). Their performances are transpositions from an African system to a Southwest Indian Ocean system, which took place in a furnace of domination and oppression. Thus the creole folktale is the place to look for multiple alternative, sometimes utopian, visions of the world. Folktale performances are a way of acting upon that world. Intertextuality of that kind—visible, traceable, and materially substantiated—illuminates the generalizations of literary theorists about textuality. Stubbornly empirical, naïvely humanistic, folkloristics pays attention to such artists.

3
Stars

NELZIR VENTRE KNEW HE WAS A STAR LOCALLY BEFORE THE MAURITIUS Broadcasting Corporation came to Poudre d'Or to film him. "He liked to sing, sing *segas,*" John Brasse explained to me. "And his *segas* were *segas* on a theme of some kind, an occasion, a story. Always he told stories . . . extraordinary things. . . ." Ton Nelzir confirmed that to a newspaper

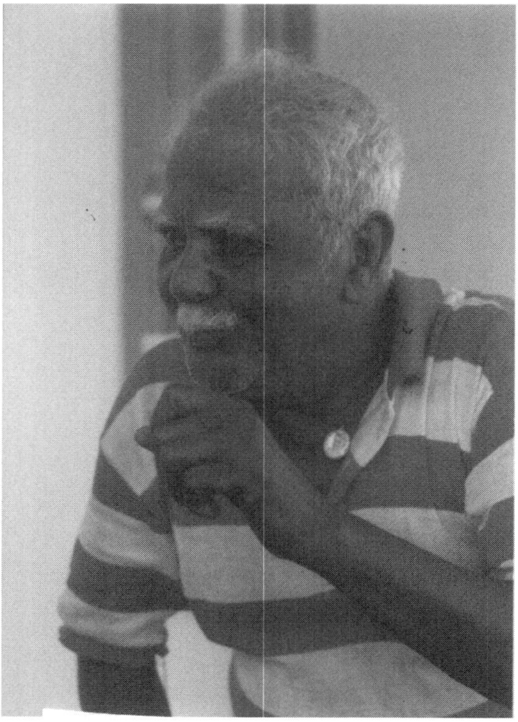

Nelzir Ventre.
Photo by Lee Haring.

interviewer: "You have to sing a *sega* of experience [*sega laventir*]." "When he sang," John Brasse continued, "I said to him, 'Sing us M. Autard de Bragard, the story of Montagne Longue.' "

73. Autard de Bragard

Nelzir Ventre, Poudre d'Or, Mauritius 1980

There was a man, an important white man. He was called Autard de Bragard. He lived at Champ de Lort. He was a keen sportsman. His passion was horse riding. In those days, there were no cars, only carts. There would be six horses with a boy behind and a driver in front. Madame, Monsieur, Grand Madame, Mamzelle—the whole family would be in that carriage to go to church, and then they'd come back to the estate. There were no big houses in Curepipe yet.

Well, this M. Autard, he liked a girl who lived at l'Ilôt in Montagne Longue. There were lots of coloreds who lived there. They had a chapel, that same chapel which was pulled down and then rebuilt, and which is known today as Notre Dame Church.

I know his story. The girl was a colored person. From time to time, M. Autard would take his cart in the afternoon to go to his fiancée and court her. Well, it so happened that there was bad weather. Long ago, we didn't say "cyclone." It was in 1892 that they started to say "cyclone" for the first time. Long ago, everybody would just say "bad weather." When there was rain and wind, that was called *burask* [strong wind]. So, this bad weather went on for four or five days. The man was getting worried because he couldn't go to l'Ilôt. When the weather got a bit better, but was still bad, there had been floods just like with [cyclones] Claudette [December 1979] and Hyacinthe [January 1980]. The sun was not out yet. He said to his mother that he would go to see his fiancée. His mother told him, "No, don't go. Wait a while more. Let the weather get better, more decent, then you should go. Wait for good weather to come back."

He said no. Well, he was thinking about his love. He kept on with his mother who was crying. He went into the stable and got the cart ready. This is why they say [in French], "Love is stronger than death."

It was love that took him to his death. The wind was still blowing, but then it got a bit calmer. When the man came, he went on Fifty Cent Bridge. (I always heard from older people that there were robbers who attacked a man on that bridge. They killed him and found fifty cents on him. So then they placed the fifty-cent coin on his belly. From that day on, that bridge was called Fifty Cent Bridge.) When M. Autard got there, it was still flooded. He, his cart, his horses: they all went in, never to come back. Up till now, they have never come back. Do you understand?[1]

For *sega laventir* and at wakes (*wit zur*), he was in demand.

> They'd invite someone who could tell stories. Well, often it was Nelzir who was there. . . . Sometimes he'd say something he had to have, something to make people pay attention to Nelzir. He had to have a pack of cigarettes there; sometimes they'd give him a cup of coffee. Every time, I'd light his cigarette. So then he'd tell a story, he talked, he talked, he talked, he talked. That gave pleasure. Everybody would laugh, laugh, laugh, so you forgot the time. The time passed fast. . . . The "eight days" usually lasted till midnight. At midnight you'd stop. Then no more. They'd tell stories there, they'd talk, you could take a chair and sleep a little—so as not to send people away.

Stardom meant he needed a group, "one called Anatole, one called Auguste," John Brasse told me.

> The only one who's still alive, René Jean-Baptiste is still alive [1990]. But he doesn't want to [perform with him] any more. There are people who don't want to go out with Ton Nelzir because . . . when it came to money, he would share very little. He'd give 25 rupees and keep most of it, because he was the author and he had gathered. So some got irritated with him.

He would also appropriate other people's material.

> He got stories from the others. Not all his stories are his own. He must have collected some of his stories from Anatole, he collected stories from Auguste, he collected stories from Armance from—from Mon Loisir. Because he has a good memory, eh? He has a good memory, he can collect, he has a good memory, he can collect (Brasse).

Wherever he got them, Nelzir Ventre's songs don't provoke laughter. They paint no brighter picture than the anecdote of Autard de Bragard. After recording the false tug-of-war (in chapter 2), Ton Nelzir said, "OK, I'll tell you another one," and went into a pathetic *sega*.

74. Little Pyang-Pyang

Nelzir Ventre, Poudre d'Or, Mauritius 1990

Now I'm going to tell you another story.

> [sings] My mother, come and see me I say
> My father, come and see me

I am staying at the king's place, earning money
and the king likes me
My mother, come and see me I say
My father, come and see me
I am staying at the king's place, earning money
and the king likes me

The narrative portrays a poor little girl who is adopted by a king, under the impression she is an orphan. Presently her song reveals that she has parents, and the king says,

"*Ma fi* [daughter], why did you tell me that you were on your own, that you had no mother, no father, and no nobody? But now, why do you say such things to me?" He says, "*Ma fi,* well, I'll give you all the things you like, and you leave. I do not need you."

With his little chorus responding five times to his calls, Ton Nelzir uses the song to transfer his heroine back to her parents, and the *sega* is over. Behind familiar elements like a munificent monarch (who may have more in mind for this girl than a mere adoption) and a heroine's unquenchable yearning to return to her parents, hunger is the prevailing theme.

75. Lasirenge, the Magic Bird

Nelzir Ventre 1983

So it is in a story he told in the 1983 television broadcast. A magic bird, King Lasirenge in disguise, steals food from Ti Zan and Ti Zann, who have been left to make lunch while their parents work the fields. Finally the parents discover the secret and destroy the monster. A more detailed version, which we recorded later, dramatizes the helplessness of the children. Once their father finds out the villain, he goes *au por,* to the harbor, and fetches *laveronik,* a poison. The children warn Lasirenge, who then says,

"I'm off. I've had enough. I know that this old man is more powerful than I am." He went out in order to leave. At the same moment the old man came back. The old man came, he just went like this, and he saw the bird ready to fly off, understand? He had become like a bird once more. Before, he had become a human being, a person, then when he is about to leave, he becomes like a bird in order to leave. He went like this, the old man saw this, the old man yelled. He said to his son, "Get my *kalaputu.*"—*Kalaputu,* what is it? It's his gun. There was a kind of gun long ago, that's an old—time gun. Well, you put gunpowder, then paper, and you pound it in. Then the lead and you pound it. You put—thing—pound again well. Well, that gun was a one-shot gun, it was called *kalaputu.*

He said, "Bring my *kalaputu* here."

Following a long exchange of call and response, the father kills the bird, but then Ti Zan wants to eat some of it. This dish turns him into a cannibal; Ti Zann calls her three faithful dogs to her aid; one eats Ti Zan, and in the most irrelevant ending imaginable, plays market woman.

He took him, then he went out to go to the market. He went to the market, he took everything to the market.

> (sings) Here is tender greens
> go to the market, clean the greens
> Go to the market, clean the greens
> Chorus: Go to the market
> Nelzir Ventre: Clean the greens

Six repetitions of the call-and-response end the *sega.*[2] Both versions are internally dissonant. In a more complete, coherent version, by Gérose Barivoitse of Réunion, slaughtering and eating the magic bird transforms the boy into a monster, and again the father must intervene (Barat, Carayol, and Vogel 80–83, 79).

76. Ti Zan the Ladykiller

In another of Ton Nelzir's stories, Ti Zan, now a "ladykiller," escapes the kind of punishment from a hostile father that he himself might throw at an ogre. At the end, he goes to church on Sunday, sees the cute Simandorin, and says,

"Do you know me, *lilot* [small island]?"

> [*sings*] *linga wen we,* do you know me, *lilot*?
> *linga wen we*
> I am myself the ladykiller, ladykiller *polipot,* ladykiller.
> I am myself the ladykiller
> Chorus: ladykiller *polipot,* ladykiller.
> Nelzir Ventre: Do you know me, *lenga we wo*?

As always, Ti Zan survives the threats.

Eh-ou. He is very happy. He is like this. As he passed he looked at her, he was very happy. So he said, "Thank you very much, God."[3]

Nelzir Ventre was quite explicit to the newspaper interviewer about the occasions when some of his tales about powerless characters were performed.

Long ago, when someone died, we would sing church songs in the house. Outside, there would be stories, singing, dancing. This is called *gro pile* [big pounding]. Many men, young men and older men, would set up bits of raffia which they would hit, *tak takatak, tak takatak,* while they would sing and dance. I was a leader in that. *Gro pile* was sung only during the night of a death, and not for just a party. And these death songs, they are the ones that many *sega* singers today have taken to make very popular hits. In *gro pile,* you have to cry too. There is singing and storytelling. . . . There was weeping too, and headbanging. And also hitting the head with stones, and eating fire. We would tell these stories at night to express our sorrow. Everybody would listen, happy to watch this. Then there would be *ku de vent*—climb on the house, take all the straw off the roof. . . . The priest would forbid this thing in those days, but we did it all the same. Old M. Giraud used to be after us, I can tell you [*laughs*].

Interviewer: "Why did the priest not accept it, according to you?"

Olivia (Ton Nelzir's wife): Well, it's no good. It's against religion. This singing and dancing, this was a custom. Our parents the Mozambicans and Malagasy, they used to do that.

Nelzir Ventre: Last time we practiced that custom was for Anatole's death, about fifteen years ago. Now we've stopped. Now we don't know this. And those who know it, we don't do it because the priests have forbidden it . . . (Ventre)

Ton Nelzir knew very well that his kind of *sega* was threatened. His response, one evening, was to emphasize his uniqueness by comparison with men one and two generations younger, who were closest to him.

John Brasse: When you are dead, this will all be over. When you are dead, this will be finished.

Nelzir Ventre (approvingly): Nobody else knows how to do this.

John Brasse: Nobody else.

Patrick Brasse (John Brasse's son): No? I can.

Nelzir Ventre: What?

Patrick Brasse: I can.

Nelzir Ventre: Is that so? You will be able to?

Patrick Brasse: Of course. I picked it up. I've picked up everything.

Nelzir Ventre: Stop talking nonsense. You? Try one song, just one. I'll find out if you know.

For the rest of that evening (14 March 1990), between the songs and stories, Nelzir Ventre sounded this theme of his stardom. Against John Brasse's advice, he insisted on recording more and more songs, as if to demonstrate his strength, endurance, and large repertoire. But Brasse later had the last word, for me, on Ton Nelzir's stardom.

And the old man, he's had lots of stuff at sea. He could make his own repairs to his net, to fix it up, repair it. And he made that net called *épervier* [cast-net]. He sewed it, for the fishermen. Great patience—because it begins with one knot, two, then it gets bigger, like that. *L'épervier.* He can do that too. A very good old man in the fishing business.

Sydney Joseph.
Photo by Lee Haring.

"Stories are not difficult to make up. If you have understood life, it's easy to make stories. Like *segas:* to create them, you observe how things go." So Sydney Joseph, another Mauritian Kreol star storyteller, described his art. Retired from factory work after an injury, Sydney Joseph was a living refutation of the fallacy that modern industrial life extinguishes oral folktales. His account of himself gives reality to the presumption of the German critic Walter Benjamin, who declared, "The storyteller takes what he tells from experience—his own or that reported by others" (Benjamin 87). The reality includes other people's art in the storyteller's experience.

In the old days, when people told stories, you would listen to them. If you have a bit of intelligence, you remember the story completely. In the old days when people told stories, I would remember them gradually so I could tell them the same way. Now when I tell stories, I invent them, to see if they are the same style, if they "rhyme" [*rime*, make sense].

The pillars of all storytelling, as Sydney Joseph said, are imitation and innovation. In creole societies they tend to be tightly interwoven. Creole creativity is shaped by a history of cultural convergence, subordination, oppression, and antagonism. The ambivalence of the word *Kreol*, which denotes both people and their language, points to the fundamental problematic for people like Sydney Joseph.[4] They are on island soil because European exploitation of empty territories populated them with slaves, who would produce export. Mauritius and Réunion received Africans of a dozen or more ethnicities, as well as Malagasy (Barker 62). They didn't all look alike. Observers from the owning class repeatedly noted the difference between the stoical but hard-drinking Mozambican slaves, with their tight curly hair and body markings, and the long-haired, insolent, unreliable Malagasy, who were always ready to desert (Barker 62–65). With so many ethnic categories, cultural goods were carried in from Anjouan (Comoros) and Seychelles, as well as from faraway Gorée, Cape Verde, Timor, and Goa. Storytellers in the islands of Mauritius, Réunion, and Seychelles speak creole languages quite distinct from each other, yet the populations share a common stock of narratives and include artists like Sydney Joseph.

His group—the creoles descended from slaves, who make up one-quarter of the population of Mauritius—were long disguised by officialdom as the "general population." But wasn't anonymity the defining characteristic of every storyteller, for Benjamin in Europe, for Lars Dahle in Madagascar, for Charles Baissac in Mauritius? Baissac, for instance, rather than reveal the names of his informants, attributed his pieces to a fictitious Mauritian Kreol narrator called "Lindor." His use of folklore to reveal his countrymen's true mentality, which entailed keeping the individual storyteller anonymous, and which was standard practice for his contemporaries, gave way, in later generations, to a grudging permission for visibility. Sydney Joseph and Nelzir Ventre in Mauritius, Gérose Barivoitse and Germain Elizabeth in Réunion, and other unnamed, yet distinct star performers in the other islands marshal multiple symbols and techniques, which define the multiple possibilities for existence in their multilingual, multicultural societies. These artists make their stories themselves, as Sydney Joseph declares, in a specific environment, which often urges them to remodel what they have heard and to point to the existing system of social relations.

Hence Sydney Joseph makes new combinations of old plots; hence Gérose Barivoitse interrupts his stories to talk about himself. Their styles and their selection of themes respond, ultimately, to the slavery and exploitation that constitute island history.

Modest and quiet though he was, Sydney Joseph remembered and could summon up many narratives, and he had extraordinary skill in combining them so that they would "rhyme" with tradition. Also, like a riddler, he could begin a story by arousing the expectations of his hearers, even a foreigner and his Kreol collaborator, whom he'd just met: "Well, there was a man and a woman in a house. They had one son." Of course my collaborator and I wanted to know what this son's adventures would be. But another story must come first.

In 1989–90, I spent a year attached to the Folklore Department of the Mahatma Gandhi Institute in Mauritius. I initiated folktale fieldwork, as an attempt to demonstrate to Mauritians that creole traditions were thriving (Haring, "Buried Treasure"). With great foresight, the director of the MGI (as it's universally called) found me a remarkable collaborator, the linguist and ethnomusicologist Claudie Ricaud, whose translations appear in these chapters.

On the morning of 27 March 1990, Claudie Ricaud and I drove from the MGI to the town of Mahébourg, in the south of the island, to call on the parish priest. We'd been told he would be a helpful contact person. In the churchyard, while he finished other business, we fell into conversation with two parishioners who were helping to repair the church as part of their Lenten resolutions. We inquired about the vitality of forms of creole folklore, in particular the *wit zur* (eight days) ceremony. This is the Mauritian creole form of wake, comparable to the "nine nights" ceremony practiced in the West Indies (Abrahams, *Man-of-Words*). At the church, Georgius and Jean-René showed us that they knew many folktales and legends, and said that *wit zur* was alive and well in their part of the island. They quickly named seven villages where it was likely to be flourishing.

Then we asked them about storytellers. They named three, most enthusiastically the watchman of the village hall at Grand Bel Air, Jocelyn Joseph, nicknamed Pion. We must ask him, Georgius said, about the story of different sexes and different cultures on the same boat (a multiethnic joke we never got to hear). Grand Bel Air is not far from Mahébourg; we went there immediately, after a short meeting with the priest.

It was easy to find Jocelyn Joseph's house by asking one or two people at Grand Bel Air, and he and his wife welcomed us cordially. Yes, he admitted, he was a pretty good storyteller, for both tales and riddles, though he'd also forgotten a good many. Usually, he said, people asked him to tell stories and told others to keep quiet. His mentor had been one Tilik, now dead, a highly praised performer. As earnest of his abilities, he went right into one story, *lezwa ek zako,* the bird and the monkey. But, he modestly said, he was not the only one: he especially recommended his mother, Elda Joseph, who lived at Bois des Amourettes. We must meet her.

We agreed to that, and we made an appointment with him. That was easy: as he started work at four in the afternoon, we could come and meet with him some morning at ten. And by the time we finished collecting stories, if we ever did, we would know the village well enough to document the *wit zur.*

But first we felt obliged to meet Mrs. Joseph. We made our way in delighted anticipation to Bois des Amourettes, which, like most Mauritian villages, lies almost invisible off a main road, this one following the south coast. Broad concrete steps lead uphill away from the sea. Ever the tourist, I turned back to admire the ocean vista opening behind me, so commonplace to the villagers. We ascended past the many houses, asking for Mme Joseph. Soon we found the house, some ten yards off the path. As we approached, an old lady came out to meet us. "Mme Joseph?" we said. Yes, she said, and ushered us in past a couple of men sitting in an outer room. But this was not Elda, it was her niece Lucia, whose house we were in. She showed us to an inner room. Elda Joseph, very old and frail, received the strangers graciously.

Her brief conversation with Claudie was deeply moving. Yes, she used to know stories, but now had great difficulty remembering any. To show what she was once capable of, she told a riddle: "I am sleeping in my house. A thief comes in. The house goes out the window. I am caught." The answer: "A fish-trap in the sea." Obviously, her age and poor health would make any attempt to collect from her a cruelty. A few weeks later Elda Joseph was dead.

What next? Always flexible, Claudie asked Lucia and the younger people in the house about *matapan,* a kind of werewolf, and Ti Zan, hero of so many tales. They all laughed. One of the men we had passed as we came in was Elda Joseph's elder son Sydney (brother of Jocelyn), who said he knew some stories he would be willing to tell us. He could come and tell some with his brother Jocelyn who, he yet insisted, was the better storyteller—a real *dyaloger,* jokester. Sydney told us he lived next door to Jocelyn at Grand Bel Air and was free all day, because he was not working.

A couple of weeks later, we returned with the tape recorder for our rendezvous with Jocelyn Joseph and were greeted by his wife. Jocelyn was not home after all. He unexpectedly had some business to attend to that day. Claudie and I looked at each other a moment, summoning up our flexibility. "Is Sydney at home, by any chance?" Yes, he was, and she disappeared for a few minutes, returning with Sydney. Remember, it was 10 o'clock in the morning, and Sydney does not work. She must have woken him out of a sound sleep. But he did not need to be reminded who we were. We faltered through greetings: we'd had an appointment with Jocelyn, you see, and he's not here, and, well, you said you knew some stories, and, well, could you by any chance—Sure, he said, settled into a chair, and said, "Well, there was a man and a woman in a house." His story would take forty uninterrupted minutes.

The shape of his hero's adventures would constitute both the form of Sydney Joseph's story and our experience as his audience (Burke 31; Goodman 1–25).[5] What rules was this storyteller following? What makes it *rime*?

77. The Siren-Girl

Sydney Joseph, Grand Bel Air, Mauritius 18 April 1990

Well, there was a man and a woman in a house. They had one son. That son, he might be around twelve, thirteen years old. Well, the mother and father, they were poor. They didn't have much. Pretty poor. Well, the father was a fisherman, he used to go fishing in the sea. Well, every time he went fishing in the sea, he didn't get enough as food. Two or three pounds of fish he would get, just enough to cook.

At any rate, one day, as he was going fishing, that little boy was always wanting to go with his father. But the father was never happy to bring him to fish in the sea. The father stopped him. He said, "No, you're a bit too weak, because in the sea you can get waves. The boat could capsize. You wouldn't be able to hold on. So how could I take you?" But that boy really liked it. That little boy was called Zan. Well, he always wanted to go fishing.

As his first *rime,* Sydney Joseph begins with a couple in poverty and a hero with the most familiar of names, who will need a wife. "One member of a family either lacks something or desires to have something," says the theorist (Propp 35–36). The poverty will be liquidated by a plentiful catch. But to "rhyme" with the genre, the boy must end, after many turnings, with prosperity and a wife. Intervening episodes will subordinate Zan to the "unfolding of the action," while the action is subordinated to the "unfolding of the verbal material" (Erlich 243). "When I tell stories, I invent them," Sydney Joseph said.

Well, one day, while his father was fishing in the sea, it was like, a wave rose in the sea. And in the sea there was a siren [*lasiren*]. She was watching him in the sea. She said to him, "Old man, I know you are poor, and you're trying to earn a living. You are fishing for your food. However, I'm going to put a *kondisyon* [magic, tabu] on you." The siren is supposed—according to the story I am giving you, she is supposed to be a power.

A woman from undersea with magic powers, who engages a man on land, is a *rime* from Madagascar's favorite legend, Ranoro (Haring, "Water-Spirits"). But it's the son the *lasiren* wants, and not for herself. Sydney Joseph innovates.

She said to him, "I know you have a son in your house over there, that he wants to come and go fishing. But you don't want to take him. I'll put a *kondisyon,* but you have to take him." Just as he was leaving, as he was going home, around midnight, she said to him, "I'll give you a boat full, overflowing with fish. You understand? And nobody should know about this." So he left the boat, let's say about this distance from the jetty. And that man, as he was going back, he was very happy because he had fish. He came in with the fish. He sold it to another boat, to fishermen. He sold the fish.

"That's finished," Sydney Joseph says at this point, marking a transition, stumbling a moment, then alluding to stories about women who can't keep secrets, darkening the sky.

The old woman—the old man—the old woman said, "But how did you get the fish?" He said, "Well, an adventure. I'm going to tell you, but it's a secret. I'm going to tell you this, because I don't trust you too much." So then and the next day, as he was about to go fishing, he said to his son like this: "You've always wanted to go fishing with me. Come, I'll take you. Let's go." And the boy, young boy, you know, when he's about to go to a new place, he's very happy. He can't sleep at night he's so happy. Then the young boy said, "Father, are you sure that you're taking me?" He said to him, "Yes. Be ready early in the morning. Get dressed and everything, and we'll go. Take everything you need for fishing."

So the father took him. They went fishing. The boy was fishing, the waves were rising. When they were in the sea fishing, it was around midday. That's when the waves started rising. The boat was rocking. The child fell, he fell into the sea. He didn't die, that child. That child, well, it was the siren who caught him. She had made a condition about this. Well, as soon as he got there, the father would get his boat full of fish, and as before would go back and sell the fish. Well, the mother, she was very anxious. She said to him, "Old man, you went fishing. Where is Zan?" He said, "Woman, you know I never wanted to take him fishing. However, Ti Zan wanted to go fishing. I took him. Well, here is what happened. Here it is. The wave in the sea hit him. He couldn't hold on. He fell into the sea."

The father knew what had happened to him, because he had made a condition with the siren, him: "Do not tell anybody where your child is." The child, he is not going to die. Then that boy, the father got his boat full of fish, went back, and told this to the old woman. To the woman he told it. He said like this—well, the woman said, "Old man!" "Woman, do not be worried. It's a child. An accident happened. We were very poor. See now how much fish we have to sell. We are rich. Now you should not be worried. Maybe one day we can—God will help us." The woman became very sad. Always mothers, they are this nature. They like to become sad and worried.

The boy will fall into the siren's power after a transition: "Now, he did things, did things. . . . Here now, we are going to tell the adventure of the siren with that boy." Sydney Joseph now reveals the principal framework of his complex tale, which folktale scholars call The Man on a Quest for his Lost Wife. This story is known all round the world, with three analogues in the *Thousand and One Nights* and three treatments by the Grimms (Thompson, *Folktale* 92).[6] A scholar can predict what's going to happen to Zan, if Sydney Joseph doesn't invent too much: A father promises his son to a sea-creature; the boy finds a princess with whom he sleeps chastely; the hero is allowed to visit home on condition that he not reveal the secret; he loses the princess by breaking a prohibition; he sets out in search, gets help, and acquires magic objects; and with their aid he retrieves and marries the princess. So Sydney Joseph "rhymes" with patterns of storytelling in Europe, Africa, and India.

Now: the siren lived under the sea. For us, we can't see it, but there was a castle. (That's what people say; they cast these stories.) So there was a castle under there. Well, that boy, he had no *korespondans* [relations] with the siren, him. As he was there, he was given food, drink—well, it's inside a palace. He didn't lack anything.

Well, that siren, she had just one daughter. The daughter was called Zann. However, she had no relations [with him]. The boy was in one room sleeping; the girl was sleeping in another room. Well, the girl was just like her mother, had power just like her. Well, it's like, that girl at night, when everybody is sleeping, she feels like having relations with that boy. But how will she do it? She was hiding from her mother and was successful in getting near that boy.

Well, that boy was sleeping. So every time as night fell and everybody is sleeping, she would not come during the day. It would be silly, because she would not get him. Because with this power business and everything, she can't make an arrangement [*tom dakor*] with a human being. So she came at night.

The boy was sleeping. Then he thought he heard, as he was sleeping at night, it's as if he heard in his—as he was sleeping, he felt on the side, just like when somebody sleeps on your arm, you understand? Well, an arm, it gets tired, that. His sleep broke. So he woke up. Now he was thinking, "Why is my arm so sore?" He was weak. It was the same every day.

One day the boy was quite sad. He was sorry. He had food, drink, still he was sad. His head was tired. Why? Because he knows someone is sleeping in his arm, but he can't know who it is. Because it's too dark. And there was no light over there. So that siren, the mother, she said to the boy, "You look quite sad." He said yes. She said, "What has happened?" He said, "No, it's like I'm thinking about my father, my mother, and I want to go and see them." The siren said to him like this: "I'll put a condition." The boy had become quite strong. He was now about fourteen years old. She said, "A condition I'll tell you. If you leave—and I am going to let you go—you must not tell anyone where you come from, understand? Or else you'll die." The boy said to her, "Yes, I respect the rules that you tell me. I accept." Well, that siren, she had power. She just took him, put him quickly ashore, and left.

Under the new rules, Zan himself becomes a storyteller.

When the boy got there, he was ashore near his mother's place. The friends he used to play with said to him, "How are you, Zan?" He said, "As you can see." "Well, it's been a long time. Where've you been, old pal?" He doesn't say anything, because he doesn't have the right to. Those are his terms. They said, "You've come here." He said, "Yes," he said, "you know, I went fishing in the sea with my father. When that wave from the sea threw me off, I fell down. Well, it's like I was thrown on to the reef; that's where I fell. I didn't die. The people who were passing by on the reef came to meet me. They had seen me. Then I went in a palace where the king lives." (Here I suppose he's telling lies to his friends, so that nobody would believe him.) "It's true. They picked me up, gave me food and drink over there. However, the terms are that I must go back, because I'm working over there." (He's not working, he's telling lies. He can't tell them the truth, what the truth is.) So that's what he said to his friends. So that's what he said to his friends standing in the street.

Sydney Joseph alludes to the Malagasy storyteller's formula, "I do not wish to tell lies, but since lies have been told to me, allow me to tell lies to you." Zan treats his mother to a fiction.

Now he goes back to his mother's place. People have been telling her, "Your son is talking to his friends in the street." So he had come back and he went to see her. His mother grabbed him. It had been such a long time, so long since they met, the mother was very happy to see her son. Well, the boy was quite strong now, he was about sixteen years old, sixteen he was. He said to his mother, "You are sad." His mother said yes. He said,

"Well, I didn't die, but a wave from the sea which—thing me, and I fell in the water. Well, it's a wave from the sea that carried me, and I fell in the reef, on an island on the corals. Well, over there, when I got there, people who were passing by picked me up. As for me, when I came to, I found myself in a palace. I suppose there must have been a king. It's not a palace, it's more like a big wooden house. He gave me work. I stayed over there. However, there is one condition. I must go back there, because I'm working there." So things went on, and he had been with his mother for fifteen days. Now he said goodbye to his father and mother and went back. So when he was about to go back, the siren knew he would come back. She already knew it. Any time he would come back, she would already know it. As he was going back, he got to the sea to get near the siren. However, he had forgotten only one thing: what had been troubling him, what had been making him tired. He came, then went back. He bought a box of matches. These matches he took with him over there. He put them in his pocket and he went.

When he got near the sea, they say, the sea opened up. He went back near the siren over there. When he got there, same thing with the siren [girl]. She came to sleep next to him at night, she came to sleep with him. It was starting to make him tired, his head was tired with all this. Then, as they were all sleeping, let's say on the fourth day, he was asleep, he pretended to be asleep. He took the matches quietly, and the stick too, and he managed, when the girl was there—he was not asleep, he was pretending to sleep. He was watching, because that was making him tired every night. When he went to sleep, let's say around eleven o'clock at night, that girl, that young siren, would come to sleep with him.

Although Zan violates a prohibition, his narrator does not. Instead he does what an African narrator does when his first episode isn't enough for him, as a great scholar noted:

> Right away he goes into a second part, which is actually another story, conforming to a different formal type from the first. Yet he has retained the same hero. So he finds himself obliged, if his tale has been moving upward, to reverse direction in this second part and move downward. This he manages either by having his hero violate an interdiction previously unknown, or by dropping that very hero into a trap that has been laid, most often, by a new adversary. . . . The listener cannot foresee the particular nature of the peril awaiting the hero, or the misdeed he will commit. (Paulme, *La mère* 43–44)

This description of West African framing uncannily anticipates what Sydney Joseph does in The Siren-Girl: Zan violates the prohibition and is thrown out.

As she put her head on his arm to sleep, the boy just lit a match. He lit the match and saw her face at night. Well, at night, when he saw her, he just grabbed her and kissed her, and he got a big shock. According to the rules, he has no right to kiss that young siren. In that castle, the mother instantly knew, and she made that castle disappear, that very night, under the sea—vanished.

Now the boy, where will he go? The sea, the waves, the sea kept on carrying him now. The sea carried him again, brought him ashore, took him to an island. On that island, let's say in the early morning, as he was very weak, he didn't know what to do. He went around that island. When the sun started rising, he kept on walking by the sea, and he found something like a dagger [*ponyar*]. He found that dagger, he kept on walking, he picked it up. He picked it up and put it in his pocket. So with this dagger, he could catch octopus. He got—he didn't have any food, so that's all he had—the octopus for eating. He took that and ate it. He also had matches, and he heated up the octopus. Also different kinds of molluscs, all those he picked out of the sea, and also fish. He took all this and ate.

Having isolated and endangered his hero, what choices does Sydney Joseph have? Usually we think that a folk narrator has relatively free choice among specific actors, objects, or incidents, so long as he obeys certain rules (Bremond, *Logique*). Sydney Joseph's choice reverses Zan's progress towards winning the siren-girl. He switches into another story, the tale of The Grateful Animals, in which a young man "earns the thanks of several animals . . . and with their help wins the princess by performing three tasks imposed upon him" (Aarne and Thompson 199–200). But the princess to be won is not the princess he has kissed.

As he kept walking around that same island—it's an island, that—as he was walking, well, where is he to go? He kept walking, walking, walking, walking, walking. He went on like that, and he saw three, like, three animals. These animals, what are they? As the story goes, apparently, we call these the *komper.*[7] There was Komper Lion, there was Komper Eagle, and there was Komper Ant, black ant. So he picked it up [the dagger]. When he had picked it up, he had seen that Komper Lion, that Komper Eagle, that Komper Ant. All three had seen that. He said, "On this island, where could I go? That lion eats people." The eagle, the ant . . . he kept thinking about that lion. "You go over there, or you go here, he will still eat you." This was on a plain, so he looked around, then he kept on walking.

That lion called him and said, "Friend! Friend," he said to him, "look around!" But he kept going. The lion came close, came close, came close, came close. He had caught a deer, but "we don't know how to share it. Well, all three of us, we were discussing how to share this—also you have a dagger with you. Please share that. Whatever you give will be all right." So he shared it, he shared it. He took the bones, the legs, the meat, the body, all that, and he said to Komper Lion, "You, your mouth is quite big. Meat you can eat and bones you eat." He opened the stomach and said to the eagle, "Look at you! You have a beak. You take all the insides for yourself." He said to the ant, "You, ant, take its head, its marrow, you eat, you eat. Then go through its nose, you dig, and you get a house for you to live in."

They said—Komper Yev [Lion] said, "*Matlo* [mate], that's a very nice way of sharing. I never saw a person share like that." Happy, they left. They thanked him.

In their gratitude, the lion, eagle, and ant offer the hero magic parts of themselves, which will impart the powers of the mammal, bird, and insect worlds. So Zan resembles the epic hero Ibonia and other Malagasy heroes, who master the non-human worlds and move from the low position of younger son, through disguise as a kingfisher, for example, and into the air astride a winged horse (Lombard).

He went, went, went, went, went. As he was going on this island, once again the lion said to him, called him, told him to come. He said, "I-yi-yi! Komper Lion has finished eating, he didn't get enough, he still wants to eat me." He said, "If I don't go, he will eat me. If I go, he will still eat me." He said, "I have to go." Well, this was on an island. Where could he go? So he came, he came, came, came, came. He met that Komper Lion. He said, "I am here."

He said, "Look, friend, I am very happy because you did good sharing for me. But I want to give you a reward." The lion turned himself straight like *this,* he looked like *this,* and he said, "Look under my whiskers. There's something like feathers that I have. You pull one of them." He said, "One day, when you are in danger, or you're having a hard time, you just say, 'By the power of my King Lion, make the biggest lion appear.' " Ah-ha! He took it, he pulled it out and left. He went, he went. He thanked him and he left. He went, he went.

Now the eagle was thinking too. He said, "Well, we were three together. You gave him a power. What about me? Can't I give him some power?" He said, "Come here," he called him and said to him, "Come here, come here, come here." He said, "I-yi-yi!" It seemed like this time he would get it; this time he wouldn't escape. The eagle told him to turn back. As he got near to that eagle, that eagle said to him, "Look, we are three friends, always together. The three of us are kings, kings or chiefs. He gave you one power, I'll give you a power too." That eagle went on the ground, as if he was asleep. He opened his wings and said, "You see a little wing in the corner there? Pull that wing out. Whenever you are in trouble, you say, 'By the power of my King Eagle, make the biggest eagle appear!' " He left. Once again he started walking, walking.

Now the ant said, "Look, friend, the three of us together, those two did something like this. Well, can't I give you a power too?" He went and called him. He said to him, "Come back here." Now, when he came back, the ant said to him, "Look, my two friends, two kings, well, all three of us are chiefs. They each gave you a power. Well, I too am going to give you a power like those." The ant went upside down as well—same thing. He said, "Can you see that little whisker that's under here? Well, you pull it out." He said, "When one day you are in trouble, you say, 'By the power of my King Ant, make the smallest ant appear!' " (The other two had given the biggest, this one gave him the smallest.)[8] So he took that. In those days, there were no handkerchiefs, so he broke a, he was walk—walking. He found a—thing—tree, he put it in there. He put it in his pocket. So he took that.

He was still on that island. Now he went, went, went, went, on that same island. He walked—walked until he was tired. He was looking for molluscs by the seaside to nibble on, to nibble on. On that island, it was flat, and in front of him there was a forest. In that forest, around over here, there was a castle. Once again, there was a king who lived in there. That king—in turn, he had people to keep watch over his animals. Billygoats, cattle, nannygoats, everything there was, all that had to be watched. Well, all those who had to keep these animals couldn't do it right. And those who couldn't do the work for him, no right behavior, they would die. So as he came near the entrance to the king's (because the king has an entrance, you know. A king's entrance, it's very long, for a castle. The castle is right at the back, and you put the entrance over here), anyway, he looked at this, he saw all this, well, and he said "I'm out of work anyway. So I'll try and see." He saw that [notice], and he said, "I'll try it and see." [obscure] It went like this, "*Celui qui* can keep all the sheep, the nannygoats and billy goats, and everything that there is: if he can keep these well without losing any, he will give him half his fortune and his daughter in marriage." The king would give his daughter. Anyway he saw that, so he went, he went.

When he got there, he said to the king, "I've seen a notice on which you had it written that I could find work, so I have come to work." The king said to him, "Look, read this notice well, and what I have written over there, or else I'll put your neck on the block. I'll cut it." He said, "Yes, I saw that, but I want to try it and see." He said, "OK." So the king's gendarmes—the king gave orders to his gendarmes. He said like this: "You know, well, take him to the place where he is to live." Well, that place where he could sleep, it's very close to where the horses sleep. That's how it is in the army. He was near where the horses sleep, very close to where the horses sleep.

Sydney Joseph is not the first Indian Ocean storyteller to combine The Grateful Animals and The Man on a Quest for his Lost Wife. Both are especially well known in Madagascar, a transshipping point for many slaves (Ferrand, *Contes* 102–13; Renel, *Contes* 1:65–76; Faublée 423–27, 435–49; Haring, "Grateful Animals"). One Malagasy narrator made the same combination in the 1870s (Dahle 250–58), but did not poise his hero between two equally desirable women, as Sydney Joseph does. "You remember stories and then you invent them," he said.

So early the next morning, when it was time to work, he gave him a little basket so he could take his food, and he left. So they gave him twenty-five goats to take on the first day, twenty-five goats to go to work and keep watch on. He took these, he left. He set forth. He kept on going very, very far, very far from the king's castle, into a desert. At that moment, now, he went up near his goats and sat down to keep watch. There was, like, a lot of tall grass forming a hedge. He sat down there. There were goats, and the goats were eating in that desert, they were eating.

Around ten o'clock, as he was sitting down eating, before he had finished eating, he heard a kind of blowing in the forest, like a cyclone. He jumped, because that kind of roaring, that was roaring. He thought about this well and he said, "What could that be? What kind of roaring is roaring like that?" He went on the rock, he stood up, he looked around, he looked in all directions, he couldn't see anybody. He had heard that noise.

Over there, those people who had been keepers for the king's goats, the ones from before—there was a lion in the forest. That's what had eaten all those goats. And that lion over there, as long as he could get food (food he could not get), he would take, bring to a place, he would keep it as a reserve for later, when there would be no food later. That was his task. Nobody could stop him. Now, those who had been working before for the king: every time they brought back the goats, there would never be twenty-five. Always only twelve, ten, eleven, thirteen would be left. The king would say, "You didn't do the job well," and kill them. That was the regular thing.[9]

Formalist criticism insisted that plot elements in folktales always occur in the same order; creole narration disregards that rule. Kissing the girl, by violating the siren's second interdiction, prolongs the lack of a wife and throws her ultimate fate into question. Meanwhile "various animals place themselves at the disposal of the hero" (Propp 45) as he "is transferred, delivered, or led to the whereabouts of an object of search." This object will be a new sweetheart, equally desirable as a wife, who is offered to him after he has accomplished the Difficult Task assigned him by her father. This picaresque movement subordinates the hero to the complexity of a suitor test and a new sort of rhyming. He will undergo no more alteration of character than Gil Blas, whose story was published the year France took possession of Ile Maurice. (Picaresque novelists owe a great deal to Sydney Joseph's European predecessors.) If the hero wants this new girl, his first task will be to protect the king's goats from a marauding lion.

Well, this keeper, when he heard that blowing coming from the forest—a big lion, a really big one. That was what was coming from the forest, that's what was ravaging in the forest. That's why no keeper could keep all the goats. So what did he say? He had seen this and he said, "That's what is devouring these ones." That is what he was thinking in his head. He said, "That's why they couldn't do anything about it." Then he thought about the power that this lion and those kings over there had given him. So he said like this: he pulled out that feather, that whisker that he had pulled out, he placed it under his tongue, and he said, "By the power of my king, King Lion, make the biggest lion appear!"

Zan accomplishes his task by staging a duel between the two, on the African model of the false tug-of-war.

Now, he got a lion. So before that lion could take any of the goats to eat, he rushed towards him. He rushed towards that one. The two of them had a fight. Fight, fight, fight, fight, fight, fight. It went on until two o'clock, until three o'clock, and the fighting stopped. Neither one could throw the other one. They were both very strong. The lion from over there, he wasn't able to take the goats, and he left.

Before the fighting was over, one had fallen on this side and the other one on that side. That lion-from-the-forest, he said like this (he could speak and answer), he said, "Look, if I get very fresh meat to eat," he said, "even dust you won't get." And this lion-who-protects-people, he said, "Me, if I get a glass of wine to drink and a girl to kiss, the dust of these bones you won't get."

So he went back, he came back, took the path back. He had finished fighting the lion-from-the-forest. He left around three o'clock. He took his goats and went back. His twenty-five goats were still there, but in his walking, as he was walking like that, he saw there were some goats. He got five more goats extra. He took these, he took them back with him. So he was thinking about this, he was thinking as he was going along. He said, "Hmmm," he thought, "so that's the rival." So he put his head to work. These goats that were extra, he ate them, and they could not get away. So what happened then? He came back, came back, came back.

Now as for the king: he was up, high up, he was watching. He saw him take the straight road like this. He could see that. He said—he was counting, he was going like this from up above. As the keeper was getting closer with the animals, closer, closer, closer, he was counting. He said, "I gave him twenty-five. How can there be thirty now?" The king himself was surprised. He was thinking about this. He said, "What kind of keeper is this keeper?" So that keeper said—he came—his daughter too came and saw this. She saw this. She was thinking, she saw that keeper who had got five more goats. So that same afternoon, that same night, the lodging where he was sleeping was changed. He got something good [*laughs*], you understand? He got something good. He had good food, really good food now. Early in the morning he would get up and go to work, the same as before. When he got there, the same as before. On the third day, he again came to work. That daughter—the king said to his daughter like this: "How can this guardian keep what he has like this? Go and find out how our keeper, how he does his job."

So on the third day, the daughter left. She followed, followed behind, behind, she went, behind, behind. He didn't know, the keeper. He kept on going. He didn't know who was coming behind him. He went, went, went. When she came near the keeper—I told you before that there was a tall grass hedge. Let's say, if you are on one side, the keeper would be up on his rock, he would not be able to see over to the other side. So the girl came near the tall grass. She was very quiet. She saw the keeper and the goats eating. She couldn't figure it out. When it was around eleven, same thing as before. They could hear that animal coming out from over there, coming in the forest, come towards them. That girl, she heard that noise blowing wherever the lion was passing. And he had that kind of tail that was moving like this, and trees would fall. That girl was trembling. Now she was scared. And she couldn't call out. She couldn't call to the keeper. She had to stay where she was. When the keeper came, when he went like this, that girl, she saw the lion.

Now she was watching to see what the keeper would do. So the keeper went up on his rock, as before. He stood up when that lion came close. He took that whisker. He put it under his tongue. He said, "By the power of my King Lion, make the biggest lion appear!" He got a very big lion. He leaped over there to fight with that other lion. Fight, fight, fight, fight, fight, fight, fight. They both spoke the same language, so, same thing again. In-the-forest one said, "If I get good, fresh meat to eat, I will eat, I will finish you." That one said, "If I get a glass of wine, and a girl to kiss, even the dust you won't get."

They each fell to one side. One fell over there, tired, weak. The lion-in-the-forest, that one, what will he do? He stayed here. The girl—before that boy, that keeper took, thing, the girl had left. She ran away, now she left. As for the boy, he came back. On the way, as he was walking, he passed, thing, and he got five more goats, as before. That was the third day he did that job.

The girl told her father what she had seen.

She too knows how to tell stories: she starts from the top.

She said "Papa, that keeper of yours: he isn't a human being [*laughs*]. Yes. Our keeper, he is not a human being, he is a lion." He said "What are you talking about, now?" She said, "Yes, that's the reason why we've been losing all the animals, in that sense. We have been killing all the previous keepers. The previous keepers were not wrong, but"—as if to say, How can you fight against that lion? "Over there, there's a lion who comes in the forest over there. He killed our goats, I suppose. Well then, our keeper, that one, when it was coming, I myself was worried, I was scared. A lion from the forest came roaring, making noise in that forest." She said, "This is what our keeper–what I saw our keeper do. He climbed on a rock, took out something from his pocket. I don't know what he said; all of a sudden on that rock I saw him disappear, and he became a big lion, just like that in-the-forest one. They both went on fighting, fighting, fighting, fighting, fighting. Then around three o'clock, each one fell on one side. That in-the-forest one said like this, 'If get good fresh meat for me to eat,' he will finish our keeper. And our keeper said like this, him, 'If get a glass of wine to drink and a girl for him to kiss, even the smoke of him there won't be.' " So the king said, "Well, daughter, you heard all this this morning. Go and do the job so we get peace, so that the animals are not lost any more."

During these three days, that boy had been watching the animals. Well, every day his pay increased, his food, drink, everything. He had good food to eat. The girl left; early morning on the third day, the girl left. She put this over there. She took her glass of wine, placed it on her tray, and she left. The boy knew nothing about any of that.

When got there, the keeper, same thing again: kept and kept [*gardyen gardyen*] the herd. At around ten o'clock, anyway during these four days, same thing, same thing happened. The keeper said—that lion-in-the-forest would fight just like before: fight, fight, fight, fight. They both fought. On the third day, the other lion said like this (they were both very weak), he said, "If I get very fresh meat to eat, I'll blow you away like smoke." That lion-keeper-of-people said, "If I get a girl to kiss and a glass of wine to drink, even dust there won't be."

Aaaaah. As soon as she heard that, the girl jumped from where she was, behind the *fatak,* the hedge. She gave him that glass of wine to drink. The lion drank it, kissed her, then he went back to fight once more. He fought once more, and he got stronger. But he did not kill him. He just went back to fight with him. He fought again, but he did not kill him. It's just like he had a fight, and that in-the-forest-one now lost, you understand. He just went and came back.

Now they both came back together. The keeper and the girl, they came back together. They had done a good job. The king said to him, "Well, I didn't know that was the kind of keeper you were. I thought you were just a keeper. Well, I made a promise, which I said like this: that whoever succeeds in keeping my animals well, I'll give him half my fortune and my daughter to kiss. Well, I'll keep my promises. You must marry my daughter, and I'll give you half my fortune."

So that keeper, Zan, said like this, "Look, king. The terms we made were well made. However, I have another path I want to follow. I'll give you a postponement. In four months I will be back. I will come back. For the time being, there won't be anything like that, that can eat your animals." The king was very happy. He agreed to that, and he said, "Go, you go."

Another path he wants to follow? At least Zan has the decency not to mention the other girl.

The story has already, by this point, become one of the most complex ever recorded in this region, comparable to Baissac's Polin and Polinn or the Sakalava Two Brothers. When Sydney Joseph embeds features of one genre within another, mixes episodes, and reflects a plurality of symbol systems, he is enacting the creole aesthetic.

Now that Zan: what do you think he was thinking, in his head? He was not thinking about the fortune, or about that girl he would marry. He was thinking about that siren girl. His mind was on that. He had to meet her.

Now in those days, as you know, there was no transport, so he went right through the forest. He was walking in the forest. He went, went, went, went, went, went in the forest. In the forest in front of him there was a hill, a bit higher, like this. He was down below, like in a hole. There was a castle (another castle, again), and a king (just like before). This time, that girl, that *lasiren,* that siren girl: now she had accepted a lion, a big lion, she had accepted that lion as her father. Now he was walking down below. He went all around near the house, and there wasn't a single way for him to go past. But he had to go in. Now how would he manage to get inside? It was something he had to do.

He went, went. They didn't see him; the keepers, nobody, nobody saw him. And that father—that girl, she was sleeping upstairs. That lion, that king lion for that girl, he was sleeping downstairs in front of the door. As if like this. What could he do? He must go through, and the only way to go through, there were guards everywhere. How could he go through? He had to go through this way, so as to be able to get inside that castle.

He walk-walked. There was a little river, which he crossed. He crossed that river and he came across some gendarmes. He managed to go through, and those gendarmes didn't see him. He came close to that lion. Now he has to go past that lion. Now he took his—that ant one. He said, "By the power of my King Ant, make me become the smallest ant that can be." Well, an ant is small. It went over the lion. It went over him. He didn't feel anything. It went on quietly. When he got to the other side over there, he became a human being just like himself.

He went through one room. He went in and he saw, he saw that girl upstairs there. Now that girl, with her too, same thing. She was in a deep sleep, she was asleep. The boy held her and kissed her. Now as soon as he had kissed her, he took that ant thing, he took that ant thing, like before. He put in his thing and he became an ant on the floor. He would walk-walk on the floor and nobody would find out. For four days he stayed in that castle, and he did the same thing with that girl.

Now the girl cried out; she said, "Papa, papa!" She called the lion; he was downstairs. She said, "Papa, papa!" she said. "There's somebody kissing me!" The lion answered her. He said, "Daughter, who could have come in? A lion like me, who could go upstairs? Wouldn't I have eaten him?" He said, "Go to sleep, there's nothing." He said to the girl, "You're dreaming."

That girl, same thing again. The boy took her once again, kissed her, same thing again. The girl cried out. For five nights he did just like that. This time, the girl pretended she was asleep, just like before. She pretended she was asleep. As soon as the boy came, he took—thing, he placed it under his tongue in order to become a human being. He held the girl and he kissed her. The girl saw him. She said, "Well! It's you who has been making me tired." The boy said, "I haven't been making you tired. Still, the first time we met, there under the water, there in your mother's castle, you did the same thing to me. And you made me tired. And me, now that I've met you—well, I've grown older. Well, now I ask you–well, we can get married."

The siren-girl responds to this proposal with the most decisive objection possible: she and he belong to different species.

She said, "Well, there's a difference between you and me. I am a siren's daughter. But you, you are not the same."

Zan has to mediate, in his fictive life, the kind of opposition between species which plays a prominent role in the structuralist-anthropological analysis of South American Indian narratives (Lévi-Strauss, *The Raw*). That mediation takes his narrator into a final story, The Ogre's Heart in the Egg.[10]

He said, "No, that doesn't matter. We can get married. However, we need to have our terms [*kondisyon*]."

So then he said to that siren's daughter, "You know, there is only one chance that I can get married to you. However . . . ," he said, "you stay down here—you stay up here, and that lion stays down there. Now if somebody kills him, who would know about it? Tell me where your father's life is placed." The girl didn't want to break the secret. She said, "No, I won't tell you where my father's life is placed. I will never tell you such a thing. You will hurt me." He said, "No, I won't hurt you. I've come here, I love you, I will marry you, because we have met already before. But now, he is a danger to you now. If somebody were to play mischief and kill that lion, he could take you away and nobody would know. These gendarmes, which way would they go? There's only one way, only one way there is. You will not know anything." Every day he was with that girl, every day he was with that girl. The girl said to him, "OK I'll go and ask my father where his life is placed. And then you'll come back." So that Zan said to her, "OK, go," Zan said to her. He went back to the king he worked for before.

That is, he goes back into the initial plot of The Man on a Quest for his Lost Wife.

Where he had been a keeper of goats, that's where he went. He stayed at the king's place over there now. He spent two months at the king's place, and the king said, "Well, we made terms, a promise that you would marry my daughter as well as half my fortune. Well, when a king has given his word, it's really his word. He can't do differently." He said, "Well, I will leave soon, but I'll come back again."

Two months went by. Once again he went back there, to that *lasiren*'s daughter's place. He went back there. The siren's daughter told him like this: "I have asked my father where his life is placed. However, don't hurt my father." He said, "No, I will not hurt your father. I will not." She said, "My father, do you know where his life is? My father—when you fight with my father, if there is any lion just like him who can fight with him, with a lion-in-the-forest-over-there," she told him, "if you succeed in killing that lion-in-the-forest-over-there (he is always fighting), over here he [father] will start getting sick, he will start getting sick, sick, sick. However, if you succeed in killing that lion-in-the-forest one, 'I [her father] will begin to die. I'll become quite weak.' Now in that lion's belly, there is an eagle. If you succeed in killing that eagle, in that eagle's belly there is an egg. Get that egg, come back, crush it on my forehead, then I will. . . ."

So now he knew all these ruses [*tiktak*]. She had told him where her father's life was placed. He spent three days with the siren, and said to the siren like this: "Well, OK, I'm leaving. Later on I'll come back."

He went back, he went back, he went. He went to the king's place over there. The king said to him, "Well, you've come to work?" He said "Yes, there's work I must do. Well, give me those goats and I'll go." Well, that lion-in-the-forest, he had never before been without food for such a long time. He was walk-walking. That one went to watch the goats, like before. He was watching.

But now there will be no glass of wine and no girl to kiss. Now they are going to fight even. Fight even, now. When the lion from over there came, they started fighting. They both fought, fought, fought, fought, same thing, fought. They both fell down. They were both weak. That lion-in-the-forest—he, he [the other lion] was a bit stronger now. He had powers, and he had become stronger than him. He succeeded in killing that lion-in-the-forest. As they were fighting, that one was feeling weak. That lion-of-the-siren one, he started to feel weak. He was weaker. They both fought. He managed to kill him all right.

Then, that lion-in-the-forest, that keeper, he took the knife, he opened that lion's belly (he was getting really weak now) to get that eagle. That eagle went and flew away, it went. Now, how could he catch that eagle, now? He was thinking, he was thinking. Now he thought about that power which the king eagle had given him. He said, "By the power of my King Eagle, make me into the biggest eagle there can be." Now he too flew, he went. He went and met him in the air. They fought, fought, fought, fought, fought, fought, struggled until he fell down. Fell down. He took his knife, he killed the eagle. He got its egg, he got that egg, took it and brought it.

Over here, that king lion (for the siren), he was very, very, very down. He was almost dying. But he had to get that egg and crush it on his forehead, for him to get well. He said to that king over here, "I am going to do a job. Later on I'll come back." And really, he left.

When he got there, he was disguised. He had become like an ant. When he came close to that lion, that lion was very weak and couldn't do anything, now. He took that egg, he crushed it on him, on his forehead. The lion died. As soon as that lion died, that *lasiren* girl, she knew about it immediately. When he went inside there, she said, "What have you done?" She said, "He was my father. You have killed my father. All you've been doing all this time was to fool me. You wanted to know where my father's life was placed. You have succeeded in killing him." She had other powers: immediately she made that castle disappear, just like before, again. He left and he went, went, went, went, went.

In a turn of his plot that nobody would predict, he manages Zan's recovery by moving the siren-girl into the cash economy of a populous town in central Mauritius.

Now this one, he was staying in the forest, with thorns everywhere. Well, what could he do? So, in the forest he went. That girl, where did she go? She went into town, let's suppose like Rose Hill, like that. She had nothing, nothing to do now. She opened a big shop and she started working. Well, she had people working with her.

Abandoning fairyland to become an entrepreneur, is she recapitulating the disappearance of old *kont,* tales, in the modern world? Alas, that there are no more fairies nowadays! Certainly the story takes on more realistic detail.

Now that keeper, that Zan, what was he doing over here? In a field of thorns, he was looking for his way; his way he couldn't find. Walk-walking in that forest, the thorns were hurting him, cutting him everywhere, until he got blisters. When you've been hurt that way and you have no medicine to put on it, well, these blisters start becoming big, big blisters. When he went—walk-walking, turning round, he met some friends. They said to him like this, "This is the first time we've seen a human being like this. As dirty as this."

He said like this, he said to them: "I have a problem. I am in a foreign country. I am in a problem. I have been walk-walking; I've got here; I am in a problem." Then the others said to him like this: "Well, now, keep walking on this road, and you'll find something like a town. When you get there, keep on walk-walking. You'll find a pharmacy. Go and ask the pharmacist for some medicine." He said to them like this: "But where will I get any money?" They said, "When they see you, in such a state . . ." Well, he had only a pair of shorts on, torn, and he had no shirt. Well what can one do? Then he told them his story. "When they see you, they will give you."

So really, he walk-walked. He came near the pharmacy on the foot-path. Kept walking till he got there. They saw him—another group of people, yet another group [*bande*]. This was that siren girl's group. It was her group of workers. They were working. Some of them were looking out, looking at the people passing by, and they saw him crossing. They took him away, they pushed him away, they said to him, "Somebody dirty like you walking near my shop, you will stop customers coming in. You think you can stay here? Walk away, get away."

Unfortunately the siren heard this and said, "Who's talking like that?" They said, "There's a man here, look at the state he's in. He's very dirty." She said, "No, do not push him away." She made him come inside, gave him a room over there, brushed him, and cleaned him clean. Washed him well, gave him clothes to wear.

Now that siren-girl, she was crying as she looked at him. She said, "All this misery you've been through because of me." The young man said to her, "Well, there's no question I'm still young, but I must say you are tiring my head ever since I was still very weak. It's gone to my head." He also said like this: "I got a girl I could marry, and also half of a king's fortune. All this I refused because of you." So she said, that siren, she said, "Well, what are you going to do?" He said like this—the siren said to him, "Well, what do I possess now? I only have this shop, I have people who work here. Well, if you agree, we'll make a *kondisyon.* We will get married. Those who live here do not know that I am a siren. You are the only one to know this. Don't tell anybody about it, or I'll leave you." They got married.

What Sydney Joseph does in The Siren-Girl illuminates what Paul Ottino, in Madagascar, has said about recursive critical readings:

> the radical transformations of signification that may not only be reversed but also return to their starting point . . . , the changes and total inversions

> of meaning they allow for, as soon as one changes one's angle of vision, point of entry, or plane of focalization, and passes from foreground to background, to the *ground* [English in original] on which the characters' actions take their support—all this constitutes an immense field of research hardly inventoried. (Ottino, *L'Étrangère* 578)

Despite the "almost kaleidoscopic variation" in The Man on a Quest for His Lost Wife, in its dissemination over Asia, Europe, and North America, it is recognizable here (Thompson, *Folktale* 91–92) and in even more radical transformations.

A verbal artist like Sydney Joseph has large responsibilities towards his countrymen, proclaimed by poets such as Ezra Pound. "Greece and Rome," wrote Pound, omitting a verb, "civilized by *language.* Your language is in the care of your writers" (Pound and Spann 338). Creole islands, where "writing" is an oral creation, have been civilized by the arts of language, and the arts are in the care of narrators such as Sydney Joseph. His Siren-Girl is a complex folktale composed and heard "against" sources such as the water-princess legend. Sydney Joseph absorbed and invented many stories in his life.

"So this means I am telling you this story now," he said. "Finished."[11]

Claudie Ricaud and I wondered when, in the ordinary course of life, he would perform such a lengthy, involved folktale. "That one?" he said.

> Let's say I would tell this story when we were working with friends. Working with friends, when you've finished eating, the last thing when you're about to go to work. . . . Each one will say, "You tell a story." So the story just goes on like that. In eight-days ceremonies, I also tell one or two.

Very well, I thought, but surely he didn't tell this lengthy piece in one factory lunch hour. Performing it over several days might explain its many episodes.

Many questions that folklorists ask weren't answered that day; we were recording only his narration, not his life story. It would have been interesting to know more about those moments when someone said, "You tell a story"–those "storytelling events," which American folklorists have erected into their main object of study (Georges; Bauman, *World*). It would also have been interesting to initiate a discussion about his favorite stories and why he liked them (Jackson). A more ambitious fieldworker might have looked for other storytellers, during lunch hour at one of Mauritius's many garment factories. Finding them would disprove the common assumption that industrial life drives out oral folklore; it might discover a special sort of performance in the factory setting. It would have been interesting, too, to organize some performances, to induce a "natural" storytelling context (Goldstein), in which we could notice audience reactions and their effect on the performer (Lord). "Oral literary criticism" might have yielded information about "an aesthetics of reception and influence" (Jauss 20; Dundes, "Metafolklore"). But that day, his main audience consisted only of Claudie Ricaud and me, with our microphone, until we spied several fascinated children peering in through his window.

If Sydney Joseph knew that Malagasy legend of the water-princess, it's no mystery how. The legend is part of the common stock. The peopling of Mauritius, Réunion, Seychelles, and the Comoros created that stock; the contact among populations ensured that many would be locally adapted. His group's history brought Sydney Joseph his material.

Sydney Joseph and Nelzir Ventre belong to the Mauritian ethnicity called "creole." Some of his ancestors will have arrived in Mauritius centuries ago. Slavery, which entails creolization, was the decisive event in the history of both Mauritius, then known as Isle de France, and Réunion, then known as Ile Bourbon. In both islands, slaves from Africa and Madagascar were imported by the French plantation owners to cut and crush the sugarcane (Mannick 32). By the beginning of the nineteenth century, the 49,000 African slaves were the majority population, telling numerous tales about deception, a vice which they were coming to understand anew. The descendants of those slaves are people like Sydney Joseph.

The Africans and Malagasy had a difficult history in Mauritius. In 1710, rebellious slaves put an end to the original Dutch colony, which was named for Prince Maurice of Nassau (Bowman 9). The ones not deported became "maroons," escapees living in the forest and raising crops and animals. In Réunion, Mauritius, and Seychelles, oppressive legal ordinances encouraged *marronage.* Ten or a dozen slaves would escape into caves or summits, which often had Malagasy names; it had long been the practice, back home, to defend a village by situating it atop a hill. *Marronage* was the most direct expression of resistance; the indirect expression was folktale, a functional substitute for running away.

From the beginning, the slaves represented a mix of cultures: "Kaffirs" from Sofala on the Portuguese East African coast, Indians from the Malabar coast, and even a few Wolof and Yoruba from West Africa (Filliot). Under the governor Mahé de la Bourdonnais (1735–1746), Indian laborers were brought from Surat and Pondichéry (Sooriamorthy; Carter and Ng Foong Kwong). The economic backwardness and political irrelevance of many creoles have helped to preserve and nurture the distinct folk cultures of the Southwest Indian Ocean.

The ending of slavery did nothing to kill folk religion, for instance, as we learned from Georgius and Jean-René. When things get tense today, witchcraft and sorcery break the surface. In early 1990, when we were recording Sydney Joseph, the villagers around Lalmatie, in another part of the island, were visited by a *lugaru,* wolf-man. Some people took him to be the invisible guard who watches over buried treasure in Montagne Thérèse at St.-Julien. The visitation was treated unkindly by the press and television. The newspaper accounts every day discounted or explained away the inherited and cherished beliefs of the locals. The cruelty of the past and their enforced Christianization have left many islanders with inherited folk religion or belief as a symbol system into which they could appropriate borrowed materials. Their sorcery today is an art of resistance (Scott), a *marronage* of the mind, much like the ceremonies of *tromba,* possession, in the Madagascar of the 1960s (Althabe; Emoff), or like the vocabulary of magic and witchcraft so uniform throughout Réunion. In February 1999, the oppressed position of creoles gave rise to riots in Mauritius. Observers attribute these to a "structure of feeling" called the *malez kreol,* or "Creole discontent" (Boswell).

Against that background, Sydney Joseph's creativity points in the opposite direction. He consciously wants to illustrate the art of fiction: "That's what people say; they cast these stories." He takes care to keep the hearer from getting confused: "Now in those days, as you know, there was no transport, so he went right through the forest"; "There was a castle. Once again, there was a king who lived there. . . . There was a castle (another castle, again), and a king (just like before)." He points to the rules of the genre: "According to the story I am giving you, she is supposed to be a power." These remarks exemplify a device familiar to western readers of Cervantes, John Barth, and Italo Calvino: "metanarration," or the "story in the story," the reflexive dimension of storytelling (Babcock, "The Story"). Oral narrators practice it too.

Zan's conflicting romances illustrate an unspoken rule. Few indeed are oral tales in which the hero is poised so long between two women, or is granted such yearning for one of them: "He was thinking about that siren girl. . . . He had to meet her." Although most men, sooner or later, want more than one woman, for most folktale heroes one woman is enough. Nor will Sydney Joseph pose the choice to the audience, as in a dilemma tale.

Zan's divided ardor reflects the divided cultural allegiances of Mauritian creoles. His movement between the two girls symbolizes the skill creoles have developed at participating in various traditions. For them, as for other peoples in Mauritius, this skill is a creative principle, a capacity for variability of language, expressive culture, and tradition. Nearly all Mauritian creoles are bilingual; many participate in both Catholic and Hindu religious observances with no fear of being culturally compromised. Analogous to language-mixing, but more conscious and deliberate, is the mixing of narrative lexicon, when Sydney Joseph inserts or rearranges story elements. And in the end, like his countrymen, Zan decides in favor of the major contender for his heart.

Are Sydney Joseph's storytelling techniques new in a multilingual society? The contrast between his audacious Siren-Girl and the Merina story of Andrianoro, who seeks a wife from heaven, reflects the fundamental difference between Malagasy conformity and Mauritian temerity. The Merina who dictated to Dahle were seen to be "constrained to respect strict rules of etiquette"; they fear any sort of departure from the words of their ancestors (Molet, "Esquisse" 32). Detailed rules and unalterable obligations, which make Merina life impersonal (Andriamanjato 45), constrain both a folktale character and his narrator. Mauritius, by contrast, is a land of *métissage,* where cultural clash produces variability in religion, dress, and cookery as well as in storytelling.

In fact, though, those two narratives are more similar than they seem. Both stories lead their hero to marriage and a permanent place in

society; both put hindrances in the way. Their most obvious difference is that Sydney Joseph throws in more devices to retard the hero's movement. These hindrances, which are essential to the charm of a folktale, are embedded in a structure that would otherwise be what a narratologist would call a "primitive narrative," that ideal type of story which is seldom found in reality, because it's too efficient to be amusing (Todorov 53–56). So in Andrianoro, when the story of The Grateful Animals comes in, the "linear narrative" of The Man on a Quest for His Lost Wife must suspend its time to accommodate the interpolated tale, which nevertheless is "pulled along by the force of the linear time of the frame," as happens in framed stories (Irwin 46). Sydney Joseph makes choices, as Shahrazad does in the *Thousand and One Nights* (Todorov 73). His very inventions make an ideological statement; they are "borrowings" in the service of a creole aesthetic, which requires appropriation of what's available. Appropriation, to one theorist, means "ridicule, subversive acts, pilfering, poaching, tax evasion and shabby work . . . , developed as a means of resistance to the dominant" (Meeks 39), but in the hands of the creole storyteller, the multiple system of symbols in Mauritian verbal art defines the multiple possibilities for people's existence.

We asked Sydney Joseph for another story.

78. Ramkalawar

Sydney Joseph, Grand Bel Air, Mauritius 18 April 1990

The one he gave us "rhymes" all right. It has a king and a prince, a love affair requiring secret meetings, and even a rival lover who tries to thwart a marriage by breaking the secrecy. But thematically it departs from the typical success story. There, Zan overcomes obstacles and gets his wife, or he rescues his sister from the clutches of her wolf-man husband; Hare tricks his dupe into getting stung by wasps, or he successfully deceives two large animals into believing he has beat them in a tug-of-war. The success in Sydney Joseph's Ramkalawar is of a different kind.

Once there was a king called Ramkalawar. That Ramkalawar, he was such a powerful, strong king, nobody could fight him. Only one chance on his side. When you are lucky, everything is good. When you are unlucky, everybody is wrong. That king, when people would hear "Ramkalawar," they would tremble, be scared. They were afraid of him. One day a weak king—each one would come and tell about his own problems, he would say, "That's what I can do for you, such and such." He had his father. His father said to him, "My son (I have left Ramkalawar), you are small. That king, he crushed all the countries, he was strong, nobody would fight against him." So the king said to him, that other king, he said to his son, "Philippe, you will take command, take the king's place. I am a bit old. You'll take my throne. What will you be able to do for the other countries?"

He said, "What I will be able to do for countries? I'll make the people become honorable. I will not dominate them. Without them, I can't do anything. If we give them death, beat them, whip them, how will anything be done? We would not be able to do anything. That's the work I would like to do. When the other king will hear this, in our country, the way we treat the people, he will be able to take the good example from us."

So the king thought about that. He said to his son, "That's your thinking?" He said, "Yes, that's my thinking. If one day you leave your throne and give it to me, that's what I will do. It's not because we are rich, and kings, that we should be allowed to do things that are not good for the people. When the people criticize us, the kings, that's very bad. It's not good."

The conflict of generations is also a conflict of values. Ramkalawar maintains his royal authority by patronage and war; Philippe, son of an enemy king, advocates peace and cooperation, saying, "I am going to fight with my mind."

His father said to him—his father was called Richard—his father [son] said to him, "You are a king, my father. Tell us what you did in your days, when you came on the throne." The father said, "Yes, I'll tell you the truth. When I came on the throne, I was not very serious. I liked to dominate. After a while, I thought over the deeds I did. It was not good. I had to change position, take a good one." He said, "You, my son, the way you are talking now, it means that you will be better than me." So the king [prince] said, "Yes, father, what I have been thinking about is even better. But for the time being, I haven't taken your throne. Let's wait until later."

Now Prince Philippe, he was not yet a king. Prince Philippe, what did he do? He went on his horse and went wandering. During his wanderings he came to the border between him and Ramkalawar. That Ramkalawar, he was so bad. He was bad, but he has his daughter. On the other side, there was the border. Ramkalawar was on this side, he was on the other side. Ramkalawar's daughter, she too. . . . The guards accompanied Ramkalawar's daughter. But him, he was a man, nobody accompanied him, so he could go where he wanted. So the other one, why was he going round and wandering? He wanted to see where his father's borders were, whether there was any cheating, people trying to cross over: that's what he was checking. He had made his first round, he had checked everything. During his round he met that girl.

These people, the daughter of Ramkalawar and Prince Philippe, they fell in love. Both are from the same lineage, same blood. She is a princess, he is a prince. So the girl spoke to the young man saying, "You, who are you?" He said, "My father is King Richard." The young man said, "And you, who are you?" She said, "My father is Ramkalawar." Ahhh. So Prince Philippe thought about it. He said, "So it's your father who kills so many people?" So he made his mind work. He was thinking carefully about this. He said to the princess, "Is there a place where we can meet?" The princess said, "Yes, we can meet any time." So Prince Philippe said to her, "I'll give a place where we can meet, on a Wednesday. You get there, we'll meet. You stay on one side, I'll be on the other side, we'll talk to each other a bit." So they met.

Now the father, King Richard, was not aware of this exchange. The young man said, "Father, you know, I am inspecting your lands." The king said, "So you've seen where all the borders are?" He said, "No, I did not see. I saw some. It will take me time to do this."

Then the young man went to meet the girl, and he said–they had met and they were talking to each other—he said to her, "Your father, with people's reactions in his country, how does he live? How is he?" She said to him, "You know, my father–you will not be able to understand him. Even I have difficulties understanding him, the way he lives. But he is my father. I cannot let him down. Furthermore he is the king." So the young man said to her, "If I ask you a question, just between us two . . . But for this to happen, for your father to stop all this, we must get married. We must get married, for your father to stop being a dictator [*dominer*]." He said, "Tell your father that you have met a young man with whom you can get married."

So the girl left and went to see her father. She said to her father, "Father, while I was walking about on your lands, as I was walking around, I met a young man near the borders. He is 'such a way,' and as we talked to each other, I have found that it would be all right for us to get married."

He said, "Oh," her father said to her, "This young man, what is his father's name? What king?" She said, "He is called King Richard." He said, "You know, that King Richard, I can't endure him. I have had fights with many, but him I have not met. I need to have a meeting with him, I have not yet succeeded. And now you say you want to get married with that young man. No, I don't agree to that."

Knowing how interested his hearers are in the art of storytelling, Sydney Joseph poses the metanarrative question, "How will she act to make the king agree?" and answers it with more metanarrative, reducing any verbatim repetition of the previous scene into "this and that."

Now the girl told the prince about this. She said, "My father said 'this and that.'" He said, "You know, in everything, the princess must get married. So if we run away, it will be a shame upon your father." The young man was making suggestions so that these habits of domineering would come to an end. So the young man too, one day, went to see his father and told him "this and that." The father too gave the same answer to his son. He said, "You know, this king Ramkalawar, he is so strong that we cannot fight against him. We will never be able to fight against him at all. You are going to get into trouble with this king. Leave him alone or else he might send his soldiers to fight against us." So Prince Philippe said, "Father, you know, in the old days he was fighting like this. But I am not going to fight with arms or anything. I am going to fight with my mind. Without blood being shed I am going to fight."

So the father said, "Explain to me how this is going to happen. Is all this true or untrue? If this is going to work, I can give you my answer too." So the young man said, "Father, you know, I have met Ramkalawar's daughter. She was walking about on her father's lands, and I was on your lands, we met on each side. She told me she was Ramkalawar's daughter. I told her who I was, she told me about her father. The only way out, as a prince, in order to avoid these catastrophes, I must marry her." The father was getting worried. He said to him, "Are you sure about what you are saying?" He said, "Yes, no problem. He will agree to it. If he does not agree, I will take her away. And the daughter has agreed to that. She loves me and she will come with me. That's how he will get this new point of view, that we are of royal descent, but that there is a difference between the two of us. We are not [unintelligible]." So the father said to his son, "Go and think this over."

Three days went by. The father thought and said, "Even though I am a king, I did not have that intelligence. That intelligence I did not have. But now my son has found a way to make us all agree. I think I should give him my support."

The prince met the girl and said, "What did your father say?" She said that her father had said "this and that." He said, "There is no other way, in this situation. We must make your father stop his way of acting, killing people, dominating them, fighting against them. And after this, everybody will say bad things about him. He will not have the dignity of a king. Everybody in his country will be against him. So the girl said, "Yes. Then come, let's meet with the king." He said to the young man, "You know, we'll go and meet that girl, so we can meet her, so that everything is clear, on which day we can run away. So the young man said "OK."

After about two months, well, every time that girl came to meet the young man and talked, there was another prince in that same country, who was also walking about, and he met that Prince Philippe and that girl. He went to tell king Ramkalawar what was happening, how his daughter had a meeting-place. "Your daughter does not respect our customs, our lineage, royal. She is talking to a young man from outside." So he told this to king Ramkalawar. King Ramkalawar said, "Oh." Ramkalawar himself went to see his daughter; he followed where she went. They crossed the border. He went this way, she went that way. So the girl came and met Prince Philippe; she crossed the border. King Ramkalawar also came and crossed, but this way. He called his daughter. He said, "How are you here?" She said, "Again and again I've told you how I met such a young man and have fallen in love with him. Well, that's that young man." Her father said to her, "Didn't I say I did not agree?" She said, "Whether or not you agree, where we are now, I'll go ahead, and you have no right to kill him, because we are not at war," she said, "We are not at war now. That's your border, that's my border. The whole country will be against you. You must accept this decision." Because of this, he agreed. King Ramkalawar has agreed. He made a big wedding without fighting.

The story finishes here, OK?[12]

Romeo and Juliet, in a similar plight, have to die to convince their parents that cooperation is better than street fighting. This prince and princess bring an end to war by marrying; in a utopian future, their children and the kingdoms will live in harmony. Even the fierce Ramkalawar is convinced in the end. Sydney Joseph, who is just one individual, has a "properly Utopian conception of what a radically different society should be and of the nature of the new social relations that might be imagined in such a system" (Jameson, "Interview" 85). He accepts folktale conventions as part of the creole "ambivalent acceptance-rejection syndrome": he combines generic conformity (his "rhyming") with a genuine utopian vision.

He inserted more explicit topical commentary in another piece.

79. The King and His Clever Minister

Sydney Joseph, Grand Bel Air, Mauritius 18 April 1990

There was a king, he thought he was such a big king that no one could touch him. What did he do? He invited all his *zandarm* [soldiers], the people who are with him, to come and see him. He was the king of that country. He told them that everything he did was for them. So the king, what did he do? He went with his soldiers, he said to them, "Everything that's here, as long as I am there, you will stay here, as long as I am the king. If one day I die, I don't know who will replace me. Maybe it will be my wife who will become queen and take my place. But as long as I am here, I'll do everything I can for you." He was a bit of a dictator, he liked to dominate the servants and expected a lot from them. . . .

The king thought that since he was so big, everybody would listen to him and approve his decisions. In some countries, some would make a revolution, a war against the king. With this king, it was not possible to be against him. The people I am talking to you about, they were a bit backward. It was not possible to argue against the king's decisions. Up to then, everything the king had done was right. But when every thing is right, and you do one thing wrong, it wrecks everything.

What did he do? He did everything well: he helped the poor; he had plenty of money, all right; when people would come to him and explain their case, their difficulties, the king would give them some money. Well, those who had land, he would give them whatever. He did everything right. But in the end he did a [injustice?] to them, he did, he acted as a dictator. He said to the king—the king said to them: "I'll put a condition to you." He said: "All the sons-in-law, kill them. We must kill them." So let's say I am married with your daughter, you know, father-in-law, mother-in-law, that's what he means by son-in-law. All of them must be killed.

Then they thought about it. He gave the order to his prime minister. He said to the prime minister that he wanted all the sons-in-law killed, hanged. What could his prime minister do? He had to listen to the king. The prime minister looked for all those who were married and had sons-in-law, he was thinking about all this. The prime minister had thought about something too. He was looking for all those who were married, he carried an inspection, he placed the rope to hang them. . . . He got eighty-two . . . eighty-two he had. Eighty-nine, ninety he did not have: he had eighty-two only. He had eighty-two sons-in-law he got. So, he had the ropes to hang them ready everywhere.

The king came and looked at everything. He said to his prime minister, he said: "That's all you got?" He said "Yes, I got eighty-two." He looked at all those who were to be hanged, and then he looked at the ropes to hang them. He counted and counted, and counted eighty-two ropes. Two of the ropes, one was of gold, and one was of silver. So the answer, he was looking for the answer: why was one of silver, and one of gold? So the king said to his prime minister, "After I finished my inspection, when I came to the silver and gold ones, it gave me a shock. What do these two mean?" His prime minister said to him: "Well, it's me and you," he said. "I am the prime minister, you are the king, you give me orders. Those ropes, the gold and silver ones: the gold one is for you, the silver one is for me."

The king said to him: "Why is that so?"

The prime minister gave him the answer: "Didn't you get married to a girl? Aren't you too a son-in-law? You gave instructions that every son-in-law should be killed. We too have a father-in-law, we too are sons-in-law like the others." So the king got a shock.

Sydney Joseph interrupts his narrative to emphasize its point to his countrywoman Claudie Ricaud, then resumes.

But it's the same nowadays, in our country. When some people earn five, ten thousand rupees, some earn fifteen hundred rupees. It makes a difference: you eat gold, the other one what will he eat? You understand the difference: it's just like today as it is going on. Some earn fifteen hundred rupees, others earn twenty-five thousand. Twenty-five thousand eat gold, fifteen hundred eat gold: what is this?

When he had done this, he got a shock. So he said to the prime minister: "Well, let's examine again what I said. But don't let anybody know that the golden rope is for me, and the silver one for you. Keep quiet. We'll make every thing go back to how it was before." The king said: "Up till now, I have not done anything against my people, I have done everything good." What he was really interested in was the rope, the golden one.

So the clever minister, like his forebears in India (Thompson and Balys 226), has distracted the king from his tyrannical order. Sydney Joseph could tell we hadn't understood his cleverest play in Kreol:

The answer comes on this: there was a pun on this. Do you get it? The rope for hanging and gold. It's not easy. The king got a shock: the answer

is on that. I made a pun on this the other day with the others. They said to me: "What is the answer?" They could not find the answer at all.

I have finished. It's not very long, only a bit.[13]

No one can deny that Mauritian Kreols, even factory workers like Sydney Joseph, are marginal. They have had their political spokesmen, like the brilliant Sir Gaetan Duval (1931–1996); they have had periods of shouting for attention, like the three days of rioting in February 1999 which followed the death of the musician Kaya in police custody (http://isuisse.ifrance.com/alternmaurit/actions/kaya.htm). But as Kaya's music and Sydney Joseph's stories prove, exclusion from political and economic power doesn't take away expressive power. Nor does it take away "ambiguities of cultural reference and of expressive and moral meaning." Like Antiguans, Mauritian Kreols play with these ambiguities "to hide and manipulate the contradictions in their cultural patterns of value and expression" (Reisman 116). Like African-Americans, they nurture a culture of contestation.

There were also star storytellers in Madagascar a century ago. Finding them is one of the joys of archival research in Southwest Indian Ocean folklore.

80. The Two Brothers

Sakalava narrator 1901–22

"There was once in a village, they say, a woman long married who could not have children." A Malagasy storyteller could always count on getting his audience's attention with this most dreaded of all Lacks. "She had consulted the most famous diviners of the neighborhood," he goes on. This neighborhood would be northwest Madagascar, where Comoran, Tsimihety, and Betsimisaraka dialects, languages, and traditions converge and sometimes conflict (Vérin, *Les Comores* 178–84). In 1898, two years after the French conquest, the Bealanana district saw an anticolonial uprising which had to be, as we say, pacified by three columns of French soldiers (Deschamps 238). Three years later, André Dandouau took up residence in Analalava (Long Forest) and founded a teacher-training school. (France has ever relied on schooling as an engine of containment.) He started collecting the district's folktales, understanding the great obstacle: "The Malagasy is hardly fond of instructing a foreigner about what intimately concerns him" (Dandouau, *Contes populaires* 9). Gradually he wore down people's resistance—all except the *mpsikidy,* diviners, who had most to hide. Dandouau may be the first folklorist in the Southwest Indian Ocean to name any of his informants, who were graduates of his school, but as he doesn't say who told which story, this potent storyteller remains anonymous.

Typically in most places, his tale, The Twins or Blood Brothers,[14] begins as two magically born brothers separate for their adventures in the world, leaving a life-token to signal that the absent one is in danger and must be rescued. At a crucial point, one brother spends a chaste night with the other's wife, which leads to bad blood until they come back together and are reconciled. Into this matrix, a narrator will insert other episodes, including the worldwide combat myth, or dragon slayer (Thompson, *Folktale* 24–33). This Sakalava star, like a great musician, so skillfully manages the movement through the adventures as to impart an impetus to the developing form of the tale. He causes each moment "to imply, by its timing and force, the timing and force of the next, so that the successive [moments] fall into place with inevitability and ease" (Haggin 281–82). I add headings to highlight those moments.[15]

There was once in a village, they say, a woman long married who could not have children. She had consulted the most famous diviners of the neighborhood. All the charms they gave her remained without effect. She decided at last to go and consult Rakakabe [the diviner, lit. "Big Beast"]. She found him in his house. "What do you want?" he said.

"I cannot have children," she said,
"and I would very much like to have some;
everyone makes fun of me in the village,
and my husband wants to put me away."

"All right," said Rakakabe.
"I know *ody* [charms] which are infallible for that.
I will give you one, on one condition:
the first of your children will belong to me.
You will give him to me as soon as he is grown,
and I shall do with him what I wish."

Promising an unborn child to an ogre is frequent in Southwest Indian Ocean tales, as it is in others around the world. The narrator gives the name of a menacing African cannibal ogre to the old Malagasy donor figure of a diviner, who will aid a childless woman in conception (Haring, *Ibonia* 73–75). Thus he can reveal the lad's exceptional qualities to the audience, while the ogre remains in the dark. She agrees.

"Yes," she said.

He gave her some leaves which she was to boil in water, so as to make a kind of tea, which she would then drink. The woman drank the infusion;

presently, she brought forth a pair of twin boys who looked absolutely alike.

Old Malagasy tradition held that twins were symbols of sovereignty and dangerous to their parents at the same time. Often they were "killed immediately after birth, and buried outside the family tomb," but, in a real-life kernel for this fictional incident, they also might be given away to a stranger (Ruud 145).

[He Eludes the Ogre]

When they were grown, Rakakabe came to see them and claimed the one from the mother, since he belonged to him. "The boys are not here," their mother said. "But tomorrow, go to our ricefield. I will put a red *lamba* [garment] on the elder one. You can see him and take him away."

But the boy, who was very clever, took the red *lamba* his mother gave him the next day, and as soon as he was in the river, he cut it up into long strips, which he gave to his comrades. Each of them made a nice loincloth out of it. When Rakakabe arrived, he did not know which one to take; all the boys were wearing a red loincloth. He went to complain to the mother. She said to him, "Tomorrow I will give my elder son a black *lamba,* so that you can recognize him." But the black *lamba* had the same fate as the red *lamba.* Rakakabe was quite baffled; he had to come back without bringing a child.

This escape from the ogre is the key episode in Gérose Barivoitse's "Ti Zan of the red rag" (Barat, Carayol, and Vogel 13–28).

A few days later, he came again and used a trick. He called the two boys and said to one of them, "Go and draw water from the big well with this coconut shell. Fill the shell up well, and be careful not to spill any." The boy set out, but on the way he spilled at least a quarter of the water he was carrying. "That's not enough," said Rakakabe. "Here," he said to the other boy, "here is another nut shell. Go fill it up at the big well, and bring it back to me carefully." The second boy came back; not a drop of water had been spilled.

"Take that one," the mother said, "since he belongs to you!"

He took him home in order to cook him and eat him. When he got home, he put him down near the hearth and went to his garden to gather some bananas, which he had decided to cook in the pot with the boy.

As a servant he had an old woman, who had been with him a long time but had little love for him. She came up to the boy and said, "Rakakabe wants to cook you in this big pot, but I want to save you. When he comes back and tells you to stir the hot water in the pot, pretend to take a stick. He will come up and try to seize you, but you push him very hard. He will fall into the boiling water and be killed."

"Yes," said the boy, "I will do that."

As soon as Rakakabe came back with his bananas, he called the boy to stir the water. He came over and bent down, as if to take a stick. Rakakabe then moved towards the pot, but suddenly the boy stood up and pushed him so hard that he fell in. The water was boiling; he was instantly killed.

Then the boy said to the old woman, "Thank you very much, grandmother, for the good advice you gave me. Without you, I would have been cooked and eaten. Now give me one of Rakakabe's nice *lambas,* and his wealth, his gun, his spears, his horse—whatever I can use." The old woman joyfully obeyed, and the young boy fitted himself out from head to foot. He turned around and saw some golden thing floating in the pot. He plunged his fingers into the water to get this thing, but he could not grasp anything. Only, when he drew his hand out of the water, it was completely gilded. He was very surprised at that. He washed it and rubbed it vigorously with sand, but the gold stuck so hard that it did not come off. Very happy, he took off his clothes and plunged all the way into the pot, with only his head and neck sticking out. His whole body was gilded; he was dazzling. He put his clothes back on, took Rakakabe's horse, gun, spears, and big sword, and he left.

[At the King's Village]

After a few hours he came in sight of a large village, where a very powerful king lived. But he dared not go forward, for this king was very evil-tempered. He went on his way and met two young birds, of a strange species named *Fitily bekopakopa,* Big-Winged Birds.[16] They were playing peacefully. Quite close to them, a large *do* [boa] crept quietly up, preparing to eat them. But the boy came up quickly and killed the *do* with one stroke of his sword. The birds thanked him, saying, "Come home with us. Our mother will thank you and give you a good reward."

"Oh no," he said, "I won't go there. I am too afraid."

"Don't be afraid. You have nothing to fear." They set forth and arrived at the house of the birds' mother. "Here is a man who saved our lives," the elder one said. "He must have a reward."

"I have no money nor jewels," the mother said, "nor anything that men seek. I have only my children. But since you saved them, take one. I give it to you."

"It will not harm me, even when it's grown?"

"No, quite the opposite. It will serve you."

In a curious reversal of his own story, the child is rewarded with magic animal children who will later play Grateful Animals. In other versions, the heroes defeat serpents (Haring, *Malagasy Tale Index* 227–31) or are rewarded with understanding the language of animals (Hébert, "Un conte"). Mixing the narrative lexicon was a valued technique even in old Analalava.

So he chose the female, got back up on his horse, and left. The bird flew over his head, followed him constantly, and with her two big wings protected him from the sun better than a parasol would have done.

A little way on, he saw two young donkeys[17] playing, and close to them there was a huge *do* which was about to eat them. He killed the *do* and saved the young donkeys. The mother donkey gave him one of her young ones to reward him; he took a female with him.

Farther on, he met two lion cubs [*simba*] and saved them the same way. The mother offered him one of her young ones; again he took a female.

Farther on, he saved two giraffes. The mother offered him one; he chose a female and added her to the other animals who were following him.

He set out with his troupe, and after they had walked a long time, he arrived near a very large village where a powerful king lived. About a kilometer west of this village there was a large cave cut into the rock. He shut his animals up there and ordered them to stay very quiet. He gave them something to eat; when they had eaten their fill, he took off his beautiful clothes and put on old, torn, dirty ones. He also took gum from a fig-tree [*adabo*] and covered his body with it. His golden radiance disappeared, and he became like a leper.

Traces of Madagascar's cultural heritage from the East appear both in the hero's shining appearance and the skin ailment that disguises it. In a Malay story, for instance, the hero's disguise will be followed by the "abrupt regeneration of the heroes, who appear at the peak of their brilliance" (Ottino, P., *L'Étrangère* 162–64).

Then he presented himself in the village and asked to see the king. At first he did not want to receive him, but then he thought better of it and said, "Bring this stranger in. Perhaps he will tell us many new things." But when he saw him enter, all filthy and tattered, looking in every way like a leper, he sent him away very quickly, saying, "Go away, go away. Lepers do not live here, they live in the village you see over there to the west. Go and join those who are leprous like you."

He left and arrived at the lepers' place. He greeted them and chatted with them. "Where do you come from?" they said.

"From Some-Place. I was at your king's place, but he sent me away and told me to come here and live with you."

"That's right. Over there is the village for people who are in good health. You have to stay with us."

They made him a place in one corner of a house. All his companions were truly pitiable. One was missing half his fingers, another was missing almost a whole foot, one had no nose, another almost no lips. Not one could walk easily or take care of himself. So the young man said, "We have nothing to eat, but have no fear. I will go and look for *ovy* [yams] for everyone. We won't eat more of these bad *kabija* [arrowroot] herbs."

He went out, entered the forest, and ran back to his animals to feed them. When he got to the cave, he undressed, removed the *adabo* gum covering his body, put his beautiful clothes back on, and chatted with his animals. When they had been fed, he again smeared himself with gum, put his rags back on, dug up several tubers—yams and manioc—and carried them to his companions. When he reached the village, he cooked and ate with them.

Modeling the behavior appropriate for a future ruler, he is unfailingly kind and honest with his animals, practices deception only temporarily with his fellow humans, and manages both communities as skillfully as the narrator manages the insertion of episodes. The woman he meets now is his equal: she follows custom as faithfully as the narrator follows storytelling tradition.

[He Marries]

He lived like that for three or four months, until a day when one of the king's daughters, wanting to get married, put out an order from her father, inviting all the young men of the country to come to the village square on the following Friday. That Friday they were all there. The young man came too, but he was pushed away by one, knocked down by someone else, and driven away by a third. Everybody wanted to get rid of him.

The girl mounted on the *fantsina* [platform[18]] with a lemon in her hand. She looked at the crowd and said, "I am going to throw this lemon. The one on whom it falls will become my husband." She threw the lemon into the air. It fell on the sham leper.

All the young men protested, saying, "You cannot marry a leper! The daughter of a great king must not choose such a husband! You must start again."

"Give me the lemon," the girl said then. "I will start again."

The young men pushed the young man behind them and the girl threw her lemon again. He was again the one it fell on. The young men protested and began to strike him. They would have overpowered him on the spot, if the king's daughter had not cried, "Let him alone, let him alone. I have to marry him, since the lemon fell on him twice!"

"Oh, princess," the young men said, "That is not possible! You cannot have a leper for a husband!" They all left, grumbling.

The king and queen were very angry, but the marriage was held. The girl led her husband to a house isolated from the village, and moved in with him there. At the end of several hours, the husband pretended to have an urgent need and went out. He ran to the lepers' place.

"I've just come from the marriage of the king's daughter," he said. "Now I will go and find a little food."

He went to give food to his animals, gathered up several tubers, and came back.

"Here," he said, "cook these *ovy* and eat them. I am going back to the feast. I can surely get some meat and rice there."

He went back to his wife's house. She served him an excellent meal, but when night came she refused to share his sleeping mat, and went to lie down in another room. She continued to do that on the following nights. It became known. Everybody made fun of them, and they all called the young man *Betaheñy,* or Big Leper.[19]

Two inserted episodes, a quest and a test, will lead to the hero's being recognized.[20]

[Curing the King]

Two months after that marriage, the king, the father of the girl, fell gravely ill; the *moasy* [diviner] was consulted. He asked the *sikidy* [divination], and declared, "In order for the king to be cured, he will have to drink ass's milk. Otherwise he will die." There was great commotion in the village. Where could such milk be procured? It had never been seen in that country. They looked for it a long time but did not find any, and the king got worse and worse. Finally the queen said, "I will give eighty piasters to the man who will bring me the milk which must cure my husband!"

Tempted by this large sum, the young men of the village took goat's milk and mixed it with cow's milk and other kinds. They took it to the *moasy,* but he recognized the deception. Betaheñy continued to visit his animals every day. One evening, he filled a bottle with pure milk from his she-ass. Then he filled another with half milk, half water and went back to his house. He hid the pure milk and gave the other to his wife saying, "Here is a liter of milk. Take it to your mother's house. Perhaps it is ass's milk!" The wife was very surprised. She thought her husband was trying to trick the diviner. Still, she made up her mind and went to her parents' house.

"Yes, that is ass's milk, but it will not do for the sick man, because a lot of water has been added to it."

The rumor spread that Betaheñy had found ass's milk. Four young men came to find him and said, "Where did you find ass's milk?"

"I found it over there."

"Give us a liter of this milk, pure, and you will have a hundred francs."

"I do not want your money," Betaheñy said, "but if you'll take a burn on the leg with a hot poker, I will give it to you right away."

"We accept," they said. He had a spear-iron heated. When it was hot, he made two burns on the left leg of each of the four young men. Then he gave them the bottle of milk he had kept in reserve. They took it to the queen's house and went in a body to consult the diviner.

"Yes," he said, "that is truly ass's milk. Go have the king drink it." Instantly he was cured. Everyone was very glad, and they held a big feast.

[War]

Two weeks after that, a king who lived not far from there sent two messengers to declare war. "I shall be there in two days," he had them say, "and I shall wait for you on the great western plain." The king took up the challenge and everybody prepared for battle. Betaheñy said to his wife, "Go ask your father for a gun for me. I too want to go and fight!"

The young woman went, but the king began to laugh: "Oh, take this old gun with no flint, it is good enough for him. What would he do with a better weapon?"

She took the gun to her husband. When he saw it, he began to laugh. "I will go find some dry grass and rice straw to load it," he said.

He left and made his way to the cave where the animals were. "Ah, ah!" he said. "I have good news to tell you. War is coming. Do you want to come with me?"

"Yes, yes!" the animals said. "We will gladly go. That is our trade." Then he threw his old gun into a corner and got his animals ready. Then he bathed carefully, so as to remove all that gum, put his beautiful clothes back on, took Rakakabe's weapons, mounted his horse, and started out, with his whole band following.

While he was getting ready, the enemies had arrived and the battle had begun. When they saw him coming, they were all amazed. The gunshots stopped, no more spears were thrown, the curses stopped. And in the two camps everyone wondered, "Who is this *Zanahary* (god) all in gold, with such incredible animals in his service?"

He made his way through his father-in-law's troops and marched upon the enemy camp. They were terror-stricken and let him pass. He went two or three hundred meters beyond their lines; then abruptly he turned round and launched himself upon them, followed by all his animals. The Big-Winged Bird struck with her wings, her talons, and her beak, and killed more than a hundred soldiers. The lioness killed more than three hundred with her teeth and claws. The giraffe struck down a good many by kicking them. The she-ass began to bray, and made such a noise that most of the soldiers took flight when they heard it. Betaheñy chased them with his horse and killed a great number of them. The rest disappeared at top speed, and the battle was won.

Betaheñy went straight back, with all his animals. No one dared to follow him, so fearful they were. He removed his clothes, smeared himself with gum, put his bad clothes back on, fed his animals, pulled up several yams for his friends, and went back to them. "How was the war?" they asked him.

"Oh," he answered, "the king had a bad gun given to me. I ran away and hid in the forest." Then he left them, saying, "I am going to the village to get news of the war and details about the battle."

When he reached his wife's house, she said to him, "Well, where were you during the war? Did you not see a god all in gold, with some extraordinary animals in his service?"

"Oh no," he answered, "your father had a bad gun given to me, and I ran away into the forest!" His wife made fun of him, but he let her talk.

A few weeks after that, the same enemy king came back to avenge his defeat. Betaheñy ran quickly to his animals, bathed, dressed, and rushed to the battlefield. "There is that god again," the soldiers said, and stopped fighting. The animals wreaked great havoc. Betaheñy too killed many enemies, but swinging his sword at random, he got a cut on his little finger. He came up to the king, his father-in-law, who did not recognize him, took the silk kerchief he had in his hand, used it to stop the blood running from the wound, and finally wrapped his finger with it. The king was afraid. "My kerchief has been taken by a god," he said. But his enemies were more afraid than he. They ran for their lives, with their king in the lead, never to return.

Betaheñy went back to his cave with his animals, took his clothes off, folded the king's kerchief with his clothes, and again disguised himself as a leper. He made his way to his friends' village, and when they asked him for news of the battle, he answered them as before, "I had bad weapons. I hid in the forest so I would not get killed!"

The lepers made fun of him and said, "You are really too fearful. When we were not ill, no one was as courageous as we were. If we had been in your place, you would have seen something!" He did not answer, and went home. His wife heaped mockery upon him, but he calmly let her talk, lay down, and went to sleep.

[He Is Recognized]

Some time later, his wife said to him, "You are too ill, my friend. You are a horrible sight to everybody. You must get cured. I am going to consult the diviner; he will give me remedies." She went to consult her father's most renowned *moasy.* After consulting the *sikidy,* he gave her two packets of herbs. With one she was to make an infusion for her husband to drink; with the other she would prepare a bath for him. She went home and said to her husband, "Do not go out. We are going to make your medicines." She called one of her serving-women and ordered, "Make an infusion with this packet of herbs the diviner gave me. Put this other packet in a big pot full of water and boil it well. We are going to wash my husband in it, so that he will be cured."

When the water was hot, she called her husband and sent him into the next room, where everything was ready. "Go and bathe my husband," she said to the servant.

"Oh no," she said. "I will not touch a leper. I am too afraid to catch his disease."

"Go quickly," the young woman said. "Obey. I, the daughter of your king, order you."

Grumbling, the servant obeyed, and began to bathe Betaheñy. She rubbed and scoured him so hard with the hot water that the gum began to come off. She saw then that her master's skin was very healthy, and what was more, it was covered with a shining layer of gold. She ran quickly to her mistress and said to her, "Pardon, O queen! Come and see what is happening. Your husband is no leper. He only has *adabo* gum on his skin, but his skin is healthy and shining like gold."

"Come, come. Just because you did not want to obey me before, don't be telling me lies now. Go back and bathe my husband."

"I am not lying. Come and see!"

"Just go. I will come see when you have finished!"

The servant continued her task, and soon Betaheñy's body appeared clean and shining, shining so much as to light up the whole room. That was how he presented himself to his wife, and she found him so handsome and splendid that she fainted away. Betaheñy tried to revive her, saying,

"If the cause of your faint is the love you have for me,
rise up and be well,
but if it is your malice and wickedness that brought it on,
do not arise, and die!"

The young woman then opened her eyes and arose. Seeing her, Betaheñy fainted away in turn, and his wife said to him,

"If it is your malice and wickedness
which have made you faint away so,
do not arise, and die,
for I have money and cattle to bury you
according to the customs of your ancestors.
But if it is your goodness and the love you have for me.
arise and live,
to enjoy with me all the riches I possess!"

Saying these words, she took a silk kerchief, moistened it in cold water and then passed it over her husband's face. He immediately came to, got up, and kissed his wife very tenderly. Then she ran happily to her parents' house and told them what had just happened. Her husband was sent for in the royal *filanjana* (sedan chair), and he was led into the *jomba* (palace). A great feast was held, and the marriage was celebrated following the traditions of the ancients.

[He Claims His Rewards]

A few days later, the young man said to the king his father-in-law, "Have all the village people brought together, I ask you. I have something to say to them!" The king gladly consented, and had them all brought together in the meeting-space. When all the crowd was there, the young man mounted on the *fantsina* and said,

> "I have had you brought together today
> to let you know about myself.
> I am no leper and I never was.
> I only put *adabo* gum on my body.
> I wanted to test you and know your mind.
>
> I was the one who provided the ass's milk
> that cured the king.
> If you do not believe it,
> send for the four young men who took it to the diviner.
> I burned their left legs with the blade of a spear,
> and you will still see the traces of the burns.
> I was the one who helped you
> in your war against the neighboring king.
> I was the one who was followed by those terrible animals
> who killed so many enemies.
> I was the one you saw appear all gilded,
> and whom you took for a god.
> And if there are any among you who do not believe my words,
> let them wait:
> I will prove that I have spoken the truth."

He quickly ran to the cave where the animals were, put his beautiful clothes back on, took his good weapons, mounted his horse, and made his way to the meeting-space, with the she-ass, giraffe, and lioness around him, and preceded by the *fitily bekopakopa* [Big-Winged Bird], which flew over him and shaded him with its wings. At sight of him, everybody bowed down and asked his pardon. He approached the king and gave him back the silk kerchief, with which he had stopped the blood from his wound. The king was convinced and solemnly recognized him. All his subjects saluted him, saying, "*Koezy, ampanjaka, koezy, ampanjaka* [We salute you, O king! We salute you, O king!"]. And the day was finished with rejoicing and a great banquet.

[The Chaste Brother]

While all these things were happening, the young man's brother was growing up in his village. One day he said to his parents, "Dear parents, I ask permission to leave you. I want to go and see what has become of my brother."

"Oh," they said, "it is no use leaving us for that. Your brother is dead; he was eaten by Rakakabe."

"No," he answered, "I do not believe he is dead. I am going to find out what has become of him." They gave him permission to leave, and he set forth.

After several hours, he arrived near the house of Rakakabe. There he found the old servant, who had remained there. He greeted her respectfully and said, "Could you not tell me, grandmother, what has become of my older brother? Rakakabe came to take him in our village several months ago."

The old lady knew all Rakakabe's charms; thanks to them, she could make out the past, present, and future. She answered, "Have no fear, grandson. Rakakabe is dead, but your brother is alive. He is in Some-Place; he has married the daughter of the king of that country." And as he wanted to leave without delay, she held him back and added, "I wish to do for you what I did for your brother. Enter that room and bathe in the water contained in the big pot. Your face is absolutely like your brother's; you will resemble him still much more."

He obeyed, and his body became all gilded. The old woman gave him magnificent clothes like the ones his brother had taken, a superb sword, a fine gun with gilded studs, and spears inlaid with yellow and red copper. He mounted a magnificent horse and set out. On the way he had the same adventures as his brother: like him, he received a *fitily bekopakopa,* a she-ass, a lioness, and a giraffe, and he took all these animals with him.

His brother went on happily living with his wife in the king's village. One day she said, "In a village over that way, to the west, I know of a very beautiful woman called Kalokatra [Game-Charmer]. She plays wonderfully well at the *katra* game.[21] She challenges all men who go to meet with her. If she wins the match, the man who lost is put in prison. If she loses, the victor shares her bed and enjoys her."

"Well!" he said. "I want to go find that woman, tomorrow morning. I will not sleep with her, but I do want to know if she plays *katra* better than I do."

The next morning, then, he set out towards the west to measure himself against Kalokatra. A few minutes later, his brother arrived from the east. The wife was quite surprised. "Hel-lo," she said, "are you back, then? Why did you not go to that place?" She took him for her husband. The brother did not want to undeceive her, but not knowing where his elder brother had gone, he did not answer her.

She went about her usual duties. She ordered her servants to put the animals out to pasture; she gave her serving-women their daily tasks; she put in place the hat and weapons of the man she thought was her husband. The servant brought rice. Before eating, the brother took a five-franc piece, stuck it into the middle of the plate of rice, and said, "Be careful. Do not eat the rice on my side. I will not eat what is on yours."

"Why are you doing that? You never did that up to now."

"Let's just eat," he answered, without saying more.

When night came, they lay down. When they were inside the mosquito-net, the brother took his large sword, put it in the middle of the bed, and said, "That is our boundary. It shall not be crossed. You must not turn over to my side, and I shall not turn over to yours."

"I don't know what is the matter with you," the wife said. "I am afraid you are going to kill me. Never since we have been married have you acted like this. And now today you are doing the strangest things!"

"Have no fear," he said. "Tomorrow I will not act like this any more. For today, let us lie down and sleep." They lay down with the sword between them, and did not turn towards each other.

The next morning, when the young man had dressed, he took his weapons and said, "I have no more fear, now, and I am going to leave." He had cleverly made the wife and the servants talk, and he knew where his brother had gone.

"Good," said his wife. "Go, and try to play a good game of *katra.*" He asked the way precisely and set forth.

The elder brother had arrived at Kalokatra's place long since, but he had been beaten and had been put in prison. When the younger brother arrived near the village, he noticed an old woman in a house apart; he wanted to question her.

"Oh, grandson," she said, "you cannot win over Kalokatra. No one plays as well as she, either at 'big *katra,*' 'deceiving *katra,*' 'first-row *katra,*' or 'laid-down *katra.*'[22] If you do not want to be beaten, here is what you have to do. You must play with her only at night. Take these four mice and put them in your pocket. If you see that you are going to lose, let the mice loose in the room. The cat will run after them to catch them, and will overturn the lamp. In the darkness you will put your pieces back in their places on the board."

"Good," he said. "Thank you, grandmother!" And he left.

Now the narrator again foreshadows Sydney Joseph, by poising the younger brother between two women. Having resisted the temptation of his sister-in-law, he resists the temptation of Kalokatra, who will sleep with any man who defeats her in the game.[23] The elder brother's plot would wind down with a conventional Malagasy recognition scene of fainting and resuscitation, but for the narrator's insertion of an Indian tale, the Cat and the Candle, which later turns up in Mauritius (Gallob 249–51).

[The Cat and the Candle]

Night was falling as he reached Kalokatra's house. He saw his brother's animals in the pasture, and he understood that he was imprisoned. He put his animals in the pasture with the others, and knocked at the door: "Hello?" "Come in!" Kalokatra answered.

He came in and proposed that they play *katra.* She agreed right away. She lit the lamp, brought the board, and the game began. A great cat came and sat curled around near the players, underneath the lamp.

The boy was, in fact, not very good at it, and in a very short time he was in a weak position. Seeing himself losing, he took the mice from his pocket and let them loose, one after another. The first one ran away, waking the cat, which was all attention. The second scurried close to it and disappeared. It made a great leap when it saw the third and fourth, but when it jumped, it overturned the lamp, and the lamp went out. Kalokatra got up to light it again from an ember on the hearth. The young man took advantage of that to pick up all his seeds and put them back into his holes.

"You are beaten," he said, "for I've 'eaten' all the seeds!"

"All right," she answered. "Let's go to bed, then."

"No. I don't want to go to bed with you. I only want you to let my brother out of the prison where you have shut him up. If you do not, I will kill you with a blow of my sword."

Kalokatra was afraid and quickly went to release the prisoner. He came, recognized his brother, and was very happy. Both embraced and told each other their story. The younger told the elder that his wife had taken him for her husband, that they had eaten rice together, and that they had slept together in the same bed. He had no time to say more. Believing that his brother had taken his wife from him, the elder flew into anger and killed him outright with one stroke. Then he left and went back to his home.

When he reached his village, he resumed his usual occupations. His wife served him rice. While they were eating, she said to him, "The other day, before you left, why did you put a five-franc piece in the rice to divide it in two? You forbade me to take what was on your side, and you would not take what was on mine. Then, when we went to bed, you put that big sword between us, and you told me I could not come near you or turn towards your side. Why did you do that?"

The husband was very upset and angry. He saw how wrong he had been to kill his brother. He went out of the house, mounted his horse, and arrived in a few moments at the foot of the bush under which he had hidden the body.

[Resuscitation]

He called a passing bee. In those times, bees were famous diviners, who had the power to revive the dead. The bee said to him, "If I revive your brother, will you give me two lengths of cloth?"

"Oh, certainly—much more, if you want it."

"All right. Go fetch me some 'life-giving vine' and we'll make a charm."

No one was there to go look for that root. He noticed a rabbit walking there[24] and said to it, "You who run so fast, go fetch me some 'life-giving vine.' "

"Will you give me some very tender grass for my trouble?"

"Yes!" said the young man. The rabbit ran off. As it entered the forest, it struck a wasps' nest. One of the wasps, furious, stung him on the end of its nose. It did not stop to scratch, though it felt very bad. But to lessen the pain, it shook it in all directions. Since then, they say, the rabbits who descended from it have kept that habit.

It found the "life-giving vine," pulled up several roots, and brought them back very fast. It received its payment, and the bee began its work.

It took the dead body and put it into a large drum. Then it crushed the vine and put it too into the drum. Then it sang and danced all around. At the end of several minutes it called the young man. He answered. It continued its dancing and singing, then called him again. He answered again, but in a stronger and surer voice. It began again a third time, then called him again. He came out of the drum. He was revived.

The bee was given the payment it was promised. The two brothers went happily back to their village. A great feast was held. Then they sent for their parents, and they lived very happy (Dandouau, *Contes populaires* 188–208).[25]

Complex, ingeniously structured, The Two Brothers is more linear and straightforward than Sydney Joseph's Siren-Girl. About its style, the collector Dandouau is contradictory. He asserts his translations to be "as rigorously exact and literal as possible," yet he writes, "Malagasy thought, which is essentially fleeting, reveals itself behind such a profusion of circumlocutions and repetitions that a literal translation would sometimes not be very intelligible, and in any case tiring for the reader" (Dandouau, *Contes populaires* 9). Is his Sakalava narrator a splendid exception, who has learned to accommodate himself to European expectations, or did Dandouau reduce his oral style to make his translation intelligible and engaging? Anyway, that cliché about redundancy, which recurs through the French colonial literature on Madagascar, is not borne out by verbatim texts from modern collectors, except when field conditions interfere with full performance—which didn't happen when Dandouau took dictation from this narrator.

More recently in Madagascar, Noël Gueunier came to know another star, locally known as *mamy amin'ny lelany,* sweet-tongued, and celebrated as a man of *matavy hiratsy,* flavored words. This artist's virtuosity, unconventionality, and fondness for paradox are all excellent qualifications for a storyteller living in modern Madagascar, which in the same period produced the new slow-and-fast music called *salegy* (Gueunier, *L'origine* 72). A summary of one narrative will show this virtuoso synthesizing the origin of kingship and a new set of Arabic etymologies for all the days of the week.

81. Origin of Kingship and the Days of the Week

Western Madagascar narrator 1980s

Earth is all dark. God decides to send light on the first day, to which the narrator gives the name *al-wahed.* Heaven separates from earth; the sun comes up. On the second day, all men but one are granted their wants from God. Hence the "real name" for Monday is "word accomplished," to denote the ending of discussion. On Tuesday (Separation), they go their various ways. On Wednesday (Alarobia), they come back to remonstrate with God: "Don't you see that the sky is separated?" Hence the narrator's "real name" for Alarobia is *Maliolanitsy,* sky away. On Thursday (day of *mani-bola,* the desire to speak), the lazy man goes to see God, who awards him the earth. On Friday, the new proprietor calls all men together and tells them to get their things off his land. The demand motivates them to go see God, and that's why Friday is called *Vonilahy,* men's decision. God explains that he has given that man the land with no regrets or restrictions. They must find ways to get along with him. They leave. Friday is the king's day, because that's the day the power was given to him. On Saturday, some who don't want to submit start away, but they are stopped on the road. That's why, concludes this inventive sage, Saturday is called *Mitsahara* among the old Sakalava.[26]

Even this bald summary demonstrates that features of myth and scripture are being synthesized. The narrator ends his myth with sympathy for the head that wears a crown:

That's the origin of the *vezaka,* punishments, of kings. . . . When the *vazaha* [Europeans] controlled us, there were no punishments. Their *vezaka* was prison. But the kings—their punishment is important—no water, a poor harvest. Because the division was done that way, each one has the part God gave him. (Gueunier, *L'origine* 93)

The best-known star performer in Mauritius had a Malagasy name. Jean Alphonse Ravaton, better known as Ti Frère, born in 1900, absorbed Malagasy, European, and Indo-Mauritian influences. The broadcast media christened him *the* representative of Mauritian *sega* singing, and he gained even more media fame than Nelzir Ventre (Putz).

And in Réunion, where the nighttime sky showers you with brilliant stars, there is a star of verbal art rightly called "the king." He will make you remember Greek mythology.

82. "Killed Seven, Wounded Fourteen"

Gérose Barivoitse, Réunion 1976

Well, once there was a king in a country. So, this king, see, he had a daughter. He was looking for a boy to marry his daughter. And every guy who tried, couldn't make it. He'd come, he'd get there—when he got there, he asked for the girl in marriage, he posed a *kondisyon.* He said, "If you can succeed in getting the giant Gran Dyab, up above, and bring him here, then I'll marry you to my daughter."[27] And all the time, every two months they had to take a girl up above to be eaten. You see, they had to. If he came down here, he'd eat everybody, so he made them bring a girl for him.

Gérose Barivoitse, of Sainte-Suzanne in Réunion, from appearing in festivals of traditional culture and on French national television, acquired enough fame to be called *le roi,* The King, and to be shown on video to French students every year. His voluble technique switches between registers of speaking and into song. Super-alert and a skillful imitator of animal sounds, he jumps up from his chair and runs a meter or two, then runs back and sits. Vocally he sounds East African; physically he looks like many Betsimisaraka men from the east coast of Madagascar, and his surname is Malagasy. Ethnically he is classed as a poor white (*petit blanc*), a member of Réunion's most oppressed, scorned, and enclaved minority. Tales like his are a window into French colonial tradition into the island, but like the Kreol language he speaks (and like other creole languages), his tales are also emergent, historically discontinuous, and autonomous, far from the assumption that they must be "hybrid" or "broken" and thus inferior to French originals.[28]

In an early interview, Gérose Barivoitse explained to Christian Barat the code that would come before these words.

Gérose Barivoitse: *Kriké!*

Christian Barat: *Kraké* the king!

Gérose Barivoitse: The key in your pocket, the shit in my bag! Always that's the habit with us, don't you find something surprising in that? Only, if people don't know, they say we seem to be talking shit. Go see if it is. Not true! Those are the words in *kreol* to begin a story.

At formulaic openings and closings, The King alternates between narrating and addressing his hearer in his own voice, or he emits several consciousnesses in a single voice (Barthes, *Critical Essays* 158). His playful alternation is a kind of miniature of the way Réunionnais speakers move among codes and channels.

Now the king had seven daughters. Of the seven daughters only one was left. Gran Dyab had eaten all of them. Not one man managed to stop him. But he thought he'd find one to take his last daughter. So he made a plan—like that gang shouting over there.[29] So guys came, every kind of guy, and he'd say, "You have to go up there and get Gran Dyab and bring him here. After that you'll marry my daughter." Guys would come, they'd go up there—Gran Dyab, *flouk!*—down the hatch. Gran Dyab didn't come, his stomach was full, why's he gonna come here? But the king saw he didn't come. Gran Dyab demanded of the king, said, "OK, it's time, I'm here to get your last daughter." Another guy, he made his speech, sent him up the mountain. But in the end, guys were afraid and didn't come any more.

Bringing on his main character, Gérose Barivoitse points to his injured leg. He must motivate the famous first incident of the tale, in which seven flies will be killed. Piquantly he connects himself to his hero, as well as other regional folktale heroes such as the scabrous Ti Zan. Well, he said,

there was one guy, he had—he was cleaning a big sore on his foot. Not like this one, 'cause I'm already cured. I got cut, I did—I couldn't have a daughter. I couldn't go to the king to marry the king's daughter. What do I have to do with that stuff? I'd rather cut him and cure myself.

Gérose Barivoitse's gesture code enlivens his performances and maintains connection with his audience (Georges; Barat, Carayol, and Vogel 103–109).

So he had a big sore like this on his foot. A nice sore! prettiest sore you could want. So he sat all day. *Vap!* the flies that came, he'd slap them down like that. The flies came; when he saw a big bunch of flies, he'd *vap!* By hitting and hitting on the sore, one day with one *vap!* he killed seven flies and wounded fourteen. So he said, "Good for me! I'll make a motto to put on my hat." He took his hat, put it on the ground, marked it like this: "Killed seven, wounded fourteen."

So he went down, down to town, put it on one side, like this—

and Gérose Barivoitse imitates his character's movement. Then, as the suitor test is imposed on the hero, he continues inserting himself into the story. No sooner does his hero get the princess's attention than Mr. Barivoitse commands his hearer's attention.

He went and passed in front of the king's house. Ah, ah! The king's daughter was up there; he gave her a wink. She said, "Here's my happiness! That's a strong man!" 'Cause he'd killed seven flies and wounded fourteen. She said, "Papa," she said, "there's a man who can go get the giant in the forest. Then he'll bring him back." So the king came down and said, "Find out who that is." Long ago they didn't need anything. The king, once he said something, that was it! He came down and asked who he was. He said, "I say—tell me your name." He said, "Me, I am Mr. 'Killed seven wounded fourteen.'" He said, "I've made war, I have." What war? The guy sat on the ground with his legs crossed.[30] He washed his legs 'cause they were so rotten, as if there were borers in his legs! So—

Kriké!

Christian Barat: *Kraké mésyé!*

Gérose Barivoitse: Let's skip his rotten legs.

But he knew how to make good. The key in your pocket, the shit in my bag!

Well, the king said, "Yes. You want to ask for my daughter in marriage?" He said, "Yes, king." "OK," he said, "if you can go get Gran Dyab up there and bring him back, I'll marry you to my daughter." He said, "Careful, King!" The king said to him, "Yes!" So he said, "Sign." The king made him a paper and everything, said to him, "Sign." "Oh," he said, "I can't sign my name." That's when signing with your thumb began. Now me, I stand up, "Hey," I say, "that guy can't read, how's he gonna sign?"

So the king said to him, "OK, wet your thumb and put it here." He wet his thumb, bap! Ah, I say, that's a signature!

Closing the episode, the narrator follows that old Malagasy tradition of using in his folktale an "etiological" tag from myth, about the origin of a custom.

Kriké!

Christian Barat: *Kraké mésyé!*

Gérose Barivoitse: The key in your pocket, the shit in my bag!

Then the guy went on his way, he went up, up, up, up, up, up, and got there. He found Gran Dyab sitting in his house, he did like this: "Mf, mf! Aaah," he said, "my food is here, my food is here." He said, "In a jiffy I'll deal with him." The guy got there, he yelled, "Anybody here?" Ah, ah! Gran Dyab—when he got close, see, he put his hat like this. His hat like this, till he couldn't see. He did this [tilted his hat forward to show the motto to Gran Dyab]. Gran Dyab gave it a look, went like this, looked at it and said, "Wep," he said, "ep—don't come in here!" he said, "hang on," he said. "What's that on your hat?"

He said, "Well, it's my name."

"Huh?"

"Killed seven, wounded fourteen."

"Uh! Don't come in here, buddy. Uh-uh-uh!"

"Yes," he said, "yes! I have to come in, I came to see you!"

He said, "What for?"

He said, "We need to take some wood down to town, need to each carry a load of wood to take it to the king down there. I need you," he said, "to carry a nice load of wood for him."

Gran Dyab said to him, "OK, let's go." Now he said, "But how to gather it?"

He said, "No need of gathering it," he said, "just cut a tree and we'll both carry it." *Kriké!*

Christian Barat: *Kraké, mésyé!*

Gérose Barivoitse: The key in your pocket, the shit in my bag, still!

So—"Well," he said, "are you ready for the wood?"

"Yes," he said, "yes, let's go! Let's go cut it right away." He said, "what are you waiting for? Do you need something else?"

"OK," he said, "let's go!"

So Gran Dyab took his axe. Man, that axe, you know? The flies light on it, *fyuk,* in two! A monster ax. The guy began to—Killed-seven-wounded-fourteen started to shake, seeing that axe, how big it was. But the guy had heart—he'd come there to get him, he had to take him. Gran Dyab gave one whack, *vap! vap!* Another whack there, *vap! vap!* A tree trunk—rrr—a tree trunk half as big as this house! Fell to the ground! Then Gran Dyab said to him, "OK, that's not it," he said, Gran Dyab said, "We'll have to break it in two," he said, " 'cause it's too big. We have to carry it," he said. Another hit, he cut it in two. Ah, the poor guy, he took his axe, gave one blow, the axe got stuck there. Gran Dyab couldn't pull it out! Nothing to do.

Kriké!

Christian Barat: *Kraké, mésyé!*

Gérose Barivoitse: The key in your pocket, the shit in my bag!

Gran Dyab fought, he tried to pull out his axe, he fought, he didn't do it, he fought. "Hey," he said, "you know," he said, "to get that thing out, you'll have to stick something in there. Take your two hands, stick them in there, like a wedge, I'll pull out the axe." So Gran Dyab, smart as he is, took his two hands and stuck them into the trunk. The guy pulled out the axe, and Gran Dyab's hands, *vap!* caught there. "Ouch," Gran Dyab said, "you—brother," he said, "what am I gonna do? Pull on my hands." He said, "No, don't pull," he said, "we'll have to carry the tree trunk like that, down below, just like that." "Aaah!" he said. He said, "What next," he said, "let's go, but don't drop it."

Gran Dyab had courage. What do you want from a beast like that? Gran Dyab with his two hands there, he lifted it and put it on his shoulder. He said, "Ah. Ready?" Gran Dyab said, "Let's go, hoist, hoist, hoist." Who's hoisting? Gran Dyab put it on his head. "Go," *vyap!* he was sitting on his four feet.

The hero plays the trickster role (was it Hare or Tortoise?)

And Gran Dyab went down, down, down. At one moment Gran Dyab said, "Stop, I'm tired."

The other guy jumped down and said, "What? Straight ahead," he said, "be careful of that turn," he said. "Go straight on!" he said, "I'm helping you the best I can and you're complaining!" So Gran Dyab resumed his pace. *Vap,* up he went and sat down. Sat, sat, sat, sat, sat.

Man! the king went like this, he jumped up and down. He saw a load of forest coming, he said, "Mama!" he said, "what's that?" The guy up there made the king see that he'd succeeded in bringing Gran Dyab. He said, "Go, go, go, forward march. Don't you understand?" He went to see, then he came down to the ground. When he got near the king's house, you see, he played big so the king's daughter would see. Y'see, he started thinking about his *pyé de ri* ["rice plant," a woman who feeds her husband], him with his big sore on his foot! He said, "Go, let's go, go! Don't you understand? You don't know me, Killed-seven-wounded-fourteen. I did what had to be done to bring him here. I'm the guy to make war! I'm the main man today!"—Him up in the air.

Success in capturing Gran Dyab by deception validates the hero as the princess's suitor, so Gérose Barivoitse can end his performance by again switching registers.

As soon as he got there, he said, "Well, king," he said, "here's your man." He said, "Where do you want your wood put?"

The king said, "My boy," he said, "I can't." He said, "Take it to the seaside and throw it in. What am I going to do with all that stuff? Take it away." He said, "Get up, go that way, cross over that way." They went in the direction of that station you see over there, the old [Sainte-Suzanne railway] station.

So Gran Dyab went on down. I was standing there looking, I said, "Fuck your mother," I said, "that bugger is strong!" What kind of strong, with that big sore? Poor bugger. Don't say it! He said, "Forward march!" Gran Dyab marched marched, got to the sea, turned over—rrr!

The narrator's final triumph of switching between voices is a quadruple closing formula, which portrays the hero's victory, fuses the fictional world with the present interaction, and pulls Gran Dyab from one world into the other.

Back on the road! The people cleaned his sores well. The guy was well decked out, he gave the orders. I found him and said, "Hey, I know everything that you've done." *Kriké!*

Christian Barat: *Kraké mésyé!*

Gérose Barivoitse: A nice story! The key in your pocket, the shit in my bag!

I said, "Give me a little something, give me—"

"A little something? Get out!" *Baf!*

I got sores there. If I hadn't been cut there, *kaf!* I got a nice sore. Well, what king's daughter am I going to kill flies for? King's daughters, there aren't any more. So I came here and told you the story. But be careful about getting sores. Try and cure them. I'm not saying you have them. If you get sores on your feet, try and cure them, because you're gonna do that, you're gonna kill seven flies, you're gonna wound fourteen! But what king's daughter will you find, what Gran Dyab either? You won't find them, because nowadays Gran Dyab goes around in his little airplane. Gran Dyab's plane goes around, he comes down at night, his two claws on his hand. People try to catch him, he gets 'em, gives 'em a hit in the face, they fall down. He takes his plane and *rrip!* That's Gran Dyab these days! Be careful!

Well, that's it. (Barat, Carayol, and Vogel 51–53)[31]

How idiosyncratic is Gérose Barivoitse's performance style? What would be different about the tale if the storyteller were someone else? Most narrators don't make such a show of stepping on and offstage. When Henri Lagarrigue, another *petit blanc,* of Ligne Paradis (near Saint-Pierre) tells The Brave Tailor, any French hearer will recognize his cowardly hero. His plot, like the plot in a 1953 version from Lower Brittany, "is centered in the series of tricks used by the tailor, whose bluffs get the better of" his adversary the king (Massignon 249). An African hearer will recognize M. Lagarrigue's string of trickster episodes: he sells the king's cattle and buries one tail in the mud to claim that they escaped underground; he sells the king's sheep and claims they all drowned; finally he enrages the king by antagonizing his child (Decros 149–59). When an anonymous narrator from Rodrigues (the small island east of Mauritius) tells the story, the hero is a drunken bum who won't even boast on his own behalf. Development experts will see this drunk as typifying Rodrigan creoles—not a mistake, since his three unwilling or accidental victories over marauding wolves connect the story to the region's other African-derived trickster tales (Carayol and Chaudenson, *Lièvre* 104–17). "Psycho-cultural plurality," whether in the Caribbean or in the Indian Ocean, means that The Brave Little Tailor will be different when told by different narrators.

What marks Gérose Barivoitse's version of The Brave Tailor as strongly different from the other two is his insistence on remaining onstage. For him, the boundary between the world of fiction and the world we live in is something to jump over, not an unbreachable wall. Take the closing formula. Henri Lagarrigue, belonging to the same ethnic group, combines the Réunionnais formula, "*Kriké, sasé!*" with the Malagasy one, "*se lé manter, pa nou l'oter, Gramoune lontan manter!*"—If it's a lie, it's not my fault, the people from far back were the liars. The Rodrigan narrator, a creole, marks the boundary by opening with the region's characteristic "*Sirandan!*" which demands a response, "*Sampek!*"[32] The formulas in their hands function to depersonalize the story, but Gérose Barivoitse demands personal recognition. After hearing him, one scholar observes, "Not only do we get episodic intrusion of the discourse into the narrative, incursions regulated by the teller and his audience with *Kriké-kraké;* the whole narrative enters *explicitly* into the narrator's [personal] history" (Vogel, "Permanence" 101). Continually varying the distance between himself and his character, he retains "the option of subverting the conventions and thwarting the operation of . . . the [listener's] cognitive tendencies" (Smith 231).

Among literary critics of fiction, the most tenacious of these tendencies is the one Mr. Barivoitse most energetically attacks: the novelistic distinction between the "I" of the work and the author himself (Smith 213–236). The distinction long held sway in criticism, after Flaubert and Henry James. What does it mean to compare an oral storyteller such as Gérose Barivoitse to a literary author?

> Often his narrative was interrupted by passages of comment in which the author expressed his views on this and that, in the manner of certain English novelists of whom at one time he had been very fond. These reflective asides, which some readers find tiresome, because they break the current of the narrative and destroy the illusion of life, were what we most liked to hear, so eager were we to know his personal thoughts, and resentful when they were concealed in one of his characters. (Proust 49)

Marcel Proust's *he* refers to a fictive novelist named C., whom he presents as the greatest novelist of his time, and whose narrative is the bulk of Proust's *Jean Santeuil.* The *we* refers to the narrator and his companion, who meet C. whilst on holiday and become enamored of his use of asides. Enamored of the asides or wearied by them, critics insist on their separateness.

What Gérose Barivoitse does, though, is not quite what Proust's C. does. Mr. Barivoitse repeatedly moves between the events the story is about and their presentation in the form of a story. Such a movement has been named "edgework," a movement between the events in the "taleworld" and the moment of performance in the "storyrealm" (Young 19–68). It is more visible in oral than in written literature, and especially vivid in The King's performance. Twice he compares himself unfavorably to the hero because he's not an eligible suitor. Repeatedly he mocks the hero's shamming and skin ailment, thus alluding to other regional folktale heroes such as Ti Zan. In the same moment he praises and deflates the hero's strength. By pointing to the king's authority, he puts the fictional world out of our reach, but then he brings the most fantastic of his characters, Gran Dyab, into postmodern air travel. He is following tradition. In West and South Africa, such "self-insertion is accepted practice in oral narrative performance" (Okpewho, "Oral Tradition" 225). It represents a "peculiar intersection of aesthetic and pragmatic imperatives," some of which are political (Okpewho, "Oral Tradition" 225–26). Videotape of Gérose Barivoitse—a specific sort of context for his presentation of self—suggests that he would make an equally assertive self-presentation to you or me, alternating between narrating and chatting with his interviewer, continually imposing on us the impression that he and only he is telling the story. He almost goes so far as to use "the narrative figure the classics called *author's metalepsis,* which consists of pretending that the poet 'himself brings about the effects he celebrates' " (Genette 234).

Although Michel Carayol, who knew him, remembered him vividly and genially to me almost twenty years later, Gérose Barivoitse might well have remained obscure. His editors withhold his name from the book of Réunionnais tales where his stories take up the majority of the space (Barat, Carayol, and Vogel 93). Instead they give us a portrait drawing of him (28), and a detailed analysis of his paralinguistic codes (93–109). Then when they identify constants and variables in Réunionnais tales, they assimilate him and three other narrators—Paul Maxime Maillot, Augustin Grondin, and Louis Grondin—into one (100). You can be on national TV and still be anonymous, if you are the voice of Réunionnais *petits blancs.*

An American anthropologist could have been imagining Gérose Barivoitse's people, the *petits blancs,* when he defined a "folk" as "an unsophisticated, homogeneous group living in a politically-bounded advanced culture but isolated from it by such factors as topography, geography, religion, dialect, economics, and race" (Greenway xii). Their forebears came from western France, bringing The Brave Tailor, Cinderella, Sleeping Beauty, and Bluebeard. Their Catholic religion and skin color, as common factors uniting them, enabled them to preserve and create French folklore. From the coastal villages of St. Paul and St. Denis, they moved into the Côte du Vent and the Côte Sous le Vent, occupying the whole coast by 1848. That was the year slavery was finally abolished in Réunion. Abolition provoked much movement. Seeking territory of their own, losing out economically to a growing bourgeoisie, the poorer whites penetrated the three huge, spectacular Cirques, which indent the island's mountainous massif. Since then, their economic, cultural, ethnic, even linguistic distinctness has drawn condescension from almost every observer (Chaudenson, *Des îles* 111–12). They are popularly defamed with ethnic slurs, mostly untranslatable: *pattes jaunes* (yellow feet), *yab, pip léo, pip la chaux, yules, litones* (Chaudenson, "Le Noir"). It would be difficult to find a group more scorned.

If they are so enclaved, and if outmoded cultural expressions are found among them, they must be a "folk." Everyone in La Chaloupe, one community that has been systematically studied,

> cleaves to folktales [i.e., legends] of the *Grand'mère Kale* or *loup-garou* [werewolf] sort, each bringing his or her style to this realm. On the border of the little path leading from the main path to Joseph's house, the garden is protected by a grill supported by tall posts. Shoes are placed atop the posts. Rose explained one day that that was done to prevent the *loup-garou* [werewolf], who comes down the path dragging his chains, from coming into the yard and knocking on the corrugated iron sheets of the house.

The writer asks the right question:

> Is this a story she believes in? Is it a story told for children? It was impossible to know whilst she was telling it in Pauline's presence. Both hypotheses are probably partly true. For the werewolf, as for Mère Kale, each person has his or her way of conceiving and telling the story.

Individuality coexists with participation in various traditions.

> Always there is the same ambiguity about each one's belief. To turn away the evil eye from a passer-by, a traditional chamber pot is placed near the pigpen, atop one post higher than the others. It is to protect the animals. That is the district's most unquestionable tradition. (Pelletier 60)

These are the people from whom Gérose Barivoitse and Germain Elizabeth (below) spring.

In performance, Mr. Barivoitse uses no narrative "voice," no imagined narrator. But he continually keeps his grasp on both plot and audience, even when spinning off Madagascar's favorite legend. His hero there is not a fisherman, but a hunter of *tenrec,* the Malagasy hedgehog, which poor people make into *kari,* stew.

83. The Hedgehog Hunter and the Magic Woman

Gérose Barivoitse, Sainte-Suzanne, Réunion 1976

Gérose Barivoitse: *Kriké!*

Christian Barat: *Kraké mésyé!*

Gérose Barivoitse: The key in your pocket, the shit in my bag! Mr. LaFoi ate his liver with a grain of salt.

One time there was an old guy—not really old, but a fairly old guy. His only trade was hunting *tang* [*tenrec,* the Malagasy hedgehog]. He hunted them, he caught a few. He had three dogs; one *tang* for him, one *tang* for each dog. He caught four *tang,* no more, he just caught that many. Every day like that. He lived all by himself.

Mr. Barivoitse leaves no doubt that this hero is really poor. He situates him in a little makeshift cabin, which no one should live in permanently.

Well, what kind of house did he have? A little *boukan* [cabin]. He'd take latania leaves, put them on wood, put his two latania leaves there. He lived there. When he got there with his four *tang,* he grilled them; he ate one, gave his dogs one each. That's how it went. So, all the time like that, all the time like that, all the time like that.

One fine day he got there, got back from hunting. Ah, ah! The place where he lived—at his latania house there, he saw a whole house built, and a lady sitting inside. Ah, ah! he went like this, he jumped. Ah! he looked hard, he went like this, he said, "Hey, hey," he said, "I've lost my way. That's not my house!" The woman came out, did like this, she saw him and said, "Come, sir, come in," she said. "Why are you running away? Are you afraid of me?"

"Oh no, ma'am," he said, "I'm not afraid of you."

"Come," she said, "this house is yours," she said. "Come in. Stay where you are," she said. "No need to run away!"

Then he came up, [all] grubby-looking, a grubby-looking guy, in rags, with his basket. And that day, he caught five *tang.* He was really surprised and said, "Damn!" he said, "and I got to catch five *tang*! Since my hunt," he said, "ah, ah! what gifts I'm getting!"

No ravishing beauty like Ranoro, no donor from under water, this *fam mazi* has already moved in and acts like the wife he must always have wanted.

Well, he went in; the woman had him go into that furnished house. And the woman was magic, a magic woman. She had her little box with her, she talked to her little box, see–her snuffbox, she called it her snuffbox—she talked to her little snuffbox, and the house was all organized—clothes for the guy, everything, everything ready. Finally she said, "Come in!" He went in. The woman said to him, "Fine, sit down!" As soon as he sat down, the guy ate. Didn't wash his feet; on his feet he had the mange, they looked like a cock's claws. So he came up, he saw a beautiful house all neat. "Well," she said, "come in!" she said. "This house is yours. Don't you get it?" "No, ma'am," he said, "excuse me, I don't get it at all." "Well," she said, "sit down."

The woman took his basket, she had to take the *tang* out, put them down. Then he said, "OK, clean those *tang* and make a *kari* [stew]." "Yes."

Only, she cleaned all his *tang;* he was ashamed, he was ashamed. He was afraid too. He said, "But how has this happened? I don't know how to act!" Then the woman took a cloth, gave it to him, took him to the back. She washed and cleaned him, took away his scabs. She couldn't take them all off; the mange was thick, and the guy never washed his feet, so imagine how thick it was! Let's say she heated a tub of water to clean him up. Then the guy started to look a bit better. Then she cooked the *tang,* she cooked them. the woman didn't throw [any] away; she cooked the *tang* and cut them in two pieces. She made a whole *kari;* the whole thing was good.

Next morning, he woke up; sleeping there he was afraid. He started to miss his old house. That night he didn't sleep. But the woman saw him, she understood his fear and said to him, "Well, sleep," she said. "What are you afraid of?"

"No," he said, "I'm not afraid," he said, "only," he said, "see, I'm not used to it, to get any sleep."

Mr. Barivoitse has to interpret, comment, and look ahead to the violation of the prohibition against speaking.

So why didn't he sleep? He was afraid it was somebody else's house. But he was in his own house. Only he didn't know the little magic woman. The woman was good, she wasn't a bad sort of woman. But only, careful, she was kind of quick, huh? [If] he talked his usual way, he could lose her in an instant.

So he thought it over. And the woman had a son. Her son, what was he? A charcoal fly![33] Ever seen a big charcoal fly? That's what the woman's son was; he was hiding in a corner out of sight.

Well, the king's house was nearby, like in town. The guy stayed a little while here up above, but people found his house, that house, I have to say—*Kriké!*

Christian Barat: *Kraké mésyé!*

Gérose Barivoitse: The key in your pocket, the shit in my bag!

So he sat, he thought it over. He wanted to go hunting. Why go hunting? They had food, the woman was magic. Nowadays, someone like that, they call her *pyé de ri,* but long ago they said *la fam mazi* [the magic woman].

Literally *pyé de ri* means rice-plant; metaphorically she is a woman who supplies her husband's needs (though in this case, she has taken away his normal occupation). Then Mr. Barivoitse breaks in to point out the alternative methods of healing, as prominent in Mauritius as in Réunion (Benoist, "Possession," "Carrefours").

She did her magicking and they ate—not like today. She, once she got her little snuffbox, at eleven o'clock, "By the virtue of my snuffbox," she said, "let me see the table set to eat and drink and everything." It came.

Long ago, there were things like that, you know. Only today, it's over. Back then, if a woman knew something like that, or a man either, well, I've seen it. Somebody would come for any sickness you had that the doctor didn't cure, but there was somebody to cure it. Ah. Yes, cure the sore. You could have a sore, I don't know, in old times never cured. But I've seen guys do it, cure the sores. Even my father himself! Because there were plenty of sores, they had sicknesses that didn't get well, ever. But my papa came, he made you a *tisane* [infusion]–it didn't bother him whatever it was—he made his herbs, he'd boil them, give it to you. Then you'd be fine—all gone! That wasn't magic. Herbs, herbal action, you see.

Kriké!

Christian Barat: *Kraké mésyé!*

Gérose Barivoitse: The key in your pocket, the shit in my bag!

Well, the king finally managed to find this guy's house. They told him it was an old *tang* hunter. He invited him. One day he gave a dance, gave a banquet. Well, he went there, he went there to eat. The woman said to him, "Are you going there?" She said, "Be careful about saying how I got here, hey. I warn you," she said, "be careful, hey."

"Ah," he said, "why do you say that?"

"Ah," she said, "it's kind of serious. A secret. If you reveal it, so much the worse for you!" Well, she talked with her charcoal fly there. She got him ready and put him to work. The woman didn't go, she sent him by himself just to see if the guy didn't talk, could hold his tongue. They had the secret, he must not reveal it.

After reinforcing the Malagasy commitment to secrecy, Mr. Barivoitse interpolates the pumpkin carriage from Cinderella (a tale he did not record). *Milor* is a calque of the English *my lord.*

They still say that. Even one person, you mustn't tell, hey! There were two things he must not tell.

Well, he harnessed his—it's called *milor*—he harnessed his *milor.* He didn't know anything about horses. He saw it come, but it was a big gourd with two big fat rats. The woman with her little snuffbox, "by the virtue of her snuffbox," she wished the rats to be two pretty horses, harnessed. Man! Two fine horses! When that guy went in there, when he got out, it went *klak!* Damn! Ip, ip, ip, ip—little blows with the whip.

He got there. The king had him come in. His horse was as beautiful as the king's, I tell you. The king said, "How can this guy have a horse like that? Where'd he get it?" He had him come in. Gave him his hand, took his horse, tied it up.

Well, the charcoal fly was hidden in his pocket. He didn't see him, didn't know he was there. He went in quietly and hid, went into the pocket of his coat. Well, he gave him a drink. That drink was bad stuff. It did something to the guy. It's good, but it destroys you! First thing, that's what he hit him with. He asked him, "So how—you're a hunter of *tang,*" he said, "what did you do to get all this stuff?"

"Well," he said, "I work," he said, "I sell my *tang.*"

"So," he said, "you sell *tang.* That's how you got all this stuff?"

He said, "A housefull—not everybody gets so much these days," he said.

"So what did you do?" He didn't say anything.

He started getting drunk—his mouth—drunk, I call that—it hit him, smashed him, smashed, smashed him! He ate and drank, he kept quiet. But the king every minute was digging at him, digging, digging. Well, little by little, that guy started to boast, you know? "Oh," he said, "I'll tell you," he said. "Only don't say I told you." (Telling would make him sick. Everything called magic, try to tell a lie. But this time, the guy was going to sell himself off!)

"Well," he said, "don't say I told you."

"Oh," said the king, "why say that to me?" The charcoal fly in his pocket went "Vyoo oo oo oo oo oo!" "Hey, hey," he said, "what's whistling like that?" said the king. "What's whistling like that?" "Oh, nothing," he said.

So he told the king, said, "You know what happened?" he said. "One day I was coming back from hunting—" The charcoal fly moved around in his pocket: "Vyoo oo oo oo oo oo," it said. "I was coming back from hunting. When I got home," he said, "I saw a nice woman." He said, "My latania house wasn't there—my cabin. There was a house. She told me not to be afraid to come in." He said, "the woman gave me her hand."

"Oh," the king said, "go on!" he said. "So why didn't you bring this woman here?"

"No," he said, "I couldn't." "Why?" "Oh," he said, "my lady, she's a pretty lady. She's pretty. I can't tell you why I didn't bring her. I don't know. I don't understand it myself." Well, the king wanted to meet her!

The charcoal fly came out of his pocket and began to sing, "Oh, hey, mama! papa said we are children of latania."

Unlike his Malagasy ancestor, this poor man denies having revealed the secret.

"Oh—" he went like this–he said, "no! I didn't tell, I didn't tell, I didn't tell!"

"Yes," it said, "you said it, you said it, you said it!" Quickly he harnessed his *milor* so as to run away. The charcoal fly, he ran to the center-post. "Oh, hey, mama! papa said we are children of latania."

"Oh no," he said, "I didn't say it, I didn't say it, I didn't say it!"

"Yes," said the fly, "yes, you said it, you said it, you said it!"

Well, the guy unfastened his horse from the post so as to mount. But what do you think, the fly got there before him. When it got there, it said, "Yes," it said, "mama," it said, "papa did say it!"

"He told?"

"Yes. He said he came, he had his latania house. He said when he came, he found you. He said the house was all built, the whole thing was ready."

He came back, he ate. Then the woman said to him, "OK," she said. "You have a bad tongue. You, a so-called man! I told you not to tell, and you told. So from now on, you stay in a house of latania! By the virtue of my little snuffbox, I am leaving. His cabin of latania must fall back into this place."

Well, the guy was furious. His latania house came back like before, and his three dogs. No more woman, no more house, no more charcoal fly! *Kriké!*

Christian Barat: *Kraké mésyé!*

Gérose Barivoitse: The key in your pocket, the shit in my sack!

So, you see, up to today, you see there are guys, they're on the road, they're beat, they're all plucked. They're there, they're insecure, they have nothing to live on, by his bad tongue, you see. No way to have anything. "Ah, such a thing as that, like that!" He was a boaster. So if he talks to anyone, a person, for example a woman or a girl, he has to tell his buddy, "Hey, never get to talk with her! But me–I'm smart. I'm a man, I am. In two–three days from now I've done it." He doesn't get anything, he [just] talks. Soon he talks some more to her. He looks, like that, he stands [there], he looks. Like a cardplayer on the side of the road. But if you don't talk, or you do your business quietly, you get along fine, you see. Nobody knows. But if you tell, "I'm talking to her, I'm talking here, I'm talking there," it's goodbye for you! 'Cause you wagged your tongue! Shouldn't say anything.

There, the story is finished. (Barat, Carayol, and Vogel 63–66)[34]

That this most voluble Réunionnais storyteller, of all people, insists on the importance of reticence shows the tenacity of the old Malagasy habit of withholding information. The vitality of Madagascar's traditions in Réunion is not something the French researchers have been keen to investigate.

Mr. Barivoitse is equally voluble in Ti Zan's many contests with the ogre Gran Dyab, as became obvious in his version of The Brave Tailor above.

84. Ti Zan's Bet

Gérose Barivoitse, Sainte-Suzanne, Réunion 1976

Ti Zan was a bad guy, a bad guy, really. Well, he made a bet, huh? There were several guys trying to marry the king's daughter, they didn't make it, they didn't score. The ones who started out to do it, Gran Dyab ate them. *Kap!* down they went.

Well, him, Ti Zan, he was kind of a do-nothing, nothing, kind of dirty, dirty, in bad shape. He thought about it, he said, "What do you have to do? All those guys, they go there, but they don't get to marry the king's daughter. Well," he said, "I'm gonna give it a try." So he went to try.

The king sent him off. "OK," he told him, "Can you go get Gran Dyab up there?[35] You bring him here. But," he said, "are you up to it?"

He said, "Yeah," he said, "I'm up to it."

So he said, "OK, off you go."

Well, he went, he climbed up, got up there, gave Gran Dyab a shout: "Hey big man! Hey big man!"

Gran Dyab was asleep. "Oh mama," he said. "Somebody's come here. As soon as they come I know. But you!" he said, "this guy like a mosquito," he said, "what did you do to get here, you?"

He said, "Now listen," he said, "there's something for us to talk over for a minute," he said. "I've come to get you to take you down below."

He said, "Down below, where?"

That Gran Dyab, he was a devil, I tell you—Gran Dyab, when I tell you Gran Dyab! A devil, really, Gran Dyab himself, he eats people, a wild beast.

He said, "Take me where?"

He said, "Down below. The king says for you to come to make a *kari*."

He said, "Me? the king said for me to go down there?" He said, "Well, who's coming to get me," he said, "the only Me?"

He said, "I tell you. Let's go cut some wood. Cut a little wood up here, and then go down. Each one take a bundle to see who carries the bigger bundle."

Gran Dyab said, "Me! I can carry a tree, I can."

"Oh," he said, "you, carry a tree? Well, I can carry more!"

"Oh," he said, "you carry more than me?"

He said, "Yes."

"Well, I bet I can carry more than you!"

So he picked up an axe and gave it to Gran Dyab. Cut a tree, cut, cut, cut—tree fell down, *fraa* . . . ! "There," he said, "Gran Dyab," he said, "we'll have to split it so each one takes one part." Gran Dyab gave one hit of the axe onto the wood, the wood opened up, the axe got stuck. Then, to pull it out, he said, "OK, pull!"

Gran Dyab said, "I'm pulling!"

"Look," he said, "you have to stick your hand in there," he said. "Take your hand, make a fist," he said, "stick it in there," he said, "then yank on it. Then you [can] take out your hand." Well, poor Gran Dyab really couldn't do it! The wood was wide open, he took both hands, stuck them in the wood, like this—the guy pulled out the axe. Gran Dyab was stuck. "Ah," he said, "now I'm pissed."

Then he said, "OK, let's go down, you'll have to carry it [like that]. Right! you look great. You have to carry it." Gran Dyab, his hand caught in there, on his head! Ti Zan climbed up into the branches at the back. They went on down. When they got there, the king was really pissed! Ti Zan said, "King, here's the guy you sent me for."

"Ah, ah, ah!" said the king, "phew!" he said, "How'd you do that? What the fuck can I do with this? What am I going to do with this? A *dyab* like that, a big tree like that? What'm I going to do with it? Take him out of here, kill him."

Right then they managed to destroy him. After that, he didn't destroy anybody, Gran Dyab. He took him down below, well, they went down—he scalded him.

Me, I passed by. I said, "Well, hey, Ti Zan! We're *kamarad* [pals]; his wedding day, huh! Well, I said, well, I didn't know. Well, I say, you got married, I said. Set me a place!

He said, "What?" he said. "You have to act like me too, huh? Go bring something from up there. Look for a strong guy, bring him here, you'll make it!"

Strong guy, guy's going to pursue me, pursue me, I tell you! I ran, otherwise the dog was set on me, I'm telling it to you today. Because back then, I used to walk pretty far. That whole Gran Dyab scene, I was with Ti Zan, I was. We were *kamarad,* Ti Zan and me!

But him, I tell you, sometimes, not a bad character, twice, you see, he's bad, you say, Look at that! Mmm-mmm. 'Cause sometimes, well, that one I tell you, Ti Zan, it's not Ti Zan, he's a liar. People in the old days, you know, in the old days; people of old days didn't want to give you the details, how it was. Well, they'd tell you a piece of Ti Zan, they'd tell you Gran Dyab and you, OK, it's not true. They tell you that so as not to—to wind up, you see. They tell you, "If that story is a lie, I'm not the liar; it was the ancestors that were the liars."

People in the old days—only sometimes it was true! Only they didn't give you the details of the thing, see. If you were a bit smart as a kid, you understood, more or less, see. Because people back then, talking in the old days, children weren't . . . Ah, no! Kids were imbeciles, see, *pas par lé paran.* So if you tried to hold a conversation, a good talk, it was "Kids, go, go out and play. Go out, go outside!" But see, there's some kids are crafty; in the old days, I was a crafty kid. When the grownups hid things, I sat a bit, quietly; I leaned in a corner, I listened.[36]

In the piece his editors consider Mr. Barivoitse's prize, Ti Zan again outwits Gran Dyab. All the interruptions are his own.

85. Ti Zan and His Red Rag

Gérose Barivoitse, Sainte-Suzanne, Réunion 1976

Gérose Barivoitse: *Kriké!*

Christian Barat: *Kraké,* sir!

Gérose Barivoitse: The key in your pocket, the shit in my bag! There's one good liver. Mr. La Foi [liver], he eats his liver with a grain of salt.

There was a little boy. His mother always wanted something. She says, "Oh, husband, go find something for me." She wanted a little water "with no frogs in it." Well, she says to his father, "Go, go look for it." And the wife was in the family way. Finally the husband, poor bugger, he went, but he didn't know what's water with no frogs. He got to some pool or other, dived in, brought it, got back to his wife, he says, "Here." The wife says, "No, that's not what I told you. Water with no frogs!" So he says, "I yelled. I asked if there was any frogs, nobody answered." He goes to see if there's any in there. Only the bugger went in a hurry to get the water, fast. He wanted to get home early. Well, before nightfall he got there. What did he do? He dived in, he arrived like to the river Sainte-Suzanne there, he dived in, he filled his gourd, went on his way. When he got there, he says to the wife, says, "There, I got it." The wife says "No, I tell you that's not it!" "OK," he says, "if that's not it, better you go yourself. I'm tired, walking since this morning."

So the wife started out. She went on the way, she climbed, more or less like into the Bagatel forest there. She got up there, ah, ah, she was tired. She did like that, she saw a little running stream, saw how small it was, two steps across. So what she did, she saw some bananas there, there were all kinds of fruit. Then she broke some off. She had a little basket. (Lots of times, I see my little basket, I think that, hey! Little basket like that, very nice.) Filled it with bananas, filled her gourd, went on her way. Went down to her house. But along comes that damn Gran Dyab. Uh-uh. He didn't see her, he looked around like this: "Ah-hah," he says, "I smell fresh meat around here." He says, "Someone's been here. Well," he says, "never mind, let 'em go, I'll catch 'em later." Well, a week later, when she got down to her house, she says to her husband, she says, "I got it." She says, "You, you didn't get all the way there. You're not a real man. Now I get to eat it, I won't give you any." With that she starts arguing with her husband. Finally the husband says, "OK, it's good. You managed to get it, good for you." Then she says, "Taste and see how good it is." The husband tasted, he says, "Hey, that's really good," he says, "is that really water?" the husband says. She says "Yeah, it's running water." The husband says, "Hey, that's not water, that's honey." She says, "Aaah, aaah, honey doesn't run like that. That's water. That's water with no frogs."

(And frogs can't get into something that way. That's oil there. Frogs'd be crazy to bathe in there, hey? Well, onward, enough.)

Next day she went back up again and got some more. But the third day, Gran Dyab says to himself, "No," he says, "they're destroying too much," he says, "I'm gonna keep watch." So he kept watch. The woman got there, did her usual, broke off some bananas. But her stomach was getting big, understand? Beginning two, three days already, getting, see? She filled her gourd with honey, took some bananas, everything she needed, started out. He caught her. He was watching, he found the place. Her basket was full. Ah, he bowed to her, Gran Dyab says, "Well, Madame," he says, "You know what you're doing?" "Oh," she says, "no, sir," she says, "I didn't know, I thought it didn't belong to anybody. I came . . ." "Yeah," he says, "you came

[here]?" She says yes. He says, "What you got in there?" "Oh," she says, "I'm in the family way, I want it." "Yeah," he says, "me too, I want it too." Then he says, "I don't know," he says, "when you have your baby, you have to give me that baby. Let's agree, OK?"

Gérose Barivoitse: *Kriké!*

Christian Barat: *Kraké,* sir!

Gérose Barivoitse: The key in your pocket, the shit in my bag! One good liver, two times Mr. La Foi eats his liver with a grain of salt. If he doesn't find it good, you have to have salt to eat it. Because if there's no salt, it's flat.

So!

Then, the poor woman, poor devil—devil's not poor—he got her baby. But Gran Dyab, two days, not yet, three days, not yet. "Ah," he says, "it—" he says, finally the woman had her baby. Well, Gran Dyab waited, eight days he had to . . .

(Nowadays a woman has her baby; she has the baby sitting down; next morning she goes out, she goes to the store, she goes to work, she goes walking. But in the old days it wasn't like that, she had to wait eight days before she went out, because . . . people in the old days said, "Ah-ah, be careful!" and it was true. Because today, there's young people who have a baby, she goes out, she comes and goes. As soon as one two three, she starts up again, see? She starts up. But in the old days it wasn't like that. If a family had a baby, ten days she stayed in. Before she'd go out, she'd wrap up well. But when she went out, she'd get her nerves back, all strong, all fixed up. Well, what the hell . . .)

Gérose Barivoitse: *Kriké!*

Christian Barat: *Kraké,* sir!

Gérose Barivoitse: The key in your pocket, the shit in my bag!

Well! So the woman got there the next day. Gran Dyab says to her, "Well, lady, did you have your baby?" She says, "Yes, I had him." "Good," he says, "that baby is for me." "Yes," she says, "OK." "So," he says, "go ahead. Take your honey, take it, it's yours. We made a deal." Then she came, she filled her thing, she went back. But Gran Dyab says to her, "No, now," he says, "tomorrow I'm coming to see your baby." "Yes," she says, "OK." "So," he says, "how'm I going to find him?" She says, "When you get there," she says, "I'm gonna put a little *langouti* [loincloth] on him."[37] She says, "When you go by all the children, ask which one is Ti Zan with the red rag." She says, "They'll show you him," she says, "yeah," she says, "take that one." Well, Ti Zan, that SOB, he was smart.

—Lots of times there's boys called Zan, they're dopes, but many times the one called Zan, mmmmm! he's serious, he's solid, he's smart!

Gérose Barivoitse: *Kriké!*

Christian Barat: *Kraké,* sir!

Gérose Barivoitse: The key in your pocket, the shit in my bag!

So, that, that's why I named my boys Zan: Zan Pyer and Zan René. So, I liked this and not that, I say, "OK, maybe, the guy will be—get lost. Finally I don't know if it'll be, if it's—because . . . not gonna break my head for Gran Dyab. That's how I am . . .

Gérose Barivoitse: *Kriké!*

Christian Barat: *Kraké,* sir!

Gérose Barivoitse: The key in your pocket, the shit in my bag!

So it went on. Gran Dyab, next morning he came down. He sharpened his teeth, he says he wanted to eat. But that Ti Zan was really smart. His mama says to him, "Zan," she says, "go, go to school, go play." He says, "Yes, mama." She says, "Don't take off your clothes, huh?" He says no. He gets there with his gang of *kamarad,* he says, "You know?" he says, "I'll tell you something," he says, "each one of you take a piece," he says, "whoever comes, asks which is Ti Zan with the red rag, then say we're all Ti Zan with the red rag." His friends are all loyal. He puts a little red cloth on all of them. "Ah," he says, "good boy!" he says. They were all playing. He ran a trick.

That damn Gran Dyab got there: "Hey kids!" They say, "Yes, big daddy!" He says, "Which one is Ti Zan with the red rag?" They say, "We're all Ti Zan with the red rag!" Gran Dyab says, "Oh, oh, oh, oh, oh, oh oh! to hassle an old fool like that! I'll eat you all, I'll eat you all, all! All Ti Zan with the red rag! But which one am I gonna eat?" Finally Gran Dyab took off, went back up. He got up there, found the lady, he says, "It's not like you said," he says. "I asked which one was Ti Zan with the red rag, they said all of them! So am I gonna eat them all? Huh?" he says, "I'm gonna eat all of them?" But the woman says, "I tell you there's only one." He says, "All of 'em there, can't tell anything—all! Aaah," he says, "change your ways, because that's not nice to me, hey! That's my honey you ate. That's my banana, all that fruit is mine that you ate, you are tricking me!"

Gérose Barivoitse: *Kriké!*

Christian Barat: *Kraké,* sir!

Gérose Barivoitse: The key in your pocket, the shit in my bag! Mr. La Foi ate his liver with a grain of salt. Nice grain of coconut! Ah, then he grilled the liver to eat. Claimed he was frying it, it took too long, he grilled it, snap!

Next day, the good lady went up, got up there, she says, "Grandfather," she says, "today you come to my house." She says, "I'll put his food out on the *farfar.* (In the old days they had the *farfar* [shelf], I don't know, a board. In the kitchen they had a little *farfar* out of bamboo, they put wood there, you could put anything on there for a while; it was a thing to put meat, all like that, she put it.)[38] So she put Ti Zan's food there. He went out to play, came back. His mother told him, "Zan!" He says "Yes?" She says

"Your food is there on the *farfar,*" she says, "go get it." Gran Dyab was waiting there to catch him and eat him. He's sitting there; Gran Dyab did like this [*gesture*]. Before he caught him, ah! he saw Gran Dyab's paw. See, Gran Dyab has a big paw. His paw stuck out, it did like this, he says, "Hey!" he says, "so that's where you are," he says, "don't move."

Uh! he turns into a rat, a big rat; he goes into the rice. He says, "There's a rat. It's coming to eat Ti Zan's food, going to eat it all." The rat comes, snap! It was that Ti Zan, only, see, he was kind of—Zan was clever. He comes and eats the whole thing. Eats his food, just like that, and leaves. "Mamma," he says, "here's the plate"—he did like this, he says "here's the plate." Ah, ah, the mother says, "Zan, you ate it?" He says, "Yes, mamma," he says, "I ate it up."

But what about it? This guy is cursed! But then Gran Dyab ate more.

Gran Dyab comes down to the place and starts to argue. "Look," he says, "lady," he says, "what's all this?" he says, "there was a big rat came to eat." "But," she says, "that was no rat," she says, "that was Ti Zan. You didn't get to eat him." He says, "Me eat an animal? Huh?" he says, "me eat a rat? Ecch," he says, "I'm changing the deal. If that's how it is, no good any more, the deal where you come to get my stuff up above." "But," she says, "I told you you had to catch the rat, had to eat him! OK," she says to him, "tomorrow I'll send him up there. Get ready—I'll tell him to go get a bag of charcoal up there, then when he comes, catch him. No—I'll send him to gather *zanbrovat* [pigeon peas] first." She says, "When he gets there, when he's gathering the *zanbrovat,* catch him." Ti Zan went up, he got there, he came back to eat—she says, "Zan," she says, "go get some *zanbrovat* up above, with—in that field." Gran Dyab hid in the tuft of *zanbrovat* there. Sat down like this, watching for Ti Zan. He sat there, sat there, watched like this. Finally Ti Zan got there with his basket. Some way away he turned into a black fly. See that bunch of big big black flies there? He stung him, like that. Gran Dyab was watching for him. He buzzed around. Gran Dyab says, "Ow, ow, ow!" he says, "Aie, aie, aie, aie, aie, aie—now—mmm, mmm, mmm! Hurts!" He fills his basket. He watched, watched, watched. He went back. Gran Dyab: "Ooh! Aie, aie, aie, aie! Brother, it hurts. Mm, mm, mm, mm, mm, mm!" He filled his basket with *zanbrovat,* got it. He got back down and says, "Mamma," he says, "here's your basket." She says, "Zan," she says, "you got it?" He says, "Oh, mamma," he says, "nothing else," he says, "I got the stuff."

Gran Dyab came there. His face was all lumpy—the black fly. He was stung, stung, his face swelled up like this. The woman said to him, "Hey," she says, "what happened to you?" "Aah," he says, "you made me get hurt," he says, "this is no good. Some animal stung me!" "Yeah," she says, "that was Zan." He says, "The black animal, I'm gonna eat that?" he says, "what do you think? You think I want to sting my tongue?" "Oh well," she says, "what am I gonna tell you? I told you to catch Zan, you don't want to do it.

"Well," she says, "last thing for you to catch him," she says, "I'll send him to fetch charcoal." She says, "You go in the sack of charcoal, then—no, say, tonight: I'll shave his head, make his head bald. I'll put him in the middle of the bed. I'll put his father in the corner and me on the outside." "Good," he says, "that'll be good."

(The papa there, the mamma on the outside; one had to be on the outside, one in the corner, one outside, him in the middle.)

She says, "When you come, feel, feel feel him. You'll find the guy with the bald head. Eat him," she says, "that's Zan for sure." Ti Zan didn't hear that, but he was watching, the way he did, chewing his piece of wood. He kept that—you understand, he liked his wood—his thing said to him, "Careful, that guy there, he might eat you tonight." So—poor Ti Zan—

Gérose Barivoitse: *Kriké!*

Christian Barat: *Kraké,* sir!

Gérose Barivoitse: The key in your pocket, the shit in my bag!

So that night Ti Zan came. His mamma plucked at his head, she says, "Here, you've got lice," she says, "we're going to shave your head clean." "OK," he says, "mamma, shave!" His mamma shaved his head really clean, done. He went to play, that night he came back to sleep. "Hey," she says, "tonight you sleep in the middle, huh?" she says, "Papa'll sleep in the corner, me on the outside." "OK," he says, "yes, mamma." She took the boy, put him in the middle. Madame on the outside, mister in the corner.

The time came. He listened well, everybody was asleep. When everyone was asleep, he took the scissors and cut his papa's hair all off. His father had a big mustache.

(Me, mine is short, but his papa, see, he had a nice mustache. If it's short like this, it's ugly, but a long time ago they cut it so it stood out. His mustache was tile colored, like Mr. Ango.)

So he cut his father's mustache all off, shaved his head, put it on his own head, and fixed everything up. Took his father's mustache, zap! Damn Gran Dyab got there, chewing his bit of curry, to put in his mouth. When he thought he caught Ti Zan, he caught the papa. Caught his father, there in the middle; he was in the corner. Gran Dyab felt, felt, felt. "Ah," he says, "I got him." Tough! Ate the father. Nowadays if you ate that, you'd say it was full-grown. "Ah, ah, ah, ah, ah!" he says, "Ti Zan wears down my teeth." The wife says, "Don't argue, just eat him!" "I'm doing it," he says, "he's like a root." So which one did he eat? The bugger! Chewed up the grownup.

In the morning, Ti Zan didn't move; he made like his papa. He put his mustache outside the covers, like this. The mamma says, "Hey, get up, get up." He didn't move, he was sleeping. The mustache was like this, the mustache stuck out. Like bad Lyev [trickster], he stayed like that all night. There he was like that, asleep.

Gérose Barivoitse: *Kriké!*

Christian Barat: *Kraké,* sir!

Gérose Barivoitse: The key in your pocket, the shit in my bag!

Next morning the woman called him to wake up. Time for him to go, she says, "Hey, still asleep, aren't you working today?" Ti Zan got up and jumped down to the ground. "Ah, Ti Zan," she says, "oh, my child, you're a curse. You've made your father get eaten by an animal!" "Yeah," he says, "mamma, the animal did what you said, not me. I don't know about it." "Eh," she says, "it was you who shaved your father's head, took his mustache and put it on your mouth!"

"Well," she says, "today you go fetch a bag of charcoal for me from up there." Then Gran Dyab spoke to her; she found Gran Dyab, told him she'd sent him for charcoal. He wanted to get this finished. But he didn't make it! So—

Gérose Barivoitse: *Kriké!*

Christian Barat: *Kraké,* sir!

Gérose Barivoitse: The key in your pocket, the shit in my bag!

Next morning she says, "Go up there," she says, "catch him in the bag of charcoal." He says, "Right." He went up. Damn Gran Dyab went inside the bag of charcoal. He sat like this. Ti Zan spied him from a distance; he got some Indian arrows. Soon as he did that, he got close, he shot him, zap zap! Gran Dyab said, "Ow, ow, ow! Aie, aie, aie, aie, aie!" He stayed in place. He didn't move. Ti Zan turned around to look; he said, "He's not dead yet." He hit him another shot, fyak! a shot with the Indian arrows. Stabbed Gran Dyab. Gran Dyab: "Oooh, uhhh," he says, "you're gonna kill me today. I'm dead." So he shot him again. Didn't move. Poor bugger, gave him one more. Looked inside. Gran Dyab rolled, he turned him, he rolled. Gave him another shot in the stomach. But before that, he put some more in his heart. Ti Zan looked at him. He couldn't get out of there. Little bugger looked at him, thwacked him, thwacked him, thwacked him. Oh well, finally, hit him some more, vyoup! Got him right in the stomach. Gran Dyab rolled in the big bag of charcoal, vap! He took and picked up the bag, put it on his back. Ah, got there, he says, "Mamma, OK, here's that bugger you were trying to have kill me. You—" Threw the bag down on mamma. The mother, ah, finished! Poor Ti Zan, he's at liberty, peacefully.

Story is finished, sir. [If] the story is a lie, I'm not the author, the grandparents long ago said it was true, that's no lie. Be careful! And Gran Dyab is still around, so be careful. Be careful with your kids, because nowadays Gran Dyab is starting up [again]. Finished.[39]

Ti Zan's mythical ancestor is Tinaimbuati (above). Given Mr. Barivoitse's ancestry, the influence of Madagascar on his pieces is no surprise (Renel, *Contes* 1:250–53; Birkeli 294–99). Farther back in Ti Zan's genealogy are Bantu stories in which trickster hides in charcoal or pumpkins, or the swallowing monster is reincarnated in a pumpkin, which then pursues people (Werner 205–21; Ottino, P., "Le thème" 219–51; Beaujard, "La lutte").

As to genre, Mr. Barivoitse's playful habit of switching between taleworld and storyrealm is a modern creole's take on the old Malagasy separation between *tantara* and *angano* (which, we already saw, was never as firm as the nineteenth-century missionaries hoped). It's difficult to know whether his realistic story about detecting a thief is fiction.

86. The Thief "Put Down Five, Pick Up Six"

Gérose Barivoitse, Sainte-Suzanne, Réunion 1976

Kriké!

Christian Barat: *Kraké mésyé!*

Gérose Barivoitse: The key in your pocket, the shit in my bag! One time M. La Foi ate his liver with a grain of salt—always, as usual, understand?

Well, there was a gang of men working to make a road. That is, to cut wood and make the road, the whole thing. There were about thirty of them or so. Well, when they came along to go to work, there was one old guy cutting wood. One of them had a good axe, you understand? *Kriké!*

Christian Barat: *Kraké mésyé!*

Gérose Barivoitse: Yup! The key in your pocket, the shit in my bag!

So he went. Regularly, every day, they did their work there. They worked, he plotted. But there was one there, he had a twisted mind. He had kind of a long hand, see. If he saw something, he had to put down five and pick up six. He was called *Poz sink, lev sis* [Put down five, pick up six].

Well, let's move along—they worked, worked, worked. A week went by with them working like that. The second week, that one gave a look at that axe; he went like this. Eleven o'clock came, time to eat. Everybody ate. He swiped the axe and hid it. He went down lower, took the axe, and went down and hid it down below.

When it came time to leave that evening, the man went looking for his axe to do his work and cut the wood. Not there! So he looked, looked, looked. He said, "Where did I put it?" *Kriké!*

Christian Barat: *Kraké mésyé!*

Gérose Barivoitse: The key in your pocket, the shit in my bag!

Finally it came time to leave. They stopped working. Then they went down the road a ways, went a little farther on. But the man who'd lost the axe went back. He went to ask the others. So he asked the foreman, said, "Foreman," he said, "in your gang, did somebody take my axe?" The gang all said "No." The foreman said, "Boys, you didn't take it?" "No," they said, "we didn't take it." "Well if you took it," he said, "tell, hey." "No." The foreman gave a look; he looked at one, his face was abashed. He said, "You didn't take it?" "No," he said. *Kriké!*

Christian Barat: *Kraké mésyé!*

Gérose Barivoitse: The key in your pocket, the shit in my bag!

Well, he stood up, made them get in line–put 'em all in line, like that. He said, "OK, I'm starting. First one," he said, "sing! And when you sing, put your arms in the air like this." He said

nothing. He said, "Go, leave here." He called the others and said, "Come!" He did that with all of them, all, all, all. Came to the last one and said, "Come here, you." The axe was under his arm, the little axe like a shingle. He sang—this was the foreman—

Tell, tell, tavalavalavalavala not me.
Tell, tell, tavalavalavalavala stole it.
Tell, tell, tavalavalavalavala pinched it.
Tell, tell, tavalavalavalavala uh, uh, uh!

Then he did it, except he lifted only one arm. The foreman said to him, "No," he said, "you have to lift both arms in the air, you can't lift one." He said, "Do like this":

Tell, tell, tavalavalavalavala . . .

"OK," he said, "the other arm, lift it." Then again,

Tell, tell, tavalavalavalavala not me.

He said, "Lift the other one."

Tell, tell, tavalavalavalavala

Bang, the axe fell. "Ah, OK," he said, so you're the thief."

Beating with a bundle of rattan–he said, "Everybody gives him two hits each. That's his punishment because he stole the axe." He said, "When I ask, you have to say yes." We had to find something hard, not a game. But . . . he didn't answer, he had the axe. Whack, whack, whack! Hit! Thirty guys. Just when they finished the whole bundle of rattan, I got there. *Kriké!*

Christian Barat: *Kraké mésyé!*

Gérose Barivoitse: Putting something in front of him to defend himself. I was too late, the guy was dead. I got there and said, "Why, why'd you beat him like that?" "Oh," they said, "he's a thief, we're disciplining him hitting him with rattan." I said, "Oh, don't hit him." Cousin, they gave me two hits on the corner of my ear! Kaf! Ee, that made me mad. Beating me. They gave me a kick and told me to come and tell it to you.

But today, these days, if you steal, the law catches you, they come after you. But long ago it wasn't like that. If you stole, they took rattan and punished you. But they punished you to death. But now, they sentence you, put you in prison, and then you'll get out. But long ago that was unknown—right away. Tan your hide!

The story is over, sir, madam. (Barat, Carayol, and Vogel 87–89)[40]

The storyteller has used folktale conventions to set off present-day reality, masking it in the language of symbol and critiquing it directly at the same time. He thereby makes his story into a text: he "entextualizes" it for Christian Barat's microphone. All performance is reflexive, but few performers, of whom Gérose Barivoitse is The King, go as far as he does in "making a stretch of linguistic production into a unit" and "put[ting] the act of speaking on display" (Bauman and Briggs, "Poetics" 73).

His countryman Germain Elizabeth, another star performer, was a more old-fashioned kind of tradition-bearer. M. Elizabeth (1899–198?), in his seventies by the time he recorded five tales for the Réunionnais research team, was more subdued. (It isn't hard to be more subdued than Gérose Barivoitse.) Nor was he a mixer of genres, or one who made up stories to "rhyme" with old ones. His family history comprised many moves from village to village; it saw the arrival in Réunion of radio, electricity, the automobile, and the airplane. His family was always poor; his biographer saw him living in a poor straw hut, which could have instantly caught fire, leaving him nothing but one cooking pot and the work clothes on his back (Vogel, "La Roche" 37). After he settled as a tenant farmer in 1926 in the village of Dos d'Ane, in the northwest part of Réunion, he raised pigs and cattle "more or less clandestinely" (Vogel, "La Roche" 38). With his neighbors he raised artichokes and garden cabbage, crops newly introduced at that time, and made his contribution to the declining *petit blanc* rural society. As a storyteller Germain Elizabeth was conservative, like his storyteller cousins the Grondins (Vogel, "La Roche" 25). They all took pleasure in honoring the French heritage of narrative. The three familiar, aspiring young women who begin his tale of Four Rose Blossoms show his respect for tradition. They are descendants of sisters found in a long-lasting European story, "The Two Sisters," found in Galland's *Thousand and One Nights* and published by the Grimms as "The Three Little Birds" (Zipes 220–305). To show similar respect, I translate his words without interruption.

87. Four Rose Blossoms

Germain Elizabeth, Dos d'Ane, Réunion 1976

There were three girls, the three were orphans. No parents, no *papa,* no *maman.* They didn't have any parents or anybody. Well, they spent their time walking, watching the people who made picnics in the forest or other places, and then they'd gather up whatever was left, a piece of bread, a jar of preserve that was left. That was how they lived. They grew up like that for a time.

One day they saw the king pass by, with his cook and his baker. When they went by like that, they followed them a little way behind. They acted so as not to be seen. When they reached the place where they were going to stop, they made a halt, the king, his baker, his cook. They stayed apart. Then the oldest one said, "How happy I'd be to marry the king's cook, and taste the soup before the king." Then they opened their ears, they heard afar off, but they didn't see.[41] The second one said, "Me, how proud I'd be to marry the king's baker, to taste the bread the cook eats." They still kept their ears open. The third one said, "Me, how proud I would be to marry the king himself, to sit at table with the king." Then when they understood the three things they'd said, the king told his cook, he said, "Tell the one who wants to marry you to come up."

So a pretty damsel arrived, nice as anything. The king said to his cook, "All right," he said, "listen, you look for a different one for you." Then he said,

"A beautiful person like this, she's not for a cook," he said. "I'm the one to marry her." And he said, "Call the one who wants to marry the baker." They called the one who wanted to marry the baker. He said to the cook, "You can keep yours; this is the one who attracts me. She's prettier, nicer, more . . . she will be for me." And then he told the one who'd wanted to marry the king himself to come up. When he saw her coming afar off, he said, "I don't know who this is," he said. "Take yours back," he said, "this, this is the one I have to have as queen, to eat at the table with me." Once they agreed, he said, "Listen," he said, "now we'll go to the palace, and then we'll have these weddings." They reached the palace: him, the king, his one, the one he'd chosen, the one he took. And each one married the one he had taken.

The king had set up two bells. He was always on the road. He said, "Listen," he said, "here's a golden bell. If my wife, if the queen bears a son in my absence, ring the golden bell. If it's a girl, ring the silver bell."[42]

It chanced that when she had her child, the king was on the road. The two sisters became jealous of their sister. So they took the boy and threw him into a stream, some way away, a bit far, and then they took a little dog and put it next to the queen. When he returned, they said to him, "Sire, the queen had a little dog." He said, "What? The queen had a little dog?" They said, "Yes, sire." They said, "You can see it for yourself, next to her, but she is still somewhat unconscious." The king came in and saw it indeed. He said, "This is not admissible! The queen! Take that little dog and bury it."

And next to the stream where they'd thrown the baby, there was an old fairy living near there. Close by, when she was drawing water from the stream, the old fairy found that baby thrown in. She picked up the baby. She took care of him, and then—"Whose baby is this?" But she gathered up the baby and took care of him.

But him, the king, he said, "The queen must not do that same thing a second time." At the end of nine or ten months, a year, she had another boy. They rang the golden bell. During that time, they went back to the baby and threw him in the same place. They took a little dog, put it with her. He arrived; they said, "Sire, the queen had a little dog." He said, "It can't be!" he said. "Second one," he said. "The queen—a queen is a human being," he said, "it can't be." They said, "Certainly, sire, go look, you have only to look."

But the king said, "Listen," he said to the queen, he said, "that's the second one." He said, "The third time you bring forth animals," he said, "the punishment you will get, if you have courage, you can bear it; if you have no courage, you will die." But the old fairy over there found the baby, by the stream where she went to draw water. She took it, gathered it up, took care of the child.

Nine months, nine, ten months, eleven months, she gave birth to a daughter. They rang the silver bell. The king was still away, and they took the little girl, they threw her in the same place. The king came back. They said, "Sire, "they said, "see, the queen had a little cat."

"Well," he said, "listen," he said. "A king has but one word. This is the punishment that must be given to the queen." He said, "Go make a hut near the gate. Put the queen in there with a guard, and let whoever goes in or out spit in her face."

Over there, the old fairy again found the baby, the little girl; she picked up the little girl, took care of her, raised her. The children grew up. The first boy got to be fourteen, his brother and his sister. They were taken to be brother and sister, that's how the children were; she had picked them up, and the old fairy saw that they were related. So the boy said to the fairy, "Fairy," he said, "allow us to call you mother," he said, "with all respect." It was the little fellow asking. She answered no. She told him the secret. She said, "You were thrown on to the bank of the stream where I went to get water, and you are foundlings."

"Well," he said, "how can we come to know who our father is, who our mother is, to tell us who our parents are if not you?" She said to him, "Well, listen," she said. "There's a place that's dangerous to go to, but it's there you have to search, eh! Only it's dangerous, dangerous. You have to follow some rules." That boy understood. "Even if it's dangerous," he said, "we have to find our parents."

"Very well," she said. "There is a place not very far from here, it's a garden where Four Rose Blossoms lives. She sleeps for six months. She has the dancing apple, the singing water, and the bird of truth," she said. "You will have to go fight with her to get those things." The boy, well, he said, "Agreed." She said to him, "Here is a horse, here is a sword. When you reach that place, you will hear your name called. You must not turn your head. When you get near that garden where you hear your name called, you must not turn your head. Go direct to the orderly. Tell the orderly you need to talk to Four Rose Blossoms. He will tell you that is impossible. Tell him that there must be a fight, but you will go in. Then he will allow you to go in. He will take you to Four Rose Blossoms.

"Ask her for the dancing apple, the singing water, and the bird of truth. She'll tell you it's impossible, you have to fight for them. Tell her, 'Let's fight.' Fight with your sword in your left hand. When she asks for mercy, demand satisfaction. If she says no, tell her you'll have to fight. She'll ask for mercy. If you tell her again that she has to give satisfaction, she will tell you no. Tell her you'll have to fight. The third time, that's when she'll give in and you'll get what you're asking for: the dancing apple, the singing water, and the bird of truth, and bringing everything in the garden back to life."

All these explanations the boy understood well, and then he left. And she said, "Now I'm setting up a glass of milk. If this glass of milk turns over, then he is [you are] staying there. Now do what I have told you to do, do what I have told you to do when you are with the dancing apple, the singing water, and the bird of truth."

He left, he took his horse. She had told him not to let his sword out of his left hand. He reached a certain distance, he heard his name called. He didn't turn his head, he went right on. He got near to the garden, he heard his name called. He turned his head. He transformed into a tomb, the horse transformed into a rosebush on the tomb.

There, the glass of milk turned over. "Your brother has stayed there," she said. "It's no good." The other brother said to the fairy, "Maybe he didn't follow the instructions, but I am going to avenge my brother and fight to find our parents. It's my part."

She said to him, "You followed what I said to your brother, everything I told him to do?"

He said yes. She said, "If I have to explain again, I'll explain again, but there's no need of explaining again if you followed well what I said to do, to reach Four Rose Blossoms there and fight." He said no, he understood everything.

So she said, "Here is your horse, go; and here's your sword, go ahead!" He got a certain distance when he heard his name called. He didn't turn his head, he didn't answer. When he got near the garden, he heard his own brother calling his name. That was too much for him; he turned his head. There he turned into a tomb and his horse into a rosebush on the tomb.

There, the glass of milk turned over. The fairy said to the girl, "Daughter, you'd better stay here by yourself—you are a lost child—rather than start again. If you don't obey the secrets I gave them, it's no good."

The girl said to the fairy, "One way or another, I have no brother any more, I have no parents either. I'm going to sacrifice my body, but," she said, "I will fight for my two brothers and fight to know if I had parents."

The fairy said to her, "Listen, if you go too, you [must] have remembered the explanations I gave." She said yes, she remembered them. "All right," she said, "if you remember the explanations, you are going to say back to me all the explanations I gave your elder brothers." She told the fairy then that on the way there would be people who would call her by her name and that she was not to turn her head. Once near the garden, they were going to call her name again, she must not turn her head. "Once in front of the orderly, tell the orderly that you need to speak to Four Rose Blossoms," she said. "He will tell you no. Tell him that if it's no, 'I'll fight.' He will obey you and he will lead you to Four Rose Blossoms."—It was her, the girl, explaining now to the fairy everything she'd given [as advice].—She said, "Once you are there, say to Four Rose Blossoms, 'I have come to get the dancing apple, the singing water, and the bird of truth.' She will tell you no. Tell her, 'Let's fight,' and fight with your left hand."

The fairy said, "Good, very good. How many times?"

"Once, twice, three times," she said. "The third time she will obey."

"All right," she said. "If that's how it is, when she goes to tell you that she is giving you Four Rose Blossoms, ask her to bring everything in the garden back to life." The fairy said, "You have understood well. If you follow well," she said, "you will find where your brothers are and you will find who your family are. There is your horse and there is your sword. Go. Done." She set up the glass of milk as encouragement.

She left, she went a distance, she heard her name called; she went on. She reached the garden; she heard her two brothers calling her name. No answer. She arrived before the orderly. The orderly stopped her. She told him that she was going in, that she needed to speak to Four Rose Blossoms. He told her that was not possible, she would not receive her. She said she was going in. He said no, that wasn't possible. She said if it wasn't possible they would have to fight, and then she would go in. The orderly said, "No, if it's necessary to fight, I'll take you to Four Rose Blossoms."

She got there. It was when she was sleeping for six months. She said to Four Rose Blossoms—Four Rose Blossoms—she asked her what she wanted. She wanted the dancing apple, the singing water, and the bird of truth. She said to her, "No, it's impossible." "Well," she said, "Let's fight!" They fought, the two of them. She cried for mercy. "Mercy? So give satisfaction." She said no. "So let's fight." For the second time she cried for mercy. She said, "Satisfaction!" "No," she said, "I cannot give satisfaction." "So let's fight." For the third time she cried for mercy. She said, "Satisfaction!" She said yes, she would give satisfaction. She said, "Here is the dancing apple, the singing water, the bird of truth—and may everything in the garden come back to life." She said, "After you pass through the gate, call your two brothers and everything there will come back to life."

She left and reached the gate. She said the names of her two brothers, and she saw them come out of the tomb, her brother with his horse the rosebush. They mounted her horse and all three set forth. Now everything in the garden was up again, like what happened to the two brothers.

They reached the fairy. The fairy said, "Your sister has more courage than you, and then she followed the instructions. . . ."[43] Now she really saw what she was given, what she had been sent for to get from Four Rose Blossoms. And now, the three, each on a horse, were turning this way and that and went a little way towards the village. But the king saw them. He saw this beautiful person, he'd never seen someone so beautiful in his kingdom. And he asked where she'd come from, how she had lived without his finding her. He came before them. He asked all three if they were of his kingdom. So they answered yes. He asked them how they had been raised. They said they had been raised by a fairy who lived near the stream over there. He said to them to lead him to the fairy so he would find out, to see if it was true. They led him to the old fairy as he asked. He asked the old fairy if these were the children she had taken in. She said yes, these were abandoned children she 'd given a home to, finally . . . there were the three, but still . . . Oh! but he said, "They are noble young people, they . . . never did I suspect there were young people in my kingdom, such beautiful, noble persons, so . . ." And he invited them to dine; he said, "If you would care to dine at the kingdom [palace] with me."

So the fairy said to them, "You could go dine with the king, since he invites you." But the fairy said to the king, "I am coming [too], only I must bring with me the dancing apple, the singing water, and the bird of truth." The king said, "Not at all. They will amuse us." He took a look, he saw them. "They will amuse us during the meal; you have only to bring them."

The day they went to dine as agreed, all three arrived on horseback at the gate. When they reached the gate, the sentinel stopped them. She said to them they must spit on that person. The apple danced, the water sang, the bird said, "One does not spit on a human being's face." The fellow listened. The others acted as if they were turning away. The king came before them, he saw them at the gate, and he came to meet them. The orderly said, "Sire, they do not want to spit on that person placed at the entry." The bird repeated, "One does not spit on a human being's face." The king too listened to the bird. The king said, "Allow them to come in." And then he said that it was he who'd invited them, that they had arrived there and were being turned away because they did not spit on. . . . But the orderly was only doing as he was told.

They went in, and the king had them pass into the salon. The king found this system admirable, the dancing apple, the singing water, and the bird of truth. They went to table. And there in the course of conversation, the apple danced, the water sang, the bird twittered and uttered some rules.

When they'd eaten and the meal was over, the bird asked the king for a melon as dessert. The king did not move, and listened. The damsel answered, "Sire, he is asking you for a melon as dessert. Once he has asked, that's a rule." A king, he'd said, can not do the contrary, and he asked for a melon as dessert.

Again the bird addressed the king, as he was cutting the melon: "Sire, what did you find in your melon?" The king said, "In a melon there are melon seeds." He repeated to him three times, "You do not find seeds of *sitrouy* [pumpkin] in your melon?" He said, "No, there can't be pumpkin seeds in a melon!" "No cucumber seeds either?" said the bird. "No, in a melon one has melon seeds."

And then it said, "Sire, how did you think that a human being could make dogs and cats?" The king stopped, surprised. The bird repeated, "You thought a human being could make dogs and cats." The king said, "I don't understand." It said, "You don't understand? Well," it said, "here are your two sons and your daughter. They are the queen's children, who were thrown out by their aunts." The king said, "That's not possible." He made the bird repeat it three times. The bird said, "That is the mother of these children who is at the gate, punished by receiving the spit of all those who pass. And she is still their mother. That is the queen whom you have put down there."

The king said he could not have done otherwise. He went over to the three children and embraced them. He went down there, he had the queen set free from her sentence, and at the same instant said to her two beautiful sisters, "The queen has undergone suffering, it is your fault. It was you who threw the children out. The old fairy gathered them up and raised them, but you, you will be burned tomorrow morning."

He went there, he took up the queen, he cleansed the queen, and she went back into the palace with her children. (Decros 267–93)[44]

Like his king and his bird of truth, Mr. Elizabeth could not act differently: he honors both social hierarchy and folktale convention, following precedents faithfully. The girls wish for husbands; the wife is calumniated; the children have adventures and are restored, all as the tale has been told in France (Delarue and Tenèze 2:633–48). Where then is the novelty we expect from creolization? A creole society is also a colonial society, which must make space for conservatism. Germain Elizabeth doesn't even localize the story, as his Malagasy predecessors did. But he does keep his own language. Merely to tell an old tale in Réunionnais Kreol is to resist the incursion of schoolroom French. Linguistic resistance is "so caught in the tissue of the work that it there takes on a new status, its immediate nature is transformed" (Macherey 297).

When he comes to tell his version of the famous tale The Smith Outwits the Devil, the European smith is not a smith, nor is the devil a devil, but the story voices creole resistance to authority. In a Mauritian version, Ti Zan, the hero corresponding to the smith, more closely resembles the Grimms' Brother Lustig (Grimm and Grimm 291–300). He lives alone, is scorned as a bad sort, and owns nothing but his deck of cards, a little bench, and a *zamalak* tree (Carayol and Chaudenson, *Les aventures* 36–63, *Contes créoles* 23–36). In all the islands, gambling at cards takes on symbolic significance in tales (Gallob 249–51). So it does in real life, where men play cards during wakes instead of listening to this performance, in which the central character is named Cardplayer (Carayol 12). Mr. Elizabeth's hero, like Ti Zan, will proclaim the victory of *petits blancs* over authority.

88. Cardplayer (The Smith Outwits the Devil)

Germain Elizabeth, Dos d'Ane, Réunion March 1976

There was a fellow, everybody called him Cardplayer. That's what he did. Every place he went, he had his cards in his pocket and he'd beat just about everybody. He'd find some fellow in the road, a child, anybody, he'd say, "Hey, let's have a card game." He played for money. Even a child going twice to the store with money, he's playing cards, he invites him, "Come on, play," and pretty soon he loses.

The universal weakling, we think; the kind of hero we recognize, who will win out over those who are stronger; supports himself only by his wits; lives alone.

Well, he had a little house, he had a kitchen, he did for himself. He had a pot, a pot to cook food for six, seven people. He took his measure of rice, put it on the fire in the morning; he played cards. Eleven o'clock came; if he won, he'd eat it all; evening, he'd put his rice back on the fire and eat it. If he didn't finish it at eleven o'clock, well, he left it for night. So he had more time to play cards.

If a Tamil (both Réunion and Mauritius have many Tamil-speaking people) could be listening, he might recognize a skillful gambler who immediately spends what he earns in a day (Thompson and Balys 192). A white Réunionnais listener would see Cardplayer differently. Living alone, cooking for himself, avoiding work, hustling everybody around him, he is a realistic portrait of a stereotype that has been alive in Réunion for at least a century and a half. He is the *petit blanc* as the bourgeois sees him, here captured in fiction. Similarly in another society of class conflict, African-Americans use the white stereotype "as an aggressive weapon against the very society which imposed it" (Abrahams, *Positively Black* 60).

So one day one fellow says to another, "Go and meet God and tell him 'God, come and get this Cardplayer here on earth,' " he says. "He's troublesome, this fellow," he says. "He's played cards everywhere in the street, he's taken four sous from children and adults alike," he says. "It would be better if God came and took him away."

The second man complains to God, who has foreknowledge.

So then one says, "I'll go see."

He gets there, he talks to God, he says, "I have come to see you," he says. "There's a man who's bothering everybody on earth," he says, "with his card games. He goes up one side and down the other. He's annoyed everybody, prevented people from working. A child going to the store, he pesters the child into playing cards. He takes money off the child."

God says, "Is his name Cardplayer?"

He says, "He's the Cardplayer."

So he said yes, he would come, he would come. He would go see if it's true.

The God of regional folktale, *Bondyé,* is an "oikotype," a local remodeling of the French *bon Dieu* on the model of the Malagasy sky-god, who sought to repress the earth hero. The eighteenth-century French word for the deity (Delarue and Tenèze 1:350; Sydow) was reshaped under the influence of nineteenth-century preachers. Their word *bon Dieu,* one historian writes, "deserves . . . a detailed study" of its "semantic transformation" (Prud'homme 26). Mr. Elizabeth's twentieth-century *Bondyé* denotes one transformation: he is a civil servant. So are the Holy Ghost and Saint Peter.

God talked to Holy Ghost and Saint Peter, he said, "Let's go see this Cardplayer," he says. "If it's true, we have to get him off the earth." When they got there, they got to him around five o'clock, they said to him, said, "Are you the Cardplayer?"

He says, "Yes, why?"

They say, "Well, we've heard about you. But," they say, "it's late," they say, "can we get hospitality from you?"

He said, "Why not?" he says, "only," he says, "you see what a small house I have," he says. "There's my pot, and," he says, "I have only one measure of rice." He says, "You can have a place to sleep here," he says, "sleep however you can. And each of us'll have a mouthful, we'll share."

"All right," they say, "that's fine."

So he took his measure of rice, washed it, put it in the pot. The others sat down and talked, he said, "Maybe that rice is cooked." OK, he looked, it was already cooked. He took a cup of water and put it in. The others were talking. When he looked, it was already cooked.

They said, "What about that rice there, isn't it cooked, then?" The rice was rising up in the pot. He went, he picked up two cups, took them out. The pot was half full.

He went to look, he said, "It's cooked, but," he said, "there's so much rice, how'd it get like that?" The others didn't answer; the others didn't say anything to him, but they took some to eat and they ate. All four got filled up. They were pleased with him. They said he was tops in politeness, in proper behavior to make sure everyone had enough to eat; and the others lay down to sleep.

Observers have always credited the *petits blancs* for their hospitality. They have often been too proud to accept assistance (Robequain 390). During World War II, when the economic isolation led almost to famine, the poverty of Germain Elizabeth's people reached a new low; he himself was impoverished. But his hero asks, instead of payment, that his little bench, his door, and his orange tree be given power to restrain at will all those who come into contact with them.[45]

Next morning, well, they said, "That's fine," they said, "how much do we owe you?"

He said they didn't owe him anything, he said. "For that little bit you ate and drank," he said, "little place to sleep, and you didn't sleep well either?" They said they'd slept fine. "Well," he said, him too, as usual, he said, he'd slept fine too.

God said to him, "If you don't demand anything," he said, "then ask me a favor."

He said, "Favor?" He said, "What kind of favor could I ask you?"

He said, "Ask for something you want," he said. "I'll give you satisfaction."

He said to God, he said, "As a favor," he said, "I ask you: see that little bench there," he said. "Anybody who sits there, they can't get up."

God said, "OK, it's done."

Holy Ghost said, "Well, me too, ask me a favor too."

He said, "Oh, you too? What can I ask you for?" Then he said, he asked for what he wanted. "Well, I'll tell you," he said. "When somebody is in that doorway there, if he leans on the door, he can't move. He's stuck." "Yes," he says, "that's done."

Saint Peter, now he said, "Me, what'll you ask me as a favor?"

He said, "All three of you want to give me a favor?" He said, "See that orange tree there," he said, "if someone climbs it without me telling him to—if he climbs it," he said, "until I tell him he can come down, he can't come down." "Yes," he said, "that's all right, done."

The three of them left, and God arrived up there. He talked to Death and said, "Say, there's a really troublesome cardplayer down there," he said. "Go and get him."

Death went and got there and called out.

He says, "Who's there?"

"Me, Death."

He says, "You, Death? You're coming after me?" he says. "Why?"

He says, "God told me to come get you."

He says, "He is crazy," he says, "that God," he says. "I'm still young!" he says, "I don't bother anybody with my cardplaying. I've had a good time on earth! Me go with God, why?"

Death becomes an apologetic petty messenger, just obeying orders.

"Well," he says, "God told me to come get you," he says. "I don't know," he says. "Get organized, and when we get there, explain to him."

He says, "It's no good."

He says, "You have to go, I'm telling you. He sent me for you!"

"OK," he says, "there's that little bench there. Sit for a minute," he says. "I'll get ready, and then we'll go." He went and sat on the little bench. "Good," he says, "you sit there. Me," he says, "I'm going. I'll go play cards."

Death is not just stuck to the bench; like any civil servant, he is stupefied at Cardplayer's lack of ambition—not to conquer or outwit anyone, as the animal tricksters do; only to go play cards.

"Hey," he says, "you're going to play cards?" He says, "I told you already, we're going to see God. You're going to play cards?"

He says, "Yeah, I'm going to play, yes."

Death says, "I'm telling you let's go!"

He says to Death, "Not me, I tell you," he says. "I'm going to play cards." He's on the little bench, he tried to get up but he was caught.

"Play cards?" he says. "God will blame me," he says. "We'll be late," he says, "I tell you let's go!"

He says, "I'm telling you no, it's no good! Especially with you, Death, taking me to God!" He says, "No good for me," he says. "I want to go play cards, I do." He tried and tried to get up, but no.

He says to the cardplayer, "Let me go," he says. "God will blame me when I get there," he says. "Let me go," he says, "I won't take you." Cardplayer says, "What, what! You'll take me with you!" He says, "No. I promise I won't take you," he says. "It's late already," he says. "I'll go up there, I'll tell God what happened to me here with you." He says, "Let me go!" Cardplayer says, "You won't take me?" He says no. OK, he says, "Move, get up, move!"

Death has become an inept intermediary between man and the impatient God.

Death went on his way, he went; he reached God. God says, "Where's Cardplayer?"

He says, "God, if you knew what happened to me with that Cardplayer! He told me to sit on the little bench while he got ready," he says. "I was stuck on the little bench. I had to make him a big promise to get free!"

God says, "Did I send you to sit on the little bench? I told you to go get Cardplayer. Go get Cardplayer!" He says, "Sit on the little bench, what for?"

"Well," he says, "God," he says, "he told me to sit there. I didn't know!" He says, "After that I was stuck there, I couldn't get up," he says. "I had to promise not to take him so he'd set me free."

"OK," he says, "I tell you, go get Cardplayer. I don't know about anything else. I command you. Go and obey."

He went back down, he got there, he called out. Cardplayer says, "What, are you back here again, Death?"

He says, "Yes, God told me to come get you," he says. "No deals."

He says, "No deals, eh?"

"You have to go."

He says, "I'm not going!"

He says, "What, you're not going?" He says, "You have to go. No deals, you have to go. He told me to come get you," he says. "Yesterday you caught me on the little bench," he says. "I told that to God. God sent me back."

"OK," he says, "never mind," he says. "Sit down a minute."

He says, "What? on that little bench?"

"OK," he told him, "just stand there a minute and wait for me," he says. He stood and the door held him; he was stuck. Then Cardplayer says, "OK," he says, "the door is holding you," he says. "I'm going to play cards."

He says, "What do you mean, play cards?" He says, "I told you, no deals. You have to go."

Cardplayer says, "I'm not going." He says, "You stay there."

Well! that fellow in the door was mad. He struggled to get free. "No more deals, Cardplayer," he says, "let me go, I tell you! God up there, second trip, he sent me to call you, bring you."

Cardplayer says, "There," he says, "don't let him go," he says. "If you're going to take me, I'm not letting you go!"

In the end, he says, "Cardplayer," he says, "let me go," he says. "I'll go tell God what happened to me, and then, then I'll go. I won't take you."

Cardplayer says, "If I let you go, you'll take me."

He says, "No, I promise not to take you," he says. "Let me go."

Cardplayer says, "If you won't take me, I let you go. Go on, get out of here. Get away from that door!"

He left the door. The fellow went on his way, Death left. He arrived up there. God says, "What's this, Death?"

"God, let me tell you what happened to me," he says.

He says, "I bet you went back and sat on that little bench."

He says no, he says, "the door held me," he says. "It held me, I was stuck in the door."

God says, "Did I send you to get stuck in a door?" he says, "I sent you to get Cardplayer," he says. "Go get Cardplayer. No deals. I need him here, I need to get him off the earth!"

He says, "God," he says, "he caught me with the door there," he says. "I struggled to get away, I couldn't do it. I had to promise him not to take him so I could get free."

God says, "Go, get out of here. Go get Cardplayer," he says. "Last trip, get it? Be careful."

So—he went down, he got there, he called out. Cardplayer says, "What? Death here again? What do you want?"

He says, "God told me to come get you. You have to go there!"

He says, "No."

He says, "What do you mean, no? You're going!"

"OK," he says, "sit on the little bench there."

He says, "What? on your little bench?"

"OK," he says, "stand there a minute by the door, and then—"

He says, "What?" he says, "and not move from there?" he says. "Let's go," he says, "you have to go!"

So he's standing outside. The orange tree there was ripe. Cardplayer says to him, "If we're really going, well," he says, "what am I gonna do? OK," he says. "Look at that orange tree, it's ripe," he says. "While I'm getting ready," he says, "go pick some," he says. "Pick four. Take two for yourself and take two for God."

So he climbs the orange tree, and when he was up there, Cardplayer says, "I'm going to play cards, I am."

He says, "No," he says, "I'm coming down so we can leave." He says, "You're not coming down from there." He says, "What, not come down?"

Cardplayer says, "No, you're not coming down."

He says, "Huh, not coming down?"

"Right," he says, "not coming down!" he says. "Wait for me," he says, "I'm going to play cards," he says, "when I tell you, I'll decide when to leave, I'll let you go."

He says, "I tell you let me go, Cardplayer," he says. "You caught me on the little bench, you caught me in the door, now you're catching me in this orange tree! OK," he says, "what do you want?" he says. "God told me it was like this, that you're a troublemaker on earth. He told me to come get you."

He says, "I don't make trouble for anybody on earth. I don't trouble God, I don't trouble—only the ones who play with me," he says. "Well let me go, I tell you, I'm going!" Cardplayer says, "No, you're gonna take me, I'm not letting you go!"

In the end he had to make a promise to Cardplayer: let him go, and he would go tell God how he'd been caught. Cardplayer says to him, "You're gonna take me," he says, "if I let you go, you're gonna take me! I'm not letting you go!"

He promised Cardplayer not to take him. Cardplayer then, he says, "Come down and get out of here!"

He got back up there with the oranges for God. God says to him, "Where's Cardplayer?" He says, "God," he says, "he caught me on his orange tree there," he says, "and wouldn't let me go," he says. "Still," he says, "he sent you two oranges and told me to give them to you." He says, "I don't need any oranges! I didn't send you to pick oranges! Did I tell you to go climb an orange tree?" He says, "I have to go get Cardplayer, that's all there is to it."

Still the petty functionary, Death resigns himself to a fourth attempt.

He had to take care of it. He went down. And he says, "You go get him. Be careful what happens there or you won't get him."

Well, he went right away. He got there, he called out. Cardplayer says, "What, is Death back here again?" he says. "Why have you come back?"

He says, "Today you have to go," he says. "God told me to come get you. No deals this time. No more bench, no more door, no more orange tree. You have to go."

Finally he says to Death, "If I have to go," he says, "wait till I get my deck of cards." He went and got his deck of cards and put it in his pocket. He took a bag, put it on his shoulder like this, and he went along. He followed behind Death.

The final episode in Germain Elizabeth's Cardplayer tale exemplifies cultural creolization. European tradition contributes Cardplayer's expulsion from Heaven (Aarne and Thompson 121); African tradition puts a familiar frame around it. Hell is forgotten, in favor of a two-sided conflict between the "little man" and constituted authority. As Mr. Elizabeth tells it, Cardplayer earns his way to Heaven.

Then he saw Gran Dyab a little way away and he says, Cardplayer says, "Wait for me a minute," he says, "till I have a game with Gran Dyab."

Death says, "I'm gonna be late!"

He says, "Just a minute. Just one hand." He gets near Gran Dyab, he says, "Gran Dyab," he says, "let's make a deal."

Gran Dyab says to him, "What?"

He says, "Let's play a game. If you win, you eat me." He says, "See, Death is over there. Either I go with Death or die in Gran Dyab's mouth, what difference?" He says, "Eat me if you win, and if I win, you give me twelve little devils."

Gran Dyab says, "Sure!" he says, "Cardplayer, you think you can play cards with me?"

To win, Cardplayer becomes an African-style trickster: he plays two strong antagonists off against each other. It's the deceptive tug-of-war again (Thompson, *Motif-Index* 4:238; Crowley, *Folktale* 14), often told in the islands as an animal tale (Baissac, *Folklore* 25–33; Goswami 1–3; Hassam and Rassool 177–80).

He played the game. He managed to beat Gran Dyab. Gran Dyab went and got twelve little devils and gave them to him. He took them and put them in his bag, put it on his back, he says, "Death, you see, we weren't playing around," he says, "let's go!"

He got to Saint Peter's gate. "Hey," he says, "Saint Peter," he says, "I got him."

Saint Peter says, "You're bringing Cardplayer?"

He says, "Yes, here he is."

"Good," he says, "bring him in." He comes in. He says, "What's that on your back?" He says, "That's what he won on the way here." He says, "He won something?" He says, "He played with Gran Dyab. He won twelve little devils." Saint Peter says, "Here? No devils coming in here!" "OK," he says, "Saint Peter," he says, "I won them," he says. "What am I gonna do with them?" he says. "Give me some place to put them, some place in a corner somewhere." He says, "No! No devils coming in here!" he says, "well," he says, "leave your little devils outside!" He says, "No, I'll put them by the door, like this."

And he put his bag of little devils on the ground.

Mr. Elizabeth gives his hero a verbal victory too, in a reproach to Saint Peter:

He sat down, and looked hard at Saint Peter, like this, and says, "Wasn't it you, a little while back, that came down and asked me for hospitality?" He says, "There were three of you."

Saint Peter says, "Yes," he says, "I was there."

"Well," he says, "the three of you, you fellows are really something," he says. "You came to my house, I took you in, I made rice, I gave it to you, I gave you a place to sleep. Now when I get here, I can't come in because I'm carrying some little devils! You're really something!" He took his pack of devils, went out of there, because he didn't want him to come in with his devils. (Barat, Carayol, and Vogel 69–74)[46]

Cardplayer has successfully played Gran Dyab off against Bondyé. Germain Elizabeth (or a predecessor) has successfully remodeled the African tug-of-war to motivate the international motif of going to Heaven but not being admitted.[47] Cardplayer has become a representative of the imperturbable *petits blancs* of la Réunion.

Similar symbolism, with fewer realistic touches, surrounds the heroes when the plot is told in other islands. The same plot in the Comoros reads like an allegory of the conflicts that have led to attempts at secession, successful in the case of Mayotte, unsuccessful for Anjouan. In a Mauritian version of the 1970s, Lucifer gives Ti Zan a place among some demons who are playing cards and smoking grass. "OK, let's play," he says. "But do you have money?" "We don't use that here. We use charcoals." "Must be a drag," he says. "I'll put one condition. Every time I win, you give me a little demon." That day and every day, Ti Zan wins fifty demons, until an angry Lucifer ejects Ti Zan from hell (Carayol and Chaudenson, *Les aventures* 36–63, *Contes créoles* 23–36). A Seychellois version, still less realistic, drawn from a different strand of European tradition, emphasizes the allegorical quality of the hero by naming him *Mizèr* (Poverty) (Delarue and Tenèze 1:346).[48] He refuses to ask for a place in heaven; Poverty will reside on earth forever after (Alsdorf-Bollée and Chaudenson 64–67). Only in Réunion is the hero such a realistic portrayal of the life of the storyteller's community.

Star performers elsewhere in the Indian Ocean islands are losing their anonymity. One is Aïsha Hussein, known as Ma Sula, who lives in the village of Sada on Mayotte and has been studied by Sophie Blanchy (Blanchy, "Lignée"). Another from Mayotte is Afiati Sufu of Mtsapere, whose energy and presence leap off the printed page (Blanchy et al.). Afiati Sufu is a postmodern Mahoraise: she sees storytelling as cinema. "*Hale halele,* Tales of old," she begins. "*Vwuka mutru nako mutru,* There was a man among men"—an oft-used Comoran formula. Her story is another version of Four Rose Blossoms, but her heroine, isolated by orphanhood and scabies, is far more aggressive than Mr. Elizabeth's tame sisters. So are her brothers, who bargain with the king for elegant clothes and money. Three times in this performance, Afiati Sufu indicates, though she doesn't always perform, the Comoran habit of repeating a whole narration from its beginning, which is doubtless influenced by Qur'anic schooling. Her adaptation of the standard closing formula is true creolization: "I left them with their nonsense. I took my cinema and all these stories of bad luck, I came home, I cultivated my rice to eat and minded my business" (Blanchy et al. 64–97).[49]

In Seychelles, the radio broadcaster Samuel Accouche is famous, indeed celebrated, for elaborating and reworking traditional materials. I return to him below. Anonymity, however, has some advantages for a performer. In Mayotte in the 1970s, where storytelling closely resembled the Sakalava storytelling of northwest Madagascar sixty years before, there was a new reason a collector would conceal the identities of narrators: the possibility of reprisal. It is common knowledge in Mayotte that performance directly criticizes social life. Anonymity meant protection (Gueunier and Said).

Specially gifted performers, building on the plurality of symbol systems imposed by history, create a "creole aesthetic." There, as Sydney Joseph illustrates, and as Caribbeanists know, creativity and imitation are inseparable (Brathwaite 16). Cultural censors to whom a response must be made, such as Nelzir Ventre's priest who forbade African-style singing and dancing, are ever present. Consequently, "new, unexpected exchanges" enter into everybody's behavior (Brathwaite 25). In verbal art, performers symbolize ambiguous or ambivalent attitudes to authority in ambiguous, ambivalent actors such as Cardplayer, objects including Ti Zan's balloon, or incidents such as killing seven flies at one blow. The creole aesthetic of the Southwest Indian Ocean serves as a model for a literary aesthetic that takes in both written and oral literatures, just as the creole islands are a microcosm that makes visible the forces behind the cultural convergences of the postmodern world (Haring, "Cultural Creolization").

4
Keys

> History . . . is not a single time span [*durée*]: it is a multiplicity of time spans that entangle and envelop one another . . . and each one of these spans is the bearer of a certain type of events. (Foucault 430)

Gérose Barivoitse continually tells you he has the key in his pocket. Sydney Joseph, telling his story of Ramkalawar, adds peacemaking and reconciliation to his hero's acquisition of a wife. His audience can perfectly well grasp the "key": narrative conventions are being transformed and reworked. Initially, Madagascar had the region's key in its pocket. That place, so consciously and deliberately conservative, was at one stage a "preliterate 'Creole' civilization'" (Ottino, P., "Mythology of the Highlands" 961). Malagasy continually assert that they change nothing in *fomban-drazana,* the customs of their ancestors. Yet those ancestors were already an Indonesian-African blend (Vérin, *Madagascar* 41–45, 48–49). Then, Indonesian ideas of kingship, Indian modes of marriage, and other "ancient and more recent symbols" came in, which "continue to influence and color one another reciprocally" (Ottino, P., *L'Étrangère* 389). The transposition of one or more systems of signs into another was the key.

Twelve years after French occupation, for example, Gabriel Ferrand discovered that the early Malagasy had creolized the Arab calendar by attaching Sanskrit names to the months (Ferrand, "Note"). Ferrand—Arabic linguist, cultural historian, diplomat—uncovered Arabic and Swahili contributions to Malagasy language, studied Muslim communities in the region, and explored the African contribution to the settlement of the island (Kent 21–22, 177). Folktales (*angano*) and other symbol systems would always reflect and remake foreign-born modes of production. The theoretical question now is whether the regularities of remodeling found among creole societies constitute a "creole narrative grammar": whether the "ambivalent acceptance-rejection syndrome; its psycho-cultural plurality," which Kamau Brathwaite finds in the Caribbean, expresses itself here in the reconstructing of borrowed narratives (Brathwaite 16); whether it is a special feature of creole narrative grammar to place "two entirely coherent but entirely incompatible readings," which the critic Paul de Man found in so much European literature, into one utterance; whether performance of creole tales is an "advanced and refined mode of deconstruction" (de Man 17). In other words, do creole societies offer a three-dimensional restatement of principles of literary theory?

In his time, Gabriel Ferrand could not, of course, let go of the chimerical search for authenticity, which had been championed by Herder, Rousseau, and the Grimms, and which continues to rule folkloristics (Bendix). When the world's best-known folktale heroine arrived in Madagascar, and her borrowed story was remodeled "to fit pre-existing cultural emphases" (Kluckhohn 168), Ferrand didn't allow himself to recognize her name. I translate and condense.

89. Cinderella 1: The Three Princesses and Andriamohamona

Antambahoaka storyteller, Mananjary, Madagascar 1880s

There were three sisters, they say, daughters of a king, living in a village. Prince Andriamohamona [Gentleman Prince], son of the king of another country of wide renown, came to marry them. He came before them carrying a golden staff.

Two favorite Malagasy moments follow: the young people reciprocally faint and have to be revived, and the girls recite their wishes for an exalted husband (Birkeli 192–95; Dubois 1307–11; Dahle et al. 99–109).

"If I marry the prince," said the eldest, "I will make a pretty mat out of little reeds and put it under the mattress both of us will rest on."

"As for me," said the next, "if Andriamohamona takes me as his wife, I will fashion a mat from fine straw to serve us as our bed."

"As for me," said Last-Girl, the youngest, "the sweet potato I am going to eat will become our child." (Ferrand, *Contes* 124)

Deciding to go find the prince at home, the sisters have a beauty competition (another favorite Malagasy event). Furious that Last-Girl always wins, the other two make her their slave.

"They even changed her name and called her Sandroy," a name Ferrand should have recognized. She is helped by a rat who not only gives her clothes and golden slippers, but restores the beautiful hair her sisters had cut off. The slipper test brings the prince to her.

"Are you really those two women's maid?" Gentleman Prince asked her.

"No, I am their little sister. They shaved my hair off and made me carry their bags like a slave, to make me ugly, because I am prettier than they are."

"Those two women were bad to you," the king's son said. "I am casting them out of my village." The two older ones set forth, pursued by people booing; on the way they transformed into little lizards. Sandroy, though, lived happily with Gentleman Prince. (Ferrand, *Contes* 123–29)[1]

The slipper test caught Ferrand's attention enough to make him cross-examine the teller, in the fear of finding borrowings from Perrault. "He is absolutely illiterate," Ferrand found with relief, "and insists he has known the tale since childhood" (Ferrand, *Contes* 129). Other storytellers in that Antambahoaka district knew it too.

If Cinderella had been imported, remembered, and remodeled, how could she be truly Malagasy? Authenticity required a tale to pass three tests: antiquity, oral transmission, and no European influence. He had already had to discredit some well-known fables that had been taken into Malagasy oral tradition.

> Tales 6, 4, and 19 so strikingly resemble the three similar fables of La Fontaine that at first I had some doubts as to their Malagasy character. Catholic missionaries did, in fact, translate a certain number of La Fontaine's fables into Malagasy, adapting them to the customs of the country. I feared these were in that number. Tale 6, The Dog and the Crow, is especially remarkable for its perfect resemblance to our great fabulist's Fox and Crow. My doubts were lifted by the assurances of aged, totally illiterate natives who knew the tales from long ago, and consequently could not have borrowed them from the collection published by the Jesuit fathers. (Ferrand, *Contes* iv)[2]

This Jesuit collection was a textbook of 1834, promoting Catholic literacy. La Fontaine was part of the program. France always attempted to implant La Fontaine in its colonies—to make him a "creole" in the old sense, a white colonist residing in the tropics. From the beginning, the *indigènes,* "natives," were to acquire a knowledge of the one book known to all French men and women. Not because there was any expectation they would become *français noirs;* rather, because the "natives" were children, they would have to pass through children's education. "From their beginnings" in France, "the Fables were used as a school textbook." Later, "the spread of compulsory education and the use of the Fables in elementary classes made La Fontaine's collection the one and only cultural patrimony common to all French people—a secular and national Pater Noster" (De Beaumarchais, Couty, and Rey s.v. "La Fontaine, Jean de"). With that patrimony, François Chrestien dutifully translated La Fontaine into Mauritian creole (1822, seven years after France lost Mauritius to Britain), Louis Héry translated him into Réunionnais creole (1828), and the Jesuit fathers translated him into Malagasy. Always the motive was to validate the local language; always the effect was to invalidate it. The tradition does not die: Lézize de Ségré's *Zistoires Missié Lafontaine dans créole Maurice* went through four editions between 1939 and 1967 (Joubert 164), and 2003 saw the publication of a collection translating several of the fables into the creole languages of Guadeloupe, Guyane, Martinique, and Haiti (*Zayann*). Thus does the French cultural patrimony enter into dialogue with the oral literature of the colonies (Marimoutou, "Louis Héry"). Yet Ferrand nurtured the chimera of authenticity by trying, and failing, to discredit his informants. The contradiction was unresolved.

The notion of authenticity has been transformed more than once. A few generations after Baissac, folktale scholars turned his criterion upside down, declaring that the warrant for authenticity was multiple existence of "the same" piece in variant forms. The single version of a tale was allowed only a local meaning, whereas Cinderella, or The Maiden without Hands—stories existing in numerous versions and variants—had international authenticity. Now the emergence of creole societies has necessitated either discarding or complexifying the notion of authenticity. Societies such as Réunion and Mauritius have particular habits of appropriation, interpretation, adaptation, treatment, rendering, rendition, paraphrase, transliteration, imitation, and parody (Haring, "Parody"), to make their products authentically creole.

Ferrand's contemporary Charles Baissac had the same longing for authenticity, but he recognized the girl (though he did not know the Indian tradition that gave his Cinderella a lecherous father).

90. Cinderella 2: The Story of Donkey-Skin

Creole narrator, Mauritius 1880s

Once there was a king who had a pretty daughter. That king was a widower. The king one day said to his daughter, "Let's get married." The daughter answered, "Oh, father, that's impossible! You are my father. I don't want to marry you." The father said, "Listen, if you consent to this, I'll give you everything you want. Ask me anything you like, I'll give it to you." The daughter still didn't want to, but he begged her for so long that she was obliged to say yes.

Then the father sent messengers all over, to fetch what he was going to give his daughter. For he had promised to make her a gift of three dresses, one the color of the sun, one the color of the moon, and the last the color of the stars. Still, when he had given her the three dresses, the princess refused to say yes, because she had a godmother who was a witch, who was stopping her.

In fact Baissac's story is a key to the recent Indian immigration.[3] On the wedding day, she shams a chill and puts off the ceremony until she can procure her grotesque disguise.

Her father said to her, "Well, let's have the wedding." The daughter said, "Give me the skin of your donkey." Because the king had a donkey that dropped gold. That was why the king was so rich. But the king said, "No, I won't do it. Never." So the girl said, "If you don't give me the skin of your donkey, I will not marry you."

The king resisted for three days. But his heart was so heavy that he had to go back to his daughter's room and say, "Very well, what can I do? I'll give you the skin of my poor donkey. But listen: tomorrow we are getting married!" He went out and slammed the door.

With her fairy godmother, she journeys to another country where she persuades the king to let her become his goose girl. The prince discovers her in this menial disguise, which Baissac's informant borrowed from another tale (The Speaking Horsehead).

They talked, they talked, they talked, eh, eh. When it came time to go to bed, the boy said, "Don't be afraid, and don't say anything to my mother. She told you to make a cake. When you go to make it, put this ring from my finger into it. I'll pretend to be choking. Then things will get confused and Mother will have to call a doctor. But we'll just see. . . ."

At the banquet, the prince bites into the piece of cake with the ring in it, cries out, and everyone jumps up. The king proclaims that any young woman who can draw out the ring can marry the prince.

Young women came, young women came, young women came, they stuck their finger in. None of them could do it. The ring stayed stuck in his throat. His mother started weeping. So the boy tried to speak, saying to his mother, "Oh, mama, how painful it is! But let Donkey-Skin try. Maybe she can do it." Donkey-Skin tried. What do you think? The ring went right on to her finger. Huh! the ring was out. The boy's mother didn't know what to say; she was speechless. The boy felt his throat and said, "Now that's what I call a cure. For sure I'm going to marry Donkey-Skin." The queen got angry and was in quite an uproar, but the boy said to her, "Well, mother, we have to do what Father said. Father is not a king with two voices, you know."

While they were quarreling that way over whether he was going to marry or not, in came Donkey-Skin's godmother. She gave Donkey-Skin a tap on the top of her head with her wand, and at once Donkey-Skin became a pretty girl in a dress the color of the sun. The queen danced for joy.

What a wedding his father gave! Everybody in that country came, they ate, they drank, they danced all night. I went to ask for a little glass of liquor, but they set the dogs on me and I ran away. (Baissac, *Folklore* 118–29)[4]

Keys here are the incestuous father, the heroine's bizarre disguise, and the ring in the cake, which combine the Indian inheritance with Perrault's famous tale (Zipes 38–46). Such motifs manage to migrate from one Cinderella to another without obscuring the plot (Thompson, *Folktale* 128), all the more in creole societies. This kind of mixing embarrassed Charles Baissac. At the end of his text, he quoted La Fontaine: "'If Peau d'âne were recited to me, I would take the greatest pleasure in it.' Yes, but Peau d'âne crossbred with Cinderella? The reader will see in this tale, perhaps better than any other, what unusual amalgams creole memory can produce" (Baissac, *Folklore* 128–29). He was right about the principle, but wrong about those amalgams, which show in European versions too, and which are not as incompatible as he thought (Zipes 26–50).

Baissac's vision of crossbreeding would have been enhanced if he had been able to hear Daniel Fontaine, of Salazie in la Réunion a century later, localize Cinderella to his island. In his first line, he signals that she is going to be transformed (Goffman 43–44).

91. Cinderella 3: Sandriyone 1

Daniel Fontaine, Réunion 1976

Sandriyone—her godmother was the Holy Virgin. She was a fairy, that godmother. The Holy Virgin was a fairy.

Most of the ensuing psycho-cultural plurality in his well-told story is recognizable. His Sandriyone is the youngest of four, not three; to transform a pumpkin (*sitrouy*) into her carriage, she must use that masculine magic wand from the Mauritian story. Her sun-colored dress she acquires from the fairy, not the king as in Perrault's version. When the prince finds her at last, Mr. Fontaine emphasizes upward social movement: "He married Sandriyone. It was Sandriyone who won. It was Sandriyone who married the king's son" (Decros 83–89).

But what if Cinderella's story is in the same reduced condition as the heroine, sitting forlornly on the stairs?

92. Cinderella 4: Sandriyone 2

Marie-Rose d'Ambelle, Réunion 1976

There was once, there was a head of family, he had several daughters, but of all the daughters Sandriyone was the prettiest. The mother didn't love Sandriyone, so she took the three or four other daughters into society, but she never took Sandriyone. She put Sandriyone on the stairs. Well, the king gave a big dance, and the other sisters went to the king's dance, but Sandriyone was still there.

Many a girl finds her monster mate at a dance; this Réunionnaise needn't be different.

So Sandriyone went out, she went crying, and she found an old fairy. The old fairy asked her why she was crying. She said that the king had organized a big dance, her sisters and her mother had gone, but they didn't want to take her. She asked her why. She said it was because she was Sandriyone, she was dirty, and like that. So she said to her, "My daughter, go to the dance."

The expression "my daughter" is so conventional that it completely masks the lingering Freudian symbolism of the donor as Sandriyone's "good" mother.

She said no, she couldn't go to the dance, she had nothing to put on, no shoes, no dress, nothing, and her mother told her she had to make the food; when she got there everything should be ready. The old fairy said to her, "No, go into the house, and in a moment you will be dressed." So she was dressed. She left with a thing with horses that came to get her, a cart. She left.

But when she got there, her sisters, her mother, they all saw her arrive without knowing it was her daughter. Well, the king's son went out of the room, he went to find the girl and danced with her. Everybody looked on. But the fairy told her, at midnight she mustn't be in the room any more. The king's son stayed with her. They talked and talked, but she saw that the time was already late and said, "No, I have to go." The young man said, "No." But see, if she didn't stick to the thing, the fairy was going to undress her in the room. Well, it was already late, she started, she left her shoe on the ground. Her carriage came to get her. The young man had to let her go. She left in her cart. But still her shoe stayed on the ground.

So the next day the young man said to the king that the person who fit this shoe, he would marry her. So everybody came back, everybody who was there that night, to try the shoe. So everybody tried the shoe, but their feet didn't go in, it wasn't theirs. So he asked if someone hadn't left a girl at home. Everybody said no. But Sandriyone's mother said, "Yes, I did leave one at home, but," she said, "she's dirty and all, she's not—whatever, she's not presentable." Then a minute later she saw the girl arrive in the same clothes as the night before, again in the cart. She came without one shoe. The mother saw that it was the same girl all right, but without knowing it was her daughter. But the king said that was her, she was the one who lost her shoe in the room, and he would marry that girl. But the mother, when she knew it was her daughter, she stayed dumb. She said how could such a thing happen, seeing her daughter was dirty. She had left her at home, and still here comes the girl present at such a party.

No more than that, I don't know any more. (Decros 23–29)

Marie-Rose d'Ambelle knows she has reduced the old story. Her demeanor towards the microphone, telling *about* the story rather than performing it, still manages to retain the elements essential to identifying a Cinderella tale.[5] Reduction, often a technique of resistance, was probably not deliberate for Marie-Rose d'Ambelle, who knew fewer stories than other members of her family such as Nicole or Jean-Max (Chaudenson, "Corpus"), but she may have been expressing an idiosyncratic attitude towards French tradition. Literary critics nowadays, though, don't scorn fragmentariness as much as they used to: "narrative discourse," one writes, "may be composed of quite brief, bare, and banal utterances as well as such extensive and extraordinary retellings as might occupy 1,001 nights or pages" (Smith 232). Studying Native American narration, a fruitful complement to Eurocentric literary criticism, has made it possible to see even the non-performance of a piece as nevertheless "one possible manner of performance of tales" (Hymes 40).

Still, reduction poses questions. What about (Mme) Théodore Fontaine's seemingly imperfect memory of another beloved story?

93. The Children and the Ogre

Théodore Fontaine, Réunion 1976

There was once a father and mother who had three children, they left them in the forest. Well, they went away. They took a loaf of bread, they gradually threw it down, they made little pellets to throw the bread on the path, and gave themselves bits to eat. They made little pellets and threw them down. They said when they went back they'd find them, so they could get back to the house. They said, "We'll look for wood and heat up some rocks." Then they waited and waited, they tasted, but it was still raw, not cooked.

But the father and mother left and the children stayed in the forest. Then they walked, walked, walked, looking for them, looking for father and mother. And they looked for those little pellets of bread they'd thrown there, didn't find them, they'd lost their way.

Where did they come to? Gran Dyab's house. When they reached Gran Dyab's house, Gran Dyab's wife said, "Children, why have you come here?" She said, "Gran Dyab is going to eat you," she said. "What are you doing here? Go back, go far, find your way, go back to your house."

They said, "But how can we do that, *granmer*? We are tired, we are hungry. How can we manage to go back?"

"Well," she said, "here's a little bit to eat, eat it quick and I'll put you to sleep." Then she said, "I'll make each one a little bonnet." She changed those with Gran Dyab's children, exchanged the bonnets. When they finished eating, one said, "I won't sleep, it's better if I leave, madame." So they left, left, left. On the way they found, like, a house that was full of food, the table was set. They went in, they ate. Done eating, they said, "This is a house to sleep in, there are good beds to sleep in." They went to sleep.

That was Gran Dyab's other house. When Gran Dyab got there, he said to his wife, "It smells of fresh meat in here, it smells of fresh meat." At the other place, when they left, the wife gave the children to Gran Dyab to eat. The children all slipped out, they went, went, went, till they found their way, then they got back to their house. But they'd become rich. The wife said to them, "Hit these sticks," she said, "you'll get everything you have to have to get what you need." And when they got there, the father, the mother saw the children coming. They said, "How did you get here?" "Oh," they said, "don't worry about it, because we have something to eat and drink." They hit the stick on the table! "Once the table is set, we'll eat good stuff," they said. "You didn't want us, you threw us out," they said. "And now we have what to eat, just watch." So they were sorry they threw their children out, but they'd got food for them. The children punished them a little. They gave them a little food, so they would not die. And they drank well, ate well—but Gran Dyab was on the point of eating them. (Decros 67–73)[6]

Giving Gran Dyab two houses is the narrator's only addition; the rest reduces the story to hunger and its consequences. Reduction is like forgetting: there's always a reason. Is Mme Fontaine only forgetting, or is she creating an allegory of the near-famine in the island at the end of World War II? Ambiguity, ambivalence. . . .

By comparison with the *département* of Réunion, with its vulnerable pastel-colored houses so like those in southern France, or the cyber-nation of Mauritius, where women in saris sit at computers, the Comoro Islands seem saturated with inherited Islam and centuries of neglect. In the light of their reputation for backwardness and their nearly indecipherable ethnic mix, it's ironic that Ngazidja (Grande Comore), Mwali (Mohéli), Ndzuani (Anjouan), and Maore (Mayotte)

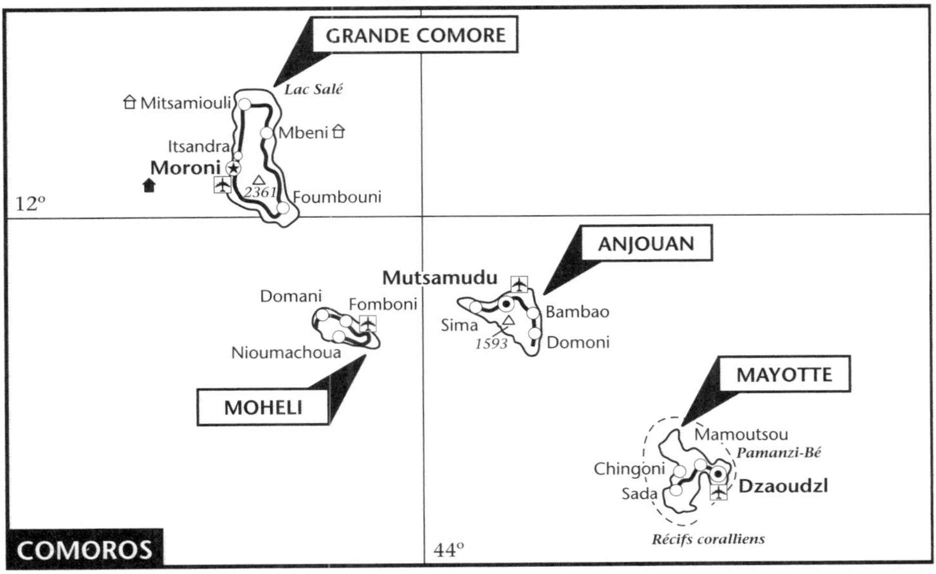

continually undergo coups d'état. Are these keys to a political plight of creole societies, another form of the ambivalent acceptance-rejection syndrome? Long ago, Africans were first to arrive in the Comoros; from the eighth century on, the dominating presence was that of the Arabo-Persians. If the ruins of their ancient mosques were signposted today, they would draw tourists from the whole Islamic world and beyond. Thenceforward came successive waves of Indonesians, Indians, Shirazi, and Arabs. In Mayotte, Swahili and Shirazi-Bantu people, two ethnicities already mixed, arrived eastward from the African coast, moving towards Madagascar while converting local people to Islam. In the opposite direction later, Malagasy moved westward towards Africa through the Comoros. What was inherited was bilingualism, in Comoran and a creolized version of Malagasy. The history of ensuing conflict brings one scholar to the point of saying, "Let us refrain from digging up the secrets of war in the Comoros" (Faurec 25). After independence in 1975, Mayotte seceded from the federation comprising the other three. Anjouan, despite a land area of only 424 square kilometers and a total lack of economic viability, has tried to secede two dozen times since 1990. Utopia lives!

Mayotte differs from the other three, being so close to Madagascar and maintaining strong connections to France. "Women play a more influential, even conspicuous role in public life, for instance, than they

The great mosque overlooks the harbor of Moroni, capital of the Comoros.

do in the stricter Koranic paternalism of the other islands" (Allen 33). In Mahorais[7] narratives too, women are certainly conspicuous. There is really only one theme: marriage.

Take the false-bride story. As this is known in Madagascar, an impostor takes the place of a wife and does away with her (Renel, *Contes* 1:261–65). Mayotte knows the impostor as a chameleon, who stows away on shipboard in woman's form. Once the true bride is rescued by *sambiny,* terns, and recognized, she refuses to live in the same house as that person of another race. Though ultimately she is taken back and the treacherous chameleon is punished, her refusal puts her in opposition to the cowering, no longer defiant girl in the canonical story (Gueunier and Said 322–33). Even when a nameless Ti Zan rescues her, the woman is the central character.

94. Falling into the Jinn's Power

El Anrif, Mayotte 1973–75

It's the story of a brother and sister. The girl was pregnant. The two of them went to gather *ambrevad* [pigeon peas], which meant a bit of a journey.[8]

They found a tall tree, in a hollow, with many eggs under its roots. Like all pregnant women, the sister took quite an interest in the eggs. She wanted to take them all. They were to take only one.

"Whose are they?" they wondered.

She put a large number of them in the basket and covered them with *ambrevad* to hide them. Then they ran off.

On the way they met the owner of the eggs. It was a jinn, who said to them, "*Wa kwendra havi pipi djuju yangu,* Where are you coming from, people?"

The boy took an interest in the *goma* [drum]. They both were very afraid of this monster. The girl trembled. The boy answered then, singing:

> *Mepwa mepwa pepingele*
> *Mepwa mepwa pepingele,*
> modulating his voice,
> *unlimbwagoma unlimbwagoma oh!*

and he beat the drum. "Get the drums ready, bring out the drums. We just cooked *ambrevad.* Dance to the sound of the drum." And the jinn started dancing on his long legs. The children took advantage of that to run away. They went to the house.

Once there, the brother told his sister to prepare the eggs, and he went fishing. As she was pregnant, she adored eggs, and she ate them all. But that's an action she wasn't responsible for; a pregnant woman's act is involuntary. At evening, the brother came back. "Where are the eggs?" he asked.

She answered that she wanted them and she had eaten them.

The second day, the very same thing happened. The third day too. The boy did not want to go there again, but still, he felt sorry for his sister and afraid the jinn would eat her if he wasn't with her. He took his drum and went to hide at the place where they met the jinn. He knew his sister would come there. She went looking for eggs and she filled her basket. The jinn found her, asked her the questions and she didn't know the answers. He put the question three times. The jinn became angry, raised his horns, his tails, and his fur. His eyes became red.

Abruptly the boy came out of his hiding place and beat the drum, for the jinn was going to eat his sister. The jinn began to dance. They ran away. (Allibert 4–5)[9]

Spinning off from the defiant-girl story, the piece points to the same tenet: a woman's birth family is her most precious possession. Marriage, as the main language of social communication in the Comoros, is always risky and fragile, never a substitute for your birth family. The foreignness of spouses is symbolized in language, which women must control.

The *grand mariage* (great wedding) is a display event for the women of the family.

People of the Comoros mix lexicons constantly, as do people in the other islands: Malagasy (Domenichini-Ramiaramanana 15–25), Mauritian Kreol (Baker 18–20), Réunionnais Kreol (Rispal-Gaba), Seychellois Kreol (Bollée and Rosalie). In this multilingual setting, the ability to understand an arcane language confers power. So in Madagascar, that ability saves a folktale hero (Hébert, *Un conte*). Reny Daosy of Kany Kely in Mayotte sings a song in two languages as part of one of her performances (Blanchy et al. 134–57). Often the ogre, jinn, or animal husband speaks a bizarre language meant to symbolize his alien status. Actually, it's derived only from a neighboring village dialect. In one Mahorais defiant-girl story, for instance, a wife who doesn't understand *shimaore* is powerless. In another version, a bilingual sister who can speak *kiunguja,* Kiswahili, effects the rescue from the monster husband. In another, the sister sings her answers to the ogre's verbalized sexual advances. He asks her all the parts of the body in turn; what stops him is a metaphor about her sex (Gueunier and Said 72–73).

Narrative and linguistic skill, for a woman, is inseparable from the magic powers she must employ against the onslaughts of males, here six times over.

95. The Mysterious Woman

Chouani, Grande Comore February 1980

There was once a man and a woman. They brought a girl into the world. She was so beautiful that her parents decided to shut her up and not send her to the Qur'an school. "Let us hire a tutor who will come and give her lessons at home," her parents said.

The tutor began to teach the girl. She was so intelligent and alert that she soon caught up with and overtook her tutor. One fine day the father and mother said to their daughter that they were going to the fields; they left the tutor and the beautiful pupil alone in the house. The man, tempted by so much beauty and charm, wanted to take the girl by force. "Mr. Teacher, stop, I beg you."

"I am not your teacher," the man said.

"Then stop, brother, I beg you, for this is impossible."

"I am not your brother."

"Then stop, O husband, for this is impossible."

"You must allow it, otherwise I will kill you, and your parents will find only your body on their return."

"Before doing such things one must purify oneself, so let us go do ablutions."

The girl took some water, made some incantations, and gave it to the tutor. The latter began to wash his hands, and as soon as he washed his face, he went blind. He began to groan, "By God and his prophet, this slut has wounded me!" The girl dashed into her room.

Her father and mother came back from the fields. The tutor called the mother and father and said to them, "Come and take away your bitch of a daughter! You said she was serious, obedient, and full of good qualities. In fact every time I come to give her lessons, I find a bunch of hooligans in her room. Today I wanted to scold her and she blinded me."

The father and mother, very angry, began to taunt and torment their daughter. The girl, very angry, wanted to explain things to her parents, but they did not want to hear. "Your tutor is a man of faith, worthy of trust. He will not have accused you wrongly." At that, the girl gathered her few things, put them in a bag, and left.

She walked to the neighboring territory. She reached the entrance of a village. There she found a very decrepit old man. She said to him, "Grandfather, will you marry me?"

"Don't make fun of me, daughter. How can a beautiful girl like you marry an old man like me, who's only waiting for death? How can I provide for your needs?"

"Just agree. I ask you."

The old man agreed and took the girl to the village. There they found the *kadi,* who married them. The girl built a house. Once the house was ready, she furnished it and lived there with her husband.

Some time after, the woman became pregnant. She brought seven children into the world. The old grandfather was rejuvenated; he looked to be 25, his wife had made him so happy. One fine day the woman said to her husband, "I mean to go pay a visit to my parents, for it is a long time since I left them." She took the children and left all her property with her husband. She started out accompanied by the children and one manservant. They walked, and arrived at a riverbank; the slave proposed they stop to rest, which everybody gladly agreed to. The slave turned towards his mistress and said, "I would like to sleep with you, and if you refuse, I'll kill you and your children too."

"If it is written, you will do it. I cannot accept such a thing from my slave."

"I'll kill this child."

"Kill him." And he killed the first child and threw it into the bush. He kept up his threats and killed the children up to the last. The slave said to his mistress, "It is your turn now. You must accept my proposition."

"In that case, go cut a few palm leaves and put them on the ground, and then we shall trust the business to God." The slave went to cut palm leaves; coming back, he bent down to spread them on the ground. The woman recited several verses of the Qur'an and blew on his back. The man tried vainly to stand up; the woman took advantage of that to leave.

She walked and walked, dragging a huge chest in which she had put all her things. As she wasn't able to carry it, she waited for someone to carry it for her. Suddenly she heard, "Oooo, oooo," the wind that wasn't wind, the rain that wasn't rain. It was a devil. "What is it?" he asked.

"I would like someone to carry this chest for me, as far as the next village." The devil took the chest and said to the young woman, "You can get up on the chest too." She got up on the chest.

They reached the entrance of the village and stopped there. She said to him, "I'm going to pay you."

"No, I don't want to be paid."

"I'm going to give you money."

"No, I don't want it."

"I'm going to give you gold."

"No, I don't want it."

"Well, what do you want, then?"

"I just want your chest. If you refuse, I'll eat you and the chest too."

"Take the chest, then!" She offered to help him put the chest on his head, and took that moment to place her hand on his head.

The devil went to his place; there he called his wife. "Wife, call the children. *Mdwauhoma mrwapvili masaidie et mze msahazi.* Have them come quick, I have a treasure." The children ran up. They vainly tried to lift the chest. Every time they tried to take the chest off the devil's head, he began crying, "Ow, ow, ow! Stop, you're pulling off my skull!" The devil stayed with the chest glued to his head.

The young woman came into the village. As she got there she found an old man, like her first husband, and proposed to marry him. She built him a house and helped him improve his life. They stayed together till the day a boat was announced. It was slave traders, who were buying men for gold. That day her servant said to the young woman, "Let's go on board." Between times the servant had plotted with the boat men to exchange his mistress for seven golden seals. The young woman and her servant mounted on board. He left his mistress in a corner. She saw her servant disembark with a first seal, a second, then a third, up to the seventh. The young woman said to her servant, "You've been working too hard, you must be tired." She lifted the seal to put it on his head, she recited a few verses of the Qur'an, placed her hand on his head, and the seal stayed glued there. He vainly tried to lift it off. He stayed like that for years and years.

During this time the boat tranquilly sailed along. One day the sailors saw this beautiful well-built girl. All those who tried to approach her were killed, so successfully that the others were afraid. They wondered, "What kind of phenomenon is this? How can it be that all those who try to approach her fall like flies?" She spoke to them like this: "I give you one chance to live, on condition you let me off on the next dry land." The boat people were so eager to get rid of the young woman that the nearest land seemed out of reach. They finally sighted land and let the strange passenger off.

Arrived in a village, she went into a mosque and disguised herself as a man. Early in the morning he called the people to prayer. The people arrived at the mosque. The king saw the handsome young man and begged him to marry his daughter. "He is the only man worthy to marry my daughter," said the king. The young man called on the king's daughter. At night he slept all dressed.

One evening "he" heard someone groaning. "He" asked his wife, "What is he suffering from, that man who groans incessantly?"

"That's someone who has a sore on his leg. For years he has tried every remedy God created, with no result. The leg is gangrenous, soon it'll separate into two pieces."

"Tomorrow morning," said the young man, "he must be summoned here. I can cure him." Next morning they had the man brought to the king's son-in-law, who tended to him, and by a miracle, his leg was cured instantly, and the sore disappeared. The man brought quantities of gold and silver to pay his heaven-sent doctor. "He" refused in these words: "It's for charity that I did that. What I want in return is that all those who are struck with incurable maladies, in the whole country, come to see me." The king sent someone to the top of the minaret to announce the good news: "All those in town and afar who are suffering, let all come, for we have found a healer who can cure all the sicknesses in the world."

When they learned this news, the parents of the young woman disguised as a man went to fetch the blind former tutor and led him to the king's place. The devil with the chest, the servant with the seal, the slave who fell in the rape attempt, this whole fine crowd came to the king's place. There was already a crowd of invalids of all kinds. The "young healer" worked wonders on all of them successfully. Came then the turn of the four last sick ones. He began with the blind man and asked him, "O father, what did you do to be like this?"

"It is divine will."

"Ah. Well, in that case, wait till divine will comes to save you. I can manage to cure an illness only when I know the profound cause and origin of the illness." So the blind man told his whole story, with the young woman whom he was tutoring and whom he wanted to rape. All four told their stories. The "young healer" said to them, "Sit there and wait for me." "He" went into his room, took off his man's clothes, and put back on his woman's clothes, did up her hair, came back to the salon, and declared, "I am the one who is at the origin of everything that has happened to you. My father and mother here are unjust; they took this gentleman as a tutor. Later he wanted to rape me. I fought well, and finally I pretended to yield and proposed we should purify ourselves first. I took water, I recited a few verses of the Qur'an, and at the moment of washing his face he went blind. That is the story, your majesty. I am no boy, but a woman like your daughter."

The father and mother started taunting the tutor.[10]

The sixfold repetition proclaims her strength. Power over speech, which she shares with her Malagasy cousins (Keenan), is her weapon. No moral need be stated, now that she operates the country's only medical clinic.

Where European fairy tales seem to be "showcasing 'women' and making them disappear at the same time" (Bacchilega 9), Comoran tales are a theater where they overcome oppression. A misogynistic king, in a 1930s story from Grande Comore, forbids immigration by women and orders all girl children executed. His antagonist is the daughter of a neighboring king, a bit like the young woman in Sydney Joseph's Ramkalawar; she presents herself in the disguise of a ship captain, accompanied by a helpful dog. Three times she avoids discovery; before a fourth test, her dog sets fire to the village, she swims to her boat, and she shouts back, "King, you are a fool. I am a woman, a woman who came to play on your stupidity."

There is more to her story. Now the king thinks to subordinate her by obtaining her hand in marriage. Little does he suspect the trickster stratagems she knows. In the wedding bed she puts a doll with a pot of honey as its head; she dons beautiful clothes and hides under the bed. The king slices the dummy, is pleased to see the goo oozing out, and runs away to his boat, only to hear her shout, "My lord, don't rejoice over your base exploits. Have a look at the blade of your sword and taste what is sticking on it." At home, when his sailors tell the people what has happened, they hang this misogynist. "Then they went to ask the Princess-Captain to come reign over their country which, thanks to the extremely intelligent new queen, who possessed the wisdom of Solomon, became peaceful and prosperous" (Fontoynont and Raomandahy 77–79). Is this a fantasy, with no hope of action, or does it hold out a Utopia of liberation for women? "In public you see only men," no women, I was told in Paris in 1982. Times must have changed: in Moroni, the capital, in 1995, I saw plenty of women in town, some wearing the bluejean costume of globalization.

If the irreplaceability of your birth family is one Comoran tenet, an ambivalent attitude to male authority is another. Comoran women learned long ago to anticipate the French writer Hélène Cixous in saying, "Woman must write her self; must write about women and bring women to writing, from which they have been driven away" (Cixous 1454). Comoran women have been writing themselves since the Middle Ages. It is hard to see them as having been driven away, when today they are principal transmitters of oral literature. The potent women in Comoran narratives invite their listeners to explore the varieties of marital experience.

The major threat to traditional culture in Mayotte is the kind of social change that can enfeeble the traditional hierarchical relationships, which set older people above younger ones. "The master-pupil relation," almost as intense as the parent-child relation, "is based on submission, obedience, services rendered, devotion, fidelity, and availability" (Djoumoi Ali M'madi 21–22). The relation is debated in a number of tales. In one Comoran version of one of the most popular of the world's tales, a magic tree is the master. Magic objects received by a poor man are stolen from him, until one of the objects enables him to retrieve the others and punish the thief. Readers of the Grimm collection know the piece as The Magic Table, the Golden Donkey, and the Club in the Sack (Grimm and Grimm 134–42). In his reduced version, Djundi Oumar sets up binary oppositions right from the beginning.

96. Magic Plate, Cudgel, North Wind, Poverty

Djundi Oumar, Mayotte 1980–81

I'll begin the story. There was once a poor man and a rich man. This poor family had no children to count on when they would be old. So the father went every day to the forest to cut wood to sell. So this poor family lived off fruits and cuttings the father could sell in the village for a low price. One day, the husband went to the forest to cut wood. In the middle of the forest, rain began to fall, fog surrounded him, and he lost his way. He walked, he walked, he walked a very long time. Several hours later, the fog disappeared. The unhappy man found himself lost. He went right, left, forward, back.

He reached a place where he saw a big tree standing in front of him. He said to himself, "A good tree to cut and make firewood out of." With his axe, he struck once, then a second time. He heard a sound that said, "Who are you? What are you doing there?" Surprised, he turned his head right and left; he saw no one. Then he hit again, again. The same voice came up, saying, "Who are you? What are you doing here?" Finally the poor peasant said, "I'm a poor peasant. For three days my family have not eaten. I came to cut wood and sell it in the village to feed my family." The voice answered, "Oh, that's how it is. Turn your head to the right." He found a big plate at the foot of the tree. "Take that, ask it whatever you want. Everything you want it will furnish." The poor peasant turned to the right, found the plate. Said, "O plate, give me something to eat right away." The plate filled with rice, meat, all sorts of food. The poor peasant ate, ate, ate his fill. He also asked for something to drink. The plate offered him clean water. He drank.

Then, paying no attention to the tree, he started for home with the plate. He said to his wife, "O, beautiful wife! Today I have brought you something extraordinary. From today on we won't be hungry." The wife said, "Aha, is it true what you say, husband?" The husband answered, "Why would I lie? Look. I found this plate in the forest. Everything we ask the plate will give us." The wife answered, "If so, I am very hungry. I want to eat and drink." Finally the plate filled with food and drink and the wife ate and drank. The family was very happy.

The poor man acts like a dependent child toward his parent. He tries cutting it at first, then "pays no attention to the tree." The magic plate is a surprise, but not a reward; it's "what is naturally expected and looked for in an established community, as the baby expects the mother's milk" (Perls 119).

After that day, that family asked everything it wanted from the plate: silver, gold, riches—and the plate got it for them. The family became one of the rich families of the village in a short time.

Envy is a tool of the hierarchical society.

Some notables of the village wondered how this family managed to become rich in such a short time. The news reached the sultan of the village. The sultan sent messengers and called the poor peasant and asked him what he had done to become rich. The peasant refused to answer. They hit him, hit him, hit him, and finally the poor peasant gave in and recounted what he had done, what happened to him in the forest, and how he managed to have a plate that gave anything it was asked for. Hearing that, the sultan said, "Aha, that's how it is. A poor peasant like you has no right to keep a precious thing like that plate. Go bring it to me."

The poor peasant, accompanied by the sultan's guards, fetched the plate and brought it to the sultan. Instead of being happy with the plate, the king ordered that all the property of the poor man be brought to the palace. The unhappy peasant was destitute. With the family he began to weep. He wept, he wept for a week.

Finally he remembered the tree. He took his axe and went to the forest. At the foot of the tree, the fog came, than lifted. The peasant began to strike the tree with his axe. Like the first time, a voice came up and said, "Who are you? What do you want?" Without hesitating, the poor peasant answered, "I am the poor peasant from before. You provided me with a plate, but the sultan took it away from me. Do something for me." So the voice answered, "Turn behind you. You'll find a cane. Take it, go to the sultan, ask him to give you your plate. If he refuses, tell the cane, 'strike.'" So the peasant turned around, took the cane, and left for the village.

When he got home, he said to his wife, "Wife, I'm back. I'm going to get back at the sultan." The wife said to him, "My poor husband! How are you going to get back at him, since the sultan has power you can't outdo?" The husband said, "I'm going to outdo him with this cane." He took the cane and left.

When he got to the palace gate, he asked to see the sultan. They asked him what he wanted. He answered, "I am the peasant from the other day. I have something interesting to show him." They let him in. He found the sultan sitting. He said to him, "Sultan, I am the poor peasant from the other day, the one you took the plate from. Give it back to me." The sultan answered, "What, you here again? Go away." He ordered his bodyguard to throw him out of the palace. The peasant said in a loud voice, "Cane, hit him! Cane, hit him!" The cane began to strike, first the king, then everyone else present. Several minutes later the king cried, "Peasant, make the cane stop." The peasant answered, "Aha! The cane will keep beating you till you give back my plate." The king said, "Oh, if that's how it is, give him back his plate and let him leave right away." They gave him back the plate, and the peasant told the cane to stop. He took the cane and the plate, and said, "OK, that's what I wanted. Goodbye, sultan."

After that day they never bothered him again, and his family again became rich. And they are still rich until today. (Daoud and Bashrahil 11–24)[11]

Ambivalent attitudes toward authority are the message. The donor tree, in a 1930s Malagasy version of the same piece, is so sympathetic to his dependent that when he has to ask for help a third time, the tree says, "Oh, is that how it is? Wait a while, we'll have some laughs!" Then it tells him where to find the magic stick that will punish the thieves who stole his magic basket and gold-producing ram (Dandouau, "Les deux époux"). Closest to Europe, the least hierarchical version comes from Michel Panofsky in Réunion. The North Wind, a real-life threat in the northern countries (Delarue and Tenèze 2:432), makes the poor mother and son even poorer by blowing away their tiny harvest; then it becomes the donor of a treasure-laying hen and a food-producing carpet. The villain is again an ambivalent woman, who is both the keeper of an inn where he sleeps and the thief of his magic objects.[12] Such ambivalences were not invented in the Indian Ocean, of course, but the island history gives them special force.

Despite the importance of women, many Comoran stories virtually exclude them.

97. Alimtru and the Buzzard

Nassor Ali, Mremani, Anjouan   February 1980

There was once a man and a woman. They had a son. His name was Alimtru. His mother offered him all the young women, but he always answered he had no need of a wife. Finally he himself went to find a wife to suit him. The day he brought her home, an old woman came to get fire, and as soon as she saw her, she fainted. The young woman got up, unfolded a *chiromani* [shawl], and struck her, saying, "Arise and go tell what you know, and the lie." The old woman got up, got some fire, went out, and just behind the house she put out the fire with water and ran to the king's. She went to say to the king, "Sire, Sire, give me a good meal to eat and beautiful clothes to dress in. I'll spit on the ground and tell you a beautiful story."

"Get away from here with your blah-blah-blah. When you want to destroy me, you'll tell me anything." He said to his servants, "Give the old lady something to eat and let her tell her story." They gave her a good meal; she ate; they gave her fine clothes, she put them on. She said to the king, "Sire, if you saw Alimtru's wife, you would make yours into a servant."

"Is that true?"

"Yes."

The king sent a first person. He came back and said it was so. The second came back and also said it was so. The third one brought the woman.

When Alimtru came to reclaim her, the king refused. He did everything to get his wife back, with no success. He stayed like that till one day desire came over him. He said to his mother, "Mother, make me seven cakes, for today I would like to go a journey." The mother prepared seven cakes. He took his horse, put on the saddle, got dressed and left. He reached the middle of the village, dismounted from the horse, cut the cake, ate half of it, and drank some water. Night fell on the way. He kept going and at dawn he arrived near a big river. He got down from the horse; he ate one cake, drank some water. He had one cake left. He took his tools and attacked an areca palm that was there. He got it to earth with blows of hatchet and axe. He worked it very well and made out of it a thing like a woman. He had brought seven *grigri* [charms, amulets]. He tied one to the first joint, then to the second, then to the third, up to the seventh *grigri.* The areca transformed into a pretty woman. Then Alimtru fainted.

The woman undid her hair and struck him with it, saying, "Get up and tell what you know of others and yourself." He got up and the two liked each other. Soon the woman got pregnant. In fact it was an areca that was transformed into a woman. He got up on his horse with his woman. When he went to fetch that woman, that took one night. The way back took one hour, and when he reached the house, he said to his mother, "Mother, this is my wife. Let no one see her, even her fingernail, much less the ends of her hair." "All right, my son." "I am going to find something to provide for the needs of this child to be born. I will look for gold."

Alimtru boarded a ship and left. He had said that he would be gone three months; in fact he would stay three days. The day he was going to come back, an old woman came to the house, to look for fire, and again seeing a woman, she ran to inform the king. He had the woman brought. They lived together, but every time the king tried to sleep with her, the woman said to him, "You made me come here to play, not to sleep with you." The third day, Alimtru came back. He saw his wife had been taken away. So he got thin, he became like a thread.

He went to see a *fundi* [diviner]. "*Fundi,* I had a first wife, the king took her from me; I had a second; he took her from me; I would like to get that second one back."

He said to him, "You won't have that woman, but you will have the *grigri.*"

"Well, tell me how."

"You will organize a big banquet and prepare seven big dishes of rice. You will call all the birds existing in the world. The bird that will go fetch the meal is the one that will go get the *grigri* back for you." He prepared the seven big dishes, and he had all the birds come. Only one bird was missing, the buzzard.

He waited till nightfall; he heard leaves falling from the trees. When he stood up he saw the old buzzard and cried, "O old buzzard!"

"What is it?"

"Come do an errand. I want to give you an errand."

"Since yesterday my children have not eaten anything."

"Come, I'll give you something to eat."

"You can give me something to eat but also something to take to my children?"

"Yes." The buzzard took the meal, ate some of it, and left one big dish. He took leaves, wrapped it into a nice bundle. He said to Alimtru, "Now entrust me with your errand."

"The king took away my wife. I would like you to go get my *grigri* [talismans] and bring them here."

"How? Give me some kind of a little song that will help me get them back."

"It's you who would know that, old buzzard." He said to Alimtru, "Listen, then."

Alimtru trundra mpe zombo rendre
Alimtru trundra mpe zombo rendre
Alimtru tsiwa djadja tsiwa mama mri kengo
Baba trendre dje mama trendre dje mama mri kongo
Nataka na zombo zantru
Nataka na roho

Then Alimtru said to him, "That's it, like that one." The old buzzard flew off, made the circuit of the king's house, went and perched on the window, and began to sing.

[song again]

The king said to his *vizir,* "Take off her stupid *grigri* and give it to him." The *vizir* went up to the woman and took off one *grigri* and gave it to the old buzzard. It flew up, flew once round, came back and sang,

[song again]

The second *grigri* got detached; a root came out of the woman's foot and pierced the floor. The king had brought his whole family there. The old buzzard sang again,

[song again]

The third *grigri* was detached. A branch of areca grew on the woman. The king said to the people, "Today you are going to see a miracle." The old buzzard chanted the song again:

[song again]

The fourth *grigri* was removed; a second branch of areca grew on the woman. When the seven *grigri* were removed, a whole areca appeared in the middle of the house, which caused the collapse of the house, the death of the king and his attendants.

The old buzzard took the *grigri* and the woman to Alimtru. As a reward he had food for his children.[13]

Nassor Ali's story recalls the first woman made out of wood, in Madagascar, and Nelzir Ventre's use of song, in Mauritius, to move the action. In Grande Comore, Mohamed Toihiri's 1992 novel *Le Kafir du Karthala* depicts a Comoran man whose revolutionary fervor is energized by his affair with a European woman (Toihiri). In creole fiction, the primary arena for mixing, however, is language. Any imaginative work born in a creole culture is mixed. So contends the Réunionnais poet and critic Jean-Claude Carpanin Marimoutou (Marimoutou, "Écrire métis" 259), pointing to novelistic characters of mixed racial background as personifications. Personifications, I would add, of the creole aesthetic.

I turn to Réunion, a French island from its beginnings, where the few storytellers who have been recorded remember French stories: Marie-Rose d'Ambelle, Théodore Fontaine, and Paul Maxime Maillot have performed them for a microphone. Daniel Fontaine knew a good many tales beyond his Cinderella: The Table, the Ass, and the Stick; a Ti Zan trickster story; and The Three Stolen Princesses. If in the following story he has only three Skillful Brothers, where the Grimms had four (Grimm and Grimm 457–61), a few readers might remember that in the 643rd of the *Thousand and One Nights,* three brothers were faced with such a dilemma. These three, after a childhood of eating, playing, and sleeping with their first cousin, all want to marry her. Their father sends them on a quest for "the thing most wondrous and marvellous of all sights"; they find a telescope that reveals the princess has fallen ill, a flying carpet that transports them homeward, and a magic apple that resuscitates her. But the king refuses to award her to any of the three, thus enabling the narrative to continue, in typical Thousand and One garrulity (Burton 3:256–313).

Given his geographical position, Daniel Fontaine is less likely to have derived his story from that book than from Breton ancestors (Delarue and Tenèze 2:559–61). It is the commonest of all dilemma tales in Africa (Bascom, *African* 7–8); these too may have influenced Mr. Fontaine. The extent of contact between the *petits blancs* and the *noirs* of Réunion has yet to be investigated. But his plot resolves the dilemma and marries off the girl. His deepest subject, another key to the creole aesthetic, is narration itself: the combining of a plurality of elements to localize the material.

98. The Rarest Thing in the World

Daniel Fontaine, Salazie, Réunion 1976

Well, there were two kings responsible for two countries, one like Mauritius, the other here in Réunion. The comparison, well, of the two countries—the king of Mauritius had a daughter, the king of Réunion had a son.

As words from different languages are thrown together in Kreol, so Mr. Fontaine throws together parts of inherited stories, calling in the precocious hero from another tale he knows well, the Three Stolen Princesses,[14] and recalling Malagasy epic heroes such as Ibonia.

One fine day his son, he grew up. He grew up, grew up. When he was born, he was eight days old, he asked his father for a *badine* [staff, wand]. Papa looked for a *badine,* gave it to him. A week later he gave it to him. Well, a week, two weeks he started walking, he was a man already.

When the two extraordinary companions (also borrowed from the Stolen Princesses tale) come onstage, they bear the names of the magic objects they will find, a bit of economy that causes the storyteller to stumble over the illogic.

He was walking on the road, he found a friend [*kopin*] who was called—Mirror, his name was Mirror, his name was Mirror, OK. So he was the one named Mirror.

He found a *kopin* named *badine*—named Wooden Horse. It was the other name, the one named Wooden Horse, it was the other name.

Well, he took along his *kopin* Wooden Horse, his first *kamarad.* They kept walking, wandering, kept going on the road. A little farther on, he found the other *kopin,* Badine, the third one. So there's the three of them. OK.

But along the way, Mirror, the son of the king of the country I just said, like Réunion for example, he looked into the glass and he saw Mauritius. The king of Mauritius, a daughter, a pretty daughter, a pretty daughter. He was hoping to marry off the daughter. But three men can't marry one girl.

There had to be one of the three to marry the girl. They had to draw cards, draw the short straw, what they call. Well, Mirror—that girl was beautiful, she would just suit him. Well, the three agreed. Wooden Horse, the second *kopin,* said, "So let's take a trip to that country." So Badine too agreed, all three go.

They got up on the wooden horse and—the wooden horse was sold by a peddler. The glass was sold by a peddler. The king's son, he bought the glass first, him. He asked the peddler what the glass was used for. The peddler answered, "The glass is used to see things now and in the future, even past, the glass."

They continued their caper.—I've skipped.—They kept journeying, they got farther along. Four days later, the same peddler came up. Wooden Horse went up to the peddler to ask him what he wanted. The peddler said he was selling the wooden horse. He said, "The wooden horse, you use it—it's faster than an airplane, even faster than a Boeing 707. It goes around the world in fifteen minutes. It goes around the world in fifteen minutes, the wooden horse [does]." He said he was buying the wooden horse from the peddler. He asked him how much for the wooden horse, how much it cost.
This ubiquitous *kolporter,* peddler, who declines to raise his prices even when invited, reflects a mode of production from the Ile Bourbon (Réunion's old name) of long ago.
The peddler told them, "A thousand francs, same price as the glass." He asked the peddler if he couldn't raise the price. "It's worth more. Something as valuable as that, you can't sell it so cheap. Only a thousand francs!" He said, "No, it's a thousand francs." He said—thanked the peddler.

They kept going on the road, got farther on. Four, five days later, they heard that same peddler yelling again. "*Badine, badine, badine, badine*!" He went up to the peddler. He asked him what he was selling. The peddler answered he was selling the *badine.* He asked the peddler, "What's that *badine* used for? How much is it?" The peddler said he was selling it for a thousand francs, the *badine.* OK. So he asked what it was used for. Well, the peddler said, "The *badine,* you use it to wake and kill living things and wake all dead things: vegetables, minerals, animals, people, like that, anything. Even dead plants it brings back to life. Even plants that are alive, it kills them and then brings them back to life."
Knowledge and power: enclaved and powerless people need both.
OK. They asked him if he couldn't sell it dearer than that. The peddler told them, "No, that's the fixed price, the *badine.*" They set off for Mauritius; the three got up on the wooden horse. The peddler explained to them how to get the wooden horse to walk. You press a button at the rear. It goes by electricity. You make the contact at twenty, the wooden horse goes up in the air, it starts off. In not even ten minutes, to the next island, the next

country. They got there. The people there had never seen these three strange young men. They were three handsome young men. They saw these three foreign guys, they were surprised, they were on the lookout. Then they went to see the authorities of the country. They asked them what country they came from, like Réunion for example. They asked them for their passports, how many days they were coming for. They learned that the king's daughter was dead. And the girl really was dead.

So the king, the queen were sad. So one of the three, Badine, he said he had a *badine* with him that would wake all dead things. Even living things it would make die and then bring back with that *badine.* So the king told him to come to his palace where the corpse was laid out, the girl was laid out. See if he could bring the girl back to life, he would be very happy, he would marry her to him, the girl, to one of the three. If the *badine* succeeded, he would marry the girl, if she came back to life, she resuscitated. That happened there. The law and the procurer general of the country were summoned in case it failed. If it failed, the three would be put in prison. The *badine* first. He called to get ready. The *badine* hit three blows on the body, the girl rose up. When the girl rose up on the couch, the candles made a cloud around her head. She got up, she walked. The people were afraid. The *badine* said, "No, don't be afraid." She got up and walked, in the courtyard of the palace there.

When she got her consciousness back, she said she would like to get married. But she would like to marry, she would like to marry the first boy there, the Mirror. But Badine [and] Wooden Horse also wanted to marry, the wooden horse with the girl. Badine too, he wanted to marry the girl. The king said, "Oh, my. What to do?" He couldn't marry his daughter to the three guys; he had to marry her to one. The other two would serve as witnesses, one beside the boy and the other beside the girl. And then the third she would marry. Yeah.

The king said he didn't agree. "Make her die again, then we'll see, with the *badine.*" Badine made the girl die, made the girl die. So the girl was dead. Wooden Horse took the girl by the foot, and Mirror took her girl by the head, they put her in the coffin. And yes, the wooden horse caught her foot, and Mirror caught the head, and Badine caught her by the middle. Badine married her. Wooden Horse and Mirror served as witnesses. So that's the end of the story of the Mirror and the Wooden Horse. *Kriké mésyé!* (Decros 109–19)

Three men are to argue over which will marry a woman just brought to life? Daniel Fontaine has revived, in a *kont,* the Malagasy myth (*tantara*) awarding the first woman to the man who turned her over. Is this creolization? The overlap and time lag of symbol systems is even clearer when he reproduces a favorite French combination: The Three

Stolen Princesses are sought by a Strong Man and his Companions. I translate most of the piece.[15]

99. The Three Stolen Princesses

Daniel Fontaine, Réunion 1976

As this piece begins, the precocious hero, Karant Milié (Forty Center), has been born, left home and acquired companions: Zan Paké d-bois (John Cordwood), Zan Palé (whose surname means quoit, a marker used in games), and Tras Montagne (Map Mountain). Then Mr. Fontaine has to go back and pick up an episode that gets the four men to a palace, which they will take over, like The Bremen Town Musicians. "I skipped, I forgot," he says. "Does it matter?" Not a bit, in the light of the rest of his lively performance, which echoes the Grimm tale of The Gnome (Grimm and Grimm 334–37).

There in the castle there were musical instruments—drums, accordion, everything, guitar, cymbals, jazz, all that was in there. Then they cooked some food and they ate. At evening, they made dinner. When they were finished, they made a *solo* [dance], there in the castle; they gave a dance for the four of them, four young men. They gave a dance. When they were tired, they lay down and slept.

Next day he said, "Gents, let's go hunting. One of us will stay as a watchman and make food." John Cordwood said, "I'll stay. I'll make food." So Karant Milié [the hero] said to John Cordwood, "When you see that it's eleven o'clock and we're in the forest hunting, ring the bell. We'll come out for mealtime. We'll have game, we'll come down." So Cordwood made food. He killed an ox, he made steaks, he peeled potatoes, he made a kari, a chicken kari, he cooked beans, he made bread. There was everything in the castle. He made fresh bread, he cooked rice, all that, he made a lettuce salad. He went down to the cellar, opened red wine, white wine, whisky. There were all those drinks in that cellar. He set the table for the four of them. When he'd finished laying the table, the meal was ready, John Cordwood looked at his watch. It was eleven o'clock. "I'll go ring the bell," he said.

He went out to ring the bell when a little Dad, as tall as this, a little dwarf with a long beard, appeared. He said, "What'd you come here to do, young man?"

He said, "I came to ring the bell. It's mealtime, and my friends left to hunt in the forest."

He said, "Young man, there's no bell to ring here."

He said, "Dad, don't play the fool with me. What do you mean, not ring the bell? I'll show you I'm going to ring it."

"Well, young man," he said, "you won't ring the bell. I'll show you, you won't ring the bell. There's no bell to ring here." The two of them mixed it up, punched each other, they beat each other black and blue and they rolled in the direction of the toilet. When they got there, the fellow got a grip on John Cordwood. He caught John Cordwood and tied him in the hole of the outhouse, tied him in the hole of the outhouse. There's poor John Cordwood in the hole of the outhouse, all smeared in shit. He tried to get out but he couldn't.

Up in the forest, the others looked at their watch. Eleven-thirty, no bell. They said, "Why is the meal late?" They put up with it, they kept hunting, they took shots at the game, at the blackbirds, the quails, and so on. They looked at their watch. Noon. No bell. "Gents," they said, "let's go down. We'll find out what happened down there." They reached the castle. They looked for him and saw that the table was set. They looked for him but didn't find him. They heard him yell outside, in there. They went to look in the outhouse. There he was, in the hole. They said, "So, comrade, how is it you're here? How did you fall in there?" They pulled him out. He was all smeared with shit! They took him, led him by the pool, they took the watering pail and doused him. They washed him with soap, with soap powder, with soap, and changed all his clothes. Once his clothes were changed, they went to the table.

Before going to the table, he said, "Gents, at least ten thousand people caught me and threw me in there. Ten thousand people caught me and threw me in there, about ten thousand people."

Said, "Ten thousand people? That's a lot!" Well, finally they ate. That night they made dinner. They made their solo, they played music, all you need to make it perfect. They were the owners of the house.

The next day they were impatient to go hunting. They said, "Gents, which of us four stays today to make food?" John the Puck said, "I'll stay. I'd really like to see who's going to throw me in the toilet hole today! I'll give him a hit with the puck and put him into the hole. I'll stay today, I'm going to see." John Cordwood came and said, "Ten thousand people threw you in there, in the toilet hole! I'm going to see who's going to fight with me today, that I'd like to see." John the Puck stayed; he made food.

Eleven-thirty came, twenty to twelve, no bell. The three guys up there, Karant Milié, John Cordwood, and Maps-Mountains-without-Compass came down. They stopped hunting. When they got there, they saw the table set and the meal ready. They looked for him, no luck. They heard him yell there in the toilet hole. They went to see him, they washed him. They bathed and changed him. Before changing, he said that today there were at least twenty thousand people who threw him there, caught him and threw him [in]. Twenty thousand people threw him in there. Ten thousand more got hold of him and threw him in there. All the time it was the little fellow with the big beard. He prevented him from ringing the bell. He tied him, beat him, and rolled him next to the toilet, he threw him in there, the little fellow.

So. They ate. Evening came. They dined, they made food, they dined. They had their dance, it was a little late. They were so tired, they would lie down and sleep; tomorrow they'd catch up.

"Gents," he said, "we have to go hunting. We need three. Which of the four of us is staying?"

Map-Mountain said, "I'll stay today. It's my turn. I don't carry a huge load of wood, I don't have a huge puck. All I do is trace a path."

OK. Map-Mountain stayed. He made food, he prepared the meal. He finished preparing the meal. Five after eleven, quarter past eleven, no bell. The three guys in the forest said—Karant Milié, the most loyal, said, "Gents, let's go down. He's in the hole, I'm sure he's in the hole, better we go down. Quarter past eleven and the bell hasn't rung. He's in the hole. He's in the toilet hole, better we go down and get him out." Finally the three men went down. Karant Milié went down. Arrived below, they went to get him out of the toilet hole. He said that twenty-five thousand people, fifty thousand people had thrown him in there. Fifty thousand people threw him in that hole. Before lunch.

They ate well, as they should. After eating, they had a little nap. In the afternoon they started preparing the meal, the dinner for the evening. The dinner finished, they played their piece a little, they had their dance, they played music as usual. When they got tired of dancing, they went to sleep.

Next morning, he said, "Which of us four stays today?" John Cordwood didn't want to. John the Puck and Maps-Mountains-without-Compass didn't want to either. Karant Milié said, "I'll stay today. Today everything's going to go right. I'll show them: I'll ring at eleven o'clock, 11:01 at the latest. I'll ring the bell. Maybe at 11:04 or 11:03, but I'm ringing that bell." Karant Milié stayed. He cooked the meal. He killed an ox, he made steaks, he killed some chickens, he made a kari, a kari with beans. He made the kari with beans and smoked meat. That was a real dinner for four! He went to the cellar, he took some wine, white wine, red wine, whisky, beer. All that he put on the table. He arranged it nicely. He looked at his watch: four minutes to eleven. "I'll go ring the bell."

The little fellow called him. He said, "No, there's no bell to ring. No, you're not ringing any bell, my friend."

"Not ring? Not ring the bell? But I am ringing the bell, my friend. I'll show you that I'm going to ring it." They punched each other. As they were fighting, they got close to some big rubber trees, like those ones in front of the town hall in Saint-André. They fought. Karant Milié held the little fellow fast by the tail of his shirt. He got a hold of the little fellow, he twisted his left arm. His beard was so long that he grabbed it with his arm. He pulled on the little fellow. With his right hand he gave a hit with the stick on the rubber tree, he opened it from top to bottom. He split the tree in two with one hit from his stick, he opened the rubber tree from top to bottom.

So he felled the tree. He tied the little fellow. He got another hold on him by the kidneys. He caught the little fellow and took him to a big branch of the rubber tree. He leaned him on it; he climbed on the little fellow's stomach. He tied the little fellow on a big branch of the rubber tree. He tied him with his beard. He tied his face to the branch so that he couldn't run away. Tied!

"So," he said, "it's you. You're the twenty-five thousand people guy? You're the fifteen thousand people man? You're the twenty thousand people man? You're the man who threw John Cordwood into the toilet hole? Ten thousand people, that's you? You? Well, let's see if you escape today!" It was all finished at 11:02. He went to ring the bell, kolong, kolong, kolong, kolong, kolong. He rang the bell.

"Ah, gents," they said, "the bell rang today! For sure Karant Milié must have caught the one who did that to us." OK, they got there. Karant Milié was at table, Karant Milié was sitting by the table. He said, "Gents, I caught that individual," he said. "Let's go see." He led them outside and said, "Is that a man? John Cordwood," he said, "that's what threw you into the toilet hole? That little moron? That little old moron, that little dwarf? That's who you're calling the man of ten thousand people, hey? Huh? John Quoit: is that the one? That's the man of twenty thousand people? And you, Maps-Mountains-without-Compass, that's the man of fifty thousand people? That? Trace mountain, that? That's what you couldn't get the better of? That's what you couldn't catch, beat, and throw to the ground? Then how did I manage? How did I tie him to the branch of the rubber tree? How did I succeed to tie him there? He didn't run away today. How is it that I could ring the bell? Well, gents," he said, "leave him there. When dinner is over I'll take care of him. I'll see what's to be done with him. There's three of us, we'll see what we have to do with him. I'll be the one to see what we have to do, what sentence we have to pass on him. Let's go eat. When we've finished eating, when we've drunk our coffee and all, we'll come back and give judgment on the branch of the rubber tree there. I'll show him how we'll fix him. Let's go eat."

They had finished eating, all three drank their coffees. Then he said, "Let's go see that guy, that little dwarf." They got there to the big branch of the rubber tree, they looked for the little fellow, they didn't find him any more. They found the skin of the little fellow's face. It had stayed glued, attached to the branch. Everywhere the beard was, the poor face was peeled off. The fellow was completely disfigured, all peeled off. It all stayed stuck to the branch. The little fellow had run off. He rolled off. They saw traces of blood. "Ah," he said, "this is too much. Let's go, gents. It's only one o'clock, half past twelve. Let's follow this trail of blood. We have to catch him. There must be a place where he's hiding."

They followed the traces a long time. They took the mountain path that they'd taken to go to the crater. They saw the same traces of blood. Right up to the edge of the crater they saw traces, drops of blood. "Oh, gents," he said, "he went down here, he went down here, the fellow! He went down there! Gentlemen, which of us goes down?" John Cordwood said he didn't want to go. He said, "Well, you, John Quoit, you go. Go!" John Quoit said, "No, I'm not going." Maps-Mountains-without-Compass didn't want to go down either. Karant Milié said, "You don't want to go down—I'll go down. Only I warn you, take the rope, carry the rope with you. When you see the rope move, take it back up. There'll be something tied to it. Take it up."

OK. He got to the bottom, Karant Milié, just him, with his fifty-thousand-kilo stick. He found the three girls there, he set them free one after another. He got them up with the rope. The three guys up above hoisted up the three girls and got them up. When the last girl was up, the three morons stayed up. They thought there were three of them and there were just three couples. Each one could get married to one girl. Karant Milié, the extra one, started up. They played him a trick, as I said before. This is what they did. They let him get halfway up the precipice. When he got more than halfway, they let him go, with his stick. He got wounded. Then luckily he found the old woman from before, the old fairy. She had a little bottle of infusion with her, she gave it to him. She told him to put it on his wound and it was going to go back to normal.

He kept walking in the bottom of the crater. But at one moment, as he was walking, there was on each side like an alley, kind of like a bed, kind of like a bed. He saw a gang of little devils sleeping, a gang of little devils sitting beside the bed. He fell on them with his stick and killed them one after another. He kept walking more, on the bottom there. He saw on a bed, the face attached, the fellow whose beard stayed caught on the branch of the tree. He beat him with the stick and finally killed that fellow on the bed.

Now, he was screwed. He was all alone at the bottom with his fifty-thousand-kilo stick. What to do? Who to turn to? The three guys had hauled up the rope and left. "Ah," he said, "what a bunch of pigs! You made fun of me, you rolled me! If I ever get back up there, watch out for me. If I get up, be careful, be careful, it won't be good!"

OK. Finally night fell, everybody went home. The white birds came, the pink-bills came, the rams, the tectec, they all came. The old woman's birds came to say their prayers and sleep. What did he say to the birds? He said, "Children, can't you manage to carry me up?"

"Oh, sir," one said, "we can't, we're too small. Your stick is heavy. Your stick weighs fifty-thousand-kilos, we are too small. I can't carry you up there. Sir, there's only one bird that can do that for you. He comes last. He'll be here in a minute. It's the eagle. The eagle can carry you up there. Make your arrangements with him." The eagle came at last. He went and talked to the eagle. The eagle said, "Comrade, I guarantee to carry you up. But I have to make one condition. You have to get some meat. With every flap of a wing, every time I go 'Pia,' one wing beat, a single shake of wing, we have to go one notch up." Then the eagle said to him, "I'll take you, but on condition that at each blow, each shake of the wing, I'll go 'Piak.' You have to put a piece of meat into my beak. And if you don't do it, if I do the last shake and you have no more meat, I bring you back down."

So he went. Down there at the bottom there were cattle, animals, there was everything. He killed two oxen, cut them in pieces with the skin, bones, and all. He put them in two big baskets, he tied—he found some rope or something—he tied the two baskets together with his stick and himself. The eagle had quite a load to carry: fifty thousand kilos, two cattle and him to take up above. It was a deep opening, quite a high precipice. They had to get up. Going down would be nothing, but there, they had to get up.

So the eagle started. First flap of his wing, "Piak!" He cut a piece of meat and put it in the eagle's beak. The eagle swallowed it. It gave another flap. "Piak!" He cut another bit of meat and put it in the beak. It gave another flap. "Piak!" He cut a bit of meat and put it in the eagle's beak. That was the last, the next to last flap. The eagle still had two flaps to go. It was also the next to last, the last piece of meat. There wasn't any more. "Oh," he said, "it's not possible." The eagle was going to make a deal with him. It was the last; the eagle was going to take him to the edge. Not much was left. Last, next to last. The eagle gave a flap. Only the height of a house to get him up there, to the edge. There was no more meat. He said to the eagle, "Comrade, there's no more meat. Do me a favor, take me up. There's almost none left."

"Oh no, comrade," he said. "The conditions were made. If you have no more meat when we get up high, I take you back down."

"Well, comrade, wait just a second." He cut a bit of meat off his thigh. Cut! He put it in the eagle's beak. There! he took him up, with his stick. He got up there, he was bleeding. He'd cut his thigh to give the eagle food. The conditions had been made like that. He plunged his hand in his pocket and took the little bottle of medicine that the old fairy had given him down below. He emptied it into his hand and passed it over his thigh. His wound closed up. He was safe and sound.

He walked there, up above. He looked for the guys and didn't find them. Very, very, very, very far towards the castle, he heard terrible cannon shots, my God! "Ah," he said, "you bunch of sons of bitches, that's how you are with me! There you're celebrating a marriage! All three of you have a girl. There's three of you. With me there, I was in the way. Wait a second, I'll show you. I'll show you in just a second."

He walked. He arrived there near the castle. He went in. The wedding procession and all was happening. The girls were already in their bridal gowns. The three boys were already dressed as bridegrooms. The witnesses were ready. The three girls, the three brides were dressed, but there was one who saw him. She said, "So-and-so, there's the gentleman who set us free." "Yes, yes," she said, "it's really him. He's the one who got us out of misery, out of prison, out of hell."

He said, "Gents, this is how you tricked me!" Everybody said that he had the power then, and "now you'll be condemned because you ought not to play such tricks. I'll show you that it's not you who will each marry one of these three virgins. I'm going to marry one, and the other two will be my sisters-in-law. But my other two friends, whether it's you, John Quoit, or you, Maps-Mountains-without-Compass, or you, John Cordwood, you're not getting married either. I'm not taking any of you even as a witness, for me or for my future wife. I'll show you. And afterward I'll condemn you. I am king. I am king of this country. I'll show you who commands you. I'm getting married."

Afterward all the gendarmes caught the three boys. They put them in jail. They caught the three boys and put each one in a cell, in prison, in a dungeon. And he said, "Young men, you'll have your heads cut off, I declare, once I'm married. One week after my marriage, the sentence will be carried out. You ought not to have tricked me like that. When I saved these three girls, you ought to have said that one of the four of us, me, would marry one, and two of my friends would have married the others. I would have had two brothers-in-law, and one could have been my witness or minister or something. But now, no minister, nothing, you'll be condemned, condemned to death by me. Right, I'm going to get married. A week after my marriage, when I've had a nice rest, you'll pay me so."

That's the end of the story. (Decros 177–213)[16]

Tales in mixed genres from Madagascar prepared the Mascareignes for mixing their symbols to symbolize injustice, as African storytellers before them had done. For instance, a Mauritian king cuts down all the *kolofan* trees to get water—not for the community water supply, but for his royal pool (Baissac, *Folklore* 16–25). The story is a Kreol spinoff of one of the most potent African metaphors, the origin of death from a falsified message. Henri Lagarrigue, of Saint-Pierre in Réunion, increases the mixed-genre effect by putting himself into the story at the beginning, and by pairing two sets of failed messengers. His five trickster incidents, chained out after the impounded water is released, follow the African pattern of alternating success and defeat. I translate his words without interruption.

100. King, *Makamouk* Tree, Hare, and Tortoise at the Well

Henri Lagarrigue, Réunion 1976

One day it got so hot that there wasn't any more water on the earth. Well, there was the king, there was his gang, me too, working—we got hired to work for the king, but there wasn't any water. So the king said, "What are we going to do?"

"My lord," they said, "you have to go around, you have to go see *Bondyé* [God] up there to get water." He said, "OK." The *boug* [guy] said, "Me, me, in just a minute!" He went up, went up, he went.

He got up there with *Bondyé.* He told him, he said, "Yes, you have to go behind your kitchen, there's a tree called *makamouk* wood. Go and cut that, you'll have water." So he left. It was high up and far away. He came down. On the way he forgot. He looked around, said, "There was a *zak* [tree], it had a spirit—he said cut that. Go hit that one, cut it!" Nothing but milk came out. The *zak* just put out a little milk. No water. Very annoying.

Another *boug* said, "Let me. He's crazy, he doesn't know anything. Let me go." He climbed up. He went up and found *Bondyé.* He got there and asked, "*Bondyé, Bondyé,* the king sent me to look for water. What day will you give me a little water?" *Bondyé* said, "Aaaah, I told you to cut that tree *makamouk* behind the kitchen."

"Oh yeah, yeah." He went back down. He sang, "*Makamouk* behind the kitchen, *makamouk* behind the kitchen, *makamouk* behind the kitchen, *maka-* . . ." When he got halfway down, didn't he forget. He found a guava tree, he cut some guava. He forgot. And then what? He said that—he didn't get anything. *I, yi, yi.* "He told you to cut that tree." He didn't know its name. But next to the place where he was, there was a pepper tree. They cut that. No water. The king said, "The whip, flog him! Get out! You're not good for anything but you still say you got it."

The hare was cleverer. He said, "Me, in a second, I'll get there all covered with dust. *I, yi, yi.* There? In just a second." "That's OK," he said, "run, go." He filled his bag and took his greens. He went. He didn't have anything to eat. When he got there, Matthew was already out with *Bondyé*. There wasn't any food. He found a plot of grass, he went into it. Ah! He forgot. He got back and said—what was it he said? "Hey, king, don't tell me I forgot!" A hiding. He left.

The horse said, "Me, me, I didn't go yet! I'll be there in a second, with my big hoofs." He said, "Go ahead up."

The tortoise, with his way of not going forward, said, "Dog, let me go."

"When are you gonna get there, with your way of walking! What day you gonna get there? Don't make me laugh."

He said, "Let me alone. I'm going."

"Yeah, what day you leaving?"

"Let me go. I'll be there in a fiddle-tune's time." Went to the ravine, cut himself a boot out of *soka* [aloe, or sisal], took his violin, went up, put down his *bertel* [backpack basket]. Only, tortoise was talking, was walking, walking ahead, only his speed was tiny. Slowly, slowly, slowly, slowly. They said, "What day's he going to get there, that idiot?" Ah. He got there and said, "*Bondyé!* Hello, *Bondyé!*"

He said, "Hello, tortoise! What'd you come for?"

He said, "I came looking for a little water. The king sends for water, you're not giving any."

He said, "I already told you what you have to do."

"Well," he said, "what tree do we have to take? Which one do we have to cut down?"

"There's no need to cut anything," he said. "Go behind your kitchen. You will find a tree, a *makamouk,* you'll cut it and water will come out."

"Ah, ah, *Bondyé,* nothing else to do but go back down." Started, "Teeleelee, teeleelee, teeleelee . . . *makamouk* behind the kitchen, teeleelee. . . ." Got there, "*Makamouk* behind the kitchen, teeleelee, teeleelee." Ah. Got there with his violin. That was his habit, he played all the time.

"What did he say?"

"What did he say? He said to take the axe and cut that *makamouk* tree."

"Ah," he said, "another imbecile." But the king has only one word. When he says something, that's it. They took the wood and cut it. *Voilà,* water! Water came out and up to now we have water.

But—he had, he had another game to play, the smart one, he was smart. He was watching. "You won, tortoise, you're a man. It's not, like, your way." He was jealous. They were jealous—brothers, even so.

One day he saw the king at mealtime, saw the king at mealtime. He didn't drink any water, that one. When he was hungry he drank the water at the table. His *kalbas* [gourd] with honey in it was in his *bertel.* He got there. He dirtied the water, dirtied the water, dirtied the water. He [king] said, "Now why's this water dirty?" It was more or less the same distance from where they put that well. What's that called, there?–Bras-de-la-Plaine. There at Bras-de-la-Plaine there's a pool. He jumped in, he bathed, he bathed, he dirtied the water, he dirtied the water. The king said, "I'm getting a watchman." One said, "Put me there." He hired that one. When he got there, he said, "There's somebody dirtying the water up here. The king put me here as watchman."

"Oh," he said, "you're crazy. Is that drinking water? Taste mine." To taste his honey. "Taste mine"–with the rope and all. "Taste mine. Mine is really water."

"Oh, give me some, *kamarad.*"

"No, wait now, I'm going to tie you, going to tie you up. Tie you up. With two hands, you could mess it up. Two hands behind your back. Go, sit there." He put him in the sun. "OK, I'm going to empty it." He didn't empty it. He left him tied up. He wrapped him up with the rope, tied him up good, left him there.

He went in the pool. He bathed, bathed, bathed, bathed.

He [king] said to the others, "What? What is that *boug* doing there?" He went up, went up there, the *boug* was tied up. He said, "What happened to you?"

He didn't say, he didn't tell anyone, he didn't tell the secret to anyone. He said, "You don't know–a man came, he tied me up. Said he was gonna give me a little water. I was going to drink his."

"Ah, you were supposed to drink his?" He untied him. On the way down he chased him away. He left.

He sent another one. Same thing. When he got there, the *boug* tied him up. He tied him, "Taste my honey," and he never tasted the honey. But nobody gave away the secret.

Békali! The ox said, "Who? Send me. A *boug* like that, I'll knock him down. I'll give him a hit in the head and send him off."

Hare was frail. He got there and said, "Hey, brother, brother! What're you doing here?"

"Oh, somebody comes here to bathe every day in the pool, but today I'm going to catch him."

"Really?" he said.

"Yeah, I'm gonna give him a hit with my horn, and the show is over."

He whistled. "Hey, I don't drink that water, not me. Isn't the king ashamed to drink that kind of water? Is that drinking water? Taste mine." He gave him just a little bit.

"Ooooh, that's good. Give me a bit of it, pal!"

He said, "Not me," he said. "Yes, I'll give you some. I'm going to fasten you, I'm going to tie your four feet, your head, everything. I'm gonna put you on the ground. Turn like that so I can pour it into you." He tied up the ox. Ox was really tied up, with his mouth to the sun. He said to him, "Don't move. In a minute I'll give you some." He went to the pool. He bathed, bathed, bathed, bathed, bathed, bathed. When he'd had enough, he sat down on a rock in the middle of the pool. He combed his hair, he dried himself. Ah! He said, "Well, goodbye boss, I'm off." He left him there. And the king drank dirty water, he drank dirty water down below.

He said, "Still like this?" He went up. He sent the horse to see what happened this time, if there was more foolishness up there. "*Koto, koto,*" the horse galloped up. He got there, the ox was fastened. The horse said, "You are really crazy, letting somebody tie you up like that! Lord, send me, me the horse. If I give him a kick, I'll finish him. Let's see if he ties me up!" He got there. "Hee, hee, hee! Oh, pal, what do you want here?"

"I want to get some water."

"Ah," he said, "every day, every day there's somebody comes to dirty the water. There's a *boug* who comes to dirty the water up here by bathing down there."

He said, "Yeah? The *boug* has nerve, huh? He dirties the water you drink?"

"The king himself drinks that," he said. "We drink it, us down there." He said, "Taste mine, taste mine. If you taste it, I'll give it all to you. It's good! I'm gonna tie you, I'm going to tie you, and after that I'll pour it all into your mouth." *I, yi, yi!* He tied up the horse and then he jumped in. He bathed.

The tortoise was the one left behind with the king. He said, "Send me, king. I'll catch him. I have to catch him."

The king said, "You? A lot of time will go by before you get there, before you catch him! Stronger *boug*s than you have not done it. And you, with your little short feet, you're gonna do it?"

He said, "I'll catch him, lord. Send me tomorrow."

So he said, "OK, I'll send you." He forgot what the tortoise did in that business of the water, the king had already forgotten it. He said, "OK, I'll send you." So, the king had already forgotten? Oh, he forgot that. He forgot that it was the tortoise who'd gone up to get water from *Bondyé.* He went to the ravine. Long time, it was full. He took seeds, crushed, crushed, crushed them on his back. He smeared himself, he put glue all over his back. He went up. He didn't know! He went up, he went up. Once he was there, he went in the middle of the pool and sat right down on the rock with the hare. He got there. "Oh, so nobody's here today? Ah, ah, oh. Hey brother! Hey brother! Hey brother!" No one. The tortoise didn't move, there in the water. He hadn't found the tortoise yet. He didn't know. "I'll show them." *Piuk!* He jumped. He bathed, bathed, bathed, bathed, bathed, bathed. He got finished bathing. Oh, he was tired, he got up on his rock. He sat down on his rock. *I, yi, yi.* He got there panting, panting, *feefeefee, feefeefee.* He came to rest, he jumped on a stone. Ah, he said, "I'm going." When he did that, *i, yi, yi!* "Hey," he said, "stop. Rock, let me go! Stop, let me go. Stop, I'll hit you one! Hey, I'll give you one, huh?" *Pow!* A hit with his fist. His hand got caught. Ah! "Stop! Let go! Stop! Let me go, rock! Stop, rock!" Right. He gave it another hit. *Kan!* His other hand was caught. "Oh, all the worse for you. I'll bite you. You're holding my hand, this time I bite you." *Ran!* His mouth was caught.

Ah, the tortoise said, "You're the master today? Let's go."

"Ah tortoise," he said, "ah, brother, let me go!" He said, "No, no, I'll turn you loose down below."

The king said, "So, hare, you're the one who's doing that!"

"No, lord, I came to drink water, I fell in, and the tortoise caught me."

"Ah! And what do you say?"

The tortoise said, "No, he's the one who's been dirtying the water. He bathes, he bathes, he bathes. Haven't you been drinking dirty water?" He said yes. "That's him. When he got through bathing, I caught him." Gone.

He said, "Stick him there in the hutch. In the hutch, to make a good stew." Ah, he was crying in there. The hare was crying.

The dog came by. The dog said, "So, brother, what's making you cry in there?"

"Ah," he said, "it's the king. He knows I don't eat meat. He caught me, put me in here, only gives me meat." The dog said, "Oh, let me take your place."

The hare said, "Open the door, open the door." He opened the door. There wasn't any meat in there, wasn't anything in there, he only said that. He opened the door, he came out. He said, "Go on in there." He closed it up. The dog was in there.

When the king came, he said to his servant, "Hey, there's a hare there in the hutch, catch it."

When he got there, he said, "So! The dog ate the hare already."

"What?" he said. "The dog ate the hare. It's him who's in there." *I, yi, yi!* He caught the dog and beat it, beat it. He said, "Well, what do we have to do?"

Finally one day, the king was eating *zariko* [beans], eating, eating. Who caught him, finally? The dog again. "*Wap! wap!* The king gave me another job. Five francs a day. *Wap! wap!*" Go see, he's caught in his *goni* [jute bag]. He's running this way, that way—he's a prisoner. What happened? The cat passed by. Said, "What's happening? Oh brother, you got a good job?"

He said, "Yes, brother, the king put me to watch his beans. *Wap! wap!* Five hundred francs a day. *Wap! wap!*"

The cat watched. He said, "Yeah, you got a good job!"

"So? You want it for yourself?" He asked the cat if he wanted the job. The cat said, "Yes," he said, "if you want, give it to me. Give it to me, brother." The dog said, "Well, untie me then. I'll give you the place." *I, yi, yi!*

When the king came, he saw the cat was caught. He said, "But cat, you don't eat beans. How'd you manage to get there, huh?" So he unfastened him. He said, "A cat, what am I going to do with a cat?" He let it go.

The cat said, "Hey you, you got me shat on, why?"

"You didn't know how to speak to the king!" he said. "Nobody could be stupider! Ah! You didn't tell him to pay you?"

He said, "Paid me with big hits with a stick!"

"Aaah, you're crazy," he said.

One day the old cat came back. He found a wasps' nest and swallowed it. One came, one came out . . . the other went, the other came. Nothing to it. Like that. "When one comes, the one behind and the one in front, I'll hit that one." He didn't hit.[17] He knew he was getting stung. He was in a tight spot with this job. He said, "How'd you get so lucky?"

"Why?" he said.

"You had a good job." He was making good money. Back then ten francs was a lot. Ten francs a day, nobody got that much then. He said, "Give me that!"

"I'll give it to you. Go to work. Hit that one!" But when does a wasp go away? When one comes out, the other goes back in. He looked. From the minute they went back in, he watched. "So, no more coming out? OK, I'm gonna hit." Bah! *I, yi, yi!* the wasp lit on him. *I, yi!* The cat's tail got swollen. He caught the nest. So, no more job? One hit with the stick! *I, yi, yi!* It got up on his back. "Aaah," he said, "old *boug,* that's bad, that's no job, that!"

Well, five days later the tortoise—one day he passed, the tortoise was sleeping under the guava tree. So as the tortoise was sleeping under the guava tree, the hare passed by. He found the tortoise's *bretel* on the ground. He had to have it. "Ah, a *bretel* for me!" The tortoise said, "No, that's my *bretel.*" He said, "No, it's my *bretel.* It's mine, I found it. So let's go to the king. I'm the one who said it, I'm the one who found it—and you said it's yours! Well, we're gonna share."

They got there. The king said, "Well, so's you'll agree, cut a piece for each one. Each one a half. A half a *bretel* for you because you found it, a half for him."

The tortoise said, "OK, I'll wait. I'll get you." Ah! Tortoise went along his way, walking, walking, quietly, quietly through the grass, *kotrok kotrok kotrok,* walking. One day around 12:30 or 1, the time the hare was asleep, he came there. He was asleep. He was asleep in the rocks. Tortoise said, "Ah, ah! a tail for me!"

"Hey, let go, that's my tail, Tortoise!"

"No now, no funny stuff, that's my tail. I found it here in the rocks. You say it's yours? No way to agree. Let's go before the king. I'll teach you. I find it in the rocks and you're gonna say it's yours!"

They went before the king. He said, "What now? What to do? You have to cut." Too bad! Up to today hares have a tail–the hare has a short tail. The king said, "You can go. The hare's tail is cut off." Well, that's finished. (Decros 237–265)[18]

Each episode preserves its autonomy, with only a transitory link to the next episode.

This kind of variation raises a broad theoretical question for the student of narrative. Variation in storytelling arises deliberately with respect to its intention, but, as in biology, "at random with respect to its effect" (Lewontin 23). It's traditional for Mr. Lagarrigue to introduce a dog or cat or particular deception without heed to the effect he may be having on "tradition." The theoretical question is, then, How is signification generated in a narrative system? Mr. Lagarrigue and other regional narrators seem to be modifying the essential elements in the folktale repertoire "from within," so to speak, by something analogous to the inflectional system of a language. Possibly an abstract level of narrative functioning, not reducible to the manifest level of a single performance, can be discovered, not merely in creole stories but in other repertoires. Possibly that abstract level is what determines the variations in story elements around the world. The sociologist Émile Durkheim, says anthropologist Rodney Needham, asked

> whether there are not certain abstract laws which are common to both [individual and collective] spheres of thought. Myths, legends, religious concepts, and moral beliefs express a reality other than that of the individual; but the way in which they attract or repel each other, unite or separate, may be independent of their content and be related solely to their common quality as representations. It is conceivable that contiguity and resemblance, logical contrasts and antagonisms, may act in the same way whatever the things that are represented. "Thus we arrive at the idea of an entirely formal psychology which would be a sort of common ground for individual psychology and for sociology" (Durkheim, *Les règles de la méthode sociologique* xviii). This formal psychology would include a comparison of the ways in which "social representations," in myths, legends, traditions, and languages, attract and exclude one another, fuse together or are distinguished, and so on. The task, in other words, would be to establish "laws of collective ideation. . . . There is a whole part of sociology which ought to seek the laws of collective

> ideation and which remains entirely to be carried out." (Durkheim, *Sociologie et philosophie* 45n; Needham 157)

If there are such laws, they will have to be discovered in the performances of narrators like Mr. Lagarrigue or Daniel Fontaine.

Or possibly there is no such system except "interperformance." Mr. Lagarrigue, Gérose Barivoitse, and other Réunionnais narrators exert no rights of private ownership over their tales, but they base every performance on previous performances by themselves and others. Even if the connections and boundaries are not visible, they exist. So, realistic details of everyday life are found in even the exchanges that look most traditional.

101. Ti Zan and His Uncle

Paul Maxime Maillot, Grand Ilet, Réunion 1976

Poor Ti Zan, I tell you, he was really pitiful. He was pitiful, 'cause he was working for his uncle. His uncle had a big—what d'ya call it—big farm, looked after lots of cattle. So one day he said to his uncle, he said, "I'm not going to work any more." He said that, that was it.

His uncle said to him, said, "Listen, my boy," he said, "work a little more."

"No, uncle, that's it."

"That's it? OK, here's a little ox." That little thing was dying of the mange, poor thing. But then, see, the uncle, a little, I don't know, thought he was giving him a nice ox, but it was dying of the mange, gave it to him.

Poor Ti Zan carried it, he had to take it, the little ox was very sick from the mange. He got there, he said, "What am I gonna do with this? A little ox like this, it's gonna die." He didn't let the ox die. He skinned it. There in the forest, he skinned the ox and took its hide. Then he took the hide, he climbed a tree—see, there was a big tree there, I don't know how tall, five, six meters tall, maybe more. He laid himself there among the branches.

There were three creoles arrived under the tree, with a nice treasure. But when he heard them, he was a little scared. He made a move with the ox's hide, he did *katatra, katatra.* The gang ran away. Hey, the gang really ran. He left the ox hide there, he came down. They'd got a little money, they left. They left the bag of money there, they all left. So then, he took his share of the money.

He found his uncle, the uncle that gave him that little ox, he said, "Uncle," he said, "the amount of beef there was there, if you'd sold it, gee, the money, you don't know what we coulda done together. 'Cause that ox's hide made a good sale. I killed your ox and went and sold the hide. See how much I got for it. Well, that money's mine. You know, last night, last night I borrowed a measuring cup from my neighbor to count it. Look, you'll see a piece stuck to the bottom. I didn't think about it, but there's a piece on the bottom. He found it. That money is mine—now I've got my bit of money to worry about."

The uncle heard that and said, "If that's how it is, Ti Zan, I'm going to kill my cattle, really." He started in, he killed three of them, killed, put the ox hides in a cart. OK, he said he was going to go sell the ox hides in town. Every corner he passed, he yelled, "Ox hides, ox hides, ox hides, ox hides!" Nobody bought any ox hides. He wasn't very happy with his nephew. He said, "If it goes on like this, I'll kill that *boug.*"

Then he came back, he said, like, he said, "Bro," he said, "those ox hides," he said, "you made me think they'd sell well. I haven't sold a single ox hide."

"Oh, uncle, listen: those ox hides, you haven't sold them. But I went to see my neighbor. You'll see the money I got, more than from an ox hide. Uncle!"

"Yes?"

"See that? That, I tell you, your ox hide, put it . . . thing . . . see that big house there, the charcoal from that sells well. If you can't make it with ox hides, tomorrow you'll make it! Set fire to that, make charcoal, you'll see how well charcoal sells!"

What did he do? Set fire to his house! To get charcoal! Goes out to sell charcoal. Charcoal doesn't sell! He yells from his cart, "Aren't you buying charcoal? Aren't you buying charcoal?" No, nobody there bought charcoal. And he said, "Hey Ti Zan!" he said, "that's enough, bro, that's enough. Two times is enough. Third time, you're finished!" He caught Ti Zan, he put him in a sack. "Ah," he said, "Ti Zan, no, you're finished!"

He was so small, he caught him, carried him in the sack, went toward the sea. He went down, then he stayed a little while up above, he came down, he came down. After a point the *boug* was pretty tired. He put Ti Zan on the ground. He found a—what do you call it?—a place to get a drink, booze, I don't know, rum, a glass of wine. He was thirsty. He put Ti Zan down by the side of the road, he went in. So he drank an aperitif; then he was [still] thirsty. I don't know how many glasses he drank, I didn't see, I don't know, wine, drank the whole thing. And he left Ti Zan on the ground there in the road.

What did Ti Zan do then, poor beggar? He managed to get going again! He made out. A *boug* [guy] came by. He was crying, crying in the sack, he cried, "Won't marry the king's daughter! Won't marry the king's daughter!" The other *boug* was going by on a horse, he heard the poor *boug* crying, so he said, "What happened to you?" "Oh," he said, "no," he said, "my boss was taking me to make me marry the king's daughter. I'm not marrying her. But," he said, "you want to marry her? If you want to marry her, get in my sack." He said, "Me, no, marry the king's daughter, I'm not marrying." So the poor *boug* he went into the sack, he let Ti Zan out. Ti Zan went off. Ehh, the *boug* came, picked up his sack like this. A little heavier it was, a little fatter, a little bigger, a little heavier. But he'd been drinking, he'd had a few. He picked it up and then went along. So he went, he got to the seaside there. He wasn't going to break his ass—he said he'd drop Ti Zan into the sea, and the sea would finish Ti Zan off. And then, after that, his heart would be peaceful. He said he'd finally killed Ti Zan.

Next day, around eight o'clock or so, he heard a gunshot go off. He said, "Who's firing a gun at this hour?" He said, "It's Ti Zan"–his friend said to him–"it's Ti Zan!"

"What," he said, "Ti Zan? No, no, no, no, no." Ti Zan, he was sure he'd dropped Ti Zan in the sea, there weren't two Ti Zans.

He said, "Sir, that is Ti Zan!"

"Ti Zan, what's he doing here? Well, really, it's Ti Zan here, now he's killed . . . He's killed three pheasants?" He went to see.

He got over there. He saw Ti Zan had killed three pheasants. "So," he said, "Ti Zan, what are you doing here?"

"Oh, uncle, look here how I kill pheasants. There's two I killed, and they fall down over there. Go have a look, go see. Go down into the hollow, you'll see, you'll find three pheasants already in the hollow. I kill them here and they fall down over there."

The uncle said to him, "Ti Zan," he said, "that—that's impossible. You can't do something like that!" he said. "No, no, no, no, no," he said, "give me one shot with your gun, I'll see."

He said, "Uncle, don't do anything stupid, huh? Watch out, you see, I'm smaller, and you, let go of my gun."

But the uncle grabbed the gun and said like this: "I'm gonna kill you." "Let go! let go!" He shot the gun, he killed the poor beggar.

And that was the end. 'Cause he was a good kid, Ti Zan. He managed to get rid of him. After the uncle caught him in the field like that, after he killed the pheasants.

Poor *boug!* (Barat, Carayol, and Vogel 54–55)[19]

Audiences know Ti Zan will bounce back, just like an animal trickster. Just like the *petits blancs* themselves, in fact: as the former president of the Université de la Réunion remarks, "the need of being anchored in a collective past, which manifests itself here as elsewhere, is a powerful stimulus for popular memory" (Carayol 7: 10).

The exemplary Réunionnais narrator might be Alfred Picard.

102. Ti Zan the Master Thief

Alfred Picard, Plaine des Cafres, Réunion March 1977

Ti Zan again. So—well—Ti Zan came, he came to ask for the king's daughter in marriage. The king said to Ti Zan, he said, "For you to marry my daughter," he said, "you have to be able to steal Lov's pillow—Lov's wife's pillow."

"All right," he said, "OK." He set out. He was sly! One night he passed through the lock like a *grélé* [cricket], passed through the lock. He went, he got close to Lov's wife's pillow. Ti Zan said like this, said, "Sleep, sleep, madame, sleep. It's just *pinèz* [bedbugs]. Sleep, sleep, wife, it's bugs, just bugs." Then he tugged a bit on the woman's pillow.

She cried out, "Lov," she said, "somebody's tugging my pillow."

He said, "Go to sleep. There aren't any bedbugs that can get under a big pillow." After a while the woman went back to sleep. He got the pillow and ran off with it. He got back and said, "Here's Lov's wife's pillow." In the morning, the woman wanted to find her pillow. No more pillow.

Well, this time he [King] said, "Now you have to go fetch Lov's horse." How was he going to do that? He said he would go to the stable that night. And he did go to the stable then. The horse was there, but he wasn't used to him. He started kicking all around the stable. Well, the king got up, went to check on his horse. He [Ti Zan] hid under the hay in the corner of the stable. The king took some hay and gave it to the horse to eat. There were still two stalks covering Ti Zan, he didn't see him. He went out quietly to see where the man was going. He caught the horse; this time he put the bit in its mouth; he went off with the horse. He said, "Here's the horse."

He came back the next evening. He told him this time he had to fetch Lov's bell. He said Lov's bell, the bell—he set out to fetch it. *I've skipped something—yes, it is Lov's bell.* He set out.

It was a big bell. I don't know how he unbolted the bell then. I don't know what he did, but he got it. He got it and wrapped it up. Next morning he [Lov] went to check, felt inside a sack, looked for a stick to kill with. He found a stick to hit with. When he got there, he yelled, he cried in the sack, said, "*Granmer, granmer,* let me out," he said. "Let me out before Lov kills me." He said "Lov is going to kill me." She opened the sack, like that. Ti Zan made a trick [*klé,* key] to catch her, put her in the sack. He caught her and picked her up.

The guy came with his stick, "Bang!" The woman yelled like this: "Lov, Lov, don't hit me," she said, "I'm your wife! Lov!" He hit her with the stick, hit and kicked. He killed his old wife—ah! ah! He opened the sack. He thought he'd killed Ti Zan; he saw his wife in there. He said, "Tricked!" He was upset, he didn't speak. He carried the bell. Just then he left.

He [King] said, "This time you have to, you're looking to marry my daughter, you have to fetch Lov himself." He thought it over and said, "How'm I going to fetch Lov?" He didn't see. Finally he said, "Give me a car, sir." He gave him a car. Then he dressed up like a rich man. He got there, he walked up and down. Old Lov was upset then, walking sadly in the road. He'd just killed his wife, his pillow was stolen, his bell was stolen, his horse was stolen, all that.

He said, "Good morning, monsieur." He said, "Why do you look so sad?"

He said, "Forget it, you're just a kid." He said "They stole my wife's pillow, they stole the horse, they stole the bell, they stole all that."

"Ah," he said, "let's go for a ride to get rid of your bad humor, get rid of your cares." He said, "Ride a ways beside me, take a ride with me." Lov said yes. They got into the car, it went "Vrrr!" He took him back there, said to the king, "Here's Lov." So the king said, "He's what I need." He took him, he hanged him, that's what the king did with him. So the story is finished—he got the girl to marry. (Decros 5–13)[20]

M. Picard is loyal to French tradition; he responds to majority culture; he projects ambiguous or ambivalent attitudes to authority; he unites creativity and imitation. Is this mixing not the creole aesthetic?

To come back at last to Mauritius: Charles Baissac was only a bit apologetic when his Kreol tales were raunchy (Baissac, *Folklore* 192–215). The ones that bothered him were the ones that seemed inauthentic, not truly creole. Looking at Polin and Polinn, which is a version of The Maiden without Hands (Zipes 506–23), he asked, "Is this a black tale?" He saw the plot and characters of this polished text being controlled by "a sure hand"—just the metaphor for a story of mutilation. The French version he knew, probably from a book by Paul Sébillot (Sébillot), seemed "hardly inferior to the creole one." So had Basile, in *Pentamerone;* implanted in Africa (Junod 266–75; Steere, *Swahili*), inserted in the *Thousand and One Nights,* it remained popular in twentieth-century France, even including the detail that identifies the two as orphans (Massignon 116–20). Worldwide distribution was for Baissac the disqualifier of Mauritian authenticity. "Creole?" he asked. "Maybe so, but black creole? I strongly doubt it . . ." (Baissac, *Folklore* 331).

Both preservation and innovation characterize Baissac's Polin and Polinn, which is no verbatim replica of oral storytelling, but a story rewritten for children. The narrator, a bit like Sydney Joseph, poises the hero between two women, but he also follows closely the vicissitudes of the banished wife of tradition. Baissac's narrator has a "sure hand" but also an eye on his or her audience: "Would you believe this? . . . Polinn, you know, was very, very pretty. . . . Let's go back to the king. . . . What else can I tell you, children? It's not hard to know what's going to happen at the end of my story." Aside from the grisly touches (Polinn has no hand to be asked for in marriage; the servant makes a joke out of Lida's punishment), what is striking in the piece is its symmetries. Polin and Polinn mirror each other; his dog balances Lida's cat and is reborn in the king's dog, named Lieutenant (Place-taker); the king is such an effectual replacement for Polin that his reappearance is an afterthought. That kind of loyalty to a romantic and complex plot is the key to one component of creolization. Out of respect for its novella qualities, I interrupt Baissac's story only by section headings.

103. Polin and Polinn (The Maiden without Hands)

Mauritian Kreol narrator 1880s

There was once a boy and a girl with no father, no mother. The boy's name was Polin, the girl's name was Polinn. Polin was Polinn's brother, Polinn was Polin's sister. Since they were very small they were always together, always *kamarad* [friends, pals]. Everything Polin got he shared with Polinn, everything Polinn got she shared half with Polin. Till they were grown up they both lived in the house their father left them.

One day, when Polin was about twenty, Polinn said to him, "Brother, you've come of age now, you must marry."

"Why marry, sister? Why should I go look for some woman we don't know? She might make trouble in our house. Let's leave our pot to cook quietly on the fire."

"Don't talk so, brother. Don't listen to chatterboxes saying a good woman is hard to find. Look at me. Get married, I tell you. I'll love your wife as much as I do you, and when you have to go out, you won't be leaving me alone in the house like now. There'll be two people waiting for you. It's not good for a girl like me not to have a woman living with her. Get married, brother."

What could Polin do? He took a wife, he got married. *I, yi, yi.*

This woman's name was Lida, and Lida was a shrew [*lagal,* skin disease]. She was jealous of Polinn: "Why does he love her? Is she his wife or am I? Is she going to be the mother of his child or am I? His sister, his sister—what's that? I have a sister too, so what?" One evening as Polin was coming into the house, instead of kissing Lida first, he kissed Polinn. You couldn't describe Lida's anger! But she didn't want to say anything for fear of bursting. The three of them ate, they went to bed. Polin slept, Polinn slept, but Lida couldn't sleep, her heart was burning so. All night she tossed and turned on the bed.

Next morning early when the cock crowed, Lida ran to her *maren* [godmother]. Lida's *maren* was an evil old *bonfam,* so evil that people called her *bonfam Laf-Labu* [Mudfish], because her tongue could kill a person like a mudfish. When an old woman wishes evil, there's not a mad dog that can get near her.

When Lida told the business to the *bonfam,* Laf-Labu gave her a lot of bad advice to make trouble for Polin and Polinn. Lida went back to the house, and right away she started. But no use making up malicious things, Polin still loved Polinn, their flour wouldn't turn into charcoal. Lida, inside, was in a lather: "I'll find a way, I'll find a way!"

Polin had a great dog named *Kas-tu* [Catchall[21]], because any stag, wild pig, any game he chased he caught. If you offered Polin two hundred piasters he'd never sell you that dog. *Kas-tu* loved Polinn so much that he'd never take food from anybody else's hand. When they tried, he'd leave the dish and didn't touch a thing.

One day when Polinn had put out *Kas-tu*'s dish, somebody called her from outside. She left the dish on the table and went out. Lida found it and quickly took a cone of white powder out of her pocket, which *bonfam* Laf-Labu gave her. She spread the powder in the dish, mixed it into the food and left. Polinn came back, took the dish, called *Kas-tu,* gave it to him; *Kas-tu* ate it all. As soon as he cleaned his dish, the poor dog started howling and howling. Lida acted angry: "Animals in people's house are really a pain!" She pushed him outside. *Kas-tu* was like a drunk, he stumbled around the yard, got to the edge of the canal, drank and drank and drank. His stomach swelled up, the water choked him, and he died.

Just then Polin came in. What did he see? His dog's dead body, with his mouth all black and his stomach like a drum. He called out; Polinn came out into the yard. He found poor *Kas-tu* dead by the water, Polinn standing next to him. She felt faint, she had to sit down so as not to fall on the ground. Polin came up and said to her, "Sister, that dog would eat only out of your hand, it's your fault he's dead!" What could Polinn answer? But her heart was heavy.

Lida had a cat. At dinnertime Polinn threw a bit of meat to the cat. Lida jumped up, grabbed the meat, and threw it out into the yard, saying to Polinn, "Here, you! You know you have a deadly hand with animals. You mustn't feed my cat, I don't want to see it dead. The day I want it killed, I'll ask you to make its meal." Polinn had to keep still.

Polinn was beginning to get quite unhappy at home, Lida hated her so much. But where could she go? Her brother was her only family. She stayed, although after the *Kas-tu* business Polin was not as nice to her as before.

[Polinn Mutilated]

Just nine months after she was married, Lida gave birth to a child, a fine little boy. Polin was happy, Polinn was happy. Lida too acted happy, but she was annoyed because day and night, the baby cried to be nursed. She couldn't sleep. When the baby began teething, as much as he kept crying, that much his mother knocked him about. Polinn took him, gave him his rattle, caressed him, quieted him.

Children, no matter how small, know which people love them and which don't love them. This one, though not yet six months old, would leave Lida's arms for the arms of Polinn. As soon as he finished nursing, he cried for Polinn to take him; Polinn took him, he would stop crying and become quiet.

Lida was furious. "What! He too loves Polinn more than his mother! Impossible! I'd rather not have a child!"

The child got ill. The doctor said to wean him, his mother's milk was no good, maybe she was pregnant. Polin took the baby from Lida's hands and gave him to Polinn. Polinn was really his mother now, took care of him, bathed him, gave him his soup to eat. Polinn put the poor little boy to sleep in the big bed with her: "This way when he needs something at night, I'm sure to hear him cry."

Lida hated Polinn so much she couldn't look at her baby any more. When the baby met his mother's eyes, he cried as if he'd been burned, her eyes were so evil.

Would you believe this? One night when everybody in the house was asleep, Lida came softly, softly next to Polinn's bed, grabbed the poor unhappy baby by the neck and strangled him. Softly, softly she went back to her room, went back to bed, listened, listened; nothing. Nobody stirred, everybody was quite asleep.

Next morning at cockcrow, Polinn got up. She went, came back, the baby didn't stir. Polinn laughed, "Hey, baby, you really can sleep!" The sun came up, baby didn't stir: "Say, baby, you missed the bell today!" Polinn came up to the bed, turned the baby over, looked at him; he didn't cry. Oh my God! she fell unconscious to the ground.

Polin heard that cry and that sound; he rushed into his sister's room. He found his poor little boy, his eyes all white, turned over, his body black; he felt him, "Oh my God, Lida, Lida, our baby is dead!" Lida came in like a whirlwind, took the baby in her arms, cried and cried. She gave Polinn a kick, still on the ground, and said to Polin, "Are you going to let this wretch kill everyone in our house?" Polin went crazy. He pulled Polinn up, loaded her up, led her into the forest, cut off her two hands with an axe. Poor Polinn, bathed in her own blood, said only, "Oh, my brother, you've cut off my hands, me, your sister! But soon you will be pricked with a truly ugly sting. Then you'll think of me!" Polin went off, leaving her all alone.

[She Marries the King]

Polinn would have died there, but she heard a sound in the bush, she looked, she saw a cute little russet-colored dog coming up to her. The dog pulled, pulled on her dress, as if to say "Come." Polinn followed him. The dog went ahead. He led her past quite a number of little paths under the trees; they reached an open space with a beautiful house next to it. The dog barked; several servants came out of the house. The dog barked again as if he were calling someone to come. Poor Polinn couldn't walk any more, she was weakened by having lost so much blood. As she fell nearly dead to the ground, the dog had the servants lift her in their arms and carry her into the house.

This was a king's house. The king was not there, he'd gone to make war in another country, but every time he went off far away, for either a big hunt or war, he left his little dog at home, and the little dog was put in his place, it was he who ordered the servants, he who knew what his master wanted people to do till he would come back.

The dog had Polinn taken care of. She was put into a fine bedroom, given a fine bed, with a mattress, pillows, everything she needed; cut the neck of a hen to make a good soup for her, gave her fine red wine, prevented noise so she could rest and sleep well; did everything she needed to get well quickly.

After two weeks Polinn was all right. But the poor girl, where were her hands?

The king came back, having had enough of war. After the dog nuzzled him a lot, he led him to Polinn's room. Polinn, you know, was very, very pretty. The king looked and looked at her; right away he was caught. He said to the dog, "Right, Lieutenant! You've done well." The dog's name was Lieutenant. He wagged and wagged his tail and barked to show how happy he was.

Every day the king came to talk and talk with Polinn. He would have liked to ask for her hand, but what hand could he ask for?

Her wrists were cut, she had no hands; he had to go without.

[Polinn Calumniated]

About a year went by like that. The king had to go back to war. Before he left, he ordered Lieutenant, "You know, Polinn will soon give birth. As soon as she has her baby, have somebody write me and give me her news, tell me if it's a boy or a girl. Take good care of her, don't let her lack anything; you're in charge when I am not here." Lieutenant wagged his tail to show he understood. The king left/went.

About two weeks later Polinn gave birth to two little boys. (When Polinn felt she was about to give birth, she called a *fam saz* [midwife] to help her.) There was a little night-light in the room which gave a little light.

The babies came, the room was all lit up: each one had a beautiful star on his forehead. The *fam saz* had to say, "No need for coconut oil with these babies! They carry their own light!"

Lieutenant had a letter written to the king to tell him all that.

As the servant carrying the letter was halfway there, he got tired; he had to go into a house to drink water and rest his feet. That was *bonfam* Laf-Labu's house. The *bonfam* made him talk. The servant told her his whole errand. Then Laf-Labu gave him food and drink, but put some kind of *feyaz* [herb] in the vegetables. When the servant ate that, sleep weighed him down, he fell to the ground and slept. Laf-Labu drew the letter out of the servant's pocket, read the letter, quickly wrote another, forged a signature and put it in its place.

When the servant awoke, he rubbed his eyes, he looked at the sun. "*Mama,* I've lost time!" He picked up his stick, thanked the old woman and ran off.

When the king read that letter, he was very sad. Here's what was written there: "King: Polinn has given birth to a little monkey and a little dog. Mother and children are doing well. We await your orders."

The king wrote in answer, "Monkey or dog, a father must love his children. Take good care of the children. When I return home, I shall see what I'll do with them.—King." The king gave this paper into the hands of the same servant, told him to go back home, he ran off.

When the servant reached in front of Laf-Labu's house, that evil *bonfam* was waiting by the side of the road. She stopped him, she said, "So, my *nwar,*[22] of course you're taking the king's answer home. I know you're in a hurry, but I wish you'd stop a minute. My relatives just sent me a an old bottle of *zamburzwa* [a tree] rum, we have to taste it together." What could the poor *nwar* do? He had to go in. Laf-Labu poured him a big glass of rum. He drank just one swallow, the glass fell out of his hand, he toppled down, he slept.

Laf-Labu took the letter out of his pocket, opened it, read it. She took a pen, ink, and paper and wrote another letter: "Listen well to what I order. Take that horror of a Polinn, throw her out with her two bastard babies. But as she has no hands to hold them with, fasten one on her back, fasten the other on her stomach. You have heard; do as I order.—King." The servant woke up; he thought it was the rum that threw him down. He was ashamed, he took his stick, he left.

When the people at the king's house learned what their master was ordering them, some were aggrieved, because Polinn was so good, others were glad, because they were jealous. But happy or jealous, they had to do as they were ordered. Lieutenant was furious. He always knew his master was too good-hearted to order such an evil deed. Never! But he was [only] a dog, with him there was no talking. He barked and barked; this time no one would listen to him.

[Her Hands Restored]

They pulled Polinn out of her bed, fastened her two babies as the letter said, led them out on to the highway, pushed them away. Lieutenant would not leave Polinn, he followed her. They walked and walked. Poor unhappy Polinn wept, Lieutenant said nothing.

They reached a big forest. Lieutenant went ahead to show the way. When they reached the side of a little stream, Polinn was thirsty, she knelt down to drink with her mouth, she had no hands to drink from. She bent down to bring her mouth to the water; the baby fastened on her back got loose and fell into the water. Polinn put her arms into the water, even though she had no hands, to catch the baby. Would you believe, it was miracle water! As she plunged her arms into the water, all at once her hands grew back! Polinn grabbed the baby, kissed him, wept, cried, "Thank you, thank you, Bondye!" Lieutenant ran, barked, rolled on the ground; he was like crazy, he was so happy.

They walked, walked, walked. After three days in a big forest, they reached an open space. At the edge of that space they found an old old house covered with *vitiver* [grass], nobody inside. They stopped there. Polinn gradually straightened up the house, gathered leaves, made a nice bed for herself and the children, a little bed for Lieutenant, she said her prayers, she stretched out, she went to sleep.

Early next morning she got up, sat on her bed and thought. "What can I do? Where can I go? I have no family; no one wants to kiss me. Better if I stay alone here in this old house; no one will come to bother me; I'll raise my children in peace; Lieutenant and I will find a way of getting food so we don't die of hunger. Right, Lieutenant?" Lieutenant barked at her, wagged, wagged his tail to show he was happy.

Let's go back to the king.

When that poor young man thought Polinn had given him a monkey and a dog instead of children, he was so upset that he didn't dare go back to his house. He stayed at war five or six years or so, his heart burned so. Then he began to feel his heart easing a little, and he returned home. "Where are my children? Where is Polinn? Where is Lieutenant?" The people stood dumb. Fortunately for them, the king's letter had been kept in a bureau drawer. They ran to fetch that letter and put it into the king's hand. The king read the letter; it was his turn to stand dumb. His eyes widened and widened, he turned the paper over and over; of course he had never written that, but he had to be surprised at how much the writing was like his! What to do? He thought and thought, then a suspicion came to him: "Call the servant who brought the letter." When the *nwar* knew the king was calling for him, his heart jumped, I tell you, but he had to come even if his legs were running away under him.

The king, by making the servant talk, drew out of him his whole story. Then it wasn't difficult to see how the whole thing had happened. *Mama!* no anger like the king's anger! The king said only one word, "Wretch!" The servant turned three times around like a top, fell down lifeless. The king grabbed him by the hair and stood him up. "Take me to that old sorceress's house! Get moving!"

When they reached *bonfam Laf-Labu*'s house, the king put guards around the house and went in by himself with the servant. Laf-Labu was sitting down, she jumped up. The king asked the servant, "Is that the one?" "That's the one, my king!" The king had the servant tie her feet and hands and put her on the dining table. He took a bottle of oil off the table and put the oil all over Laf-Labu. The servant thought, "Is the king going to make a salad out of her? But there's no salt, or pepper, or vinegar."

They went out into the yard. The king ordered the guards to set fire to the four corners of the house. Laf-Labu inside yelled and yelled; the fire reached her she caught fire just like those torches the fishermen light on the reefs. She gave a great light, she died. May the wind scatter her ashes!

The king sent a company of people to search out news of Polinn everywhere, everywhere. They went in different directions, looked, asked, found nothing. They had to return to the king's house and say that. The poor king was so upset he got thin.

Two years or so went by. One day, when the king was hunting in the forest, the dogs raised a stag. The king fired and wounded him. But the stag didn't fall, he had wings, he flew. He went, went, went; the dogs had to let him go, they were so tired, only the king had the strength to stick with him. The stag ran and ran; when he knew he'd left the king some way behind, he stopped for a second to rest and breathe; the king came up, the stag rushed off. They stayed at it for two days; at sundown they reached the edge of an open place. The ground was open before him, the stag took off; the king looked far, far ahead; no use keeping on trying; the king took off his hat to him, he had to laugh, he cried, "Hey, you really can run! You can boast of it. OK! Maybe we'll meet another day." The stag was far off and didn't answer.

There was the king by himself at the edge of the plain. He looked, didn't recognize anything, he'd never come this way. But maybe he would find a house to rest for the night, or even a little something to eat. After two days his stomach was starting to feel hunger. He walked, walked, then he saw a light afar off. He kept walking; it was a little house covered with *vetiver.* The house was shut; the king knocked, knocked on the door. He heard someone quietly, quietly walking inside, like someone afraid. He cried, "Open,

open, if you have a good heart! I'm hungry, I am tired: help me, and Bondye will help you!" The door opened, the king went in.

In the room there was just a young woman. It was starting to get dark; the king couldn't make out her face, but he thought it was a face he knew, a face, how to say, Polinn's face. "Oh, oh, poor Polinn, where is she now?" The king asked the young woman for something to eat; from her cupboard the young woman took *patat* and manioc, with a piece of roast hare. She put the dish before the king on the table. "Poor Polinn, with no hands to serve me!"

While he was eating, the king watched this young woman coming and going in the room. But the young woman dared not speak to him, as if she were afraid of him. While the two of them were there, the king heard a dog barking, barking afar off. "Not possible—but I know that voice. That's Lieutenant's voice!" The dog's voice came closer, the king kept listening. The dog wasn't alone; two little boys were with him, having a good time barking back at the dog. The king jumped up and went to the door. Night had fallen, it was very dark outside. But the king had to keep rubbing his eyes, because he was seeing something he'd never seen before. On the foreheads of these two little boys who were following the dog there were stars. The stars gave off so much light that the whole outside was lit up like day, I tell you. As the king was being surprised at this miracle, suddenly the dog with the boys caught his scent. The dog leaped into the house, jumped on the king, wept, licked him, barked, wagged his tail, rolled around, licked his feet, jumped up to his face to lick him some more, he was out of breath, crazy. "Lieutenant, Lieutenant, it's you, Lieutenant!" The king took him in his arms, they both wept for joy.

The king turned around, he went towards that young woman, took her in his arms: "Polinn, Polinn! It's really you, my Polinn!" Kissed and kissed and kissed her. But enough now, enough of making people jealous. What else do I need to tell you, children? It's not hard to know what'll happen in the rest of my story.

Early next morning before cockcrow, they all left that old house to return to the king's house. What though the sun wasn't up yet? The stars on the children were there to light their way! On the third day they reached the king's house. The people were happy, they sang and yelled and yelled. The ones who were jealous of Polinn sang the loudest; that's how things are, children, you'll understand some day.

Thanks to that miracle water, Polinn had hands now, she had a finger to put a wedding ring on. The king asked for her hand, the king put the ring on her finger. They made a banquet, children! What a banquet! Open your baskets, I tell you, open your vest, I tell you! Leave your pants unbuckled behind.

As we were sitting down to the table, a poor beggar came into the room to ask for charity. He dragged his body with sticks, his eyes were red with weeping, his mouth all twisted like a fish torn by a hook. Polinn looked at this poor beggar, went to him, and kissed him. "It's you, Polin, it's you, my brother!" They told their story quick, quick, for fear the soup would get cold. Lida drugged him to kill him, because that shrew was tired of having a husband; that's what twisted up his mouth. But Lida, one day, as she was having an argument with somebody, took a major blow to the head with a stick and fell down dead. Polin had to run away in case people would believe it was he who'd killed his wife. "Aïa, it was the stick that killed you."

"Let's eat, brother. You will stay with us, nothing to worry about."

Just as I was going to sit down at table with them, they pulled my chair out from under me. I fell down and rolled and rolled; I stopped here to tell you the story. (Baissac, *Folklore* 290–331)[23]

After the full, detailed performance, with all its European touches, the typical Mauritius closing formula effectively shows how well on its way the creole folktale was, in the 1880s, to being installed as children's literature.

A century later, Polin and Polinn's two sons reappear in Mauritius, with their stars, but also with major changes. In his first line, Marcel L'Allouette establishes a link to his audience.

104. Two Brothers Become Rich

Marcel L'Allouette, Port Louis, Mauritius 1980

Once upon a time, in a country, guess what there was? There was a king and his queen. Life went on, then the queen died. All those who worked in the castle got very sad. This king's two sons, Fis [Son] and Batyan, told their father to get married again, or else they would leave the country. The king answered, "If you insist that I should remarry, find me the wife of your choosing."

The following day, the two young men and some other people from the castle went out to look for a princess for the king. Each one said they'd like this one or that one, until finally they agreed on one princess. So the marriage took place, and everybody was very happy.

But a few months after the ceremony, the two sons had some very hard times with the new queen. As long as the king was present, she pretended to like them and be nice to Fis and Batyan. But as soon as the king went out, she would keep turning like this, turning and twisting. . . . And one day she tore her clothes with a pair of scissors, while the king was visiting people on his land far away. As soon as he came back, she rushed up to him saying, "Look what Fis and Batyan did to me. They tried to rape me."

The king got so angry that he asked his guards to bring him two white horses. On the forehead of the first one he ordered a moon to be placed, and on the second one a star. He gave one horse to Fis and the other to Batyan. Then he ordered two executioners to take them far away into the forest and kill them. He also told them to bring back their liver as proof that they had done what he ordered. But the two executioners had very fond memories of the dead queen, so they decided not to kill her two sons. One of the two men told them, "As soon as we let you go, just go, keep going, and never come back to this country." On their way back, the two executioners killed two animals and brought their liver back to the king.

The two brothers walked straight ahead. They went, they went, they went. Night fell. They sat under a *vakwa* [screw pine] tree and fell asleep. Batyan immediately went into a very deep sleep, while Fis was thinking about what to do the next day.

In the tree were a couple of martins. The female said to the male, "Look at these two boys, so tired, and they are sleeping, and they haven't had any food. Let's give them our life. The one who eats you, the fatter of us two, he will become rich on the following morning. The one who eats me, the thinner, he will become rich late in life." Fis, who was not really asleep, listened. The male said to the female, "Can't you keep quiet? Have you gone crazy? You think I'll give them my life?" As it was very cold, Fis started a big fire under the tree. The female kept saying the same thing to the male. But the male wouldn't agree, and said, "I tell you, leave me alone, leave me in peace."

Hearing this, the female got very angry, pounced on the male, and both fell into the fire and died immediately. Fis, who had been on the watch ever since they started talking, wasted no time. He took them out of the fire, cleaned them, woke his younger brother, and offered him the fatter bird, thinking that he had all the time to become rich. After this unexpected meal, they both fell asleep until next morning.

The next day, they started walking, each one in his own direction, with the condition that the first one to find a river, or water, would whistle to let the other one know.

Half a mile on, Batyan came into a country where the king had just died. There was a little monkey there who had a crown on his head. Before he died, the king had told the little monkey that the first one whose head he would put the crown on would become king. As soon as the little monkey saw Batyan, he ran up to him, grabbed him by the neck, and put the crown on his head. So Batyan became king.

After he had wandered for many years, Fis reached that same country. Having nothing to eat, he sold his horse, the one that had a moon on its forehead. Well, the person who bought that horse, he kept on walking with the horse so much that the king noticed him. The king called him and asked him to bring him the person who had sold him the famous horse. When Fis came, they didn't recognize each other. It was such a long time ago, and each one had grown a beard that long. Despite all the explanations that Fis gave, the king wouldn't believe him. He ordered his executioners to go to the plain of death.

While waiting for the sentence, Fis was locked in prison. Fis fell asleep, and his heart was full of sadness. But during his sleep, he saw his dead mother, who showed him a magic ring, and also gave him this advice: "Before they kill you, call the king. Tell him that you can put that big boat, which has been sleeping for twelve years, into the sea." The king had had a big ship made, but nobody had been able to put it afloat for twelve years.

On the day of the sentence, the prisoner told this to the king. The king was very surprised that his prisoner could promise to succeed where everyone else in the kingdom had failed. So he called all the people, from his castle and from the country, to the sea, in order to watch the prisoner at work. Before taking the prisoner, he promised him freedom if ever he succeeded in putting the ship afloat. To the great surprise of everyone, Fis just touched the boat and it went straight into the sea, so quickly that everybody jumped. So the king, Batyan, declared that Fis was free on the spot, and also made him captain of the ship.

His first voyage brought him to a country where there was a sign saying [in bad French], "The one who succeeds to ring the bell with a spiderweb rope, I'll give him half my fortune and also my daughter." The sailors, who were in a hurry to get rich, and get married to the nice princess, rushed up to ring this famous bell. But as soon as they touched the spiderweb rope, it would break. So last of all was Captain Fis. On the very first try, he managed to make the bell ring with such force that it shook the whole country. So he became rich on the spot.

Back to the country of King Batyan, he introduced the princess to him and started saying him the story of Fis and Batyan. The two brothers recognized each other. So they had a big feast.

I was spying through the door and *kutna* went to tell this to the king, they gave me a good kick in the ass, and I fell here to tell you this story.

Philippe Christian: What is a *kutna*?
Marcel L'Allouette: A big fly.
Philippe Christian: What fly?
Marcel L'Allouette: Not a real fly, somebody who's kind of a talebearer.
(Christian, "L'Allouette" 6)[24]

Ti Zan transforms into that spying fly which Gérose Barivoitse used in his story of the red loincloth (above). M. L'Allouette's refashioning of traditional motifs is another key to the creole combination of creativity and innovation.

Mauritian creoles had no monopoly on combining memory and innovation, especially after the abolition of slavery in 1835. They had rivals. The British, having acquired the island twenty years before, now had to face the French plantation owners, who never dreamed the slaves would simply walk off the plantation. Obliged to import labor to protect the island economy, the British turned to the Raj. From 1834 to 1839, 25,458 "coolies" from Bihar, Bengal, Tamil Nadu, and other parts of India immigrated, bringing religion, songs, myths, and costume, and building scores of temples. As the Indian population grew by the thousands, Mauritius came to supply most of the Empire's sugar in the Victorian age (Toussaint). The Indian indentured laborers cared little for their role in allowing the control of Mauritius by international business. In time they came to dominate demographically, then politically: they led the island to independence from the British in 1968. Today they are the leaders.

Two generations after indenture began, Charles Baissac had to allow a tale from India, Sabour, into his collection. Seen simply as an instance of folktale variation, Sabour is easily comprehended. Its first episode structures the plot as a riddle: a daughter says "Sobur" (wait) to her father when he asks what to bring from his journey, and until he finds Prince Sobur, he does not know that his daughter will make a rich marriage. Romantic twists and turns take the lovers apart and bring them together, as in Bengali and other Indian versions (Day 124–37). At the end, in an un-Indian closing formula, as the king gives the wedding banquet, "I wanted to put some of the cake in my pocket for my children, but they beat me, threw me out into the yard, kicked me, and I fell here" (Baissac, *Folklore* 130–45).

The story also reached Mayotte. By the time Claude Allibert recorded it there in the 1970s, it had acquired a strongly Mahorais episode to explain the casting-out of the heroine.

105. Swaburi n'Swali

Mahamudu Abiamri, Mayotte 1973–75

There was once, by the seaside, a widowed king who was very rich. He had six daughters. The sixth was the most beautiful. Her name was

Fatima. They lived in a large palace on the top floor. On this floor there were six bedchambers without windows, and each chamber was occupied by one daughter and her servant woman. They spent their youth in this palace. Their father had given each one a mirror, which they were to look at all their lives, and said to them: "I absolutely do not wish you to go out of here. If you like, you can amuse yourselves inside the house with your servants. The mirrors I have given you are my watchmen. Every morning, you will gather here and I will check your mirrors. If, as bad luck would have it, I find that one among you has her mirror covered with smoke and that it does not shine like the others, that will mean that she has gone out—and then let her beware. She will see what will happen to her. I will only spend the morning checking the mirrors. Behave yourselves!"

Then he went. Several months went by. The six young women lived happily in their palace with their friends; they played inside the house. One day, a *grand mariage* was announced for the village. The couple were well-known people. Their parents organized a great *chigoma* [celebration] which took place in the public square. All those who wished could participate in the *chigoma.* People were also invited from foreign lands. Monumental posters were stuck up everywhere to announce what time this game would begin. A messenger was sent to the palace where the young women were. The eldest sister said to the others, "We all have to go together to see this *chigoma* tonight. Our father will not know!" All the young women agreed except Fatima. She refused, saying she was afraid of her father. But the five others decided to go, each one wanting to make herself more beautiful than the others. That evening at nightfall, when everything was finished in the house, they made their way to the town. They went about everywhere they wanted, had a good time with the other young women, chatted with the young men, while Fatima slept by her servant's side.

In the morning, at first cockcrow, the young women came back to the house. There each one became worried at seeing her mirror, which was now clouded over. They ran to Fatima's chamber, went in, grabbed the shining mirror and put another in its place, while their sister was asleep. Then they wondered how they would manage with one mirror. The eldest said, "Today we'll have to go see our father one at a time. The first one called will take this mirror. When she comes back, she'll give it to the next without our father seeing, and so on!"

It was already daylight. Quickly their father arrived and sat down on a chair. He called his daughters. The eldest went first. The father told her to call one of her sisters. She hurried to the door and gave the mirror to the next one. This the five young women passed before their father. Fatima, who had awaked at the last minute, got up and, took her mirror without looking at it. Without washing her face, she hurried to her father. "Good morning, father!" she said as she gave him the mirror. The king took one glance at the mirror and brutally broke it on his daughter's face. Saying nothing to her, next he kicked her. He slapped her face, and the young woman could not even cry out. Her body was covered with blood. Finally, weary of striking her, he drove her out of the house.

The poor pretty young woman went her way in despair. She walked along the shore. Far from the young woman, very far from the house, she was attracted by a puff of smoke rising from a big rock. She went up to it and knocked. "Come in," said someone living in the rock. A door opened and the young woman went in.

She saw an old woman coming towards her. She welcomed her politely, asking her her news and where she came from. The poor young woman calmed down and told her her experience from the beginning. The old woman would keep the young woman in the rock, where there was a house with two chambers: the bedroom and the kitchen, with the yard. The old woman told her that she lived like this: "If you see an ant carrying a grain of rice, pick it up quickly, put it in a pot, add some water, make a fire. Then the pot will fill up with cooked rice. If you see a mouse carrying a bone, pick it up, put it in a pot, add everything needed, a good sauce, and you'll find pieces of good meat in the pot. That's how you'll do everything!"

A few months later, the king embarked on a sea voyage. He went to sell his goods. He asked each of his daughters what she wanted him to bring her back from his voyage, and each one said what she wanted: one wanted a gold bracelet, another, another jewel, and so on. The next day, early, he left in company with other voyagers. Out at sea, the boat stopped short. Not a puff of wind. Nothing but sea stretching on all sides! Everyone was worried. Then the *mwalimu* [diviner] said to the king, "You have one daughter who does not know that you have embarked on this voyage. You did not ask her what she wanted as you did with the others. We must go back to our starting place, otherwise we'll always stay here!" The king himself made the boat take a half-turn. Soon he found himself at the shore. The king already knew what was up and where his daughter was. He sent a messenger to ask her what she wanted. The messenger ran up to the rock. When he got there, he found the young woman getting ready for prayer. He immediately said to her, "Your father has sent me to announce that he is going to go away on a voyage. If you want something, tell me quickly, I'll tell it to him, and when he comes back, you will have it!" The young woman said, "*Swaburi n'swali,*" which means "Wait, I'm going to pray first." The envoy ran back to the king and told him, "It seems she wants *swaburi n'swali.*" Without asking what that was, they again departed.

This time the boat reached its destination. The king disembarked with his goods. He sold them, and going from shop to shop he bought what he had promised to his daughters. Only the *swaburi n'swali* was left to find. He looked everywhere but didn't find it. He went to the king of the country he was visiting and spoke to him of his daughter's request. The other king told him, "It is my son who is called Swaburi n'Swali. But I don't know if he will agree to go with you!" He was called and asked if he would agree to go with the king. He did agree, but before anything else he went to dig out a tree trunk and planed it down so no one could see the opening. Then he gave the trunk to the king and asked him to take it to his daughter's house. The king was not very happy to have this tree trunk to take, but he well knew that without it, he would not get back to his own country.

On his return, he paid two men to carry the tree trunk to his daughter's house. When she received the trunk, Fatima questioned the two men. "Where does this kind of tree come from?" she said in surprise. "Your father gave it to us to bring you." "I thank God!" she said. The two men put the trunk in the yard and left.

One day when the two women had no more firewood in the house, her grandmother said to her, "Take the axe and try cutting the trunk, so that we

The great social and cultural event in the Comoros is the *grand mariage,* which brings together hundreds of celebrants.

can make something to eat." The young woman did as she was asked. At the third blow of the axe, a gold piece fell to the ground. She quickly called her grandmother and gathered up all the gold. She put it in their room, which almost filled up completely with it. She then read the letter: "If you need me, take the fan and put it against your face. I will come immediately." No sooner read than done! Swaburi n'Swali arrived. Each one questioned the other one. "Know that Swaburi n'Swali is a prince." He was very handsome, and his father was as rich as the king who was the princess's father. He became red with rage when he learned of the girl's misadventure, and he decided to take his fiancée and the grandmother home with him. He married the young woman, and he invited the wicked king, who was ashamed before everyone. They say the other five young women never got husbands. (Allibert 82–85)[25]

It is no accident that such a romantic Indian tale has remained in tradition, in an island where so many people are bilingual. But if it is antique in genre, its theme is alive. Jokes in modern multilingual Mauritius, and doubtless elsewhere in the region, often turn ironically on such misunderstandings of language.

106. Say It in French

Kreol narrator 1984–85

There was a boy who dressed up. He put his suit on, very correct, and he went into a bakery where they make cakes. He's dressed up, with a necktie. He wants to play gentleman, so he decides to speak French today. He wants to eat a cake, but he's forgotten whether you say, in French, *un gateau* or *une gateau.* How is he going to say he wants to eat a cake? So he says, "Sir, give me two cakes minus one." (Gallob 311–12)[26]

Speaking to an American, another joke-teller switches from English to Kreol to Hindi to make the point. It helps to know that in Hindi, *dadi* means grandmother.

107. Dadi

Trilingual narrator, Mauritius 1984–85

You know, especially in Europe, in your country, kids have the custom of calling their father Daddy, but here in Mauritius we don't say Daddy, we say Papi or Papa. Once in a poor family a father sent his son to study medicine in England. After completing his course he returned to Mauritius. He wore a pair of spectacles now. He has completed his course now. He was at the airport here, Plaisance Airport, and his father has gone to pick him. The doctor, seeing his father, ran to his father saying, "Hello Daddy! Hello Daddy!" The father replied in Creole, "I sent you to become a doctor, now you come back, you wear spectacles, you don't recognize your father, you are calling me your grandmother." He gave him two slaps. (Gallob 264)[27]

Not only are words in English heard as insults, but the voice of the homeland condemns foreign influence for corrupting family relations. Thus creolization in language is both performance and critique. It is here that Mauritius holds the key: through performance and poetics comes the critique of the world's sociopolitical ills (Bauman and Briggs, "Poetics").

One way of viewing creolization would see it as merging cultural forms that have family resemblances. For instance, in a Mauritian tale of Hare and Tortoise, African fictive kinship (the *komer* and *konper*) merges with European godparentage (Dorothy Noyes, personal communication). Afro-Mauritian trickster stories glorify verbal deviousness, but so also do tales rooted in the European Middle Ages. Baissac perceived one *fabliau* to be "an adaptation to creole of a story brought complete from the *grand terre*" (Baissac, *Étude* 140–41), but any fan of Ti Zan or Soungoula would applaud the wife's quick thinking.

108. Clever Dealing 1: The Corpse; or, The Dead Man on the Ass

Mauritian Kreol narrator 1880s

A woman was in her house with her lover. Her husband had gone out that evening without saying when he'd be back. Early in the morning the wife hears knocking at the door. She asks, "Who's there?"

Her husband says, "Me."

So the wife says to her lover, "Quick, go hide in that big jar in the corner of the house." He goes and hides. When the woman opens the door, her husband asks her if she's put water on the fire to make coffee. His wife says to him, "I'm just going to do it. But why did you come back so soon?"

"I found the person I went to see and came back right away, that's all."

Meanwhile the water is boiling. She pours the water on the coffee. The rest of the water—I don't know what she was thinking of—she pours it into the jar where her lover went to hide. The poor *boug* [guy] doesn't say a word, he's seized by this boiling water, he has a fit, he dies. In death his mouth stays half open as if he were laughing.

In the morning, when her husband goes to work, the woman says to her lover, "Quick, come out, he's gone, careful lest he come back." Lover doesn't move. "Hey, come out quick, I tell you! Ah, ah, I'm talking to you and you're laughing!" She sees he doesn't stop laughing, she grabs him by the hair, pulls him out of the jar. Only then she sees he's dead. "Great God, great God! Mama! What am I going to do with a dead body in the house?"

She thinks, she thinks. There's an old donkey going up and down in the yard. She takes the dead man, ties him to the donkey, and lets the donkey go. The donkey runs off, he goes to the field of an old man who has planted maize. The donkey does nothing but chew, he who never had anything but wheat grass to eat. As he is chewing, the housewife sees a man on a donkey and the donkey eating. "Hey you, sir! What are you doing? You're letting your donkey eat my corn and you're on his back! Can't you stop him from doing damage?" The man doesn't answer anything, he laughs. "What! I speak fair to you and you make fun of me!"

So the goodwife is furious, she calls "Husband!" The husband comes with his stick. The goodwife says to him, "Can you believe I am talking to that Monsieur there, I tell him not to let his animal eat my maize, he makes fun of me, he only laughs." So the husband gives a hit to that man on the donkey. *Bouf, Msié* falls off.

So the husband sees that, he says "God, God, wife, what have we done? We've killed a man. What are we going to do?" The wife thinks, she says, "Don't be afraid." She takes a bundle of old old clothes, she ties the dead man up in the bundle of clothes. She acts as if when she got to the river, she's forgotten the soap. She puts down the bundle, she runs as if she were fetching the soap. Behind her some thieves come, take the bundle, run off.

That's how the goodwife found the way to get out of a bad spot.

Thieves are thieves, they'll even steal a dead body. That's how the story ends. (Baissac, *Étude* 141–46)[28]

Stories like this connected nineteenth-century Mauritius to medieval Europe (Baissac, *Folklore* 14–15). Anticipating later creolization theory, Baissac saw the creole folktale as "a highly plastic material, which everyone is free to take up and refashion to his taste." He attributed this freedom to the absence of European laws: "Where literary property is unknown, everything belongs to everyone," but he didn't remark on another key to the plasticity of the material: its applicability to real life. Self-preserving quick thinking was undoubtedly just what a creole needed in post-emancipation days.

109. Clever Dealing 2: The Priest

Rev. Patrick Beeton, Mauritius 1850s

A priest in the country had had his poultry-yard cleared at different times of all its feathery tenants, from the speckled guinea-fowl to the tender turkey which he had reserved for his own Christmas dinner. Suspecting that the thieves were among his own flock, he assembled his *brébis noirs* [black sheep] for confession. The first penitent was the man who had stolen the turkey, with which he had feasted his friends there assembled. After some time he came forth, perspiring at every pore, and panting with excitement. The contest had been a keen one, and he had to relate his experience to the others, who had to pass through the same fiery ordeal. "Him say, 'Do you ever steal ducks?' Me say, 'Never, father; me never steal ducks.' 'Do you ever steal geese?' 'Never, father; me never steal geese.' 'Do you ever steal guinea-fowls or chickens?' 'Never, father; me never steal guinea-fowl or chicken.' 'Good; me absolve you. Go.' But (here there was a shout of laughter, heartily shared in by the audience), the good father! he never ask if me stole turkeys";—("Mais li bon père! li n'a pas demandé, si moi fin volé di' dindes"). (Beeton 92–93)[29]

The clergyman was a fine ethnographer.

Baissac also expected that the linguist Hugo Schuchardt would appreciate the creole's mastery of language, and so he did.

110. Clever Dealing 3: The Planter

Hugo Schuchardt 1880s

A planter whose house I dined at ordered his cook to make an excellent *kari* [stew] from one of the capons he had been fattening for two months. The order was carried out, but in serving it, the planter noticed that one of the fowl's legs was missing. "Call Charlie," he said. "Tell me, Charlie, since when do capons have only one leg?"

"Don't know, sir. Maybe that capon is sick."

"Sick or not, he had to have two legs."

"Bugger, sir, it comes back to me. He broke his foot, so [obscure]."

"You ate the capon's leg?"

"May God punish me, sir, if I ate it."

"If you tell me the truth, nothing will be done to you."

"Ah, sir, a big misfortune happened. I was starting to boil the pot, you know. Just then the leg of the capon jumped out of the pot and fell into the fire. I said, 'My white master, he doesn't eat ashes, it'll make him sick, I'll take it out.' Sir, aftar that I tasted it."

"After that you ate it?"

"That's it, master, you said it, the devil tempted me. Forgive me!" (Chaudenson, *Textes* 55)[30]

Baissac's other tale of multilingualism transcribes one narrator's mix of Mozambican, Malagasy, Indian, and Chinese pronunciations (not consistently as to orthography), and gives attention to his paralinguistic codes, or what ordinary folk call gestures.

111. Clever Dealing 4: The Boss

Kreol narrator 1880s

I was one of M. Gambriesse's blacks. I guarded the manioc. Every day I passed by the henhouse to go to my work. Every day I saw a big turkey. Coo!
At this exclamation, which Baissac translated *bonne affaire,* "lucky break," he noted a ten-second pause.
Sir, you know what that turkey said to me? "Chongor, eat me, eat me, eat me!" You know, sir, since I was a child I always had a good heart. I never liked hearing anyone ask for anything. Just to please him, I cut his throat, I put him in the pot, I ate him.

Next day, M. Gambrièce, my boss, he gets me, he asks me how I stole his turkey. I say to him, "I didn't steal him. I did something to please him. He asked me like this, 'Chongor, eat me, eat me, eat me!'" M. Gambrièce's heart was hard, not like mine. He called to people, "Catch this *nwar* for me, put him on the ladder, give him fifty hits with the whip."
"Again he shakes his head for a good minute," Baissac interjects. "Then while his left hand stays level over his head, his right arm strikes with big blows and his fingers make the sound of the whip. He shakes his head, he groans dully. Finally he reaches the end of the torment and goes on, his eyes full of tears":
Those weren't the people of old days! Thanks to the queen, thanks, she is the true God! The blood was coming out of my body. "Take some pepper and salt, put them in those wounds," says M. Gambrièce. Dee dee dee dee, dee dee dee dee dee.
"And he bends down, straightens up, twists himself, jumps up and down and weeps, to make you understand the horrible burning he went through. This is pronounced from the throat and teeth, with clenched jaws." Baissac continues discussing the language (Baissac, *Étude* 105–108).[31]

If creole narrative was plastic material, crossing the line between fiction and fact, as Gérose Barivoitse does, is another technique for working the material. In Mauritius, third-person *zistwar,* including the Siren-Girl, Ti Zan, and Polin and Polinn, are complemented by first-person accounts. Henri Bernardin de St.-Pierre (1737–1814) put Mauritius on the literary map with the most popular and most critically despised of all French novels, the pre-romantic *Paul et Virginie,* in the year of revolution, 1789. Earlier, he witnessed and wrote about Mauritian slavery, in a decisive testimony that blacks and Indians were already mixing (Bernardin de St. Pierre 397–403). Two centuries later, other eyewitness accounts of slavery began coming to light (Nagapen 116); so did accounts of interaction between settlers and slaves (Chaudenson, *Textes* 100–103). Poignant first-person testimonies from nineteenth-century Indian immigrant women (Carter), as well as letters, depositions, and petitions of Indian, Chinese, Malagasy, Comoran, and African laborers (Carter and Ng Foong Kwong), all recently uncovered, call attention to the genre of personal narrative.

So do dream stories.

112. A Curious Adventure at Albatros

France Laval Jean-Baptiste 1880

"I'm told you had a curious adventure at Albatros," says an interviewer. "Is that so?" The interviewer, Philippe Christian, is visiting a 44-year-old *chef-grévier,* a salter of fish on the island of St.-Brandon. Unvisited by tourists or most Mauritians, Albatros Island lies north of the Cargados Carajos Shoals. "Albatros is a nice memory for me," says Mr. Jean-Baptiste, putting himself at center stage and arousing his hearer's expectations. He worked for a member of a prominent family.

France Laval Jean-Baptiste: A long time ago, I salted fish for M. Guy Quenette. When he left for Mauritius, he left me alone on the island to take care of his business. A few Seychellois who were there also left, after a fight that had broken out among them. For three months I lived all alone on that island.

A person who has never been alone on a tropical island, but who has read *Robinson Crusoe* or seen Tom Hanks's film *Cast Away* (2000), will have no trouble visualizing such solitude, without envying it. What happens to a man all alone on an island? Robinson Crusoe finds a companion to serve and help him, and to point up the superiority of his colonizing culture.[32] Chuck Noland (the Tom Hanks character in *Cast Away*) creates a household god by painting a face on a volleyball; now he has that "someone to talk to." France Laval Jean-Baptiste will have a supernatural visitation.

Well, you know how these places are, where there were these old French people of a certain era, who died there. Also there was this terrible cemetery, with a tomb that nobody exactly knew [where it was]. One minute it appeared, one minute it disappeared; no way to know what it was. It was in dense bush. Albatros is a very big island, bigger than Raphael, Pirelo—cocos double double![33]

Mr. Jean-Baptiste comes to what a rhetorician would call his "proof," or "confirmation."

One night, towards midnight, when I was sleeping in my cabin, the big door opened. Then I couldn't tell what was behind the door. In my sleep I saw a very beautiful girl coming towards me. She had blonde, blonde hair, white trousers, a white jacket. She was about seventeen, admirable, terrible! She came and placed herself at the side of my cot. She tried to put a gold chain around my neck. I woke up with a start, I looked in all the corners, but I didn't see anybody. I couldn't sleep any more, my mind was working.

The "admirable, terrible" seventeen-year-old blonde resembles the fairy of European folktale like an illustration in a children's book. Her other model is the French beach tourist who visits Mauritius in large numbers, though to Albatros she comes only in dream. The combination of folk, popularized, and commercial images begins the "primary sequence" or surface structure of the narrative, the five failures Mr. Jean-Baptiste will narrate (Labov and Waletzky 31–32). The fairy's attempt to give the dreamer a magic object, which would ensure later success in his adventures, is the first failure. For that night, the dream is incomplete.

Day came and everything went on as usual. I went to work without really thinking about that business. Night came, I went to sleep again. The girl showed herself again in my sleep. This time she spoke to me and said, "There are three cocks which I like best on this island. Kill them and give them to me, and I'll have you dig up a pile of money." And she was talking French to me!

Like any folktale fairy, she assigns him a task and gives him instructions; like the tourist, she talks French to him. European women sometimes seek local lovers for holiday flings on the islands, knowing they will leave them behind, and ignoring their susceptibility to a sexually transmitted disease. Since *cock* means the same in Kreol as in English, the interviewer might wonder whether it's really a dead fowl this temptress wants. Discovering a treasure in a dream is a frequent motif not merely in Mauritian folktale (Ramsurrun 95–100), but also in regional legends (Thomas 131–39). Echoing island treasure-hunters and reinforcing belief, the teller adds,

It's true that there are a whole lot of chickens, cocks, and rabbits on that island.

Still in folktale mode, the fairy gives the hero his instructions for securing the prize.

She also said to me, "That money is easy for you to get. Over there, near that little pond where those people swim, over there there's a tree. Under its third branch you just dig, and you'll find a pile of money." And all that really is there, the little pond, the tree. I heard about money, no need to tell you more!

His attempt to pursue the quest that has been assigned in the dream leads to the second failure.

About one in the morning I went out with a spade, a hoe, and a pick. I also took a gunnysack. But when I got near the first cock, I got scared. I went quietly back to my bed. The two following days the girl didn't show herself. I thought it was a really stupid dream.

Were this a traditional folktale, the hero would find the prize, get the girl, and ascend the throne. But it is also legend and fantasy, in which the fairy will scold him as no folktale fairy ever would.

Well! the third day I saw the girl again in my sleep. She was shaking her head and looking at me. She said to me, "Don't you want to go? You are scared." I sent her to hell, I took no notice of her.

The anger with which he covers his admission of failure brings him a second donor figure, who will assign him the same task more forcefully in the fourth episode of failure. Europeans, even in dreams, dress in white; the picture of the old colonial even refers to someone the interviewer is presumed to know.

The fourth day, I then met an old Frenchman. He had a white dog with him, that big. He was all dressed in white, he wore shorts and long socks. He went back and forth, smoking a pipe, sort of like Mr. Davidson.

Philippe Christian attempts a reality check, and a curious skirmish erupts.

> *Philippe Christian:* Did you see him in flesh and blood, like me?
> *France Laval Jean-Baptiste:*—I am talking sleep with you. I bet your girlfriend is probably making you tired.

The interviewer has gone too far. Mr. Jean-Baptiste has revealed himself so openly that he assimilates Philippe Christian to the dream state, and admonishes him for violating the conventional respect expected in an interview (Robinson 84) (which, of course, Philippe Christian may have done deliberately). To regain control of the dialogue, the narrator must dismiss any contrastive view.

> He came closer to me, holding a big book in his hand. That book, it was a Buddhist book.
> *Philippe Christian:* But what have Buddhist priests to do with the French?
> *France Laval Jean-Baptiste: Way-ee,* the tin Buddhist priest. The book too was made of tin, but it's just like paper. The man said to me, "Go and get these three cocks for me. The first time you go, you will meet

a black cat that high. Don't be scared, keep on going. Farther ahead, a white dog will cross the road. Keep on going, you'll find a little pond near a tree. You dig and take all the money in front of you. However, don't forget to kill the cocks right there."
After that, I went out with my hoe, pick, spade, and bag, just like the first time. But once again I got scared. I threw my tools in the shed and went back to bed.

Only in the fifth dream episode does he finally show any sexual assertiveness, but he has violated the taboo against offending a fairy. With a change of costume, the fairy signals that she is no longer available to him. So the rejected male must reject this female.
On the fifth day, the woman showed herself to me, all dressed in black this time. She threatened me in my face. She was very angry. Ah well, women, when you don't take notice of them, they get very angry. She didn't even sit next to me. I tried to take her in my arms but she turned her back on me. I called her in vain. Before disappearing, she threatened me once more and said to me, "You will regret this later."
She threatens revenge for being slighted. At this point, after the tension between interviewer and narrator, the complication has peaked. The narrator reveals just how crucial this incident was in his life. To resolve the plot, he blames only himself for the sequence of failures. After explaining how his life was *not* changed, he has had to resign himself to doing without that treasure, as many creoles have had to do after not winning a lottery.

Philippe Christian: Do you regret this chance today?
France Laval Jean-Baptiste: Well, those words came true. I am a humble worker, I've worked for so many years, and I'm still a very poor man.
Philippe Christian: Why don't you go back to this place and pick up the treasure of your dreams?
France Laval Jean-Baptiste: A person's luck, it's like smoke. When it has passed, it disappears. For a very long time, I felt very sad to have let such a chance go by. But gradually this feeling is disappearing. But every time I have hard times, I think of that treasure I didn't get because of my stupidity. I think that by turning her back on me, the girl wanted me to understand that I was condemned to always toil in the sun to earn my living. I have even stopped thinking about her. You know, you can go crazy with that story. Sometimes it can get to your head. Luckily God gave me a little place in the sun, so I can make it, if God gives me courage. (Christian, "Jean-Baptiste")[34]

The immediacy and skill of Mr. Jean-Baptiste's narrating indicate that the "memorate," or personal experience narrative, is another key to Mauritian national identity (Haring, "Personal Narrative").

Even in Mauritian jokes, the overwhelming issue which the defiant girl faced, through the centuries of storytelling, is still alive. How shall I avoid marrying the wrong person?

113. The Wrong Bed

Bhojpuri narrator 1984–85

A young man went courting a girl. Some people like to stay overnight, some people don't like to stay overnight. He had a little money, he would go in his car. So, one day he was obliged to stay, stay, stay, stay. They gave him a bed in a room in the girl's house. They thought, the girl thought, "Maybe he will go in the night, taking his car." So what did they give him in the room, they put a bed with a wall on it so that if he left, they would know.

So from there he called out, "I don't sleep alone." So there was a two-year-old child, they said, "Look, here's this child, take him and sleep [in the same room]." So he went to sleep.

[Then] he was feeling he had to pee. "What'll I do? It'll wake them up." He was ashamed, his sister-in-law, all of them sleeping on that side, his father-in-law, wife's brother would wake up and know he went out to pee. So, what he did, there was the child's bed, and he put the child in his bed. (He was there to keep him company, so he would know that somebody else was sleeping there.) So he slowly went and lifted the child out and peed there, so they would think that it was the child who peed. But the child shat in his bed. He couldn't face them, he took his car key, opened the door, and left, and till today he hasn't gone back there. (Gallob 275–78)[35]

Mauritius today, like poorer countries, situates itself in world politics through jokes like the one on *bomli,* or "Bombay duck," translated above. Where stereotypes are as common as ethnicities, the "folk" see them from the underside, inventing multi-ethnic jokes as their form of comparative study (Dundes, "Study" 190–91; Abrahams, *Deep Down* 231–32). The key example, told in English, illustrates the persistence of a folktale convention like magic transportation. Most prominent and most politically relevant of the conventions is the grateful fairy, who grants any boon that may be asked as a reward.

114. The Shipwreck

Creole narrator, in English 1984–85

Well, this boat sank, and then there were these three chaps. There was a banker, manager of a bank, a manager of an insurance, and an unemployed Mauritian that found himself on a small island with only coconut trees on it. They were hungry. The manager said, "There is just one thing, and every day one will climb on a coconut tree and break three coconuts. And we'll eat it, drink the water, and survive. Today I will climb."

So the banker climbed on a tree and broke three coconuts and shared it. Second day, the insurance manager climbed on a tree and broke three coconuts. The third day came the turn of the unemployed Mauritian. He said, "I have been unemployed all my life, never worked in my life, you know. Now you want me to climb a tree to get the coconuts. No, I am not. I will sleeping, relaxing."

The banker climbed again. The insurance manager climbed again. When the turn came for the Mauritian unemployed, "No, I am not." And he went on like that for two months. He didn't climb once a tree. And then one day he saw a bottle floating, and inside that bottle there was a fairy. And the fairy said, "Get me out of that bottle, please, and I will give you anything you want." So he got the bottle, and the fairy was out, and she said, "Okay, if you ask one thing, I'll do it."

So the manager of the bank said, "I was in New York, in my big office, and a big car. Please send me back there." So he disappeared. He was in New York in his office.

The insurance manager said, "Send me back to New York also. I had a big car, looking for a holiday with my family. Everyone is waiting for me now. You know, please take me." And he went.

And then come to the Mauritian unemployed. He said, "Oh my God, going back to Mauritius, where there is so much trouble, you know, and here I was just relaxing, and these two chaps were just feeding me. So can you get these two chaps back." (Gallob 306–308)[36]

The joke is a key to people's awareness of the dependence of their 720-square-mile sugar plantation and tourist paradise on foreign investment and support. If "humor depends upon the perception of . . . an 'appropriate incongruity'" (Oring ix), the humor of a creole society has plenty of incongruities to draw on. Mauritius with its stars holds the key to the ambiguity and ambivalence of the creole aesthetic, as increasing "development" moves it towards being one huge city where jokesters will continue to perform such stories. Already only a tiny patch of forest shows what the Mauritian landscape looked like at the time when Flacourt attempted to settle in Madagascar. All the islands are fragile, both ecologically and culturally. The dodo—friendly, flightless, ungainly, the ambivalent symbol of Mauritian identity—symbolizes one possible future for cultural heritage. What happened to him? Monkeys, rats, and pigs imported by the Dutch destroyed the poor bird's nests; when the forest was cut down to export ebony, his habitat went the same way. What song the dodo sang, or what name it assumed among human beings—though puzzling questions, as Sir Thomas Browne foresaw about other mythical creatures—are not beyond all conjecture, but its esteem among Europeans foreshadowed the fate of the islands. The Dutch called it *walckvögel,* disgusting bird (Quammen 265). Immortalized by Lewis Carroll and John Tenniel, the dodo suffered the same fate as the folktale—relegated to children's books as a means of keeping it alive (though none, so far, show the dodo in Kreol). We did not hear Jocelyn Joseph's stories or meet his mentor Tilik; we don't know what storytelling in Réunionnais *petit blanc* communities used to be like; no one has even begun to carry out folklore research in Anjouan. Yet "the eleventh hour is always with us" (Kirshenblatt-Gimblett 300), and there are stars and keys in the smallest of the nations, the Republic of Seychelles.

5
Postcolonial Seychelles

"There was once a cat and a rat who were good friends." So begins a storyteller in Seychelles in the late 1960s. The islands, no longer a dependency of Mauritius, are still a colony of Britain. His ancient voice echoes his African forebears: "One day, the hyena made friends with the hare" (Mbiti 109); "A long time ago, hyena and squirrel were great friends . . ." (Njururi 28). But in his fiction, cat and rat won't be good friends for long. Speaking out of the Afro-Seychellois past, their narrator presages the future. Characters such as Cat and Rat and their plot of false friendship are ancient symbols. How shall Cat and Rat and their false friendship be treated now, after independence—as outmoded relics, dull museum objects, quaint anthology pieces, or promising materials for reworking? In the past, dominance and oppression made it necessary for Seychellois, as for the other islanders in their region, to remodel their language and renegotiate their culture. What will globalizing influence do to inherited traditions? Will these old stories evoke a nostalgic call to return to the inherited past, or will they become tokens in a free play of cultural goods without substance—in other words, in a postmodern Seychelles? This pre-independence narrator foreshadows the answer.

He gives Cat and Rat the label *konper,* which marks them in Seselwa language as fictional characters (D'Offay and Lionnet 174).[1]

115. Cat and Rat

Samuel Accouche, Seychelles 1960s

Konper Cat was a big planter, while *konper* Rat was a big lazybones. Every time *konper* Cat would do planting in his plantation, Rat would declare his stomach was bad.

Ignoring their difference, they make a deal.

Cat would tell his friend the rat, "You're going to come give me a hand watching over my plantations at night, in case thieves come in and steal." The rat would say, "Yeah, pal." But the rat started thinking: he would start eating the manioc and sweet potatoes that Cat had under his feet, but when Cat wanted him to guard, the rat was working his mind a different way. In the place that Cat told him to stand guard, the rat dug a little hole in the maize plot. There were many tunnels under all the biggest maniocs and sweet potatoes. In the evening, when Cat would guard his spot, rat would do his thing and go down to his basement and start eating his friend's maniocs and sweet potatoes. He ate everything down there in such a way that there was no sign of it visible on the ground.

In a Sakalava version of "Cat and Rat," collected before this storyteller was born (Dandouau, *Contes populaires* 80–83), it was Cat who volunteered to steal manioc and sweet potatoes. This narrator makes Rat the active character.

From time to time Cat came to ask him if he'd found a thief passing by. Rat said, "I found just one mouse, but when I chased him, he ran away." Cat said, "So everything is all right?"

Rat answers him in English, *"All right everywhere."*

When Cat turned his back, the rat went down into his hole and ate the plants without his friend knowing. The time came when the melons got ripe. The Rat didn't say anything to his friend, but his plan was to eat two or three melons. But though he did his best, it was difficult, because Cat was watching his melons so carefully, and when the melons were above ground, then he couldn't eat them without Cat seeing. Still, the rat wanted to eat the melons, now that they were ripe and pretty. He worked his mind.

Rat and Cat live in a country where the government nowadays seeks to promote fisheries, and where a principal industry is the export of tuna to Europe.

One day he said to Cat, "My friend, why don't we go do a bit of fishing?" Because he knew Cat liked fish. So Cat said to him, "Yes, my friend, we could go do a bit of fishing, but it's too bad we have neither a *pirog* nor a *katyolo*."[2] The Rat said to the Cat, "But it's easy for us to make a little *katyolo;* we have all the stuff [for it] ready." Cat asked, "Where's the stuff?" The Rat told him, "We have a lot of ripe melons at our feet, and with my teeth I can scoop out a *katyolo* for us to go fishing in. And I won't even make you pay me for my trouble."

The model for this invented dialogue, indeed for the whole plot, is the Afro-Malagasy passion for verbal duels. Always ready with a trickster-like scheme for common benefit, Rat says, "We can break two of the larger hard melons and scoop them out for the *katyolo,* and with the other we'll make our paddles, oars, *tyak* [deck], and the rest." Cat, not displeased with his good friend, turns over to Rat two of the melons he has been planning to steal. The narrator addresses his audience directly: No need to tell you, everything that came out of those two melons went into friend Rat's little stomach, the self-styled carpenter. So when the melon *katyolo* was all ready, Cat bought all the things needed and they went to fish.

The two don't go far offshore.

As they would do their fishing off Saint Anne, they didn't bring along anything to eat. Cat wanted to bring food, even though they weren't going far out to fish, but his good friend the rat told him, "No need, we won't be late." When they started fishing, some bad weather came up and hit them; it wet the *katyolo,* which broke, and they started making for Dry Island. When it got dark, they were both getting hungry. The rat said to Cat, "My friend, I can't take this much cold. I['ll] have to hide under the *tyak.*"

We interrupt this program to ask, "Who is speaking?" Is this text a bit of village ethnography? No: it's a radio script by the best-known storyteller in Seychelles history, Samuel Accouche. Between 1966 and 1973, Samuel Accouche broadcast about three dozen oral tales, elaborating many of them from Afro-Malagasy-Seychellois oral tradition. For radio, employing a technique of creolization, he would augment dialogue, which a face-to-face audience would have understood. In the terms of performance analysis, he "decontextualized" and "recontextualized" his stories for an audience "unfamiliar with the contextual details familiar to the author" (Shuman 117). It was only towards the end of his broadcast career that the recording of village performances began (Bollée and Chaudenson). So electronic technology brought inherited traditions into the twentieth century before village ethnography began.

Back to his story. Rat continues his path towards the breaking of friendship.

When he saw water starting to pour into the *katyolo,* he came out from under the *tyak* and sat on the end of the *katyolo.* Poor Cat didn't notice that water was pouring into the *katyolo* till he found the *katyolo* full of water. He said, "Rat my friend, what's happening that our *katyolo* is filling up with water?" The rat said, "Maybe a *marto* [fish], or else a fierce shark, was chewing under our *katyolo.*"

A trickster can always invent someone else to take the blame.

Cat said to him, "But my friend, we are in danger all around. If we keep on like this, we could break up on Dry Island. Better we jump into the sea and we'll swim to Dry Island." The rat said, "My friend, I can't swim to shore. I'll drown." Friend Cat said to him, "Get up on my back, I'll carry you to land." When they got to Dry Island, both of them were cold. They went under a rock to hide from the cold.

As Samuel Accouche moves through trickery, deception, discovery of the trick, escape, and the breaking of friendship (Haring, *Malagasy Tale Index* 297; Haring, "Pattern"), he interpolates an episode to make Rat more aggressive. Not content with eating their common conveyance, he now attacks his supposed partner.

When it got to be about two in the morning, the rat couldn't sleep, and he was still hungry. He looked to see whether Cat was sleeping soundly. He said to himself, "All clear." He started eating the bottom of Cat's foot, and he blew as he was eating, to make a breeze so cat wouldn't feel it. In the morning when they woke up, poor friend Cat almost couldn't walk on one edge of his foot. He said to his good friend the rat, "My friend, was something eating the bottom of my foot?" The Rat told him, "Maybe when you were swimming to land, some little fish or other ate the bottom of your foot without you knowing." So what was poor Cat going to do, suffering from hunger and also the edge of his foot? But the rat wasn't hungry at all.

As there wasn't anything to eat on that island, they kept looking to see if a fishing boat would pass by and come for poor them on that island. Night came again, and the rat thought he'd eat the other side of his friend Cat's foot. In the night the rat looked to see if cat was asleep, to take his meal again. But Cat was acting as if he was asleep, because he had an idea to watch out for rat playing his trick under his foot. He didn't really think his good friend was capable of that, he thought maybe it was another rat, but all the same he didn't sleep, and he also had quite a pain. As Cat was lying quietly, he saw his friend the rat go up to the other side of his foot. He stayed quiet to see what was going to happen. The rat soon started blowing on his foot and took a first little bite. Cat told him, "Rat, my brother! Friends as we are, you are eating the bottom of my foot. From today on, we are finished, us two." Cat then was really angry, for he'd never thought his good friend would go so far as to eat the bottom of his foot.

Samuel Accouche ends his broadcast in the most traditional way imaginable, with two etiological markers, but without an "I was there" formula.

He swam to St. Anne and left his false friend on Dry Island. The rat, there on Dry Island, went around looking for food, because he no longer had the skin of cat's foot to eat. He met two–three rat friends and they stayed together there in Dry Island. That's how Dry Island got its rats, and that's also how Cat doesn't want to catch sight of rat without killing him. (Accouche 79–80; Bollée and D'Offay 41–44)[3]

It took another twenty years before ecologists shone a scientific light on the effect of the rat population on other species in the outer islands. Now, even the casual tourist knows they have been effectually excluded from the bird sanctuaries on Cousin and Bird islands.

While appropriating modern technology, Samuel Accouche looks back to Africa to recreate the Creole past. He uses the African-Malagasy making-and-breaking pattern (Accouche 68–73); his narratives contain social critique. Many of his pieces with human characters are moralities: for instance he will castigate a busybody's interference with a married couple (distantly echoing Polin and Polinn). Marriage comes in for realistic treatment, even unspoken dialogue, when a defiant girl with the odd name of Serpentine captures the rich, handsome Totor. In time, bored with her marriage, she lives with another man, Macassar, until, bored again, she conceals her opinion of him as *un grand imbecile* with a lying speech to him: "Believe what I tell you, my heart will never change, I'll never love another, my heart is fixed on you." To herself she says, "I'm going to do you the same way I did Totor." Macassar, quoting to himself the English proverb "Prevention is better than cure," sends her away (Accouche 64–67). The story evidently intends the same lesson as the proverb.

He was not the only narrator to portray fathers who give Polonius-like advice to their children: a narrator of La Digue, Seychelles' third island, has told a pseudo-myth in which Father Rat tells his six children how to conduct depredations against human beings (Diallo, Rosalie, and Essack 8–9).

Seldom taciturn, Samuel Accouche tends so much towards verbosity that one wonders whether there was a red light in the studio at Radio Seychelles. In one wordy piece, modeled on the debate of the belly and its members as the framework,[4] he brings on all a king's workers, who quarrel over which of their trades is supreme. A doctor, a nurse, a driver, a scientist; dentists, electricians, masons, carpenters, plumbers, shoemakers, seamstresses, washerwomen, fishermen, cooks, policemen, merchants, carters, woodcutters, and laborers all advance their claims; obviously this is a performance piece. Called in to make peace, old Justin preaches on the debate of the belly, convincing the assembled workmen that they're all equally important (Accouche 27–29). In another script, faithful to the Afro-Malagasy infatuation with the word, a boy's clever answers to a king are the model: the young hero wins thousands of rupees by guessing a nickname and a true name. He learned his craft, he says (speaking for his author), by listening to older people (Accouche 77–78). The lengthy "Zistwar Gaspar ek Ti Dyak" (so lengthy it may not have been broadcast) parodies those stories in which a powerless hero gets to marry the queen or princess by accomplishing tasks. Ti Dyak's true task is to induce boss Gaspar to break his vow not to speak angrily. Ti Dyak's final task is to escort Gaspar's wife round the tennis court. "But if I don't make your wife happy," says Ti Dyak, "will you get angry?" "No." Ti Dyak pleases the lady so much that when Gaspar sees them, he faints away, and his evil heart breaks. Madam marries Ti Dyak, who has killed off the blustering father figure without ever provoking the hoped-for speech act (Payette, *Kont* [1990] 137–46).[5] Samuel Accouche was a man of words.

Samuel Accouche voices that plurality of symbol systems that is at the heart of creolization, and, some say, of postmodernism. Soungoula, in one of his scripts, masquerades as a French Canadian gambler with extensive foreign holdings. "I have a factory that makes automobiles. A big shipping company called Cunnard-line [*sic*], a big factory that makes airplanes, Canadien Air-Ways Co., and a bigger company Train Electric that's in Canada, all that is mine. What am I going to do with my money?" (Bollée 47). Samuel Accouche takes him through several successes and threatened defeats, puts him in modern hotels and taxis, and ends the piece parodying the myth formula: ever since then, all hotelkeepers look for a passenger called by either of the fake names Soungoula used (Bollée 45–49; Payette, *Kont* [1990] 33–45).

Is it the influence of detective stories that inspired another narrator, a few years after Samuel Accouche, to conceal from his audience the identity of a trickster, or will everybody recognize him anyway?

116. Mister François Poncé

Praslin narrator 1980–81

There was a man named François Poncé. He was a *gran blan* [big white man] with big moustaches and very white hair. Well, one day he heard that there was a big party at the king's. He got the idea he would go have a look at that party. So he went over to the river where the washerwomen did the clothes and got a nice outfit. The day of the party, he stood in front of his door, very straight, and he looked inside.

At the party, the king sat with his madame and his daughter. He looked outside, he saw that gentleman standing so nicely gotten up. But that gentleman had nice little side whiskers! He was sorry he didn't know that gentleman so he could invite him to the party. He went up to the gentleman and said, "Sir, who are you? What is your name?" The gentleman answered, "I am Monsieur François Poncé, white outside."

The king then was not slow to have another party so he could invite that gentleman. The day of the party he sent an invitation for "Monsieur François Poncé, white outside." Quite early, the friends he had invited arrived.

But Monsieur François Poncé came late. The king occasionally checked if the gentleman hadn't come. At last he saw the gentleman coming. The king went to the entry to meet the gentleman and have him come in. The king saw that this was a *gran msye blan,* was more interested in him than the other guests. He even served the gentleman a drink himself. At evening when dinner was over, everybody got ready to dance. At the first round, Monsieur François Poncé took the queen, madame king, to waltz with. All the people were surprised at how well the gentleman danced. The girls started checking if he wouldn't come ask them, but the gentleman preferred dancing with the princess.

The others whispered in their friends' ears about that gentleman always dancing with the princess. Sometimes they said a word in the princess's ear. The king saw them, but he acted as if he didn't, he was so happy that that gentleman might marry his daughter. The gentleman also had daring, gave the princess two–three little kisses on the cheek. When the princess turned her cheek for him to give her, she gave him a little one on the side. The king acted as if he didn't see clearly. When the dancers went in to drink rum, the gentleman had some more. Then he was feeling drunk. But then they gave him some drink.

At four o'clock in the morning, he said to the princess he was leaving. He thanked the king and all his guests, gave the princess a little kiss, and left. Then he fell on the doorstep and couldn't go any farther. He went to sleep. The sun came up and struck him. He kept his hair straight with wax. When the sun hit it, it melted, and all his straight hair fell all over his shoulders all over his face. On his head there was just some crinkly grains. His pretty moustache and his side whiskers all came unstuck. Soungoula himself it was, sleeping on the corner of the doorstep.

Nennenn [the servant] then swept the doorstep, she looked in the corner, she saw Soungoula sleeping. She ran to Mamzel: "Mamzel, last night you were dancing with an animal." The princess came to look. When she saw Soungoula, she ran to tell her father. The king, when he saw the packet of wax running down Soungoula's face, his straight hair unstuck on the ground, and just the grains of pepper on his head, became angry. He had the soldiers called to kill Soungoula. He called out, "Come, come shoot it, come kill this animal . . ."

He made so much noise that Soungoula jumped out of his sleep and ran up on to a big rock and said, "King, who's there?" The king said, "I'm who's here, today I'll show you your place. You made an oath to come and make a fool of me again."

Soungoula said, "King, you can't talk me a miracle, I danced with your wife, I kissed your daughter, whatever you say." The king stopped short. He yelled murder for his soldiers to come more quickly. Soungoula jumped on a rock and left, "Vreeeeeet" (as if he was) going after the murderer. Nobody could catch him. (Diallo et al., *Veyez 2* 71–73)

The narrator adapts old devices of trickster narrative to treat the class barrier in Seychelles, which could not be acknowledged in real life (though pre-independence British anthropologists met it in field work [Benedict and Benedict]).

Samuel Accouche—adopting and polishing the mix of Seselwa and English that constitutes ordinary street talk, punning interlingually (as Comoran narrators do) to call one Indian character Telepati and another Mirabo, embedding features of modern popular fiction within a remembrance of African narration, localizing Soungoula at La Mizer (a village not far from the capital)—Samuel Accouche refashions, invents, and influences other artists. Evoking African-Malagasy tradition for his plot, he shows how rapidly Seychellois storytelling left behind that setting of performance under a tree which André Dandouau witnessed in Madagascar. Here is no old grandparent enrapturing village children; here is a media figure, whose audience does not need literacy, creating the hybrid genre of broadcast folktale. Samuel Accouche's imitation and his creativity are inseparable.

He was not the only broadcast narrator. Around that time, some two hundred radio scripts were sent in to Radio Seychelles for possible broadcast. Eighty-four of these are now stored in the National Archives. Some were Seselwa translations of literary texts, such as the Grimms' Freddy and Katy, no. 59 (Grimm and Grimm 225–30), omitting the later episodes, and Perrault's Puss in Boots (Perrault 16–25; Zipes 397–401). One is the French folktale Our Lady's Child in Seselwa, a story otherwise unknown in the islands;[6] another is Baissac's Polin and Polinn ("Creole Stories" 113–14, 7–10); another is his Sabour. The writers drew plentifully on oral tradition. Many of their scripts were oral tales, reproduced faithfully or elaborated and revised,[7] including the Mauritian-Réunionnais story of Ti Zan and the red rag. One, which almost rivals Sydney Joseph's Siren-Girl in magnitude—and with lions and tigers too!—is a tale featuring a compassionate executioner.

117. A Hundred and One Thieves

Contributor to Radio Seychelles 1970s

Well, one time there was a king. But in the place the king lived, there were no girls. He had them all killed. But one day Mrs. King had a little daughter. The king said to his whole band of soldiers, "My wife has had a daughter.

She must be killed." But the king also had a son, and he was also a soldier. He said to his father, "Give me my little sister. I'll go kill her myself." The king said, "Here's your sister. Go kill her, only bring me her heart here." The boy said, "Yes, father."

He went with his baby sister. He arrived in the forest, he found an old *tantin* [old lady]. He said, "*Tantin,* father has sent me to kill my little sister, but, *tantin,* I'm going to give my sister to you. You'll be able to take care of her." *Tantin* said, "Yes, my son." The boy said, "But *tantin*, father told me to take the heart to him." *Tantin* had a goat. She sacrificed her goat, killed it, took out the heart and gave it to the boy. She said, "Here, give this to your father." The boy said, "Very well, *tantin*, but only you have the *esprit*."

The writer echoes the ancient Malagasy myth showing God and the earth dividing the spirit and body of someone who dies.

The boy took a thousand rupees out of his pocket and gave it to the *tantin* to take care of his sister and buy whatever was necessary.

The boy went to his father and said, "Papa, here is my sister's heart." His father said to him, "Good, my son, you are a brave soldier." One day the boy took leave. He went to the *tantin*'s place to see his sister. When he reached the *tantin*'s place, he said, "Hello, *tantin.* I've come to see my sister." *Tantin* said to him, "Your sister's asleep." The boy so much wanted to see his sister that he went and woke her up. He started embracing his sister. He said, "*Tantin,* how she's grown. Mama will want to see her daughter." Still, before he left, the boy gave the *tantin* another 2,000 rupees.

He made his way to his father's place. When he got there, he said to his mother, "Do you want to see your daughter?" His mother said, "Yes, but your father had her killed." The boy said nothing. Another day he took leave. Again he went to the *tantin*'s and said, "*Tantin,* my sister must have gotten big." *Tantin* said to him, "You wouldn't recognize her." But his sister was sitting inside. *Tantin* went and called her. She came; the boy stayed dumb when he saw his sister, she'd grown so much. He said, "*Tantin,* do you know how old she is?" The *tantin* said, "She's fifteen." The boy said, "Well, today I'm taking her to see our mother." *Tantin* said, "The king will kill her there." All the same, the boy said to his sister, "We're going to go see our mother." The girl went with her brother.

When he reached the street by the king's place, his mother looked out the window and saw her son with a girl. She started weeping. The king heard his wife weeping and went to see; in the street he saw his son with his sister. The king called his band of soldiers. The boy and his sister started running away, the band of soldiers behind them. Soldiers could not catch up with them. The boy and his sister got very tired running, and they missed the path to go back to the old *tantin*. They fell down in the forest.

When they could walk [again], the girl said, "Brother, I am tired, I am hungry." The boy saw a big pond filled with watercress. He told his sister to wait for him till he'd go cut some watercress for them to eat. The boy cut a big bunch of watercress and told his sister to eat it. When they finished eating, the girl said, "Brother, I'm tired. Let me sleep for a minute in your lap." Her brother sat under a big *danmyen* tree; his sister put her head in his lap.

As she was doing that, she looked up the *danmyen* tree and saw something hanging in the air. She said, "Brother, look up there in the tree." Her brother climbed the *danmyen* tree and saw a bunch of keys tied to a branch. He took the bunch of keys and climbed down. When he got to the ground, he counted and found there were a hundred and one keys. He said to his sister, "Let's go follow that path that goes up over there. There must be someone living up there."

They climbed up. When they reached the top of the mountain, they saw a big house, but all the doors were shut. The house had 101 doors. The boy said to his sister, "The 101 keys are for this very house!" He opened one of the doors of the house. He told his sister to go upstairs and sleep and make no noise. Only the boy stayed downstairs near the big door where there was a trapdoor. He took out his sword and held it in his hand.

In an instant he heard an argument in the road. A hundred and one thieves were arguing amongst themselves: "Where's the keys?" The head thief said, "You left them in the yard." The band of thieves said to the chief, "We say we did not leave the keys in the yard." When they got to the house, they saw the door open. The head thief said, "Didn't I tell you you left the keys here? See for yourselves."

No need to say, the boy was waiting in the corner for them to come in. The band of thieves started coming in one after another. The boy started cutting them one at a time, till he was done and only the head thief was left. He managed to cut just one bit of the head thief's ear. The whole band of thieves fell down the trapdoor. The head thief fell in too.

The boy roused his sister and said to her, "Sister, you can use all the keys, but that one key you see on the table, that's the key to the trapdoor. You mustn't touch it. I don't want you to touch it." But for all that, you know the way of women, they're stubborn and nosy. They'll always want to see for themselves so they can believe. The boy took his gun and went hunting. His sister, back there, took the key of the trapdoor and opened it. As soon as she opened it, the head thief said to her, "I'm hungry, I'm thirsty." The girl took him a little food and a little water, which she put in a bag and tied it up with a rope, let it down into the trap that was hiding the thieves. The head thief said to her, "Thank you very much. But there's one word I must say to you: are you happy?"

The girl said, "Sure I am." The head thief said to the girl, "Let's kill your brother and the two of us will get married."

The girl said to the head thief, "All right, we'll kill him." The head thief said to the girl, "Well! As soon as you go to sleep, sham illness. Tell your brother you dreamed that someone told you to drink tiger's milk to be cured." The girl told the head thief yes. She closed the trapdoor, put the key in its place, and went to bed.

Her brother came back and saw his sister asleep. He said to his sister, "What's the matter?" She answered, "I'm sick." Anyway it was getting dark. The boy went to bed. When he was asleep, his sister started complaining, "Ay, ay, ay, you people."

The boy asked her, "Are you hurting a lot?"

His sister said, "Yes, but I dreamed that somebody told me to drink a little tiger's milk to make me well." The boy loved his sister so much that he didn't hesitate. Even in the middle of the night he got up, took his gun and a bullet, and went into the forest. When he reached the forest, he heard a bunch of tigers yelping. He stood up to listen. He saw a lion go by, going to eat that bunch of tigers. The boy took one shot at the lion and the lion died. The bunch of tigers said, "Thank you, sir. The greatest service you ask us, we'll do it for you." The boy said, "I have to have a little of your mother's milk." Just then the mother tiger was going by and said to her children, "I smell fresh meat here." Her children said to her, "Stay still, let us tell you what's coming. There's a boy who's killed a lion that was going to eat us. The boy needs a bit of your milk."

The tiger told her children to call the boy. They called the boy and he came. Mama Tiger told him, "Take milk and go. Take one of my children with you. The greatest service you need we'll do for you." The boy left.

He got to where his sister was, gave his sister the milk, she drank, she slept. At day he got her up. His sister told him, "I'm all right, brother." Her brother went hunting again. The head thief asked the girl, "Did your brother bring you the milk?" The girl said, "Yes, he did." The head thief said, "He's funny, he succeeded in getting it. But now ask him for a little lion's milk. This time the lion will eat him." The girl said, "All right." Girl closed the trapdoor and put the key in its place.

The boy came, they started cooking and ate. They ate, then they went to sleep. When they were asleep, the boy heard crying, "Ayo, ayo, ayo, ayo, ayo!" The boy asked his sister what was the matter. He said, "Are you sick again?" His sister told him yes: "This time I dreamed someone said to me to drink a little lion's milk." As she said that, the boy took his gun and a bullet and went back into the forest. When he got into the forest, he heard lions growling. There was a big tiger going by; he killed the tiger. The band of lions said to him, "Thank you, sir. The greatest service you ask of us, we'll do it for you." The boy said, "I need a little of your mother's milk." Big lion came along saying to her children, "I smell fresh meat here." Her bunch of children told her, "Stay here, Mama, let us tell you. There's a boy who killed a big tiger, that big tiger was coming to eat us. We asked him what he wanted as a reward, the boy answered, 'I want a little of your mother's milk.'" The lion told her children to call the boy. The bunch of lions called the boy. The boy came. The lion told him to draw the milk he needed from her, and to take one lion child with him and leave quickly. The boy left with his little lion. He got to where his sister was, he gave her the milk. The girl drank, they slept. Day came. The girl said to her brother, "I'm all right now." The boy took his gun and again went hunting. The girl, behind, took the key and opened the trapdoor. The head thief said to her, "Did your brother bring you the milk last night?" The girl said, "Sure he did." The head thief said, "How did he do it?" Then he said to the girl, "Be sick again, ask for a little *divet* [venom] from a snake's tongue." The girl shut the trapdoor, took the key, put it in its place.

Boy also reached home later. They ate. Night fell, they went to bed. When they were asleep, the boy heard his sister crying, "Ayo, ayo, yo, brother, I'm dying." Her brother asked her, "Are you sick again?" His sister answered, "I dreamed someone told me to eat a little *divet* from a snake's tongue." The poor boy saw that his sister really looked sick, he took his gun and went.

He arrived at the bank of a stream. He heard a snake crying. The boy saw a lion going to eat the troop of snakes. He killed the lion. The troop of snakes said to him, "Thank you, sir. The greatest service you ask of us, we'll do it for you."

The boy said, "I need a bit of *divet* from your mother's tongue." The big snake came along saying to her children, "I smell fresh meat today." The band of snakes said to her, "Mama, stay still, let us tell you what's happened. There was a big lion coming to eat us. A boy killed him and he says he needs a little *divet* from your tongue." The snake told them to call the boy. They called the boy, the boy came. The snake said to him, "Go ahead and take from my tongue, scrape it, and go. Take one of my children with you." The boy left. He reached where his sister was and gave her the *divet.* Then they slept. At day he got her up. The girl said, "Brother, I'm well now."

The boy took his gun and again went hunting. The girl, behind, took the key, opened the trapdoor. The head thief asked her, "Did your brother bring you *divet* last night?"

"Sure, he brought it," the girl told him. The head thief thought a bit and said, "This time act as if you're dead. Before you do that, tell him, 'I'm going to die today. I dreamed someone told me I'd have to have a leaf of the tree called Raise-the-Dead.'" The girl said yes. She closed the trapdoor, she put the key in its place. Later her brother arrived. When night fell, he had them go to bed. In the middle of the night, the boy heard his sister complain, "Ayo, ayo, ayo, yo!" Her brother asked her, "Are you sick again?" Girl told him, "Yes, I dreamed someone told me to sniff a bit of leaves of Raise-the-Dead." The boy ran into the forest with his gun, in the middle of the night. He saw a tree with branches touching the earth. He broke off a branch of that tree. Three men under the tree answered, "Thank you, sir." Then the boy asked those three men what they were doing under that tree. One answered, "We have been cursed by Bondye [God] to guard that tree. Bondye told us if some day, someone came and broke off a branch of the tree, we would get our speech back and become as we were before." The boy said to that band of men, "Come with me."

They followed the boy. They walked together. The boy got to where his sister was. He said to the three men each to take one room to sleep in. He went to look at his sister. His sister wasn't moving. She was acting dead. Poor boy thought his sister really was dead. He took the leaf of that tree with him, had his sister sniff it, he passed it under her nose. The girl took a big breath, she got up, she said, "Brother, never forget where that tree is." The boy took the bunch of leaves of the tree and threw them out the window.

Day came, the boy took his gun, and went hunting with the three men, his lion, his tiger, and his snake. There behind, the girl took the key and opened the trapdoor. The head thief said to her, "Did your brother bring those leaves?" Girl told him, "Yes, he brought them." Head thief told her to go look in the trap. The girl went and looked, and he sent her down into the trap with head thief. As he sent her, all those hundred thieves who were dead got up. They climbed into the air and said to the girl to go up to her room and go to sleep. The girl went up. Then all the 101 thieves stood outside waiting for the poor boy to come to kill him. The boy came along the road. His three men said to him, "Look in the road, that crowd of men that's there." The boy looked and saw that whole band of thieves having got up. He said to his three friends, "My sister has raised that whole band of thieves with those leaves." Then the boy said to lion, tiger, snake, "You always told me you would save me one day from whatever great misfortune might come. So do your duty now, on that band of thieves you see over there." With a little blow and a big one, the three animals went screaming at that whole family, and YLOUP! In an instant all the band of thieves were dead.

The three men went together with the boy to the house. The boy called to his sister. The girl came and said, "Pardon, brother, the head thief made me do it." Her brother said to her, "I told you you must not touch the key on the table. But you did touch it. You were willing for me to lose my life so you could stay with the head thief. I say to you, sleep there on that table." The girl went to sleep. The boy took his sword and cut his sister into three pieces. He gave the head to the snake, he gave the tiger the middle piece, and he gave the lion the lower piece. The boy stayed there with the three men and his three animals too.

One time I went to that boy's place, I asked him for a job. He told me, "What my sister made me go through, I'll do the same to you," but he only took long enough to give me a kick, and I arrived here with my *kannson* [pants] torn." ("Creole Stories" 115–17)[8]

Like other star narrators far away, this one, whose identity we don't know, assembles "a treasury of magical themes" (Dorson, *Folktales* 10).

Transmitting oral style just as successfully, another radio narrator puts the heroine in the position of the defiant girl, echoing Gérose Barivoitse's woman who took water from Gran Dyab.

118. Sililinn

Contributor to Radio Seychelles before 1978

Well, once there was an old wolf named Zalumbe. He stayed in a house in the forest. Next to his house there was a big lemon tree that was always full of lemons. Not too far from his house was a lady who lived with her little daughter. The little girl was named Sililinn. She was an obstinate girl. She did everything her mother told her not to do. She had a passion for going and picking Zalumbe's lemons every day. Every time she came back, her mother argued with her, "Sililinn my child, you're a bad child, stop stealing lemons. Some day Zalumbe's coming to catch you." She didn't stop.

Sililinn said to herself, "Every day Mama argues with me, but today so she doesn't smell it, I'll eat the lemons over there, by myself." So Sililinn took everything she needed [for] salad, such as her knife, plate, salt, sugar, pepper, vinegar, chili, and went.

So she got to the lemon tree. She looked around a bit, she didn't see anyone. She quickly climbed the lemon tree. She looked everywhere, still nobody. She took her position on a branch and started on the lemons. In just a minute she heard a noise in the straw. She looked, who could it be? Zalumbe! Ahhh! Yes, Zalumbe came with a big sack on his back and an axe in his other hand. Sililinn shook. She remembered her mother's words. She wanted to cry out, she wanted to jump, but it was too late. Then she heard Zalumbe and his big voice saying, "Hmmm! Fresh meat here! There's fresh meat here!" Wow! Then Sililinn made herself small, small, she thought Zalumbe couldn't hear her. Then Zalumbe said, "Sililinn, Sililinn, come down out of there."

Sililinn answered, "You'll eat me if I come down." Zalumbe told her two more times to come down. Sililinn didn't come down, she said, "Zalumbe, you might eat me, I'm scared."

Zalumbe said, "I'm going to cut down the lemon tree." So Zalumbe took his big axe and started cutting, *Tok, tok, tok, tok!* He cut down the lemon tree. Sililinn shook. The lemon tree fell over, it went *Weeeeeeeeeyyyaaa!* So Sililinn tried to run, but Zalumbe jumped on her, put her in his big sack, ran with her to his house, and put her in a concrete bed of coconut leaves which he filled with all kinds of insects—bedbugs, centipedes, cockroaches, scorpions, millipedes, mosquitoes, spiders, rats, and so on. He covered Sililinn with a big mat, blocked his door with a coconut stick, and was very happy.

Zalumbe ground his teeth, he started lighting a big fire and then thought, "I don't want to eat Sililinn all alone. Better I go find my whole pack of pals to make us a good party." He went looking for the whole herd of wolves, Matumak, Songor, Kapiler, Chimite, Yoyote, Budume.[9] He told them all to bring their wooden forks. So they made their way to go to the party at Zalumbe's to go eat Sililinn's flesh.

Meanwhile Sililinn's mama went searching for her child. When she got to the woods, she saw the lemon tree cut, her heart went up in her neck, she put he hand on her head and said in her heart, "Must be Zalumbe has caught Sililinn." She ran to Zalumbe's house, saw the coconut stake blocking the door. She took courage and opened the door. She saw Sililinn covered with the mat, only picked up a basket. She put Sililinn in it, she took a banana trunk and put it in Sililinn's place. Going into the woods, she met the crowd coming to party with Zalumbe. Zalumbe said to her, "Madame, we're going to party at my place." Just then he didn't know Sililinn was in the basket. The lady told him, "I'm in a hurry, I can't turn back."

So when Zalumbe got home with his pals, he had them come in. They didn't lift up the mat, they just started jabbing it with forks. They said it was the meat. One jabbed it and said, "But thin." Another said, "Yeah, it is." So Zalumbe lifted up the mat, what did he see but a banana trunk. His gang of friends said to him, "We get you now." They started beating him till he was half dead.

During that time Sililinn arrived home. Her mother gave her two rotten eggs. She told her, "Go back in the woods before Zalumbe comes looking for you and when you hear him, run, and throw the two eggs behind you, and after running, come back here." Sililinn went, she heard Zalumbe come running. Sililinn threw those two rotten eggs, she started running. The two eggs became a big river. Zalumbe cried, "OK, Sililinn, I'm catching you!" He started making a bridge out of coconut poles across the river to go reach Sililinn. When he went on the bridge, it broke, everybody into the water. Sililinn was very happy to get home all right. Me, I ran to see what was happening and me too, I fell in the river. ("Creole Stories" 51)[10]

The narrator's debt of Seychelles to Africa and Madagascar is obvious. Nothing "postmodern" there.

Literary hybridization may explain the fullness of a Seychelles version of The Language of Animals, a story from India which has always been appropriate to multilingual societies.

119. The Language of Animals

Contributor to Radio Seychelles before 1978

Once there was a boy called Ti Zan. He worked as a planter. Well, one day he had been hoeing and he threw his dirty clothes down by a cedar tree . . . and he set fire to the straw. There was a snake came out of the burning straw, and that snake said to Ti Zan, "Ti Zan, Ti Zan, save my life." Ti Zan asked the snake, "How can I do that?" The snake said to Ti Zan, "Put me on that stump, where I was, I'll slide out from there."

The snake came down. When it got to the ground, it said to Ti Zan, "Take me to my papa." Ti Zan answered he couldn't take him to his father, because he would bite him. The snake said, "No, nobody's going to bite you." They went along, both of them. Part way there, the snake said to Ti Zan, "When we get to my father's, Papa is going to ask you what you want for saving my life. You'll say that for your reward, to reveal the language of animals." The snake went on to say, "If Papa doesn't want to give you that reward, tell him you don't want anything but that."

When they got near the place where the snakes stay, the snake said to Ti Zan, "Wait for me." As Ti Zan was waiting, he could hear the snakes, and when Ti Zan saw the number of snakes coming out to greet that little snake that was coming, Ti Zan got scared and climbed a tree. The little snake told them what had happened to him and who saved his life, and he told them the boy had come with him.

The little snake's father called him. The little snake called Ti Zan, and Ti Zan came down the tree frightened, shaking, and the little snake told him he shouldn't be afraid. Ti Zan went with a troubled heart. When he got to the little snake's father, he said to him, "Ti Zan, thank you very much for saving my child," and he asked Ti Zan what he wanted for the trouble of saving the little snake. Ti Zan told him he wanted nothing except that he should make him able to know the language of animals.

The big snake told Ti Zan that it was impossible to tell him all animal languages. Ti Zan answered, "If you can't, thank you very much, there's nothing else I want." The little snake was there, and when he heard his father say that, he began crying. The snake's father cried at Ti Zan to see his child weeping.

He said to Ti Zan, "All right, here's the language of animals, but if one day you tell it to someone, that very day you are dead." Ti Zan said yes, he wouldn't tell anyone, and the big snake told Ti Zan to open his mouth and he blew into Ti Zan's mouth. When he had blown into Ti Zan's mouth, Ti Zan understood everything animals said.

Ti Zan thanked the big snake and went off. Two–three days later, Ti Zan found a girl and married her. One day Ti Zan said to his wife, "Let's go for a ride." At that time, Ti Zan's wife was in the family way. Each of them went in a carriage drawn by a horse. The horse that drew Mme Ti Zan was a female, and she was expecting a baby too. The one drawing Ti Zan was a male. Ti Zan went behind and his wife in front. When they got on to the road, Ti Zan sped up and overtook his wife.

As the horse drawing Ti Zan got in front, he said in horse language to the one drawing Madame, "See, I was behind you and I could pass in front of you." The horse answered, "You can go in front of me, you're pulling just one *bourgeois,* but I'm pulling four."

When Ti Zan heard that, he understood, and he started to laugh, and all the way along, the horse kept saying the same thing and Ti Zan kept laughing all the way. His wife became angry to see Ti Zan laughing, and she didn't know why Ti Zan was laughing.

Ti Zan's wife said to Ti Zan, "Let's go back to our place." They turned around. Then they got to their place, Mme Ti Zan asked her husband, "Now tell me what you were laughing at as we were riding." Ti Zan didn't answer. But she kept asking Ti Zan all the time till he said, "You want to know what was making me laugh, make my coffin. After that I'll tell you what was making me laugh." Right away his wife sent for carpenters and made Ti Zan's coffin, and when the coffin was ready, his wife said to him, "Here's your coffin, now tell me what was making you laugh." Ti Zan said to his wife, "Wait a minute, later I'll tell you."

Before Ti Zan told her, he took a piece of bread and moistened it. Ti Zan had an old dog. That dog, all his teeth had fallen out, he had only one left. Ti Zan took the bread and gave it to his old dog. The dog smelled the bread and cried and went off. A big cock came out and that big cock ate all that bread. The old dog said to the cock, "You've got heart." The cock said, "With reason." The dog said to the cock in his language, "My boss could die, that's the last thing he gave me, and you have the heart to eat it." The cock flapped his wings, crowed once, and said to the dog, "My boss is stupid. Look how many hens I have under my command. If one of 'em starts to fight another, I give them a hit with my beak and it all stops. He has just one wife and he lets his wife dominate him. When his wife asks him what was making him laugh, all he has to do is take his stick and give her two–three hits, and the wife will swear never to ask him a question again."

So Ti Zan laughed and said many thanks. He raised his hand and picked up his stick and said to his wife, "Come on and tell me what was making me laugh." Ti Zan began following the instructions with the stick. The wife cried, she asked pardon, and she'd never ask again the cause of his laughing. After that, when they went out together and whenever Ti Zan would laugh, she never asked Ti Zan again, because he knew what to do to win. ("Creole Stories" 16–17)[11]

By leading his fellow script-writers across the border between oral and written styles, Samuel Accouche energized a pro-*Kreol* movement, which favored research. Yet there was still ambivalence towards vernacular culture. Criticism said his tales were not "traditional" (Neumann 72n8). The new government of 1977 established a cultural section "to promote cultural activities as a means of enriching the people" (René 67). Until the recent invigoration of Lenstiti Kreol, the enrichment was limited to a few publications which pass on results of field recording in the islands of La Digue and Praslin (Diallo, Rosalie, and Essack). These yield some stories translated above: Soungoula as schoolmaster and Soungoula with the king's whale, Tizan ek Gran Dokter (Haring, *Indian Ocean* 117–19). One narrator from Praslin brilliantly combined Cat and Rat with Aesop's fable of the Hare and the Tortoise (Aesop, *Complete* 257).

120. Soungoula and Tortoise's Swimming Contest

Narrator of Praslin 1980–81

Soungoula and Tortoise were never on good terms. Each one thought he was braver than the other one. One day as they were talking, Tortoise said to Soungoula, "You talk so much about being better at everything. I assure you, you cannot match me for swimming!"

Soungoula answered, "My *boy* [English in original], I'm better on land, I'm better in the sea, every place."

"Soungoula, you run your mouth all the time but you don't have much to say. No matter what, you do it better. Now, if you are willing to see that I swim better than you, tomorrow get ready, we'll go from La Digue here and swim to Mahé." Soungoula thought a bit. He knew perfectly well he couldn't swim. But he would not let Tortoise play him for a fool. He said, "Five o'clock tomorrow morning I'll show you, we'll start. Don't make me wait or not come."

Tortoise said, "Tomorrow from four o'clock on I'll be there. I'll be patient, I'll wait till five. Then whoever has come, that's it."

Instead of the agreement to start at five o'clock, they started at 4:30 in the morning. As soon as Soungoula got there, Tortoise said, "Let's start right away, we'll finish earlier." Soungoula said, "What are you waiting for? Let's go." Tortoise launched. Soungoula took the air and jumped. At the signal he jumped on Tortoise's back, who opened the water, they went.

He didn't feel the load on his back. He didn't see that Soungoula was coming behind him. The more the swells tried to hit him, the faster Tortoise went. Soungoula held on to Tortoise on both sides. His eyes were getting red as the waves wetted him. Once or twice he almost lost his breath. After a while Tortoise called out, "Soungoula, where are you?" Soungoula answered quietly, "Don't look for me, brother, I'm right on you" [*obor ou,* pun]. Tortoise didn't turn around. Then he went through some big big swells. He really thought he'd left Soungoula a good distance behind him, while then he heard Soungoula talking just near him. Still he didn't lose confidence. He glided [along], his back above the water. Then, Soungoula in his head started considering he might get seasick. Despite that, he brought out all his strength to catch Tortoise. Arriving near to Ros Kayman, Tortoise called out, "Soungoula, where are you?"

Soungoula answered quietly, "Keep going! Don't look for me, I'm right on you [*obor ou*]!" As Soungoula said that, Tortoise put out all his effort to go a little faster. He didn't think to turn back and see if Soungoula was really coming behind him. Tortoise said to himself, "Shoot! Never did I think Soungoula could swim like that. I'll have to push harder, otherwise he'll get to Mahé before me and talk too much."

All that while, Soungoula was praying he would make it to Mahé. Cramps were engulfing him. Twice he vomited, and at any moment he might get seasick again. His throat was full of salt water which was making him thirsty. He said to himself, "Not reached Mahé yet?" It was still a long way. Arriving at Manmel, Tortoise called out, "Soungoula, where are you? Don't tell me you are right on me [*obor mwan*]." This time Soungoula didn't answer. A big wave almost knocked him off Tortoise's back. His fear mounted and he acted as if he didn't hear what Tortoise said to him. Still, he did hear inwardly, [but] Soungoula decided not to answer. Tortoise called out again, "Brother Soungoula, where are you? Are you coming?" Tortoise heard a sound in the sea around him. Soungoula stayed quiet where he was hanging on. Tortoise finally thought that he'd left Soungoula a good distance behind. He got more courage to go a little faster. More, when he noticed that he was getting close to Mahé, Tortoise slid faster yet. Just before Tortoise reached the jetty on Mahé, he called out with all his strength, "Brother Soungoula, where are you? I got there! You didn't drown back there!" At that point Soungoula saw the jetty in front of him, he took more courage, his head wasn't spinning any more; so he jumped on to the jetty. When he reached the jetty, he answered, "Hey! Tortoise, you're just getting here now? I had time on land at the Dauban bar, I knocked back a couple of quick ones! I had some of the *vin du pays* because I doubted that you were a good swimmer and risked drowning."

Tortoise didn't want to believe what he was seeing and hearing. He looked for an answer to a stack of questions that suddenly were coming into his head. When he climbed up on the jetty, his eyes were so black with astonishment that Tortoise said, "Soungoula, where are you?" Soungoula answered, "Right here, brother. I got here a long time back, I've been waiting for you. If I'd wanted, I could have swum back to La Digue, I could have returned to Mahé, and you hadn't even crossed yet. Tortoise, look here, you walk slowly, you swim slowly, but try flying, maybe you will appreciate speed!"

Tortoise lowered his head. When he raised his head, he saw Soungoula. Tortoise started laughing. He said to Soungoula, "Now let's make a bet from here to La Digue. If you beat me again, you're a better clown than me."

Soungoula wasn't slow to answer, "Let's start right away, if you like." Tortoise agreed. Soungoula said to him, "Go ahead. I'll give you a little distance." Tortoise obeyed. He went down into the water. As he started swimming, Soungoula jumped on his back. This trip, he felt that his weight was greater, and he knew why. Only he acted as if he didn't know anything was happening. He was thinking so much about how he was going to fix Soungoula that Tortoise forgot he was on a bet, and so he had to swim fast. When he passed the beacon, Tortoise dove down. He started eating down there. For quite a while he swam under water. Then he came up for air. When he arrived on the surface, Tortoise called out, "Brother Soungoula, where are you?"

Soungoula then, his eyes were popping out. He started vomiting the salt water he'd swallowed while Tortoise was eating down there. In his weakness he got courage to answer, "What? You swam under water and still I was on you! But first you were swimming on top of the water. If you go have the courage down there in the depth, count on me giving time to arrive at La Digue. We made a bet to swim there. But we didn't make a bet to kill our bodies."

Tortoise didn't say anything to Soungoula. In his heart he said, "There's more to come, wait, brother!" Just as Tortoise felt that he was approaching a place where there was a lot of big coral, he dove down again. Before his foot touched some big, big corals, Tortoise turned his body and started swimming on his back. When his shell touched the coral, he didn't feel anything and most of the coral broke off. But Soungoula was in a bad spot; his whole body was encircled, his little trousers were all torn; he'd drunk big big mouthfuls of water; his guts were popping! Then Tortoise kept swimming on his back.

When there was no more coral in front of him, Tortoise decided to go up and take a little air. He turned over and started up. Just as his head came above the water, he called, "Brother Soungoula, where are you?" When Soungoula caught his breath, he managed to answer, "Brother, I'm right on you. Only something bad has happened to me. My stomach is starting to burn, from the water a sickness is proclaiming itself on me. Brother, I have to jump on your back and you take me back to Mahé, I'll go to a doctor." Tortoise said to him, "Where were you? Not in the water . . . ?" Before Tortoise finished speaking, Soungoula answered, "I'll jump, I'll arrive on your back."

Tortoise said, "I won't take you back to Mahé where I got to. I'll hurry to take you to La Digue. Only I have to swim under water. Watch out, here I go!" Soungoula didn't have time to say anything to Tortoise. On the contrary he started swallowing mouthfuls of salt water one after the other until he felt he was losing his strength fast. Little by little his hand lost its hold on Tortoise. In a moment, in his delirium, Soungoula felt that he wasn't on Tortoise's back any more but he was descending on his own into the deep. His guts slowly exploded and Soungoula's body started slowly, slowly coming up till he was just floating on the top of the water. At the same moment, Tortoise broke the surface a little farther on. When he didn't feel any weight on his back, he continued swimming on the surface all the way to La Digue, without taking any account of what direction the current was taking his pal. (Diallo et al., *Veyez 2* 41–47)[12]

Equally classic is a joke from La Digue in which the narrator plays trickster on the audience with a somber cliché. In old times, the "normal" use of a childless couple, at the outset of a tale, was to anticipate the birth of the hero. So it happens, for instance, in Edméa Crispin's Sen Dispare, from Praslin. That strangely episodic piece brings in the snake who gets the hero the knowledge of animal languages, a pearl necklace about which the husband lies, a baby whom the wife does not in fact give birth to, and a shift of point of view that points to some literary source in the background (translated as Saint Passaway in Haring, *Indian Ocean* [125–29]). The La Digue narrator misdirects his audience like a magician.

121. Letandir

Narrator of La Digue 1980

Mr. and Mrs. Fany lived a long time together, but in all that time they didn't have any children. It was a big problem. In spite of that, Mrs. Fany had another difficulty, her husband was too fond of making money. One day she asked her husband, "Why are you piling up all that money? We don't have any children. When death takes us, we'll leave all that money behind. So what's the use of making a pile and then leaving it all behind for I don't know what?"

"It doesn't matter. I'm piling it up to increase it [*pu letandir,* punning on *les temps durs,* hard times]." Mrs Fany kept quiet and stopped talking about that subject. She did talk [about it] to people in the village.

In that same village there was a guy named Letandir. When Mr. and Mrs. Fany were talking about the money question, that Letandir was passing by and he heard their conversation. At evening he couldn't sleep for thinking how he could get hold of that money. Finally he came upon a solution. He knew Mrs. Fany was a little dumb, and so he thought he could make his plan work. Next morning, when Mr. Fany had left for work, Letandir presented his face before Mrs. Fany. "Good morning, madame. I am Mr. Letandir."

"Good morning, sir. Just so, my husband left some money here for you. Wait for me a minute, I'll go fetch it." After a little while Mrs. Fany came back out on the verandah with a little packet in her hand. "There, sir."

"Thank you, madame. Tell him I came by, eh?" Letandir didn't stay long, because he was afraid Mr. Fany would come back and spoil his good fortune of that day. Several times he looked behind him, thinking Mrs. Fany might change her mind, but each time, there was no one following him, and in his heart Letandir thought he was in the clear.

Evening came and Mr. Fany came home. That day Mrs. Fany was very happy to see him and she leapt on Mr. Fany, kissed him, saying, "You mustn't worry. I paid all your debt. Mr. Letandir came and I gave him the money you piled up for him." Mr. Fany didn't know what he would do. After, in his rage, he leaped on his wife and began beating her with a stick he found around there. In his rage, Mr. Fany jumped outside saying, "The day I find a wife stupider than you, I'll come back to you." Since that day Mr. Fany began putting his money in the bank. (Diallo, Rosalie, and Essack 16–17)[13]

After independence, some local Seychellois were trained in collecting folklore (Barre and Vogel). Then, with the movement toward stabilizing the orthography of Seselwa, writing complicated the picture of tradition.[14] Advocates of the new, government-sponsored system, in an effort to found a literary tradition, illustrated Seselwa with six formerly oral tales, now rewritten by named authors (Bollée and D'Offay). The Lenstiti Kreol, which had been recently constituted, published twenty-eight signed narratives (Payette, *Kont, Kont 2,* and *Kont 3*). The new program, which scholars of folkloristic history elsewhere call "imagining the nation and making it seem to be real," included "producing and consuming traditional texts," but only in rewritten form (Bauman and

Briggs, *Voices* 224). The novelist Antoine Abel became Samuel Accouche's literary counterpart, publishing written versions of The Princess Who Cannot Solve the Riddle, Hare at the Animals' Well, and Soungoula's tricking a fisherman into taking his place in a sack (Abel, *Contes et poçmes* 11–17, 19–20, 25–27). Oral and written came together in a nostalgic-modernizing effort to establish cultural identity. In a country where universal primary education is the pride of the government, and in a time when people regularly consult books to refresh their memory, print and oral storytelling now collaborate to create new traditions. Before independence, Samuel Accouche's broadcasts might have been a form of consciousness-lowering, but his free reworking of old symbols in a modern medium pointed forward.

Postcolonial societies create something new, which they romantically call old or imagine to be precolonial. In their sense of a new context in which old values have lost their function, they reaffirm egalitarianism or democracy and hope for socioeconomic progress. From their new position, they record and codify old vernacular culture, as "the basis of a new ethnically defined sense of nationality, which was to become the new basis of politics" (Gellner 76). Samuel Accouche used radio as his medium to generate "a new kind of form . . . The production of the sentence [on radio] becomes itself a new kind of event *within* the work" (Jameson, *Marxism* 393–97). The new event looked back to the oppressive past and forward to postcolonial Seychelles. The determining marker of Seychelles history was not colonialism (McClintock 293); it was the mixing, assemblage, and convergence of cultures. Now, as more and more people move to Victoria, the capital, where a huge land reclamation project to the north and east will create more housing, more traffic congestion, and more cultural convergence, the mixing is bound to continue. The country displays all the "flows" of globalization which have been delineated by the anthropologist Arjun Appadurai: *ethnoscapes*, "the landscape of . . . tourists, immigrants, refugees, exiles, guest workers"; *mediascapes*, the spread of information media and "the images of the world created by these media"; *technoscapes*, the shape and movement of technologies; *financescapes*, the movements of global capital; and *ideoscapes*, the organization of political cultures around inherited and borrowed concepts (Appadurai 33–37). What is to become of the inherited and remembered?

What oral narrators represent to some authorities in Seychelles—the voice of tradition, poetic knowledge, fictional knowledge, literary knowledge—lies deeper than any rewriting or any chronicle. Cultural experts have called on Seychellois people "to inventory their culture, assimilate, preserve, develop, exploit, and spread it on both the national and international plane" (Diallo, "Avant-Propos"), and these responsibilities have been undertaken by Lenstiti Kreol, National Heritage, and the annual Festival Kreol. Across the oceans there is a similar call: three Caribbean writers demand a similar restoration of a lost consciousness through tradition. They champion a contrived, sophistical notion of identity named "créolité" (Bernabé, Chamoiseau, and Confiant), which is supported in Mauritius by the prominent novelist Lindsey Collen (Hookoomsing 150; Collen). Transported to Seychelles, the *créolité* writers would encourage schoolchildren to read the twenty-four stories collected in La Digue and Praslin, which require no translating and which reflect the islands' history (Diallo, Rosalie, and Essack; Diallo et al., *Veyez 2*), side by side with Greek mythological stories in Seselwa (Choppy) and recently published *zedmo*, verbal arts (Diallo et al., *Zedmo*).

Some Seychellois seem to need to create a folkloristics of nostalgia, or to proclaim "folklore" as something receding into the past, but their products look postmodern. The "free play" of symbols, the postmodern disregard of history, explains a thirty-two-page book on slick paper published in 2001, titled *Telegraf Mouswar*, Gestures of the Kerchief (Barbé, *Télégraphes*). Posed, black-and-white photographs in this book illustrate the symbolism of thirty-one ways of carrying or displaying a kerchief (*mouswar*), in your hand, on your arm, your wrist, or your head. Each photograph is captioned, in French and Kreol, with a verbal translation of the pose. The introduction attributes this symbolism of the kerchief to French tradition of a century ago. More grandiosely, the writer attributes *all* the cultural traits of Seychellois, not merely this kerchief symbolism, to France (Barbé, *Télégraphes* 1). The authority for these revelations is neither the social-political history of Seychelles (Scarr; Shah), which is well documented, nor the African-Malagasy storytelling of a Samuel Accouche. Nor is there any evidence that people today are actually wearing *mouswar* in these ways. The authority is the testimony of a single seventy-seven-year-old informant.

Whether as social history or cultural study, this book, like its companion book on flower symbolism from the same informant (Barbé, *Lanblenm fler*), is wantonly misleading. To promulgate a minority ideology, and to call today's population culturally ignorant, is to assert French hegemony over a society which from its beginnings was a classic case of creolization and mixing. The slave trade ensured that Europeans and Africans would be living in the closest contact (Benedict 13); later, Indian and Chinese merchants added to the mix, all bringing their languages, traditions, and ideologies. Where a ruling minority, such as the French in Seychelles, has positioned itself over a subjugated population, conflicting interests express themselves in different ideologies. Subversive characters, including Soungoula or the Rat, express the everyday resistance of the majority, which perpetuates itself in ambiguous and ambivalent attitudes to authority. Ideology works and is heard through imaginative constructs, symbols, signs, and images like those in oral tales. Thus if the kerchief book and flower book are held up to standards of evidence, they are only a pastiche of cultural research, which hides the ethnic and cultural mixing of which Seychellois are so proud. Such reactionary Eurocentrism does more than flatten out a diverse culture; it tries to conceal the central facts about Seychelles behind "Vacations, Holidays, Honeymoons, Romance, Scuba, Sailing, and Paradise on Earth" (http://www.sey.net).

The enormous amounts of money that flow into Seychelles, and which flow out right away into the international hotel chains, have done almost nothing to defend "tradition." Hotels almost never consult the Division of Culture to help them find village performers. Not long ago, one of the beach hotels engaged a Philippine dance troupe, instead of local dancers, to entertain its foreign guests. Although National Heritage and Lenstiti Kreol both have cultural displays in their beautiful historic buildings, they attract far fewer visitors than the beach hotels. After eating the delectable dishes at the Vye Marmit restaurant, no diner can go away with the beguiling trilingual cookery book (*Dekouver*); it's not sold there. It's as if the nation has somersaulted over the nostalgias of "folklore" and a *folklorique* past, from which the bourgeoisie could distance itself, and catapulted into the postindustrial world.

Simultaneities which might be called postmodern are present in Seychelles. When Lenstiti Kreol sponsored annual writing contests, some of the submissions were written versions of oral tales (Payette, *Kont* [1990]). Such "close replicas of oral texts" (Dorson, "Use" 473) acknowledged the coexistence of orality and literacy. Other submissions were "elaborations and revisions of oral tales . . . literary inventions based on oral folklore," and "literary invention based on literary folklore" (Dorson, "Use" 474–75), all of which Samuel Accouche practiced in his broadcasts. Modernism would prefer oral, "traditional" folktales over the "un-traditional" rewritings of Antoine Abel and Samuel Accouche, but postmodernism abolishes the distinction as artificial. Maybe it is. In some touristed islands in the world, people present their culture ironically, so as to protect the "real" and the "authentic," and also to profit from the commodification that tourism requires. Their fragmented way of managing the public domain reflects the fragmentation of everybody's life. Ideology in a creole society seldom welds people into the postcolonial harmony seen among the people of Seychelles. But there, as in all the Indian Ocean islands, the real ideology expresses itself in the ambiguity, ambivalence, and skill in manipulating traditions that storytellers practice.

Those who study creole societies practice similar skills. Inherently, ethnology and folklore are creolizing disciplines. They require their observers to be "compulsive poachers. Border transgressions and forays into uncharted lands are in fact the essence of their calling, which is the discovery and constant renewal of cultural relativism" (Feuser 380). Such poaching is a true interdisciplinarity. Creolized scholarship is what occurs when thinkers of different disciplines and orientations are forced together by the nature of what they are looking at: ethnoscapes, mediascapes, and the rest of the global flows. Scholars, imagining themselves to be students or analysts, inevitably participate in intellectual flows. With self-awareness, they will see that the cultural creolization visible in places such as the Southwest Indian Ocean offers a model wherewith to understand the cultural convergences of Europe and the rest of the postmodern world. *Postmodern,* if it means "contextual and self-reflexive," characterizes creole literatures, whether oral or written. Writing about the United States, Ralph Ellison remarked that any viable theory of part of a culture obligates us to fashion a more adequate theory of the whole of that culture (Krupat 173). Now, any viable theory of world culture obligates us to assemble facts about cultural convergence, transgressing intellectual borders and foraying into uncharted lands.

If what I have said is not true, I am not the liar (not here, anyway); it was the storytellers of long ago who invented these tales.

Appendix

INDIAN OCEAN VERSIONS OF THE "DEFIANT GIRL" (*LA FILLE DIFFICILE*), CROSS REFERENCED TO NUMBERING IN GÖRÖG-KARADY AND SEYDOU 2001

Madagascar

Mcar1 (Renel 1910, 2:310–311). Haring, *Malagasy Tale Index* 2.1.311.
Mcar2 (Ferrand 1893, 119–122). *Malagasy Tale Index* 3.1.311A.
Mcar3 (Dandouau 1922, 200–225). *Malagasy Tale Index* 3.1.311B.
Mcar4 (Renel 1910, 1:275–277) *Malagasy Tale Index* 3.1.311C.
Mcar5 (Renel 1910, 1:77–81). *Malagasy Tale Index* 3.1.311D.
Mcar6 (Renel 1910, 2:261–264). *Malagasy Tale Index* 3.1.311E.
Mcar7 (Renel 1910, 2:265–267) *Malagasy Tale Index* 3.1.311F.
Mcar8 (Birkeli 1922–1923, 240–245). *Malagasy Tale Index* 3.1.311G1.
Mcar9 (Decary 1964, 99–101). *Malagasy Tale Index* 3.1.311G2.
Mcar10 (Michel 1957, 177–179). *Malagasy Tale Index* 3.1.311G3.
Mcar11 (Birkeli 1922–1923, 272–275). *Malagasy Tale Index* 3.1.311H.
Mcar12 (Dahl 1968, 87–91). *Malagasy Tale Index* 3.1.311I.
Mcar13 (Dahl 1968, 92–96). *Malagasy Tale Index* 3.1.311J.
Mcar14 (Mamelomana 1968, 889–892). *Malagasy Tale Index* 3.1.311K.
Mcar15 (Grandidier 1932, 180).

Mcar16: Listed as Beaujard Mo1 in (Görög-Karady and Seydou 2001, 239–240). Similarly: Mcar17: Beaujard Mo2; Mcar18: Beaujard Mo3; Mcar19: Beaujard Mo4; Mcar20: Beaujard Mo5; Mcar21: Beaujard Mo6; Mcar22: Beaujard Mo7; Mcar23: Beaujard Mo8; Mcar24: Beaujard Mt1; Mcar25: Beaujard Mt2; Mcar26: Beaujard Mt3; Mcar27: Beaujard Mt4; Mcar28: Beaujard Mt5; Mcar29: Beaujard Mt6.

Mcar30 (Fanony 2001, 56–73).

Mauritius

Mts1 (Baissac 1887, 146–153; Goswami 1987, 20–23; Baissac 1989, 118–121).

Mts2 (Baissac 1887, 154–161; Baissac 1989, 122–125).

Mts3 (Baissac 1887, 162–179; Baissac 1989, 126–135).

Mts4 Nelzir Ventre, Mauritius Broadcasting Company television broadcast, 2 January 1983.

Mts5 Nelzir Ventre, recorded at Poudre d'Or by Claudie Ricaud and Lee Haring, 27 February 1990.

Mayotte (Comoros)

May1: Trans. Zaharia Soilihi and Sophie Blanchy, *L'Espoir* 2, August 1989, 20–31.

May2–23: N.-J. Gueunier collected 22 versions in Malagasy language in Mayotte (Beaujard 2001, 240).

May24 (Allibert 1977, 66–68).

May25 (Blanchy 1991:72–103).

Réunion

Rn1 (Gamaleya 1977, 18–27).

Rn2 (Barat, Carayol, and Vogel 1977, 29–32).

Rn3 (Barat, et al. 1977, 33–34).

Rn4 (Barat, et al. 1977, 34–35).

Rn5 (Barat, et al. 1977, 35–37; Carayol, Chaudenson, and Doomun 1978, 68–79).

Rn6 (Barat, et al. 1977, 37–38).

Rn7 (Barat, et al. 1977, 38).

Rn8 (Decros 1978, 57–65).

Seychelles

Se1 (Bollée and Neumann 1984, 57–79).

Se2 (Creole stories, 1978, 42).

Notes

In this book, the actors, incidents, and objects which scholars call motifs are referenced by their numbers in Stith Thompson's *Motif-Index of Folk-Literature*. Recurrent plots, which scholars call tale types, are referenced by AT and a number from Antti Aarne and Stith Thompson, *The Types of the Folktale*. Tales from Madagascar are referenced to my *Malagasy Tale Index*.

Preface

1. Historian Paul Ottino is one scholarly model for this alternation of text and comment (Ottino, P., *L'Étrangère*), but every parent reads to a child.

1. Land of the Man-Eating Tree

1. Collected by a schoolteacher, 1907–10. Tale 1.1.06 in Haring, *Index*. Motifs: A810, Earth covered in water; A812, Earth-Diver; A816.3, God causes primeval sea to roll back; A827, Earth made by drying up of primeval water; A1263, Man created from part of body; A1270, Primeval human pair; A1724.1, Animals from body of slain person.

2. Reprinted as "Man-Eating Tree a Myth" in the youth periodical *The Pathfinder*, 14 June 1930, 15. My thanks to Ann Wollock for this citation.

3. Motifs: A1241, Man made from clay (earth); F162.2.1, Four rivers of paradise; G303.9.4, Devil as tempter; C621, Forbidden tree (fruit); A1331, Paradise lost because of one sin; A1275.1.1, Deity creates princess from prince's body and gives her to him; T541.16, Birth from knee; S73.1, Fratricide; A1010, Deluge; A960, Creation of mountains; A1484, Origin of reading and writing; T547, Birth from virgin; P715.1, Jews; M301, Prophets; D1856, Death evaded.

4. Flacourt does not identify his informants; I assume arbitrarily that the two accounts were given him by the same person. I preserve Flacourt's spellings of caste names. Motifs: G303.11.1, The devil's wife; G303.11.2, The devil's son; Z71.5.6.2, Seven deadly sins; A1120, Establishment of present order: winds; A1135, Origin of wintry weather; A1142, Origin of thunder; A1341.3, Origin of thefts and quarrels; A1384, Origin of evil inclinations; A1343, Origin of lying; A102.16, Justice of God; Z127, Sin personified; G303.8.8, Devil lives in the water.

5. Motif A960, Creation of mountains. Tale 2.1.07 in Haring, *Index* (234).

6. "Nikasa hiady tamy ny lanitra ny tany," Dahle 268–69; Dahle and Sims 193. Trans. Ferrand (182–83); Dahle et al. (309–10). Tale 2.1.08 in Haring, *Index* (234–35). Motifs: A162, Conflicts of the gods; A969, Origin of mountains and hills.

7. "Ny voro-manidina nifanaiky hanao mpanjaka," Dahle 290. Type 221, Election of the Bird-King, in Aarne and Thompson; Uther (1:138–39). Motifs: A2491.2, Why owl avoids daylight; A2493, Friendship between the animals; A2494, Why certain animals are enemies; B236.0.1, Animal king chosen as result of contest; B242.1.5, Shrike as king of birds (Haring, *Index* 188–89).

8. *Dicrurus forficatus.*

9. Motifs: A2489.1, Why cock wakes man in morning; A2477.2, Why hen scratches in ground.

10. Motifs: A1443, Origin of domestic animals; A2275, Animal cries a reminiscence of former experience.

11. "Le mari et ses deux femmes," Betsileo, collected 1887–1893. Tale 1.2.81 in Haring, *Index* (126–27). Motif A1585, Origin of laws of division of property within a family.

12. Fitzgerald is famous for saying, "The test of a first-rate intelligence is the ability to hold two opposed ideas in the mind at the same time, and still retain the ability to function" (Fitzgerald 69). By his criterion, most creole societies display first-rate intelligences and creatively exploit the oppositions.

13. Motifs: A1270, Primeval human pair; A1331, Paradise lost; A63.6, Devil in serpent form tempts first woman.

14. A more recent instance: In 1932, a Merina pastor published a story on the origin of healing arts in the Protestant magazine. To one reading sixty years later, he seems conflicted: he shows loyalty to the world of the ancestors by playing the role of the traditional storyteller, but he recoils from friends and compatriots who after all were nearly naked savages. The tale, which the pastor got from a healer-diviner, brings together Biblical and Qur'anic accounts of Dama and Hova (Arabic names for Adam and Eve) and the dispute between herding and agriculture, personified by their two sons. The herdsman son, no fratricide, is dismissed by the end of the story in favor of the farmer, who acquires the healing arts from God's son Ratompo (Lord). After living fifty years on earth, Ratompo ascends to heaven, delivering to his healer disciples a prayer to God and his son, a pair familiar from ancient religion. The pastor-collector apparently suggested adding the third term of the Trinity, so that the formula would say, "You are strong, strong, strong, Andrianahary [God], Ratompo [Lord], Ramanitse [Ruler]" (Gueunier, *L'origine* 41n3). The farmer's three sons, who of course have no Bible source, have Islamic names: Babamino, "Believer-Father," Makarailo, from the Qur'anic-Biblical angel Michael, and Tsarafailo,

from Asrafel who will sound the trumpet on the day of resurrection (Gueunier, *L'origine* 34–45).

15. Motifs: C31.9, Taboo: revealing secrets of supernatural wife; F420.1.2.1, Water-maidens are of unusual beauty; F420.6.1.4, Water-maiden goes to home of mortal and marries; C952, Immediate return to other world for broken taboo. The piece has innumerable versions (Haring, *Index* 358–60).

16. Tale 1.1.22 in Haring, *Index* (86). Motifs: A288, Rainbow goddess; A1275, Creation of first man's mate; T111.1.2, Man marries the daughter of a god; A1653, Origin of kings; A1555, Origin of marriage; A1319.9, Origin of bodily attributes.

17. "Origin of Burial." Tale 1.1.11 in Haring, *Index* (80–81). Motifs: A1210, Creation of man by creator; A1252.1, Mankind from vivified wooden image; A1275, Creation of first man's mate; A1277, Offspring of first parents; A1591, Origin of burial; A1537.1, Sneezer wished long life.

18. Motif A736.1.4, Sun and moon married.

19. Jacques Faublée collected three versions from his Bara informants (Faublée 354–59; Haring, *Index* 91–92), commenting on the wide distribution of motif A1252.1, Mankind from vivified wooden image, and noting versions from other parts of the island (Le Barbier, "Notes" 149–50; Dandouau, *Contes populaires* 93, 374). The pun appears also in a Betsileo creation story (Dubois 1331; Haring, *Index* 89–90), which Faublée comments on: "Only among the more developed Malagasy populations is the motif of the turned-over woman justified with an etymological pun" (Faublée 359).

20. "Les trois hommes," Betsimisaraka, collected at Antanambao in Betsimisaraka-du-Sud. Tale 1.4.653A in Haring, *Index* (161). Type 653A, Repairing an Egg, in Aarne and Thompson. African in origin (Bascom, *African Dilemma Tales* 52).

21. Motifs: H621, Skillful companions create woman: to whom does she belong?; R111.7, Joint rescuers quarrel over rescued princess. Outside Madagascar the dilemma is enclosed in Type 945, Luck and Intelligence (Aarne and Thompson). Indian narrators in antiquity may have invented the debate among the three suitors with magic powers, who show up in the collections of Straparola, Basile, and the Grimms (Zipes 335–46).

22. "Ny akanga," Dahle 298; Dahle and Sims 194. Trans. Sibree, "Oratory" (314). Tale 2.1.121 in Haring, *Index* (261). Motif J229, Choice between evils.

23. The Four Skillful Brothers, Type 653 in Aarne and Thompson (228–30). Motifs: P251.6.2, Four brothers; R166, Brothers having extraordinary skill rescue princess; H621.2, Girl rescued by skillful companions; to whom does she belong?; Z16, Tales ending with a question.

24. Tale 2.1.03 in Haring, *Index* (232–33). Motifs: A625.2, Raising of the sky; A1420, Acquisition of food supply for human race; A1437, Acquisition of clothing.

25. The Bara diet, as Michel observed it, was largely vegetarian–manioc and yam. Being herdsmen, however, they ate beef nearly every day, though they would do the killing only on a fixed day. All customs had to be observed before an ox could be killed. Then part was dried and powdered for seasoning the manioc or other food (Michel 143–44).

26. Motif A2430, Animal characteristics: dwelling and food.

27. Motifs: A2433.5.2, Why fly lives amid filth; A2450, Animal's daily work; A2489, Animal's periodic habits.

28. Motifs: B244, King of reptiles; A2433.6, Haunts of reptiles. Tale 1.5.41 in Haring, *Index* (171).

29. Motifs: A2345, Origin and nature of animal's teeth; A2345.7, Why animal lacks teeth.

30. Motifs: A1420, Acquisition of food supply for human race; A1430, Acquisition of other necessities; A1614.4, Origin of tribes from choices made; A1650, Origin of royalty. Tale 1.2.13 in Haring, *Index* (109).

31. Motifs: A400, God of earth; A511, Birth and rearing of culture hero; A520, Nature of the culture hero; H1510, Tests of power to survive; A1414.1, Origin of fire, rubbing sticks; D1380, Magic object protects; A1540, Origin of religious ceremonials; A962, Mountains from ancient activities of hero; A920.1, Origin of lakes; T111.2, Woman from sky-world marries mortal man; A625.1, Heaven-mother, earth-father; A1420.4, Food originally obtained without effort; A1423.2, Acquisition of rice; A1421.0.1, Hoarded rice made available to men by culture hero (Haring, *Index* 220–21; Dandouau, "Folk-lore sakalava et tsimihety" 453–59).

32. This Sakalava version (1901–1907) is one of the earliest to have been written. Others from other groups show the importance of the ideologeme of powers in conflict (Renel, *Contes* 1:215–23, 268–74; Birkeli 290–93; Dandouau, *Contes populaires* 149–53; Faublée 412–53, 496–500). When the earth-god and sky-god overcome their antagonism and cooperate in creation, the tradition overlaps another, in which mankind is created from a vivified image of wood or clay (Dandouau, *Contes populaires* 92–94, 154–56; Renel, *Contes* 3:11–12, 17–18, 39–41, 45, 89–91, 95–96, 97, 98, 107–108, 119–21; Dubois 1331–32; Faublée 344–45, 347–48, 366–68; Michel 175–77).

33. Dandouau's footnote: "In another version, the man and *Rakakabe,* after leaving the ox, appeal to a *fody* (Cardinal, Foudia Madagascariensis Passereaux), who says to the man, 'Isn't it you who catches me in your traps, when you are sowing your ricefields? Don't you drive me away, with the help of your children, when your rice is ripe, throwing sticks and stones at me, saying, 'Go away, accursed bird!' Why would I defend you now? You are getting only what you deserve'" (Dandouau, *Contes populaires* 369n).

34. "L'homme et le rakakabe" is a version of The Ungrateful Serpent Returned to Captivity, Type 155 in Aarne and Thompson; Uther (1:107–108). Tale 4.155 in Haring, *Index* (407–408). Ultimately the tale type was of Indian origin, judging from the seventeen references in Thompson and Balys (262). Motifs: A165.2, Messenger of gods; B19, Mythical animals; W154.2.1, Rescued animal threatens rescuer; K551, Respite from death granted until particular act is performed; J1772.3.2, Animals render unjust decision against since man has always been unjust to them; J1172.3, Ungrateful animal returned to captivity. Dandouau collected a similar story in which a different mythical beast is entrapped by man, with God's connivance (Dandouau, *Contes populaires* 299–301).

35. The tale is derived from Type 533, The Speaking Horsehead, in Aarne and Thompson (191–92), where the cut-off head of the girl's helpful horse speaks to reveal the treachery (motif B133.3). Other versions have been found in Madagascar (Haring, *Index* 151–52, 391–92, 474–75). Motifs in Rusillon's text: P236, Undutiful children; K2251, Treacherous slave, or K2251.1, Treacherous

slave-girl (inexplicably, Rusillon translates the slave as a male); B211.9, Speaking bird; B131, Bird of truth; H1574, Tests of social position; H74, Recognition of royalty from personal characteristics or traits.

36. My translation preserves Faublée's unusual orthography, which despite its logic has never usurped the place won by the British missionaries' efforts of the 1820s.

37. Tale 7.554.1 in Haring, *Index* (475–77). Motifs: A165.1, Bird as messenger; H961, Tasks performed by cleverness; H882, Riddle: top and bottom of staff; H161, Recognition of transformed person among identical companions. AT554, The Grateful Animals, begins: H1260, Quest to the upper world; D670, Magic flight; B360, Animals grateful for rescue from peril of death; D210, Transformation into a vegetable form; D1312, Magic object gives advice; D270, Transformation: man to object; H335, Tasks assigned suitors; H1149, Miscellaneous superhuman tasks; B571, Animals perform tasks for man; E121.1, Resuscitation by a god; H1132, Task: recovering lost objects from sea; B548.2, Fish recovers object from sea; H1023.2, Task: carrying water in a sieve; H952, Reductio ad absurdum of task: counter-impossible obligation; K605, Cannibal sent for water with vessel full of holes, victim escapes; H162, Recognition of disguised princess by bee lighting on her. End of AT554. K527, Escape by substituting another person in place of the intended victim; E80, Water of life; A1438, Origin of medicines; Z64, Proverbs.

38. Type 326, The Youth Who Wanted to Learn What Fear Is, in Aarne and Thompson. Tale 1.7.326 in Haring, *Index.* Motifs: H1376.5, Quest for trouble; H1360, Quest for dangerous animals; D440, Transformation: object to animal; K567, Escape by pretending to perform errand for captor; H1440, The learning of fear.

39. "A Malagasy seldom visits a superior without taking some present or offering" (Sibree's note).

40. Sibree's note: "The literal translation of the original here is, 'Let us catch the ticks [of the oxen],' an operation which could only be performed with very gentle animals. Games with oxen were formerly favourite amusements of the Hova [Merina], and are still so with other Malagasy tribes. Bull-fighting was a favourite pastime of the chiefs, and wrestling with oxen, and bringing them down by sheer strength is also practised at funerals among the Betsileo, and is also as common among the Sihanaka, and probably with other tribes as well" ("Malagasy Folk-Tales" 53n).

41. Tale 7.35.3 in Haring, *Index* (464–66). Motifs: D1610.2, Speaking tree; L215, Unpromising magic object chosen; T548.3, Magic elixir to produce a child; T61.5.3, Unborn children promised in marriage to each other; A511.1.2.2, Culture hero in mother's womb indicates direction to be taken by her; T584.1, Birth through the mother's side; F601, Persons of extraordinary powers; E761.3, Life token: tree fades; K1941, Disguised flayer; D471.2.1, Transformation: house door to stone; D1960, Magic sleep; C400, Speaking tabu (Haring, *Index* 464–65). Sibree published his Malagasy folklore materials first in the (London) *Folk-Lore Journal* for 1883, in five installments, then in the periodical he edited, *Antananarivo Annual,* for 1891, and finally in his *Madagascar Before the Conquest.*

42. The errand foreshadows one in a Réunionnais tale collected a century later, where again a pregnancy is implied but not stated (Barat, Carayol, and Vogel 13–18).

43. Motifs: D1925.3, Barrenness removed by prayer; F525, Person with half a body; H1385, Quest for lost persons; H57, Recognition by missing member. Related tales have been collected in Madagascar (Renel, *Contes* 1:209–14; Decary, *Contes et légendes* 129–33; "Voatovo"; Faublée 391–94). The word tay, which Mr. Barivoitse uses in his formula even when he isn't telling Malagasy tales, is also of Malagasy derivation.

44. Excerpt from a summary of the story by the LMS missionary James Sibree. "Ilaisambilo sy iampelaman anoho," Dahle 170–78. "Isilikolona," Dahle et al. 186–95; Haring, *Index* 398–400; Ottino, P., *L'Étrangère* 248–54. Motifs: F525, Person with half a body (cf. T551.4, Boy born with one side flesh and one iron); H1221, Quest for adventure; H1331.1, Quest for marvelous bird; H1360, Quest for dangerous animals; E761.3, Life token: tree fades; D1444, Magic object catches animal; E761.7.5, Life token: dogs pulling on leash; B29, Other combinations of beast and man; G691, Bodies of victims in front of ogre's house; H1023.2, Task, carrying water in a sieve; D672, Transformation flight; F910, Extraordinary swallowings; G522, Ogre persuaded to drink pond dry bursts; D481, Transformation: stretching cliff; K678, Cutting rope to kill ogre who is climbing the rope to reach his victim; H1242, Youngest brother alone succeeds on quest; G514, Ogre captured.

45. Motifs: C321, Taboo: looking into box; C915.1, Troubles escape when forbidden casket is opened. Tale 2.2.09 in Haring, *Index* (275).

46. Rakoto's mother echoes the wonderworking mother of the Merina epic hero Ibonia (Haring, *Ibonia*).

47. One of six versions of The King and the Peasant's Son, Type 921 in Aarne and Thompson, collected in Madagascar (Haring, *Index* 210–14). Motifs: H583, Clever youth answers king's inquiry in riddles; J1675, Clever dealing with a king; Q91, Reward for cleverness; H1024.1, Task: milking a bull; J1533, Absurdities concerning birth of animals; H1021.3, Task: making a ship of stone; H1543, Contest in remaining under water; K231.1, Refusal to perform part in mutual agreement; J1191.7, Rice pot on pole, fire far away; J1536, Ruler's absurdity rebuked; K607.1, The cave call; K842, Dupe persuaded to take prisoner's place in a sack: killed; K843, Dupe persuaded to be killed in order to go to heaven.

48. Theoretical studies of this problem include the articles by Lüthi; Dégh and Vázsonyi; Abrahams; and Ben-Amos in Ben-Amos, *Folklore Genres.*

49. Motifs: H1024.1, Task: milking a bull (cf. H1361, Quest for lion's milk); J1530, One absurdity rebukes another.

2. Diaspora

1. Motif D1415.2 in Thompson, *Motif-Index.*

2. Motifs: D1315, Magic object locates lost person; H1385, Quest for lost persons.

3. The use of bark as a garment was already obsolete in Madagascar when Jacques Faublée, conducting fieldwork there before World War II, was told a story narrating the invention of this mode of clothing (Faublée 484).

4. Motifs: H12, Recognition by song; K500, Escape from death or danger by deception.

5. In translating, I adopt Joel Chandler Harris's "Brer" as Soungoula's title.

6. Recorded 15 February 1990 at Poudre d'Or by Claudie Ricaud and Lee Haring. Trans. Claudie Ricaud and Lee Haring.

7. Interview at the house of Ngoma, Machakos district, Eastern Province, Kenya, 6 January 1968. Trans. P. David Matolo.

8. Type 175 in Aarne and Thompson; Uther (1:120–21).

9. Recorded at Poudre d'Or on 27 February 1990, trans. Claudie Ricaud and Lee Haring. Type 175, The Tarbaby and the Rabbit (Aarne and Thompson 63–64). Motif K741, Capture by tarbaby, in Thompson, *Motif-Index.*

10. Motif H162, Recognition of disguised princess by bee lighting on her, in Thompson, appears in many Malagasy tales (Beaujard, *Mythe et société* 428–29).

11. Hare's excessive punishment of his victim echoes a European tale, The Bear and the Honey, in which the trickster fox leads bear, his dupe, to a wasp-nest (Type 49 in Aarne and Thompson). The simultaneous evocation of a European tale and an African episode is what is meant by creolization.

12. Type 72 in Aarne and Thompson. Motifs: K1110, Deceptions into self-injury; K1241, Trickster rides dupe horseback; K1042, Water bird takes dupe to sea: shakes him off into water.

13. Types 4, Carrying the Sham-Sick Trickster, and 72, Rabbit Rides Fox A-Courting, in Aarne and Thompson; Uther (1:65). Motif K1241, Trickster rides dupe horseback.

14. "Le chat et le rat d'eau," Betsimisaraka, 1886–93, collected from a female informant at Mananjary (Ferrand, *Contes* 1–2; Haring, *Index* 296–97). Motif A2494.1.4, Enmity between cat and rat. Ferrand commented that in his time in Madagascar, the phrase "let's eat him, let's kill him" was in common use for any enemy, man or beast, and could be heard in public speeches.

15. Motif K1251, Holding up the rock.

16. Motif K1251; found also in a *sungura* story of the Nyamwezi. As elephant demands payment of a debt, "'I was just going into the hole there to get it, said the rabbit, but I am afraid of the hill falling on me, do you lean against it and hold it still while I go and fetch the money.' The elephant leant against the hill till his friends came by and jeered at him, and the rabbit went into the hole, but did not come out again. The same tale is told among the Yaos in a similar form" (Steere, "On East African" 150–51).

17. Motif K607.1 in Thompson, *Motif-Index.*

18. Motifs: H1543, Contest in remaining under water (Malagasy); J1191.7, Rice pot on pole, fire far away; J1536, Ruler's absurdity rebuked. Also in Abdallah Paune (103–105); Hatubou (41–44); Ahmed-Chamanga and Ali Mroimana (41–47).

19. K139, Other worthless animals sold; X1826.5, Disguise as priest; K1240, Deception into humiliating position; K1400, Dupe's property destroyed; (cf. G93, Cannibal breaks wind as means of attack;) X700, Humor concerning sex; K1315.2, Seduction by posing as doctor; Q583, Fitting bodily injury as punishment; K842, Dupe persuaded to take prisoner's place in a sack: killed; L161, Lowly hero marries princess.

20. Motifs: H931, Tasks assigned in order to get rid of hero; H336.2, Suitor required to catch wild animals; H1273, Quest to devil for objects; K330, Means of hoodwinking the guardian; B325.1, Animal bribed with food; H1151.3, Task: stealing sheet from bed on which person is sleeping; K439, Thief loses his goods or is detected; K841, Substitute for execution obtained by

trickery; S139.2, Slain person dismembered; H1272, Quest for devils in hell; K710, Victim enticed into voluntary captivity or helplessness; L161, Lowly hero marries princess. A Réunionnais version was collected in 1976 (Decros 5–13), with many similar elements: Ti Zan steals Lov's pillow, horse, and bell at command. By exchanging places in a sack with Lov's wife, he tricks Lov into beating her to death, and then escorts him to his king and his death.

21. "Association de Kotofetsy avec Mahaka," collected from a Merina narrator on the east coast. Other versions are found in Dahle and Sims (39–40) and Longchamps (95–97), with the addition of motif K444, Dream bread. Tale 2.3.127 in Haring, *Index.* Motifs: K132, Sale of worthless animals + K140, Sale of worthless objects = J1530, One absurdity rebukes another.

22. The head of the clan has this responsibility.

23. The story combines Types 1525, The Master Thief, and 1737, The Parson in the Sack to Heaven (Aarne and Thompson; Uther 2:242–54, 404–405). Tale 2.3.1525 in Haring, *Index.* Motifs: K527, Escape by substituting another person in place of the intended victim; K842, Dupe persuaded to take prisoner's place in sack.

24. Some editors, like Ferrand, omit the prefix *I,* which signals a proper noun.

25. "Comment Kotofetsy et Mahaka trompèrent le roi," tale 2.3.38 in Haring, *Index.* Motif K1833, Disguise as ghost.

26. "Ny nanandratany sampy," Dahle et al. 72–73; Dahle and Sims 47. Previous translations found in Sibree, "Oratory" (339–40) and Dandouau, "Contes malgaches" (30). Tale 2.3.42 in Haring, *Index.* Motifs: K1961, Sham churchman (or K1963, Sham magician); K1970, Sham miracles; K110, Sale of pseudo-magic objects.

27. "Nifamono reny Ikotofetsy sy Imahaka" (Ikotofetsy and Imahaka kill their mothers), Dahle 362–63; Dahle et al. 78–80; Dandouau, "Contes malgaches" 28–29; Longchamps 121–23. Tale 2.3.135 in Haring, *Index* (339). Motifs: J261, Loudest mourners not greatest sorrowers; K1875, Deception by sham blood; K944, Deceptive agreement to kill wives/children.

28. Motif K2321.1, Man who killed mother uses her corpse to get presents.

29. Adapted in colonial days as an indicator for French readers of Malagasy culture (Leblond 239–40). The tale echoes ATU Types 1536, 1537, and 1655 (Uther 2:269–73, 359–60). Motifs: K2321, Corpse set up to frighten people (cf. K1383, Trickster throws corpse in river and accuses princess of the murder).

30. "Tromperie de Kotofetsy et Mahaka envers un homme riche," Ferrand, *Contes* 213–15; Dahle et al. 68–70. Trans. Chapus (66–69). Tale 2.3.44 in Haring, *Index.* Motif: K111.1, Alleged gold-dropping animal sold.

31. The *sakoririka* is an insect inhabiting banana and sugarcane plants, sometimes eaten in Betsileo country.

32. "Le sakoririka devenu boeuf," Betsileo, 1907–10. Collected at Fiadanana, Fianarantsoa district. Type 1415, Lucky Hans, in Aarne and Thompson. Tale 1.3.2034C B in Haring, *Index.* Motif N421.1, Progressively lucky bargains, in Thompson, *Motif-Index.*

33. "Celui qui crut être plus rusé que Kotofetsy et Mahaka," Ferrand, *Contes* 233–34. Tale 2.3.37 in Haring, *Index.* Motifs: G230, Habitat of witches; G247, Witches dance.

34. Motifs of Baissac's version: H936, Tasks assigned because of longings of pregnant woman; S222.1, Woman promises her unborn child to appease

offended witch; K500, Escape from death or danger by deception; K602, "Noman"; D1254.1, Magic wand; D855, Magic object acquired as reward; D642.1, Transformation to escape captivity; D117.1, Transformation: man to mouse; K620, Escape by deceiving the guard; K521, Escape by disguise; F577.2, Brothers identical in appearance; (cf. K1611, Substituted caps cause ogre to kill his own children;) D231, Transformation: man to stone; D700, Person disenchanted (Baissac, *Folklore* 98–111).

35. I reproduce Baissac's nineteenth-century orthography of Kreol.

36. Motif H936 in Thompson, *Motif-Index.*

37. *Nwar,* black, has some of the same effect as *nigger* in African American vernacular speech, permitted to members of the in-group when they address each other.

38. Type 563, The Table, the Ass, and the Stick, in Aarne and Thompson; Uther (1:331–33). Motifs: D1470.1, Magic wishing-object; D1601.5, Automatic cudgel; D1401.1, Magic club (stick) beats person; D1651.2, Magic cudgel works only for master; D861.1, Magic object stolen by host; D881.2, Recovery of magic object by use of magic cudgel. The goat's defecation obliquely refers to the motif of a gold-producing ass in European versions—for example, the Grimms' no. 36.

39. *Sideroxylon grandiflorum.*

40. Motifs: L112, Hero of unpromising appearance; K1918, Monster disguises and wins girl; G82, Cannibal fattens victim; D1118.1, Magic air-riding basket; D1532, Magic object bears person aloft.

41. The appendix lists at least some of its versions in Madagascar, Mauritius, Réunion, Seychelles, and the Comoros, supplementing the comprehensive listing in Görög-Karady and Seydou.

42. Thanks to Marie-Josée Baudot, who interviewed him for the broadcast and made the transcript available to me and my collaborator, Claudie Ricaud. Nelzir Ventre's words are presented here in full.

43. The three types in Aarne and Thompson are 900, King Thrushbeard; 311, Rescue by the Sister; and 312, The Giant-Killer and his Dog. Attempts to classify the defiant-girl story are made by Biebuyck and Biebuyck; Haring, *Index* (363–71).

44. The editor translated the name as "he who overturns everything" (Grandidier 180). In Mauritian Kreol, the Malagasy *lolo* (spirit, revenant) fuses with French-derived *loup* (wolf) to produce a creole prince.

3. Stars

1. From a 1980 interview in the Mauritius periodical *Weekend,* trans. Claudie Ricaud. Motifs: T91.6, Noble and lowly in love (cf. T83, Lover drowned as he swims to see his mistress, and P613, Putting coin in dead person's mouth).

2. Recorded 27 February 1990 at Poudre d'Or. Trans. Claudie Ricaud. Motifs: D169, Transformation, man to bird, miscellaneous; G512, Ogre killed; D551.3, Transformation by eating flesh.

3. Recorded at Poudre d'Or on 27 February 1990. Trans. Claudie Ricaud.

4. In this book, *Kreol* denotes the language and *creole* the people.

5. Trans. Claudie Ricaud and Lee Haring. Some hesitations and petty mistakes are rectified, such as "He gave him his, a little basket," or "Well, the keeper, this keeper, when he went like this, when he heard that blowing coming from that wood . . ." Others are retained, in our attempt to reproduce Sydney Joseph's oral style in Kreol.

6. Type 400, The Man on a Quest for His Lost Wife, in Aarne and Thompson (128–31); Uther (1:231–33). Grimm nos. 92, 932, and 193.

7. Sydney Joseph wants his hearer to note that he is giving his animal characters conventional folktale names (Baker and Hookoomsing 155). The fictive kinship of being a *komper* appears in a Seychelles tale above. France and Central America too have systems of fictive kinship, which open the possibility of making claims on those more powerful than you are (Donothy Noyes, personal communication). In Central America, *compadrazgo,* or godparent ritual, is a well-established social institution.

8. These motifs are as traditional as the word *komper.* B392, Hero divides spoil for animals; B431.2, Helpful lion; B455.3, Helpful eagle; B481.1, Helpful ant; B501, Animal gives part of its body as talisman for summoning its aid; D1421, Magic object summons helper.

9. The task is to guard the herd; motif H1199.17 in Thompson, *Motif-Index.*

10. Type 302 in Aarne and Thompson; Uther (1:180–83). Similar episodes occur in a nineteenth-century Mauritian tale (Baissac, *Folklore* 358–89), and in a Radio Seychelles broadcast of the 1970s ("Creole Stories" 19–20).

11. Recorded on 10 April 1990 at Grand Bel Air, Mauritius. The Man on a Quest for His Lost Wife is Type 400 in Aarne and Thompson, well known in India. A Marofotsy version (Madagascar) is very different (Renel, *Contes* 1:65–76; Haring, *Index* 410–11). Motifs: B81.0.2, Woman from water world; S211, Child sold (promised) to devil or ogre; F320, Fairies carry people away to fairyland; F133, Submarine otherworld; F127.1.1, Submarine palace (Indian); N711.2, Hero finds maiden in (magic) castle; T350, Chaste sleeping together; F374, Longing in fairyland to visit home; C423.3, Tabu: revealing experiences in other world; F377, Supernatural lapse of time in fairyland; F235, Visibility of fairies; C120, Tabu: kissing; D1810.0.5, Magic knowledge of witches; D705.1, Castle disenchanted, another Indian motif. When Sydney Joseph creates a new Lack for the hero, he interweaves two more plots, each corresponding to an international tale type. The first, The Wise Carving of the Fowl (AT1553, H601), which in Madagascar demonstrates the hero's cleverness (Dubois 1341–1343), provides Sydney Joseph with a transition to the second, The Grateful Animals (AT554, B350), where he incorporates several Indian motifs: D1421.0.1, Magic bell summons helper; D1421.0.2, Magic ashes summon helper; D1421.0.3, Magic hair when thrown into fire summons supernatural helper. Then follow motifs H1471, Watch for devastating monster; B431.2, Helpful lion; Q135, Wine as reward; Q93, Reward for supernatural help; D55.2, Person becomes magically smaller; D700, Disenchantment; N476, Secret of unique vulnerability learned; D1024, Magic egg; D152.2, Man transforms to eagle; C31.9, Tabu: revealing secrets of supernatural wife.

12. Recorded at Grand Bel Air on 18 April 1990. Trans. Claudie Ricaud and Lee Haring. Motifs: P12.2.1, Tyrannical king; P17.0.2, Son succeeds father as king; A1101.1.1, Reign of peace and justice (under certain king).

13. Recorded 18 April 1990 at Grand Bel Air. Trans. Claudie Ricaud, revised by Lee Haring. The pun was not clear to us; perhaps *kord,* rope, and *or,* gold? Motifs: H561.5, King and clever minister; P12.2.1, Tyrannical king; M2, Inhuman decisions of king; J1115.10.2, Clever minister; J1500, Clever practical retort; J1521.5, Catching by words; J810, Policy in dealing with the great.

14. Type 303 in Aarne and Thompson; Uther (1:183–85), tales 60 and 85 in Grimm and Grimm.

15. Other versions and cognates are included in Birkeli (258–69); Barat, Carayol, and Vogel (13–28); Carayol and Chaudenson, *Les aventures* (94–99), *Contes créoles (97–99); Baissac,* Folklore (98–111).

16. "Legendary birds with huge wings, still larger than the Aepyornis" (Dandouau, *Contes populaires* 191), which is Madagascar's favorite extinct bird.

17. The informant said *farasy:* horse in Swahili; donkey in Ndzwani, the variety of Comoran spoken in Anjouan. Horses, donkeys, lions, giraffes, and camels are known in Madagascar only in fiction (Dandouau, *Contes populaires* 192n).

18. The *fantsina,* a regular stage for storytelling sessions, is a platform roofed with leaves and mats to shade people from the sun.

19. "*Betahegny* [Dandouau's spelling] properly signifies a person stricken with swelling or with many *tahegny,* skin sores that look like leprosy" (Dandouau, *Contes populaires* 195n). These skin ailments are the African-derived symbol of alienation.

20. The narrator is glancing at, but not going into, Aarne-Thompson Type 551, The Sons on a Quest for a Wonderful Remedy for Their Father (Aarne and Thompson 197).

21. This game is known all over Africa, under such names as *bao, wari,* or *omweso* (Zaslavsky 116–36). Stones are moved and gathered in four rows of eight holes each. In Madagascar it exists in variant forms. In Dandouau's time (1901–10) it was a men's game in his northwest districts and a women's game in the highlands.

22. Varieties of the game.

23. Motif H332.1.2, Suitor test: to defeat bride in game.

24. Since, as the collector Dandouau noted, the rabbit (Oryctolagus cuniculus) had been introduced into Madagascar relatively recently as a domestic, not a wild animal, the East African motif (A2476.1, Why rabbit continually moves mouth), which refers to the hare (Lepus) was not far to seek.

25. "Les deux frères," Type 303 in Aarne and Thompson. Motifs: D2161.3.11, Barrenness magically cured; S211, Child promised to ogre; T512, Conception from drinking; F577.2, Brothers identical in appearance; G461, Youth promised to ogre visits ogre's home; G530.5, Help from old woman in ogre's house; G513.3.2, Ogre burned in his own oven; D1467, Magic water furnishes treasure; B31.6, Giant birds; B364.4, Bird grateful for being saved from attacking serpent; K1818.1, Disguise as leper; W11, Generosity; H316.1, Orange, lemon thrown to indicate princess's choice; L161, Lowly hero marries princess; T288, Wife refuses to sleep with detested husband; H1212, Quest assigned because of (feigned) illness; K1821, Disguise by changing bodily appearance (H61, Recognition of twins by golden chain under their skin); B350, Grateful animals; B571.3, Animals fight together with their master; E52, Resuscitation by magic charm; H55, Recognition through branding; H84, Tokens of exploits; H332.1.2, Suitor test, to defeat bride in game; T351, Sword of chastity; G551.4, One brother

rescues another from ogre; N342.3, Jealous and overhasty man kills his rescuing twin brother; B291.4.1, Bee as messenger from heaven to earth; B512, Medicine shown by animal; A2474, Why some animals continually shake head; E55.1, Resuscitation by song; E105, Resuscitation by herbs; E122, Resuscitation by animals. A similar Sakalava tale was published forty years later (Hébert, "Le Cycle Légendaire").

26. Motifs: A1412, Origin of light; A625.2, Raising of the sky; A710, Creation of the sun; A1653, Origin of royalty.

27. "Up above" translates Réunionnais Kreol *lao* (French *là-haut,* up there), which in tales indicates the dwelling-place of adversaries.

28. Robert Chaudenson very kindly arranged for me to see videotapes of Gérose Barivoitse and Germain Elizabeth, now deceased, who both spoke the Réunionnais Kreol that French standardization is seeking to extirpate.

29. Political campaigners were making noise during the recording.

30. A window into French tradition. Since the cross-legged posture alludes to the Brave Tailor's occupation, Mr. Barivoitse probably knew French versions of it.

31. Type 1640, The Brave Little Tailor, in Aarne and Thompson; Uther (2:342–44). Motifs: G11.2, Cannibal giant; S262, Periodic sacrifices to a monster; H310, Suitor tests; L112.7, Skin-sore as hero; K1951.1, Boastful fly-killer; (cf. H335.3.1, Suitor task: to kill dragon to whom the princess is to be sacrificed;) A545, Culture hero establishes customs; G84, Fee-fi-fo-fum; J2131.5.3, Numskull sticks his head in the branches of a tree; K71, Deceptive contest in carrying a tree: riding; G512.11, Ogre drowned; T68, Princess offered as prize; L161, Lowly hero marries princess; T121.3.1, Princess marries lowly man.

32. Malagasy examples are found throughout the history of collecting (Dahl; Ramamonjisoa et al.; Renel, *Contes* 1:45, 49, 88–89, 153).

33. *Hymenoptera* is a large black fly that digs into trees. The same Transformation: man to fly (motif D185.1 in Thompson, *Motif-Index*) is undertaken by Ti Zan and other young male characters. For Marcel L'Allouette in Mauritius (see below) as for Mr. Barivoitse, the charcoal fly has the character of a spy.

34. Recorded in 1976 at Sainte-Suzanne by Christian Barat. Motifs: F346.2, Fairies build house for mortal; D1470.2.2, Supplies received from magic box; T111, Marriage of mortal and supernatural being; C31.9, Tabu: revealing secrets of supernatural wife; F348.5.1, Mortal not to betray secret of fairies' gift; D411.2, Transformation: rat to another animal; D411.6.1, Transformation: mouse to horse; D1111.1, Carriage produced by magic; F861.4.3, Carriage from pumpkin; C930, Loss of fortune for breaking tabu; Q585, Fitting destruction of property as punishment.

35. *Up* and *down* in Kreol languages roughly mean away from and towards whatever center is relevant, such as the village, but *lao* (French *là-haut)* in tales is the adversary's dwelling-place. The contrast echoes the old African opposition of forest/savage and village/civilized, often found too in European fairy tales.

36. Recorded in 1976 at Sainte-Suzanne by Christian Barat. Ti Zan's capture of Gran Dyab recalls Type 38, Claw in Split Tree, where the clever animal or man persuades the bear to stick his claw into the cleft of a split tree. Motifs: L101, Unpromising hero; M146, Vow to marry a certain woman; K100, Deceptive bargains (recalling the making and breaking of friendship in previous chapter); K1111, Dupe puts hand into cleft of tree; (cf. G561, Ogre tricked into carrying his prisoners home in bag on his own back;) G512.3, Ogre burned to death.

37. The langouti or *langout* (*languti* in Mauritian Kreol) was the loincloth worn by indentured Indian laborers imported to the Mascareignes. The red color of the garment evokes the bitter times (*tan margoz*) of slavery and indenture.

38. The word is derived from Malagasy *farafara,* "anything made level and high, like a bedstead . . .; the stone shelves in native tombs on which corpses are laid," as well as derivative senses (Richardson 169).

39. Motifs: H1212.4, Quest assigned through longings of pregnant woman; G84, Fee-fi-fo-fum; S12, Cruel mother; S211, Child promised to devil (ogre); K527, Escape by substituting another person in place of the intended victim; D117.3, Transformation: man to rat; D185.1, Transformation: man to fly; (cf. K1611, Substituted caps cause ogre to kill his own children;) Q410, Capital punishment.

40. Motifs: K341, Owner's interest distracted while goods are stolen; K439, Thief loses his goods or is detected; Q212, Theft punished; Q458, Flogging as punishment.

41. The pronoun *zot* is used for both the girls and the men; I translate literally.

42. This is a reference to a curious Indo-Mauritian story, in which a bored wife rings a copper, a silver, a gold, and a diamond bell in turn, each time summoning her unforgiving husband. She is swallowed by a wolf for violating his order, but finally must be rescued. "Very poor in invention," said Baissac (Baissac, *Folklore* 190–91).

43. Inaudible moment on the recording.

44. "Kat fler d-roz" was recorded by Germain Elizabeth for Christian Barat in March 1976, as the very first of the 120 narratives recorded by the Réunionnais research team. M. Barat transcribed and published the text in the journal *Fangok,* 1 August 1978 (24–33). The Three Golden Sons (or Children) is Type 707 in Aarne and Thompson (242–44); Uther (1:381–83). At least six versions of the type have been recorded in Madagascar:

1. Merina, 1864–75 (Callet 1:16–17n15). Tale 4.707A in Haring, *Index.* The folktale plot is framed into a clan origin legend.
2. Merina, 1872–76. "Andriambahoaka sy ny zanany" (Dahle 259–67), trans. Dorian and Molet (Dahle et al. 99–109) under title "Haitraitra an'olombelona, zaka an'nanahary." Omitted from Haring's 1982 Index. A quite elaborated version of AT707.
3. Betsileo, 1886–1893, collected at Fianarantsoa. "Le mari et ses trois femmes" (Ferrand, *Contes* 184–91). Tale 4.707B in Haring, *Index* (417).
4. Sakalava, 1907–22. "Ramikiloke" (Birkeli 192–95). Tale 4.707C in Haring, *Index.* The sections Wishing for a Husband and Calumniated Wife are present, but the children don't grow up or have adventures. The story focuses on a husband and two jealous sisters.
5. Sakalava, 1907–22. "The speaking bird" (Birkeli 278–83). Tale 4.707D in Haring, *Index.* Two sections of AT510, Cinderella, come in at the beginning, The Persecuted Heroine and Meeting the Prince, taking the place of the Wishing for a Husband episode. Once she is married, The Calumniated Wife, The Children's Adventures, and Restoration of Children episodes follow.
6. Betsileo, 1913–38. "Andriabohoemanana and the unfortunate Rafaravavy" (Dubois 1307–11). Tale 4.707E in Haring, *Index* (419–20). A quite complete version of the type. A seventh version from Mayotte is discussed in the chapter "Keys."

45. Motif Q115, Reward: any boon that may be asked.

46. The Smith Outwits the Devil is Type 330 in Aarne and Thompson. Christian Barat recorded Germain Elizabeth at Dos d'Ane, inland from La Possession, near Rivière des Galets, in March 1976. Motifs: N221, Man granted power of winning at cards; K1811, Gods in disguise visit mortals; Q115, Reward: any boon that may be asked; D1413.5, Bench to which person sticks; D1413.16, Magic door holds person fast; D1413.1, Tree from which one cannot descend; Z111.2, Death magically bound to tree; Q565, Man admitted to neither heaven nor hell. Robert Chaudenson has kindly pointed out to me that a version from Lorraine closely resembles Mr. Elizabeth's (Delarue and Tenèze 1:346–49). Most frequently in French versions, the hero goes back and forth between heaven and hell. In Réunion, the *petit blanc,* at least in Mr. Elizabeth's day, didn't have that choice.

47. Motif Q565, Man admitted to neither heaven nor hell.

48. This Seychelles version derives from a separate strand of European tradition, Type 330D (Aarne and Thompson 123; Uther 1:219–21).

49. Afiati Sufu's extraordinary piece re-creates Type 707, The Three Golden Sons (Aarne and Thompson 242–44), retaining the episodes of wishing for a husband, the calumniated wife, the children's adventures, and the restoration of the children.

4. Keys

1. Type 510, Cinderella, in Aarne and Thompson; Uther (1:293–96). Tale 1.6.510 in Haring, *Index* (207–208). Motifs: T24.2, Swooning for love; H1596, Beauty contest; K2212, Treacherous sisters; L52, Abused youngest daughter; L131, Hearth abode of unpromising heroine; B431.1, Helpful rat; D1050.1, Clothes produced by magic; N711.6, Prince sees heroine at ball; H36.1, Slipper test; Q551.3.2, Punishment: transformation into animal; L162, Lowly heroine marries prince.

2. Ferrand's tale 6 is well known as Aesop's fable no. 124, Raven with Cheese in His Mouth (Aesop 6), and is closer to Aesop than to La Fontaine. See also Type 57 in Aarne and Thompson; Uther (1:52–53). His tale 4, The King of the Frogs, is no. 44 in Aesop and no. 4 of La Fontaine's Book Three (Aesop 62). Ferrand's Malagasy version ends with a proverb with no parallel in either European author. The third tale, Election of the Bird-King (Type 221 in Aarne and Thompson; Uther [1:138–39]), probably reached the Jesuit fathers from no. 171 in the Grimm collection (Grimm and Grimm 548–50). Ferrand translated it from Dahle, again after authenticating it among his east coast informants.

3. Type 510B in Aarne and Thompson (177–78) and Uther (1:295–96), The Dress of Gold, of Silver, and of Stars (known in English as Cap o'Rushes), has long been told in India (Thompson and Roberts 73; Thompson, *Folktale* 128).

4. Motifs: T411.1, Lecherous father; K521.1, Escape by dressing in animal skin; T311.1, Flight of maiden to escape marriage; F311.1, Fairy godmother; D1473.1, Magic wand furnishes clothes; H94.2, Identification by ring baked in bread; L162, Lowly heroine marries prince.

5. To qualify, in the eyes of scholars, as a version of Type 510, a tale must contain a persecuted heroine, magic help, meeting the prince, proof of

identity, and marriage with the prince (Aarne and Thompson 175; Uther 1:293–94).

6. Type 327, The Children and the Ogre, in Aarne and Thompson; Uther (1:211–16); a "supertype" or framework for many Indian Ocean narratives (Haring, *Index* 380–91). Motifs: S321, Destitute parents abandon children; S301, Children abandoned (exposed); S143, Abandonment in forest; R135, Abandoned children find way back by clue (breadcrumbs . . .); G401, Children wander into ogre's house; G532, Hero hidden and ogre deceived by his wife when he smells human blood; G84, Fee-fi-fo-fum; K1611, Substituted caps cause ogre to kill own children; Q280, Unkindness punished.

7. The French name of the island is Mayotte, the local name Maore; hence the adjective is *Mahorais.*

8. The *ambrevad* is the pigeon-pea plant: in Malagasy, *amberivatry* or *ambaravatry;* in Mauritian Kreol, *ambrevad;* in Réunionnais Kreol, *zanbrevat* or *zanbrovat.*

9. Motifs: T571, Unreasonable demands of pregnant women; D1415, Magic object compels person to dance.

10. "La Femme Mystérieuse," collected and translated into French by Abdallah Daoud; made available by the kindness of the Centre National de Documentation et Recherche Scientifique, Moroni. Motifs: L142, Pupil surpasses master; T471, Rape; T323, Escape from undesired lover by strategy; T321.5, Magic sickness prevents lover from raping woman; Q451.7, Blinding as punishment; K2112, Woman slandered as prostitute; P210, Husband and wife; T121, Unequal marriage; T586.1.2, Seven children at a birth; K2251, Treacherous slave; S302, Children murdered; D1413, Magic object holds person fast; Q551.2.1, Magic adhesion to object as punishment; K1826, Disguise as churchman (cleric); D2161, Magic healing power; H11.1, Recognition by telling life history; Q551.7, Magic paralysis as punishment; D2091.9, Magic paralysis drawn down on foe; D2171, Magic adhesion; K1837, Disguise of woman in man's clothes; D2161.2, Magic cure of wound; N270, Crime inevitably comes to light; Q210, Crimes punished; Q244.1, Punishment for attempted rape.

11. The Table, the Ass, and the Stick, Type 563 in Aarne and Thompson; Uther (1:331–33). Motifs: D1610.2, Speaking tree; D1470.1, Magic wishing-object; D1472.1.20, Magic plate supplies food; D862, Magic object taken away by force; D1601.5, Automatic cudgel; D881.2, Recovery of magic object by use of magic cudgel. I am very grateful to the Director of the Centre National de Documentation et Recherche Scientifique, of the Federal Islamic Republic of the Comoros, for permission to use this piece and others, and to her colleague Moussa Issahaka for translation.

12. Motifs: B103.2.1, Treasure-laying bird; D861.1, Magic object stolen by host at inn; D1472.1.8, Magic tablecloth supplies food and drink; D1601.5, Automatic cudgel; D1401.1, Magic club beats person. One or two other versions of this tale type, still unpublished, were collected by the same research team.

13. One of the few folktales collected in Anjouan. Translated by the collector, Damir ben Ali. I am grateful to the Centre National de Documentation et Recherche Scientifique for permission to use the piece. Motifs: F1041.1.6.1, Fainting away at sight of goddess; T11.1.1, Woman's beauty reported to king causes quest; P19.2.1, King abducts woman to be his paramour; D435.1.1, Transformation: statue comes to life; B322.2, Helpful birds demand food; B172.2, Magic bird's song; D215, Transformation, woman to tree; P16.7, King

slain in revenge; D1560, Magic object performs services for owner. *Grigri* is the Kreol word for the wooden charms or amulets called *ody* in Madagascar.

14. The Rarest Thing in the World is Type 653A, and Three Stolen Princesses is Type 301 in Aarne and Thompson (Uther 1:176–79). Typically, the hero is precociously strong and quickly finds two companions with extraordinary powers. The popularity of AT301 among Réunionnais poor whites (Decros 161–75) is no less than its huge popularity in France and the French-speaking Caribbean, not to mention Arab tradition (Delarue and Tenèze 2:108–33). An episode in which a nonhuman antagonist, such as a malevolent dwarf, punishes the companions but is defeated by the hero (H1471, Watch for devastating monster, hero alone successful) has its own popularity, as other texts in this book attest (see also Schrive, *Contes* [1992] [100–13]). A related Betsileo tale, Three Princes Sons of the Same Mother, was published by Henri Dubois (1313–16). Mr. Fontaine knew both and recorded them for the Réunionnais research team in 1976.

15. This type frequently "combines various introductory episodes with a common main part" (Uther 1:176); thus the combination is no creole invention.

16. The Strong Man and His Companions often combines with the Quest for a Vanished Princess (Massignon 155–60). Motifs: T615, Supernatural growth; F601, Extraordinary companions; H1471, Watch for devastating monster, youngest alone successful; F451.5.2, Malevolent dwarf; F102.1, Hero shoots monster and follows it into lower world; N773, Adventure from following animal to lower world; F92, Pit entrance to lower world; F80, Journey to lower world; B455.3, Helpful eagle; B542.1.1, Eagle carries men to safety; R111.2.1, Princesses rescued from lower world; K1931.2, Impostors abandon hero in lower world; K963, Rope cut and victim dropped; Q262, Impostor punished.

17. Mr. Lagarrigue was a bit unclear at this point. Evidently the dupe is again to be deceived into taking trickster's place.

18. The impounded water motif (A1111) is prominent in the Mauritian version (Baissac, *Sirandann* 40–45, *Folklore* 16–25). Other motifs: K981, Fatal deception: changed message from oracle; B291, Animal as messenger; K741, Capture by tarbaby (parodying K1241, Trickster rides dupe horseback); K714.2, trickster twice deceives the dupes, dog and cat, into taking his place, each time with physical punishment (a diluted version of K842, Dupe persuaded to take prisoner's place in sack; killed); J1171.1, Solomon's judgment on the *bretel;* J1170, Clever judicial decisions; A2378.4.1, Why hare has short tail.

19. Type 1535, The Rich and the Poor Peasant, including AT1737, The Parson in the Sack to Heaven (Aarne and Thompson 440–41; Uther 2:267–72, 404–405). Baissac's "Flanker" is a Mauritian version of the same type (Baissac, *Folklore* 44–57). The Malagasy trickster Imahaka does a similar series of trades (Renel, *Contes* 2:60–63); so does a Sakalava trickster noted by Dandouau (Dandouau, *Contes populaires* 359–66; Haring, *Indian Ocean* 27–32). Motifs: K335.1, Robbers frightened from goods so that trickster can steal them; N630, Accidental acquisition of treasure or money; K941.1, Cows killed for their hides when large price is reported by trickster; J2415, Foolish imitation of lucky man; K941.2, Dupe burns house because trickster reports high prices paid for ashes; J2094, Expensive wood burned to make charcoal; K842, Dupe persuaded to take prisoner's place in a sack: killed.

20. Motifs: H335, Tasks assigned suitors; H1151.3, Task: stealing sheet from bed on which person is sleeping; H1154.8, Task: capturing magic horse; H1172, Task: bringing an ogre to court; L161, Lowly hero marries princess. Alfred Picard, of Plaine des Cafres, knew stories about Ti Zan and Gran Dyab, Puss in Boots, versions of international tales such as The Table, The Ass, and the Stick (Chaudenson, "Corpus"), and one he couldn't finish, about a wedding ring swallowed by a fish. This last might be The Ring of Polycrates, Type 736A in Aarne and Thompson (253), known by Herodotus as seen in tales 3.40–43 (Hansen 190n) but not often reported from France.

21. Probably also a pun on *sas-tu,* Hunts Everything.

22. *Nwar,* black, is a Kreol in-group expression.

23. "Zistoire Paulin av Pauline, Histoire de Paulin et de Pauline" belongs to Type 706, The Maiden without Hands, in Aarne and Thompson (240–41); Uther (1:378–81). It has been previously translated in Baissac, *Sirandann* (202–25). Motifs: P253.10, Great love of brothers for sister; Q451.1, Hands cut off as punishment; S161, Mutilation, cutting off hands; B421, Friendly dog; N711.1, King (prince) finds maiden in woods and marries her; L162, Lowly heroine marries prince; B530, Animals nourish men; H71.1, Star on forehead as sign of royalty (from Type 707); K2115, Animal-birth slander; K2110.1, Calumniated wife; K2117, Calumniated wife: substituted letter (falsified message); D2161.3.2, Magic restoration of severed hand; E782.1, Hands restored; S451, Outcast wife at last united with husband and children; Q414, Punishment: burning alive.

24. Trans. Claudie Ricaud and Lee Haring. It seems appropriate to multilingual Mauritius that M. L'Allouette's plot resembles a predominantly European tale, The Three Languages (Type 671 in Aarne and Thompson; Uther [1:367]). There, a youth who has learned the languages of dogs, birds, and frogs employs his knowledge to cure a sick princess or discover a treasure; as a linguist he makes his fortune. Yet M. L'Allouette's tale is a new creation. Motifs: S31, Cruel stepmother; K2111, Potiphar's wife; K512.2, Compassionate executioner: substituted heart; D1815.2, Magic knowledge of language of animals; N451, Secrets overheard from animal conversation; J2351, Animal betrays himself to his enemies by talking; H171, Animal or object indicates election of ruler; E323, Dead mother's friendly return; E323.4, Advice from dead mother, an Indo-African motif; F841, Extraordinary boat; H32, Recognition by extraordinary prowess; H1023, Task contrary to the nature of an object; Z210, Brothers as heroes.

25. Motifs: D1163, Magic mirror; C567, Tabus of princesses; E761.4.3, Life token: mirror becomes misty; C955, Banishment from heaven for breaking tabu; N825.3, Old woman helper; D931, Magic rock; D1552, Mountains or rocks open and close; D1393, Magic object helps fugitive; D1472.1.9, Magic pot supplies food and drink; H946.1, Task assigned from misunderstanding: search for prince named Sabr ("wait"); J1805.2.1, Daughter says "Sobur" (wait) to her father when he asks what to bring from the journey; T135, Wedding ceremony. I thank Claude Allibert for his permission to translate.

26 My re-translation from Dr. Gallob's text and her two versions. I am grateful to her for translation permission.

27. Motif J1802, Words in foreign language thought to be insults.

28. Type 1536c, The Murdered Lover, in Aarne and Thompson (442); Uther (2:271–72). Motif K2151, The corpse handed around. A Seychelles reader later made a radio script out of Baissac's story.

29. Motifs: J1160, Clever pleading; J1280, Repartee with ruler (judge, etc.).

30. Motifs: J1169, Clever dealing, miscellaneous; J1390, Retorts concerning thefts (cf. K402, The lamb without a heart).

31. It is Baissac who spells the white man's name so irregularly. Motifs: J1144, Eaters of stolen food detected; J1160, Clever pleading; Q458, Flogging as punishment.

32. I was told in Seychelles that part of *Cast Away* was filmed there; other information situates it on the uninhabited island of Monu-riki, in Fiji. Tom Hanks's sister, however, continues to operate the Splash Café, at Baie Lazare on Mahé, the main island of Seychelles. The journalist Brendon Grimshaw acquired the island Moyenne, in Seychelles, and reworked it into his living place with the aid of a single companion.

33. Mr. Jean-Baptiste refers to the "coco de mer," the rare palm tree, which produces a uniquely shaped nut that reminds sex-starved men of what they've been missing. It grows mostly in Seychelles.

34. Motifs: D1814.2, Advice from dream; N531, Treasure discovered through dream; N511, Treasure in ground; D1148, Magic tomb.

35. My re-translation from Dr. Gallob's interlinear translation. I am grateful to her for permission to translate. Motifs: J2600, Cowardly fool, with a strong reminder of the oft-told Malagasy motif K525.1, Substituted object left in bed while intended victim escapes.

36. Motifs: F330, Grateful fairies; Q115, Reward: any boon that may be asked; F341, Fairies give fulfillment of wishes; D2120, Magic transportation; D2074.2.3, Summoning by wish; J1116, Foolish person becomes clever. Thanks to Dr. Gallob for reprint permission; I've added only punctuation.

5. Postcolonial Seychelles

1. Modern orthography spells the name of the language, in French *Seychellois*, as *Seselwa* (Bollée and D'Offay).

2. A *pirog* is the handmade canoe of the Southwest Indian Ocean region; a *katyolo* is a small skiff.

3. Motifs: A2494.1.4, Enmity between cat and rat (cf. S131.1, River carrier throws passenger off and drowns him). Translated from a typescript in the National Archives by permission of the Director.

4. Type 293 in Aarne and Thompson.

5. AT1000, Bargain Not to Become Angry (see AT650A, incident III c, and AT1351), perhaps of African origin, analogous to motif K263, Agreement not to scratch (Dundes, "African and Afro-American Tales" 38). Motifs: K172, Anger bargain; F613.3, Strong man's labor contract: anger bargain: first to become angry shall receive blow. Samuel Accouche's version is written; an oral version was collected in 1980–81 (Diallo et al., *Veyez 2* 57–70).

6. Our Lady's Child is Type 710 in Aarne and Thompson, with a forbidden-chamber motif (C611) recalling Bluebeard (Delarue and Tenèze 2:662–65).

7. Examples from the typescript in the National Archives: AT910A, Wise through Experience, pp. 4–7; AT706, The Maiden without Hands, pp. 7–10; AT1168A, The Demon and the Mirror, p. 13; AT670, The Animal

Languages, pp. 16–17; AT1381C, The Buried Sheep's Head, pp. 17–18; AT302, The Ogre's Heart in the Egg, pp. 19–20; AT571–574, Making the Princess Laugh, combined with parts of AT563, The Table, the Ass, and the Stick, pp. 20–21; AT763, The Treasure Finders Who Murder One Another, pp. 25–26; AT155, The Ungrateful Serpent Returned to Captivity, pp. 26–27; AT1408, The Man Who Does His Wife's Work, pp. 32–33; AT563, The Table, the Ass, and the Stick, pp. 34–35.

8. Motifs: B350, Grateful animals; K512, Compassionate executioner; Q285, Cruelty punished; H1361, Quest for lion's milk.

9. The wolves have an assortment of obscure nonhuman names, except for Songor, probably a male person of African appearance (Baker and Hookoomsing 301). Kapiler is the name for a maidenhair fern; Chimite might allude to *simityer,* cemetery; Yoyote is Kiswahili for "everything"; Budume, who knows?

10. Translated, without attribution, as "Pa Loulou and Sililinn" in Carayol and Chaudenson, *Lièvre* (158–65) and *Contes créoles* (149–53). Motifs: G610, Stealing from ogre; G84, Fee-fi-fo-fum; G421, Ogre traps victim; G11.18, Cannibal tribe; K525.1, Substituted object left in bed while intended victim escapes; D672, Obstacle flight; R111.1.4, Rescue of maiden from giant (monster). Thompson lists no motif for "mother rescues daughter," which should follow R153.4 as R153.5, echoing here the importance of the mother-daughter relation in Comoran tales.

11. "Ti Jean avec language zanimaux," "Ti Zan and the animal languages," *Creole Stories,* 16–17. Type 670, The Man Who Understands Animal Languages, in Aarne and Thompson (233–34); Uther (1:365–66). Motifs: B350, Grateful animal; B491.1, Helpful serpent; B165.1, Animal languages learned from serpent; B216, Knowledge of animal languages: person understands them; C425, Tabu: revealing knowledge of animal languages; N456, Enigmatic laugh reveals secret knowledge; T253.1, Nagging wife drives husband to prepare for suicide; K2213, Treacherous wife; N451, Secrets overheard from animal conversation; B469.5, Helpful cock; T252.2, Cock shows browbeaten husband how to rule his wife.

12. Type 275A, The Race between Hare and Tortoise (Aarne and Thompson 81; Uther 1:157); motif K11.3 in Thompson, *Motif-Index.*

13. Type 1541, For the Long Winter, in Aarne and Thompson (444–45); Uther (2:279–80). Motifs: K362.1, For the long winter, with a lead into the readily attached Type 1384, The Husband Hunts Three Persons as Stupid as His Wife (Aarne and Thompson 412; Uther 2:191–92).

14. Nor did the new orthography receive enthusiastic acceptance from the most eminent creole linguist: "Ill-considered changes carried out by incompetent technicians (provided at the time by French cooperation) and without integration of the action into a global project, brought absurd modifications into the previously existing system, in which some tools for the instrumentalization of the language had already been worked out."

Works Cited

Aarne, Antti, and Stith Thompson, translated and enlarged by. *The Types of the Folktale: A Classification and Bibliography.* 2nd rev. ed. FF Communications 184. Helsinki: Suomalainen Tiedeakatemia, 1961.

Abdallah Paune, Kamaroudine. "Cultural Traditions in Comoro Islands." Master's thesis (mémoire de maîtrise d'anglais), Université de Paris III, 1977.

Abel, Antoine. *Contes des Seychelles.* Paris: CLE International, 1981.

———. *Contes et poèmes des Seychelles.* Paris: Pierre Jean Oswald, 1977.

Abinal, R. P., and Victorin Malzac. *Dictionnaire malgache-français.* Paris: Éditions Maritimes et d'Outre-Mer, 1963 (1888).

Abrahams, Roger D. *African Folktales.* New York: Pantheon Books, 1983.

———. *Deep Down in the Jungle: Negro Narrative Folklore from the Streets of Philadelphia.* Rev. ed. Chicago: Aldine, 1970 (1963).

———. *The Man-of-Words in the West Indies.* Baltimore: Johns Hopkins University Press, 1983.

———. *Positively Black.* Englewood Cliffs, N.J.: Prentice, 1970.

Abrams, M. H. "Orientation of Critical Theories." *Twentieth Century Literary Criticism: A Reader.* Ed. David Lodge. London: Longman, 1972. 1–26.

Accouche, Samuel. ["Creole Stories"]. Unpublished. In Seychelles National Archives.

Aesop. *Aesop's Fables.* Trans. V. S. Vernon Jones. Intro. by G. K. Chesterton. Illus. Arthur Rackham. New York: Avenel, 1975.

———. *The Complete Fables.* Trans. Olivia and Robert Temple. Harmondsworth: Penguin Books, 1998.

Ahmed-Chamanga, Mohamed, and Ahmed Ali Mroimana. *Contes comoriens de Ngazidja, au-delà des mers.* Paris: L'Harmattan, 1999.

Allaoui, Masséande Chami. "Genres of Comoran Folklore." Trans. Lee Haring. *Journal of Folklore Research* 34.1 (Jan.–Apr. 1997): 45–57.

Allen, Philip M. *Security and Nationalism in the Indian Ocean: Lessons from Latin Quarter Islands.* Boulder, Colo.: Westview, 1987.

Allibert, Claude. *Contes mahorais.* Archives Orales Mahoraises. Paris: Académie des Sciences d'Outre-Mer, 1977.

Alsdorf-Bollée, A., and R[obert] Chaudenson. "Deux contes populaires seychellois: texte, traduction et notes." *Te Reo* 16 (1973): 60–86.

Althabe, Gérard. *Oppression et libération dans l'imaginaire: les communautés villageoises de la côte orientale de Madagascar.* Paris: Maspéro, 1969.

Althusser, Louis. *For Marx.* Trans. Ben Brewster. New York: Pantheon Books, 1969.

Ancelet, Barry Jean. *Cajun and Creole Folktales: The French Oral Tradition of South Louisiana.* Jackson: University Press of Mississippi, 1994.

Andriamanjato, Richard. *Le tsiny et le tody dans la pensée malgache.* Paris: Présence Africaine, 1957.

Appadurai, Arjun. *Modernity at Large: Cultural Dimensions of Globalization.* Public Worlds. Minneapolis: University of Minnesota Press, 1996.

Arewa, E. Ojo. "A Classification of the Folktales of the Northern East African Cattle Area by Types." Ph.D. diss., University of California, 1966.

Ashley, Leonard R. N. "Rhyme and Reason: The Methods and Meanings of Cockney Rhyming Slang, Illustrated with Some Proper Names and Some Improper Phrases." *Names* 25.3 (Sept. 1977): 124–54.

Babcock, Barbara A. "The Story in the Story: Metanarration in Folk Narrative." In *Verbal Art as Performance.* By Richard Bauman. Prospect Heights, Ill.: Waveland, 1977. 61–80.

———. "Taking Liberties, Writing from the Margins, and Doing It with a Difference." *Journal of American Folklore* 100.398 (Oct.–Dec. 1987): 390–411.

Bacchilega, Cristina. *Postmodern Fairy Tales: Gender and Narrative Strategies.* Philadelphia: University of Pennsylvania Press, 1997.

Baer, Florence E. *Sources and Analogues of the Uncle Remus Tales.* Helsinki: Suomalainen Tiedeakatemia, 1980.

Baissac, Charles. *Étude sur le patois créole mauricien.* Geneva: Slatkine, 1976 (1880).

———. *Folklore de l'île Maurice.* Paris: G. P. Maisonneuve et Larose, 1887.

———. *Sirandann sanpek: zistwar an kreol.* Port Louis (Mauritius): Ledikasyon Pu Travayer, 1989.

Baker, Philip. *Kreol, a Description of Mauritian Creole.* London: C. Hurst, 1972.

Baker, Philip, and Vinesh Y. Hookoomsing. *Diksyoner kreol morisiyen, dictionary of Mauritian Creole, dictionnaire du créole mauricien.* Paris: Éditions L'Harmattan, 1987.

Barat, Christian, Michel Carayol, and Claude Vogel. *Kriké kraké: recueil de contes créoles réunionnais.* Travaux de l'Institut d'Anthropologie Sociale et Culturelle de l'Océan Indien. Paris/St Denis: CNRS, 1977.

Barbé, Marinette. Intro. to *Lanblenm fler/Les emblèmes de fleurs.* Victoria (Seychelles): Arsiv ek Mize Nasyonal, Minister Gouvernman Local, Sport ek Kiltir, 2001.

———. Intro. to *Télégraphes de Mouchoir/Telegraf Mouswar.* Victoria (Seychelles): Archives Nationales et Musées Nationaux/Arsiv ek Mize Nasyonal, 2001.

Le Barbier, Camille. "Contes et légendes du pays des bara." *Revue d'Ethnographie et des Traditions Populaires* 6 (1921): 119–37.

———. "Notes sur le pays des bara-imamono." *Bulletin de l'Académie Malgache,* n.s., 3 (1916–17): 63–162.

Barker, Anthony J. *Slavery and Antislavery in Mauritius, 1810–33: The Conflict Between Economic Expansion and Humanitarian Reform Under British Rule.* New York: Macmillan, St. Martin's, 1996.

Barre, Jacques, and Claude Vogel. "Les stages de formation pour la collecte des traditions populaires des Mascareignes et des Seychelles." *Études Créoles* 79.2 (Dec. 1979): 64–77.

Barthes, Roland. *Critical Essays.* Trans. Richard Howard. Evanston, Ill.: Northwestern University Press, 1972.

———. "The Death of the Author." *The Rustle of Language.* Trans. Richard Howard. New York: Hill and Wang, 1986 (1968). 49–55.

Bascom, William R. *African Dilemma Tales.* The Hague: Mouton, 1975.

———. "The Forms of Folklore: Prose Narratives." *Journal of American Folklore* 78 (1965): 3–20.

———. "Four Functions of Folklore." *The Study of Folklore.* Ed. Alan Dundes. Englewood Cliffs, N.J.: Prentice, 1965. 279–98.

———. *Ifa Divination.* Bloomington: Indiana University Press, 1969.

Bauman, Richard. "Conceptions of Folklore in the Development of Literary Semiotics." *Semiotica* 39 (1982): 1–20.

———. *A World of Others' Words: Cross-Cultural Perspectives on Intertextuality.* Oxford: Blackwell, 2004.

Bauman, Richard, and Charles L. Briggs. "Poetics and Performance as Critical Perspectives on Language and Social Life." *Annual Review of Anthropology* 19 (1990): 59–88.

———. *Voices of Modernity: Language Ideologies and the Politics of Inequality.* Cambridge: Cambridge University Press, 2003.

Beaujard, Philippe. "La fille difficile malgache (Madagascar et Mayotte)." *La fille difficile, un conte-type africain.* Ed. Veronika Görög-Karady and Christiane Seydou. Paris: Editions CNRS, 2001. 239–62.

———. "La lutte pour l'hégémonie du royaume à travers deux variantes d'un même mythe: le serpent-à-sept-têtes." *ASEMI* 7.3–4 (1977): 151–204.

———. *Mythe et société à Madagascar (Tanala de l'Ikongo): le chasseur d'oiseaux et la princesse du ciel.* Paris: L'Harmattan, 1991.

———. *Princes et paysans: les tanala de l'Ikongo. Un espace social du sud-est de Madagascar.* Paris: L'Harmattan, 1983.

Beck, Brenda E. F. "Frames, Tale Types and Motifs: The Discovery of Indian Oicotypes." *Indian Folklore 2.* Ed. Peter J. Claus, Jawaharlal Handoo, and D. P. Pattanayak. Mysore: Central Institute of Indian Languages, 1987. 1–51.

Beeton, Patrick. *Creoles and Coolies; or, Five Years in Mauritius.* 2nd ed. London: James Nisbet, 1859.

Beidelman, T. O. "Four Kaguru Tales." *Tanganyika Notes* 61 (Sept. 1963): 135–46.

———. "Hyena and Rabbit, a Kaguru Representation of Matrilineal Relations." *Myth and Cosmos: Readings in Mythology and Symbolism.* Ed. John Middleton. Garden City, N.Y.: Natural History Press, 1967. 287–301.

Belsey, Catherine. "Constructing the Subject: Deconstructing the Text." *Contemporary Literary Criticism: Literary and Cultural Studies.* Ed. Robert Con Davis and Ronald Schleifer. New York: Longman, 1994. 354–70.

Ben-Amos, Dan, ed. *Folklore Genres.* Austin: University of Texas Press, 1976.

———. "Folklore in African Society." *Forms of Folklore in Africa: Narrative, Dramatic, Gnomic, Dramatic.* Ed. Bernth Lindfors. Austin: University of Texas Press, 1977. 1–34.

Bendix, Regina. *In Search of Authenticity: The Formation of Folklore Studies.* Madison: University of Wisconsin Press, 1997.

Benedict, Burton. *People of the Seychelles.* London: Her Majesty's Stationery Office, 1966.

Benedict, Marion, and Burton Benedict. *Men, Women, and Money in Seychelles.* Berkeley: University of California Press, 1982.

Benjamin, Walter. *Illuminations.* New York: Schocken, 1968.

Benoist, Jean. "Carrefours de cultes et de soins à l'île Maurice." *Soigner au pluriel: essais sur le pluralisme médical.* Paris: Éditions Karthala, 1996. 89–113.

———. "Possession, médiation, guérison: un chamanisme sud-indien à l'île de la Réunion." *L'Ethnographie* 87–88 (1982): 227–39.

Ben-Porat, Zvi. "The Poetics of Literary Allusion." *PTL* 1 (1976): 105–28.

Benveniste, Émile. *Problems in General Linguistics.* Miami: University of Miami Press, 1971.

Bernabé, Jean, Patrick Chamoiseau, and Raphaël Confiant. *Éloge de la créolité.* Trans. Patrick Chamoiseau, Raphaël Confiant, and M. B. Taleb-Khyar. Paris: Gallimard, 1993.

Bernardin de St. Pierre, Henri. *Voyage à l'Isle de France.* Ed. Robert Chaudenson. Mauritius: Éditions de l'Océan Indien, 1986.

Berthier, Hugues. *Notes et impressions sur les moeurs et coutumes du peuple malgache.* Tananarive: Imprimerie Officielle, 1933.

Bhabha, Homi K. *The Location of Culture.* London: Routledge, 1994.

Biebuyck, Daniel P., and Brunhilde Biebuyck. *"We Test Those Whom We Marry": An Analysis of Thirty-Six Nyanga Tales.* Budapest: African Research Program, Lorand Eötvös University, 1987.

Birkeli, Émile. "Folklore sakalava recueilli dans la région de Morondava." *Bulletin de l'Académie Malgache,* n.s., 6 (1922–23): 185–417.

Blanchy, Sophie. "Lignée féminine et valeurs islamiques à travers quelques contes de Mayotte (Comores)." Mémoire, Université de la Réunion, 1986.

———. "Mères et filles dans les contes de Mayotte (Comores)." *L'enfant dans les contes africains.* Ed. Veronika Görög-Karady and Ursula Baumgardt. Paris: CILF, 1988. 131–68.

———. "Le tambour." With Zaharia Soilihi. *L'Espoir* (Réunion) 2 (Aug. 1989): 20–31.

Blanchy, Sophie, Zaharia Soilihi, Noël J. Gueunier, and Madjidhoubi Said. *La maison de la mère: contes de l'île de Mayotte.* Illus. Gilles Joisseaux. Paris: L'Harmattan, 1993.

Bloch, Maurice. *From Blessing to Violence: History and Ideology in the Circumcision Ritual of the Merina of Madagascar.* Cambridge: Cambridge University Press, 1986.

Bloom, Harold. *The Anxiety of Influence: A Theory of Poetry.* New York: Oxford University Press, 1973.

Bollée, Annegret, ed. and trans. *Ti anan en foi en Soungoula: creole stories from the Seychelles.* By Samuel Accouche. Köln: Privately published, 1976.

Bollée, Annegret, and Robert Chaudenson. "Deux contes populaires seychellois: texte, traduction et notes." *Te Reo, Journal of the Linguistic Society of New Zealand* 16 (1973): 60–86.

Bollée, Annegret, and Danielle D'Offay. *Apprenons la nouvelle orthographe. Proposition d'une orthographe rationnelle pour le créole des Seychelles avec six contes créoles seychellois.* Cologne; Mahé: The authors, 1978.

Bollée, Annegret, and Ingrid Neumann. "Le créole des Seychelles et la littérature orale." *Les Seychelles et l'Océan Indien.* Ed. Bernard Koechlin. Paris: L'Harmattan, 1984. 57–79.

Bollée, Annegret, and Marcel Rosalie, eds. and trans. *Parol ek memwar: récits de vie des Seychelles.* Hamburg: Helmut Buske Verlag, 1994.

Booth, Wayne C. *The Rhetoric of Fiction.* Chicago: University of Chicago Press, 1961.

Boswell, Rosabelle. *Slavery, Blackness and Hybridity: Mauritius and the Malaise Créole.* New York: Columbia University Press, 2005.

Bouillon, Antoine. *Madagascar, le colonisé et son "âme": essai sur le discourse psychologique colonial.* Paris: L'Harmattan, 1981.

Bowman, Larry. *Mauritius: Democracy and Development in the Indian Ocean.* Boulder, Colo.: Westview, 1991.

Brasse, John. Interview by Lee Haring. Poudre d'Or (Mauritius), 1990.

Brathwaite, Edward. *Contradictory Omens: Cultural Diversity and Integration in the Caribbean.* Kingston (Jamaica): Savacou Publications, 1974.

Bremond, Claude. *Logique du récit.* Paris: Éditions du Seuil, 1973.

———. "Traitement des motifs dans un index des ruses." *Le conte: pourquoi? comment?* Ed. Geneviève Calame-Griaule, Veronika Görög-Karady, and Michèle Chiche. Paris: Éditions du CNRS, 1984. 35–53.

Burke, Kenneth. *Counter-Statement.* Chicago: University of Chicago Press, 1957 (1931).

Burton, Richard F., trans. and ed. *Supplemental Nights to the Book of the Thousand Nights and a Night, with Notes Anthropological and Explanatory.* 5 vols. The Burton Club, 1888.

Cagnolo, Fr. C. "Kikuyu Tales, Part 4." *African Studies,* June 1953, 63–66.

Caillois, Roger. *Man, Play, and Games.* Urbana: University of Illinois Press, 2001 (1961).

Calame-Griaule, Geneviève. *Ethnologie et langage: la parole chez les Dogon.* Bibliothèque Des Sciences Humaines. Paris: Gallimard, 1965.

———. "L'art de la parole dans la culture africaine." *Présence Africaine,* Third Quarter 1963, 73–91.

Callet, R. P. *Tantaran'ny andriana.* Originally *Tantara ny andriana eto Madagascar* (1908). Trans. G.-S. Chapus and E. Ratsimba. 3 vols. Antananarivo: Librairie de Madagascar, 1958.

Cameron, James. "Ikotofetsy and Imahaka, Two Rogues from Madagascar." *Cape Magazine* (Cape Town), Dec. 1871, 334–44.

Carayol, Michel. "La littérature orale réunnionaise." *L'encyclopédie de la Réunion.* Ed. Robert Chaudenson. Vol. 7. Saint-Denis: Livres-Réunion, 1980. 9–36.

Carayol, Michel, and Robert Chaudenson, compilers. *Les aventures de Petit-Jean: contes créoles de l'Océan Indien.* Paris: EDICEF, 1978.

———. *Contes créoles de l'Océan Indien.* Paris: Conseil international de la langue française; EDICEF, 1979.

———. *Lièvre, Grand Diable et Autres.* Paris: EDICEF, 1978.

Carnell, W. J., trans. "Four Gogo Folk Tales." *Tanganyika Notes and Records* 40 (1955): 30–42.

Carter, Marina. *Lakshmi's Legacy: The Testimonies of Indian Women in 19th Century Mauritius.* Stanley, Rose-Hill (Mauritius): Éditions de l'Océan Indien, 1994.

Carter, Marina, V. Govinden, and Satyendra Peerthum. *The Last Slaves: Liberated Africans in 19th Century Mauritius.* Port Louis (Mauritius): Centre for Research on Indian Ocean Societies, 2003.

Carter, Marina, and James Ng Foong Kwong. *Forging the Rainbow: Labour Immigrants in British Mauritius.* Port Louis (Mauritius): Privately published, 1997.

Chagnoux, Hervé, and Ali Haribou. *Les Comores.* 2nd ed. Paris: Presses Universitaires de France, 1990.

Chapus, Georges-Sully. *Les imériniens dans les "contes des anciens."* Montpellier: Imprimerie Causse, Graille et Castelnau, 1930.

Chaudenson, Robert. "Corpus des contes réunionnais retenus en vue de l'analyse." Personal communication. Saint-Denis, 1977.

———. *Des îles, des hommes, des langues: essai sur la créolisation linguistique et culturelle.* Paris: L'Harmattan, 1992.

———. "Le noir et le blanc: la classification raciale dans les parlers créoles de l'Océan Indien." *Revue de Linguistique Romane* 38.149–152 (1974): 75–94.

———. *Textes créoles anciens (La Réunion et Ile Maurice): comparaison et essai d'analyse.* Kreolische Bibliothek. Hamburg: Helmut Buske Verlag, 1981.

Chaudenson, Robert, and Salikoko S. Mufwene. *Creolization of Language and Culture.* New York: Routledge, 2001.

Chauvicourt, J. and S. *Fanorona, the National Game of Madagascar.* Ed. and trans. Leonard Fox. Charleston, S.C.: International Fanorona Association, 1984.

Choppy, Penda, trans. *Lezann Klasik: Lagres Ansyen: Vol. 1.* O-Kap (Au Cap) (Seychelles): Lenstiti Kreol, 2002.

Christian, Philippe A. "Interview with France Laval Jean-Baptiste." *L'Express* (Mauritius), 7 July 1980.

———. "Interview with Marcel l'Allouette." *L'Express* (Mauritius), 26 July 1980: 6.

Cixous, Hélène. "The Laugh of the Medusa." *The Critical Tradition: Classic Texts and Contemporary Trends.* 2nd ed. Ed. David H. Richter. Boston: Bedford Books, 1998. 1453–66.

Clarke, Kenneth Wendell. "A Motif-Index of the Folktales of Culture Area V, West Africa." Ph.D. diss., Indiana University, 1958.

Collen, Lindsey. *The Rape of Sita.* Port Louis (Mauritius): Ledikasyon pu Travayer, 1993.

Cosentino, Donald. *Defiant Maids and Stubborn Farmers: Tradition and Invention in Mende Story Performance.* Cambridge: Cambridge University Press, 1982.

Cousins, William E. "The Ancient Theism of the Hova." *Antananarivo Annual* 1 (1875).

Cousins, William E., and John Parrett. *Malagasy Proverbs, Printed for the Use of Europeans Interested in the Study of the Language.* Antananarivo: By subscription, 1871.

"Creole Stories from Various Contributors, Vol. 1." Unpublished, 1978. In Seychelles National Archives.

Crowley, Daniel J. *Folktale Research in Africa.* Legon: University of Ghana, 1971.

———. *I Could Talk Old-Story Good: Creativity in Bahamian Folklore.* University of California Publications: Folklore Studies 17. Berkeley: University of California Press, 1966.

Dahl, Otto Chr. *Contes malgaches en dialecte sakalava.* Oslo: Universitetsforlaget, 1968.

Dahle, L[ars]. *Specimens of Malagasy Folk-Lore.* Antananarivo: A. Kingdon, 1877.

Dahle, L[ars], and John Sims. *Anganon'ny Ntaolo.* Antananarivo: Trano Printy Loterana, 1971.

Dahle, Lars, collector, John Sims, ed., Denise Dorian and Louis Molet, trans. *Contes des aïeux malgaches (anganon'ny ntaolo)*. Paris: Institut des Langues et Civilisations Orientales, 1992.

Dandouau, André. "Contes malgaches: Histoire de Benandro, etc." *Revue de Madagascar*, Jan. 1907, 25–32, 199–202.

———. *Contes populaires des sakalava et des tsimihety de la région d'Analalava*. Algiers: Jules Carbonel, 1922.

———. "Les deux époux." *Revue de Madagascar*, Apr. 1934, 63–67.

———. "Folk-lore sakalava et tsimihety." *Revue de Madagascar (Paris)* 9.10 (Oct. 1907).

Daoud, Abdallah, and Amina Kassim Bashrahil. *Zamani: hale za shikomori, hadisi za kikomori*. Moroni (Comoros): Centre National de Documentation et de Recherche Scientifique, 1983.

Day, L. B. *Folk-Tales of Bengal*. London: Macmillan and Co., 1883.

De Beaumarchais, J. P., Daniel Couty, and Alain Rey, eds. *Dictionnaire des littératures de la langue française*. Paris: Bordas, 1984.

de Man, Paul. *Allegories of Reading: Figural Languages in Rousseau, Nietzsche, Rilke, and Proust*. New Haven: Yale University Press, 1979.

de Silva, Hazel (Mugot). *Séga of Seychelles*. Nairobi: East African Publishing House, 1983.

de Voogt, Alex. "Bao." *African Folklore, an Encyclopedia*. Ed. Philip M. Peek and Kwesi Yankah. New York: Routledge, 2004. 18–19.

Decary, Raymond. *Contes et légendes du sud-ouest de Madagascar*. Paris: G.-P. Maisonneuve et Larose, 1964.

———. *La faune malgache*. Paris: Payot, 1950.

———. *Moeurs et coutumes des malgaches*. Paris: Payot, 1951.

Decros, Marie Christine. "Contes réunionnais, textes et traductions." Mémoire de maîtrise, Centre Universitaire de la Réunion, 1978.

Dekouver marmit: traditional food of Seychelles. La cuisine traditionnelle seychelloise. Victoria: National Heritage, 2001.

Delarue, Paul, and Marie-Louise Tenèze. *Le conte populaire français. Catalogue raisonné des versions de France et des pays de langue française d'outre-mer*. 3 vols. Paris: G.-P. Maisonneuve et Larose, 1964, 1976.

Delivré, Alain. *L'histoire des rois d'Imerina: interprétation d'une tradition orale*. Paris: Klincksieck, 1974.

Derive, Jean. "Les filles difficiles." *La fille difficile, un conte-type africain*. Ed. Veronika Görög-Karady and Christiane Seydou. Paris: CNRS Editions, 2001. 263–97.

Derrida, Jacques. *Speech and Phenomena*. Trans. David B. Allison. Evanston, Ill.: Northwestern University Press, 1973.

Deschamps, Hubert. *Histoire de Madagascar*. 4th ed. Paris: Berger-Levrault, 1972.

Detienne, Marcel. "The Interpretation of Myths: Nineteenth- and Twentieth-Century Theories." *Mythologies*. Comp. Yves Bonnefoy. Prepared by Wendy Doniger. 2 vols. Chicago: University of Chicago Press, 1991. 1:5–10.

Diallo, Abdourahmane. "Avant-Propos." *Veyez 2*. Ed. Abdourahamane Diallo, Marcel Rosalie, Gabriel Essack, and Eudoxie Labiche. Victoria (Seychelles): Ministère de l'Éducation et de l'Information, 1983.

Diallo, Abdourahamane, Marcel Rosalie, and Gabriel Essack, eds. *Veyez: zistoir kreol seseloi*. Division de la Culture, Ministère de l'Éducation et de l'Information, 1981.

Diallo, Abdourahamane, Marcel Rosalie, Gabriel Essack, and Eudoxie Labiche, eds. *Veyez 2.* Victoria (Seychelles): Division de la Culture, Ministère de l'Éducation et de l'Information, 1983.

———. *Zedmo sesel: devinettes et jeux de mots des Seychelles; riddles and conumdrums [sic] of Seychelles.* Victoria (Seychelles): Ministry of Local Government, Sports and Culture—Culture Division (National Heritage), 2001.

Dieterlen, Germaine. "Twins, a Dominant Theme in West African Mythologies." *Mythologies.* Comp. Yves Bonnefoy. Prepared by Wendy Doniger. 2 vols. Chicago: University of Chicago Press, 1991. 1:33–35.

Djoumoi Ali M'madi. "Transmission traditionnelle des savoirs et des savoir-faire à Ndzaoudze." Dissertation, Ecole Nationale d'Enseignement Supérieur, M'vouni, 1989.

D'Offay, Danielle, and Guy Lionnet. *Diksyoner kreol-franse/Dictonnaire créole seychellois-français.* Kreolische Bibliothek. Hamburg: Helmut Buske Verlag, 1982.

Doke, Clement M. *Lamba Folk-Lore.* New York: G. E. Stechert, 1927.

Domenichini-Ramiaramanana, Bakoly. *Le malgache, essai de description sommaire.* Langues et Civilisations de l'Asie Du Sud-Est, de l'Océan Indien et de la Réunion. Paris: SELAF, 1977.

Dorson, Richard M., ed. *The British Folklorists, a History.* Chicago: University of Chicago Press, 1968.

———. *Folktales Told around the World.* Chicago: University of Chicago Press, 1975.

———. "The Use of Printed Sources." *Folklore and Folklife: An Introduction.* Ed. Richard M. Dorson. Chicago: University of Chicago Press, 1972. 465–77.

Dubois, Henri. *Monographie des betsileo.* Paris: Musée de l'Homme, 1938.

Duffy, Karen M. "Tracing the Gift: Aurelio M. Espinosa, 1880–1958." *The Folklore Historian* 12 (1995): 39–53.

Dumézil, Georges. *Mythe et épopée 2: Types épiques indo-européens: un héros, un sorcier, un roi.* Paris: Gallimard, 1971.

Dundes, Alan. "African and Afro-American Tales." *African Folklore in the New World.* Austin: University of Texas Press, 1977. 35–53.

———. "African Tales among the North American Indians." *Mother Wit from the Laughing Barrel: Readings in the Interpretation of Afro-American Folklore.* Englewood Cliffs, N.J.: Prentice, 1973. 114–25.

———. "Folk Ideas as Units of Worldview." *Journal of American Folklore* 84.331 (Jan.–Mar. 1971): 93–103.

———. "The Making and Breaking of Friendship as a Structural Frame in African Folk Tales." *Structural Analysis of Oral Tradition.* Ed. Pierre Maranda and Elli Köngäs Maranda. Philadelphia: University of Pennsylvania Press, 1971. 171–85.

———. "Metafolklore and Oral Literary Criticism." *The Monist* 50.4 (Oct. 1966): 505–16.

———. "A Study of Ethnic Slurs: The Jew and the Polack in the United States." *Journal of American Folklore* 84 (1971): 186–203.

Durkheim, Émile. *Les règles de la méthode sociologique.* Paris: Presses Universitaires de France, 1947 (1898).

———. *Sociologie et philosophie.* Paris: Presses Universitaires de France, 1951.

Eagleton, Terry. *After Theory.* New York: Basic, 2003.

———. *Ideology: An Introduction.* London: Verso, 1991.

———. *Literary Theory: An Introduction.* Minneapolis: University of Minnesota Press, 1983.

Eastman, Carol M. "An Ethnography of Swahili Expressive Culture." *Research in African Literatures* 15.3 (Fall 1984): 313–40.

Edmonson, Munro. *Lore, an Introduction to the Science of Folklore and Literature.* New York: Holt, Rinehart and Winston, 1971.

Emoff, Ron. *Recollecting from the Past: Musical Practice and Spirit Possession on the East Coast of Madagascar.* Middletown: Wesleyan University Press, 2002.

Erlich, Victor. *Russian Formalism: History, Doctrine.* 3rd ed. The Hague: Mouton, 1969.

Fanony, Fulgence. *L'oiseau grand-tison et autres contes des betsimisaraka du nord (Madagascar).* Paris: L'Harmattan, 2001.

Faublée, Jacques. *Récits bara.* Paris: Institut d'Ethnologie, Musée de l'Homme, 1947.

Fauconnier, Gilles, and Mark Turner. *The Way We Think: Conceptual Blending and the Mind's Hidden Complexities.* New York: Basic, 2002.

Faurec, Urbain. "Histoire anecdotique de l'archipel des Comores." Antananarivo (Madagascar), n.d.

Feeley-Harnik, Gillian. "Divine Kingship and the Meaning of History among the Sakalava of Madagascar." *Man,* n.s., 13 (1980): 402–17.

———. *A Green Estate: Restoring Independence in Madagascar.* Washington: Smithsonian, 1991.

Ferrand, Gabriel. *Contes populaires malgaches.* Paris: Ernest Leroux, 1893.

———. "Note sur le calendrier malgache et le fandruana." *Revue des études ethnographiques et sociologiques,* 1908.

Feuser, Willfried. "Review of Ige's *Comparative Literature as a Distinct Discipline: A Superfluity.*" *Research in African Literatures* 19.3 (Fall 1988): 377–80.

Filliot, J.-M. *La traite des esclaves vers les Mascareignes au XVIIIe siècle.* Paris: ORSTOM, 1974.

Finnegan, Ruth. *Oral Literature in Africa.* Oxford Library of African Literature. Oxford: Clarendon Press, 1970.

Fitzgerald, F. Scott. *The Crack-Up.* New York: New Directions, 1945.

Flacourt, Etienne de. *Histoire de la Grande Isle Madagascar.* Paris: Gervais Clouzier, 1661.

Fokken, H. A. "Erzählungen und Märchen der Larusa." *Zeitschrift Für Kolonialsprachen* 7.2 (1917): 81–104.

Fontoynont, Maurice. "Le folklore et les coutumes." *L'Encyclopédie coloniale et maritime: Madagascar,* 1947.

Fontoynont, Maurice, and Raomandahy. *La Grande Comore.* Tananarive (Madagascar): Imprimerie Moderne de l'Émyrne, Pitot de la Beaujardière, 1937.

Foucault, Michel. *Aesthetics, Method, and Epistemology.* New York: New Press, 1998.

Fox, Leonard, ed. and trans. *Hainteny, the Traditional Poetry of Madagascar.* Lewisburg, Pa.: Bucknell University Press, 1990.

Frye, Northrop. *Anatomy of Criticism, Four Essays.* Princeton: Princeton University Press, 1957.

Gallob, Karen W. "An Anthropological Study of Incongruity, Play, and Identity in Mauritian Verbal Humor." Ph.D. diss., University of Colorado, 1987.

Gamaleya, Boris. "Contes populaires de la Réunion." *Bardzour Maskarin* 1 (1974).

———. "Contes populaires de la Réunion." *Bardzour Maskarin* 4 (1977): 18–27.

Gecau, Rose. *Kikuyu Folktales.* Nairobi: East African Literature Bureau, 1970.

Gellner, Ernest. *Language and Solitude: Wittgenstein, Malinowski and the Habsburg Dilemma.* Cambridge: Cambridge University Press, 1998.

Genette, Gérard. *Narrative Discourse: An Essay in Method.* Trans. Jane E. Lewin. Ithaca: Cornell University Press, 1980 (1972).

Genovese, Eugene D. *Roll, Jordan, Roll: The World the Slaves Made.* New York: Vintage Books, 1976.

Georges, Robert A. "Toward an Understanding of Storytelling Events." *Journal of American Folklore* 82 (1969): 313–28.

Glassie, Henry. *All Silver and No Brass: An Irish Christmas Mumming.* Bloomington: Indiana University Press, 1975.

Goffman, Erving. *Frame Analysis: An Essay on the Organization of Experience.* Harmondsworth: Penguin Books, 1975.

Goldstein, Kenneth S. *A Guide for Field Workers in Folklore.* Hatboro, Pa.: Folklore Associates, 1964.

Goodman, Paul. *The Structure of Literature.* Phoenix Books. Chicago: University of Chicago Press, 1962 (1954).

Görög-Karady, Veronika. Intro. to *Le mariage dans les contes africains: études et anthologie.* Comp. and ed. Veronika Görög-Karady. Hommes et Sociétés. Paris: Éditions Karthala, 1994. 5–15.

Görög-Karady, Veronika, and Christiane Seydou, comps. and eds. *La fille difficile, un conte-type africain.* Paris: CNRS Éditions, 2001.

Goswami, Keshava. *More Folktales from Mauritius.* Quatre Bornes (Mauritius): Pandit Ramlakhan Gossagne Publications, 1987.

Gow, Bonar A. *Madagascar and the Protestant Impact: The Work of the British Missions, 1818–1895.* London: Longman; Dalhousie University Press, 1979.

Grandidier, Guillaume. "À Madagascar, anciennes croyances et coutumes." *Journal de la Société des Africanistes* 2 (1932): 153–207.

Greenway, John. *Literature among the Primitives.* Hatboro, Pa.: Folklore Associates, 1964.

Griaule, Marcel. *Conversations with Ogotemmêli: An Introduction to Dogon Religious Ideas.* London: Oxford University Press for the International African Institute, 1965.

Grimm, Jacob, and Wilhelm Grimm. *The Complete Fairy Tales of the Brothers Grimm.* Trans. Jack Zipes. New York: Bantam Books, 1987.

Gueunier, Noël J. *L'oiseau chagrin: contes comoriens en dialecte malgache de l'île de Mayotte.* Collected by Noël J. Gueunier and Madjidhoubi Said, trans. Noël J. Gueunier. SELAF No. 346. Paris: Peeters, 1994.

Gueunier, Noël [J.], trans. and intro. *L'origine des choses: récits de la côte ouest de Madagascar.* Antananarivo: Foi et Justice, 1991.

———, and Madjidhoubi Said, eds. *La belle ne se marie point: contes comoriens en dialecte malgache de l'île de Mayotte.* Trans. Noël J. Gueunier. Asie et Monde Insulindien. Paris: Peeters, 1990.

Gutmann, Bruno. *Volksbuch der Wadschagga.* Leipzig: Verlag der evangelisch-lutherischen Mission, 1909.

Haggin, B. H. *Music in the Nation.* New York: William Sloane Associates, 1949.

Hansen, William. *Ariadne's Thread: A Guide to International Tales Found in Classical Literature.* Ithaca: Cornell University Press, 2002.

Haring, Lee. "African Folktales and Creolization in the Indian Ocean Islands." *Research in African Literatures* 33.3 (Fall 2002): 182–99.

———. "Buried Treasure." *Journal of Mauritian Studies* 4.1 (1992): 22–35.

———. "A Characteristic African Folktale Pattern." *African Folklore.* Ed. Richard M. Dorson. Garden City, N.Y.: Doubleday Anchor, 1972. 165–79.

———. "The Classification of Malagasy Narrative." *Research in African Literatures* 11.3 (1980): 342–55.

———. "Cultural Creolization." *Acta Ethnographica Hungarica* 49.1–2 (2004): 1–38.

———. "Eastward to the Islands: The Other Diaspora." *Journal of American Folklore* 118.469 (Summer 2005): 290–307.

———. "Folklore and the History of Literature in Madagascar." *Research in African Literatures* 16.3 (Fall 1985): 297–318.

———. "The Grateful Animals in Morondava, Analysis of a Malagasy Tale." *Le conte, pourquoi, comment? Actes des journées d'études en littérature orale.* Ed. Geneviève Calame-Griaule, Veronika Görög-Karady, and Michèle Chiche. Paris: Centre National de la Recherche Scientifique, 1984. 151–67.

———. *Ibonia, Epic of Madagascar.* Lewisburg, Pa.: Bucknell University Press, 1994.

———. *Indian Ocean Folktales: Madagascar, Comoros, Mauritius, Réunion, Seychelles.* Chennai (India): National Folklore Support Centre, 2002.

———. "Interperformance." *Fabula* 29.3–4 (1988): 365–72.

———. "Interpreters of Indian Ocean Folktales." *Fabula* 44 (2003): 98–116.

———. *Malagasy Tale Index.* FF Communications. Helsinki: Suomalainen Tiedeakatemia, 1982.

———. "The Multilingual Subaltern: Creolization as Agency." *Estudos de Literatura Oral* 5 (1999): 109–19.

———. "Parody and Imitation in Western Indian Ocean Oral Literature." *Journal of Folklore Research* 29.3 (Sept.–Dec. 1992): 199–224.

———. "Personal Narrative in Mauritian Studies." *Journal of Mauritian Studies*, n.s., 2.2 (2004): 1–19.

———. "Pieces for a Shabby Hut." *Folklore, Literature, and Cultural Theory.* Ed. Cathy Lynn Preston. New York: Garland Press, 1995. 187–203.

———. *Verbal Arts in Madagascar: Performance in Historical Perspective.* Philadelphia: University of Pennsylvania Press, 1992.

———. "The Water-Spirits of Madagascar." *Cross Rhythms* 2 (1985): 157–75.

Harris, Joel Chandler. *Nights with Uncle Remus: Myths and Legends of the Old Plantation.* Boston: Houghton Mifflin, 1883.

Harvey, David. *The Condition of Postmodernity: An Enquiry into the Origins of Cultural Change.* Oxford: Blackwell, 1989.

Hassam, S., and A. Rassool. *Contes et légendes de l'Océan Indien.* Paris: Fernand Nathan, 1979.

Hattingh, S. C. "The Tar-Baby Story in Africa (Die Teerpopsprokie in Afrika)." *Tydskrif Vir Volkskunde en Volkstaal (Johannesburg)* 1.1 (Aug. 1944): 13–19.

Hatubou, Salim. *Contes de ma grand-mère (contes comoriens).* Paris: L'Harmattan, 1994.

Hébert, J. C. "Un conte malgache: le langage des bêtes." *Revue de Madagascar* 32 (1957): 46–51.

———. "Le cycle légendaire de Tandrokomana." *Revue de Madagascar* 21 (1963): 13–26.

Heseltine, Nigel. *Madagascar.* Praeger Library of African Affairs. New York: Praeger, 1971.

Holbek, Bengt. "Games of the Powerless." *Unifol (Kobenhavn)* (1977).

Honko, Lauri. "The Problem of Defining Myth." *Sacred Narrative: Readings in the Theory of Myth.* Ed. Alan Dundes. Berkeley: University of California Press, 1984. 41–52.

Hookoomsing, Vinesh Y. "(Re)Constructing Identities: Creole and Ancestral Connections." *Globalisation and the South-West Indian Ocean.* Ed. Sandra J. T. Evers and Vinesh Y. Hookoomsing. Réduit: University of Mauritius, 2000. 149–55.

Houbert, Jean. "Colonization and Decolonization in Globalization: The Creole Islands of the Indian Ocean." *Globalisation and the South-West Indian Ocean.* Ed. Sandra J. T. Evers and Vinesh Y. Hookoomsing. Réduit (Mauritius): University of Mauritius, 2000. 191–211.

Houlder, J. A. *Ohabolana, ou proverbes malgaches.* Trans. H. Noyer. Tananarive (Madagascar): Imprimerie Luthérienne, 1957.

Huizinga, Johan. *Homo Ludens: A Study of the Play-Element in Culture.* London: Routledge and Kegan Paul, 1949.

Hymes, Dell. "Breakthrough into Performance." *Folklore: Performance and Communication.* Ed. Dan Ben-Amos and Kenneth S. Goldstein. The Hague: Mouton, 1975. 11–74.

Irwin, Bonnie D. "What's in a Frame? The Medieval Textualization of Traditional Storytelling." *Oral Tradition* 10.1 (Mar. 1995): 27–53.

Jackson, Michael. *Allegories of the Wilderness: Ethics and Ambiguity in Kuranko Narratives.* Bloomington: Indiana University Press, 1982.

Jameson, Fredric. "Interview with Leonard Green, Jonathan Culler, and Richard Klein." *Diacritics* 12.3 (1982): 72–91.

———. *Marxism and Form: Twentieth-Century Dialectical Theories of Literature.* Princeton: Princeton University Press, 1971.

———. *The Political Unconscious: Narrative as a Socially Symbolic Act.* Ithaca: Cornell University Press, 1981.

Jauss, Hans Robert. *Toward an Aesthetic of Reception.* Minneapolis: University of Minnesota Press, 1982.

Johnson, Barbara. "Melville's Fist: The Execution of Billy Budd." *The Critical Tradition: Classic Texts and Contemporary Trends.* Ed. David H. Richter. Boston: Bedford Books, 1989. 1036–56.

Johnson, John William, ed. and trans., Fa-Digi Sisoko, narrator. *The Epic of Son-Jara, a West African Tradition.* Collaborators, Charles S. Bird et al. Bloomington: Indiana University Press, 1986.

Joubert, Jean-Louis. *Littératures de l'Océan Indien.* Vanves (France): EDICEF, 1991.

Jung, C. G., and C. Kerényi. *Essays on a Science of Mythology: The Myth of the Divine Child and the Mysteries of Eleusis.* Trans. R. F. C. Hull. Princeton, N.J.: Clarendon-Oxford University Press, 1969.

Junod, Henri A. *The Life of a South African Tribe.* New Hyde Park, N.Y.: University Books, 1962.

Kabira, Wanjiku Mukabi, and Kavetsa Adagala, eds. *Kenyan Oral Narratives, a Selection.* Nairobi: Heinemann Kenya, 1985.

Kabira, Wanjiku Mukabi, and Karega wa Mutahi. *Gikuyu Oral Literature.* Nairobi: Heinemann Kenya, 1988.

Keenan, Edward Louis, and Elinor Ochs. "Becoming a Competent Speaker of Malagasy." *Languages and Their Speakers.* Ed. Timothy Shopen. Cambridge: Winthrop, 1979. 113–58.

Keenan, Elinor Ochs. "Norm-Makers, Norm-Breakers: Uses of Speech by Men and Women in a Malagasy Community." *Explorations in the Ethnography of Speaking.* 2nd ed. Ed. Richard Bauman and Joel Sherzer. Cambridge: Cambridge University Press, 1989 (1974). 125–43.

Kent, Raymond K. *Early Kingdoms in Madagascar, 1500–1700.* New York: Holt, Rinehart and Winston, 1970.
Kirshenblatt-Gimblett, Barbara. "Folklore's Crisis." *Journal of American Folklore* 111.441 (1998): 281–327.
Klipple, May Augusta. "African Folk Tales with Foreign Analogues." Ph.D. diss., Indiana University, 1938.
Kluckhohn, Clyde. "Recurrent Themes in Myths and Mythmaking." *The Study of Folklore.* Ed. Alan Dundes. Englewood Cliffs, N.J.: Prentice, 1965. 158–68.
Knappert, Jan. *Myths and Legends of the Swahili.* Nairobi: Heinemann Educational Books, 1970.
Kolchin, Peter. *American Slavery, 1619–1877.* New York: Hill and Wang, 1993.
Kristeva, Julia. *Desire in Language: A Semiotic Approach to Literature and Art.* Ed. Leon S. Roudiez. Trans. Leon S. Roudiez, Thomas Gora, and Alice Jardine. New York: Columbia University Press, 1980.
———. *Revolution in Poetic Language.* Trans. Margaret Waller. New York: Columbia University Press, 1984.
Krohn, Kaarle. *Bär (Wolf) und Fuchs: eine nordische Tiermärchenkette.* Journal de la Société Finno-Ougrienne, no. 6. Helsingfors: Société Finno-Ougrienne, 1889.
Krupat, Arnold. "Post-Structuralism and Oral Literature." *Recovering the Word: Essays in Native American Ethnopoetics.* Ed. Brian Swann and Arnold Krupat. Berkeley: University of California Press, 1987. 113–28.
Labov, William, and Joshua Waletzky. "Narrative Analysis: Oral Versions of Personal Experience." *Essays on the Verbal and Visual Arts.* Ed. June Helm. Seattle: American Ethnological Society, 1967. 12–44.
Lacan, Jacques. "The Mirror Stage as Formative of the Function of the I." *Écrits.* Trans. Alan Sheridan. New York: W. W. Norton, 1977. 1–7.
Lakoff, George, and Mark Johnson. *Philosophy in the Flesh: The Embodied Mind and Its Challenge to Western Thought.* New York: Basic, 1999.
Lambrecht, Winifred. "A Tale Type Index for Central Africa." Dissertation, University of California, Berkeley, 1967.
Leblond, Marius. *Les îles soeurs, ou le paradis retrouvé. La Réunion—Maurice, Eden de la mer des indes.* Paris: Alsatia, 1946.
Lefevere, André, ed. *Translation/History/Culture, a Sourcebook.* London: Routledge, 1992.
Lentricchia, Frank. *After the New Criticism.* Chicago: University of Chicago Press, 1980.
Leroy, Louis. *Les français à Madagascar.* Paris: Ch. Delagrave, 1884.
Lévi-Strauss, Claude. *From Honey to Ashes.* Trans. John Weightman and Doreen Weightman. Vol. 2 of *Introduction to a Science of Mythology.* New York: Harper Torchbooks—Harper and Row, 1974.
———. *The Raw and the Cooked.* Trans. John Weightman and Doreen Weightman. Vol. 1 of *Introduction to a Science of Mythology.* New York: Harper Torchbooks—Harper and Row, 1970.
Levine, Lawrence W. *Black Culture and Black Consciousness: Afro-American Folk Thought from Slavery to Freedom.* Oxford: Oxford University Press, 1977.
Lewontin, R. C. "Darwin's Revolution." *New York Review of Books,* 16 June 1983, 21–27.
Limon, José E. *Dancing with the Devil: Society and Cultural Poetics in Mexican-American South Texas.* Madison: University of Wisconsin Press, 1994.

Lindenberger, Herbert. *Opera, the Extravagant Art.* Ithaca: Cornell University Press, 1984.
Linton, Ralph. *The Tanala, a Hill Tribe of Madagascar.* Anthropological Series 22. Chicago: Field Museum of Natural History, 1933.
Lombard, Jacques. "'Zatovo qui n'a pas été créé par dieu': un conte sakalava traduit et commenté." *ASEMI* 7.2–3 (1976): 165–223.
Longchamps, Jeanne de. *Contes malgaches.* Paris: Éditions Érasme, 1955.
Lord, Albert Bates. "Avdo Mededovic, Guslar." *Journal of American Folklore* 69 (1956): 320–30.
Macdonald, D. "Yao and Nyanja Tales." *Bantu Studies* 12 (1938): 251–85.
Macdonald, Duff. *Africana.* London: Simkin Marshall, 1882.
Macherey, Pierre. *A Theory of Literary Production.* Trans. Geoffrey Wall. London: Routledge and Kegan Paul, 1978.
Mamelomana, Edmond. "Recueil de contes antesaka." *Bulletin de Madagascar* 269 (Oct. 1968): 853–905.
Mannick, A. R. *Mauritius: The Development of a Plural Society.* Nottingham, U.K.: Spokesman: Russell Press, 1979.
Marimoutou, Jean-Claude Carpanin. "Écrire métis." *Métissages I: Littérature, Histoire.* Comp. Jean-Claude Carpanin Marimoutou and Jean-Michel Racault. Publications de Centre de Recherches Littéraires et Historiques de l'Université de La Réunion. Paris: L'Harmattan, 1992. 247–60.
———. "Louis Héry et la créolisation des fables."*Études Créoles* 24.2 (2001): 71–103.
Massignon, Geneviève. *Folktales of France.* Chicago: University of Chicago Press, 1968.
Mbiti, John S. *Akamba Stories.* Oxford: Clarendon, 1966.
McClintock, Anne. "The Angel of Progress: Pitfalls of the Term 'Post-Colonialism.'" *Colonial Discourse and Post-Colonial Theory, a Reader.* Ed. Patrick Williams and Laura Chrisman. New York: Columbia University Press, 1994. 291–304.
Meeks, Brian. *Narratives of Resistance: Jamaica, Trinidad, the Caribbean.* Barbados: University of the West Indies Press, 2000.
Michel, Louis. *Moeurs et coutumes des bara.* Mémoires de l'Académie Malgache. Antananarivo: Institut Scientifique de Madagascar, 1957.
Michel-Andrianarahinjaka, Lucien X. *Le système littéraire betsileo.* Fianarantsoa: Éditions Ambozontany, 1986.
Mills, Margaret. *Rhetoric and Politics in Afghan Traditional Storytelling.* Philadelphia: University of Pennsylvania Press, 1991.
Mitchell-Kernan, Claudia. "Signifying." *Mother Wit from the Laughing Barrel.* Ed. Alan Dundes. Englewood Cliffs, N.J.: Prentice, 1973 (1971). 310–28.
Molet, Louis. *La conception malgache du monde, du surnaturel, et de l'homme en imerina.* 2 vols. Paris: L'Harmattan, 1979.
———. "Esquisse de la mentalité malgache." *Revue de Psychologie des Peuples* 14.1 (Jan. 1959): 25–40.
Mvula, Enoch S. Timpunza. "Chewa Folk Narrative Performance." Paper presented at Seventh Congress of the International Society for Folk Narrative Research. Edinburgh, 1979.
Mwakasaka, Christon S. *The Oral Literature of the Banyakyusa.* Nairobi: Kenya Literature Bureau, 1978.

Nagapen, Amédée. *Le Marronnage à l'Isle de France—Île Maurice: rêve ou riposte de l'esclave?* Port Louis (Mauritius): Centre Culturel Africain (Centre Nelson Mandela pour la Culture Africaine), 1999.
Needham, Rodney. *Belief, Language and Experience.* Chicago: University of Chicago Press, 1972.
———. *Reconnaissances.* Toronto: University of Toronto Press, 1980.
Neill, Stephen. "The Missionary Contribution to Ethnology." *Wort und Religion/Kalima na dini. Studien zur Afrikanistik, Missionswissenschaft, Religionswissenschaft. Ernst Dammann zur 65 Geburtstag.* Ed. Hans-Jürgen Greschat and Herrmann Jungraithmay. Stuttgart: Evangelischer Missionsverlag, 1969. 192–200.
Neumann, Ingrid. "Les contes créoles seychellois." *Études Créoles* 2.2 (1980): 41–53.
Nietzsche, Friedrich. *On the Genealogy of Morals.* Ed. and trans. Walter Kaufmann. Trans. R. J. Hollingdale. New York: Vintage–Random House, 1967.
———. *The Portable Nietzsche.* Ed. and trans. Walter Kaufmann. New York: Viking, 1954.
Njururi, Ngumbu. *Agikuyu Folk Tales.* London: Oxford University Press, 1966.
Noiret, François. *Le mythe d'Ibonia.* Arts et Culture Malgaches: Angano Malagasy/Contes de Madagascar. Antananarivo: Foi et Justice, 1993.
Okpewho, Isidore. *African Oral Literature: Backgrounds, Character, and Continuity.* Bloomington: Indiana University Press, 1992.
———. "Oral Tradition: Do Storytellers Lie?" *Journal of Folklore Research* 40.3 (2003): 215–32.
Olrik, Axel. "Epic Laws of Folk Narrative." Trans. Jeanne Poyntz Steager and Alan Dundes. *The Study of Folklore.* Ed. Alan Dundes. Englewood Cliffs, N.J.: Prentice, 1965. 129–41.
Oring, Elliott. *Jokes and Their Relations.* Lexington: University Press of Kentucky, 1992.
Osborn, Chase Salmon. *Madagascar, Land of the Man-Eating Tree.* New York: Republic Publishing Co., 1924.
Ottino, Arlette. "First Settlers, Rice-Cultivation and the Alliance with Nature Spirits: Agrarian Rituals and the Reproduction of the World-Order in Madagascar." *L'étranger intime: mélanges offerts à Paul Ottino.* Saint-Denis: Université de la Réunion, 1995. 117–41.
Ottino, Paul. "Les aventures de Petit Jean: les aspects bantous et malgaches." *Notre Librairie* 72 (Oct.–Dec. 1983): 33–41.
———. *L'étrangère intime: essai d'anthropologie de la civilisation de l'ancien Madagascar.* Paris: Éditions Des Archives Contemporaines, 1986.
———. "The Mythology of the Highlands of Madagascar and the Political Cycle of the Andriambahoaka." *Mythologies.* Comp. Yves Bonnefoy. Prepared by Wendy Doniger. 2 vols. Chicago: University of Chicago Press, 1991. 2:961–76.
———. "Un procédé littéraire malayo-polynésien: de l'ambigüité à la plurisignification." *L'Homme* 6.4 (Oct.–Dec. 1966): 5–34.
———. "Le thème du monstre dévorant dans les domaines malgache et bantou." *ASEMI* 8.3–4 (1977): 219–51.
Paulhan, Jean. *Les hain-teny merinas, poésies populaires malgaches.* Paris: P. Geuthner, 1913.
Paulme, Denise. *La mère dévorante: essai sur la morphologie des contes africains.* Paris: Gallimard, 1976.

———. "Quelques procédés du conteur africain." *La statue du commandeur: essais d'ethnologie.* Paris: Le Sycomore, 1984. 79–97.

———. *La statue du commandeur: essais d'ethnologie.* Paris: Le Sycomore, 1984.

Payette, Flavienne, ed. *Kont ek lezann seselwa.* By Samuel Accouche, Marietta Hoarau, and others. Anse aux Pins (Seychelles): Instìti Kreol Lans-o-pen, 1990.

———, ed. *Kont ek lezann seselwa 2.* By Samuel Accouche, Marietta Hoarau, and others. Anse aux Pins (Seychelles): Instìti Kreol Lans-o-pen, 1991.

———, ed. *Kont ek lezann seselwa 3.* By Samuel Accouche, Marietta Hoarau, and others. Anse aux Pins (Seychelles): Instìti Kreol Lans-o-pen, 1992.

Pelletier, Joseph. "La Chaloupe: une société créole." Ph.D. diss. Paris: EHESS, 1983.

Perls, Laura. "Notes on the Psychology of Give and Take." *Recognitions in Gestalt Therapy,* ed. Paul David Pursglove. New York: Funk and Wagnalls, 1968. 118–28.

Perrault, Charles. *Perrault's Complete Fairy Tales.* New York: Dodd, Mead, 1961.

Pound, Ezra, and Marcella Spann, eds. *Confucius to Cummings, an Anthology of Poetry.* New York: New Directions, 1964.

Propp, V. *Morphology of the Folktale.* Austin: University of Texas Press, 1968.

Proust, Marcel. *Jean Santeuil.* Trans. Gerard Hopkins. New York: Dell Publishing, 1961 (1955).

Prud'homme, Claude. "Le catholicisme à la Réunion: histoire et mécanismes d'une implantation." *Le mouvement des idées dans l'Océan Indien occidental.* Saint-Denis: Association Historique Internationale de l'Océan Indien, 1985. 5–39.

Puhvel, Jaan. *Comparative Mythology.* Baltimore: Johns Hopkins University Press, 1987.

Putz, Lucien. *Ile Maurice: hommage à Ti Frère.* Singer, Alphonse Ravaton. Paris: Ocora/Radio France C 560019, HM 83, 1991. Compact disc.

Quammen, David. *The Song of the Dodo: Island Biogeography in an Age of Extinctions.* New York: Simon and Schuster, 1997.

Rabezandrina. *Ikotofetsy sy Imahaka, sy tantara malagasy hafa koa.* Tananarive: John Parrett, 1875.

Raison-Jourde, Françoise. *Bible et pouvoir à Madagascar au XIXe siècle: invention d'une identité chrétienne et construction de l'état (1780–1880).* Paris: Karthala, 1991.

Ramamonjisoa, Suzy, Maurice Schrive, Solo Raharijanahary, and Velonandro [Noël J. Gueunier]. *Femmes et monstres 1: tradition orale malgache.* Paris: Conseil International de la Langue Française; EDICEF, 1981.

Ramsurrun, Pahlad. *Folk Tales of Mauritius.* Rev. ed. Port Louis (Mauritius): Twentieth Century Marketing Ltd., 1987 (1982).

Rattray, R. Sutherland, comp. *Some Folk-Lore Stories and Songs in Chinyanja.* New York: Negro Universities Press, 1969 (1907).

Reisman, Karl. "Contrapuntal Conversations in an Antiguan Village." *Explorations in the Ethnography of Speaking.* Ed. Richard Bauman and Joel Sherzer. New York: Cambridge University Press, 1989. 110–24.

René, France-Albert. *Seychelles, the New Era.* Victoria: Ministry of Education and Information, 1982.

Renel, Charles. *Contes de Madagascar.* 2 vols. Collection de Contes et Chansons Populaires. Paris: Ernest Leroux, 1910.

———. *Contes de Madagascar.* Vol. 3. Collection de Contes et Chansons Populaires. Paris: Ernest Leroux, 1930.

Richardson, John. *A New Malagasy-English Dictionary.* Antananarivo: The London Missionary Society, 1885.
Rigaud, L. ["Radama II"]. *Bulletin Mensuel de l'Enseignement (Tananarive)* 13.9 (Sept. 1911): 311–14.
Rispal-Gaba, Nicole. "Alternance codique et stabilité identitaire." *Cuisines/ identités.* Ed. D. Baggioni and J. C. C. Marimoutou. Saint-Denis: UA 1041 du CNRS, 1988. 103–20.
Robequain, Charles. *Madagascar et les bases dispersées de l'union française (Comores, Réunion, Antilles et Guyane, Terres Océaniennes, Côte des Somalis, Saint-Pierre et Miquelon, Iles Australes, Terre Adélie).* Pays d'Outre-Mer. Paris: Presses Universitaires de France, 1958.
Robinson, John A. "Personal Narratives Reconsidered." *Journal of American Folklore* 94.371 (Jan.–Mar. 1981): 58–85.
Rossetti, Carlo Giuseppe. "*Folklore by the Fireside,* by A. Falassi." Review. *Man,* n.s., 17.1 (Mar. 1982): 174.
Rusillon, H[enri]. *Un petit continent, Madagascar.* Paris: Société des Missions Évangeliques, 1933.
Ruud, Jorgen. *Taboo, a Study of Malagasy Customs and Beliefs.* Oslo: Oslo University Press, 1960.
Said, Edward W. *Culture and Imperialism.* New York: Knopf, 1993.
Scarr, Deryck. *Seychelles since 1770: History of a Slave and Post-Slavery Society.* Trenton, N.J.: Africa World Press, 1999.
Scheub, Harold. *A Dictionary of African Mythology: The Mythmaker as Storyteller.* New York: Oxford University Press, 2000.
Schoffeleers, J. M., and Adrian Roscoe. *Land of Fire: Oral Literature from Malawi.* Limbe (Malawi): Popular Publications, 1985.
Schott, Rüdiger. "La Fille Difficile Bulsa (Nord-Ghana)." *La fille difficile, un conte-type africain.* Ed. Veronika Görög-Karady and Christiane Seydou. Paris: CNRS Editions, 2001. 109–37.
Schrive, P. Maurice. *Contes betsimisaraka.* Antananarivo: Alliance Française de Madagascar, 1989.
———. *Contes betsimisaraka: contes du nord-est de Madagascar.* Antananarivo; Tamatave: Foi et Justice; Alliance Française, 1992.
Scott, James C. *Domination and the Arts of Resistance: Hidden Transcripts.* New Haven: Yale University Press, 1990.
Sebba, Mark. *Contact Languages: Pidgins and Creoles.* Modern Linguistics Series. New York: St. Martin's, 1997.
Sébillot, Paul. *Contes populaires de la haute Bretagne.* Paris, 1880.
Seitel, Peter. "Proverbs and the Structure of Metaphor among the Haya of Tanzania." Ph.D. diss., University of Pennsylvania, 1972.
———. *See So That We May See: Performances and Interpretations of Traditional Tales from Tanzania.* With Sheila Dauer. Bloomington: Indiana University Press, 1980.
La Selve, Jean-Pierre. *Musiques traditionnelles de la Réunion.* 2nd ed. Saint-Denis: Azalées Éditions, 1995.
Seydou, Christiane. "Du mariage sauvage au mariage héroïque." *Le mariage dans les contes africains.* Ed. Veronika Görög-Karady. Hommes et Sociétés. Paris: Karthala, 1994. 85–134.
———. "La fille difficile peule I (du Sénégal . . . au Nigeria)." *La fille difficile, un conte-type africain.* Ed. Veronika Görög-Karady and Christiane Seydou. Paris: CNRS Éditions, 2001. 23–64.

Shah, Kantilal Jivan. "Les premiers éléments de connaissance sur les Seychelles." *Les Seychelles et l'Océan Indien.* Ed. Bernard Koechlin. Paris: Éditions L'Harmattan, 1984. 31–42.

Shuman, Amy. *Storytelling Rights: The Uses of Oral and Written Texts by Urban Adolescents.* Cambridge: Cambridge University Press, 1986.

Sibree, James, Jr. *Madagascar and Its People.* London, 1870.

———. *Madagascar Before the Conquest.* London: Fisher Unwin, 1896.

———. "Malagasy Folk-Tales." *Folk-Lore Journal (London)* 2 (1884): 45–57.

———. "Malagasy Folk-Tales." *Folk-Lore Journal (London)* 2 (1884): 129–38.

———. "The Oratory, Songs, Legends, and Folk-Tales of the Malagasy." *Folk-Lore Journal (London)* 1 (1883): 210–11.

———. "The Oratory, Songs, Legends, and Folk-Tales of the Malagasy." *Folk-Lore Journal (London)* 1 (1883): 337–43.

Smith, Barbara Herrnstein. "Narrative Versions, Narrative Theories." *Critical Inquiry* 7.3 (Autumn 1980): 213–36.

Smith, Edwin W., and Andrew Murray Dale. *The Ila-Speaking Peoples of Northern Rhodesia.* 2 vols. New Hyde Park, N.Y.: University Books, 1968 (1920).

Sooriamorthy, Ramoo. *Les tamouls à l'île Maurice.* Port Louis (Mauritius): The Standard Printing Establishment, 1977.

St. Jorre, Danielle de, and Guy Lionnet. *Diksyonner kreol-franse/Dictionnaire créole seychellois-français.* Bamberg and Mahé: 1999.

Steere, Edward. "On East African Tribes and Languages." *Journal of the Anthropological Institute* 1 (1871): 143–54.

———. *Swahili Tales as Told by Natives of Zanzibar.* London: Society for Promoting Christian Knowledge, 1889.

Sumner, William Graham. *Folkways: A Study of the Sociological Importance of Usages, Manners, Customs, Mores, and Morals.* New York: Dover, 1959.

Sutton-Smith, Brian, and John M. Roberts. "The Cross-Cultural and Psychological Study of Games." *The Folkgames of Children.* By Brian Sutton-Smith. Austin: University of Texas Press, 1972. 331–40.

Sydow, C. W. von. "Folktale Studies and Philology: Some Points of View." *Selected Papers on Folklore.* Copenhagen: Rosenkilde and Baggar, 1948. 189–219.

Szwed, John F. Review of *Creole Drum,* ed. Jan Voorhoeve and Ursy M. Lichtveld. *Research in African Literatures* 9 (1978): 495–98.

Theal, G. McCall. *Kaffir Folk-Lore.* London: Swan Sonnenschein, 1886.

Thomas, Athol. *Forgotten Eden: A View of the Seychelles Islands in the Indian Ocean.* London: Longmans, 1968.

Thompson, Stith. *The Folktale.* New York: Holt, Rinehart and Winston, 1946.

———. *Motif-Index of Folk-Literature: A Classification of Narrative Elements in Folktales, Ballads, Myths, Fables, Mediaeval Romances, Exempla, Fabliaux, Jest-Books and Local Legends.* Revised and enlarged ed. Bloomington: Indiana University Press, 1955–58.

Thompson, Stith, and Jonas Balys. *The Oral Tales of India.* Bloomington: Indiana University Press, 1958.

Thompson, Stith, and Warren E. Roberts. *Types of Indic Oral Tales: India, Pakistan, and Ceylon.* FF Communications. Helsinki: Suomalainen Tiedeakatemia, 1991.

Todorov, Tzvetan. *The Poetics of Prose.* Trans. Richard Howard. Ithaca: Cornell University Press, 1977.

Toihiri, Mohamed. *Le kafir du Karthala.* Paris: L'Harmattan, 1992.

Toussaint, Auguste. *Histoire de l'île Maurice.* 2nd ed. Que Sais-Je? no. 1449. Paris: Presses Universitaires de France, 1974.

Tutuola, Amos. *The Palm-Wine Drinkard and His Dead Palm-Wine Tapster in the Dead's Town.* New York: Grove, 1953.

Uther, Hans-Jörg. *The Types of International Folktales, a Classification and Bibliography.* FF Communications 284. Helsinki: Suoamalainen Tiedeakatemia, 2004.

Velde, H. te. *Seth, God of Confusion: A Study of His Role in Egyptian Mythology and Religion.* Leiden: E. J. Brill, 1967.

Ventre, Nelzir. Interview. *Weekend* 1980: 12–13.

Vérin, Pierre. *Les Comores.* Paris: Éditions Karthala, 1994.

———. *The History of Civilisation in North Madagascar.* Rotterdam: A. A. Balkema, 1986.

———. *Madagascar.* Paris: Karthala, 1990.

"Voatovo, ou calébasse." *Revue de Madagascar,* Oct. 1958, 41–48.

Vogel, Claude. "Permanence et changement: la prolifération du récit (1)." *Kriké-kraké, recueil de contes créoles éunionnais.* Comp. and ed. Christian Barat, Michel Carayol, and Claude Vogel. Saint-Denis: Centre Universitaire de la Réunion, 1977. 93–101.

———. "La roche qui roule ramasse pas de limon." *Études Créoles* 4.2 (1982): 20–39.

Volosinov, V. N. *Marxism and the Philosophy of Language.* Trans. Ladislav Matejka and I. R. Titunik. New York: Seminar Press, 1973 (1930).

Walen, A. "The Sakalava." *Antananarivo Annual* 7 (1883).

Werner, Alice. *Myths and Legends of the Bantu.* London: Frank Cass, 1968 (1933).

Williams, Raymond. *The Long Revolution.* Rev. ed. New York: Harper and Row, 1961.

Wong, Kate. "The End of Eden?" *Scientific American,* 10 Oct. 2000.

Woodward, H. W. "Makua Tales." *Bantu Studies* 9.2 (1935): 115–58.

Young, Katherine G. *Taleworlds and Storyrealms: The Phenomenology of Narrative.* Dordrecht (Netherlands): Martinus Nijhoff, 1987.

Young, T. C. *Notes on the Customs and Folklore of the Tumbuka-Kamanga Peoples in the Northern Province of Nyassaland.* Livingstonia (Malawi): Mission Press, 1931.

Zaslavsky, Claudia. *Africa Counts.* Boston: Prindle, Weber and Schmidt, 1973.

Zayann. Guadeloupe: Éditions PLB, 2003.

Zipes, Jack. *The Great Fairy Tale Tradition: From Straparola and Basile to the Brothers Grimm.* New York: W. W. Norton, 2001.

Index

LEE HARING is Professor Emeritus of English at Brooklyn College of The City University of New York. He is author of *Verbal Arts in Madagascar: Performance in Historical Perspective, Ibonia: Epic of Madagascar,* and several other books.